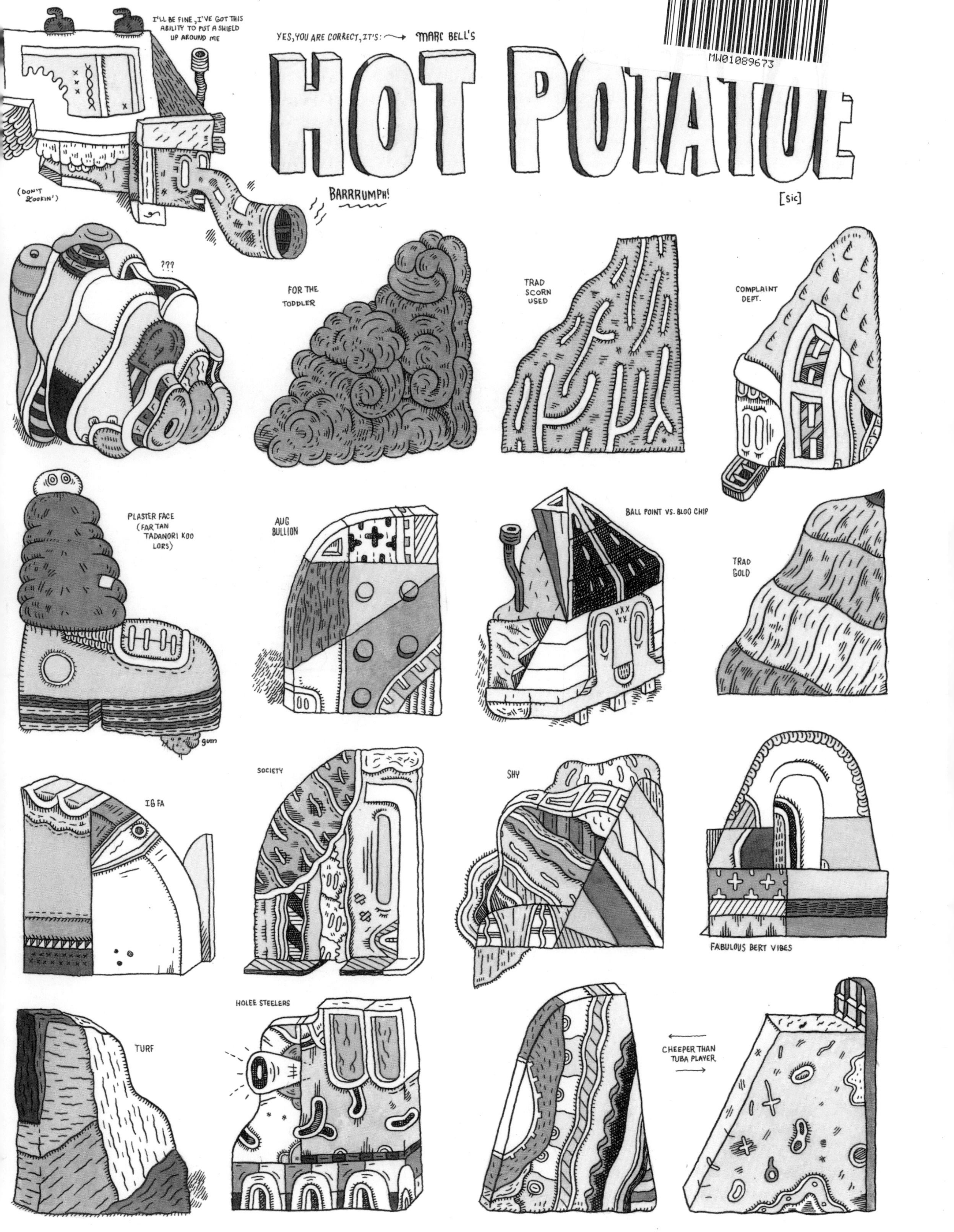
I'LL BE FINE, I'VE GOT THIS ABILITY TO PUT A SHIELD UP AROUND ME
(DON'T LOOKIN')
YES, YOU ARE CORRECT, IT'S: → MARC BELL'S
HOT POTATOE
BARRRUMPH!
[sic]
???
FOR THE TODDLER
TRAD SCORN USED
COMPLAINT DEPT.
PLASTER FACE (FAR TAN TADANORI KOO LORS)
AUG BULLION
BALL POINT VS. BLOO CHIP
TRAD GOLD
gum
IGFA
SOCIETY
SHY
FABULOUS BERT VIBES
TURF
HOLEE STEELERS
← CHEEPER THAN TUBA PLAYER →

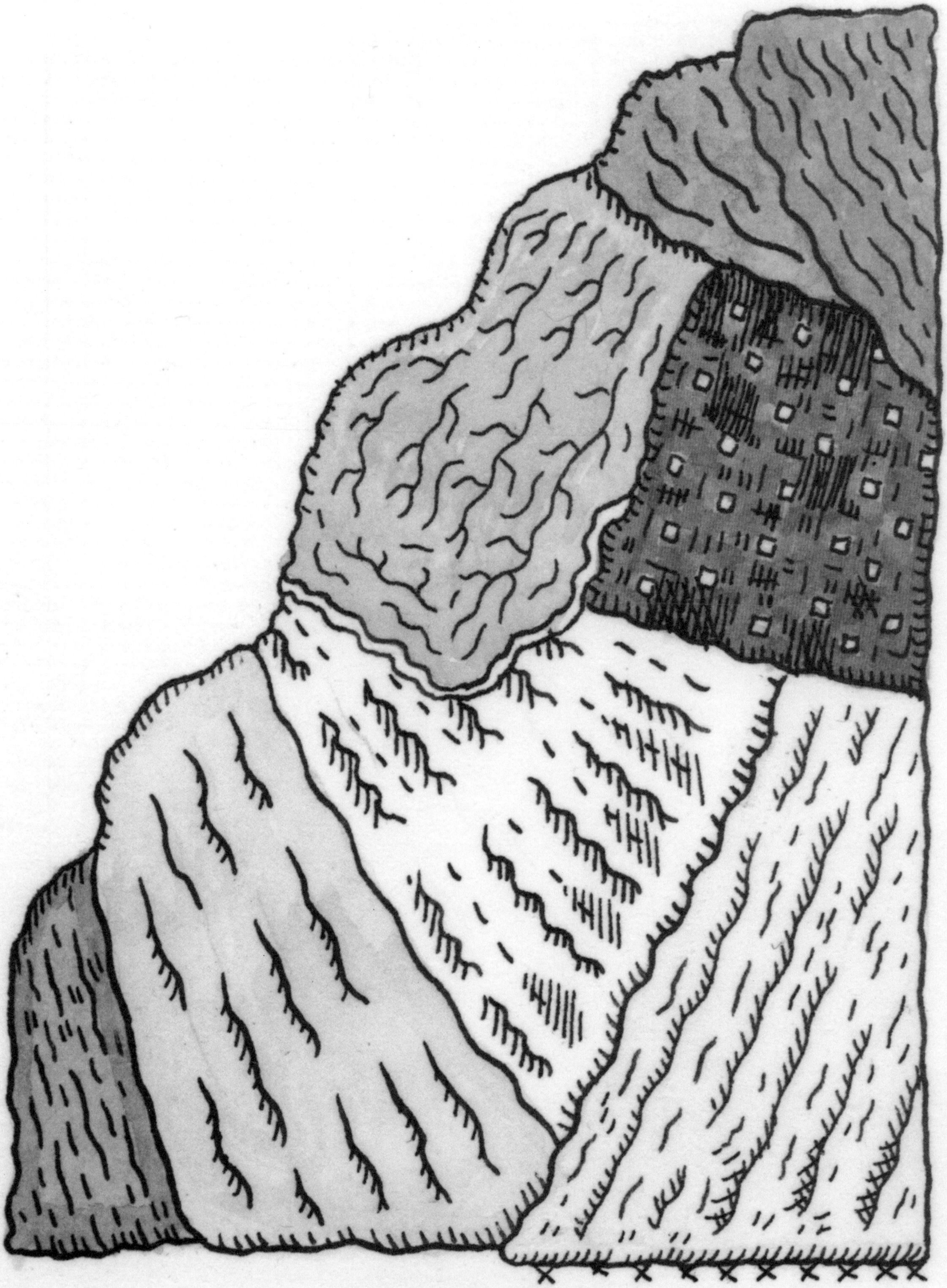

MARC BELL's

HOT POTATOE

[sic]

INCLUDING: AUG BULLION, THE STORY OF THE PILE OF BACON, COMPLAINT DEPT.,
HUDSUN MACK TURBIDITY, BELL'S TRAD (LOOKED LIKE), CHEEPER THAN TUBA PLAYER,
PHEW! COMICS AIN'T BUTTAH, FRESH FROM THE SILVER PUMPKIN, CONFIRMED,
TO: GNOSTIC PIZZA esq., MY INNER FOOT SAYS (THE FUNDEMENTALS ARE OUT OF WACK),
AND MORE...

DRAWN & QUARTERLY

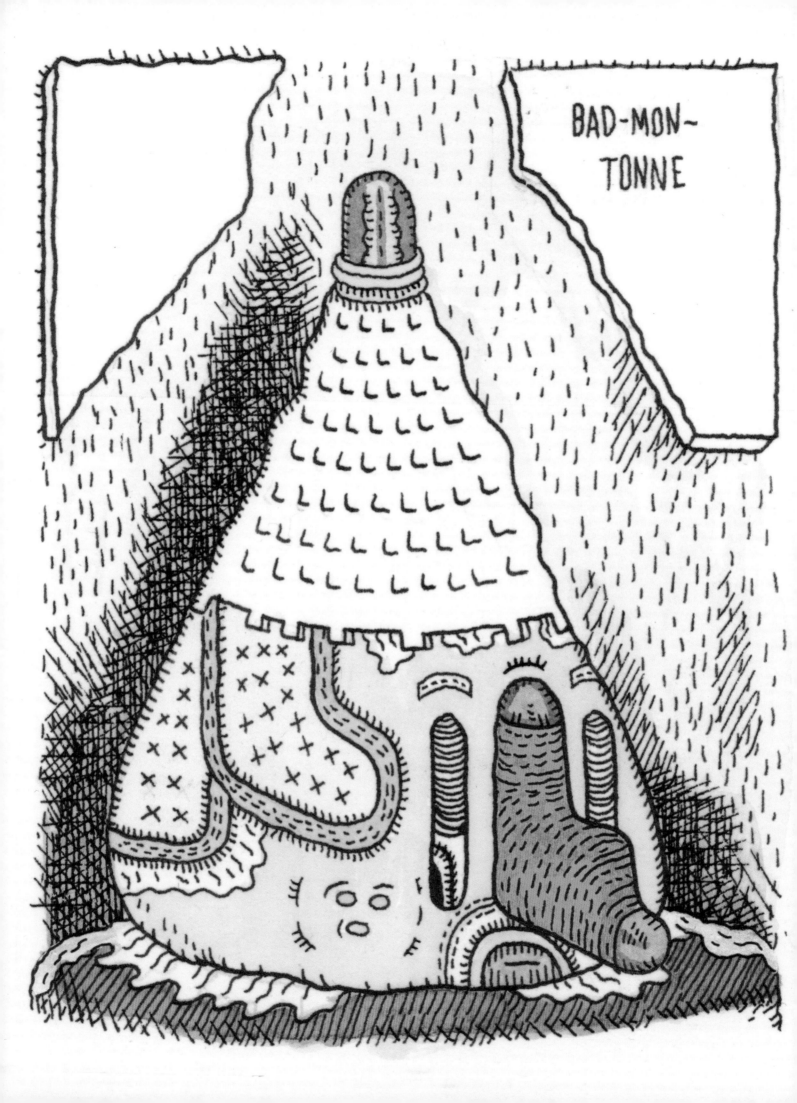

BAD-MON-
TONNE

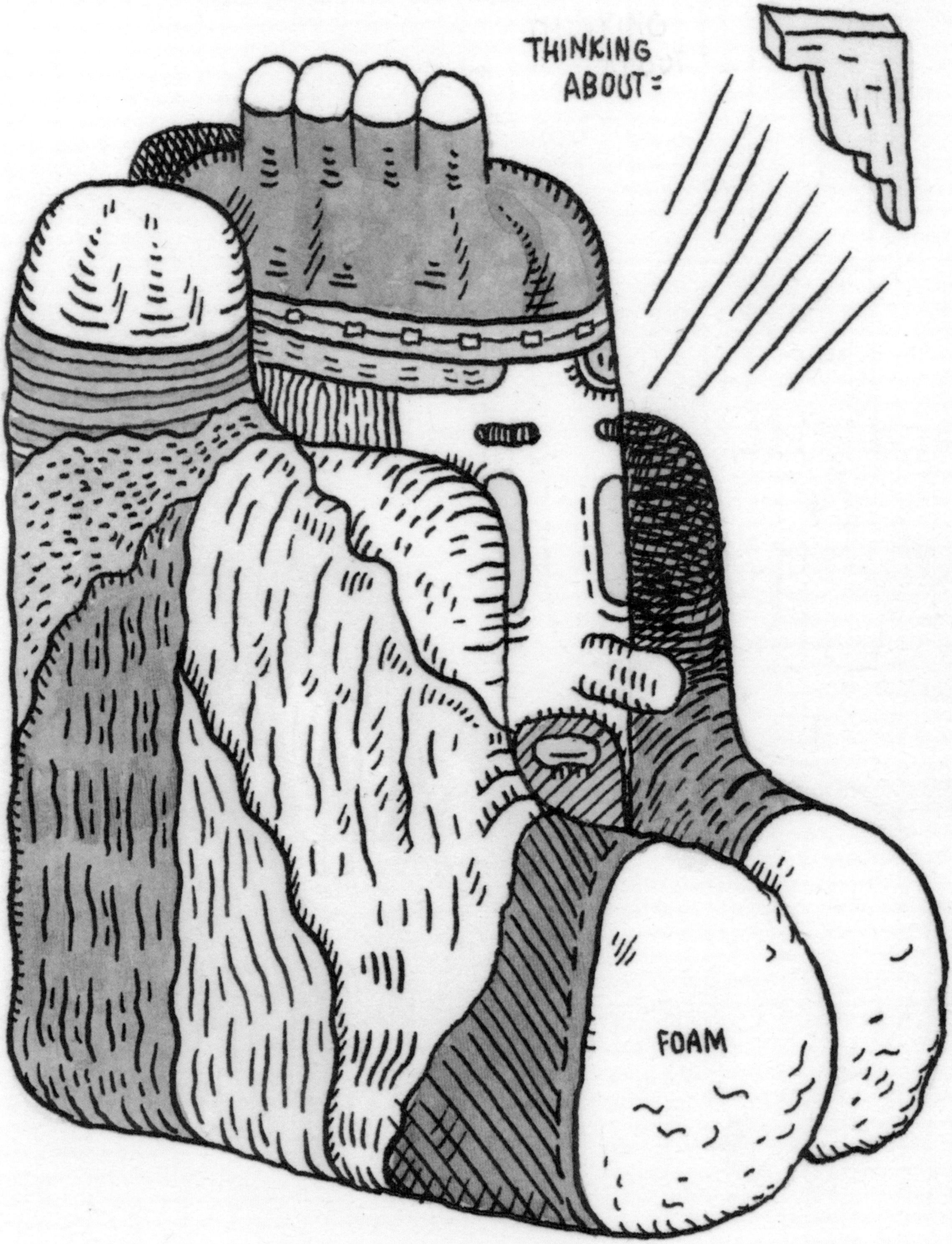
THINKING
ABOUT=
FOAM

Entire contents © copyright 2009 by Marc Bell (unless noted). All rights reserved. No part of this book (except small portions for review purposes) may be reproduced in any form without written permission from Marc Bell or Drawn & Quarterly. Drawn & Quarterly; Post Office Box 48056, Montreal, Quebec, Canada H2V 4S8. www.drawnandquarterly.com; First Hardcover Printing: September 2009. Printed in Singapore. 10 9 8 7 6 5 4 3 2 1; Library and Archives Canada Cataloguing in Publication; Bell, Marc, 1971- ; Hot potatoe / Marc Bell.; Includes articles by Dirty Debbie, Tommy Lacroix, Matthew P. Soucie, Swanson "Dinner" Newbury, Mark Slutsky, Balsam Adhesives, Tom Devlin, Snow Cone Schnauzer, Lulu Peabody-Sherman. ISBN 978-1-897299-89-0; I. Title. II. Title: Hot potatoe. PN6733.B45A6 2009 741.5'971 C2009-901648-6; Drawn & Quarterly acknowledges the financial contribution of Owens Art Gallery, Mount Allison University, Sackville, New Brunswick. Drawn & Quarterly also acknowledges the financial contribution of the Government of Canada through the Book Publishing Industry Development Program (BPIDP) and the Canada Council for the Arts for our publishing activities and for support of this edition. Distributed in the USA by: Farrar, Straus and Giroux; 18 West 18th Street, New York, NY 10011; Orders: 888.330.8477; Distributed in Canada by: Raincoast Books; 9050 Shaughnessy Street, Vancouver, BC V6P 6E5; Orders: 800.663.5714

Details from *Fresh From Kiev #2,* 2006, ink and watercolour on paper (this page and other pages at front of book)

Bell and Amy Lockhart at Julia's in Sackville, NB, 2006, photo by Shayne Ehman (after contents page)

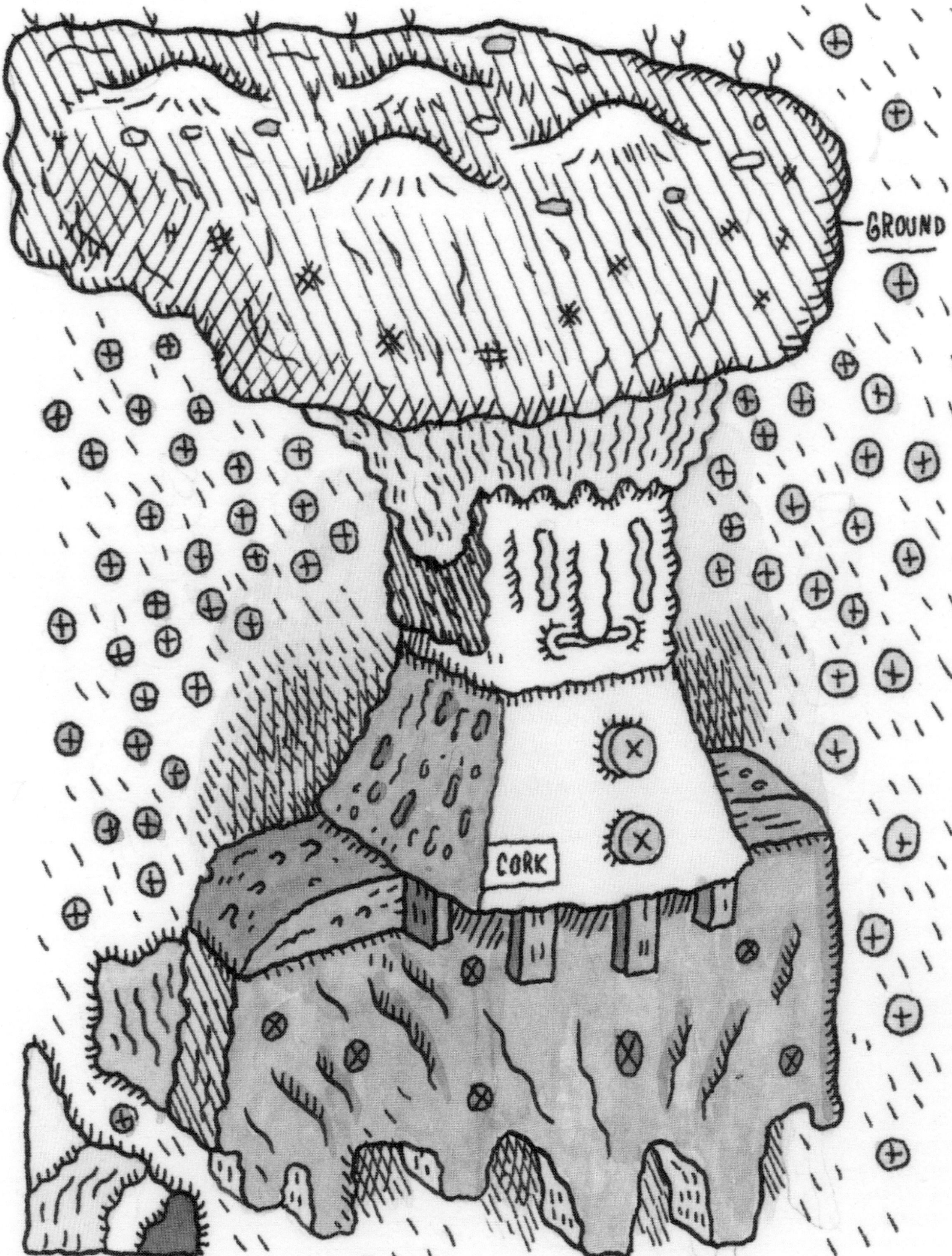
GROUND
CORK

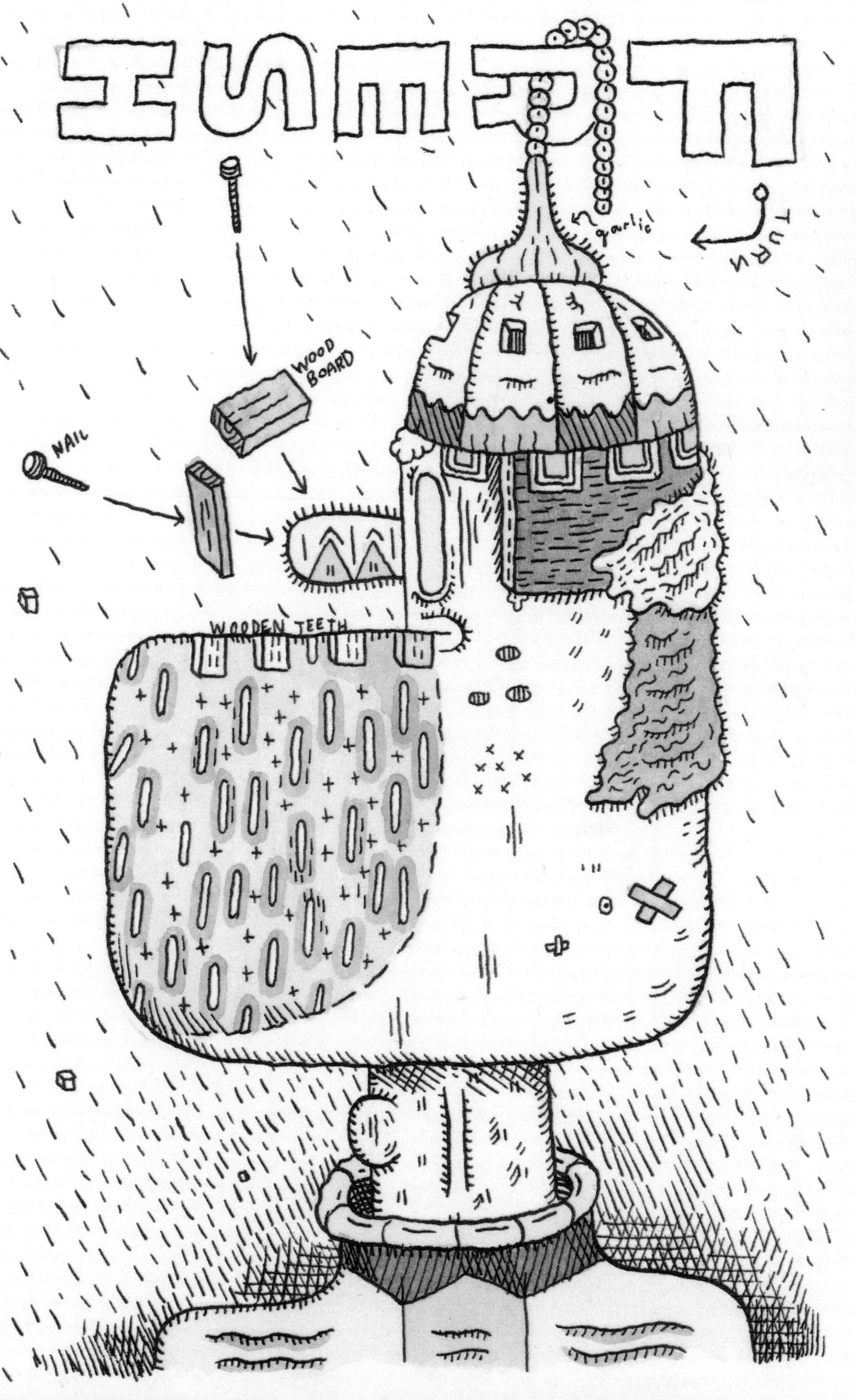
garlic
TURN
WOOD BOARD
NAIL
WOODEN TEETH

HOT POTATOE

CONTENTS

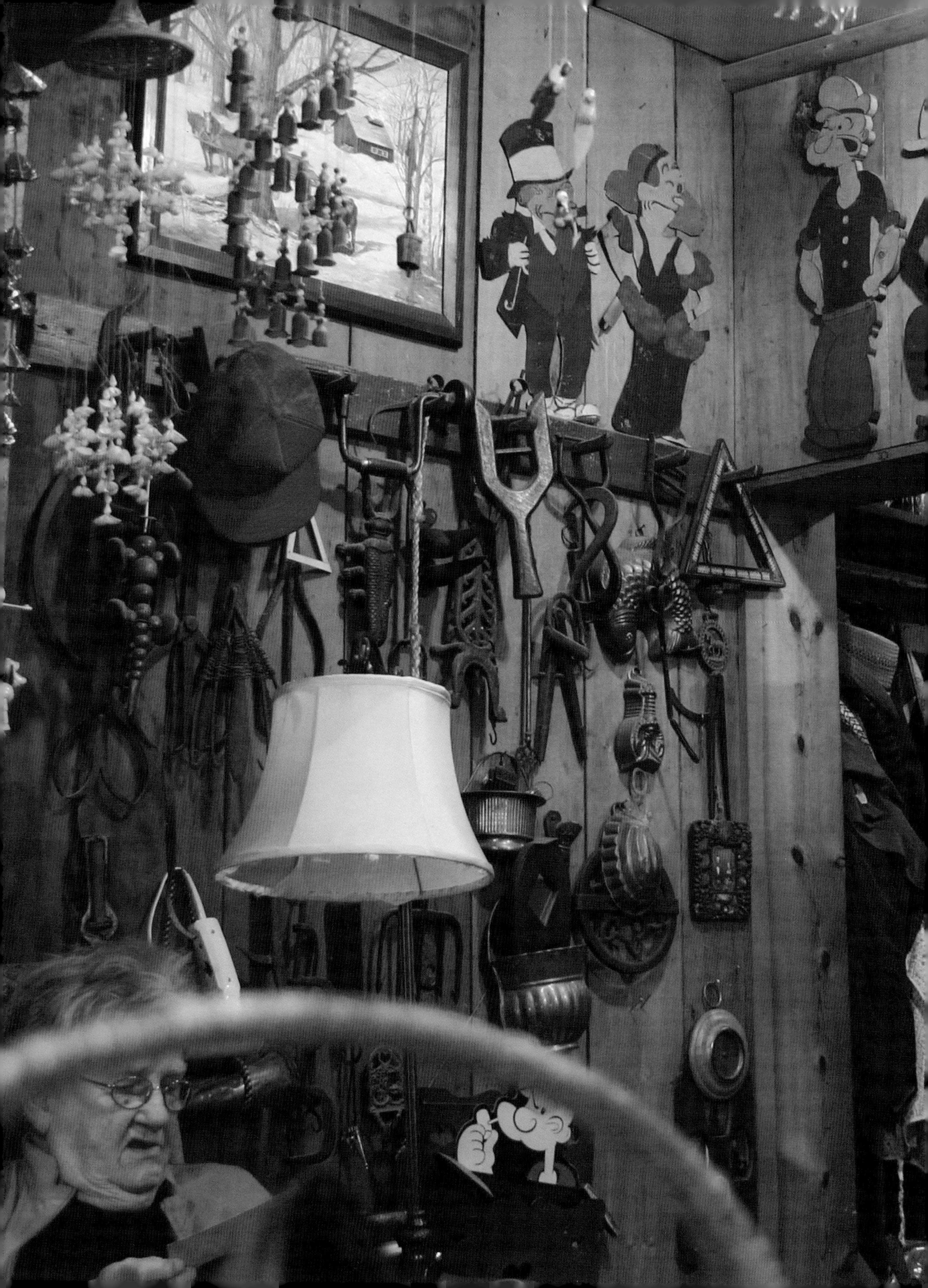

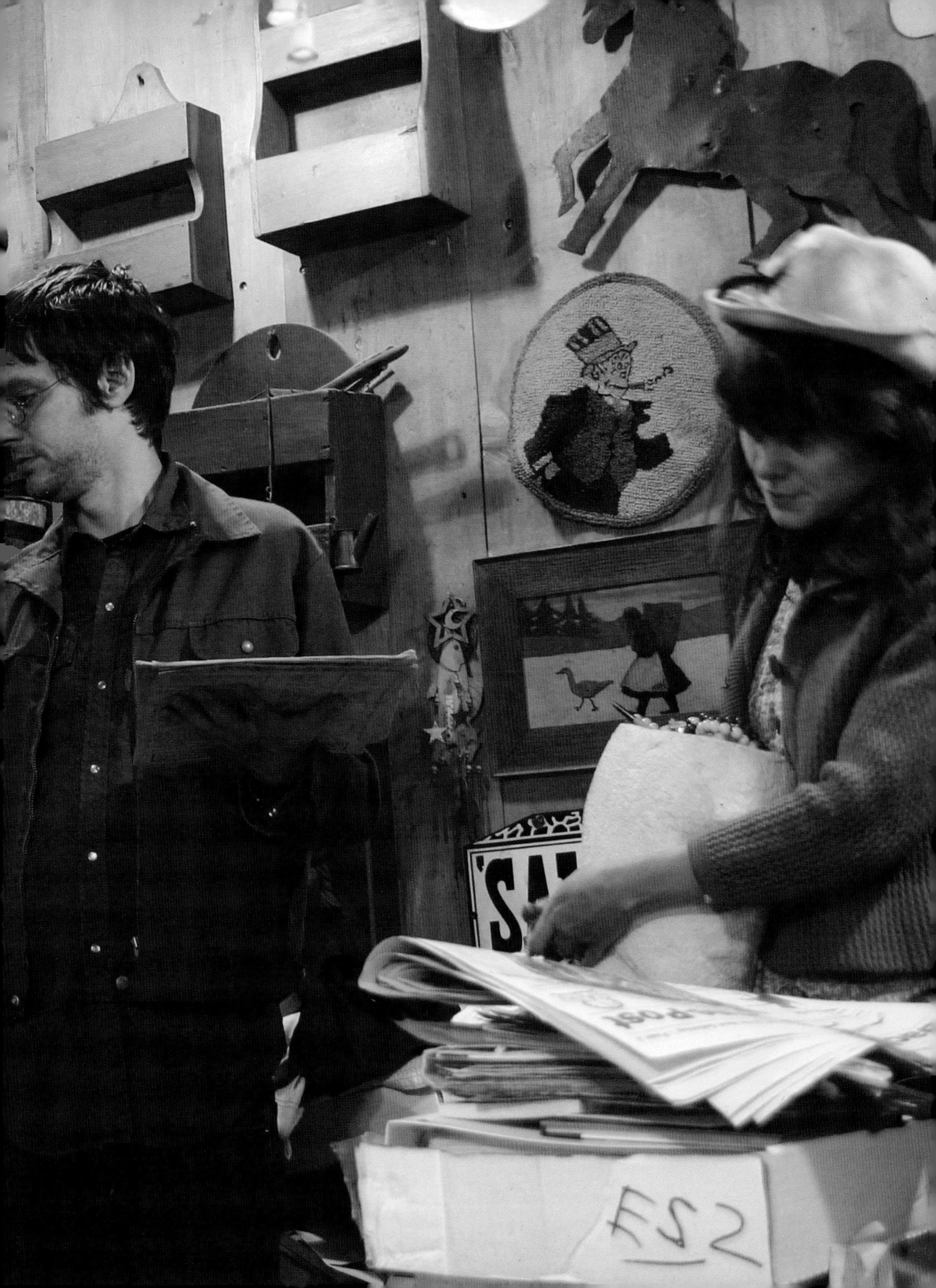
ES2

Who the Hell is *Dirty Debbie?*

by Dirty Debbie

Several weeks ago I was approached by a group of esteemed editors and publishers with a request that I tap out a few words regarding Marco Bell (or, quite simply, The Marco, as in *The* Marco). I assume this task was put to me not for any talent that I might have as a wordsmith; rather, the powers–that–be hoped that I, as a reluctant witness to the many ups and downs in the The Marco's storied career, could provide some insight, some explanation, some way to understand the man.

It is true that I have known The Marco for 15 years. I have seen him pass through many phases and chapters on the way to becoming the man he is today. From absurdist to geopolitical prophet; from his early monk–like aesthetic to his post–fame flamboyance and conspicuous consumption; from angry young iconoclast to amateur metallurgist (including his bizarre and lesser known foray into the world of speculative gold mining). Yet despite having observed this vast and varied life firsthand, I find there is no easy answer to the question: "Who is *The* Marco?"

When I first met The Marco he was just another struggling young artist, like so many of us were in those early troubled times. To say he was down on his luck would be too dramatic; his existence was more unremarkable than anything. He lived in a dilapidated old house with a smattering of other vaguely artistic types. I can still remember the parties, attended by aspiring beardos, aging hippy art teachers and other hangers–on. In the midst of it all there was The Marco: sullen, disheveled, crammed in the corner taking a whiff of the stink and uttering his patented "ew gawd" in a general expression of disdain for the whole affair.

It was around this time that The Marco struck up an instant friendship with a witty young classmate called Dirty Debbie. It was a friendship that ultimately would rescue The Marco from the precipice of artistic irrelevance. And, in retrospect, it becomes clear that the answer to the original question begs another perhaps more important question: "Who the Hell is Dirty Debbie?"

Over the years, many have sniveled at his sometimes nonsensical writings, his yankee–doodle–dandies and scribbles. Time and time again, the proponents of corporate artdom have cast Dirty Debbie aside, favouring the more marketable works of Marco Bell. Only The Marco, ironically, has a true appreciation for the genius of the man in all his unpolished glory. Only The Marco knows that no one has come closer to creating a complete parable for these difficult economic times, indeed for the entirety of the human condition, than Dirty Debs.

Virtually all of The Marco's most engaging concepts have come directly from Dirty Debbie in one fashion or another. *The Birthday Moustache*, a powerful metaphor for these trying times, was of The Debbie's creation. Likewise, the saga of Sweet Powder and Farmer Henry IV was a Dirty Debs original. Monsieur Picklepants? The Debs. Mister Baloney Man And His Picadilly Park Peyote Picnic? Yup, The Debbie. Even The Marco's prophetic best–selling book on the real estate bubble titled *Submitting to Learn from the Crow: How to Swoop in after the Crash* was inspired by Dirty Debbie's own musings on the topic.

There are influences everywhere, from musical side projects (Dirty Debbie founded Blue Pooch in the early 1990s, after which time The Marco fronted the more commercially viable but less interesting Red Bunny…in addition, The Marco sung the lead vocals in *Bogman*, Dirty Debbie's incredibly ambitious rock opera about a Norwegian peasant cast into the bog in the 1500s only to return to life in the 20th century as a beatnik poet) to journalistic concerns (such as Debbie's witty and irreverent column "The Daily Durt," copied by The Marco in his pedestrian broadsheet publication *Who Gives a Fuck Weekly*), to cinematography (such as the Chaplainesque silent feature titled *Man in Blue Suit Pokes at Trash* which starred The Marco but which was conceived and directed by Dirty Debbie), even right down to Marco's patented frown and even his favourite sayings (take for instance "ew gawd" and "get the fug oot," both Marco trademark sayings coined by Debbie).

Despite their longstanding friendship, these days they barely speak. Precisely what lead to the rift is unclear. Much has been written about "The Document." The details aren't exactly clear but it was purported to be some kind of contract or legal paper which Dirty Debbie would not sign, despite The Marco's repeated request. Suffice it to say that this refusal was seen by The Marco as a colossal betrayal. It is speculated that The Marco's obsession with the whole event precipitated his growing tendency to mumble. It has also resulted in his apparent inability to be without his "personal papers" as he calls them. These are, it is supposed, various papers including legal papers and documents of little or no significance, which The Marco carries by his side and which he guards with extreme jealousy. Some of these papers may even be nonsensical writings authored by The Marco himself. Though it can't be confirmed, one unnamed source in The Marco "Inner Circle" claims to have glanced through a scroll–like document called "Hot Potatoe [sic]: The Optional Protocol to the International Convention on the Rights of Thee Honourable Chunky Floors and Hair Farmers," a bizarre quasi–legal treatise created, one assumes, by The Marco in a fit of madness.

The Debs, for his part, has remained tight–lipped about the controversy, and stoic in his own lack of recognition. Rumours abound that the two have been trying to patch up their differences, perhaps even going so far as to complete *Barnyard Beardos*, the much–anticipated follow–up to *Birthday Moustache*. Not incidentally there have also been rumblings that the two might try and finally come to some agreement on how to wrap up their unfinished *magnus opus*, *Sweet Powder Steals an Eggiwegg, or: The Betrayal of Pepites*. We dare to dream.

Whether the two are friends or foes, whether they collaborate anew or remain on opposite sides of the artistic fence, the work they have produced together speaks for itself. And if imitation is the highest form of flattery, this collection serves as a long awaited and much deserved tribute to the myth behind the man: Dirty Debbie.

Facing page: detail of *Notification of Baggage Inspection (Bologna Made Me Lonely And Thin)*, 2005, mixed media on board

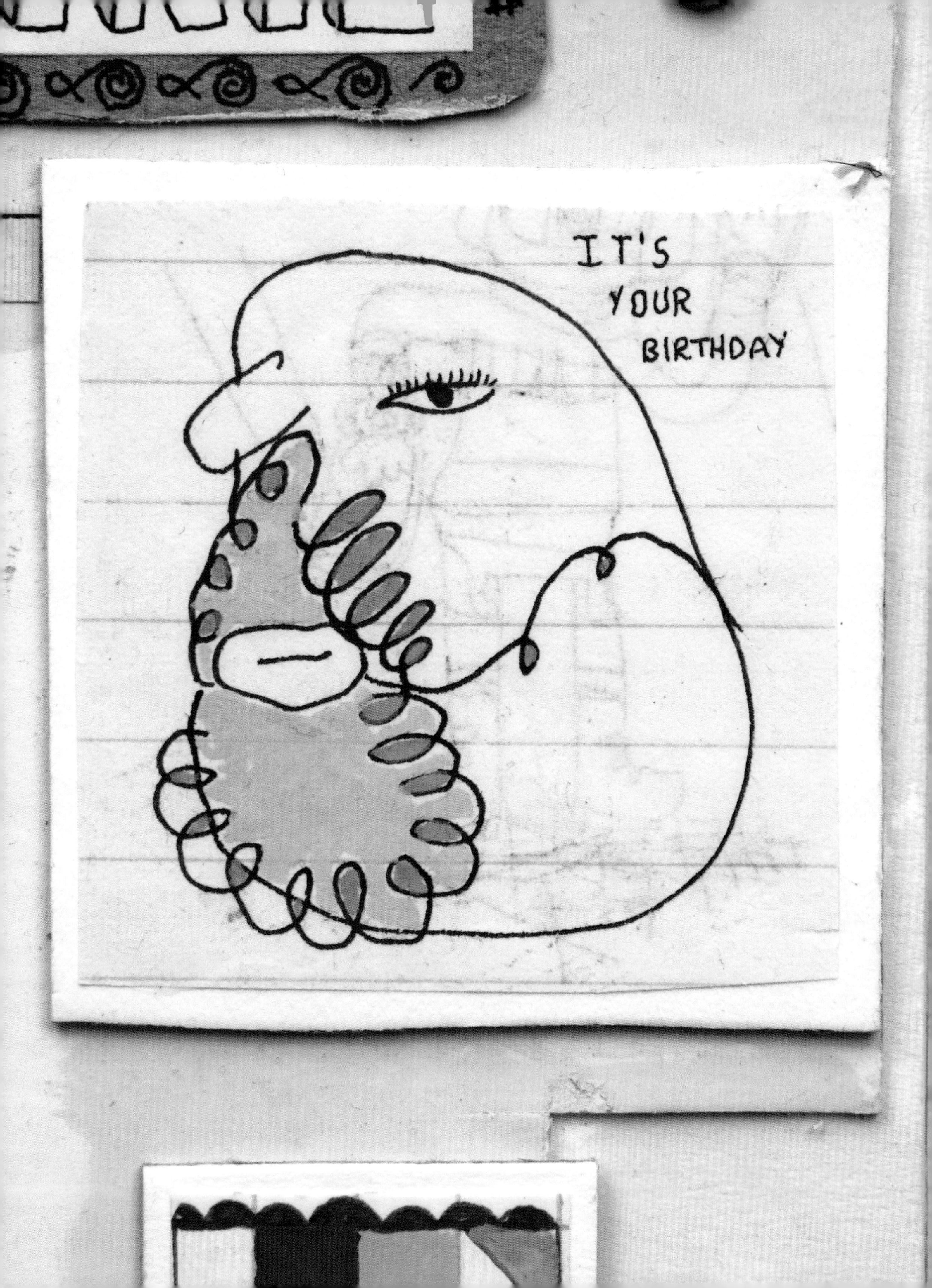
IT'S
YOUR
BIRTHDAY

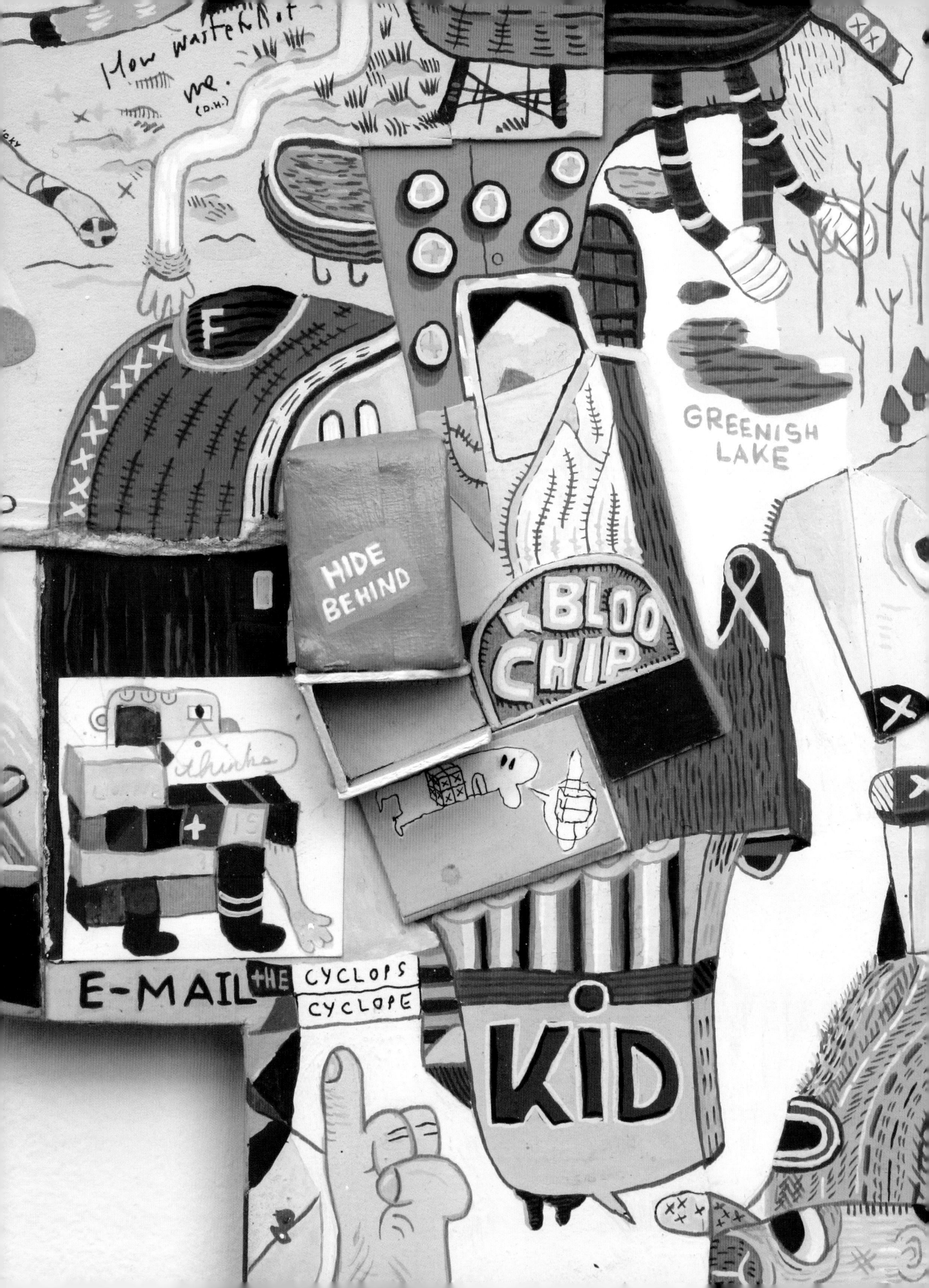
GREENISH LAKE
HIDE BEHIND
BLOO CHIP
E-MAIL
THE
CYCLOPS
CYCLOPE
KID

See You In The Funny Pages
Marc Bell: A *Highly* Organized Guy

by Tommy LaCroix

Former director of The Ministry of Casual Living, a fully accredited, licensed hairdresser, creator of *www.gogxmagog.blogspot.com*

I first became aware of Marc Bell, and his work, when he and I both lived in Vancouver, BC, in the late nineteen–nineties. I knew him and that he drew and made little self–published 'zines, but I didn't pay much attention to any of it. That is, not until one day he showed me a poster he had designed for some sort of film festival or the other. He had some sort of a career in the arts or something, and I figured I had better check it out.

He presented the thing to me and proudly pointed out that I had been included in it. Now my (self) interest was peaked. My inclusion in it was represented simply by a tin can with an arrow pointing to it, like a Chester Gould gimmick, and labeled, clearly, "Tommy." To be honest, it took me aback. I wasn't sure if I should be flattered or not. I mean, this was coming from a guy who I already knew was known to sort of fetishize mentally ill people, so, just what was I supposed to think? He used to hang around with these other similarly perverse artists, Jason Mclean, Owen Plummer, and Shayne Ehman. They spent endless hours at a snack bar in the back of Save–on–Meats right in the heart of the city's infamous skid row district. What was I supposed to think? The very idea of this snack bar was all wrong; I would never eat there. A civilized person would naturally assume it was rock bottom and with dubious sanitary conditions. Eating there was beyond out of the question and strictly for those who could only do no better. It was, in fact, primarily patronized by society's cast–offs, the damaged, and insane. Plus these guys. They sat there all day drinking terrible coffee and soaking up the atmosphere, passing drawings in various states of completion between each other, adding to their combined draughtings. He claimed the hamburger sandwich they served there was actually pretty good, but the very thought of eating it made me sick. Artists and mental illness are often not far from each other, but while I do not share Marc's questionable culinary choices, his work is far too informed to be confused with of the scrawlings of a madman. While an afflicted individual could be found endlessly filling pages with nonsensical scratches, it is doubtful that an organized mind would give them such deftly executed composition, practiced hand and fine degree of finish. Even so, all his work (and he is very prolific) is uniformly absurd. They are fine art but they are also comics. They are supposed to be funny, but what the heck are they about? He covers the things in writing—words and script (from the narrative comic strip tracts, to giant–fonted gibberish exploding all over the page). This becomes the representation, the subject itself, invading the figurative subject matter's space, crowding it inward and out. And what do these words say? Non–sequiturs, phonetical colloquialisms, misspelled, borborigmic glossolalia and fractured onomatopoeia. It opens an insight to drawing as pathology, not so much the workings of a sick mind but the locating of an abstract state within a formal construct. It just looks like a psychotic made it. It's weird with these artists who are so inspired by *Art Brut*. You can't blame them for being inspired. There's so much great work: Martin Ramirez, Henry Darger, Justin Green. It's more of a spirit that it translates through an autonomy that is provided by craft. A D. I. Y. ethic. Even the Naive Artist becomes masterly with constant practicing of his craft.

It is difficult to know where to begin when describing the art of Marc Bell. The work is busy, intricate, detailed to the point of obsession. The subject matter and styles are so diverse, ranging from pure abstraction to finely rendered representationalism, often within the same piece. Abstractions meld into and out of figurative form in trippy fashion. There is text, yet it is a sort of concrete poetry and usually confounds interpretation. One almost has to step back from each piece in order to take in all that goes on. With reference upon reference and new influences around every turn, neat descriptions of Marc's drawings are difficult at best. He is part of an enormously popular school of like artists pursuing a similar post–modern absurdist vision informed by pop culture, comics, and the urban experience. It is almost a type of sociological fragmentation resulting in the distillation of a barrage of stimuli, and appearing like a comic book deconstructed into a postmodern still life meant to represent the actual experience of reading the comics. Certain characteristics, mainly the comic style fine line pen and ink, and the comic tropes that are the language of these images, mark the work. There is an improvisational element to the pictures, but this is designed into the composition, and similarly, collaboration is frequently employed. It always retains integrity. The dedication to the practice of collaboration leads Marc and his cohorts to send works back and forth through the post. A tradition of mail–art, especially that of Ray Johnson, comes into play, and even the work that Marc completes entirely on his own is informed by this. The built up layers of collaged surfaces on his constructions, afterthoughts and revisions, are each a comment on the last. Like the *cliché*—"A difficult job to know when finished"—it becomes painterly.

When I look at Marc's work and try to crack the code behind it, I inevitably begin to imagine the process by which it is made. I can envision him in a little mid–century not–quite ghetto character apartment, not unlike the ones he so often places his scenarios. Detailing away at his things, intense in concentration, filling in every blank space with penned in filigree. He becomes a filter for the city he lives in and any bit of it may come out of his subconscious mind at any time and land directly on the paper. It is almost like a stream of consciousness diary. The world around him as well as the input and ideas of his many collaborators provide him with a bottomless pit of fresh material. This is not to say the work is random or formless. Each piece is intricately composed; he means to cover the entire surface from the outset, I would suppose, because he does. He must build the thing in pieces and make his decisions as he goes along, again like a Jazz Musician improvises. Or a Garage Rock Hippy. Or some crazy Dub Reggae Dude. There's an ideal of structure held in mind as the artist "plays" and the results, no matter the subjects held therein, are fanciful, dancing freak jams. They speak

Previous page: detail of *(Hide Behind) Bloo Chip Kid*, 2005
Mixed media construction (detail)

JCHEERUPP
PYLON
HOWARD PAVILION
VIN
YOU PARANOID FREAK
KNOZE
LORENCE

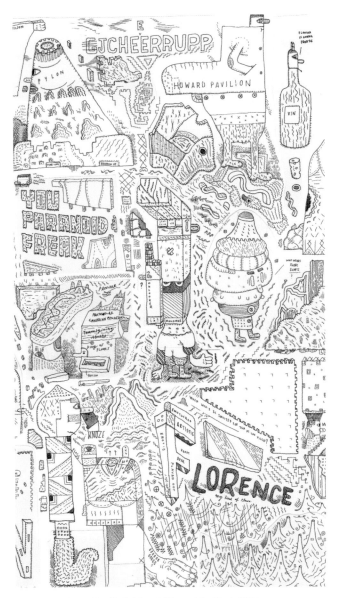

Detail of *Jcheerup (Howard Pavilion)*, 2006
Mixed media on paper

of the surreal. Also like a musician, he has refined his "fills," his "licks," so to speak. Shading a background or the pattern between two forms takes on intricacies and stylistic peculiarities that remind me of a Cool Jazz or Heavy Prog Rock Player's constantly evolving interpretation of a standard, bent and personalized so often that the original all but disappears to make way for the new structure. Of recent, some of Marc's fills are reminding me, a bit, of Miro: cubist lines suggesting space. Sort of like the disintegrating bits of landscape in George Grosz's city views, just the tip of a corner or one angle of a windowpane, criss–crosses and zigzags, but again like Miro with added curlicues and decorative flourishes extending around. These works are definitely informed by fine art masters of the 20th–Century but at the same time there is the combined canons of cartoons, children's illustration, and character logos out of the advertising industry. Then there is the seemingly intentional childishness of the whole vision. It's gentle and playful, full of houses with faces on them and cartoon people with impossible anatomy. Even the crazy words, phonetical jokes, and naughty graffiti come off as silly, facile, kindergartener's word play. They are never mean. And though you will never see an overt joke told in his strips, paintings, drawings, constructions or collages, the gags are piled on so deep the amusement continues to take on new levels the longer you look. They are funny in an inventive way. It is a type of intrigue, which invites the patron for fun and games. He is often compared to Robert Crumb, and there is an unmistakable influence in his line, shading and the textures he draws. There's also the old–fashioned 1920s–30s look to many of the scenes. Characters that appear like twisted Max Fleisher drawings high–step across two–bit rooms, windowpanes reflected in their bugging out eyes. Rubber legs stamping down on floorboards with every wood grain plank and neatly placed cracked lath and plaster drawn in lovingly. Exaggerated lips pucker into a whistle, blowing puffs of steam as giant sweat droplets spring from uncoiling celluloid collars. These gestures, all typical of jazz age comedy, are a huge part of the standard by which cartoonists glean their lexicon. It goes back to R. F. Outcault and his Yellow Kid. There are absurd anachronisms and an overarching jolliness to it all. Cute, innocuous in its way, maybe these drawerers need a title, say: "The New Wimpy"—like Popeye's buddy, ever with clouds of dust puffing out of his heels and every gesture completed with a juicy "splat" noise written above his head. Anywhere else these things could come off as cornball, but in comic art they are tradition. They have formed into a language specific to the medium, and exploited to the degree we see here, they take on a more intense and self–referential commentary. Part of the mechanics and higher meaning of satire.

As in comics, and conversely children's art, everything possible has been anthropomorphized. The trees, buildings, food, dirt, have faces all, and engage in human activities. This pretty much defines what a cartoon is. Look back to Ancient Egypt, to the earliest examples, painted on tombs. A couple of lions play chess. One of them is cheating. It's a bona fide classic! Who'd cheat at chess? Never fails to crack me up. So overabundant are these type of tropes in Marc's visions that he winds up creating this goofy netherworld, this halfway point where the whole universe he creates hangs between both inanimate and sentient. It becomes absurdly neither. He is steeped in the comics and his work embodies so much more than their mere influence. Besides, you should meet the guy. He reminds me a little of a cartoon character himself, something out of a Walter Lantz cartoon, Doobily Doodler or Droopy Drawerer. In his cardigan sweater and "mi–oh my–oh" demeanor, all he is missing is the speech impediment.

Marc tells me that recently he has been very enamored of the work of a group of artists described under the rubric of the Chicago Imagists. Several links can be drawn to his and their careers. The Chicago Imagists worked just outside the accepted circle of high–art New York artists. They practiced in America's "Second City." They worked in a hybrid of painting and illustration, which, while still separated today, were seen as two different, diametrically opposed classes of importance altogether in the art world of the 1950s. After pop art, comics, illustration, and *brut* sensibilities began to gain acceptance in the fine art circles, the two

FOR RENT

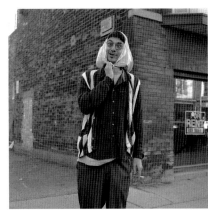

Photo of Marc "Droopy Drawerer" Bell in Toronto, 1997, by Neil Rough

gradually coming together. Yet, illustration still bears some residual historic stigma of being overly populist, too plebian, somewhat beneath "High Art." The Chicago group rebelled against this tyranny and banded together to create a new and fanciful visual language that reflected the experience of modern life. The critic Ken Johnson said they worked in "the post–war tradition of fantasy–based art making." The lines of correlation to Mr. Bell's situation are quite clear. Marc came out of London, ON and spent some later formative time in the East Coast and Vancouver, BC. These Canadian places, both secondary to Toronto, mirror the relationship between "Second Cities" in America, like Chicago, and the art centre of NY. His roots in London, specifically, relate because the group of London artists a generation ahead of Marc: Greg Curnoe, The Nihilist Spasm Band et al, were outside of Toronto, the "high art mecca" on the landscape of the Canadian identity. Because of this, these are some of Marc's historical and cultural forebears.

Marc makes "Fine Art." It is rooted in comic book art, yet crosses that well–worn line. And his work is fantastical. You can say he creates a world with its own well drawn out geographic, but that would be redundant, as are the comparisons to R. Crumb. True, he is in a league with Crumb, and has been influenced, but it's like saying the Stones are influenced by Howlin' Wolf. It is too easy, it is obvious, not a secret, and not necessary to dwell on. It is not even that interesting. They are simply of like mind. However in Marc's case I would probably choose to compare Budgie and Rush as an analogy, because, you know—the Stones—they're gross.

PLASTIC
UNIQUE
ILLUSTRATION BOARD
27
PILLOW
HANDMADE
PREMIUM PLUS
GARBANZO
100% ORGANIC

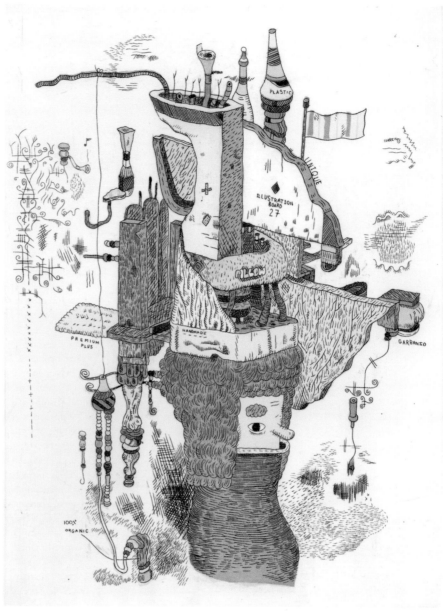

Hers Unique Headwear, 2005
Two colour etching with hand watercolouring, edition of 30

His drawings look like cityscapes, bird's eye views of urban blocks, with avenues and alleyways all bristling with activity. In so many ways his work reminds me of how children draw. They enter the task as an activity, a game. They are filling up time. Then their involvement produces an inner growth of the creative imagination and becomes motive to its own craftsmanship. The drawings flourish and the ideas proliferate. Where to house these myriad things and situations? Buildings opening to reveal their many compartments, apartment blocks and tenement rows, characters and situations framed by every windowsill, city streets populated with all the new follies sketched. The page gets filled, no square inch left undoodled. We see a population explosion in Cartoonland. Much of his work evolves the same way, and he is a busy kid.

Now I'm fishing around endlessly in this junk box of writing trying to come up with some Carny's game–of–chance trick. I'm coming up pretty trinket–less, and, like, I'm not catching no "big muskies." All I'm getting is "consolation prizes." It's the "Fishin' Hole Game" where everyone's a winner. So, cast your magnet on the end of a string, into the greasy tank, and "PLOP!" That's it! The magazine! Basil Wolverton's almost–forgotten legacy, where Mad Magazine SHOULD have progressed. We fall back to the Underground Comics. The heavy pen and ink and "Head" Art of the Sixties.

Within underground comics, primarily those from the 60s and 70s, we begin to see illustration for the comic strip format as an art–object of itself. Rick Griffin's single sheets and panels, devoid of linear meaning, appear as a painterly exercise in black and white. They exist merely for the viewer to have something to stare at when high on drugs. Looked at objectively it is so much about the craft of pen and ink, however what it accomplishes is far greater. It becomes psychedelic. Like something out of Michael Furtado. Stare long enough and you are transported somewhere else, somewhere that exists only in the imagination. You see this in Marc's work as well; the whole page comes into play, the story unfolds in every direction. It's overwhelming, and the little characters inside it proclaim that, too! Their hats pop off their heads, they ejaculate with astonishment, eyebrows wiggle and toes burst forth from crummy old shoes. It is comedy as mimetic chain reaction and the overall nonsensicality makes sense. And it's giddy, goofy, sometimes perplexing, but always in motion. Stoned.

Again, too deep, and I feel overwhelmed. This time, a step back leaves me to consider the overall filled–in–ness of his designs. He must fall in love with his creations, for every little bit of the page is attended to with details and addendums. I would like to see him commit etchings, for the same techniques abound here (see previous page). Go look at Hogarth. Anything from that period. It is early poster art. Satirical, overwrought, and captivating in its ingenuity. They spent so much time on producing the thing that they simply had to fit in as much action as they could; just to get their, and your, money's worth. These are things you are meant to buy and spend a lot of time with, just like any good art. Self published, easily obtainable editions, today's art 'zine is akin to the etchings of Georgian England. Also, *Head Comics* of the 1960s. Similar as well is the extent of the further hilarity upon hilarity, revealed with novelty, more so even, upon deeper and prolonged inspection. But there you go. References. You might as well reference a computer store that gave you shitty service (no. 119) or "The Space Channel" (no. 21). Take a wild shot, Already Been Chewed gum, stinky socks, how about "Mammy's home cookin'?" It's probably in there too…somewhere. As long as it's spelled wrong—the sky's the limit! You could shut your eyes and stick a pin in a retarded version of Funk & Wagnall's. Go ahead, get mad! What are you going to do? Grab the little guy by his skinny arm and force coherence out of him? It won't work! I've tried. I need cogence. I want semiotic normalcy. But, I'm fucked. At the end of the day it matters not. Because ol' Marco is doing what is expected of him, he is doing the job of an artist. He takes in the world, digests it, and regurgitates the truth of it all out as something to which is his own, yet to which any viewer can relate. I think. Actually, now, I'm confused. Maybe that's the Artist's job…to be giving me a headache.

GUSTON
BLUEBERRY JUICE
MOLECULE
ARMS

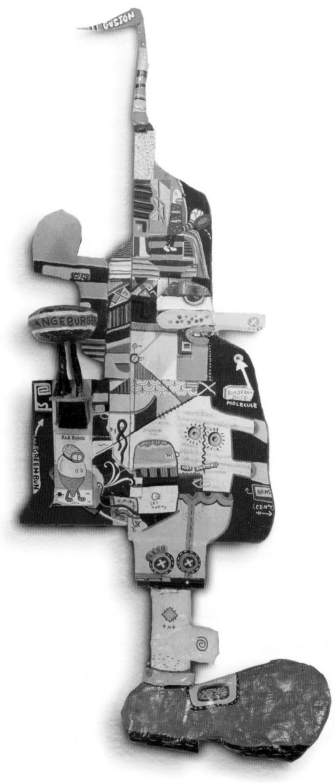

Blueberry Juice Molecule (Guston), 2003
Mixed media construction

All these ramblings bring me back to another illustrative anecdote relating to my relationship with Marc, the man. I was standing, yet again, in front of the previously mentioned Save–on–Meats market. Looking up at the signage, seeing the mascot (flying dollar bills and winged pig leaping not over the moon but through actual Jupiter's own rings) I flash back on the many faces of this acquaintanceship we have forged. Through the years I have seen many faces of Marc Bell the Artist. His hobbling hobo man in Dirty Debbie's super 8 movie *Man in Blue Suit Pokes at Trash*, his participation in the All–Star Schnauzer Band's International Waffle Day Parades in Vancouver and his current, more introverted, activity. But our fortunes have traveled different roads. I see him, like horseshit used to be, all over the place. He is always friendly and responsive, but I am afraid I have become not much so. I'm standing there in front of Save–on and I'm thinking about the irony. For, before, I would make fun of him for choosing to eat there. Only now, I only wish I was able to. I have gone crazy from alcoholism and crack, and am starving, at the brink of ruin, wishing I had something to eat, eyeing a half–eaten portion of a pogo corn–dog resting temptingly on top of the public garbage can. I'm dirty with filth and am wearing the same black satin funeral dress and ratty child's wig that has become my permanent costume of late. No shoes. I'm so fucked on crack and bent on partying that I've adopted the persona of a Sicilian widow to camouflage how fucked up I really am. It isn't working on most of the population, but Marc is no guy to judge. He's nice to me anyway. Around the time of all this I had been trying to self–publish my methamphetamine journals, and he was flatly, totally supportive. I expected people to want to punch me in the face for what I was trying to say in my little zines, but not old Marco Bello. He would always point me in the direction of the zine swap meets that he would be involved in. I was included just on his recommend. That means a lot to me now, but back then it mostly confused me. I would still attend. I did appreciate meets that he would be involved in. I was included just on his recommend. That means a lot to me now, but back then it mostly confused me. I would still attend. I did appreciate the opportunity to disseminate my mental illness. I guess my motives were kind of attention deficit anxieties or something. Like I said, by now I had turned into a full–blown crackhead and things were no longer as they seemed. He and Jason were the organizers and he told me to go to this thing.

I got it together especially for this important zine fair. It was to take place at an underground tranny bar that was attached to a bathhouse, Ms. T's Cabaret. I believe it has since burned down, but it was sideways and I loved going there. The thing about tranny bars is that they don't mind if you're really fucked up; they even make more sense that way and are more fun if you are. I made special resolutions and was determined to attend this event, even going so far as to plan, execute, and debut a special full–colour edition of a new title for the occasion. I had made what I believed to be so profane a story that it defied written language and had morphed into entirely meta–visual representation. It was called *The Beauty of Life*. Like I said, I had kind of lost my mind by this point.

So anyway, I make sure to put aside enough change from my welfare check to get to this thing and get my drink on, and its right after welfare day, so I'm cool. I've got a bit of money, and maybe people will buy this cheaply produced, overpriced booklet I've made. Micro Economics in action.

It's the night of the bookfair, which is downtown, so I get on the bus in my ragged dress, filthy wig and bare feet, and I'm shining, holding the public at bay, anxious to get there. On the #22 Downtown there's this jabbering shit–eyed drunk, coarse and caustic, a total goof. He's harassing a pair of young girls. If there's anything a fucking loser can't stand it's the sight of another, bigger, fucking loser, beaking off and bringing everybody down. Especially to ladies. This asshole was gooned, stinking drunk and being particularly disgusting and lewd to these two teenaged girls. I'm standing at the back doors, hanging onto the pole glaring at him. I see a bottle sticking out of his shirt as he hovers over the girls, grinding his crotch at them and drooling obscenities as well as actual drool. The bottle is 26 oz. and nearly full. It's my stop now, and as he wavers stupidly and the bus pulls up I move into action. I yank the bottle free and mad dash out the door and down the block. Liberation. I can hear the whole bus cheer as it pulls away, the wino's groaning defeat clownishly drowned away.

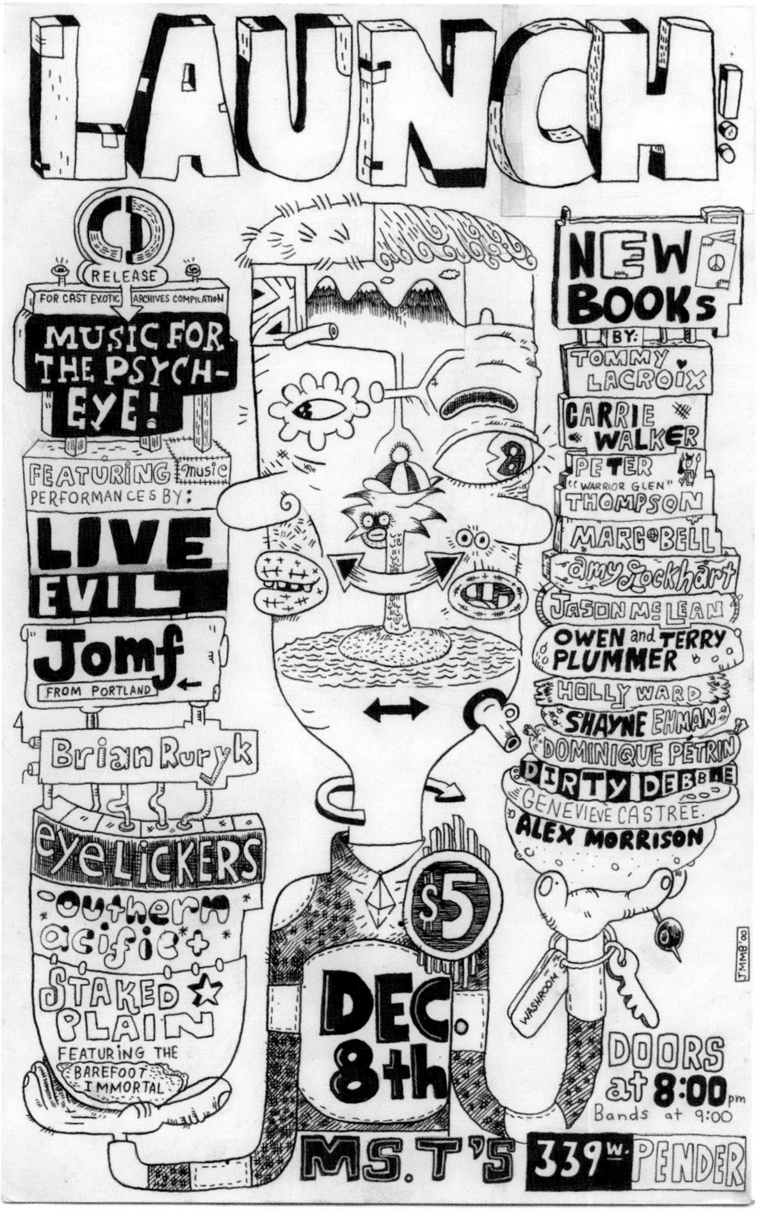

LAUNCH!
RELEASE
FOR CAST EXOTIC ARCHIVES COMPILATION
MUSIC FOR THE PSYCH-EYE!
FEATURING music
PERFORMANCES BY:
LIVE EVIL
Jomf
FROM PORTLAND
Brian Ruryk
eyelickers
STAKED PLAIN
FEATURING THE BAREFOOT IMMORTAL
NEW BOOKS
BY:
TOMMY LACROIX
CARRIE WALKER
PETER "WARRIOR GLEN" THOMPSON
MARC BELL
amy Lockhart
JASON MCLEAN
OWEN and TERRY PLUMMER
HOLLY WARD
SHAYNE EHMAN
DOMINIQUE PÉTRIN
DIRTY DEBBIE
GENEVIEVE CASTREE
ALEX MORRISON
$5
DEC. 8th
WASHROOM
DOORS at 8:00pm
Bands at 9:00
MS. T'S 339 W. PENDER

Poster design for book launch at Ms. T's Cabaret by Bell and Jason Mclean, 2000

Now I had a 26er of Rum! Libations! I celebrated right then and there by starting to drink it on the street before proceeding to sneak it into the club, then commencing to sneak it into empty glasses, surreptitiously at first, but then pretty quickly, not hardly bothering to sneak it at all, until the last thing I remember is just swilling away at the jug right in front of the staff, laughing and spinning around before collapsing between the back wall and the pinball machine that stood in the corner there. Bally's Fembot pounding into my brains until I blacked out. The whole thing, if I had to describe it, would be like one of Marc's drawings. A shattering cacophony of disintegrating fragments and bent socio–cultural signifiers, flying around my head like so many stars and planets, and my head itself comprised of a pile of old credenzas and dressers, drawers yawning open, barfing wet garbage, oozing submarine sandwiches, etc. Marc—he throws a good party. The ancient queen bartender roused me, literally, from under a table hours later. It was after closing and nobody else was there. The flashing lights weren't so rosy anymore. They were fucking grim.

Of course, that is a part of it…the world is a confusing place. Too much is going on. Really the only way to accept it, the only way to be at peace with it, the only way to enjoy it, to thrive in it, is to laugh. Laugh or start crying. However, if you do choose to bawl, you may just become another hapless, ridiculous, only semi–human caricature. A one–legged head on a pair of dungarees, the bastard child of Philip Guston's Rudimentary Man and Richard Scarry's Lowly Worm. Squirting out obscene, gigantic crocodile tears, a concentrated idea of what "cry–baby" might mean. Weeping, alone, and without an umbrella (or snowsuit.) There is the threat! Look too close and you just might recognize your own personal satire of your own human condition. The ol' switch–er–oo.

"Big smoked fingers wave, come hither…come hither…"

—Don Van Vliet

Hello, Is Peter Gabriel There?

An Overview of Recurring Memes and Utterances in the Marc Bell Oeuvre

by Dr. Lulu Peabody–Sherman

Puddington Scholar and Red Bull Keynote Speaker

For initiates to the movement within Canadian art circles loosely dubbed "psychedoolia," some of the prevailing tropes in Marc Bell's catalogue probably seem commonplace and even strangely comforting. His manifold bunscapes and intricately networked ecosystems are generously rendered if circuitous, and the jocular non–sequiturs and calculated misspellings that comprise his shambolic "prose" are disarming and, dare I say, sweet. To an outsider however, the labyrinthine topographies and bacon worlds that unfold within Bell's "fine ahtwerks" can seem impenetrable. Congested with a recurring cast of characters, themes and exhortations that flummox and taunt with their apparent detachment from everything, Bell's werk hints at a plethora of subterranean plots while simultaneously resisting affiliation with conventional narrative methodologies. "Aug Bullion." "Flug Tag." "Gnee–O–Gneppotism." "Foistoid." Surely, or as Bell might say "verily," such otherworldly vernacular must be aligned with some esoteric allegorical tradition...but then again, maybe not. Perhaps, if I may appropriate an obsolete Bell–ism, the artwerks are mere "Theatre Absurd–O,"[1] turbulent visual diatribes that dazzle and engross, but, like a "bespoke Brazilian suit covered in gorgeously skewed circus mirrors," serve ultimately to obscure meaning or distract from a dearth thereof.[2] It might also be suggested that by leaving certain key questions unanswered (Who wears the white denim? Is Peter Gabriel there?), Bell promulgates a series of absurd riddles far more central to his werk than any conclusive "answers." As an an avowed admirer of Bell's compositional acumen and a generally sensible person, I refuse to subscribe to this *reductio ad absurdum*. Thus, at risk of giving away the answers to the sixty–four–thousand–dollar–questions at the crux of this puzzling but rewarding werk, let's dive into some of the dominant motifs and quotations in *Hot Potatoe*. We may even find out whether the elusive Peter Gabriel is indeed "there."

Constructions With Paper Cups: Continental Stone World, Hot Bun Parachute, Gravy World & Friends

The predominance of stupid paper cups on shelves in Bell's mixed media construction is impossible to ignore, and no appraisal of his werk should overlook this important recurring theme. One might speculate that Bell is simply an artist who really enjoys his soft drinks, and this assessment would be fair, but I'm afraid it would only scratch the surface of Bell's elaborate relationship with take–away beverages. The branding strategies and allusions to companies real and imagined that populate the surfaces of these crudely rendered cups are what really stand out here, and in my estimation, are what distinguish these constructions from lesser works in the sub–genre (see M. P. Soucie's *Fresca? Moi?*).[3] "Continental Stone World" (detail, right) is an actual business on Venables Street in Vancouver B.C that presumably sells "stone" to clients across the continent, and is, according to my British colleague and self–styled Bell expert Morris Twance–Morris, "a place Marc would often scoot by in a stolen electric wheelchair when he lived in Vancouver."[4] "Hot Bun Parachute" (no. 10) is a prototype for a restaurant conceived by Bell and some of his Vancouver colleagues wherein sandwiches would be shot from small overhead cannons inside the establishment and float to assigned tables attached to small parachutes. Bell is currently involved in discussions with the Brazilian government, which has asked him to set up a modular, outdoor Hot Bun Parachute in Sao Paulo's Ibirapuera Park, its second biggest, but most relevant public space. "Gravy World" (no. 8, p. 199) is a fictional theme park, originally conceived by Bell in conjunction with Toronto architectural firm Tripp, Thompson and Tripp. Although plans for its construction were halted due to interference from the Toronto Board of Health, Bell continued to include "Gravy World" in his werk and may very well do so again. You never know.[5]

FRAGILE
C/O ARTHUR SELENT
MAPLE
CANADA
ALSO AVAILABLE
SMALL JOBS ?????
-3778
GREEN BUN
CANAD-IAN AZTEC
CONTINENTAL
STONE WORLD

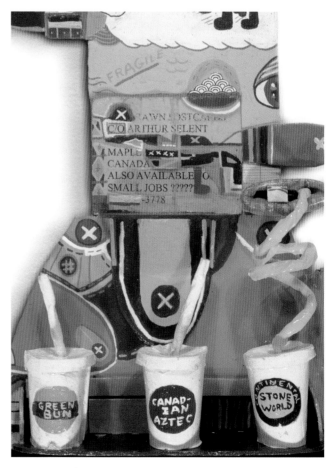

Detail of *Greenbun, Canadian Aztec, Continental Stone World,* 2003
Mixed media construction

Bloo Chip

A misspelled reference to the most expensive chip in poker and to the stocks of companies with stable earnings and no extensive liabilities, the "Bloo Chip" figures prominently in Bell's werk and symbolizes his growing obsession with the effects of indifferent market forces on the art and real estate worlds. As an artist known more for his peculiar spelling of pants (ponts) than for his ability to fuse diamonds to human skulls and sell the end product to hedge–fund managers and Sheiks, Bell's concern seems warranted in light of today's precarious economic climate. Diagnosing the speculative buying frenzy that occurred during Vancouver's real estate boom as an early symptom of worldwide economic collapse, Bell once exclaimed "the Bloo Chips fell" (no. 117). When the economy did indeed lapse into decline, Bell was hailed as a soothsayer, but only by three people, one of whom was my sycophantic British colleague, Morris Twance–Morris. The others were the professional American skateboarder known as Sean the Humpback Whale Poodlesnake and a ticket scalping vagabond known only as "Barb Rouge."[6] *Bloo Chip*, appropriately, is also the title of Bell's second solo show at the Adam Baumgold Gallery in New York's Upper East Side, a neighborhood that houses numerous "blue–chip" galleries and consequently, numerous designer cupcake shops.

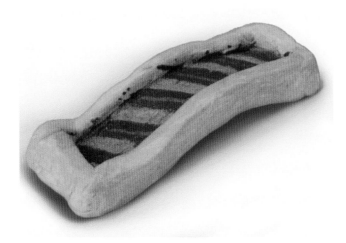

Piece Of Bacon, 2007, paint and oven–baked Sculpey

Bacon & Waffles (Marc Bell's Werk is the Most Transubstantiated Meal of the Day)

The importance of bacon in any worthwhile discussion of Bell's werk has been probed ad–nauseum, and while its significance and prevalence is crucial, I would be remiss if I did not first examine the aesthetic and mutative properties of the slabs themselves. Three–dimensional and chunky, Bell's trademark bacon defies formal expectations, shifting its physiognomy to suit the composition at hand. Bacon is employed as a bridge, as asphalt, and, frequently, as a component in the headgear of "Balsam Adhesives Guy" (no. 32). It can mimic a simple textile or swoop through the arteries of a drawing like a magic carpet. It can also be nailed to your Knoze.[7] In fact, Bell's bacon rarely behaves like proper bacon at all. In typically evasive fashion, Bell had only this to say about the matter: "I came up with a way to draw bacon that interested me and so I started to repeat it. It looks like an abstracted, boxy form of bacon." Indeed. So, while bacon seems to be a relatively new stylistic device, making its début in 2005, the waffle's place in the Bell canon can be traced back to the early 90s, when the first posters for the All–Star Schnauzer Band were assembled. Waffles were a go–to visual element as Bell, assuming the identity of "On/Off Schnauzer," and Jason McLean as "Libby Schnauzer" struggled to promote their semi–legendary semi–band. Since then, Bell's waffles have evolved steadily, undergoing a crispy, golden–brown series of transmogrifications and appearing, often alongside bacon, in situations that leave normative perceptions of wafflehood in the dust. Says Bell: "I do like the look and shape of waffles." Enough said.

Dear G.P. esq.
I TALKED TO THE
G.D.P.
IT WANTED TO
SET UP A MOVIE
SET OUTSIDE
MY DOOR
(OUTSIDE MY DOOR)
MORE SPECIFICALLY:
UH, THEY
I WUZ A BEELEVER IN GNOSTIC PIZZA PAJAMAS TILL THE PEPPERONI KILLED ME WITH THE BEER ELEVATOR
KING OF PIZZA
TURF
PETE WAS THERE, ON THE NEXT PAGE OR (THE PREVIOUS ONE)
PITZA
WOOL/ACRYLIC BLEND

Detail of *August 10th to: Gnostic Pizza Esq.,* 2006
Ink and watercolour on paper

Gnostic Pizza & Egypt Buncake

Not to be confused with Donald Petrie's 1988 film *Mystic Pizza* starring Annabeth Gish, Julia Roberts and a young Vincent D'Onofrio as Bill, the term "Gnostic Pizza" punctuates no fewer than 3 seminal Bell pieces and adds to an already relentless barrage of scrumptiousness in his body of werk. Yet another example of Bell's provisional experiments with fictitious restaurants, "Gnostic Pizza" appears on the label of a soda–pop cup in Bell's mixed media construction *Koff (Japan)* (no. 7). It seems apropos to mention here that Bell workshops thousands upon thousands of these counterfeit eating establishments, but does not consider one "ready for the big show" until it appears on a cup in a mixed media creation. Among these "restaurants," "Gnostic Pizza" is remarkable for its versatility, making prominent appearances in less overtly food–oriented contexts. The drawing, *Aug. 10th to: Gnostic Pizza Esq.* (no. 97) for instance, states abstrusely, "I wuz a beleever in Gnostic Pizza Pajamas till the pepperoni killed me with the beer elevator." This quotation is ludicrous but epigrammatic, not only for its bold re–branding of "Gnostic Pizza" as a type of pajama that one might believe in, but also for its allusion to "Beer Elevator," which is currently the operative title of Bell's unfinished, semi–autobiographical screenplay.[8] A reference to the sequel *Beer Elevator II* can be found in *Egypt Buncake (Lazer Illustration Board)* (no. 21).

Of course, it is almost impossible to grasp the full significance of "Gnostic Pizza" without careful scrutiny of its close relative, "Egypt Buncake." These two recurring leitmotifs are inextricably linked due to confusion that arose when Bell was naming his third solo show. Leaning heavily toward "Gnostic Pizza" as a title for the show, Bell was asked whether this was in fact an homage to the aforementioned Donald Petrie film. Unfamiliar with the film, but "quite frankly, vexed" by the suggestion, Bell turned his back on "Gnostic Pizza," opting for the *(continued on p. 140)*

UNDER THIS DESTRUCTION, SCIENCE AND GOV'T SEEMED TO FLOURISH.
"LIFE'S RICH VARIETY" WAS IMPLEMENTED
GET BACK TO THE STANDARD
SCIENCE DEVELOPED
EVERYTHING HAS FEET. HAVE YOU EVER SEEN ANYTHING WITHOUT FEET ?
AGAINST MR. DUCK
the DESTRUCTION SUBSIDED AS the IBUDS DISCOVERED NEW WAYS to

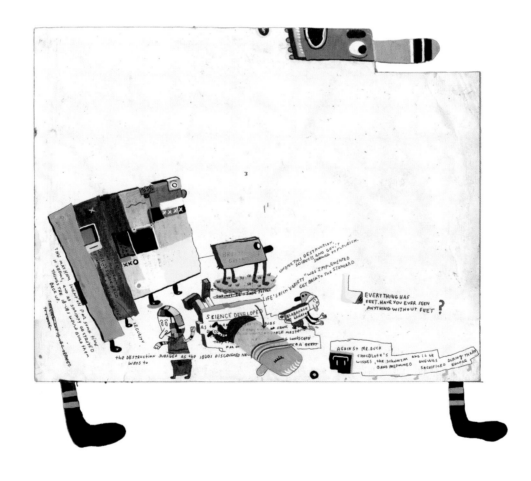

1. *Everything Has Feet,* 2003
Mixed media on board, 10 x 11-½ x ¾ in.

MIXED MEDIA
WERKS

AND MIXED MEDIA
CONSTRUCTIONS

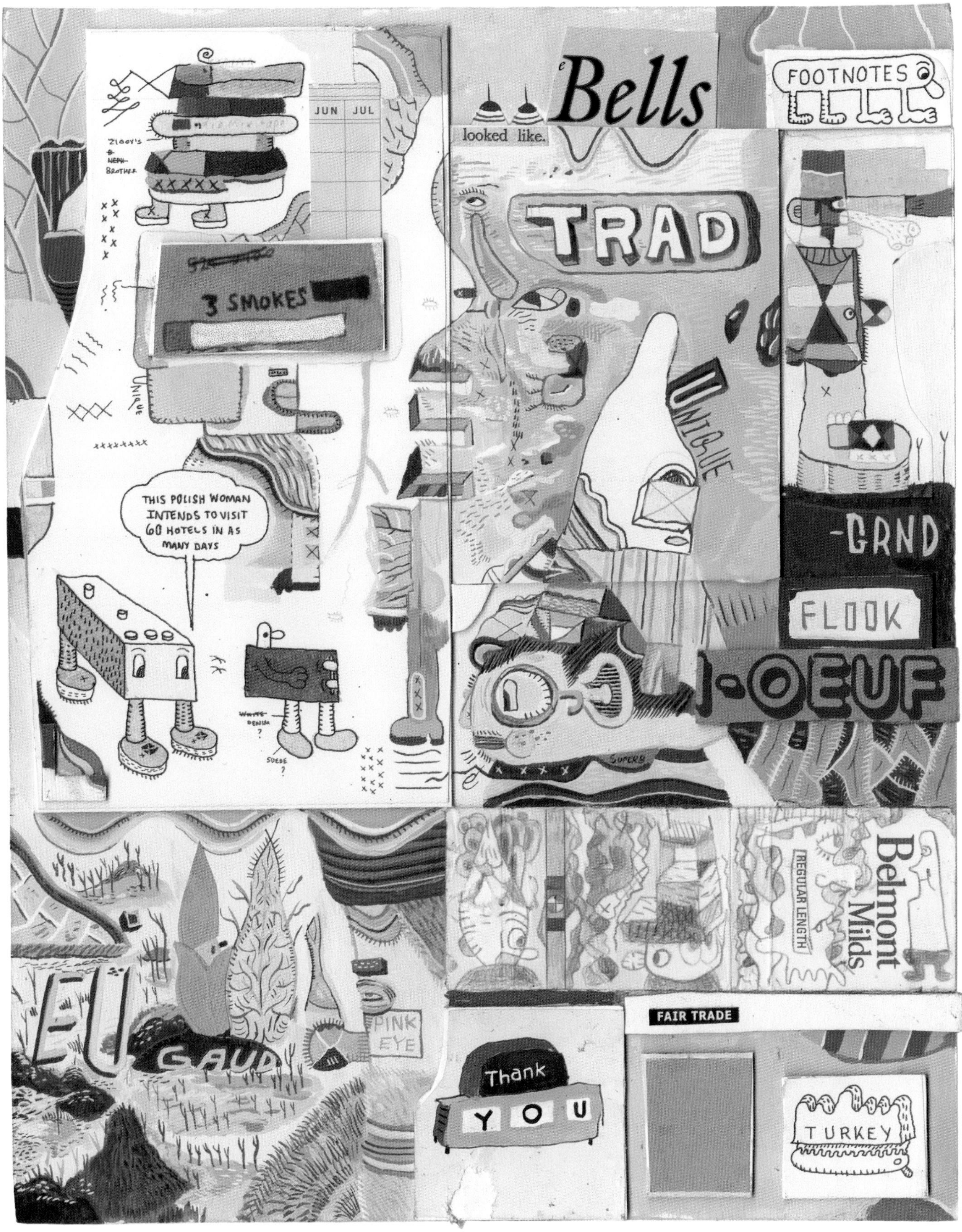

JUN
JUL
3 SMOKES
THIS POLISH WOMAN INTENDS TO VISIT 60 HOTELS IN AS MANY DAYS
UNIQUE
Bells
looked like.
FOOTNOTES
TRAD
UNIQUE
-GRND
FLOOK
-OEUF
GAUD
PINK EYE
Belmont Milds
REGULAR LENGTH
FAIR TRADE
Thank
YOU
TURKEY

2. *Bell's Trad (Looked Like),* 2005
Mixed media on board, 10 x 8 in.
Includes: "3 smokes" ink jet scrap, egg carton clipping and Belmont Milds matchbook

3. *Trad Gold,* 2005
Mixed media on reverse of sketchbook cover, 11–⅛ x 8–⅛ in.
Includes: segment of acrylic paint box

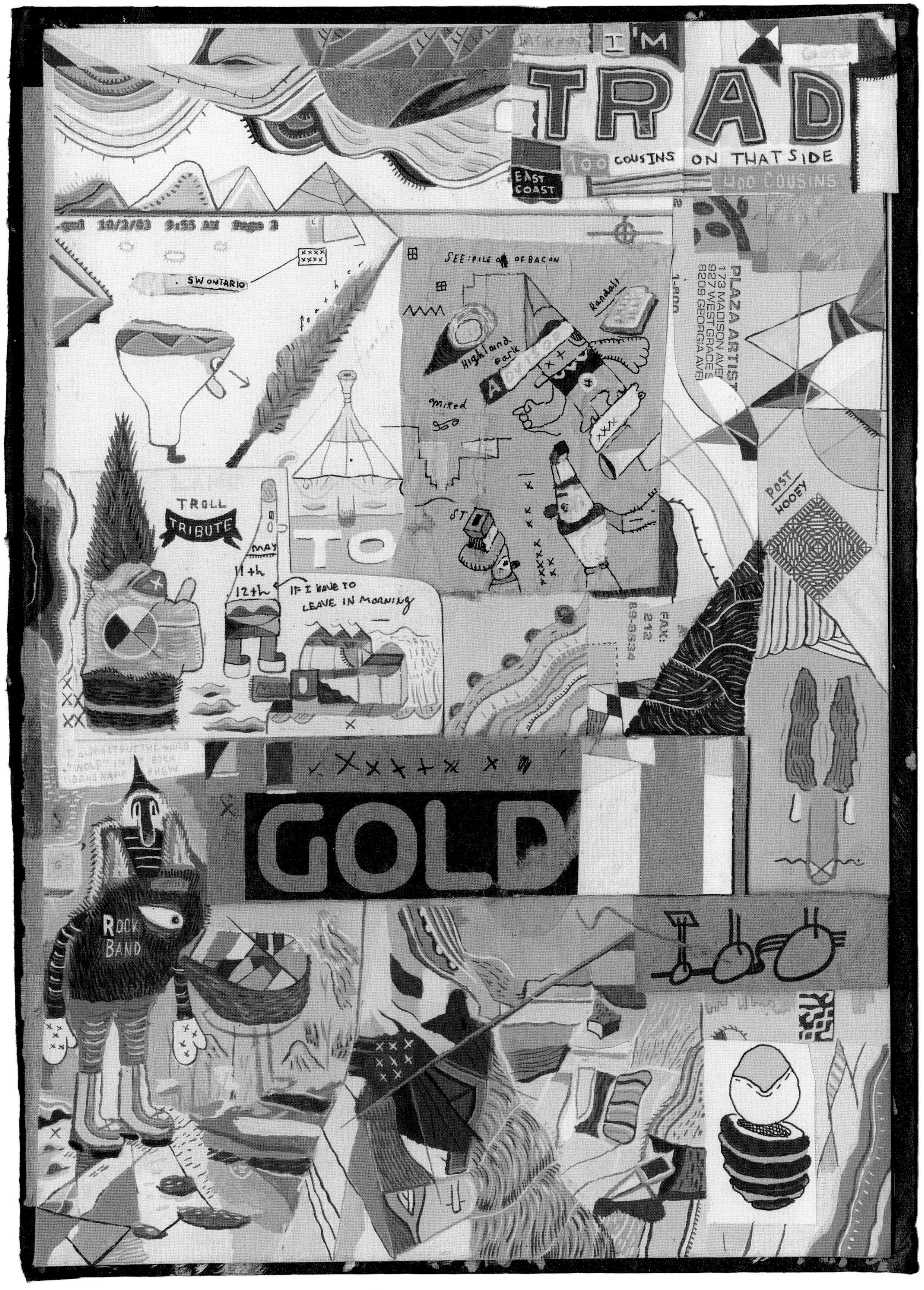
JACKPOT
I'M
TRAD
100 COUSINS ON THAT SIDE
EAST COAST
400 COUSINS
.qxd 10/2/03 9:55 AM Page 2
SW ONTARIO
feather
SEE: PILE OF BACON
Randall
Highland park
ADVISOR
mixed
PLAZA ARTIST
173 MADISON AVE
927 WEST GRACE S
8209 GEORGIA AVE
1-800
LAME
TROLL
TRIBUTE
MAY
11th
12th
IF I HAVE TO
LEAVE IN MORNING
TO
FAX:
212
POST
HOOEY
GOLD
ROCK
BAND

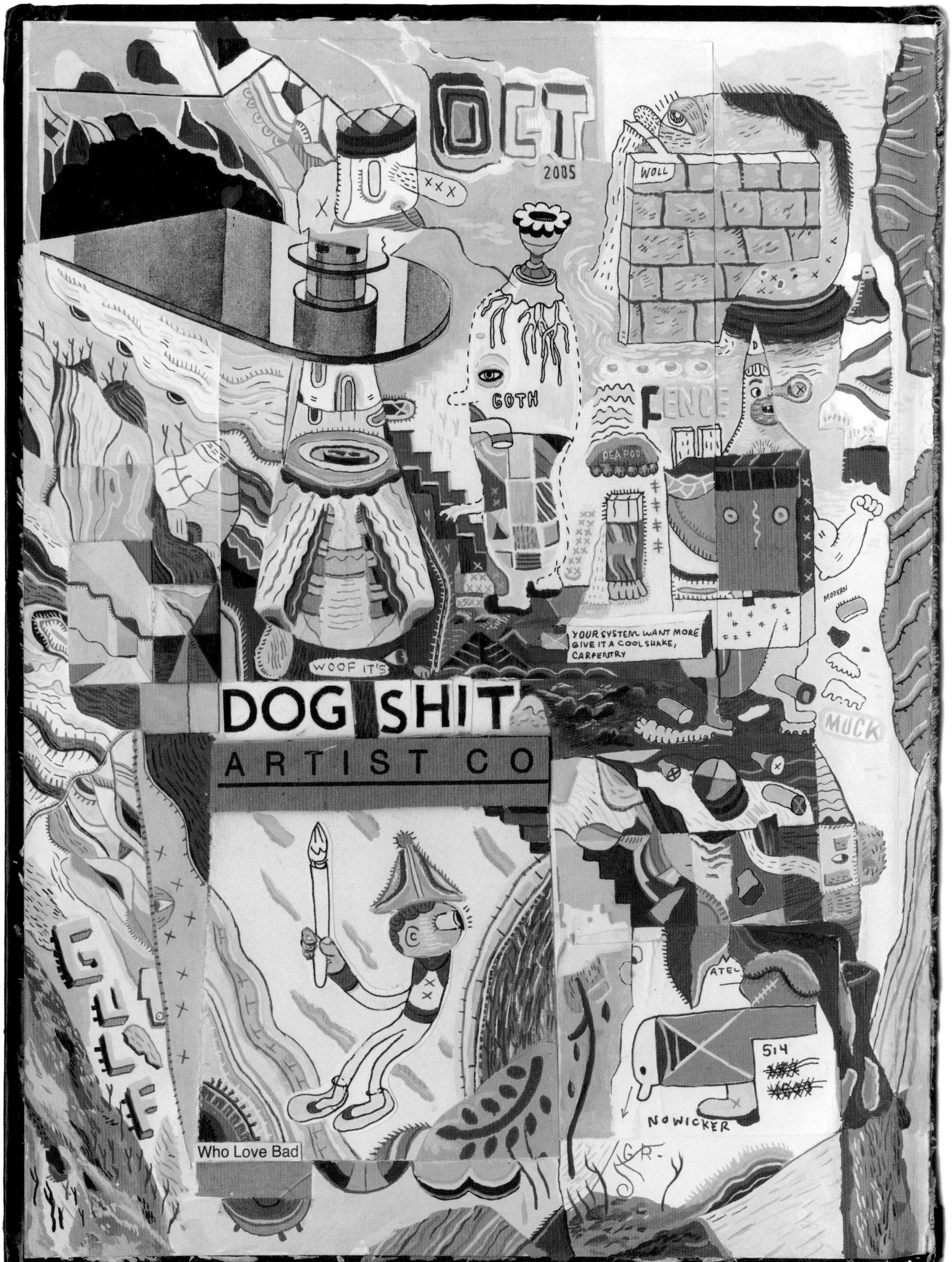
OCT
2005
WOLL
GOTH
FENCE
PEAPOD
YOUR SYSTEM WANT MORE
GIVE IT A COOL SHAKE,
CARPENTRY
MODERN
MUCK
WOOF IT'S
DOG SHIT
ARTIST CO
ATEL
514
NOWICKER
Who Love Bad
G.R.

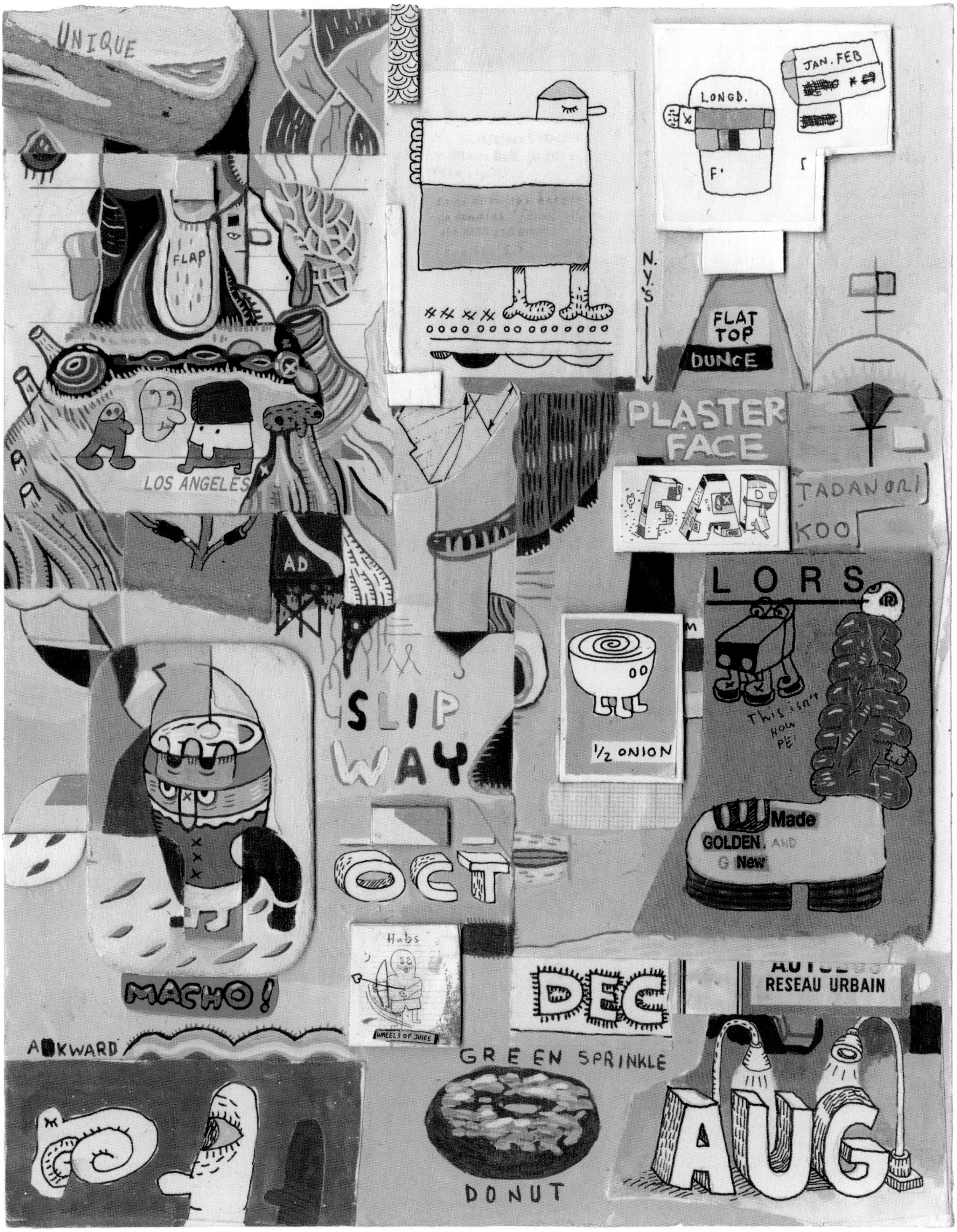
UNIQUE
FLAP
LOS ANGELES
AD
LONGD.
JAN. FEB
N.Y.'S
FLAT TOP
DUNCE
PLASTER FACE
FAR
TADANORI
KOO
LORS
SLIP
WAY
1/2 ONION
Made
GOLDEN. AND
New
OCT
MACHO!
Habs
WHEELS OF JUICE
DEC
RESEAU URBAIN
GREEN SPRINKLE
DONUT
AUG

4. *(Woof It's) Dog Shit Artist Co.*, 2005
Mixed media on reverse of sketchbook cover, 11–½ x 8–½ in.
Includes: segment of acrylic paint box

5. *Plaster Face (Far Tadanori Koo Lors)*, 2005
Mixed media on board, 10 x 8 in.
Includes: Wheels Of Juice reference, segment of acrylic paint box

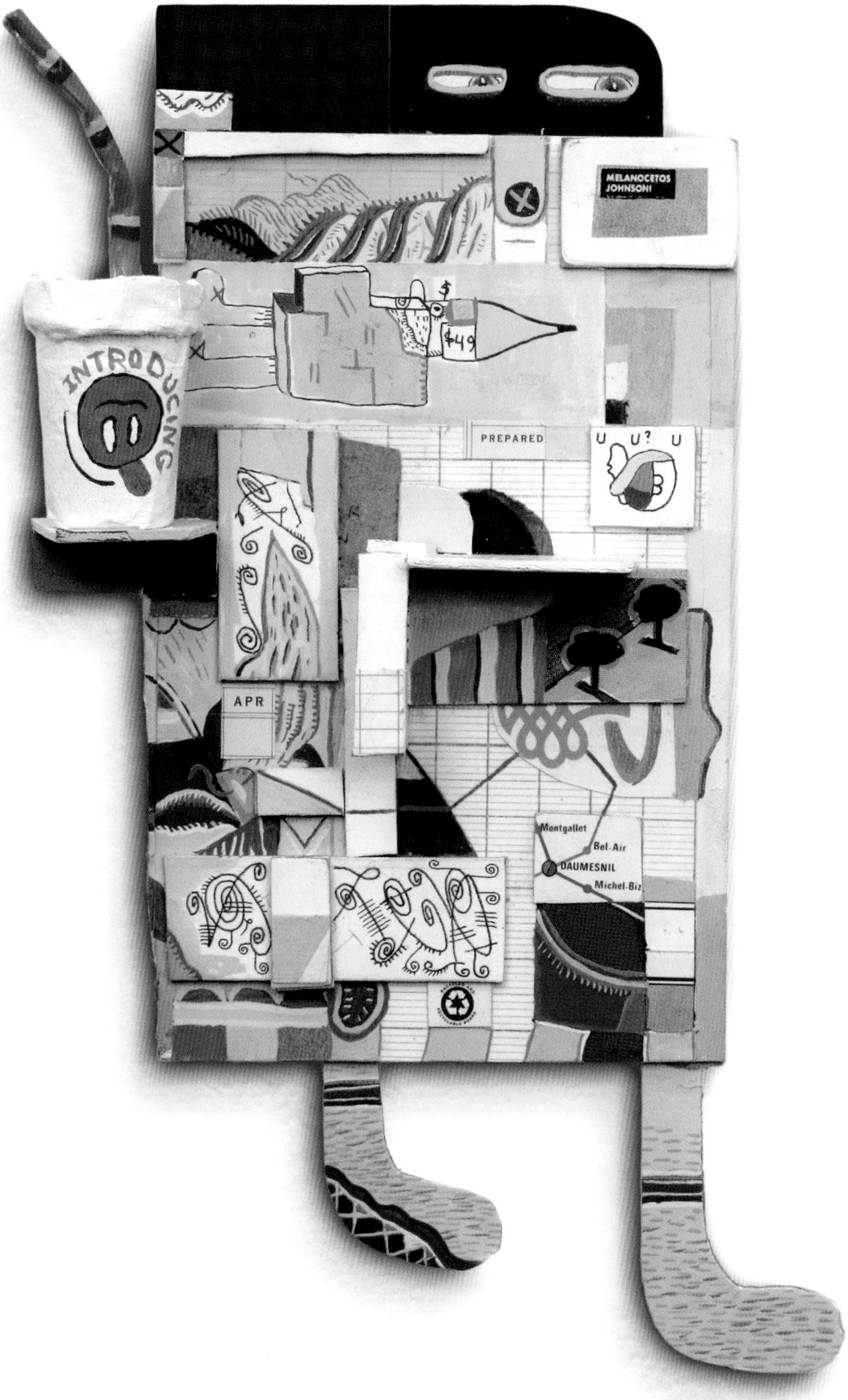
MELANOCETOS
JOHNSONI
$49
INTRODUCING
PREPARED
U U? U
APR
Montgallet
Bel-Air
DAUMESNIL
Michel-Biz

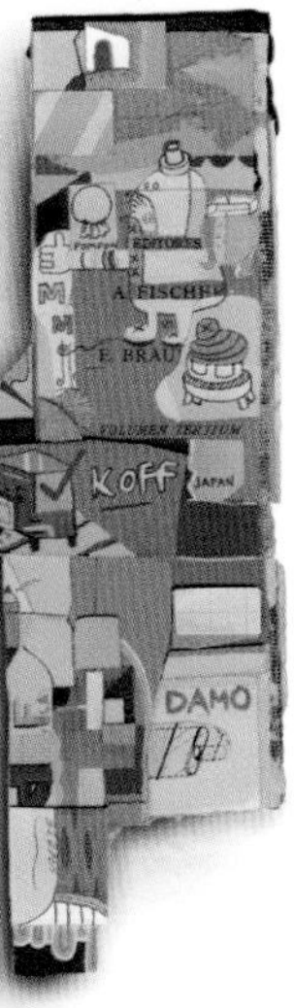
A. FISCHER
E. BRAU
VOLUMEN TERTIUM
KOFF
JAPAN
DAMO

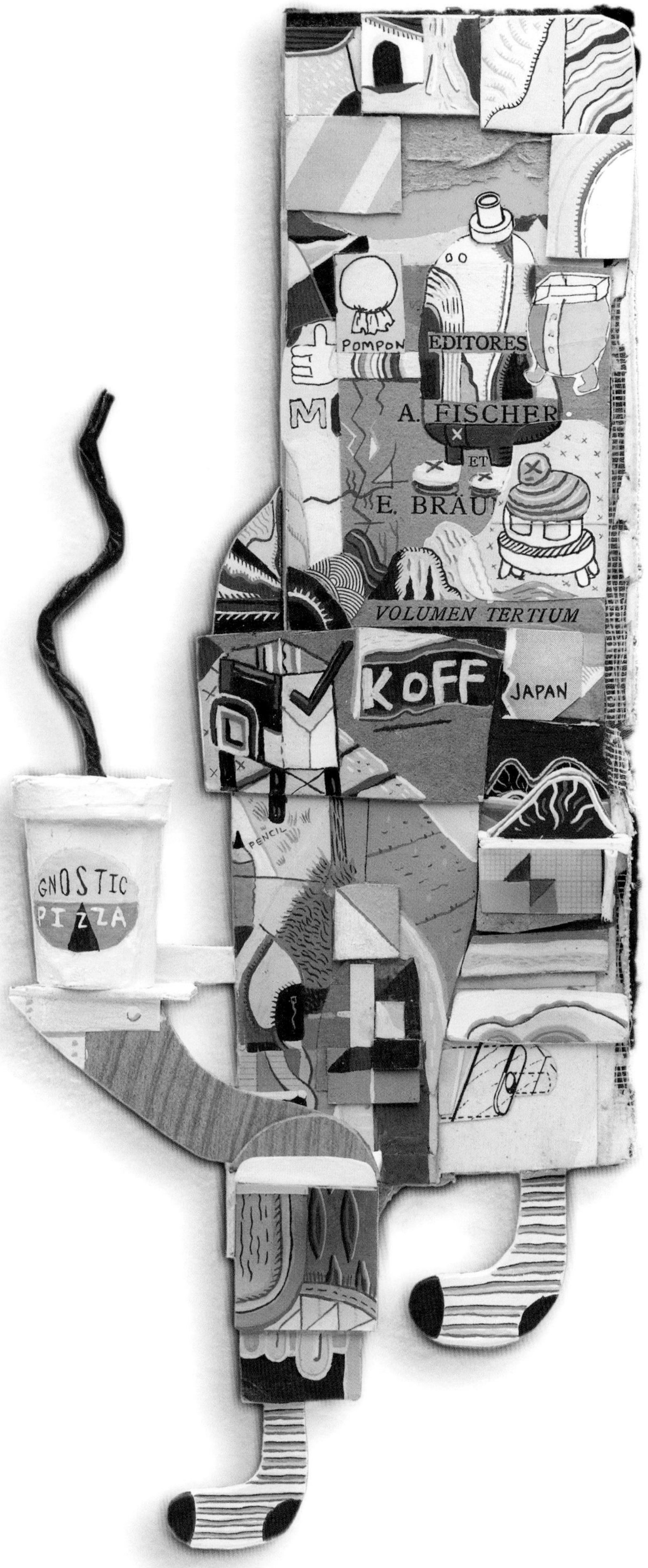
POMPON
EDITORES
M
A. FISCHER
ET
E. BRÄU
VOLUMEN TERTIUM
KOFF
JAPAN
PENCIL
GNOSTIC
PIZZA

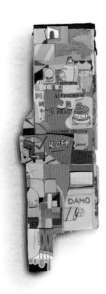

7. *Koff (Japan),* 2006
Mixed media construction,
11–½ x 5 x 1–⅜ in.

Shown at top left:
Koff (Japan)
in a previous state

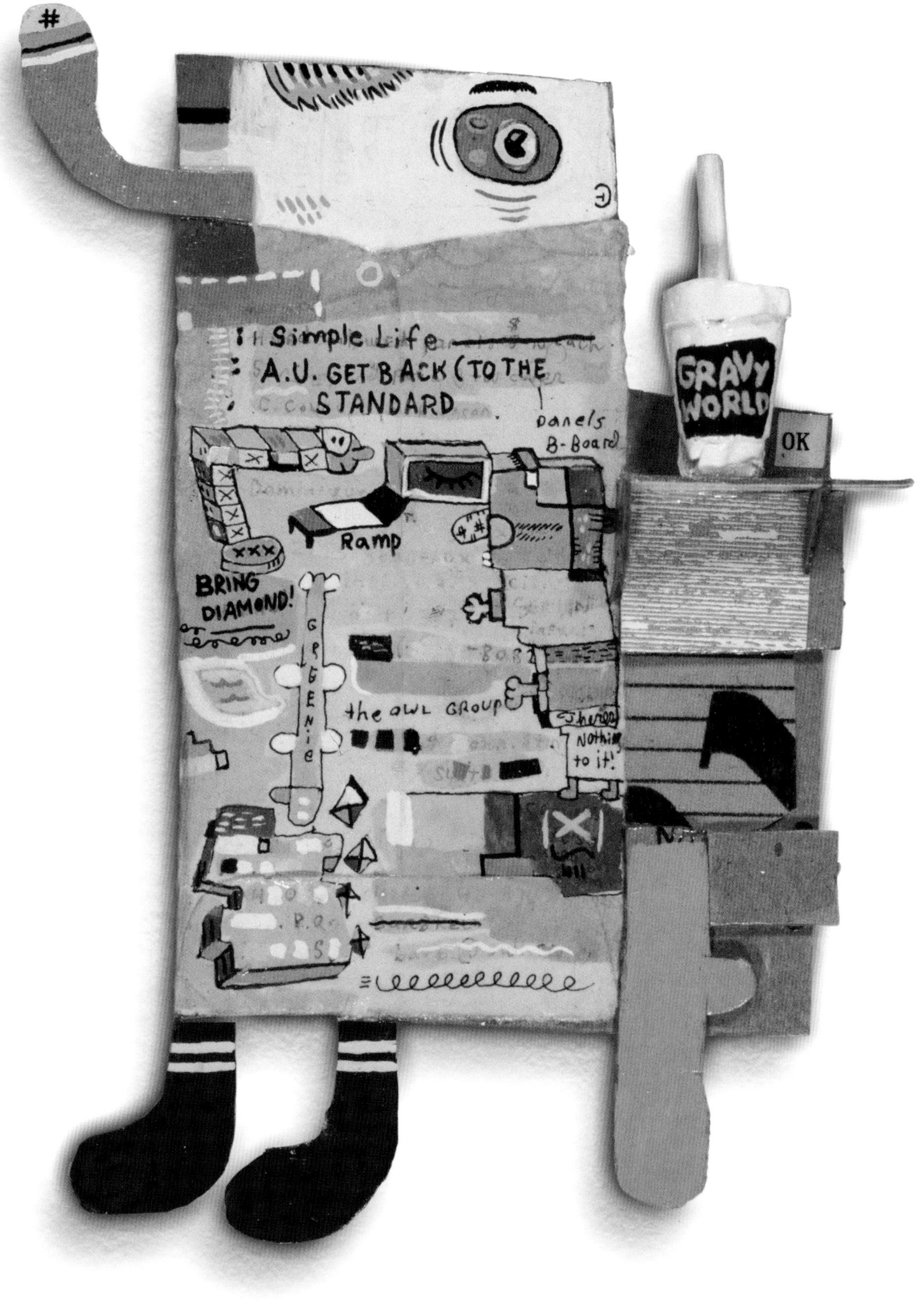
Simple Life
A.U. GET BACK (TO THE
STANDARD
danels
B-Board
GRAVY
WORLD
OK
Ramp
BRING
DIAMOND!
the OWL GROUP
to it!

8. *Gravy World,* 2001
Mixed media construction, 6–⅜ x 4–⅞ x ¾ in.
Includes: slogan: "A. U.—Get Back To The Standard"

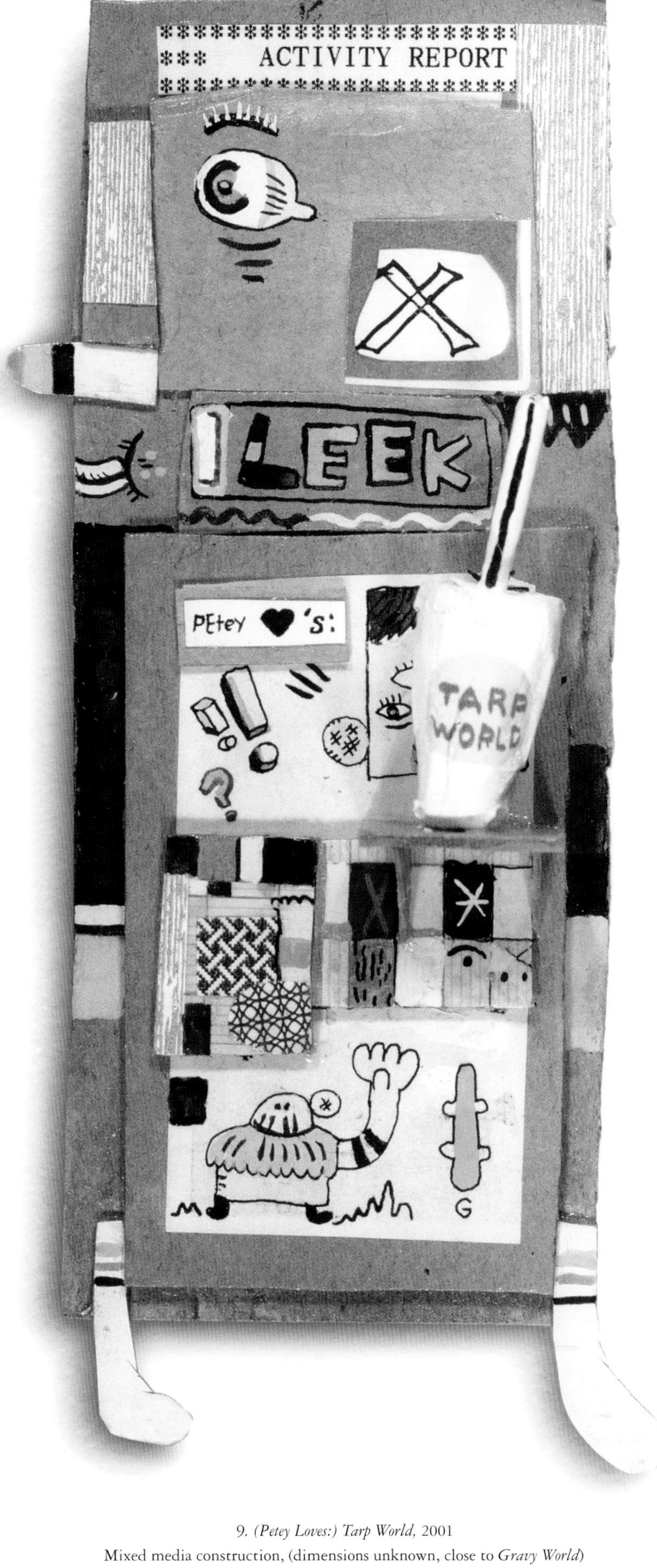
ACTIVITY REPORT
LEEK
PEtey ♥'s:
TARP WORLD
G

9. *(Petey Loves:) Tarp World,* 2001
Mixed media construction, (dimensions unknown, close to *Gravy World*)
Includes: sports socks

ZUKI
FRESHCOD
FOR THE PAST 24. YEARS
I HAVE BEEN HARRASSED:
HECKELED: BOYCOTTED:
LIED TO: LIED ABOUT: STOLE
FROM: TOLD TO GET OFF
THE STREET: ALL OF
THIS BY BOTH "WHITES"
AND BLACK'S: AND I AM "JUST
STICKING AROUND TO SEE WHAT THE
H" WILL HAPPEN NEXT.
JESSE-HOWARD
HOT
BUN
PARACHUTE
TOWN
MISSOURI
LON

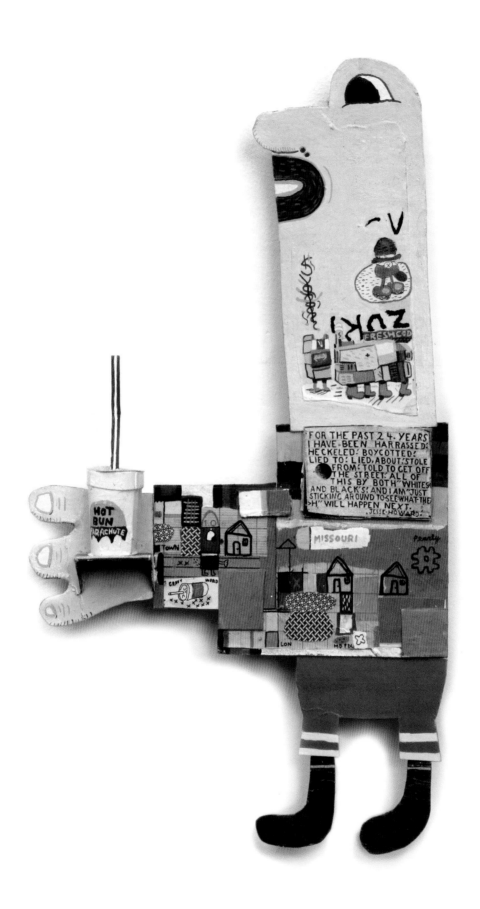

10. *Zuk (Hot Bun Parachute),* 2003
Mixed media construction, 12 x 7–½ x 1–½ in.
Includes: photocopied "samples" of Jesse Howard artwork

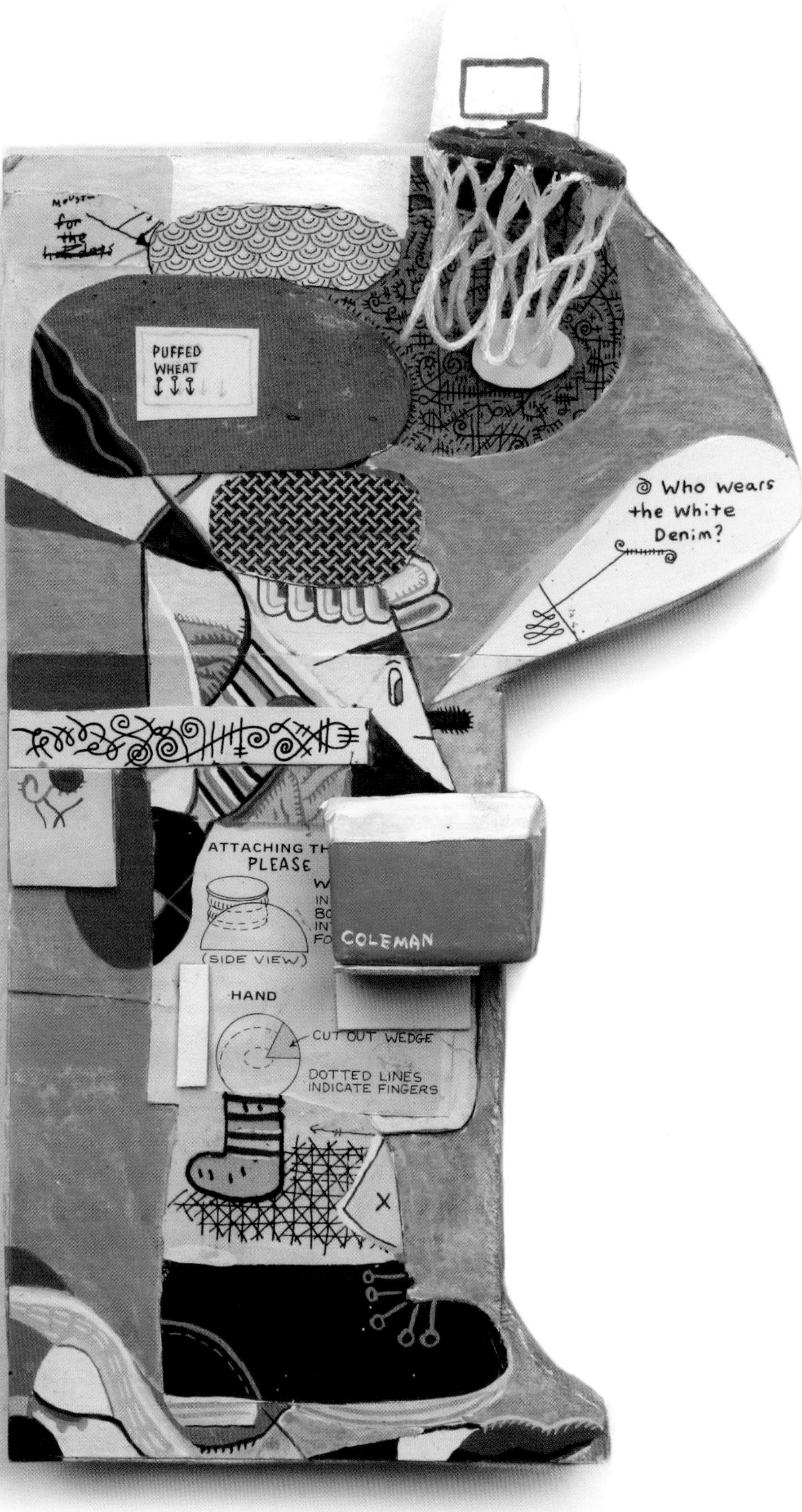
PUFFED WHEAT
Who wears the White Denim?
ATTACHING TH
PLEASE
(SIDE VIEW)
COLEMAN
HAND
CUT OUT WEDGE
DOTTED LINES INDICATE FINGERS

11. *Puffed Wheat (Coleman)*, 2005
Mixed media construction, 10-¼ x 5-¾ x 1-¾
Includes: basketball hoop built by Amy Lockhart

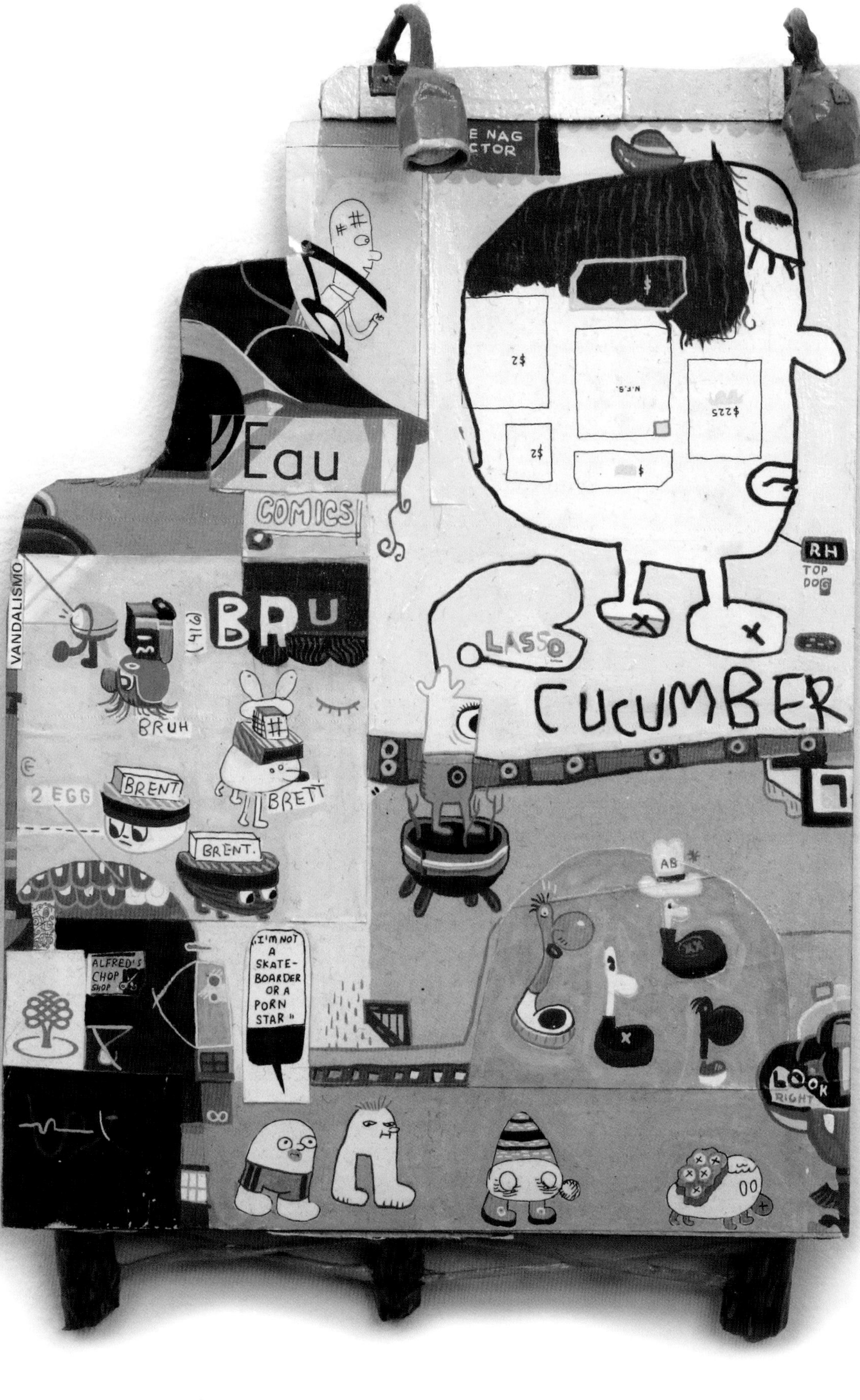
E NAG
CTOR
Eau
COMICS
VANDALISMO
BRU
BRUH
BRENT
BRETT
2 EGG
BRENT.
LASSO
CUCUMBER
RH
TOP
DOG
AB
"I'M NOT A SKATE-BOARDER OR A PORN STAR"
ALFRED'S CHOP SHOP
LOOK
RIGHT

12. *Cucumber,* 2003
Mixed media construction, 14 x 9 x 1–½ in.
Includes: "the nag factor" (partially hidden), variations on name of new nephew
(**also see:** detail on p. 263)

GREENISH LAKE
ORANJ LAKE
HIDE BEHIND
BLOO CHIP
Envelope Buildings
E-MAIL
THE CYCLOPS
CYCLOPE
KID
This quaint pajama bag hobo
A LOCAL
Witch Pinata

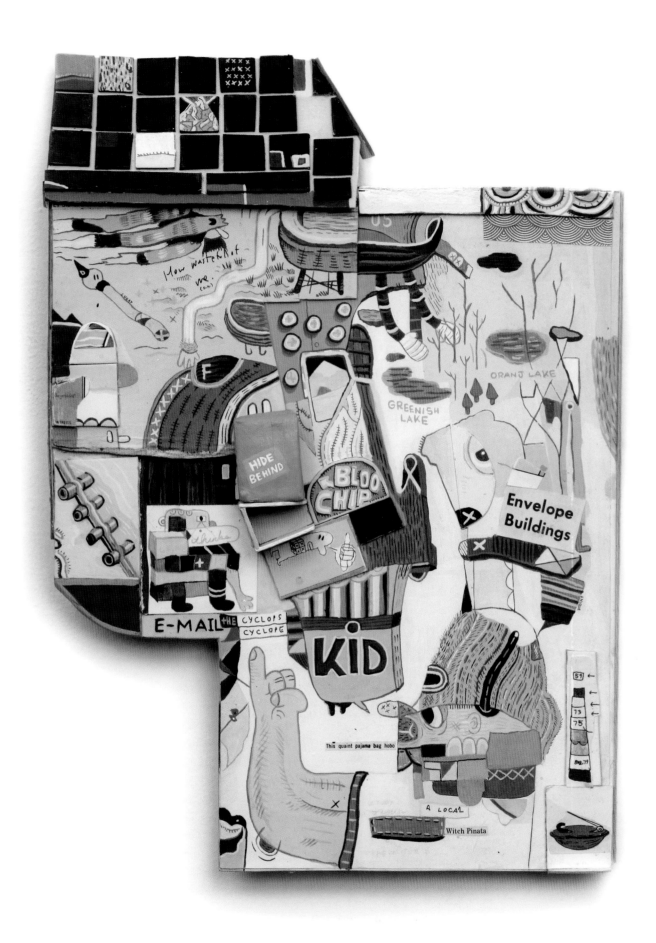

13. *(Hide Behind) Bloo Chip Kid,* 2005
Mixed media construction, 14 x 9–⅞ x 2 in.
Includes: clippings from "scrap craft" magazines and envelope patterns

This is your number
Nº 4
SHOWN
SWISS ARCHICTECTURE

FER SHORE, FRIENDS
Paint the platform
IS HE A
SCIENTIST
?

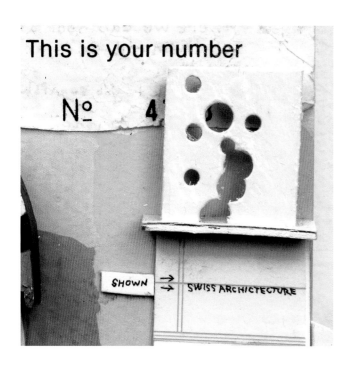

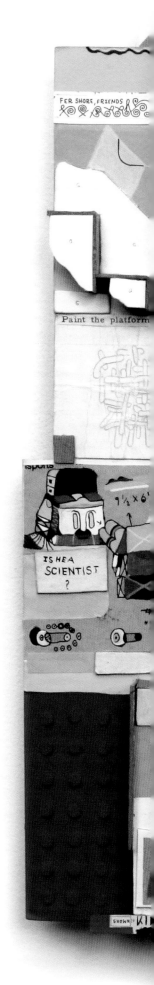

14. *Farm Equipment,* 2005

Mixed media construction, 17–½ x 15 x ⅞ in.

Includes: swiss cheese (**see detail above and p. 260**), faux red Lego, King Of Floors, The Olde Foundry receipt

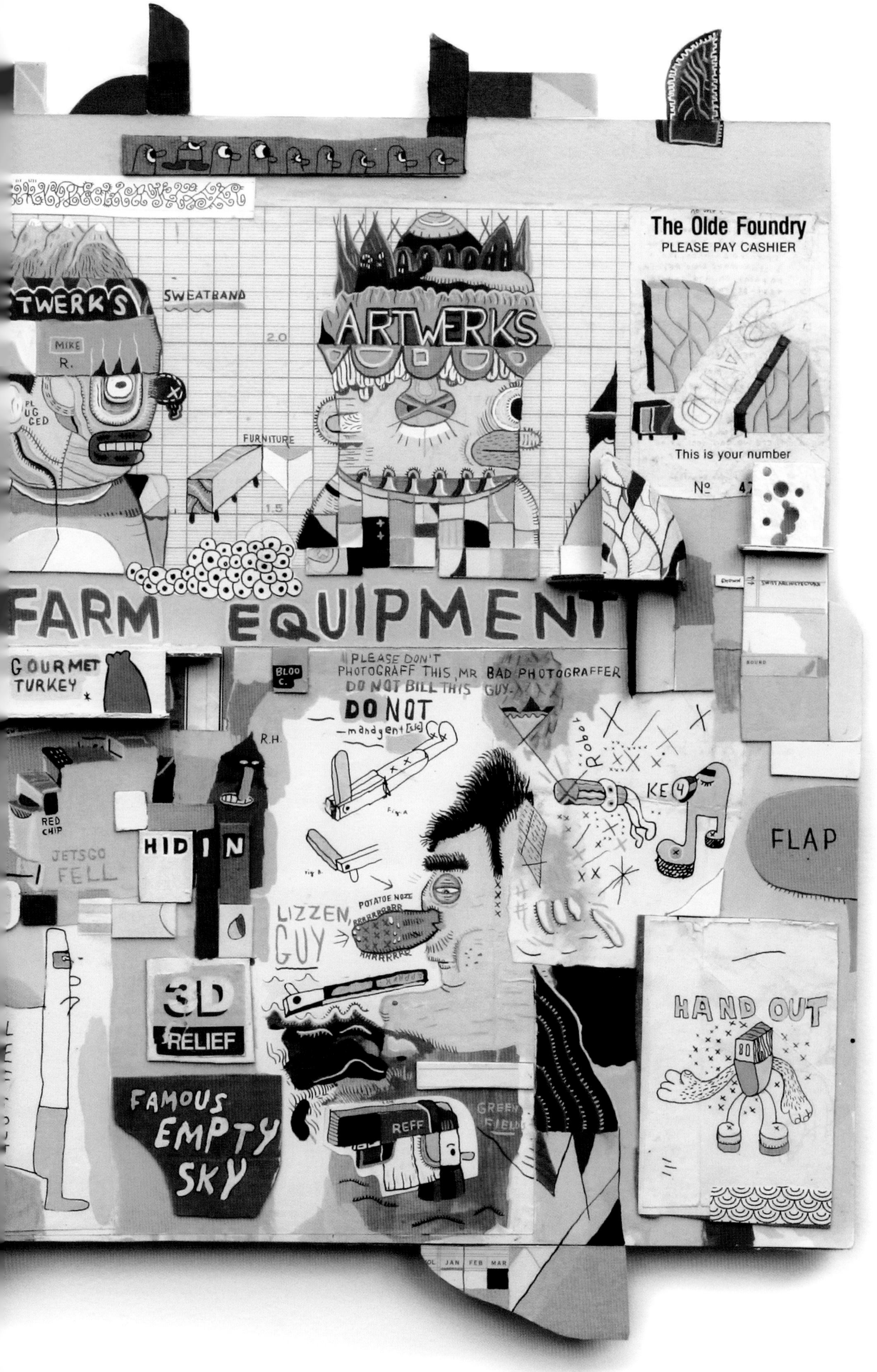

TWERK'S
SWEATBAND
MIKE R.
2.0
ARTWERKS
FURNITURE
1.5
The Olde Foundry
PLEASE PAY CASHIER
This is your number
№
FARM EQUIPMENT
GOURMET TURKEY
BLOO C.
PLEASE DON'T PHOTOGRAFF THIS, MR BAD PHOTOGRAFFER
DO NOT BILL THIS GUY.
DO NOT
R.H.
ROBOT
KEY
RED CHIP
JETSGO FELL
HID IN
FLAP
POTATOE NOZE
LIZZEN, GUY
3D RELIEF
HAND OUT
FAMOUS EMPTY SKY
REFF
GREEN FIELD
JAN FEB MAR

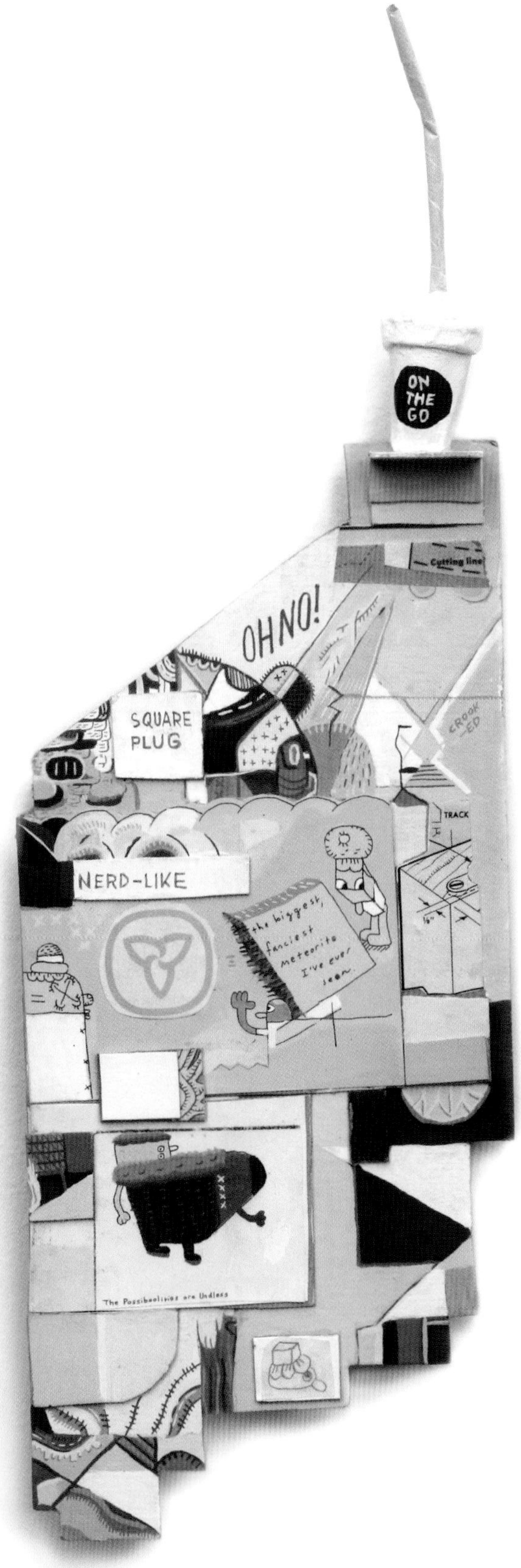
ON THE GO
OHNO!
SQUARE PLUG
NERD-LIKE
the biggest, fanciest meteorite I've ever seen

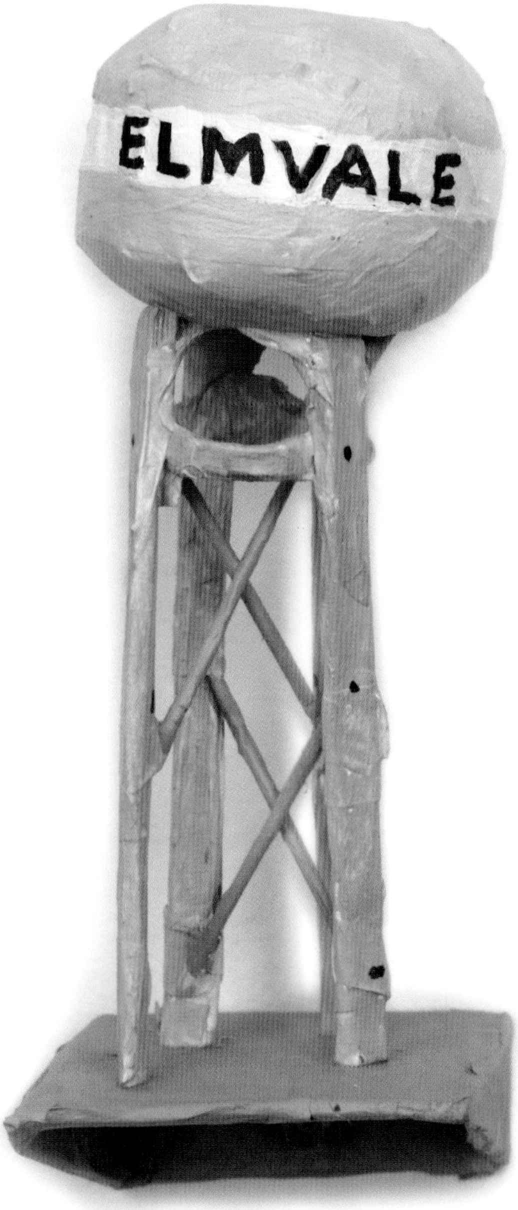
ELMVALE

15. *On The Go (Nerd–Like),* 2005
Mixed media construction, 17 x 6 x 3 in.
Includes: official logo for the Province of Ontario

16. *Elmvale,* 2001
Mixed media construction, 7 x 3–½ x 3–½ in.

Facing Page:

17. *Ontario, Get Your Blanket (Florida),* 2005
Mixed media on reverse of sketchbook cover, 11 x 8–½ in.
Includes: sand traps, rec room, potato chip, tighty whities, house key

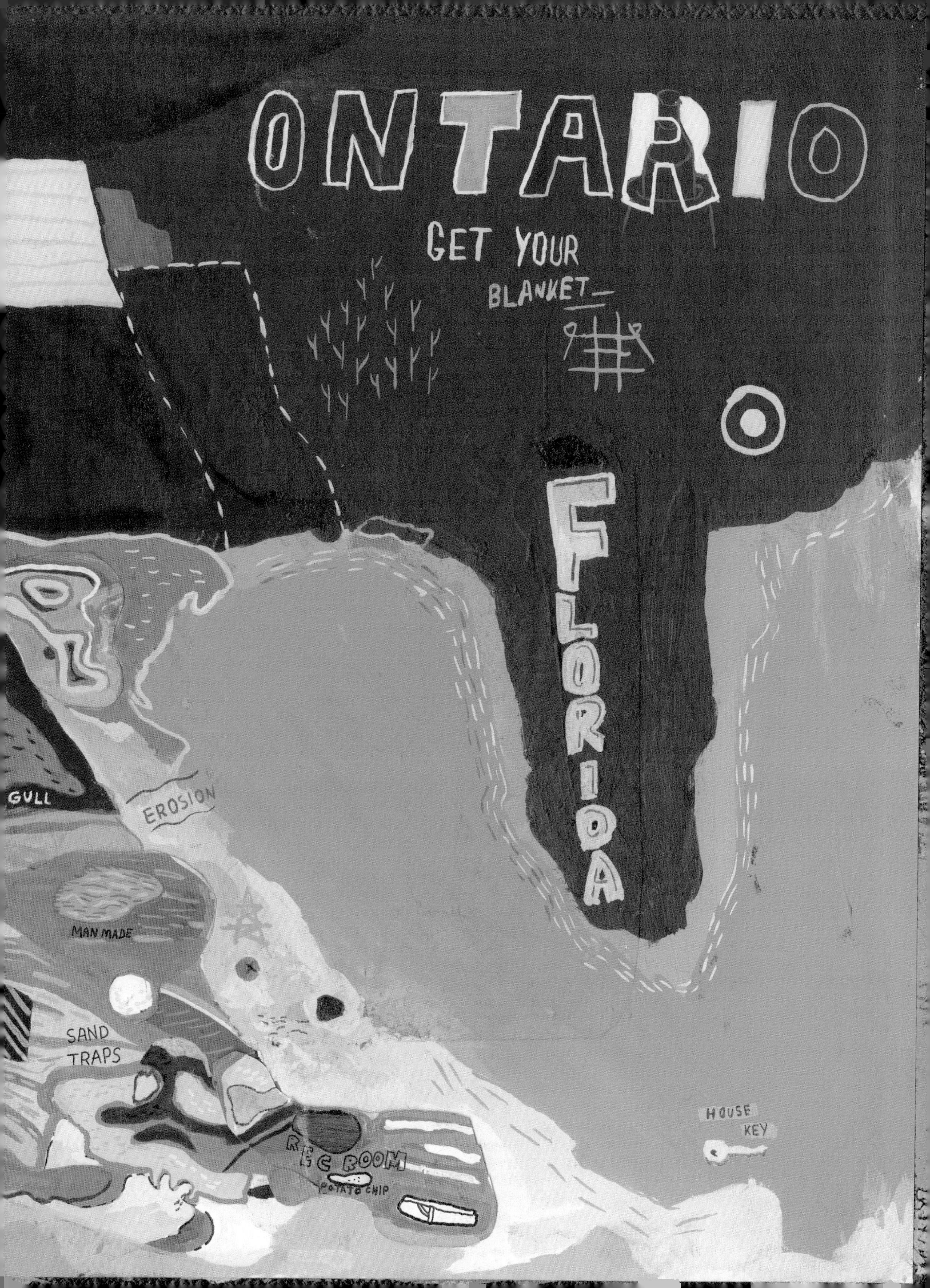
ONTARIO
GET YOUR
BLANKET
FLORIDA
GULL
EROSION
MAN MADE
SAND
TRAPS
REC ROOM
POTATO CHIP
HOUSE
KEY

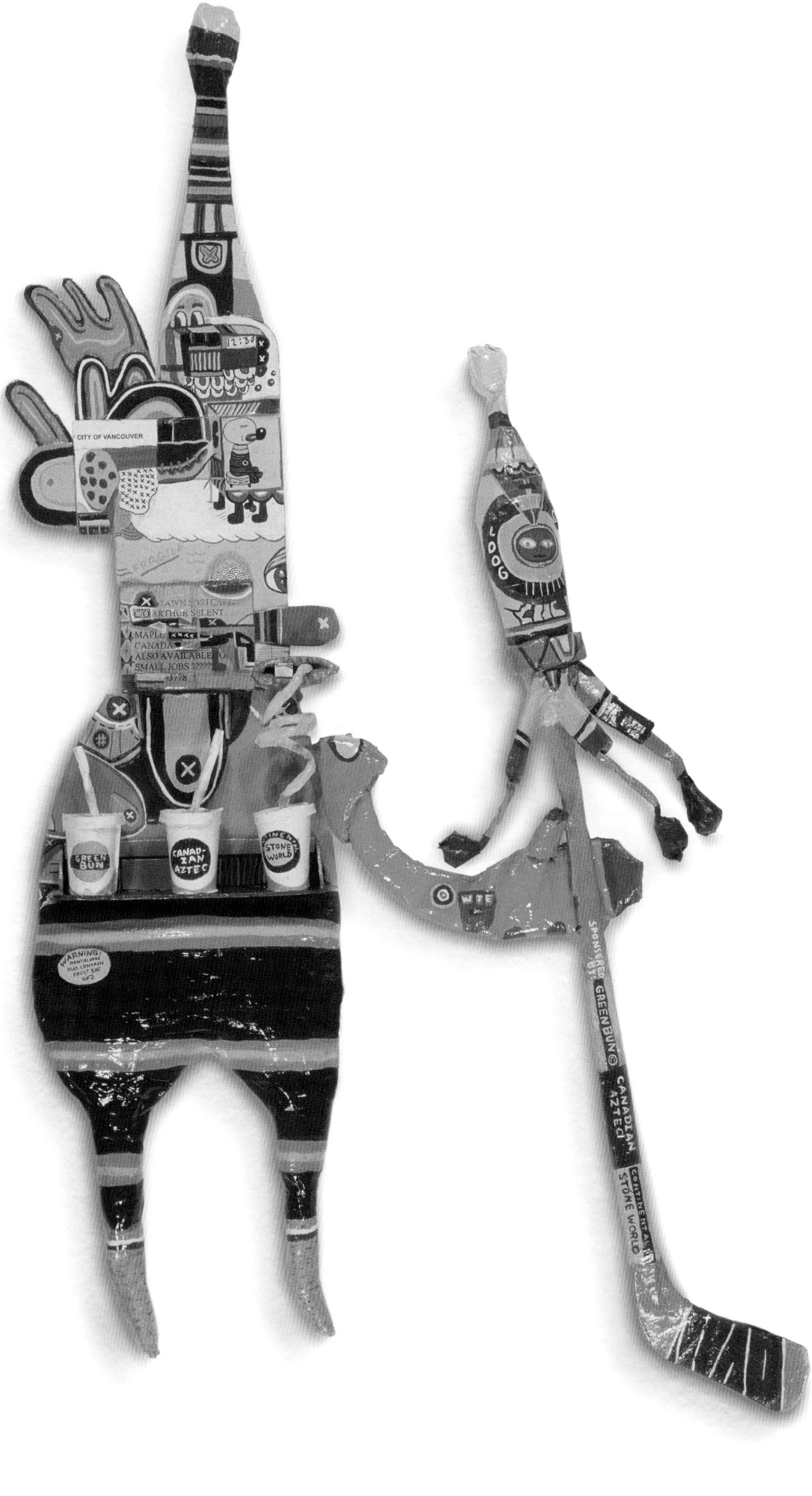
12:30
CITY OF VANCOUVER
GREEN BUN
CANADIAN AZTEC
STONE WORLD
WARNING: PANTALOONS MAY CONTAIN FRUIT SAC
SPONSERED BY: GREENBUN©
CANADIAN AZTEC
CONTINENTAL STONE WORLD

18. *Greenbun, Canadian Aztec, Continental Stone World,* 2003
Mixed media construction,
27 x 14 x 2–½ in.
Warning: "pantaloons may contain fruit sac"

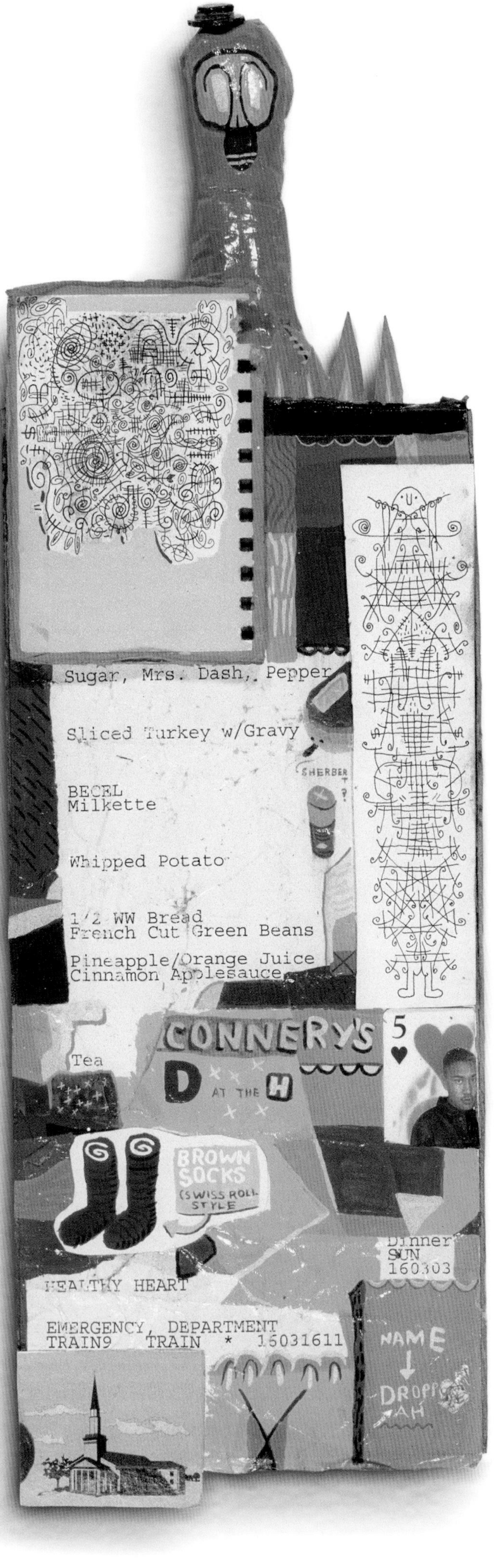
Sugar, Mrs. Dash, Pepper
Sliced Turkey w/Gravy
SHERBER
BECEL
Milkette
Whipped Potato
1/2 WW Bread
French Cut Green Beans
Pineapple/Orange Juice
Cinnamon Applesauce
CONNERY'S
D AT THE H
Tea
5
BROWN SOCKS
(SWISS ROLL STYLE
Dinner
SUN
160303
HEALTHY HEART
EMERGENCY DEPARTMENT
TRAIN9 TRAIN * 16031611
NAME
DROPP
AH

19. *Connery's D,* 2003
Mixed media construction,
17 x 5–¾ x 1–½ in.
Includes: old address book cover,
Connery's dinner menu

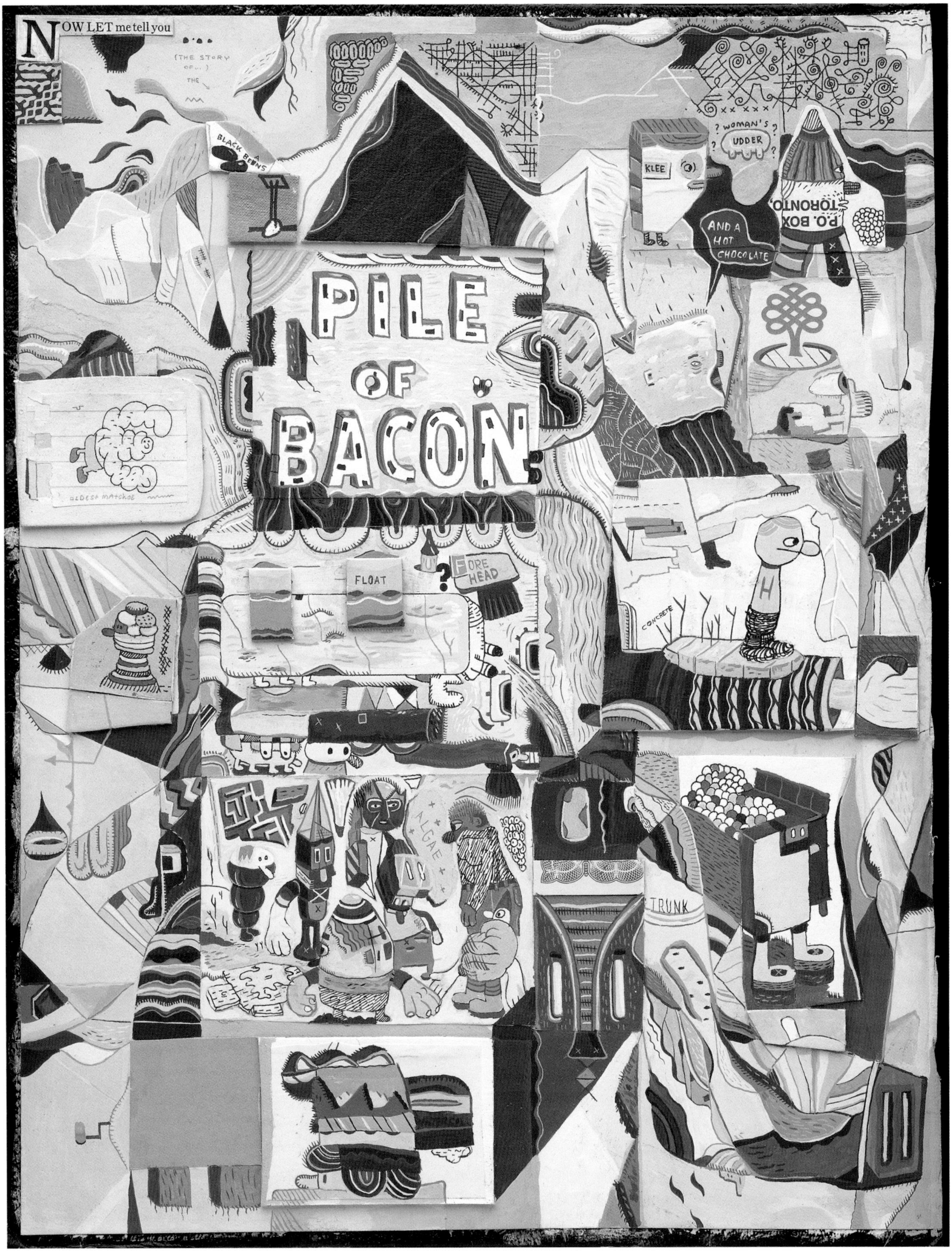
NOW LET me tell you
(THE STORY OF...)
THE
BLACK BEANS
? WOMAN'S ?
UDDER
KLEE
P.O. BOX
TORONTO
AND A HOT CHOCOLATE
PILE OF BACON
OLDEST MATCHOE
FLOAT
FORE HEAD
CONCRETE
H
ALGAE
TRUNK

20. *The Story of the Pile of Bacon,* 2006
Mixed media on reverse of sketchbook cover, 14 x 10–7⁄8 in.
Includes: "Oldest Matcho," no pictoral depictions of bacon, Paul Klee and "woman's udder?"

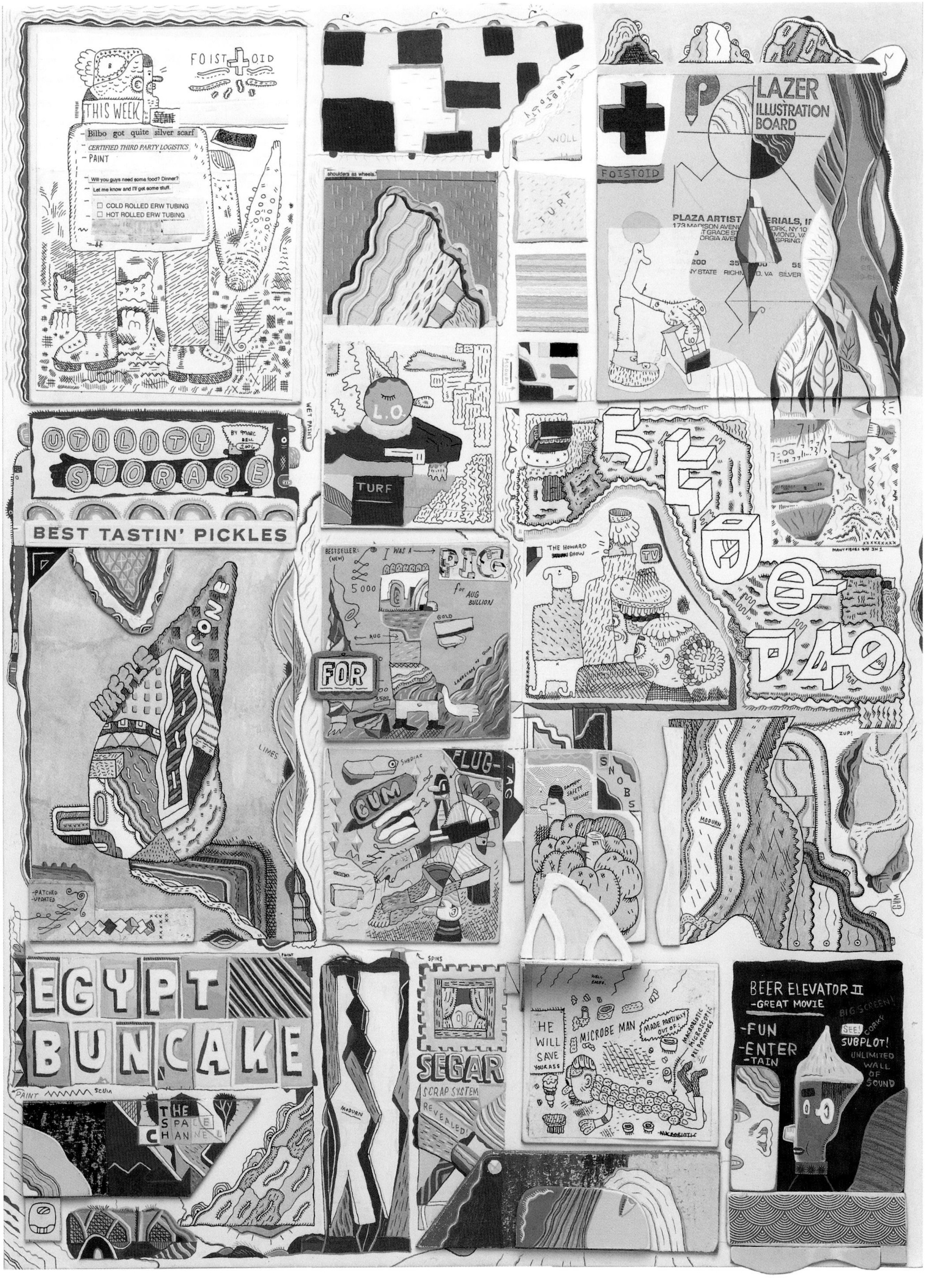
FOIST OID
THIS WEEK
Bilbo got quite silver scarf
CERTIFIED THIRD PARTY LOGISTICS
PAINT
Will you guys need some food? Dinner?
Let me know and I'll get some stuff.
COLD ROLLED ERW TUBING
HOT ROLLED ERW TUBING
WOLL
FOISTOID
LAZER
ILLUSTRATION
BOARD
PLAZA ARTIST
shoulders as wheels.
TURF
WET PAINT
UTILITY
STORAGE
BEST TASTIN' PICKLES
L.O.
TURF
BESTSELLER: (NEW)
I WAS A
PIG
5000
FOR
AUG BULLION
THE HOWARD SHOW
TV
WAFFLE CONE
LIMES
PATCHED UPDATED
GUM
FLUG-TAG
SNOBS
MODURN
ZUP!
GUM
EGYPT
BUNCAKE
PAINT
THE SPACE CHANNEL
SPINS
SEGAR
SCRAP SYSTEM
REVEALED!
MODURN
HE WILL SAVE YOUR ASS
MICROBE MAN
MADE PARTIALLY OUT OF
MACROBIOTIC MICROSCOPIC POTATOES
BEER ELEVATOR II
-GREAT MOVIE
BIG SCREEN!
-FUN
-ENTER
-TAIN
SEE!
CORKY
SUBPLOT!
UNLIMITED WALL OF SOUND

21. *Egypt Buncake (Lazer Illustration Board)*, 2006
Mixed media on board, 20 x 15 x 1 in.
Includes: Best Tastin' Pickles, Microbe Man, "Ad" for *Beer Elevator II*

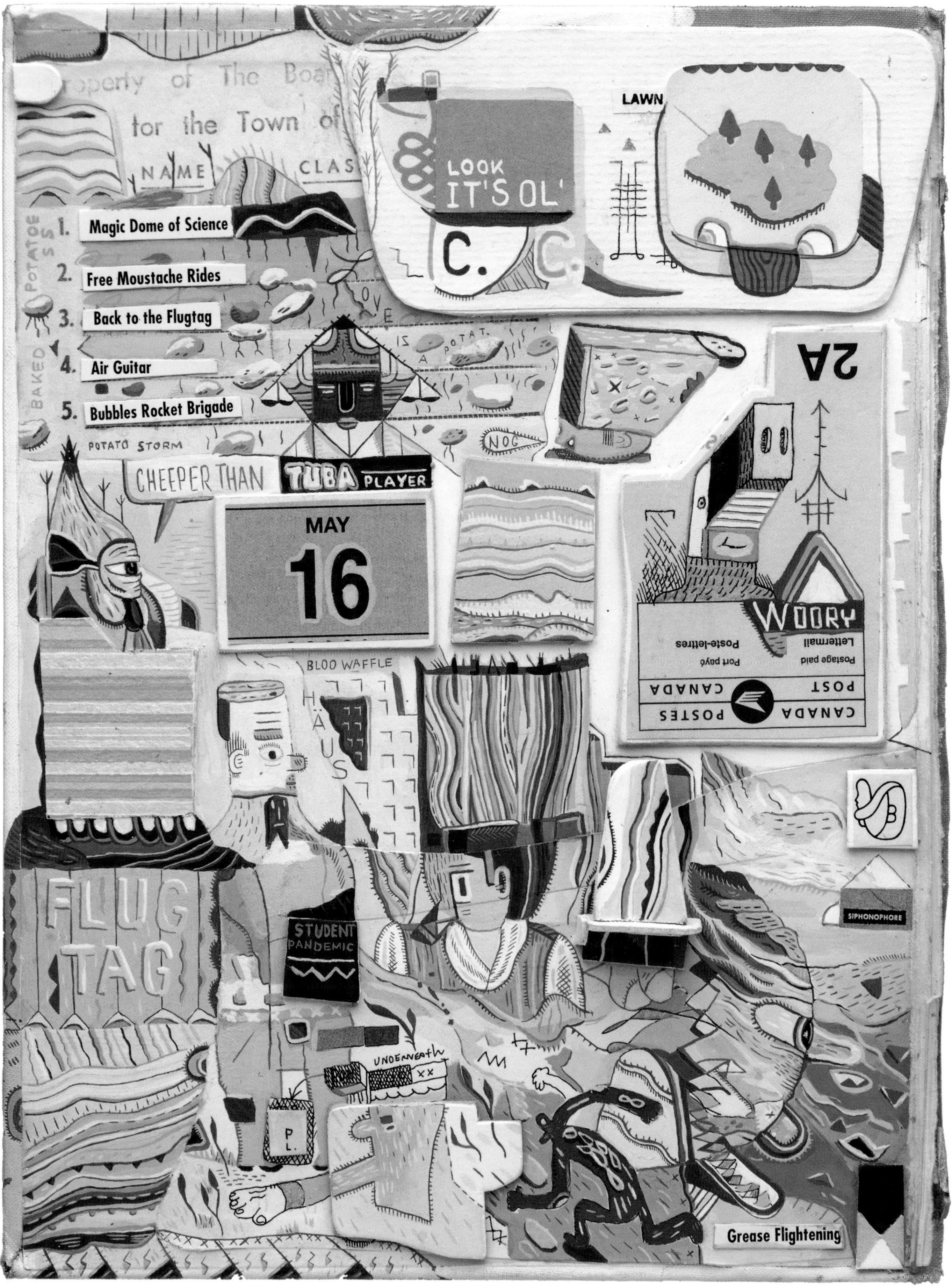

roperty of The Boa
for the Town of
NAME
CLAS
1. Magic Dome of Science
2. Free Moustache Rides
3. Back to the Flugtag
4. Air Guitar
5. Bubbles Rocket Brigade
BAKED POTATOES
POTATO STORM
LOVE IS A POTAT.
NOG
CHEEPER THAN
TUBA PLAYER
LOOK IT'S OL'
C. C.
LAWN
2A
MAY
16
BLOO WAFFLE
HÄUS
WOORY
Postage paid Port payé
Lettermail Poste-lettres
CANADA POST
POSTES CANADA
FLUG TAG
STUDENT PANDEMIC
UNDERNEATH
P. L.
SIPHONOPHORE
Grease Flightening

22. *Cheeper Than Tuba Player (May 16th Flugtag),* 2006
Mixed media on book cover, 10 x 7–⅝ in.
Includes: London Transit bus transfer, Canada Post label, Flugtag texts, wallpaper

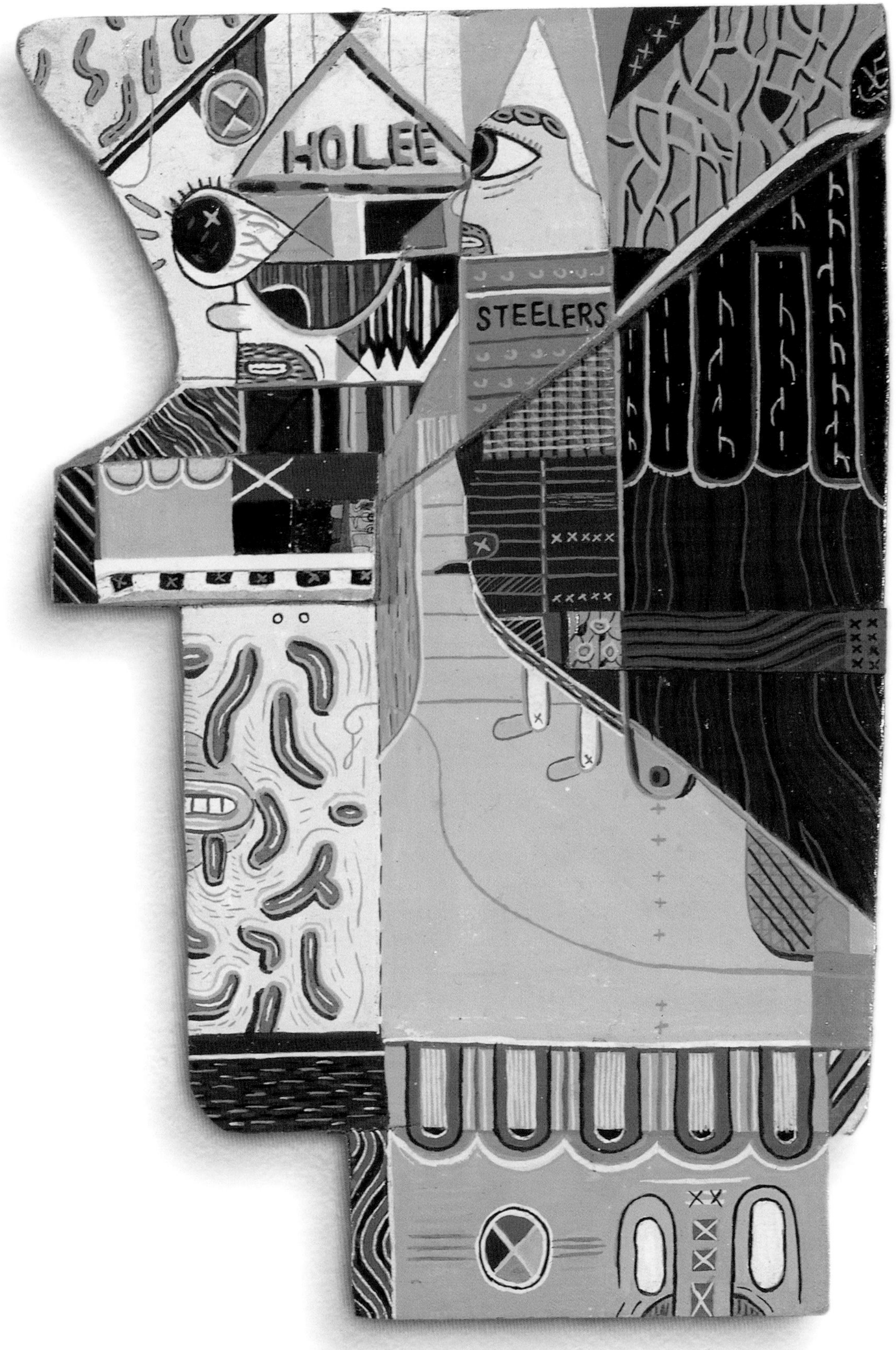
HOLEE
STEELERS

23. *Holee Steelers,* 2004
Mixed media on board, 9 x 6 in.

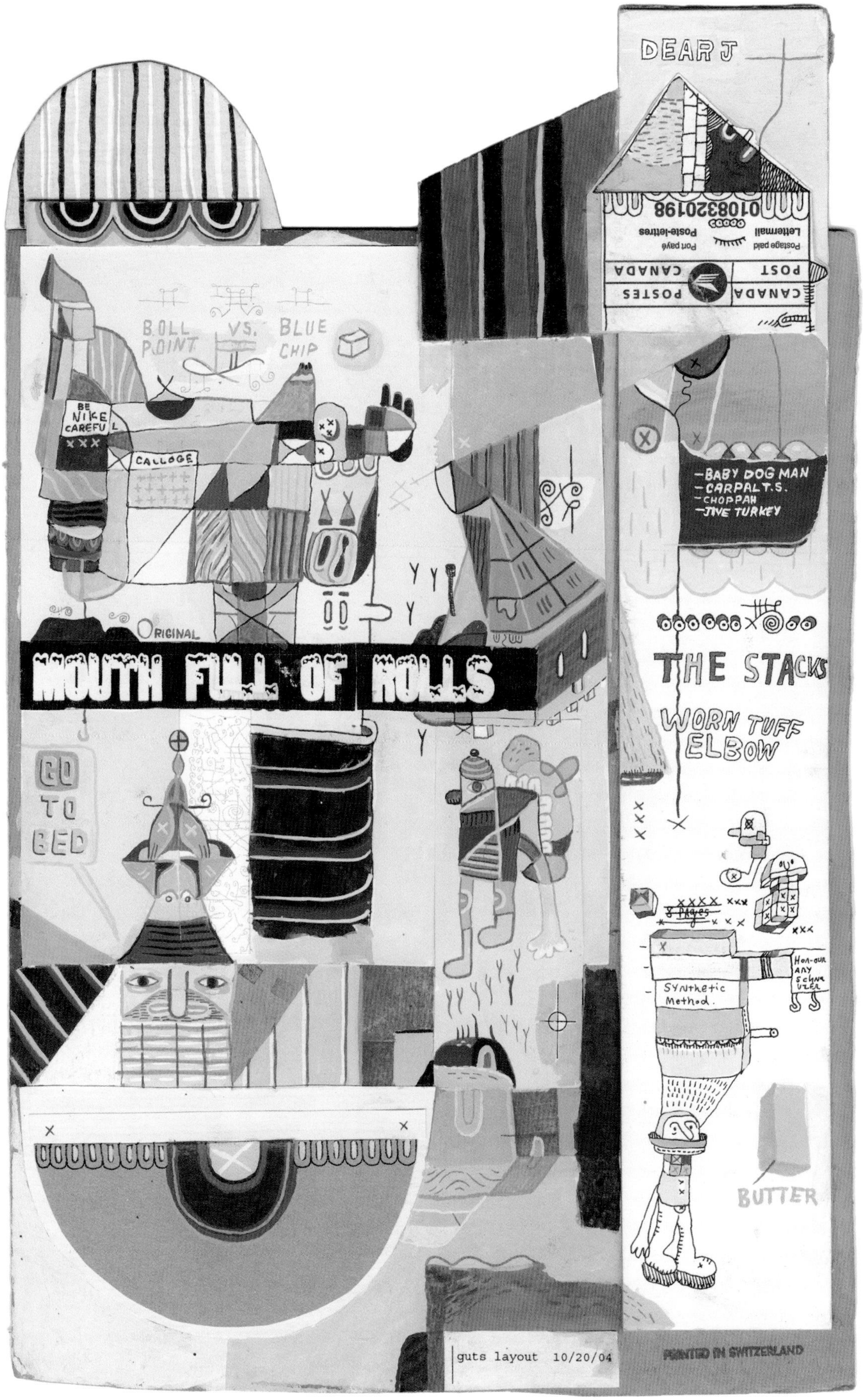
DEAR J
B.OLL POINT VS. BLUE CHIP
BE NIKE CAREFUL
CALLOGE
ORIGINAL
MOUTH FULL OF ROLLS
GO TO BED
-BABY DOG MAN
-CARPAL T.S.
-CHOPPAH
-JIVE TURKEY
THE STACKS
WORN TUFF ELBOW
Synthetic Method.
BUTTER
guts layout 10/20/04
PRINTED IN SWITZERLAND

24. *Ball Point Vs. Blue Chip (Go To Bed),* 2004
Mixed media on board, 12 x 7–½ in.
Includes: "butter" and titles of other works: *Baby Dog Man, Choppah, Jive Turkey, The Stacks, Worn Tuff Elbow, Synthetic Method* and *Mouth Full Of Rolls*

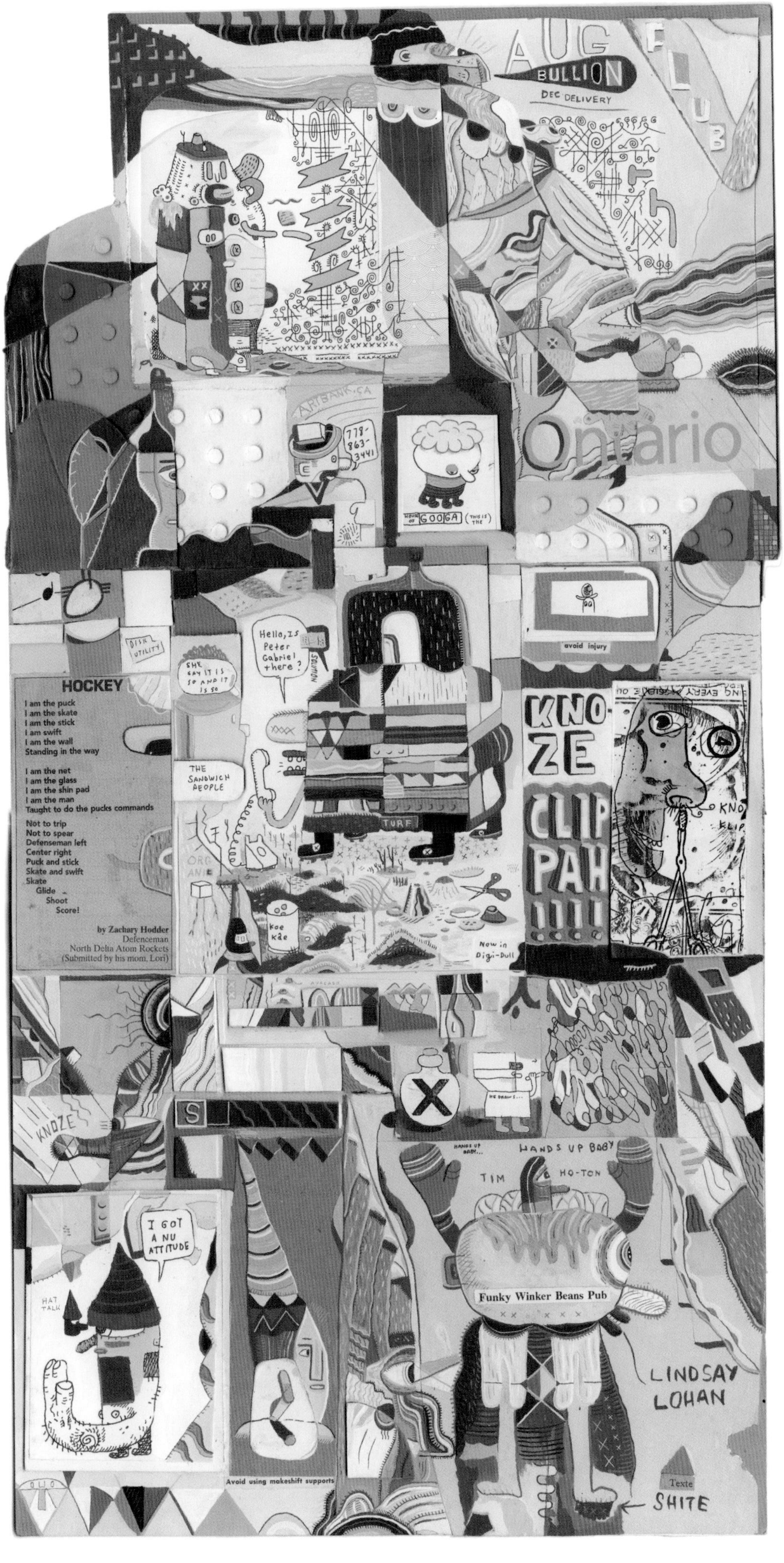
AUG
BULLION
DEC DELIVERY
CLUB
778-863-3441
HOUSE OF GOOGA (THIS IS THE)
Ontario
DISK UTILITY
avoid injury
Hello, Is Peter Gabriel there?
SHE SAY IT IS SO AND IT IS SO
HOCKEY
I am the puck
I am the skate
I am the stick
I am swift
I am the wall
Standing in the way
I am the net
I am the glass
I am the shin pad
I am the man
Taught to do the pucks commands
Not to trip
Not to spear
Defenseman left
Center right
Puck and stick
Skate and swift
Skate
Glide
Shoot
Score!
by Zachary Hodder
Defenceman
North Delta Atom Rockets
(Submitted by his mom, Lori)
THE SANDWICH PEOPLE
TURF
KNOZE
CLIPPAH!!!!
Now in Digi-Dull
KNOZE
HANDS UP BABY
TIM HO-TON
I GOT A NU ATTITUDE
HAT TALK
Funky Winker Beans Pub
LINDSAY LOHAN
Avoid using makeshift supports
Texte
SHITE

25. *Aug Bullion,* 2006
Mixed media on board,
22–⅛ x 11–⅜ in.
Includes: *Knoze Clippah!* clipping, faux blue and white Lego, "Hockey" by Zachary Hodder, peter gabriel phone call, Lindsay Lohan reference, a 778 area code phone no., egg carton clipping

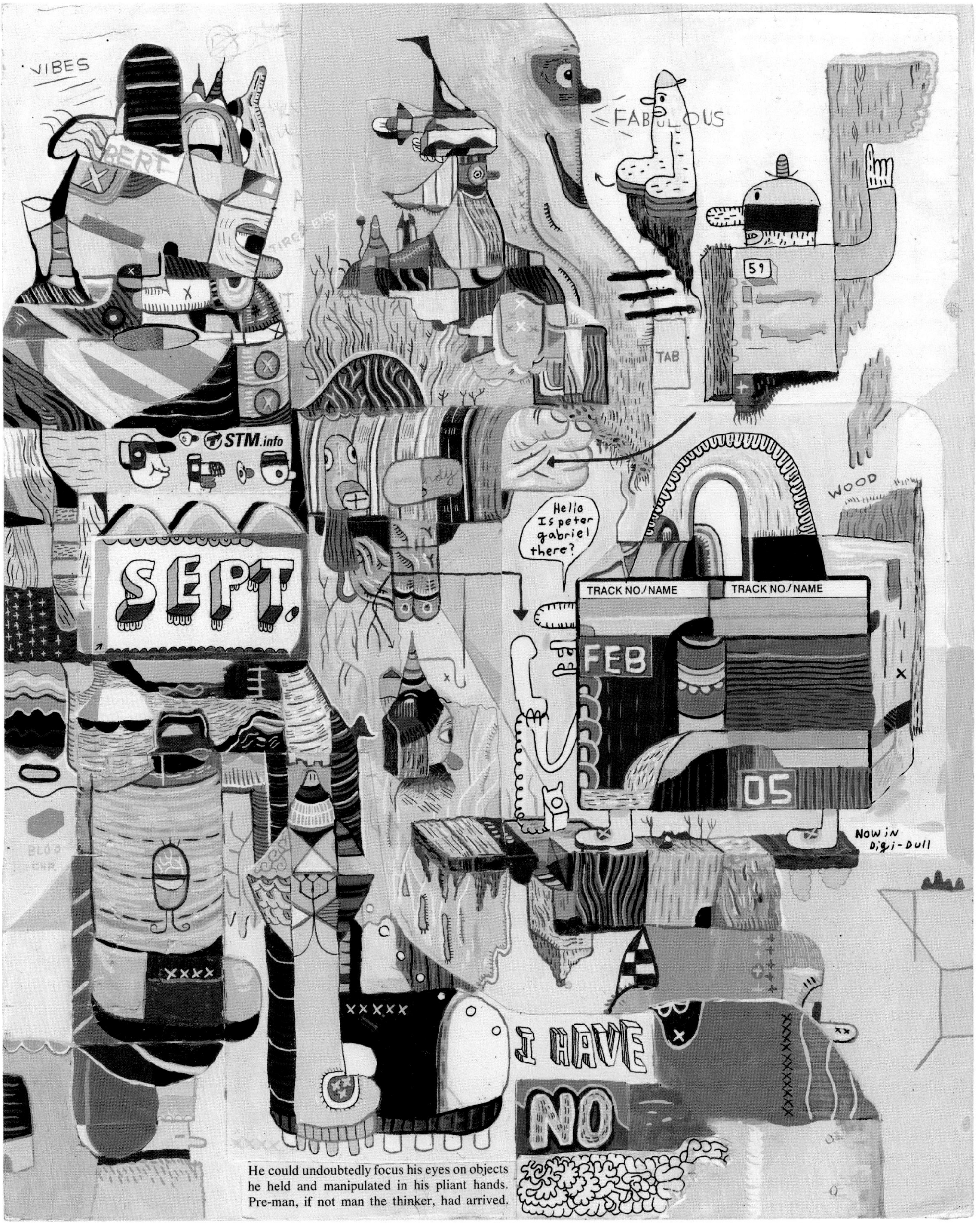
VIBES
BERT
FABULOUS
TAB
59
STM.info
WOOD
Hello Is peter gabriel there?
SEPT.
TRACK NO./NAME
TRACK NO./NAME
FEB
05
NOW IN Digi-Dull
I HAVE
NO
He could undoubtedly focus his eyes on objects he held and manipulated in his pliant hands. Pre-man, if not man the thinker, had arrived.

26. *Fabulous Bert Vibes,* 2005

Mixed media on board, 13 x 10–¾ in.

Includes: peter gabriel reference created on cdr sleeve

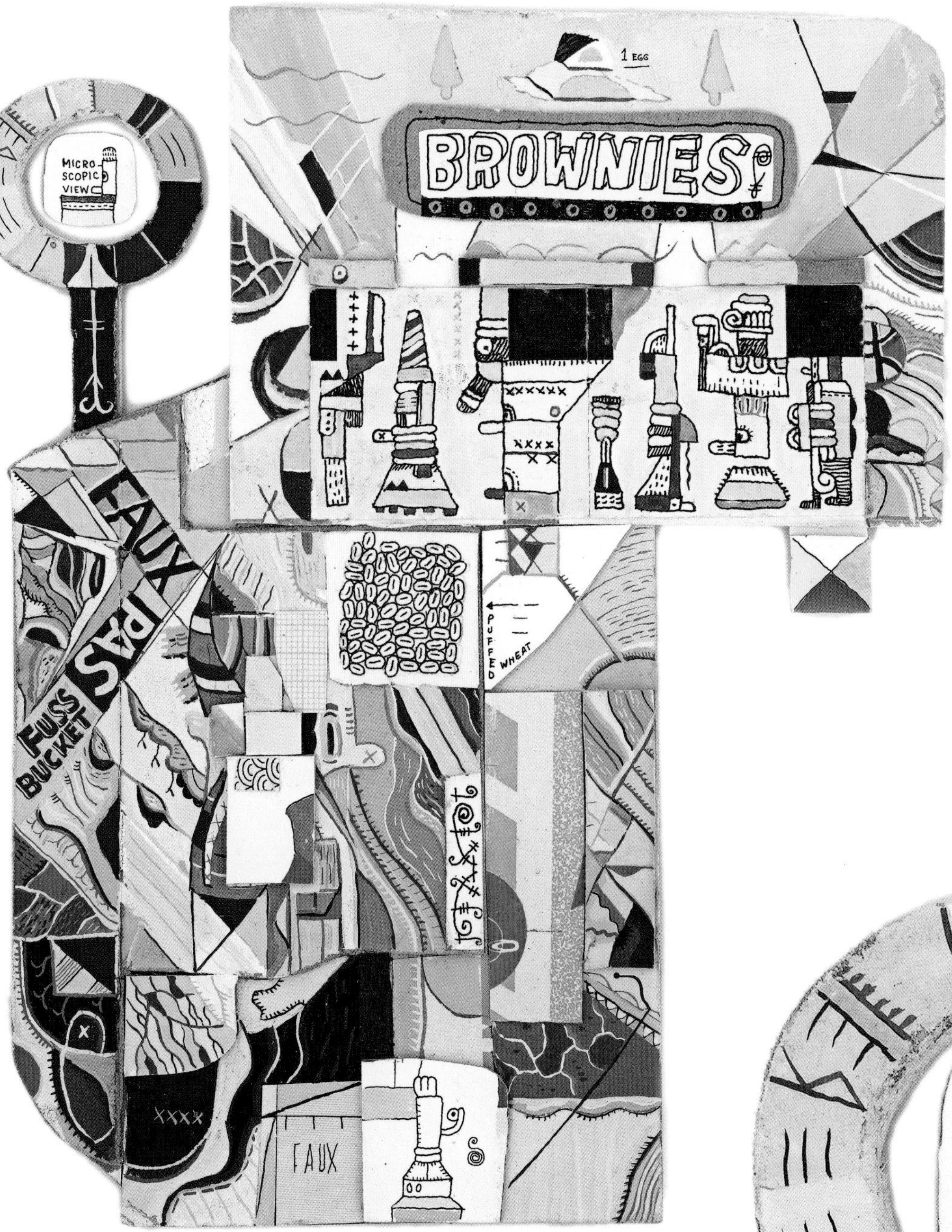
1 EGG
BROWNIES
MICRO-
SCOPIC
VIEW
FAUX
PAS
FUSS
BUCKET
PUFFED
WHEAT
FAUX

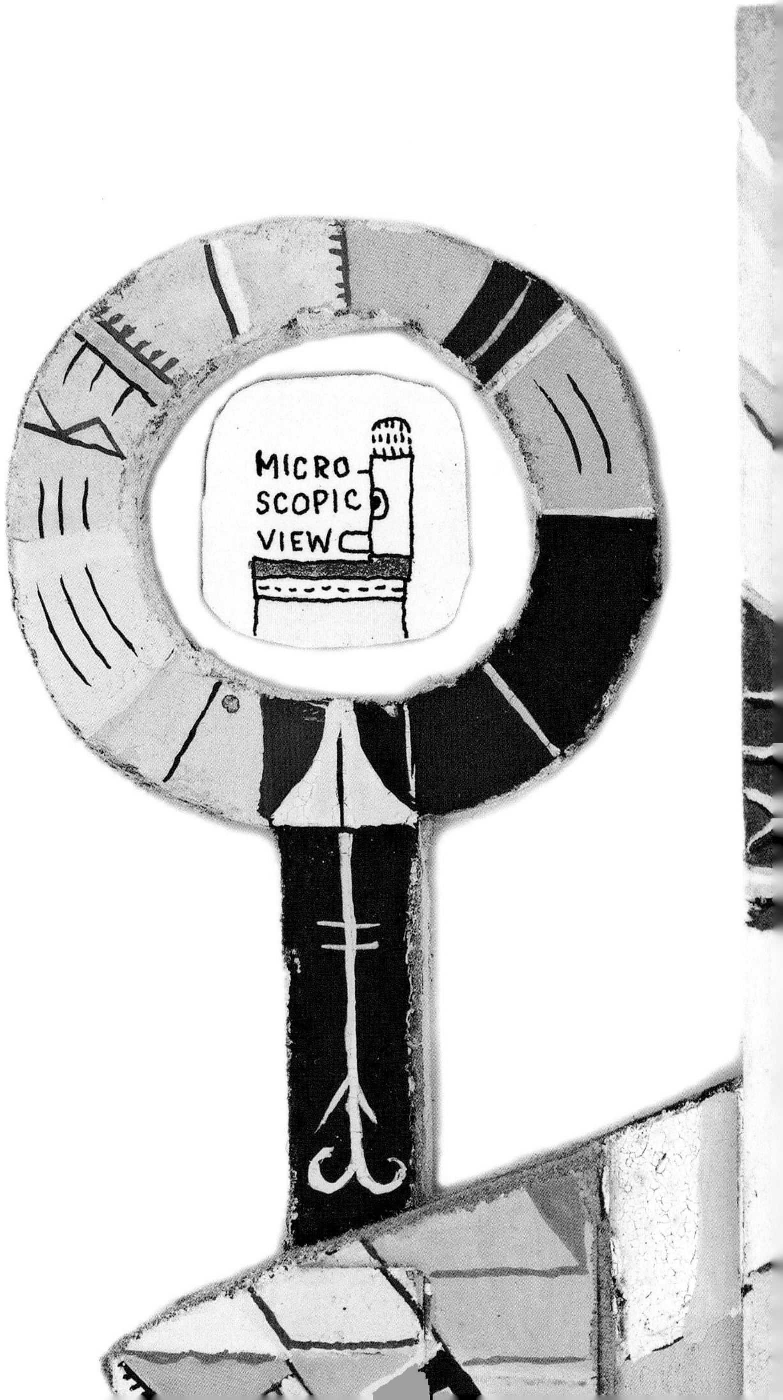
MICRO-
SCOPIC
VIEW

27. *Faux Pas Fuss Bucket (One Egg Brownies),* 2005
Mixed media on board, 9 x 7 in.

Shown at right: microscopic view

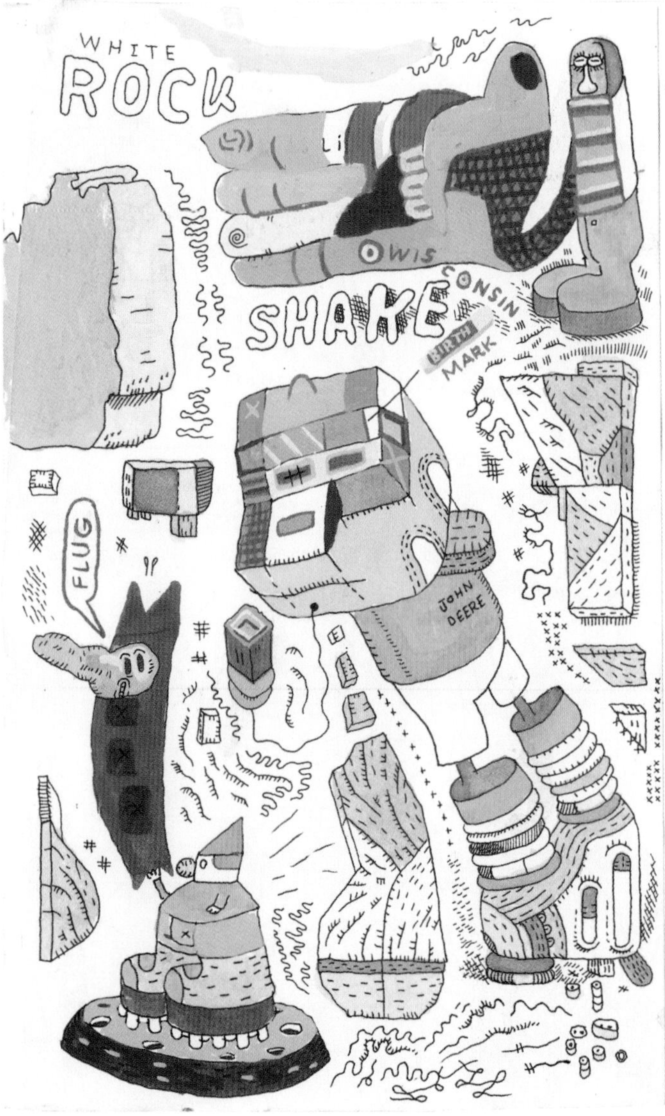
WHITE
ROCK
SHAKE
WIS CONSIN
BIRTH MARK
FLUG
JOHN DEERE

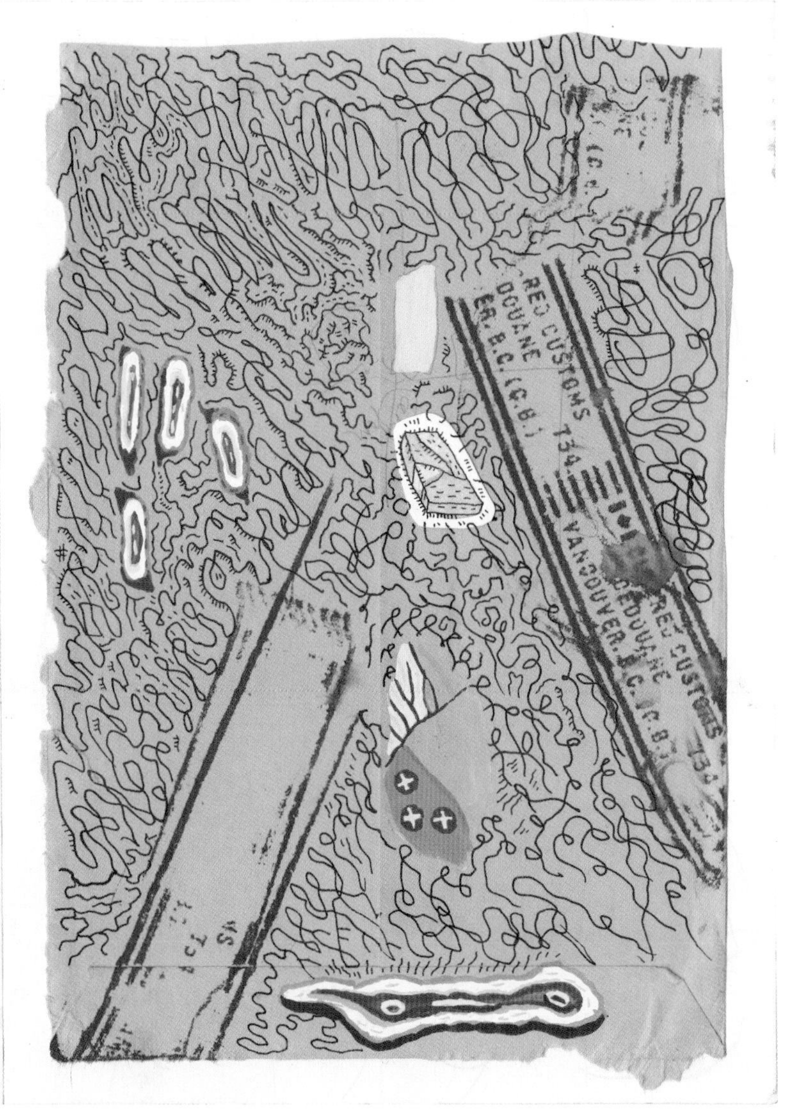
RED CUSTOMS
DOUANE
ER. B.C. (C.B.)
734

28. *White Rock Shake,* 2005
Mixed media on board, 7–½ x 10 in.
Includes: piece of envelope that cleared Canadian Customs

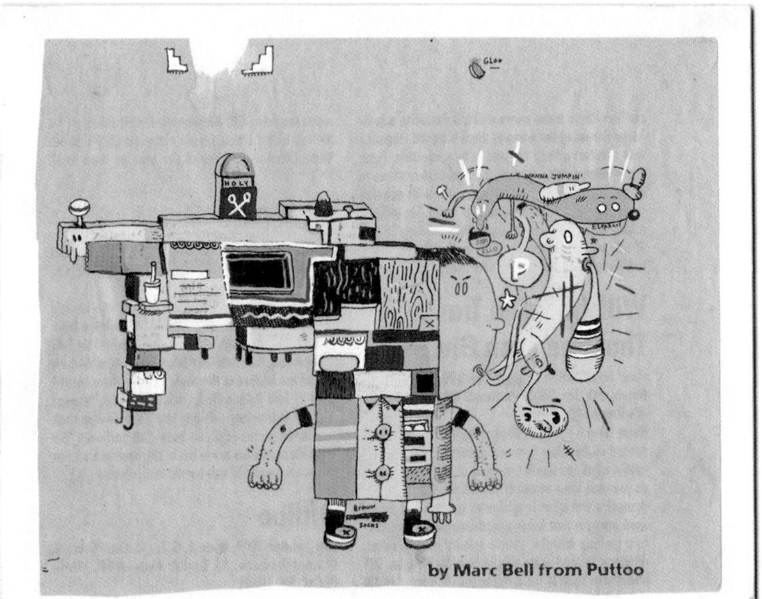
HOLY
by Marc Bell from Puttoo

29. *By Marc Bell From Puttoo,* 2003
Mixed media on clipping from *Broken Pencil Magazine*
Includes: "holy scissors"

30. *Shoo Slog,* 2008
(Facing page), mixed media on board, 20 x 15 in.
Includes text: SHOE SLOG, Sloe Gin Fizz, flap, Scissors, Famous New Brunswick Artists, The French Frie Person Invited Us To The Party The Bouncer Wouldn't Let Us In, GREENIE (upside down), BLOO CHIP, Moustache Mondays, SLOGGIE please, Sour Grapes?, I See C.C., PLASTIC HORMONES, we are not connected with Snyder of Berlin, FW Acrylic, 08 so far, nuttins comin in–it's all goin' out, SLOPPY, hypergraphica, philoctetests centre, thin buttah ain't comics, damm straight–belly boy, Silver Fizz, six additional buses, some busses in the pocket, Ecomomy Stimulus Package Dept, Total Destruction: BUY, SELL, BUY, SELL, Fuzzy Pink Beret, bloo chips falling, stable–izer, Zonked: TIRED, WHERE WITHOUT WITHALL, MELT SNOW IN A PAN!, some disturbing patterns, LITMUS TEST: who will stuck round, BUTTAH (dis ain't comics), if you really want me to see it–put it under my chin, Miles Goodwin, balanced? neurotic?, SLOE SLOG

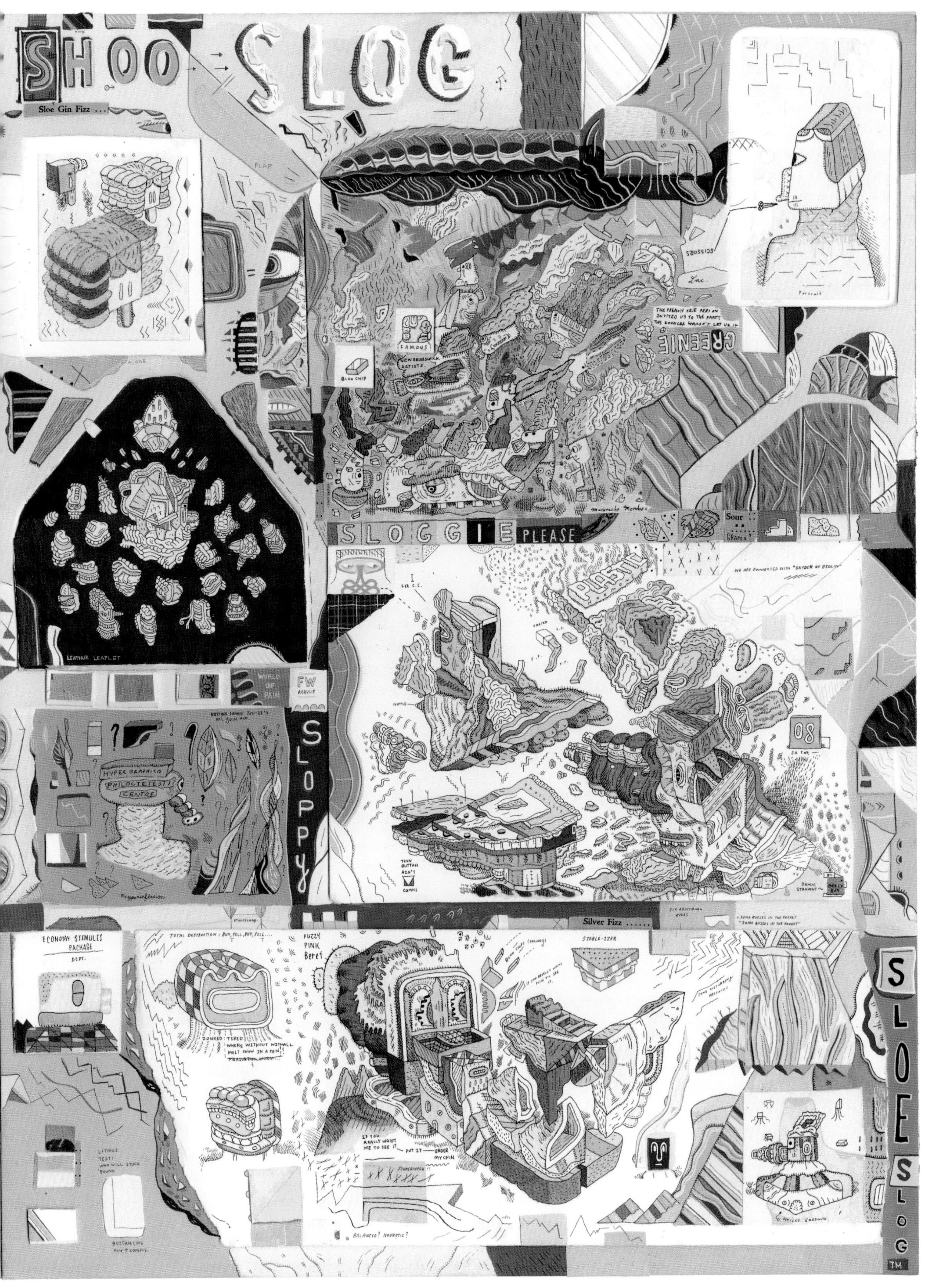

SHOO
SLOG
Sloe Gin Fizz . . .
FLAP
SCISSORS
Portrait
THE FRENCH FRIE PERSON INVITED US TO THE PARTY THE BOUNCER WOULDN'T LET US IN
GREENIE
FAMOUS
NEW BRUNSWICK ARTISTS
BLOG CHIP
Moustache Mondays
SLOGGIE PLEASE
Sour GRAPES?
WE ARE CONNECTED WITH "SNYDER OF BERLIN"
PLASTIC
LEATHUR LEAFLET
WORLD OF PAIN
FW ACRYLIC
NUTTING COMIN' IN—IT'S ALL GOIN' OUT
HYPER GRAPHICA
PHILOCTETES'S CENTRE
SLOPPY
08
SO FAR
THIN BUTTAH AIN'T COMICS
DAMM STRAIGHT~
Silver Fizz . . . . . .
ECONOMY STIMULIS PACKAGE
DEPT.
TOTAL DESTRUCTION: BUY, SELL, BUY, SELL....
FUZZY PINK Beret
STABLE-IZER
ZONKED: TIRED
WHERE WITHOUT WITHALL MELT SNOW IN A PAN!
IF YOU REALLY WANT ME TO SEE IT PUT IT UNDER MY CHIN
LITMUS TEST: WHO WILL STICK 'ROUND
BUTTAH CDIS AIN'T COMICS.
BALANCED? NEUROTIC?
SLOES
SLOG
TM

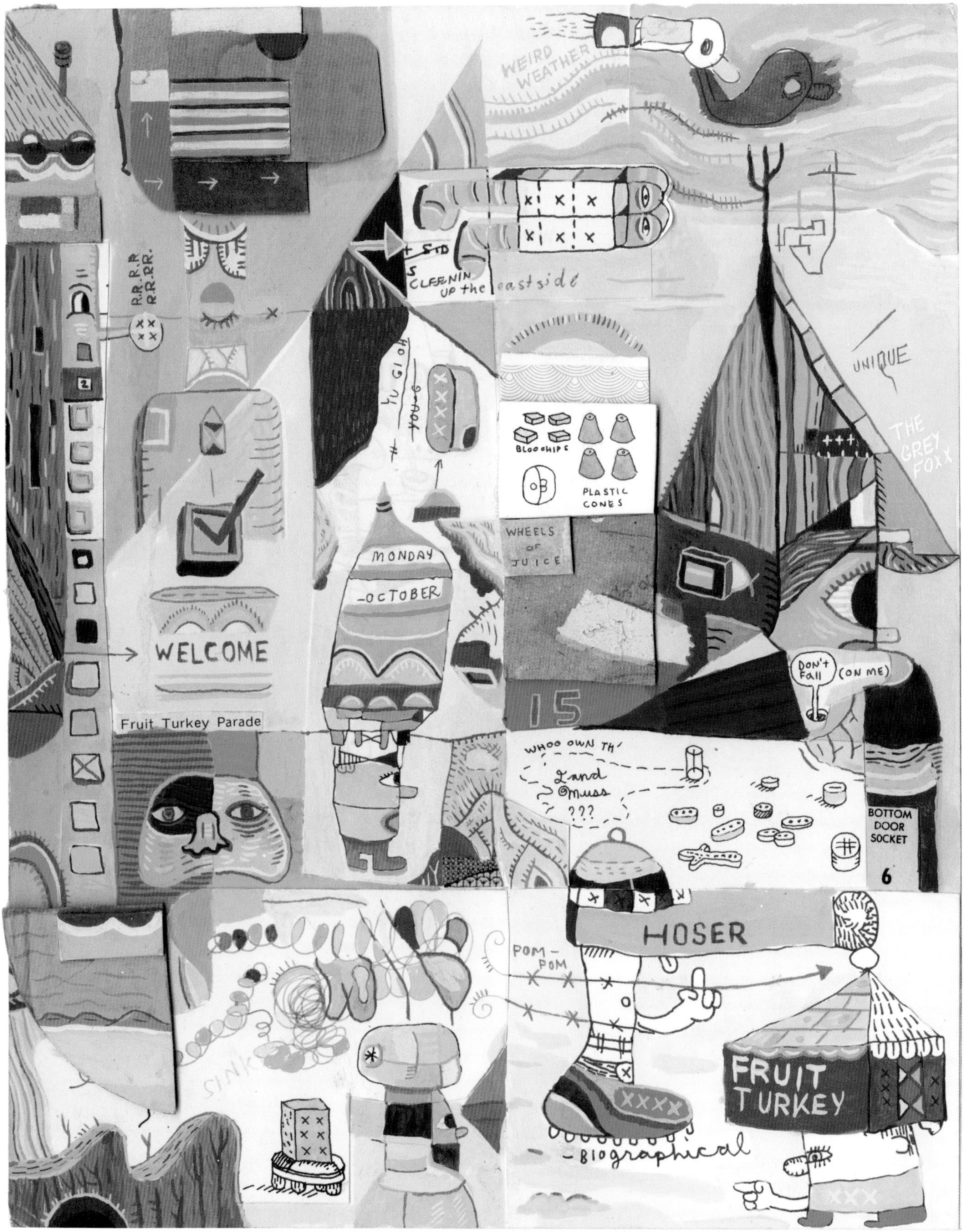
WEIRD WEATHER
+ STD
CLEENIN UP the eastside
R.R.R.R R.R.RR.
UNIQUE
THE GREY FOXX
BLOOCHIPS
PLASTIC CONES
WHEELS OF JUICE
MONDAY
-OCTOBER
WELCOME
Fruit Turkey Parade
15
Don't Fall
(ON ME)
WHOO OWN TH'
Land Muss
???
BOTTOM DOOR SOCKET
6
HOSER
POM-POM
FRUIT TURKEY
-Biographical

31. *Fruit Turkey Parade,* 2005
Mixed media on board, 10 x 8 in.
Includes: Ron Regé, Jr. nose reference, Wheels of Juice promotional item, reference to *Cleenin' Up The East Side* (no. 33)

32. *Balsam Adhesives,* 2007
Mixed media on board, 20 x 15 in.
Includes: swiss cheese

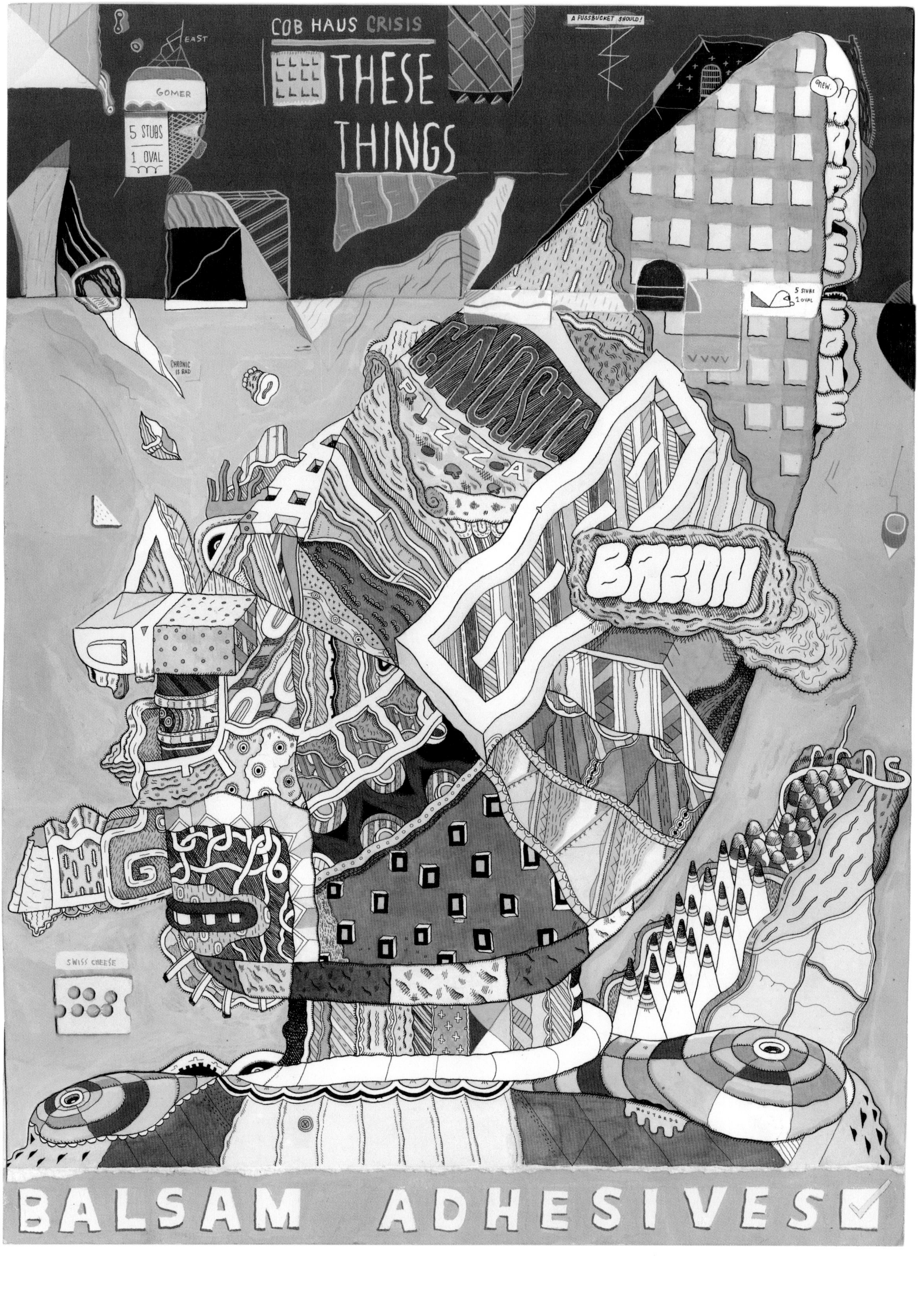
COB HAUS CRISIS
THESE THINGS
A FUSSBUCKET SHOULD!
EAST
GOMER
5 STUBS
1 OVAL
NEW.
5 STUBS
1 OVAL
CHRONIC IS BAD
PIZZA
BACON
SWISS CHEESE
BALSAM ADHESIVES

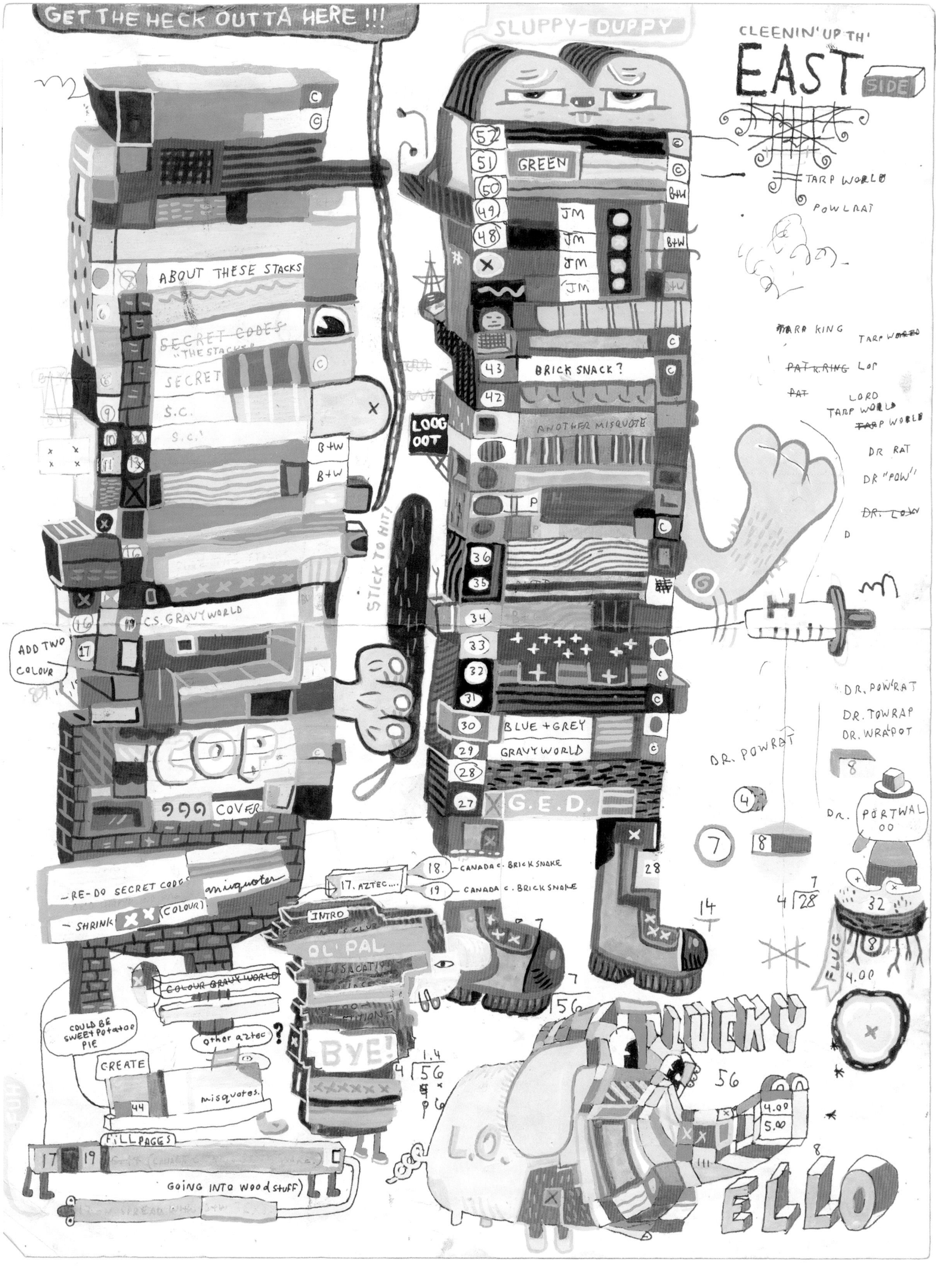
GET THE HECK OUTTA HERE !!!
SLUPPY-DUPPY
CLEENIN' UP TH' EAST SIDE
TARP WORLD
POWLRAT
GREEN
B+W
JM
JM
JM
JM
B+W
ABOUT THESE STACKS
SECRET CODES
"THE STACKS"
SECRET
S.C.
S.C.
B+W
B+W
BRICK SNACK?
ANOTHER MISQUOTE
LOOG OOT
TARP KING
TARP WORLD
PAT K.RING
LOP
PAT
LORD
TARP WORLD
TARP WORLD
DR RAT
DR "POW"
DR. LOW
STICK TO HIT!
C.S. GRAVYWORLD
ADD TWO COLOUR
BLUE + GREY
GRAVYWORLD
G.E.D.
COVER
DR. POWRAT
DR. TOWRAP
DR. WRAPOT
DR. POWRAT
DR. PORTWAL
RE-DO SECRET CODES
misquotes
SHRINK
(COLOUR)
17. AZTEC....
18. CANADA C. BRICKSNAKE
19. CANADA C. BRICKSNAKE
INTRO
OL' PAL
BYE!
COLOUR GRAVY WORLD
COULD BE SWEET POTATOE PIE
other aztec ?
CREATE
misquotes.
FILL PAGES
GOING INTO WOOD STUFF)
PLUG
LUCKY
L.O.
4.00
5.00
ELLO

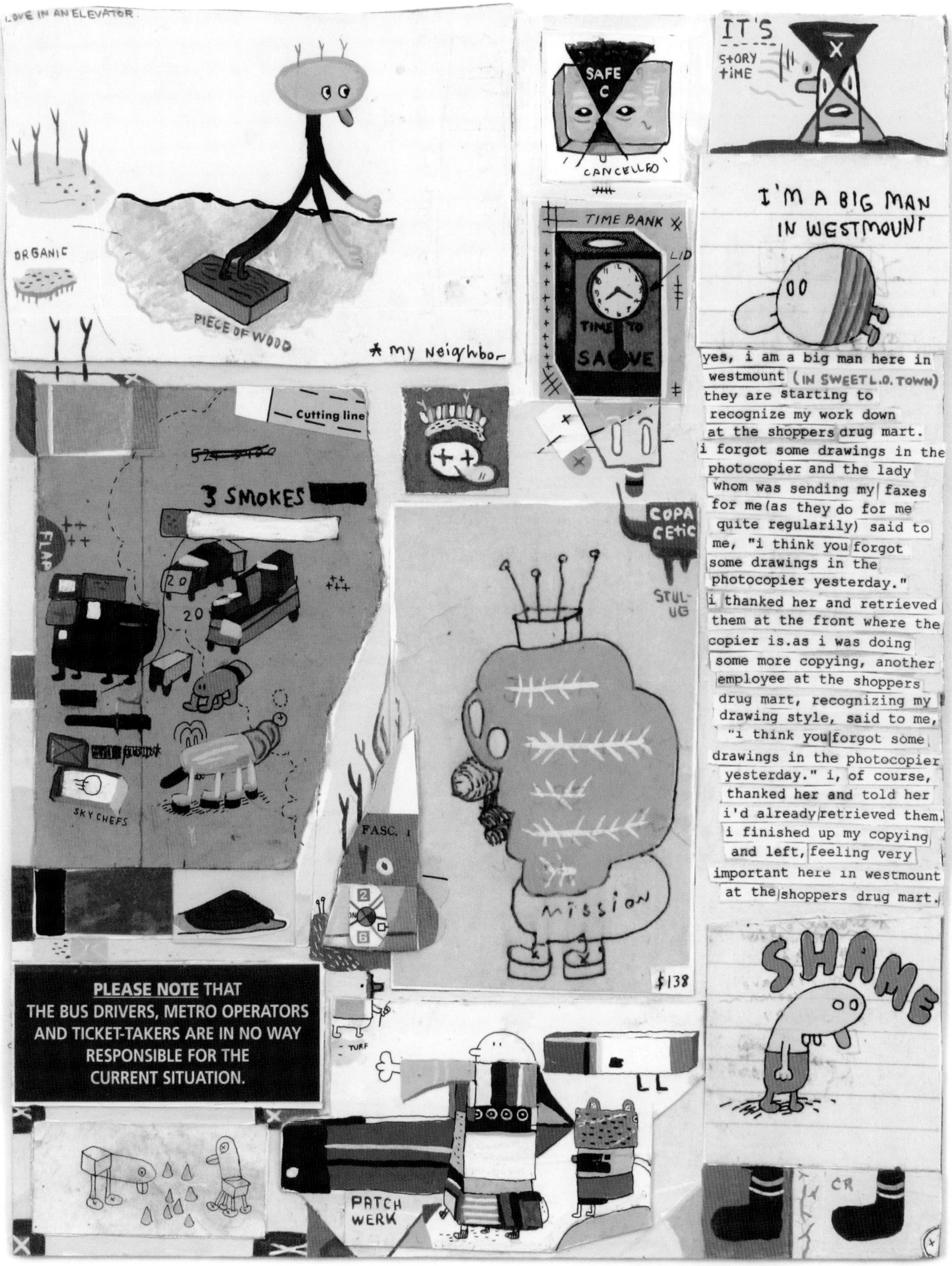

LOVE IN AN ELEVATOR
ORGANIC
PIECE OF WOOD
* my Neighbor
SAFE C
CANCELLED
IT'S
STORY TIME
TIME BANK
LID
TIME TO SAVE
I'M A BIG MAN IN WESTMOUNT
yes, i am a big man here in westmount (IN SWEET L.O. TOWN) they are starting to recognize my work down at the shoppers drug mart. i forgot some drawings in the photocopier and the lady whom was sending my faxes for me(as they do for me quite regularily) said to me, "i think you forgot some drawings in the photocopier yesterday." i thanked her and retrieved them at the front where the copier is.as i was doing some more copying, another employee at the shoppers drug mart, recognizing my drawing style, said to me, "i think you forgot some drawings in the photocopier yesterday." i, of course, thanked her and told her i'd already retrieved them. i finished up my copying and left, feeling very important here in westmount at the shoppers drug mart.
Cutting line
3 SMOKES
FLAP
SKY CHEFS
COPA CETIC
FASC. 1
MISSION
$138
PLEASE NOTE THAT THE BUS DRIVERS, METRO OPERATORS AND TICKET-TAKERS ARE IN NO WAY RESPONSIBLE FOR THE CURRENT SITUATION.
SHAME
TURF
PATCH WERK
CR

33. *Cleenin' Up The East Side,* 2003
Mixed media on board, 11–½ x 8–½ in.
Includes: Lucky Ello

34. *I'm a Big Man in Westmount,* 2003
Mixed media on board, 11 x 8–½ in.
Includes: 3 smokes, official apology

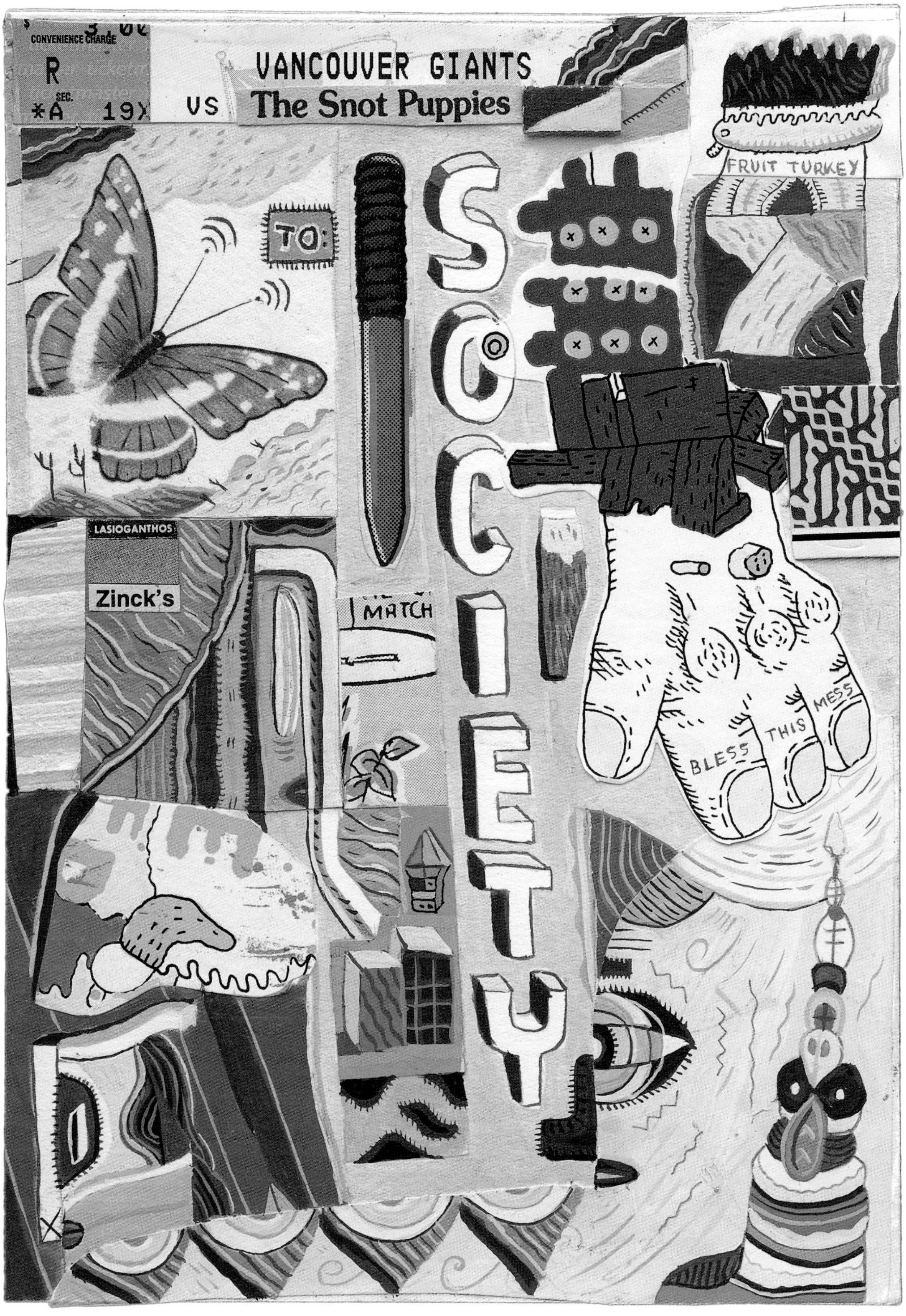
CONVENIENCE CHARGE
R
SEC.
*A 19
VANCOUVER GIANTS
VS
The Snot Puppies
FRUIT TURKEY
TO:
SOCIETY
LASIOGANTHOS
Zinck's
MATCH
BLESS THIS MESS

35. *Society (Stub #4, Vancouver Giants Vs. The Snot Puppies),* 2006
Mixed media on board, 7 x 5 in.
Includes: Vancovuer Giants ticket (unused)

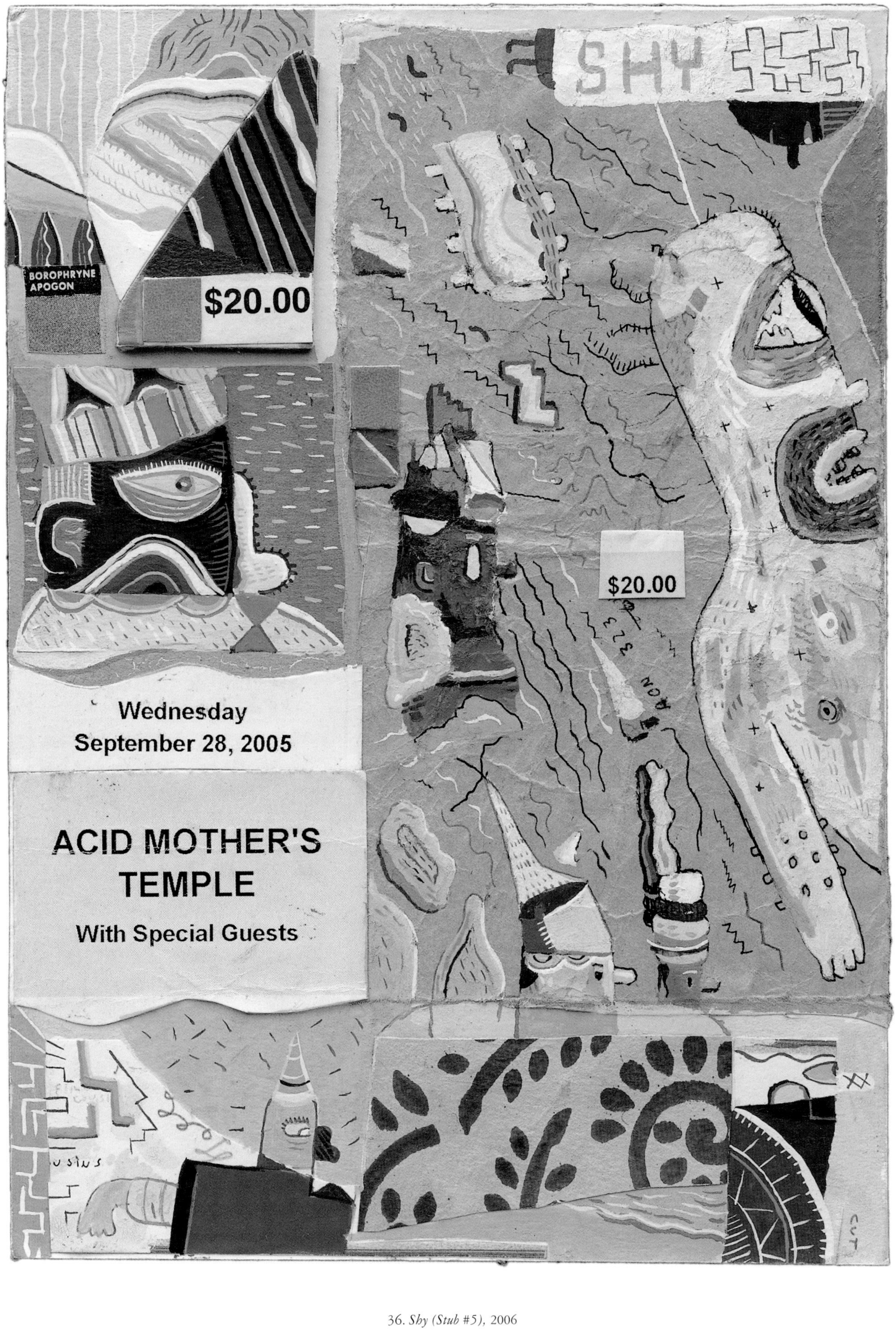
SHY
BOROPHRYNE
APOGON
$20.00
$20.00
Wednesday
September 28, 2005
ACID MOTHER'S
TEMPLE
With Special Guests

36. *Shy (Stub #5)*, 2006
Mixed media on board, 7 x 5 in.
Includes: Acid Mother's Temple ticket stub

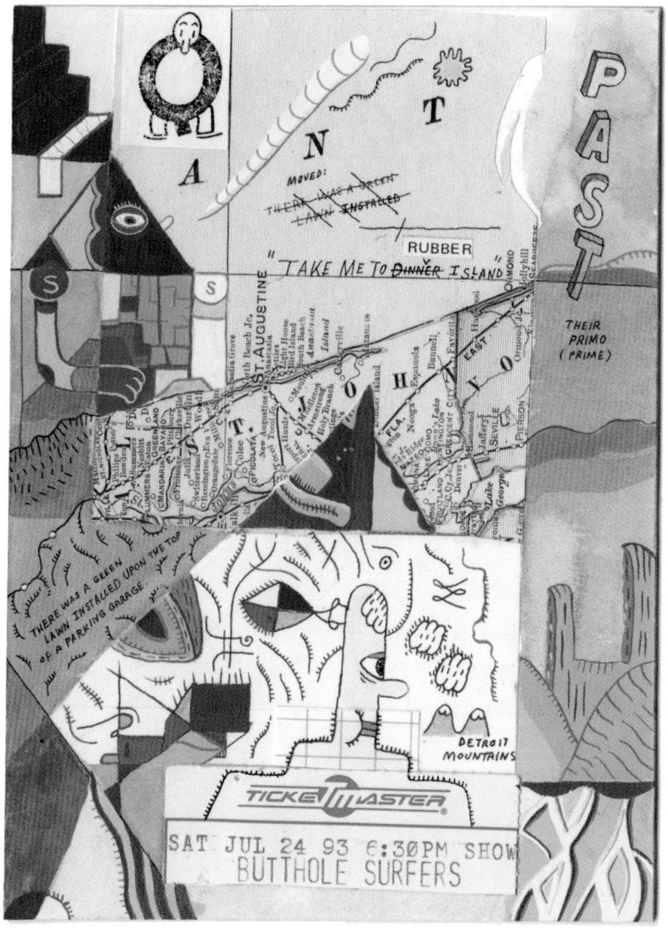
PAST
MOVED:
THERE WAS A GREEN LAWN INSTALLED
RUBBER
"TAKE ME TO DINNER ISLAND"
THEIR PRIMO (PRIME)
THERE WAS A GREEN LAWN INSTALLED UPON THE TOP OF A PARKING GARAGE
DETROIT MOUNTAINS
TICKETMASTER
SAT JUL 24 93 6:30PM SHOW
BUTTHOLE SURFERS

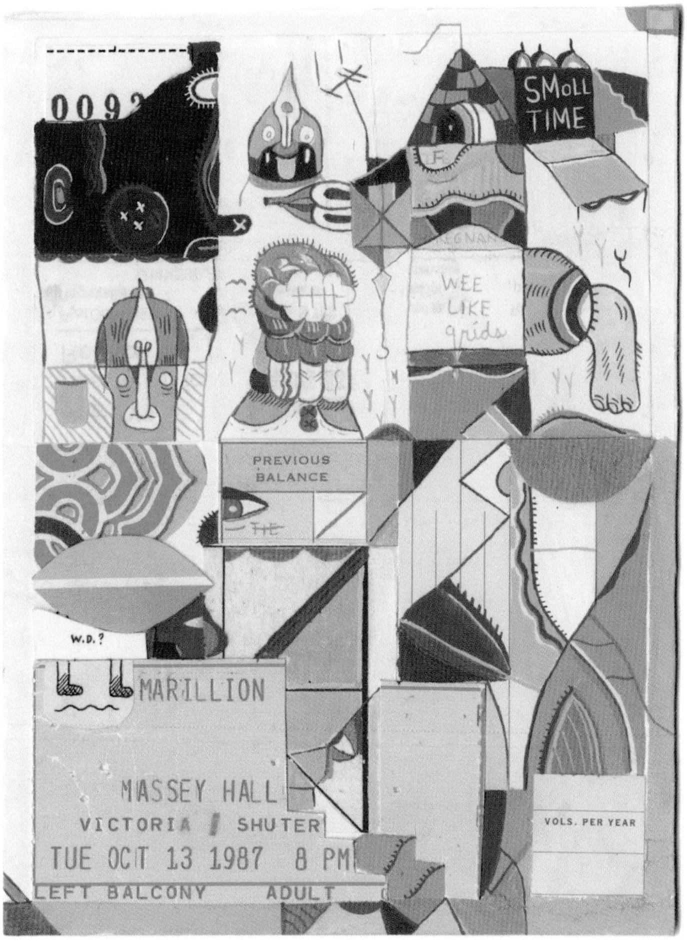
SMoll TIME
WEE LIKE grids
PREVIOUS BALANCE
W.D.?
MARILLION
MASSEY HALL
VICTORIA / SHUTER
TUE OCT 13 1987 8 PM
LEFT BALCONY ADULT
VOLS. PER YEAR

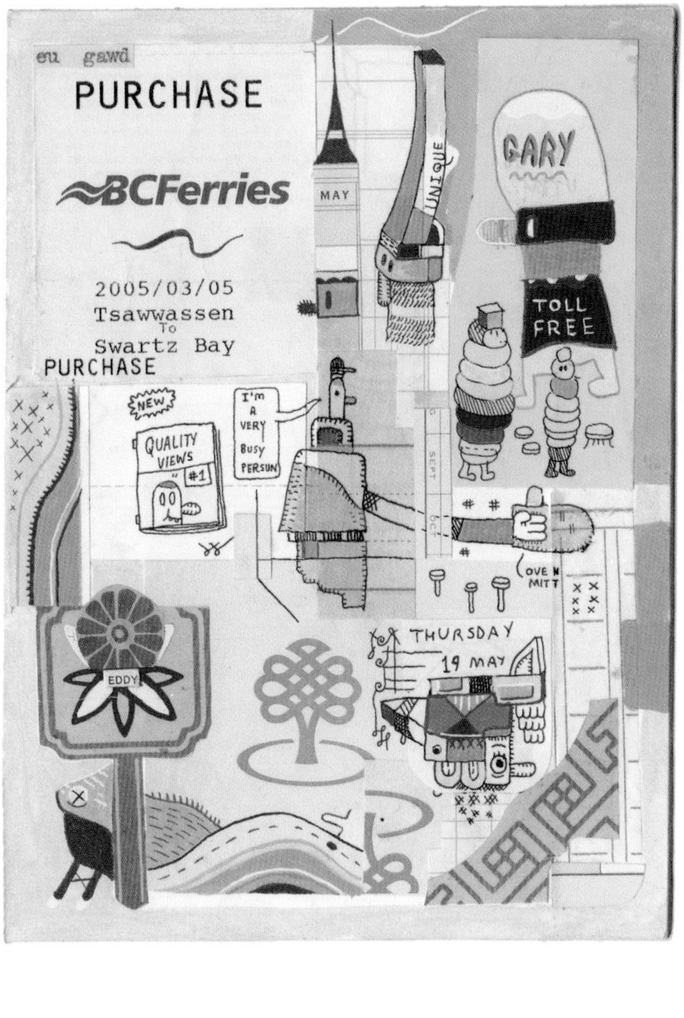
eu gawd
PURCHASE
BCFerries
2005/03/05
Tsawwassen
To
Swartz Bay
PURCHASE
MAY
UNIQUE
GARY
TOLL FREE
NEW
QUALITY VIEWS #1
I'm A VERY BUSY PERSON
OVEN MITT
THURSDAY
19 MAY
EDDY

37. *Ant (Stub #2)*, 2006
Mixed media on board, 7 x 5 in.
Includes: Butthole Surfers ticket stub

38. *Wee Like Grids (Stub #1)*, 2006
Mixed media on board, 7 x 5 in.
Includes: Marillion ticket stub

39. *Quality Views (Stub #3)*, 2006
Mixed media on board, 7 x 5 in.
Includes: B.C. Ferries ticket stub

Facing page:

40. *Turf*, 2005
Mixed media on board, 7–⅛ x 5 in.

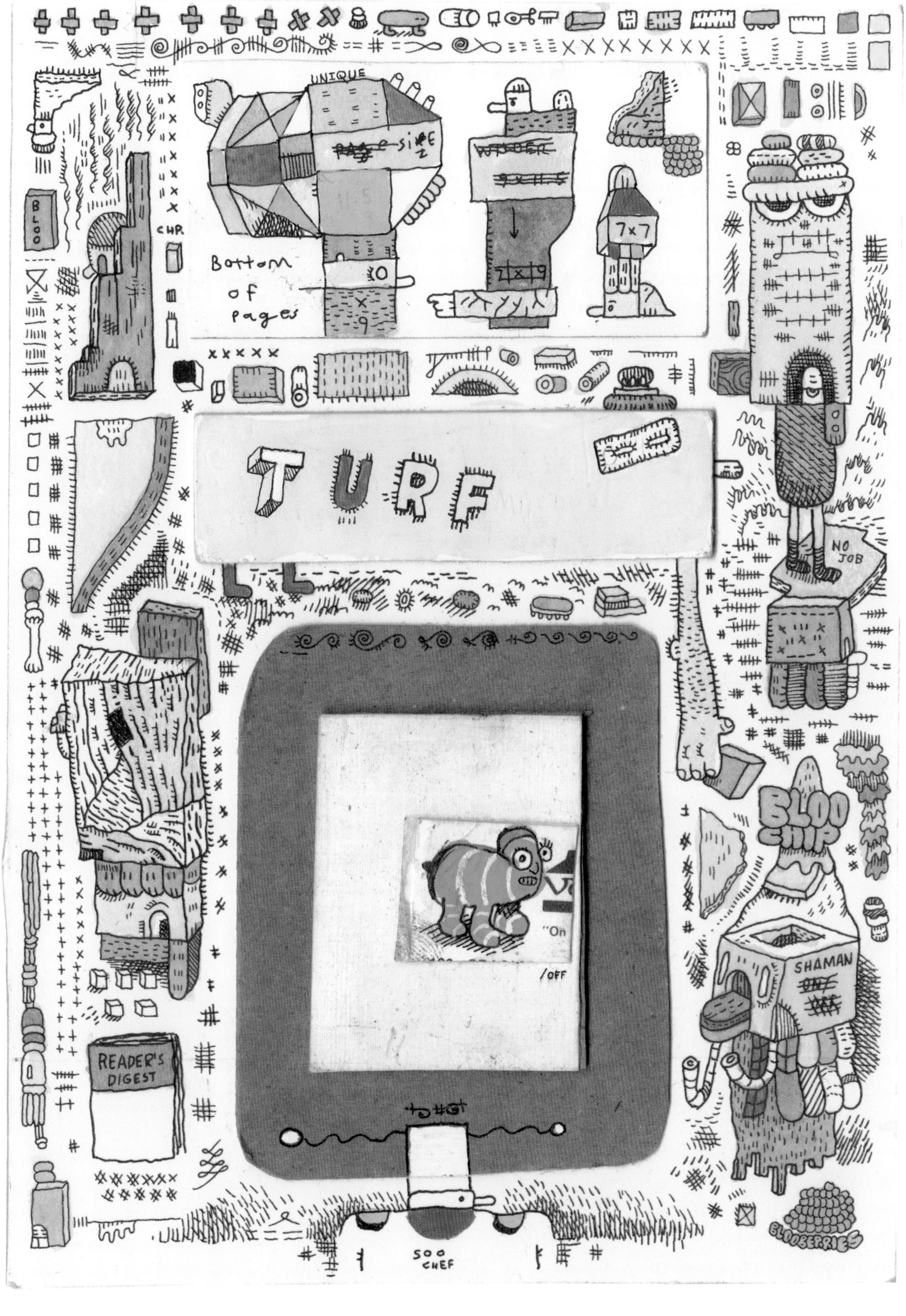
UNIQUE
PAGE SIZE
WIDER
Bottom of pages
7x7
7x9
BLOO
CHP
TURF
NO JOB
BLOO CHIP
SHAMAN
"On
/OFF
READER'S DIGEST
SOO CHEF
BLOOBERRIES

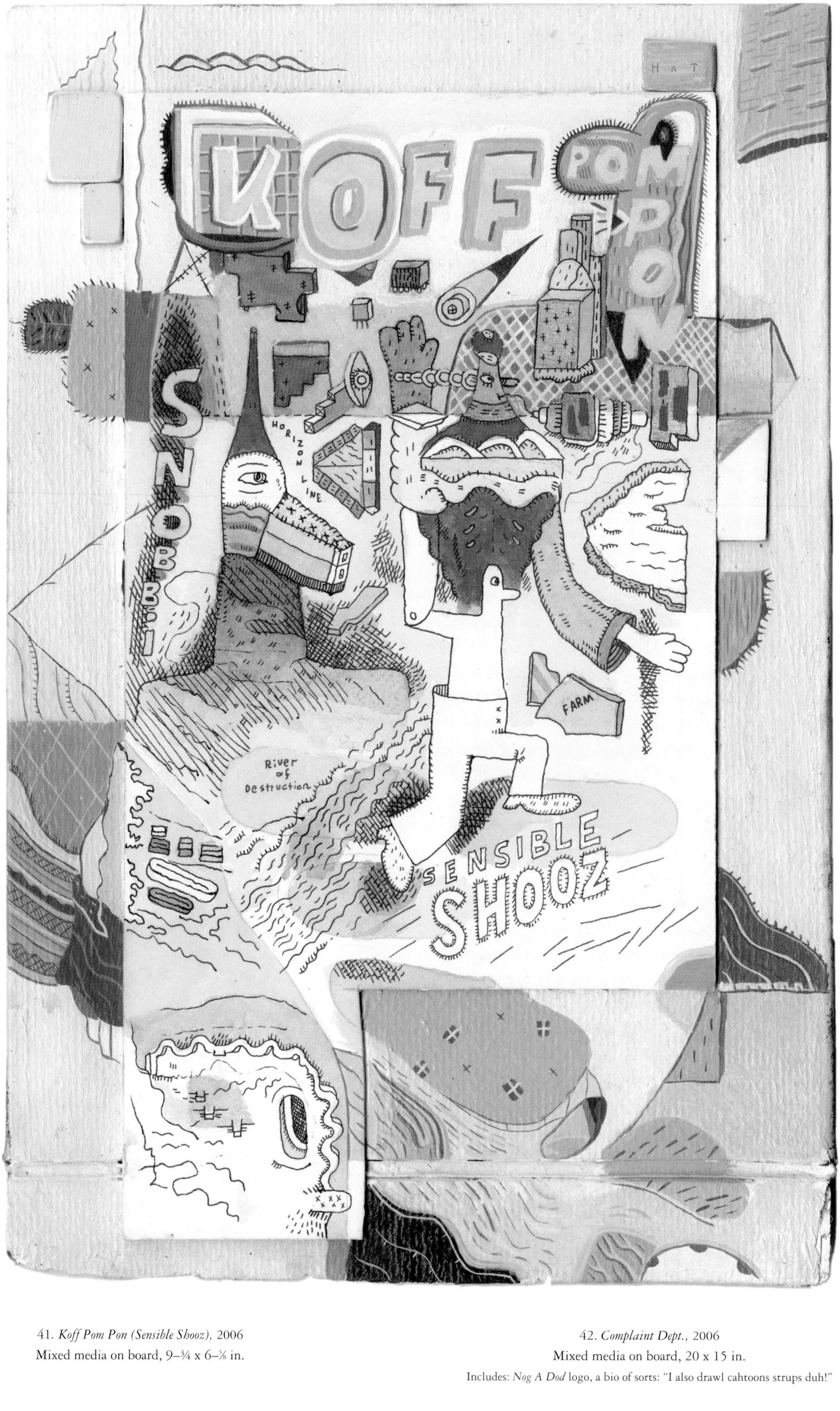
HAT
KOFF
POM
PON
SNOB
HORIZON LINE
FARM
River of Destruction
SENSIBLE
SHOOZ

41. *Koff Pom Pon (Sensible Shooz),* 2006
Mixed media on board, 9–¾ x 6–⅜ in.

42. *Complaint Dept.,* 2006
Mixed media on board, 20 x 15 in.
Includes: *Nog A Dod* logo, a bio of sorts: "I also drawl cahtoons strups duh!"

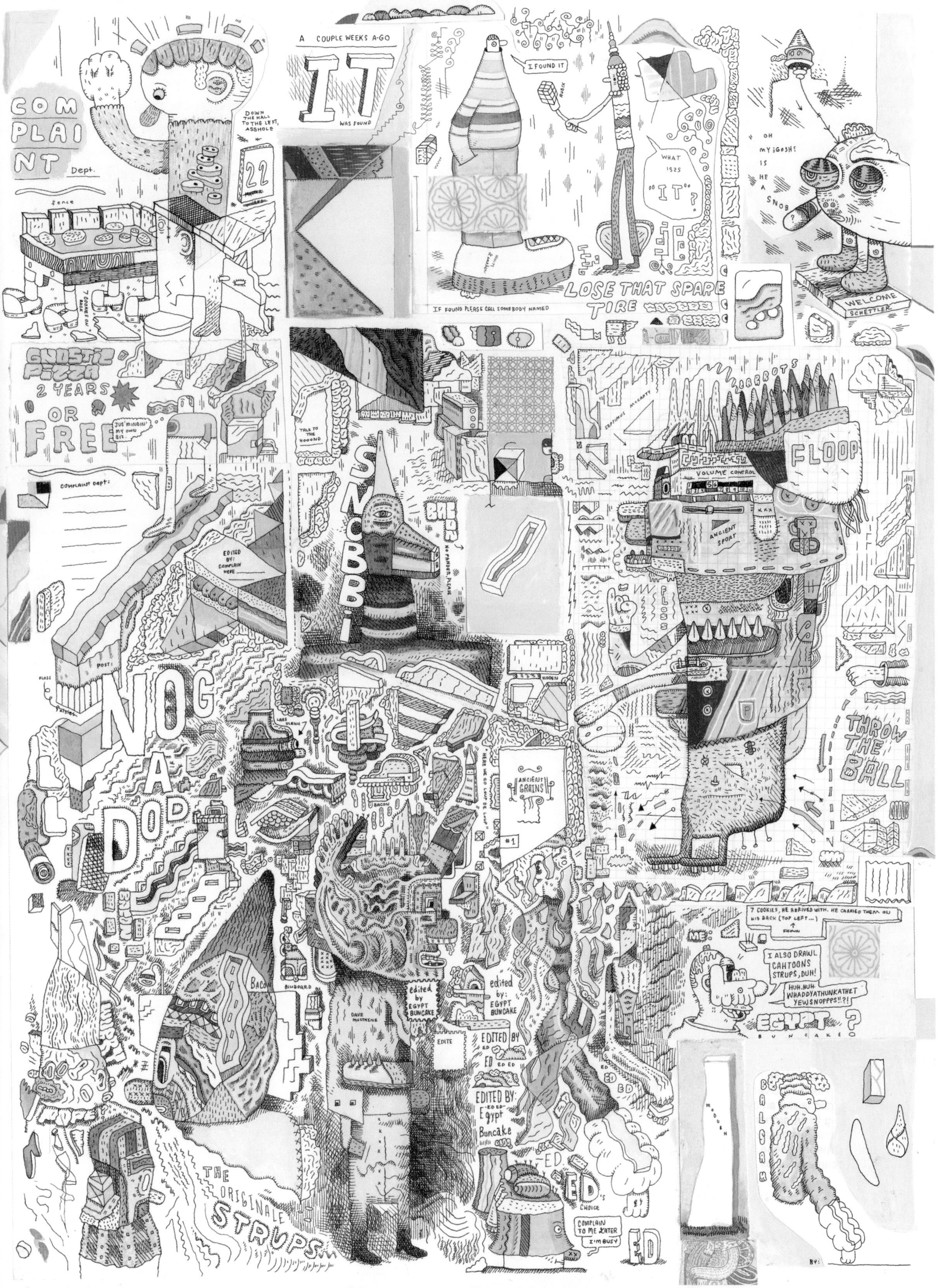

COMPLAINT Dept.
fence
DOWN THE HALL TO THE LEFT, ASSHOLE
22
A COUPLE WEEKS A-GO
IT
WAS FOUND
I FOUND IT
WHAT ISIS "IT"?
OH MY GOSH! IS HE A SNOB
WELCOME SCHETTLER
LOSE THAT SPARE TIRE
IF FOUND PLEASE CALL SOMEBODY NAMED
GNOSTIC PIZZA
2 YEARS OR FREE
JUS' MINDIN' MY OWN BIZ.
TALK TO THE HOOOND
COMPLAINT DEPT:
EDITED BY: COMPLAIN HERE
SNOBBI
BACON
NO PANDER, PLEASE
CARROTS
SEPTIMUS MCCARTY
FLOOP
VOLUME CONTROL
ANCIENT SPORT
FLOSS
NOG LA DOD
ANCIENT GRAINS
#1
THROW THE BALL
7 COOKIES, HE ARRIVED WITH. HE CARRIED THEM ON HIS BACK (TOP LEFT...)
SHOWN
ME:
I ALSO DRAWL CAHTOONS STRUPS, DUH!
HUH HUH WHADDYATHUNKATHET YEWSNOPPPS!!?!
EGYPT ? BUNCAKE
edited by EGYPT BUNCAKE
edited by EGYPT BUNCAKE
DAVE MUSTAINE
EDITED BY ED
EDITED BY: Egypt Buncake
NOPE
THE ORIGINALE STRUPS
ED's CHOICE
COMPLAIN TO ME LATER I'M BUSY
ED
MODERN
BALSAM
BY:

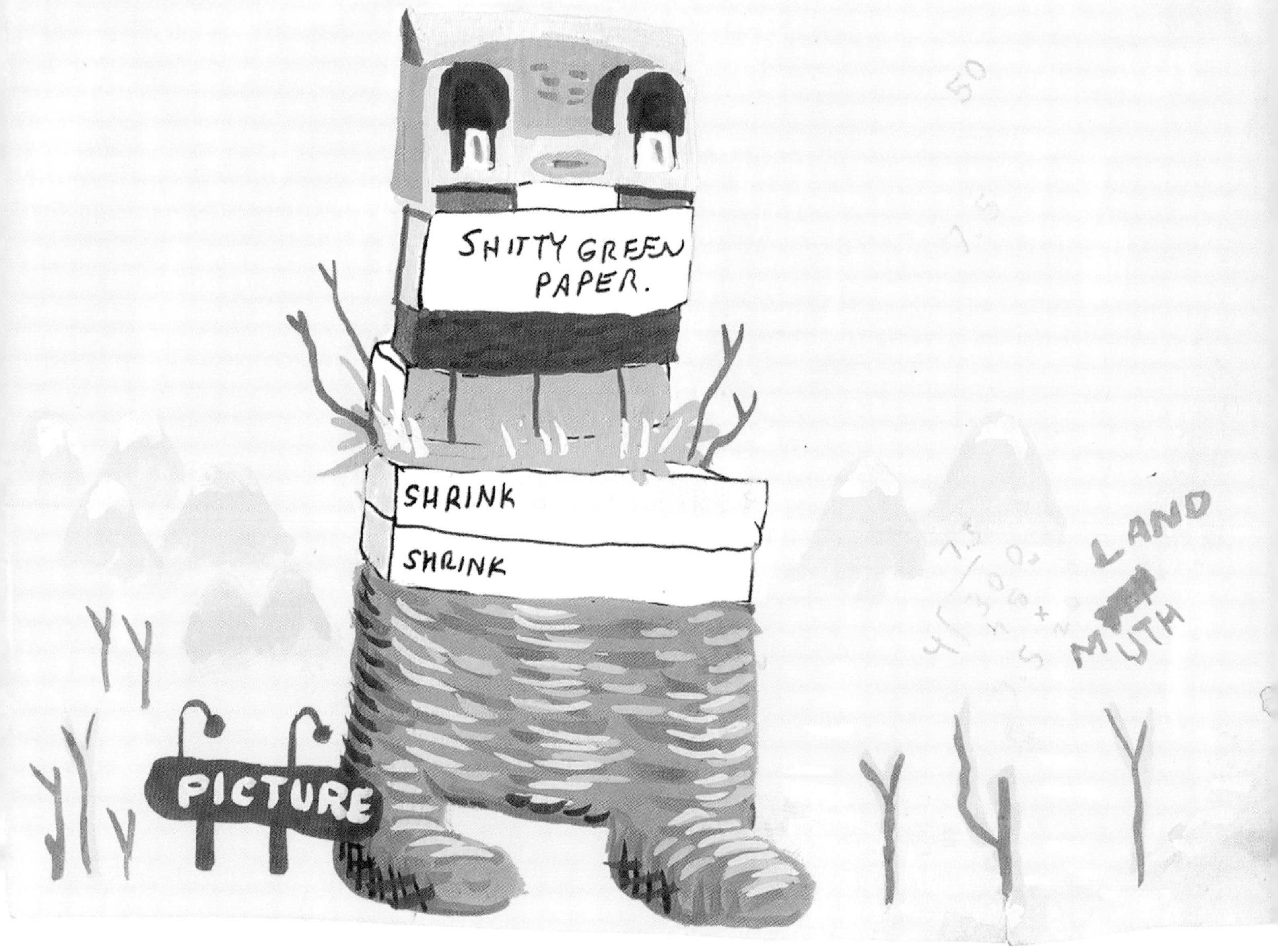
SHITTY GREEN PAPER.
SHRINK
SHRINK
PICTURE
LAND

43. *Shitty Green Paper,* 2003
Mixed media on paper, 4 x 5 in.

44. *They Me,* 2003
Mixed media on board, 4 x 5–¾ in.
Includes: "Sky Chefs" logo, accounting

Facing page:

45. *The Boys (Oven Mitt),* 2002
Mixed media on board, 6 x 4–½ in.
Includes: ad for "Giant Masher"

46. *Dog Whelks Periwinkles Up! (Air Goes Up),* 2000
Mixed media on board, 9 x 6 in.
Includes: Amy L. t–shirt design, french for "eat my balls," Ontario logo pattern, Flag (CAD)

47. *Us Them,* 2005
Mixed media on board, 3–¾ x 6 in.
Includes: more accounting

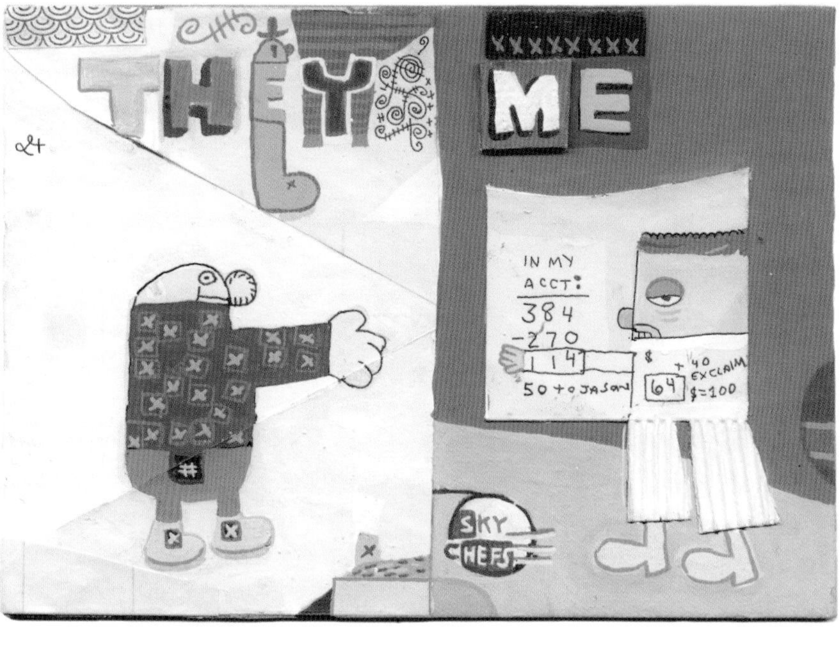
THEY
ME
IN MY ACCT:
384
-270
114
50 + to JASON
64
+40 EXCLAIM
$=100
SKY CHEFS

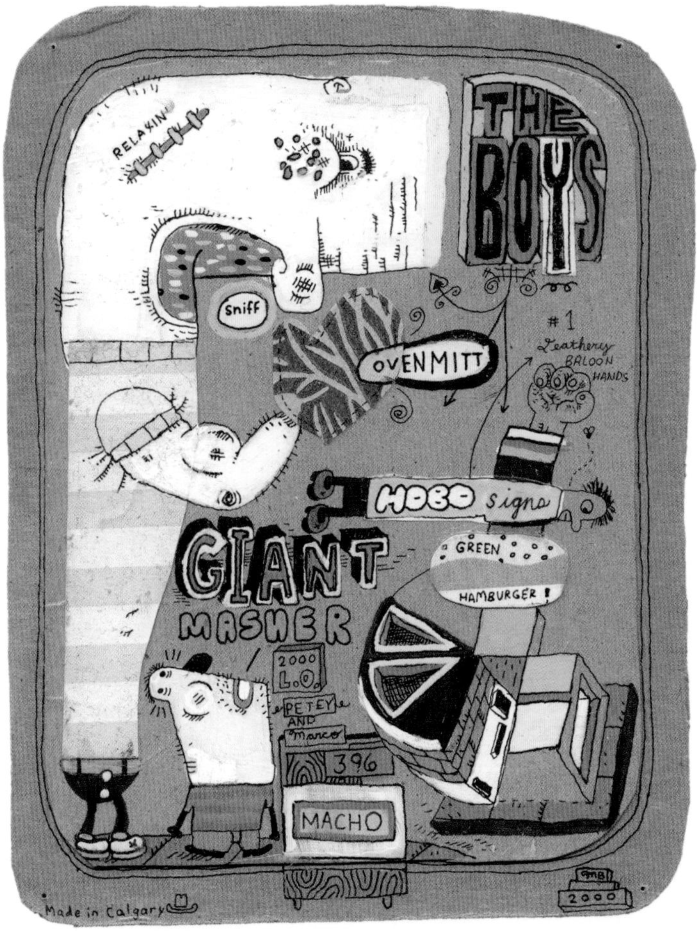
RELAXIN'
THE BOYS
sniff
OVENMITT
#1
HOBO signs
GIANT
MASHER
GREEN
HAMBURGER!
2000 L.O.
PETEY AND
396
MACHO
Made in Calgary
MB 2000

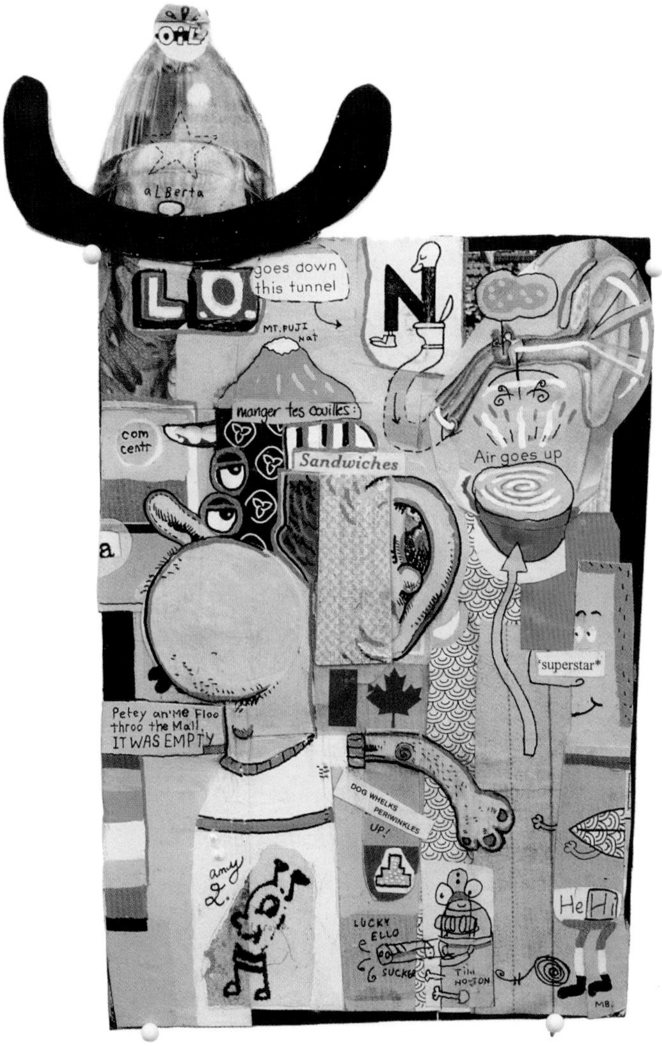
alBerta
L.O.
N
goes down this tunnel
MT. FUJI
manger tes ouilles
Sandwiches
Air goes up
superstar
Petey an'me Floo throo the Mall. IT WAS EMPTY
DOG WHELKS
PERIWINKLES
UP!
HeHi
MB.

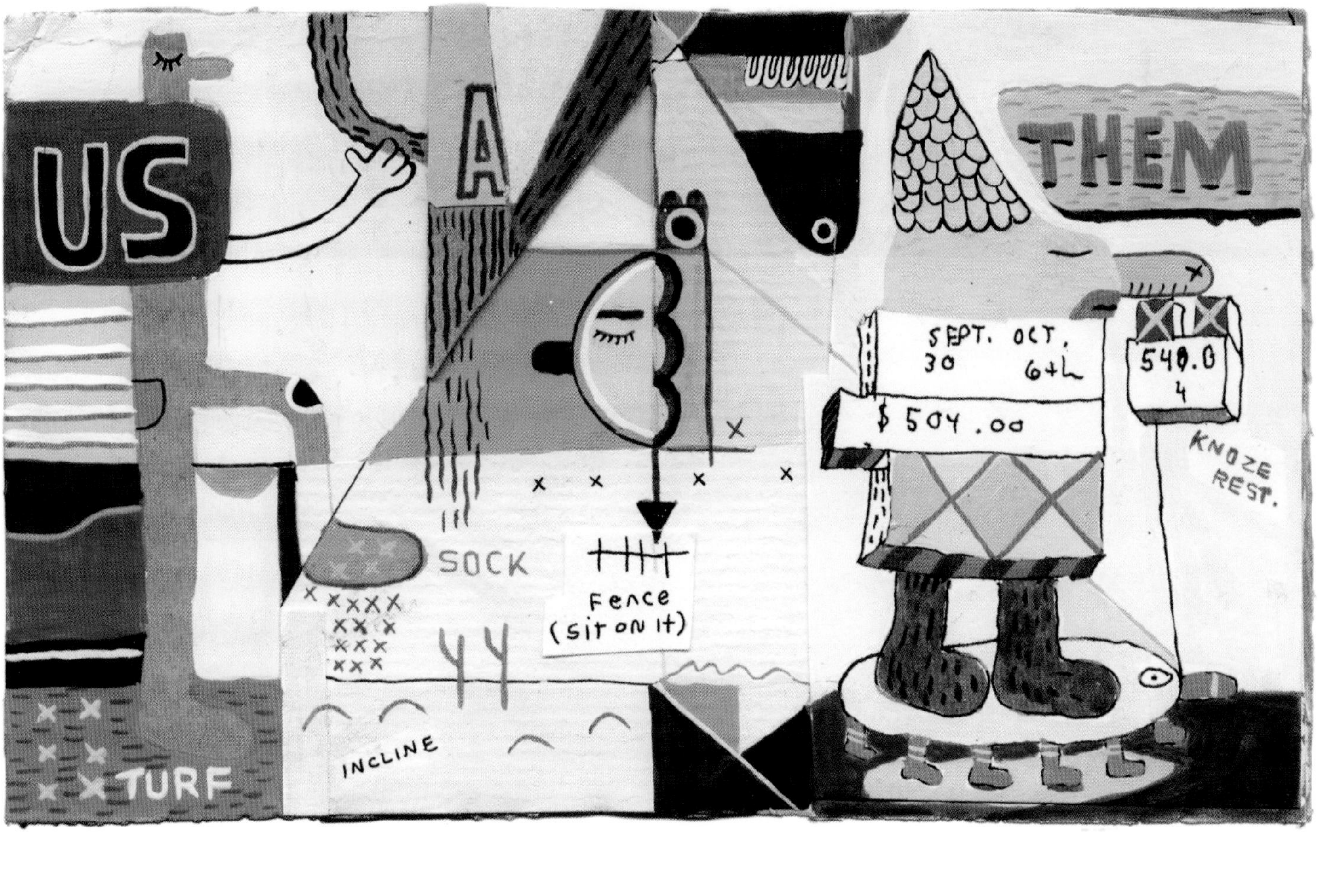
US
A
THEM
SEPT. 30
OCT. 6+L
$ 504.00
540.0 4
KNOZE REST.
SOCK
Fence (sit on it)
INCLINE
TURF

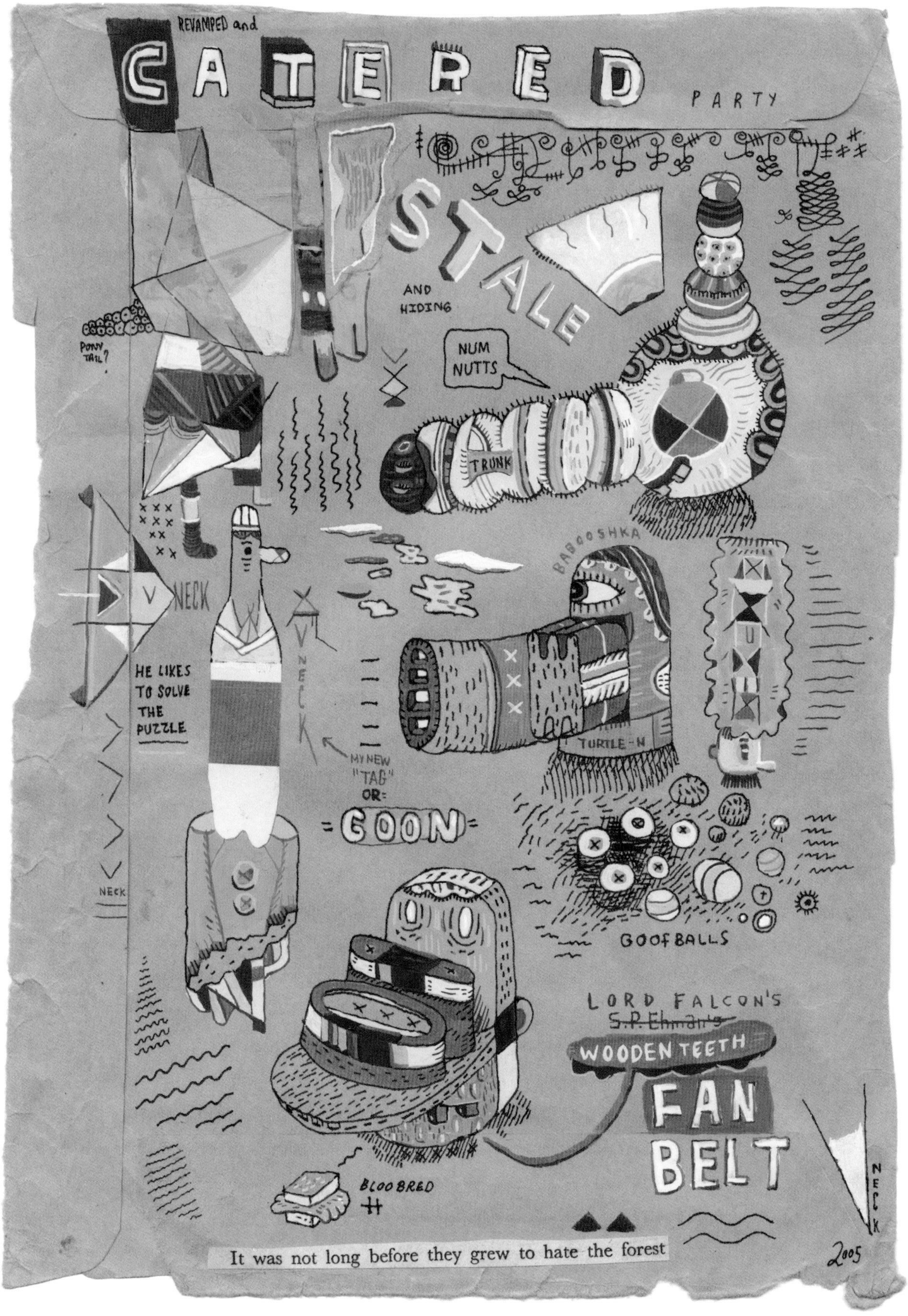
REVAMPED and
CATERED
PARTY
STALE
AND HIDING
NUM NUTTS
PONY TAIL?
TRUNK
BABOOSHKA
NECK
HE LIKES TO SOLVE THE PUZZLE
NECK
MY NEW "TAG" OR:
GOON
TURTLE-N
GOOFBALLS
NECK
LORD FALCON'S
WOODEN TEETH
FAN BELT
BLOOBRED
NECK
It was not long before they grew to hate the forest
2005

48. *Catered Party (Stale and Hiding),* 2005
Mixed media on envelope, 9 x 6 in.
Includes: phrase clipped from *The Hobbit*

Facing page, top: *Catered Party (Stale and Hiding)* in previous state

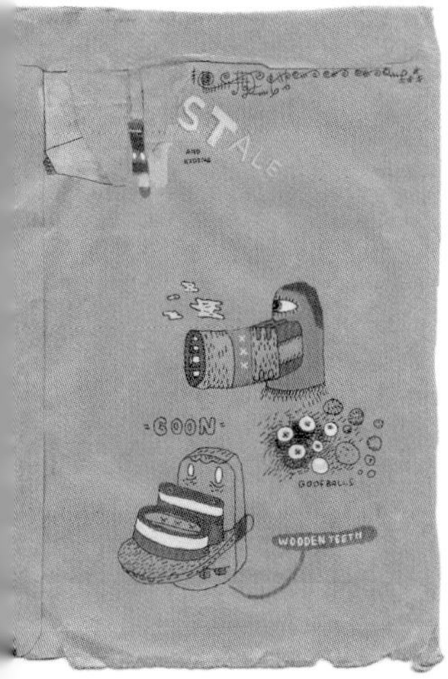
STALE
GOON
WOODEN TEETH

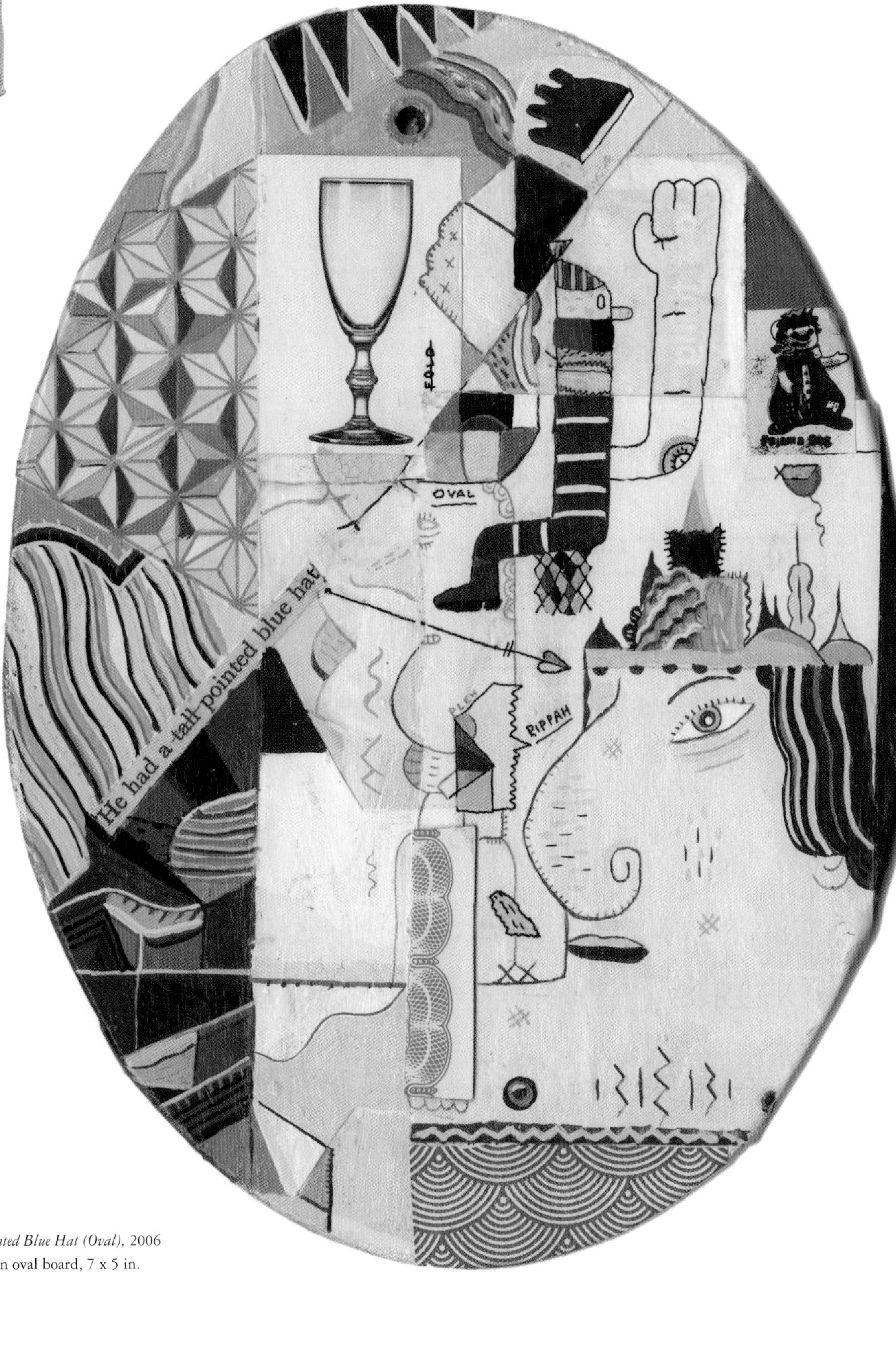
He had a tall pointed blue hat
FOLD
OVAL
RIPPAH

49. *He Had A Pointed Blue Hat (Oval),* 2006
Mixed media on oval board, 7 x 5 in.

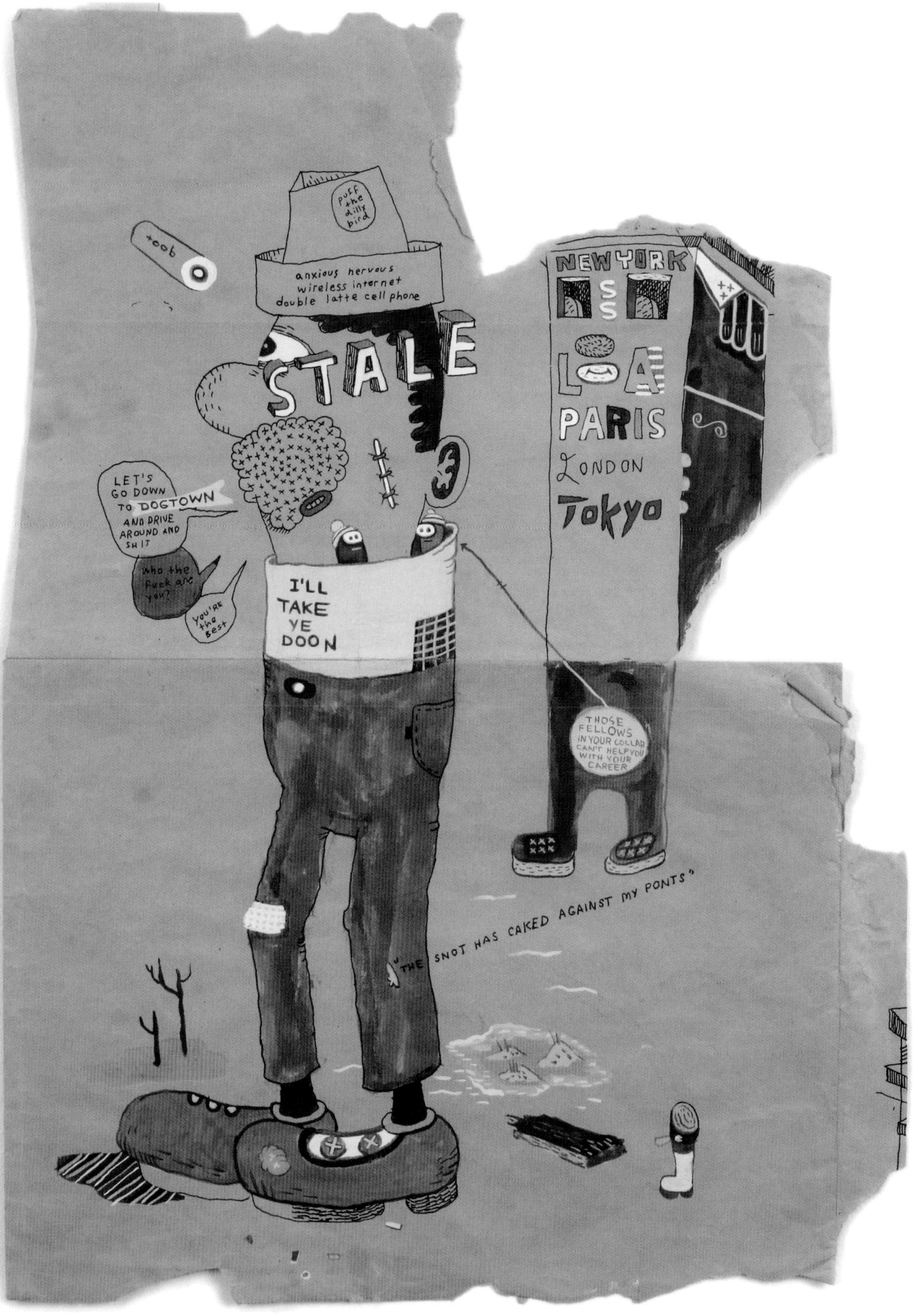
puff the dilly bird
toot
anxious nervous wireless internet double latte cell phone
STALE
LET'S GO DOWN TO DOGTOWN AND DRIVE AROUND AND SHIT
Who the fuck are you?
You're the best
I'LL TAKE YE DOON
NEW YORK
LA
PARIS
LONDON
Tokyo
THOSE FELLOWS IN YOUR COLLAR CAN'T HELP YOU WITH YOUR CAREER
"THE SNOT HAS CAKED AGAINST MY PONTS"

50. *Stale,* 2003
Mixed media on envleope, 17 x 12 in.
Includes: Arthur Lee (Love) lyric reference

51. *To "Hell" With Tomorrow Attitude,* 2005
Mixed media on board, 11 x 8–½ in.
Includes: clipping from bankruptcy counseling program literature ("things to avoid"), characters here are reused in *Floor Folk* drawing (no. 53) and "Floor Folk (It Is Explained)" (p. 72)

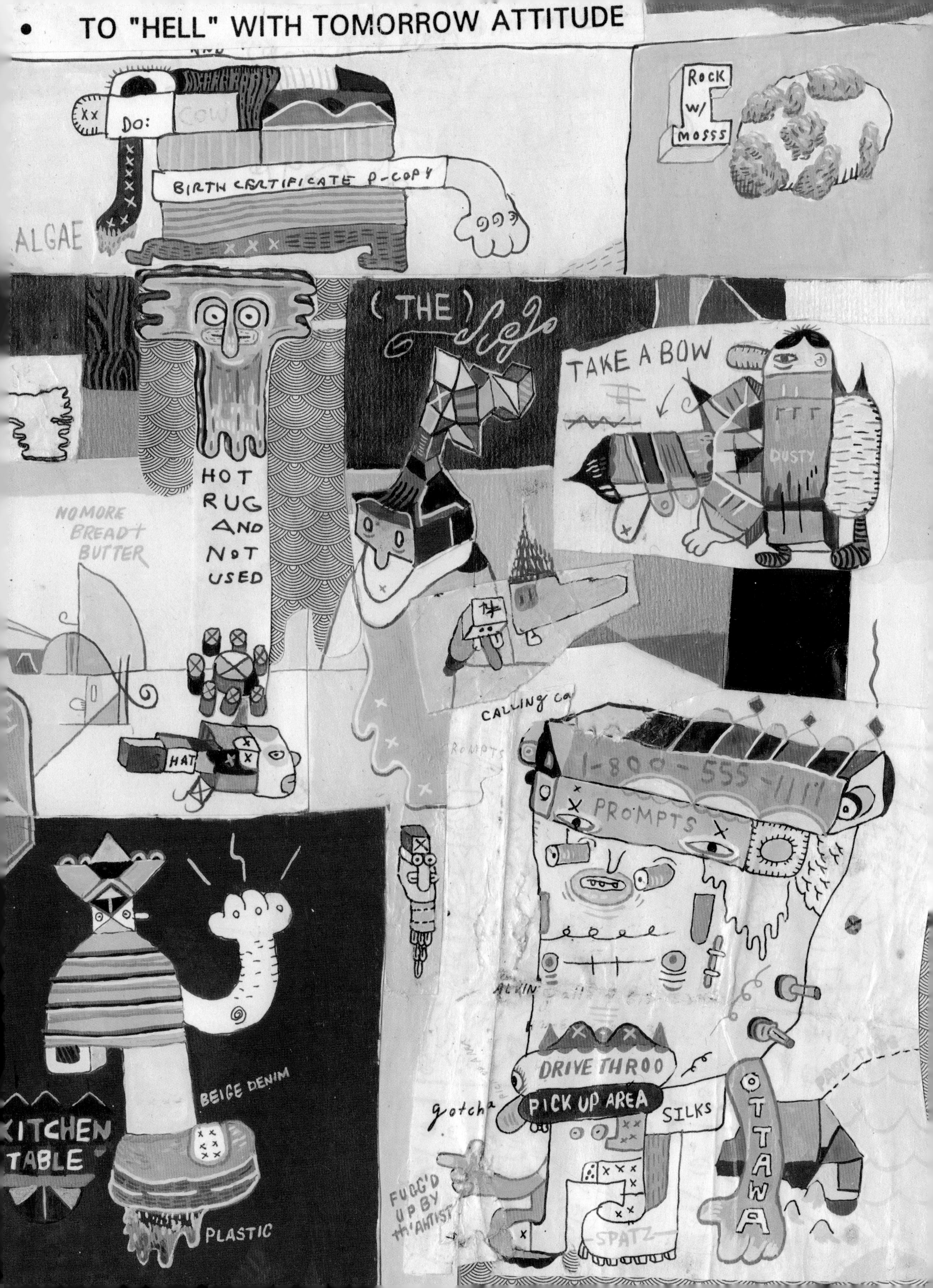
TO "HELL" WITH TOMORROW ATTITUDE
DO:
COW
BIRTH CERTIFICATE P-COPY
ALGAE
ROCK W/ MOSSS
(THE)
TAKE A BOW
DUSTY
HOT RUG AND NOT USED
NO MORE BREAD + BUTTER
HAT
CALLING CA
PROMPTS
1-800-555-1111
PROMPTS
ALVIN
DRIVE THROO
PICK UP AREA
gotcha
SILKS
OTTAWA
FUGG'D UP BY TH'AHTIST
SPATZ
BEIGE DENIM
KITCHEN TABLE
PLASTIC

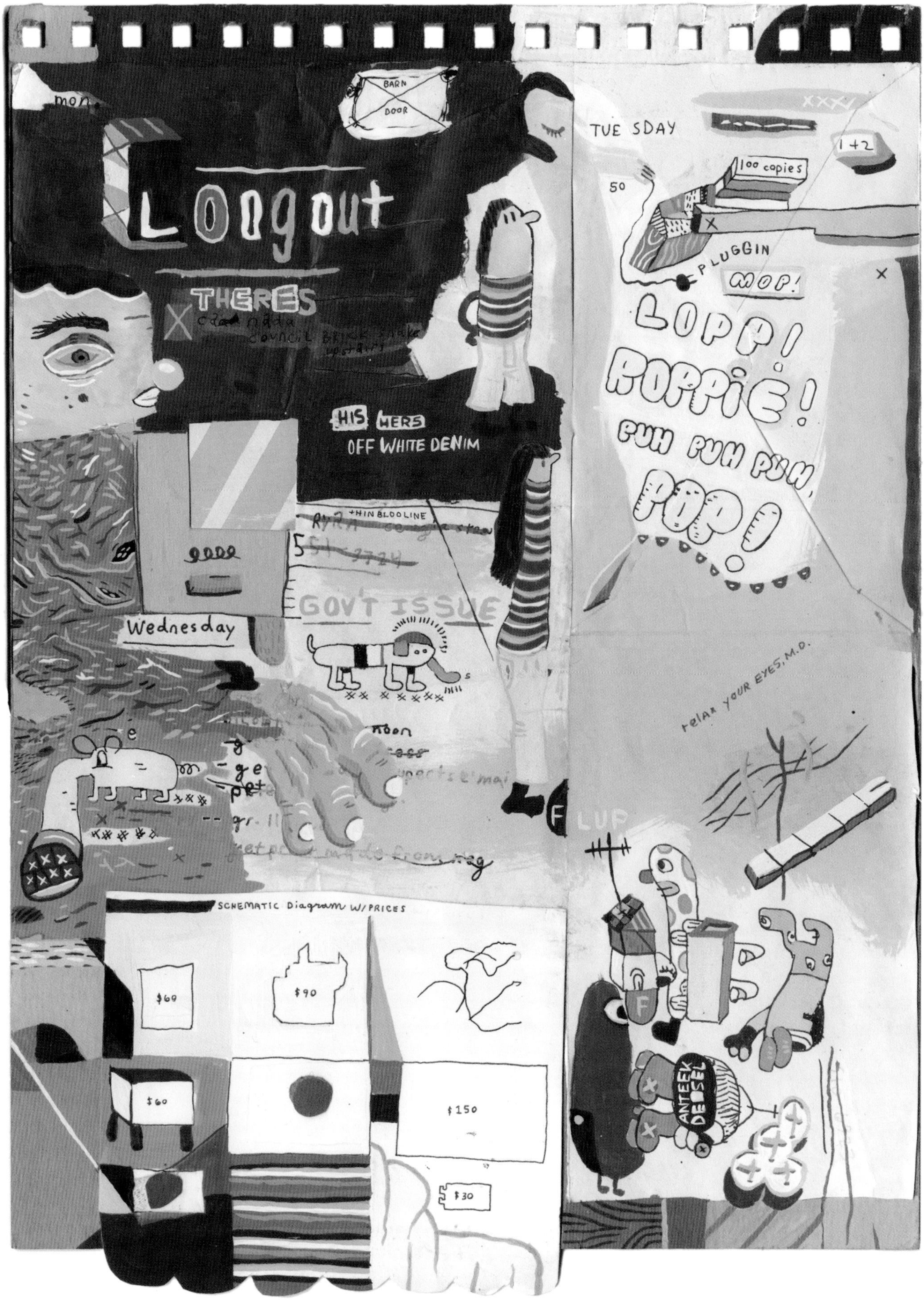
BARN DOOR
mon
Loogout
THERES
HIS HERS
OFF WHITE DENIM
+THIN BLOODLINE
GOV'T ISSUE
Wednesday
TUE SDAY
100 copies
1+2
50
PLUGGIN
MOP!
LOPP!
ROPPIE!
PUH PUH PUH,
POP!
relax YOUR EYES, M.D.
FLUP
SCHEMATIC Diagram W/PRICES
$69
$90
$60
$150
$30
ANTEEK DEESEL

52. *Loogout,* 2004

Mixed media on board, 12–¼ x 8–¾ in.

Includes: schematic drawing with prices

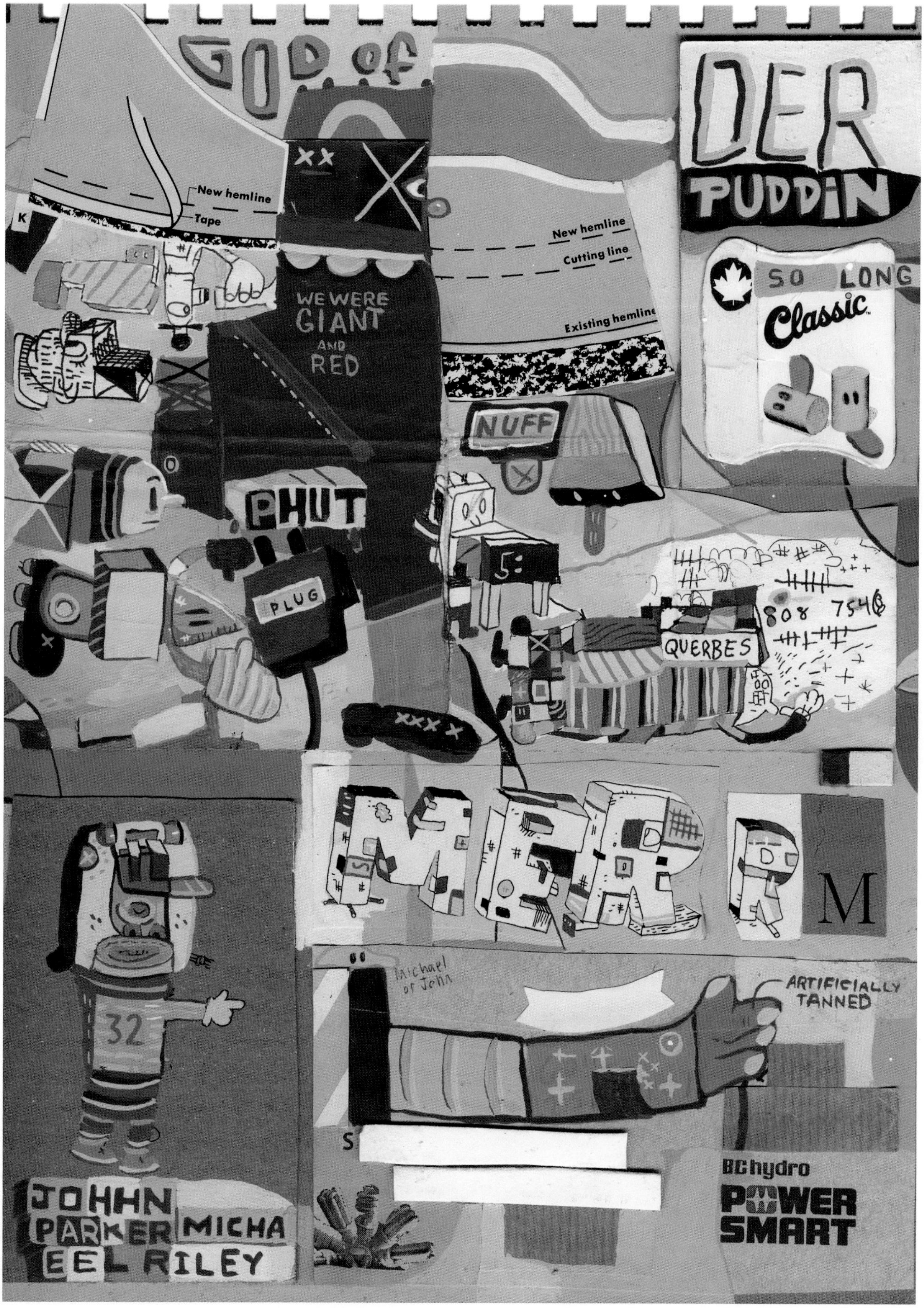
GOD of
DER
PUDDIN
New hemline
Tape
K
New hemline
Cutting line
Existing hemline
WE WERE
GIANT
AND
RED
SO LONG
Classic
NUFF
PHUT
PLUG
5:
808 754
QUERBES
XXXX
MERR
M
Michael or John
ARTIFICIALLY
TANNED
32
S
JOHHN
PARKER MICHA
EEL RILEY
BC hydro
POWER
SMART

53. *God of Der Puddin,* 2004
Mixed media on board, 12 x 9 in.
Includes: ear plug packaging, BC Hydro envelope

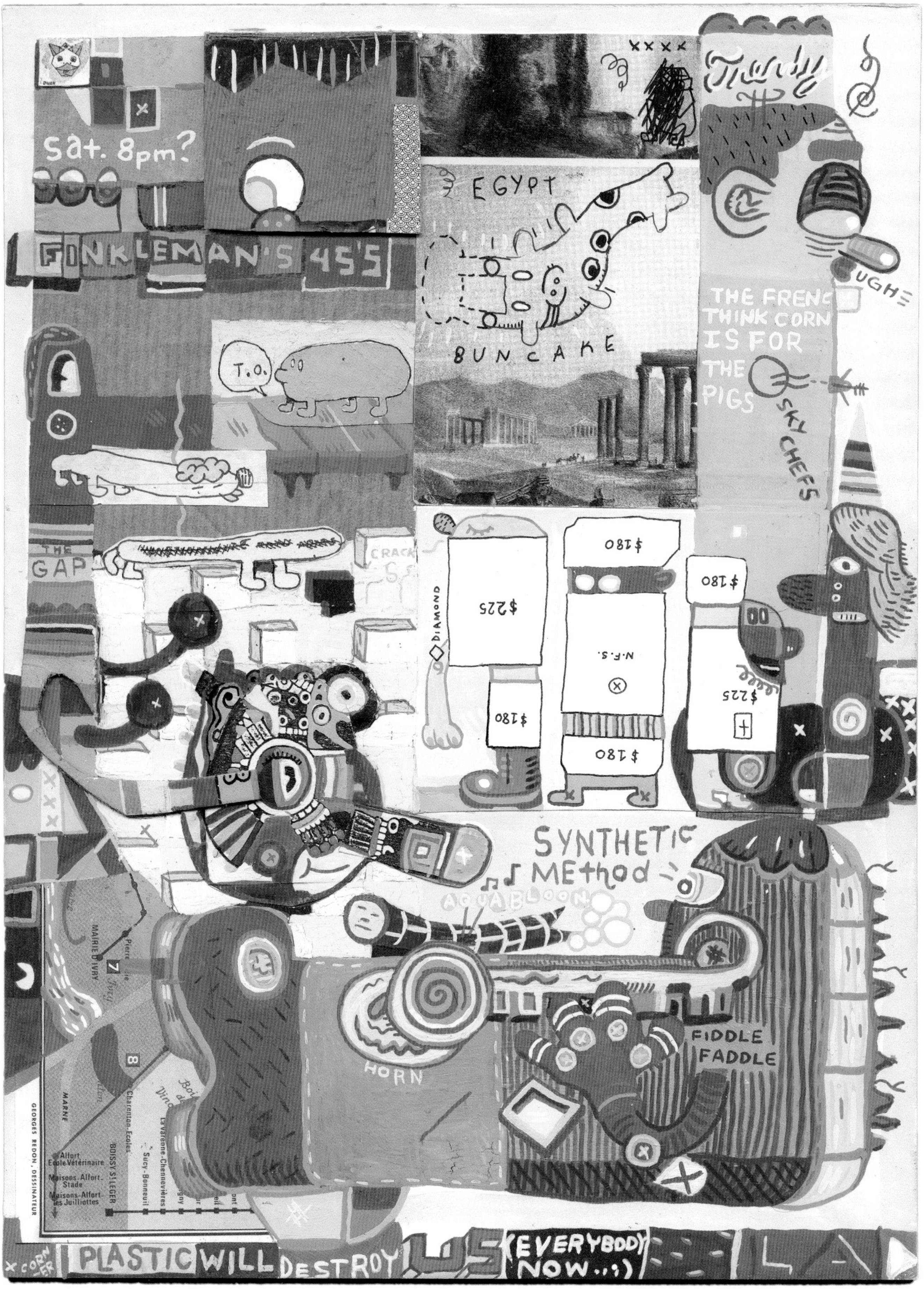
sat. 8pm?
FINKLEMAN'S 45'S
EGYPT
BUNCAKE
T.O.
THE FRENC THINK CORN IS FOR THE PIGS
SKY CHEFS
THE GAP
CRACK
DIAMOND
$225
$180
N.F.S.
SYNTHETIC METhod
AQUABLOON
HORN
FIDDLE FADDLE
MAIRIE D'IVRY
Charenton-Ecoles
MARNE
Alfort Ecole Vétérinaire
Maisons-Alfort Stade
Maisons-Alfort les Juilliottes
BOISSY St LEGER
Sucy-Bonneuil
La Varenne-Chennevières
GEORGES REDON, DESSINATEUR
PLASTIC WILL DESTROY US (EVERYBODY NOW..:)

54. *Synthetic Method,* 2003

Mixed media on board, 9–½ x 7–¼ in.

Includes: schematic drawing with prices

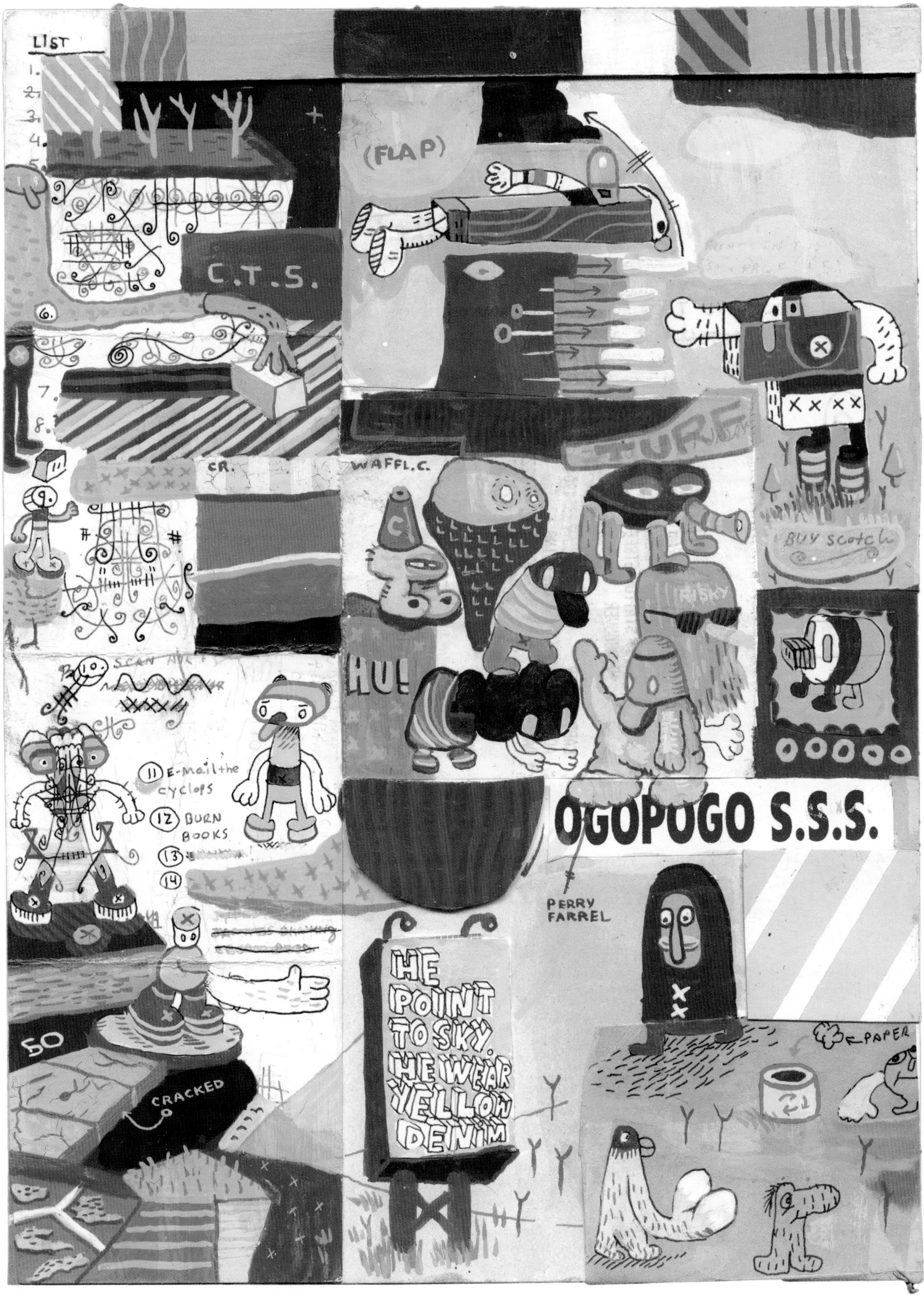
LIST
1.
2.
3.
4.
5.
(FLAP)
C.T.S.
6.
7.
8.
CR.
WAFFL.C.
TURF
BUY scotch
RISKY
HU!
9.
10.
11 E-mail the cyclops
12 BURN BOOKS
13
14
OGOPOGO S.S.S.
PERRY FARREL
HE POINT TO SKY. HE WEAR YELLOW DENIM
PAPER
50
CRACKED

55. *Ogopogo S.S.S.,* 2003
Mixed media on board, 10 x 7–½ in.
Includes: Perry Farrel

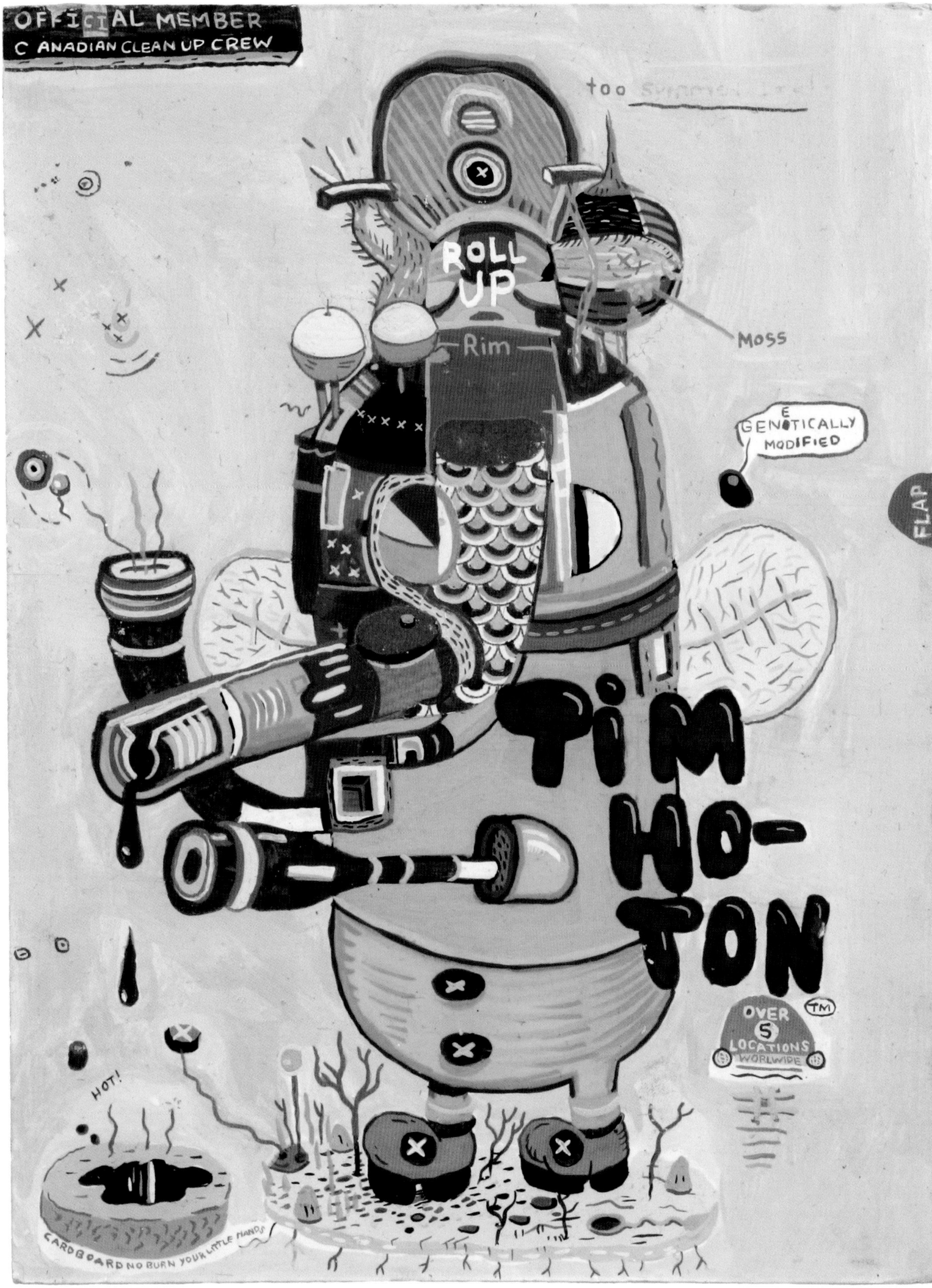
OFFICIAL MEMBER
CANADIAN CLEAN UP CREW
too
ROLL UP
Rim
MOSS
GENETICALLY MODIFIED
FLAP
TIM HO-TON
TM
OVER 5 LOCATIONS WORLWIDE
HOT!
CARDBOARD NO BURN YOUR LITTLE HANDS

56. *Tim Ho–Ton,* 2003
Mixed media on board, 9–¾ x 7–¼ in.

57. *(P)LUPAG (Fruits are of no use),* 2003
Mixed media on board, 11 x 8–½ in.
Includes: character that is used in a comic strip on the following page

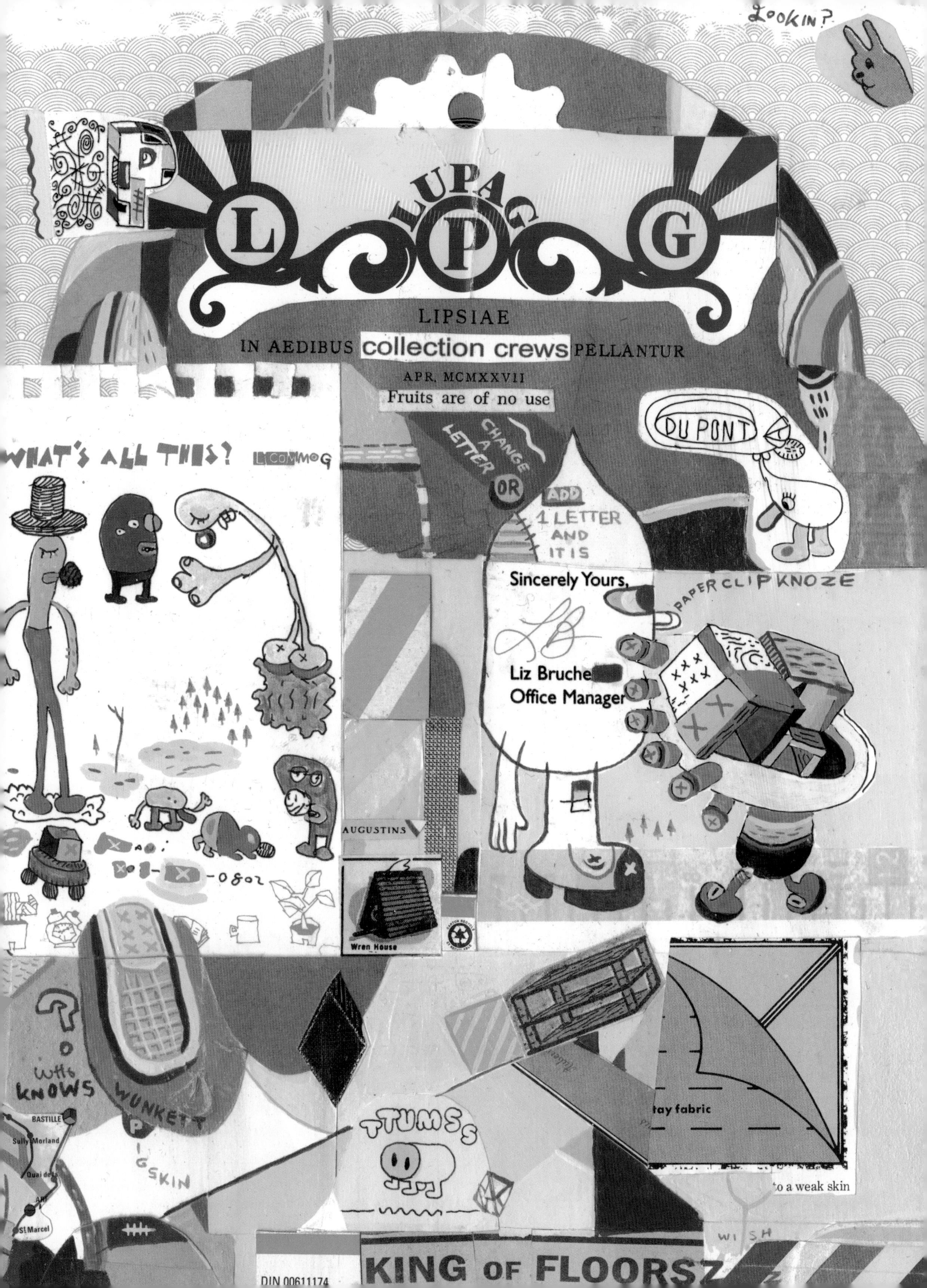
LOOKIN?
LUPAG
L P G
LIPSIAE
IN AEDIBUS collection crews PELLANTUR
APR. MCMXXVII
Fruits are of no use
DU PONT
CHANGE A LETTER
OR
ADD 1 LETTER AND IT IS
WHAT'S ALL THIS?
Sincerely Yours,
Liz Bruche[redacted]
Office Manager
PAPERCLIP KNOZE
AUGUSTINS
Wren House
WHO KNOWS
WUNKETT
PIGSKIN
BASTILLE
Sully Morland
St Marcel
TUMSS
tay fabric
to a weak skin
WISH
DIN 00611174
KING OF FLOORSZ

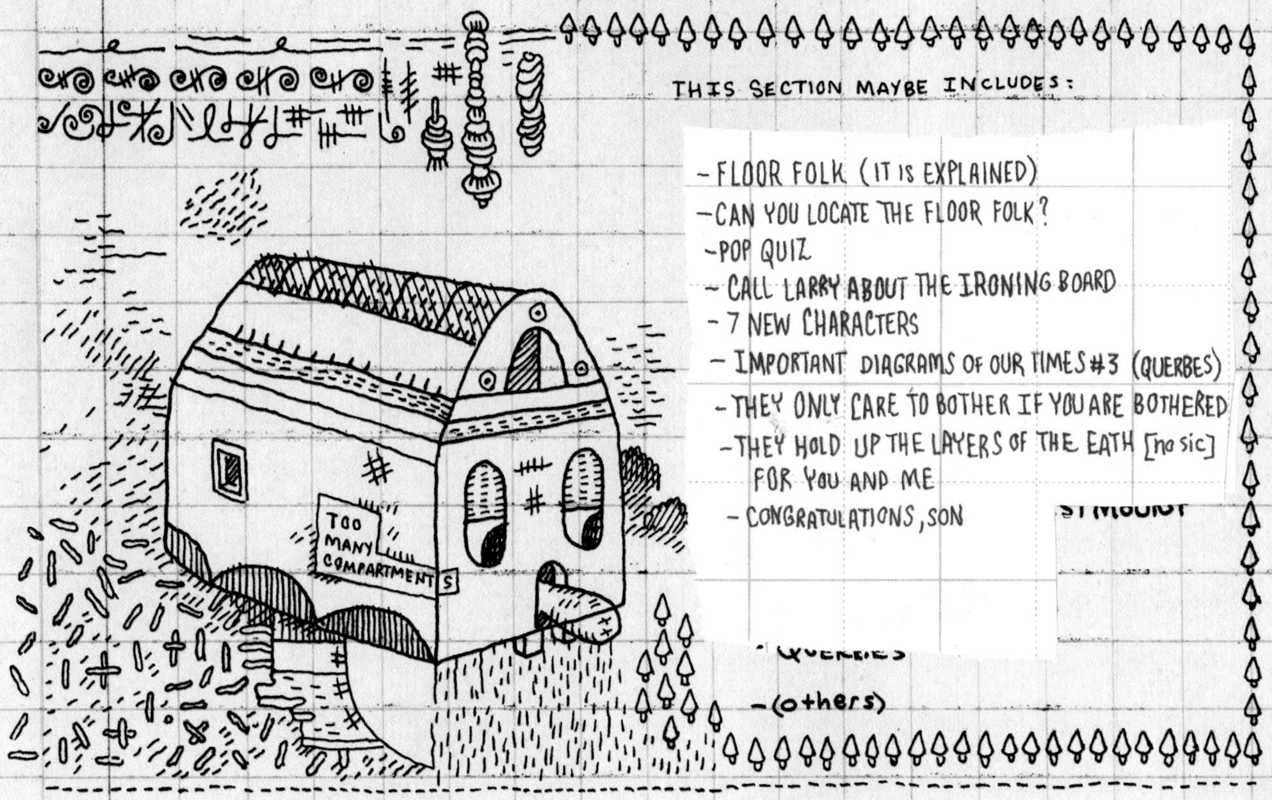
THIS SECTION MAYBE INCLUDES:
- FLOOR FOLK (IT IS EXPLAINED)
- CAN YOU LOCATE THE FLOOR FOLK?
- POP QUIZ
- CALL LARRY ABOUT THE IRONING BOARD
- 7 NEW CHARACTERS
- IMPORTANT DIAGRAMS OF OUR TIMES #3 (QUERBES)
- THEY ONLY CARE TO BOTHER IF YOU ARE BOTHERED
- THEY HOLD UP THE LAYERS OF THE EATH [no sic] FOR YOU AND ME
- CONGRATULATIONS, SON
-(others)
TOO MANY COMPARTMENTS

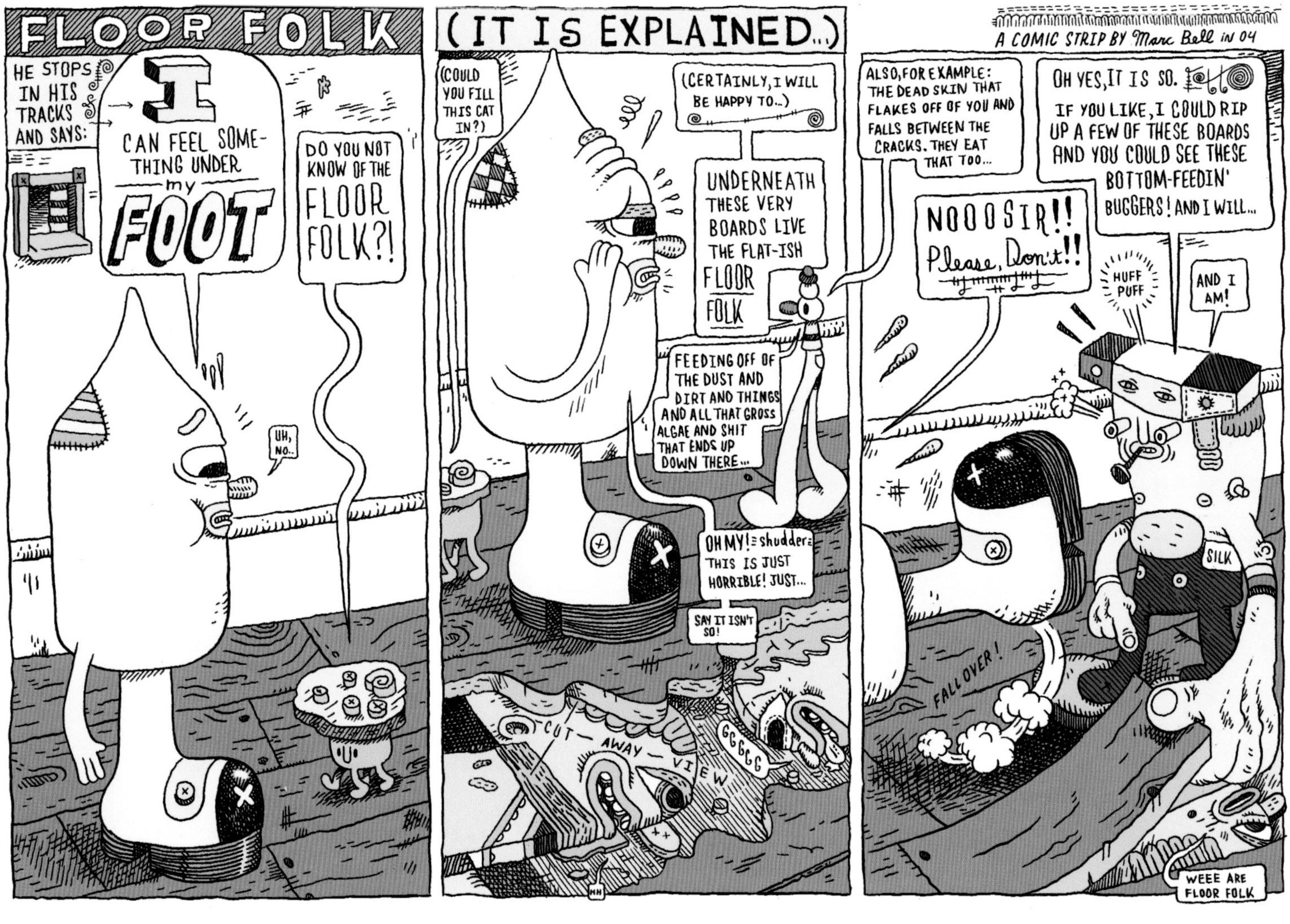
FLOOR FOLK
(IT IS EXPLAINED..)
A COMIC STRIP BY Marc Bell IN 04
HE STOPS IN HIS TRACKS AND SAYS:
I CAN FEEL SOMETHING UNDER my FOOT
DO YOU NOT KNOW OF THE FLOOR FOLK?!
UH, NO..
(COULD YOU FILL THIS CAT IN?)
(CERTAINLY, I WILL BE HAPPY TO..)
UNDERNEATH THESE VERY BOARDS LIVE THE FLAT-ISH FLOOR FOLK
FEEDING OFF OF THE DUST AND DIRT AND THINGS AND ALL THAT GROSS ALGAE AND SHIT THAT ENDS UP DOWN THERE...
OH MY! shudder THIS IS JUST HORRIBLE! JUST...
SAY IT ISN'T SO!
CUT—AWAY—VIEW
GGGGG
ALSO, FOR EXAMPLE: THE DEAD SKIN THAT FLAKES OFF OF YOU AND FALLS BETWEEN THE CRACKS. THEY EAT THAT TOO...
OH YES, IT IS SO.
IF YOU LIKE, I COULD RIP UP A FEW OF THESE BOARDS AND YOU COULD SEE THESE BOTTOM-FEEDIN' BUGGERS! AND I WILL...
NOOOSIR!! Please, Don't!!
HUFF PUFF
AND I AM!
SILK
FALL OVER!
WEEE ARE FLOOR FOLK

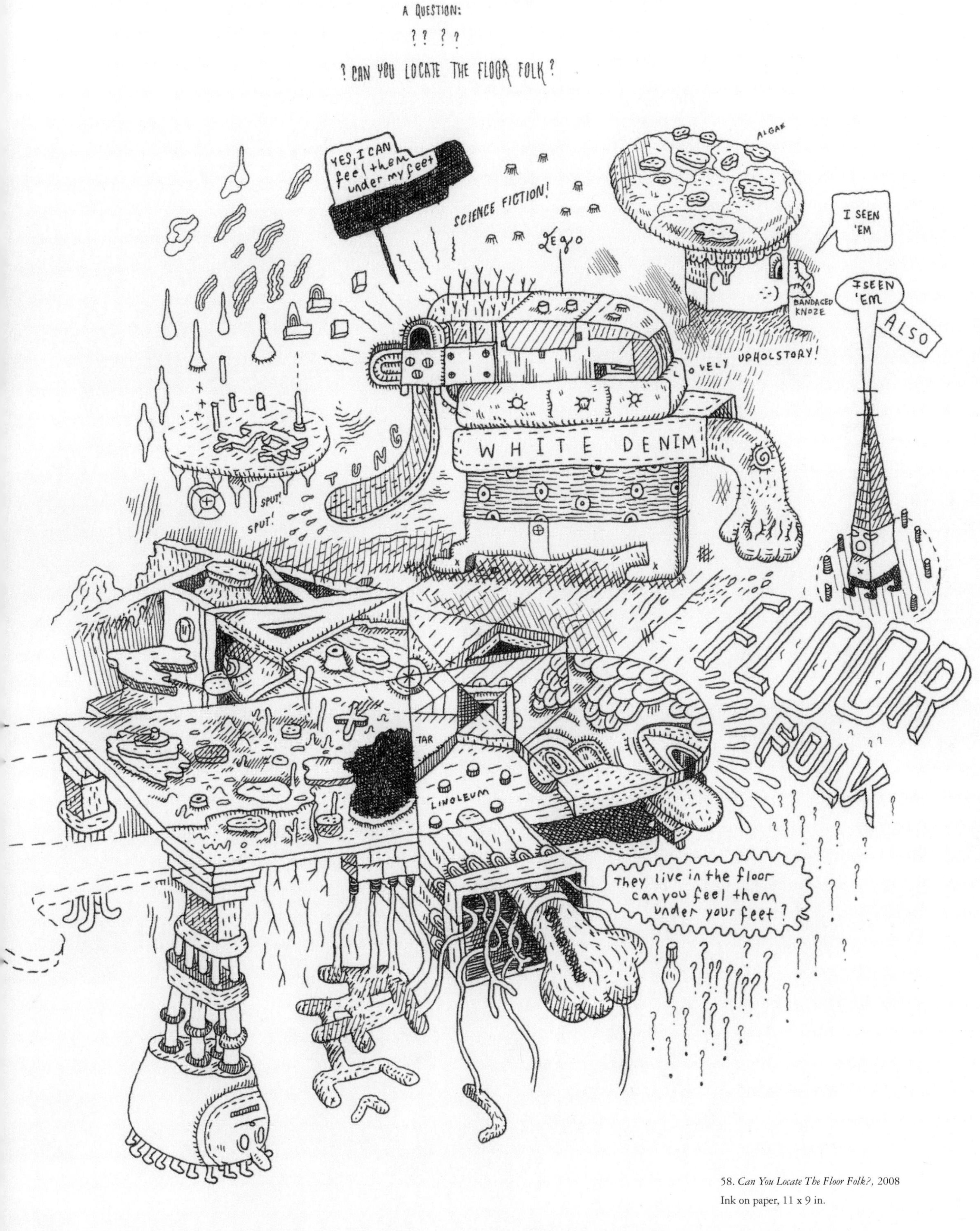
A QUESTION:
?? ??
? CAN YOU LOCATE THE FLOOR FOLK ?
YES, I CAN feel them under my feet
SCIENCE FICTION!
Lego
ALGAE
I SEEN 'EM
I SEEN 'EM
ALSO
BANDAGED KNOZE
LOVELY UPHOLSTORY!
TUNG
WHITE DENIM
SPUT!
SPUT!
FLOOR
FOLK
TAR
LINOLEUM
They live in the floor can you feel them under your feet?

58. *Can You Locate The Floor Folk?,* 2008
Ink on paper, 11 x 9 in.

POP QUIZ

LET'S SEE IF YOU'VE BEEN PAYING ATTENTION SO FAR

1. WHEN ONE CLAIMS TO BE "BIG IN WESTMOUNT," IT MEANS
   (check one)
   - ☐ THE RIVER OF DESTRUCTION EMPTIES INTO LAKE INFERIOR
   - ☐ PIECE OF WOOD IS AT THE TOP OF THE CHARTS
   - ☐ DRAWING ON GRAPH PAPER IS TRANDY [no sic]
   - ☐ THEY ARE KNOWN BY THE EMPLOYEES DOWN AT THE SHOPPERS DRUG MART

2. YOU ARE INVITED OVER TO THE ART DIRECTOR'S HOUSE BUT YOU ARE NOT SURE WHY. IT IS CLEAN AND WHITE WITH LOTS OF EMPTY SPACE. HE TALKS TO YOU ABOUT THE LABEL DESIGN THAT HE IS WORKING FOR A NEW BRAND OF MAYONAISE THAT IS COMING ONTO THE MARKET. YOU ARE NOT SURE IF HE IS INFERRING THAT HE MIGHT WANT YOU TAKE PART IN THIS PROJECT OR NOT. HE GOES ON TO EXPLAIN WHAT SOME OF HIS IDEAS ARE SO FAR.
   DRAW A PICTURE OF HIM IN THIS BOX:
   (PLEASE):

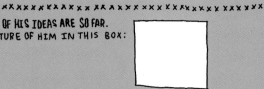

3. MY NEIGHBOR PRYS OPEN SOME OF HIS FLOOR BOARDS TO DISCOVER SEVERAL FLAT-ISH PERSONS LIVING UNDERNEATH THEM. THEY HUM AND HISS AND STARE AT HIM BUT DON'T SAY ANYTHING. IN A PANIC, MY NEIGHBOR STRIKES THEM WITH A HAMMER HE BORROWED FROM ME 6 MONTHS AGO. IT IS AT THIS POINT THAT YOU ARE ARRIVING. HE LETS YOU IN AND EXPLAINS THE SITUATION.
   YOU SUGGEST:
   - ☐ CALLING LARRY ABOUT THE IRONING BOARD
   - ☐ RETURNING MY HAMMER TO ME (CLEANING IT FIRST)
   - ☐ BORROWING A JAR OF MAYONAISSE FROM THE ART DIRECTOR DOWNSTAIRS
   - ☐ THAT THESE ARE THE MIGHTY FLOOR FOLK AND THEY FEED OFF OF THE FILTH THAT FALLS BETWEEN THE CRACKS!

ANSWERS: 1. YOU KNOW 2. IN YOUR HEART 3. WHAT IS RIGHT

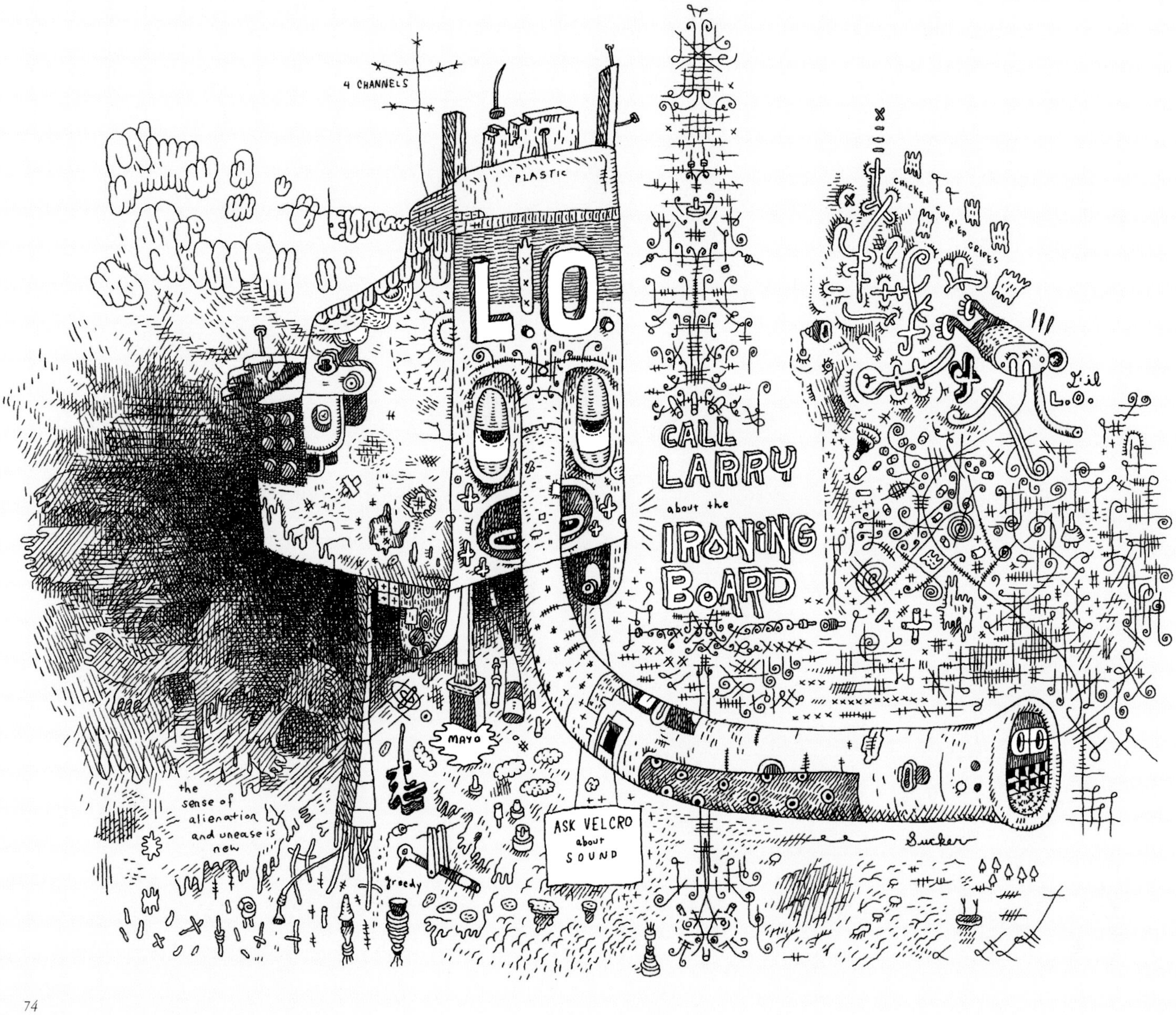

4 CHANNELS
PLASTIC
L.O
CHICKEN CURRIED CRIPES
Lil L.O.
CALL LARRY about the IRONING BOARD
MAYO
the sense of alienation and unease is new
ASK VELCRO about SOUND
greedy
Sucker

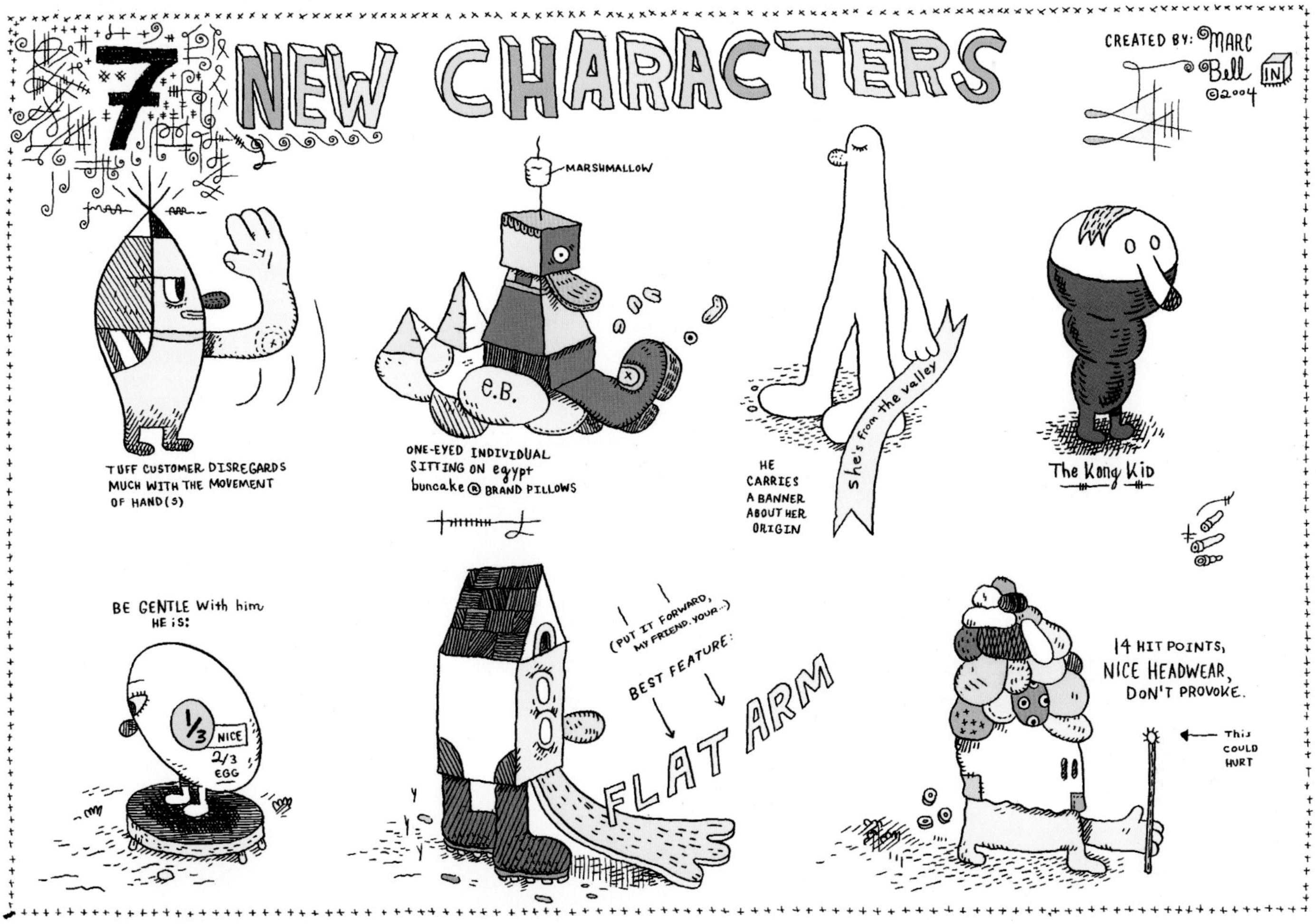
7 NEW CHARACTERS
CREATED BY: MARC BELL IN ©2004
MARSHMALLOW
TUFF CUSTOMER DISREGARDS MUCH WITH THE MOVEMENT OF HAND(S)
e.B.
ONE-EYED INDIVIDUAL SITTING ON egypt buncake ® BRAND PILLOWS
she's from the valley
HE CARRIES A BANNER ABOUT HER ORIGIN
The Kong Kid
BE GENTLE With him HE iS:
1/3
NICE 2/3 EGG
(PUT IT FORWARD, MY FRIEND. YOUR...)
BEST FEATURE:
FLAT ARM
14 HIT POINTS, NICE HEADWEAR, DON'T PROVOKE.
This COULD HURT

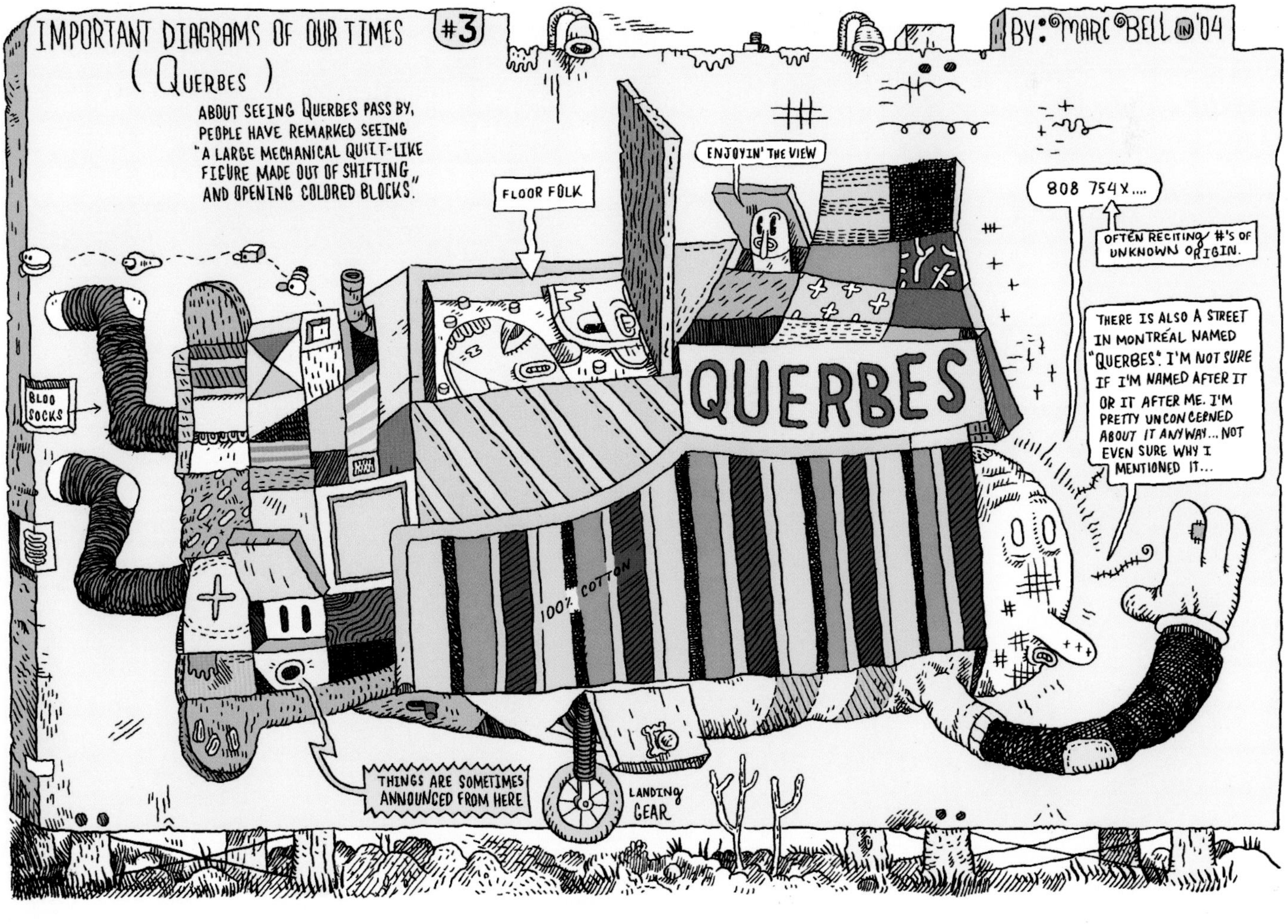
IMPORTANT DIAGRAMS OF OUR TIMES #3
BY: MARC BELL IN '04
(QUERBES)
ABOUT SEEING QUERBES PASS BY, PEOPLE HAVE REMARKED SEEING "A LARGE MECHANICAL QUILT-LIKE FIGURE MADE OUT OF SHIFTING AND OPENING COLORED BLOCKS."
ENJOYIN' THE VIEW
FLOOR FOLK
808 754X....
OFTEN RECITING #'S OF UNKNOWN ORIGIN.
THERE IS ALSO A STREET IN MONTRÉAL NAMED "QUERBES". I'M NOT SURE IF I'M NAMED AFTER IT OR IT AFTER ME. I'M PRETTY UNCONCERNED ABOUT IT ANYWAY... NOT EVEN SURE WHY I MENTIONED IT...
BLOO SOCKS
QUERBES
100% COTTON
THINGS ARE SOMETIMES ANNOUNCED FROM HERE
LANDING GEAR

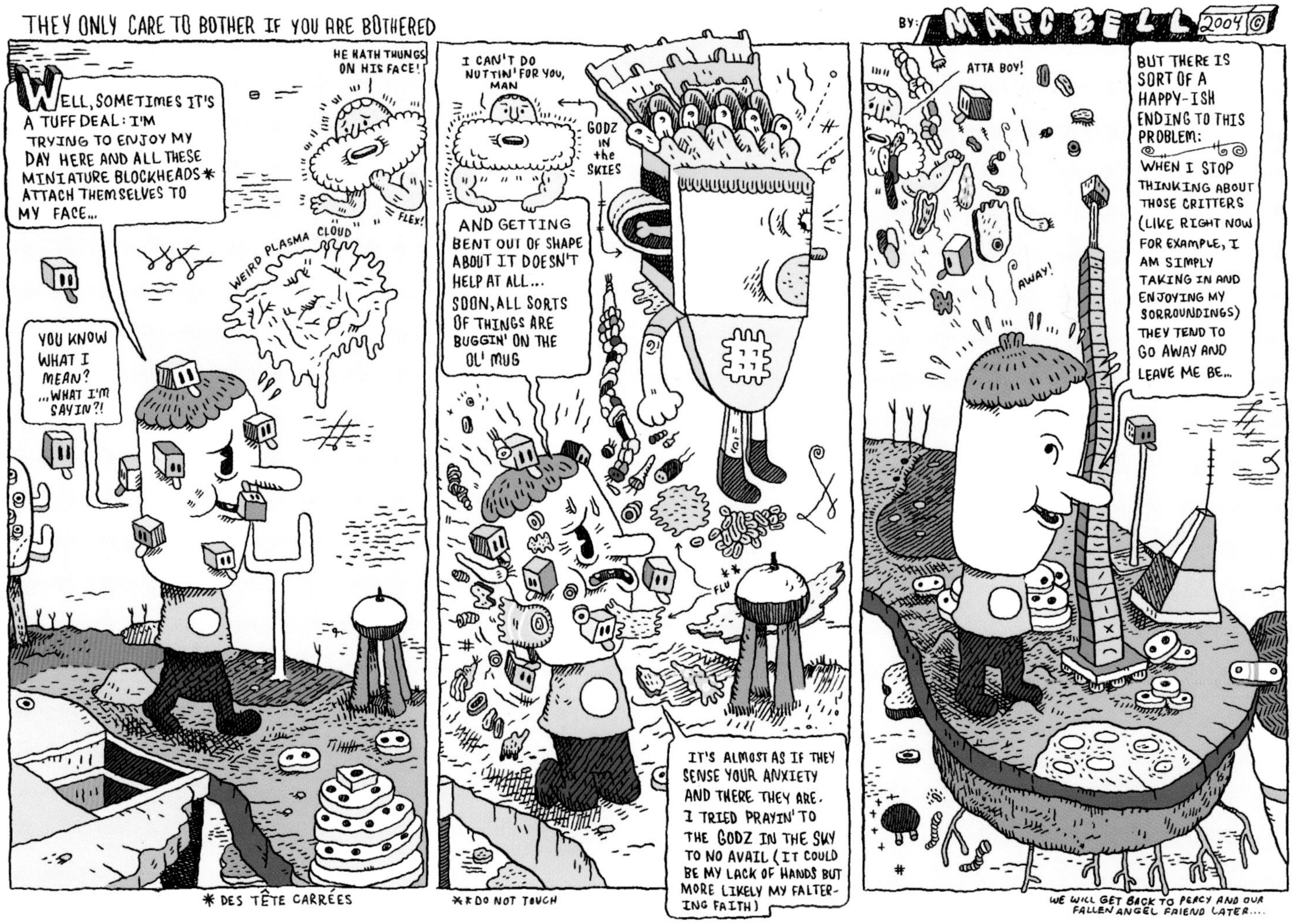
THEY ONLY CARE TO BOTHER IF YOU ARE BOTHERED
BY: MARC BELL 2004 ©
WELL, SOMETIMES IT'S A TUFF DEAL: I'M TRYING TO ENJOY MY DAY HERE AND ALL THESE MINIATURE BLOCKHEADS * ATTACH THEMSELVES TO MY FACE...
HE HATH THUNGS ON HIS FACE!
FLEX!
WEIRD PLASMA CLOUD
YOU KNOW WHAT I MEAN? ...WHAT I'M SAYIN'?!
* DES TÊTE CARRÉES
I CAN'T DO NUTTIN' FOR YOU, MAN
GODZ IN the SKIES
AND GETTING BENT OUT OF SHAPE ABOUT IT DOESN'T HELP AT ALL... SOON, ALL SORTS OF THINGS ARE BUGGIN' ON THE OL' MUG
FLU **
IT'S ALMOST AS IF THEY SENSE YOUR ANXIETY AND THERE THEY ARE. I TRIED PRAYIN' TO THE GODZ IN THE SKY TO NO AVAIL (IT COULD BE MY LACK OF HANDS BUT MORE LIKELY MY FALTERING FAITH)
** DO NOT TOUCH
ATTA BOY!
AWAY!
BUT THERE IS SORT OF A HAPPY-ISH ENDING TO THIS PROBLEM:
WHEN I STOP THINKING ABOUT THOSE CRITTERS (LIKE RIGHT NOW FOR EXAMPLE, I AM SIMPLY TAKING IN AND ENJOYING MY SORROUNDINGS) THEY TEND TO GO AWAY AND LEAVE ME BE...
WE WILL GET BACK TO PERCY AND OUR FALLEN ANGEL FRIEND LATER....

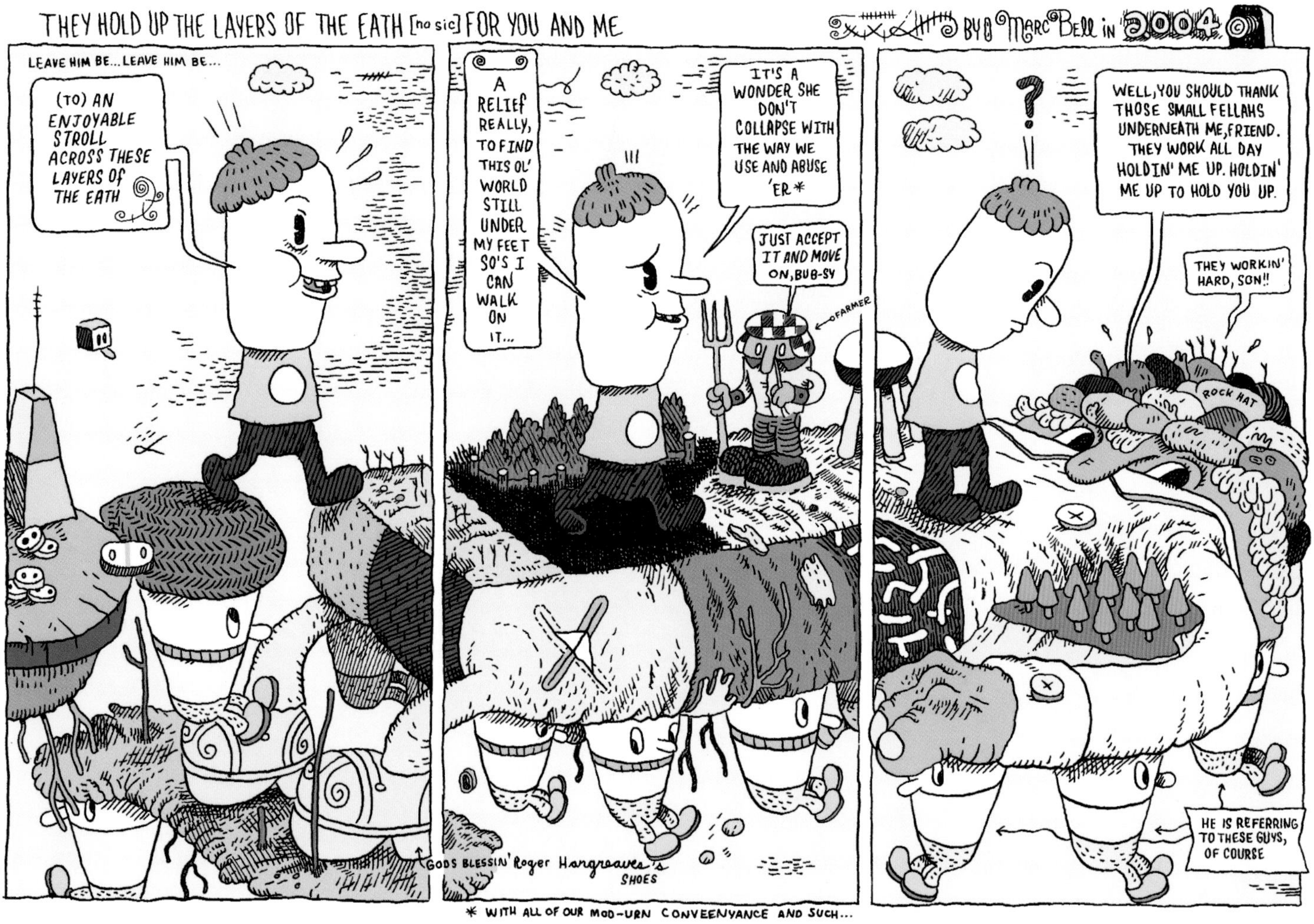
THEY HOLD UP THE LAYERS OF THE EATH [no sic] FOR YOU AND ME
BY MARC BELL IN 2004
LEAVE HIM BE... LEAVE HIM BE...
(TO) AN ENJOYABLE STROLL ACROSS THESE LAYERS OF THE EATH
GODS BLESSIN' Roger Hargreaves's SHOES
A RELIEF REALLY, TO FIND THIS OL' WORLD STILL UNDER MY FEET SO'S I CAN WALK ON IT...
IT'S A WONDER SHE DON'T COLLAPSE WITH THE WAY WE USE AND ABUSE 'ER *
JUST ACCEPT IT AND MOVE ON, BUB-SY
FARMER
* WITH ALL OF OUR MOD-URN CONVEENYANCE AND SUCH...
?
WELL, YOU SHOULD THANK THOSE SMALL FELLAHS UNDERNEATH ME, FRIEND. THEY WORK ALL DAY HOLDIN' ME UP. HOLDIN' ME UP TO HOLD YOU UP.
THEY WORKIN' HARD, SON!!
ROCK HAT
HE IS REFERRING TO THESE GUYS, OF COURSE

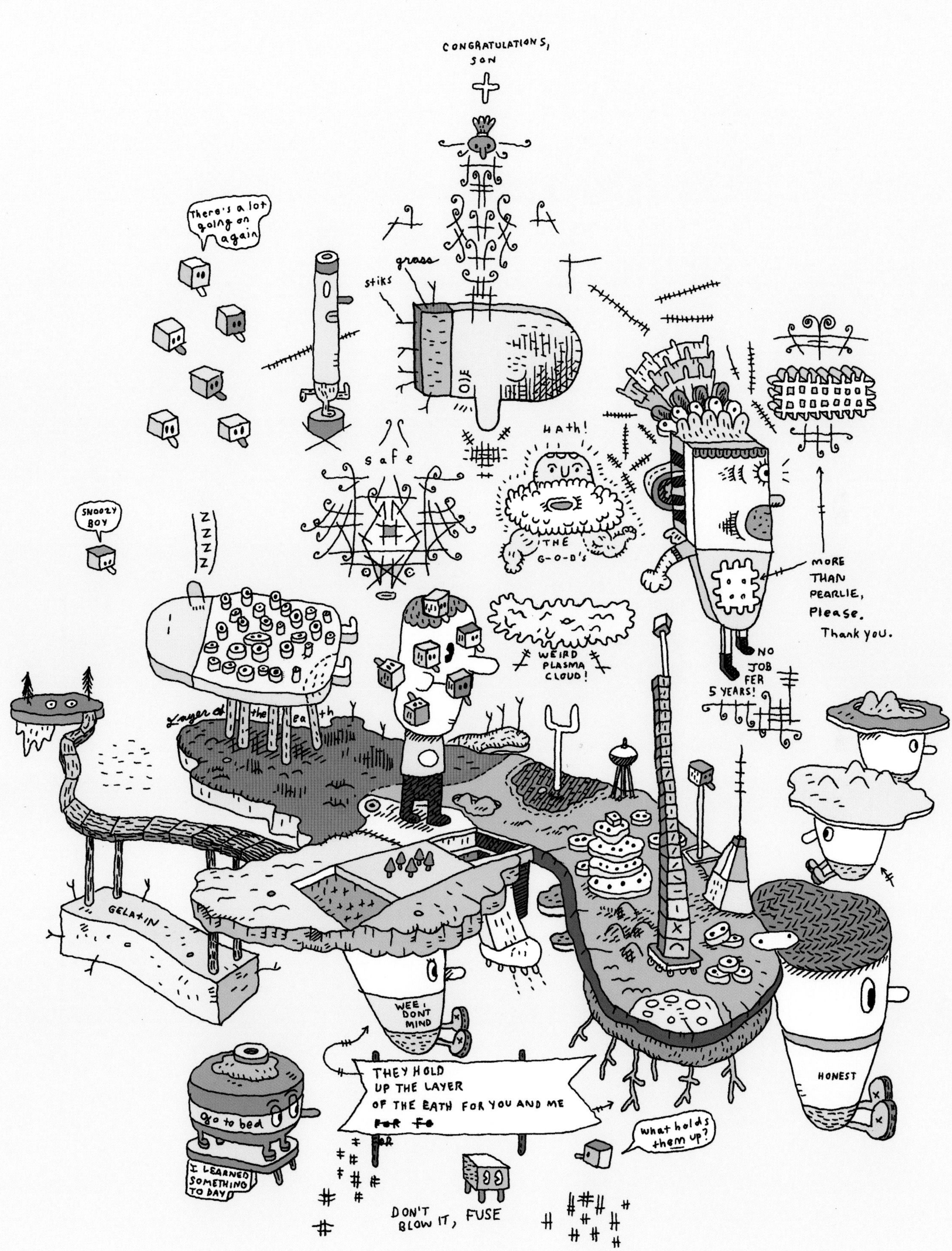

CONGRATULATIONS, SON
There's a lot going on again
grass
stiks
safe
HAth!
THE G-O-D's
SNOOZY BOY
ZZZZ
MORE THAN PEARLIE, Please. Thank you.
NO JOB FER 5 YEARS!
WEIRD PLASMA CLOUD!
GELATIN
WEE, DONT MIND
HONEST
THEY HOLD UP THE LAYER OF THE EATH FOR YOU AND ME
go to bed
I LEARNED SOMETHING TO DAY
what holds them up?
DON'T BLOW IT, FUSE

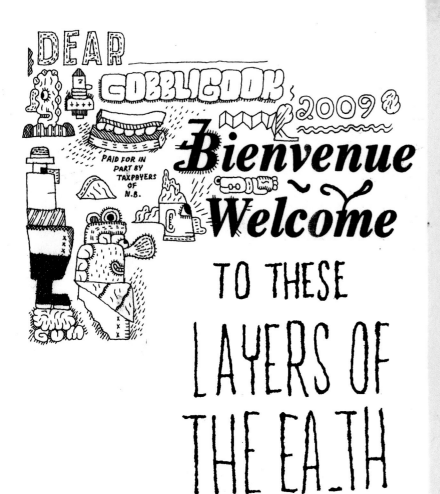

DEAR GOBBLIGOOK, 2009 &

Bienvenue ~ Welcome

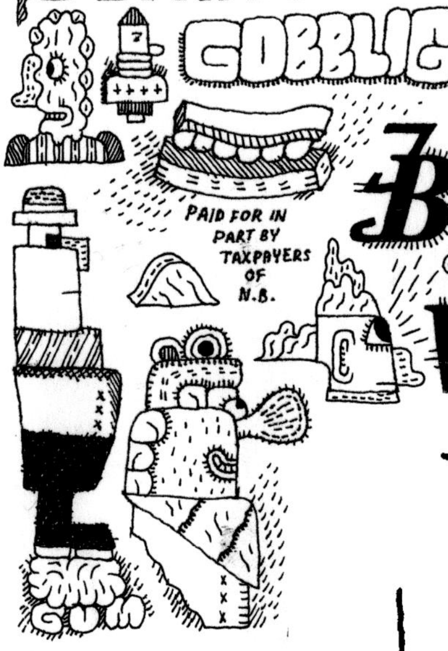
PAID FOR IN PART BY TAXPAYERS OF N.B.
GUM

TO THESE LAYERS OF THE EA_TH

THESE DRAWINGS
WERE CREATED
BETWEEN 03-08

MANY OF THEM WERE
EXHIBITED AND/OR
REPRODUCED IN SELF-
PUBLISHED BOOKLETS
(eg: "CALL LARRY ABOUT
THE IRONING BOARD")
AND THEN RE-WORKED RE-WORKED
AGAIN AGAIN. LATER.

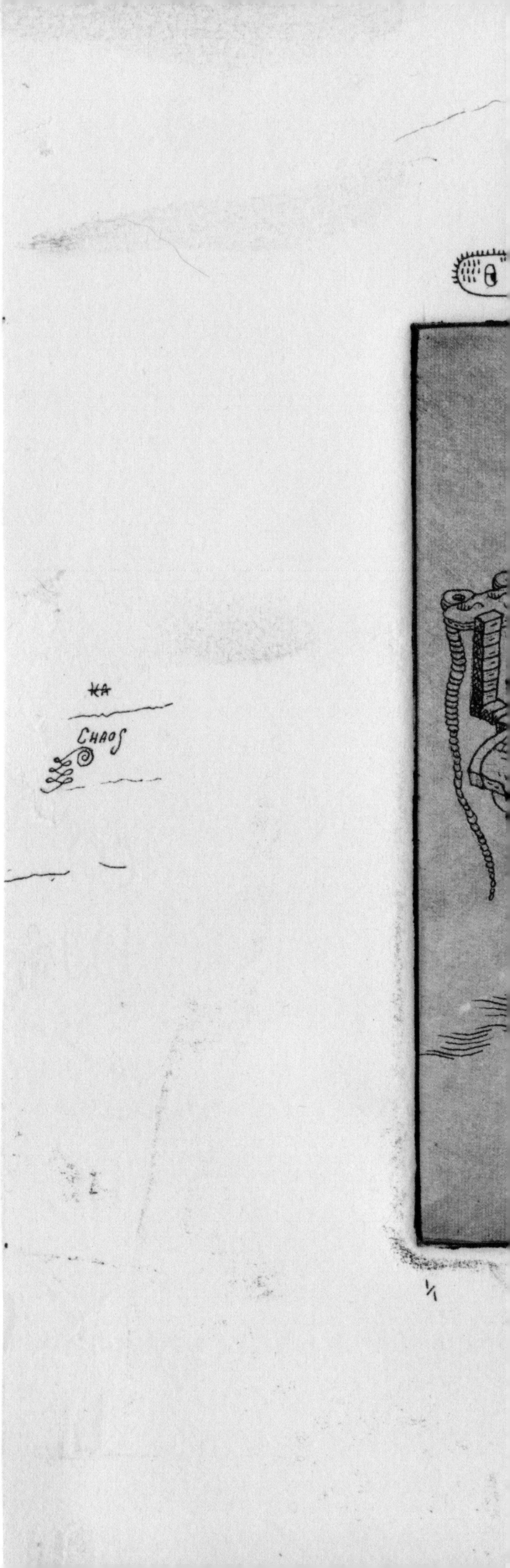
KA
CHAOS
1/1

59. *Above, Below,* 2005
Mixed media on un–editioned intaglio print, 9 x 10 in.

Above,

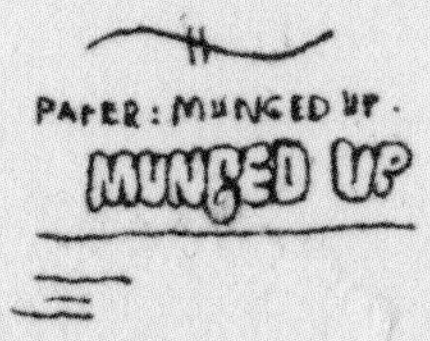
PAPER: MUNGED UP.
MUNGED UP

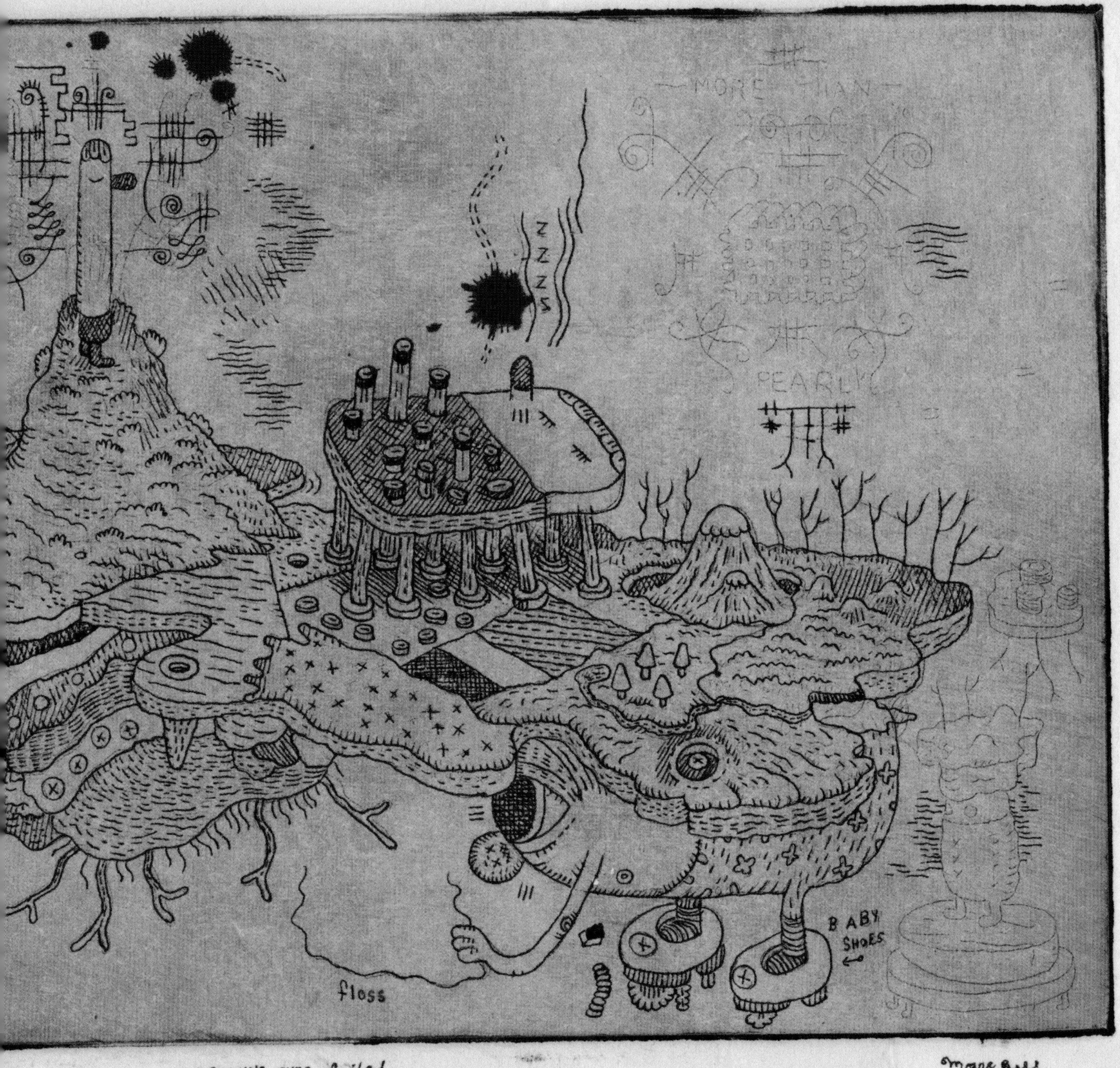
MORE THAN
PEARL
BABY SHOES
floss

DRAWING OVER failed intahglio [no sic]

Marc Bell
2005

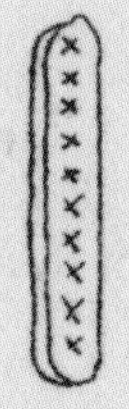

Below,

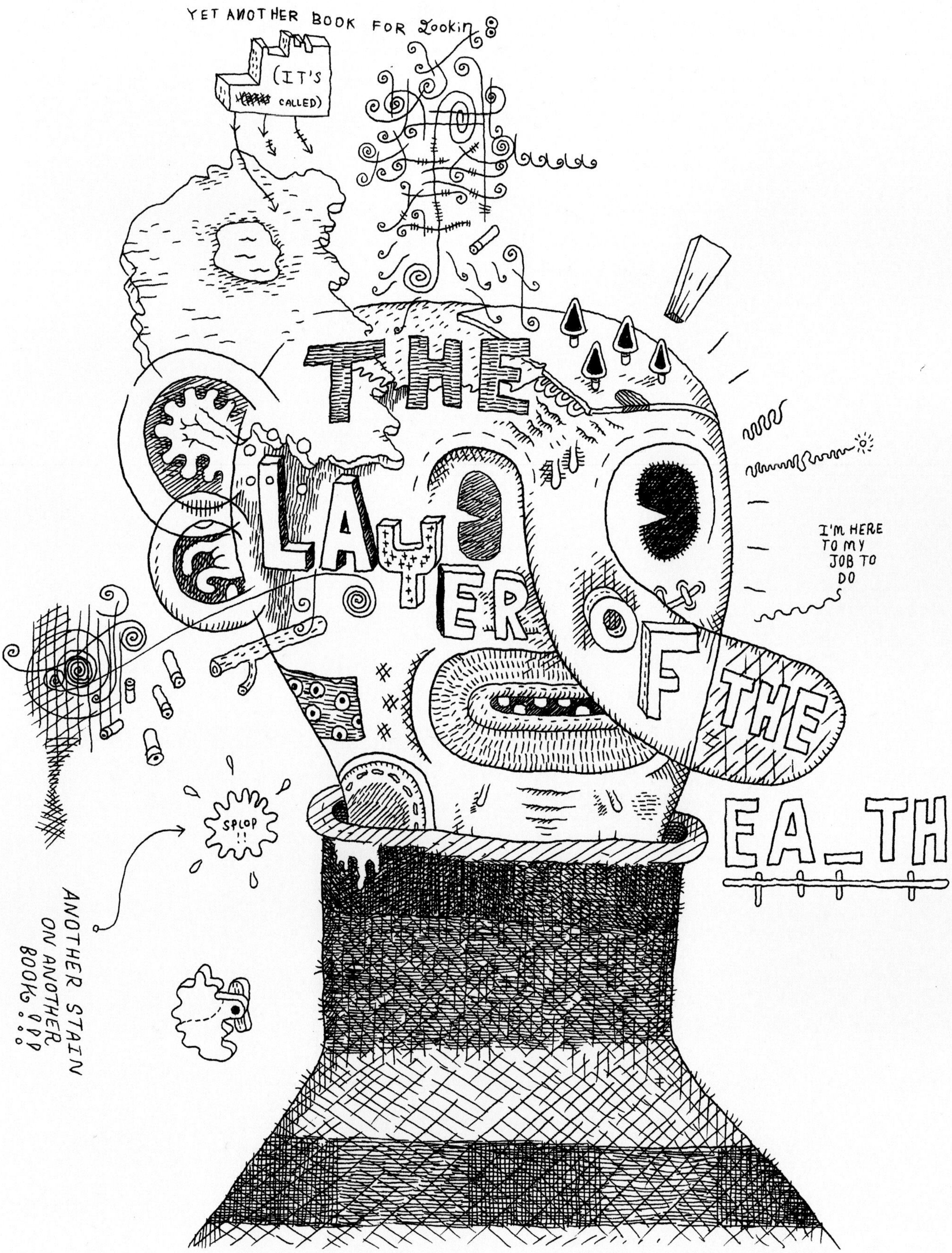
YET ANOTHER BOOK FOR Lookin
(IT'S
CALLED)
THE LAYER OF THE
EA_TH
I'M HERE TO MY JOB TO DO
SPLOP !!
ANOTHER STAIN ON ANOTHER BOOK

60. *Layer Of The Ea_th*
(This was the cover for vol. 2 of a photocopied booklet of the same name)

61. *Nowicker (Strong Wind)*

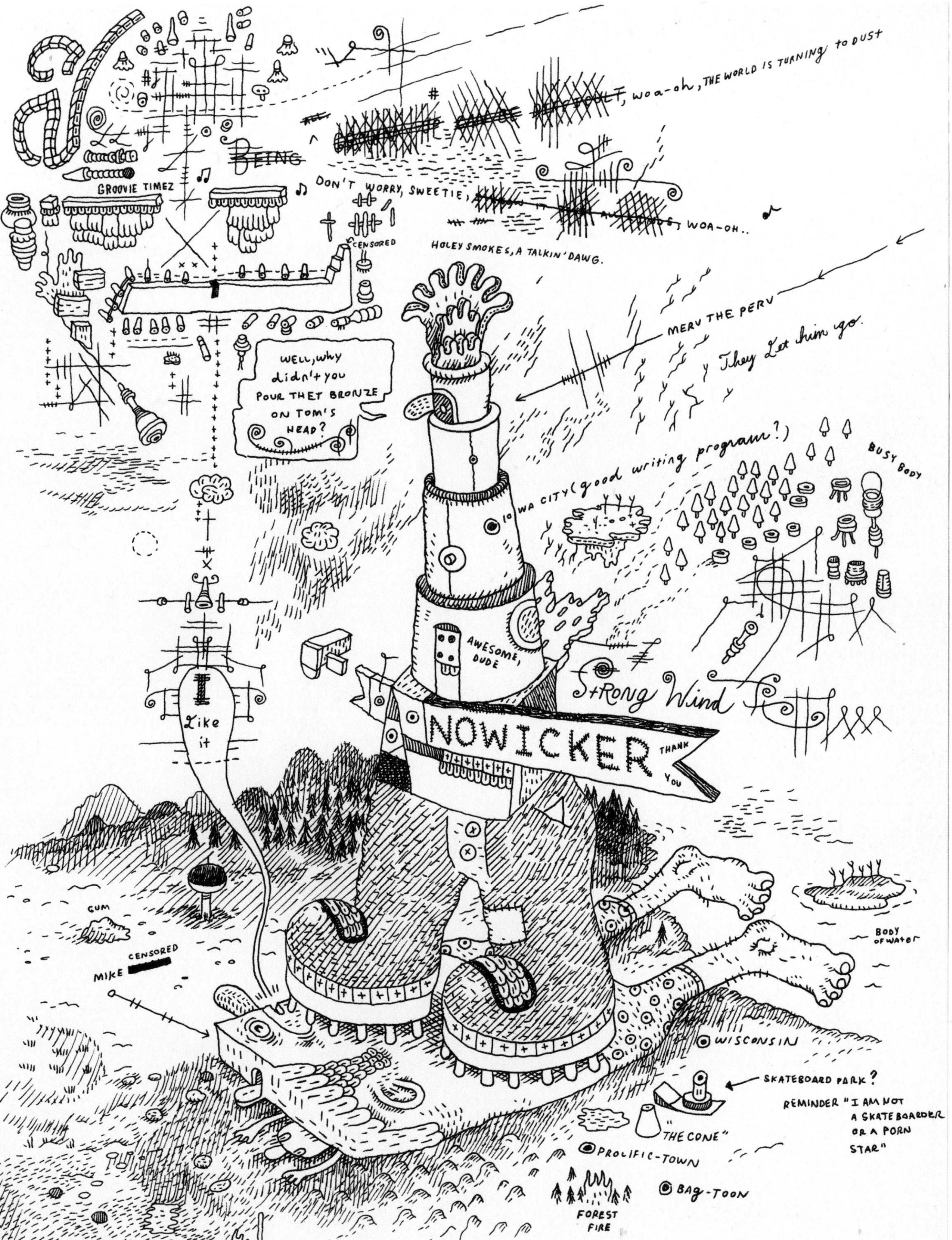

WOA-OH, THE WORLD IS TURNING TO DUST
BEING
GROOVIE TIMEZ
DON'T WORRY, SWEETIE,
WOA-OH..
CENSORED
HOLEY SMOKES, A TALKIN' DAWG.
MERV THE PERV
They Let him go.
WELL, why didn't you POUR THET BRONZE ON TOM'S HEAD?
IOWA CITY (good writing program?)
BUSY BODY
AWESOME, DUDE
Strong Wind
NOWICKER
THANK YOU
I Like it
GUM
CENSORED
MIKE [redacted]
BODY OF WATER
WISCONSIN
SKATEBOARD PARK?
REMINDER "I AM NOT A SKATEBOARDER OR A PORN STAR"
"THE CONE"
PROLIFIC-TOWN
BAG-TOON
FOREST FIRE

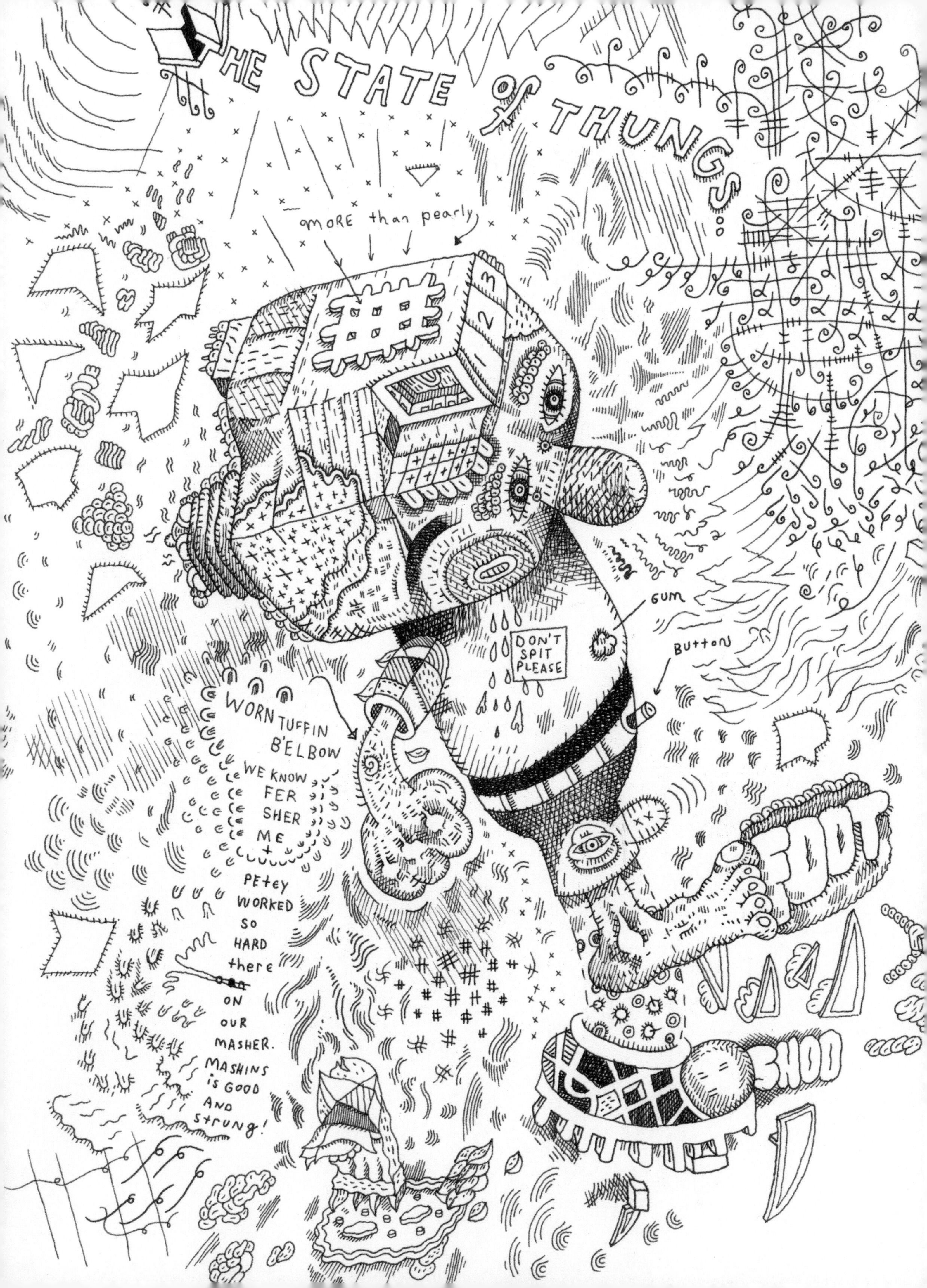
THE STATE of THUNGS
more than pearly
GUM
DON'T SPIT PLEASE
BUTTON
WORN TUFFIN B'ELBOW
WE KNOW FER SHER ME
Petey WORKED so HARD there ON OUR MASHER. MASHINS is GOOD AND strung!
FOOT
SHOO

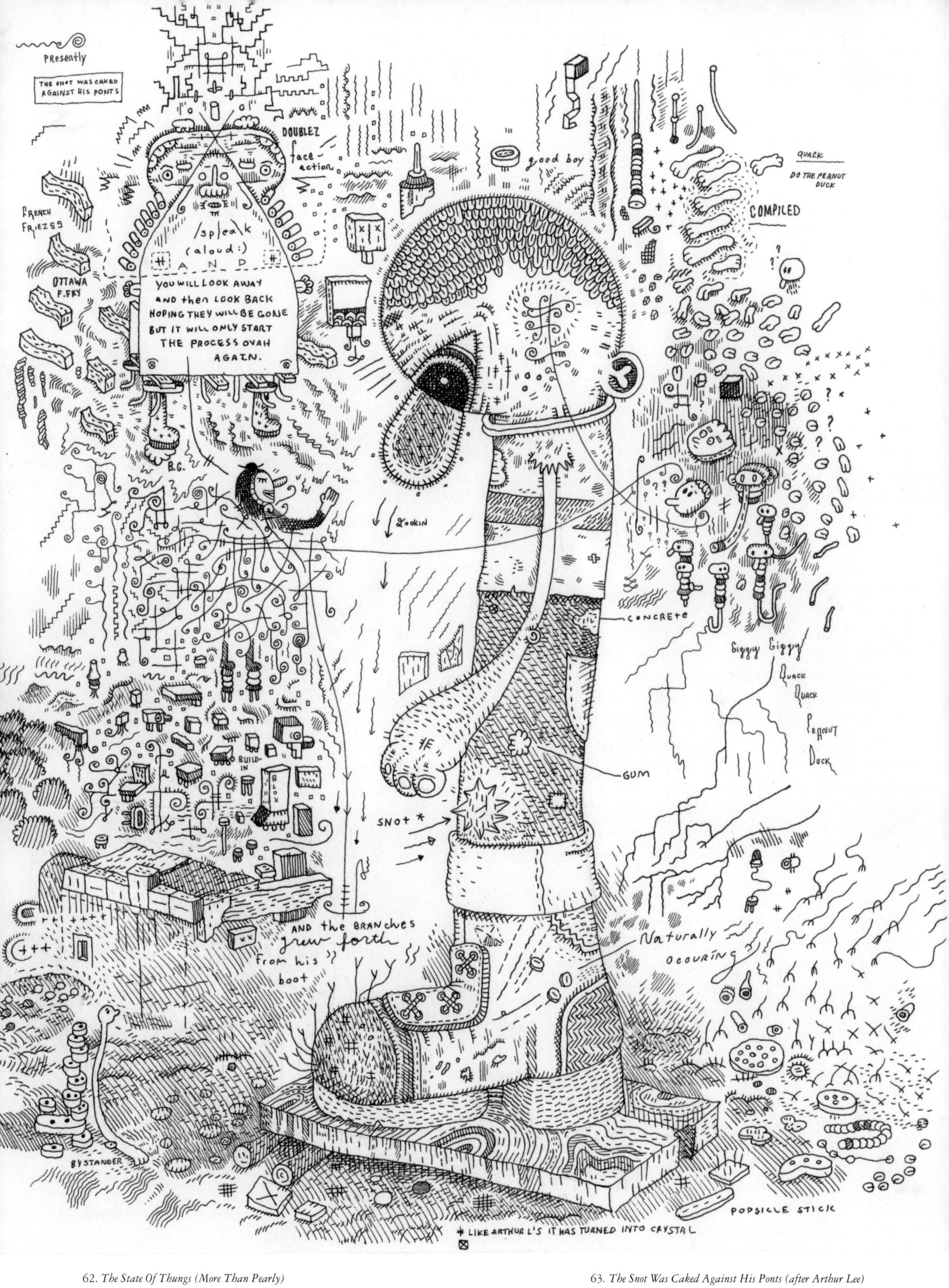
Presently
THE SNOT WAS CAKED AGAINST HIS PONTS
DOUBLEZ
face-action
good boy
QUACK
DO THE PEANUT DUCK
COMPILED
FRENCH FRIEZSS
OTTAWA F.FRY
/sp/ea/k (aloud:)
AND
YOU WILL LOOK AWAY AND then LOOK BACK HOPING THEY WILL BE GONE BUT IT WILL ONLY START THE PROCESS OVAH AGAIN.
B.G.
Lookin
CONCRETE
Giggy Giggy
Quack
Quack
Peanut
Duck
BUILD-IN
BLOX
GUM
SNOT *
AND the BRANches grew forth from his boot
Naturally occuring
BYSTANDER
POPSICLE STICK
* LIKE ARTHUR L'S IT HAS TURNED INTO CRYSTAL

62. *The State Of Thungs (More Than Pearly)*

63. *The Snot Was Caked Against His Ponts (after Arthur Lee)*

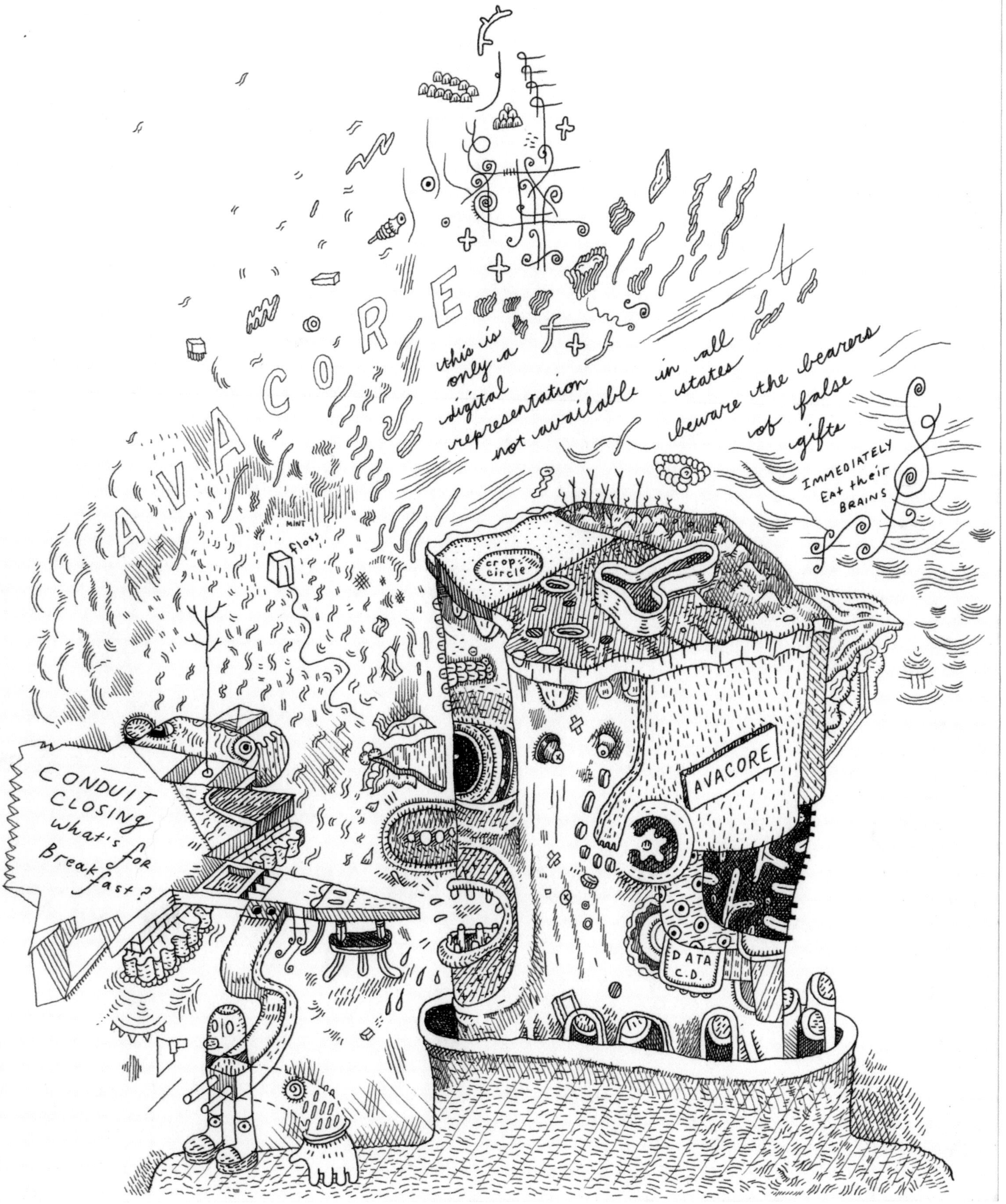
AVACORE
this is only a digital representation
not available in all states
beware the bearers of false gifts
IMMEDIATELY Eat their BRAINS
MINT
floss
crop circle
AVACORE
CONDUIT CLOSING
what's for Breakfast?
DATA C.D.

64. Avacore (This is only a Digital Representation)

65. Greetings From Calgary

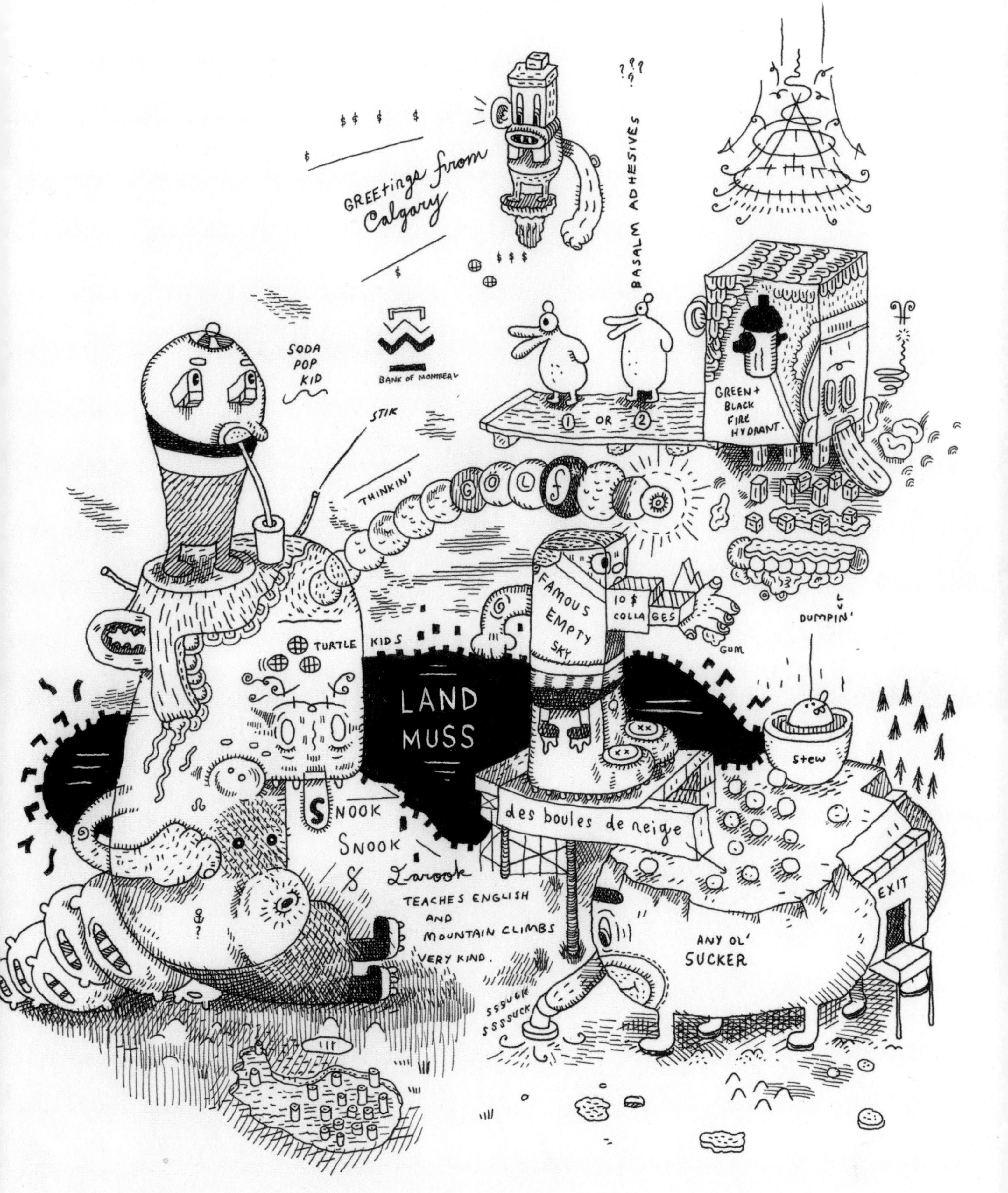
GREEtings from Calgary
BASALM ADHESIVES
SODA POP KID
BANK OF MONTREAL
STIK
THINKIN'
GOLF
1 OR 2
GREEN + BLACK FIRE HYDRANT.
DUMPIN'
FAMOUS EMPTY SKY
10 $ COLLAGES
GUM
TURTLE KIDS
LAND MUSS
stew
SNOOK
SNOOK
& Zarook
TEACHES ENGLISH AND MOUNTAIN CLIMBS VERY KIND.
des boules de neige
EXIT
ANY OL' SUCKER
SSSUCK SSSUCK

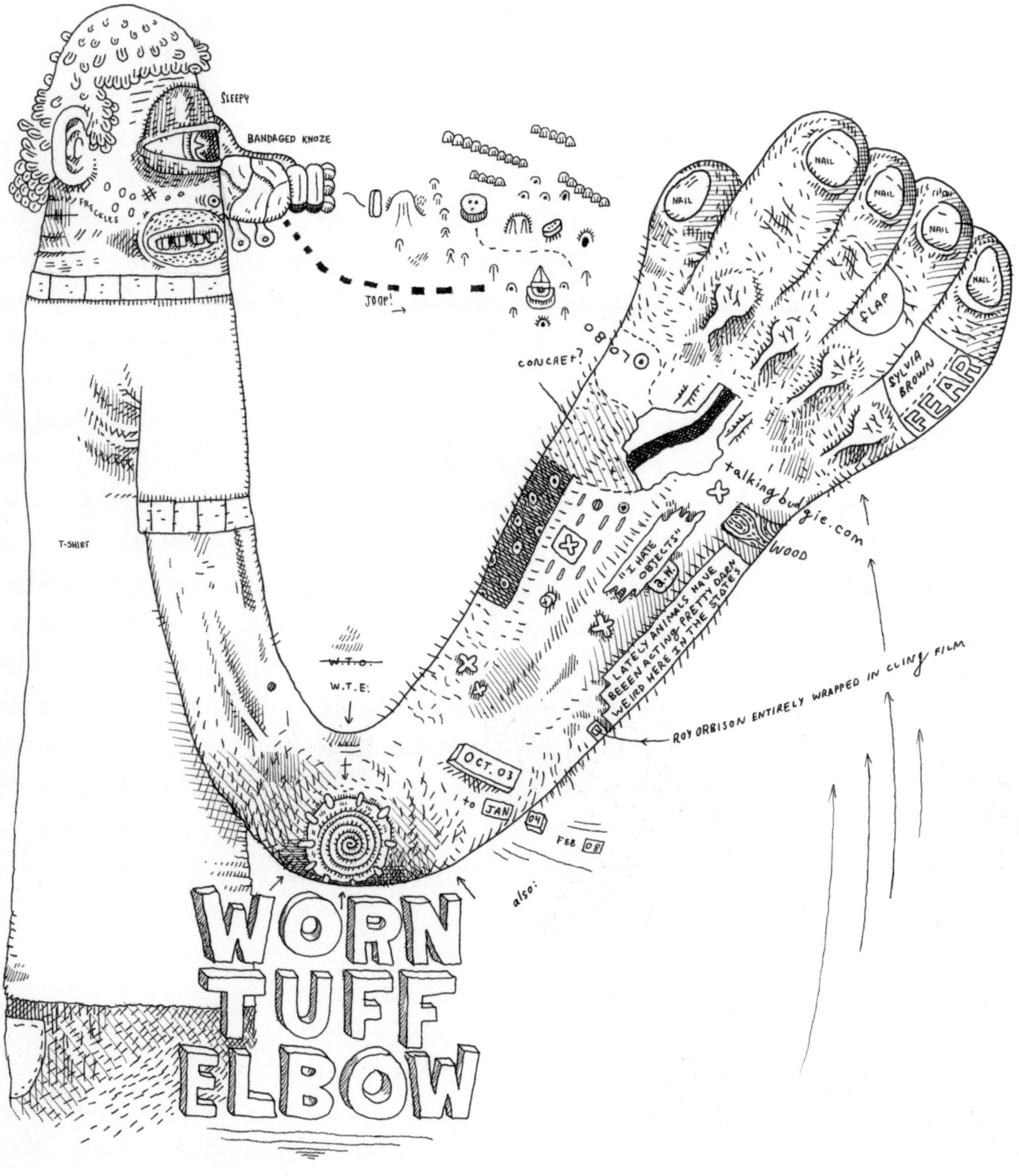
SLEEPY
BANDAGED KNOZE
FRECKLES
JOOP!
NAIL
NAIL
NAIL
NAIL
NAIL
FLAP
SYLVIA BROWN
FEAR
CONCRET?
talkingbudgie.com
WOOD
"I HATE OBJECTS" A.H.
LATELY ANIMALS HAVE BEEEN ACTING PRETTY DARN WEIRD HERE IN THE STATES
ROY ORBISON ENTIRELY WRAPPED IN CLING FILM
T-SHIRT
W.T.O.
W.T.E.
OCT. 03
to JAN 04
FEB 08
also:
WORN TUFF ELBOW

66. *Worn Tuff Elbow (Bandaged Knoze)*

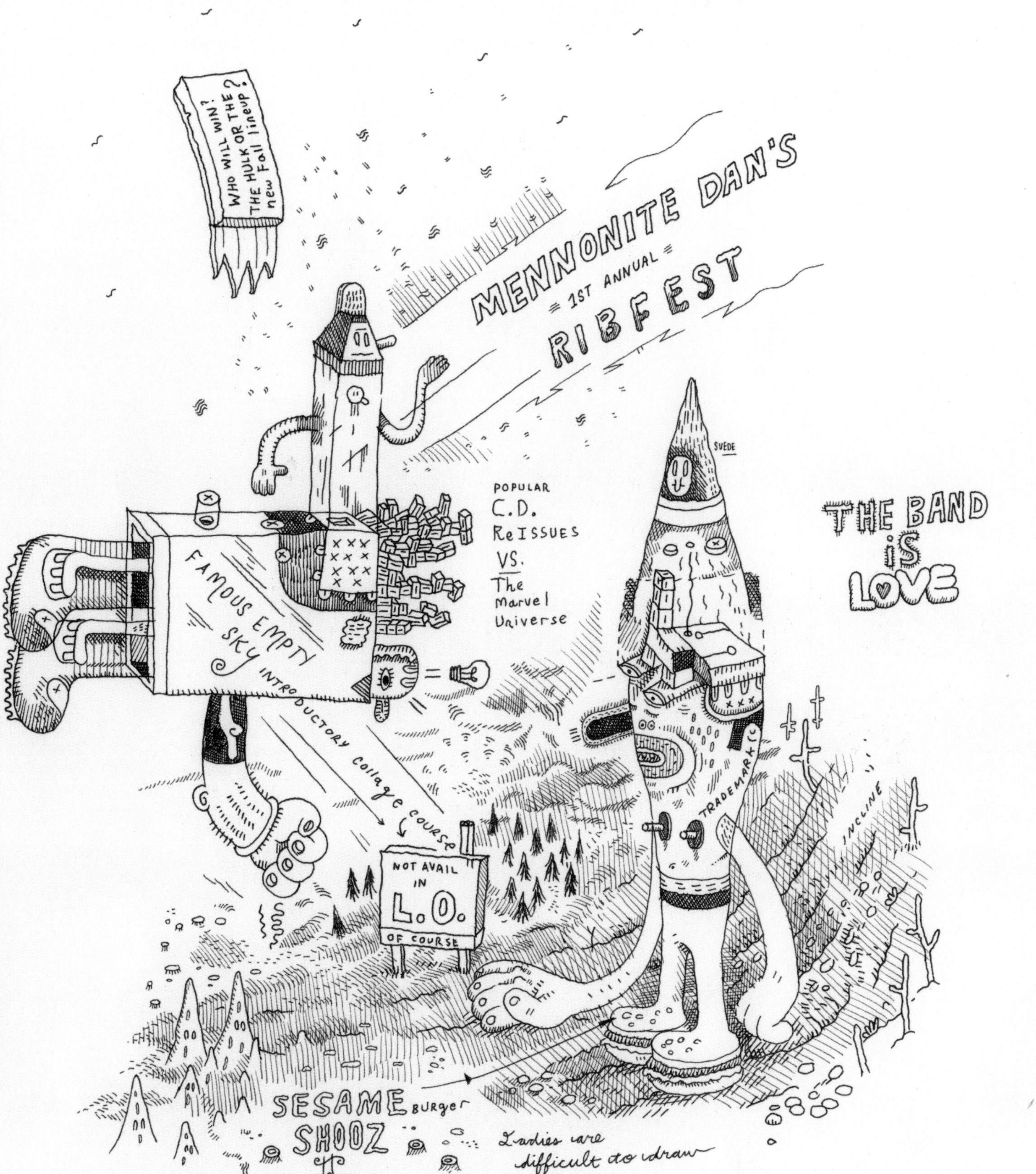

WHO WILL WIN? THE HULK OR THE? new Fall lineup?
MENNONITE DAN'S
1ST ANNUAL
RIBFEST
SUEDE
POPULAR C.D. ReISSUES VS. The Marvel Universe
THE BAND is LOVE
FAMOUS EMPTY SKY
INTRODUCTORY collage course
NOT AVAIL IN L.O.
OF COURSE
TRADEMARK
INCLINE
SESAME burger SHOOZ
Ladies are difficult to draw
(They weren't there anyways)

67. *Mennonite Dan's 1st Annual Ribfest*

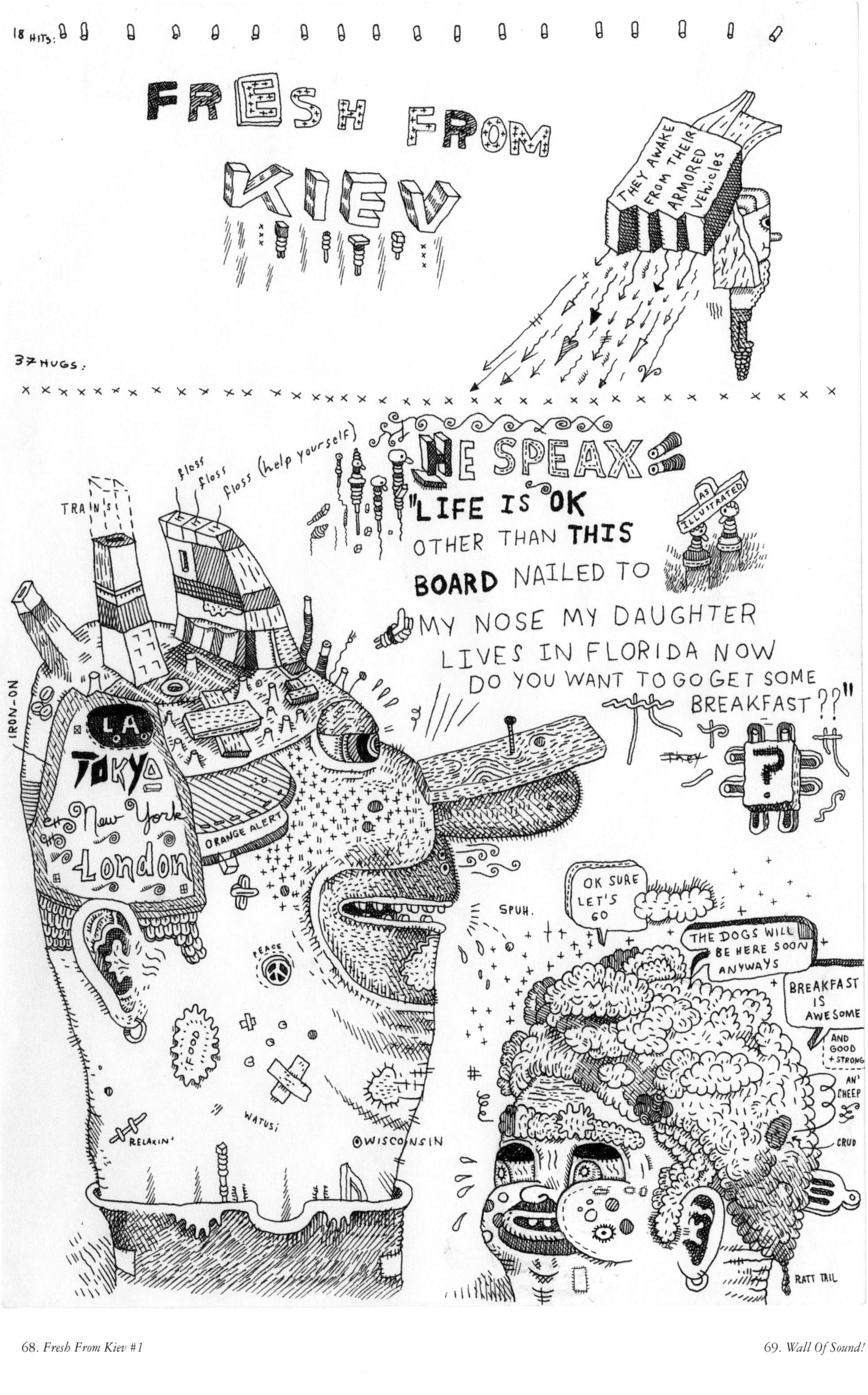
18 HITS:
FRESH FROM KIEV
THEY AWAKE FROM THEIR ARMORED VEHICLES
37 HUGS:
HE SPEAX
"LIFE IS OK OTHER THAN THIS BOARD NAILED TO MY NOSE MY DAUGHTER LIVES IN FLORIDA NOW DO YOU WANT TO GO GET SOME BREAKFAST??"
AS ILLUSTRATED
floss floss floss (help yourself)
TRAINS
IRON-ON
LA
TOKYO
New York
London
ORANGE ALERT
OK SURE LET'S GO
SPUH.
THE DOGS WILL BE HERE SOON ANYWAYS
BREAKFAST IS AWESOME
AND GOOD + STRONG
AN' CHEEP
CRUD
PEACE
FOOD
WATUSI
RELAXIN'
WISCONSIN
RATT TAIL

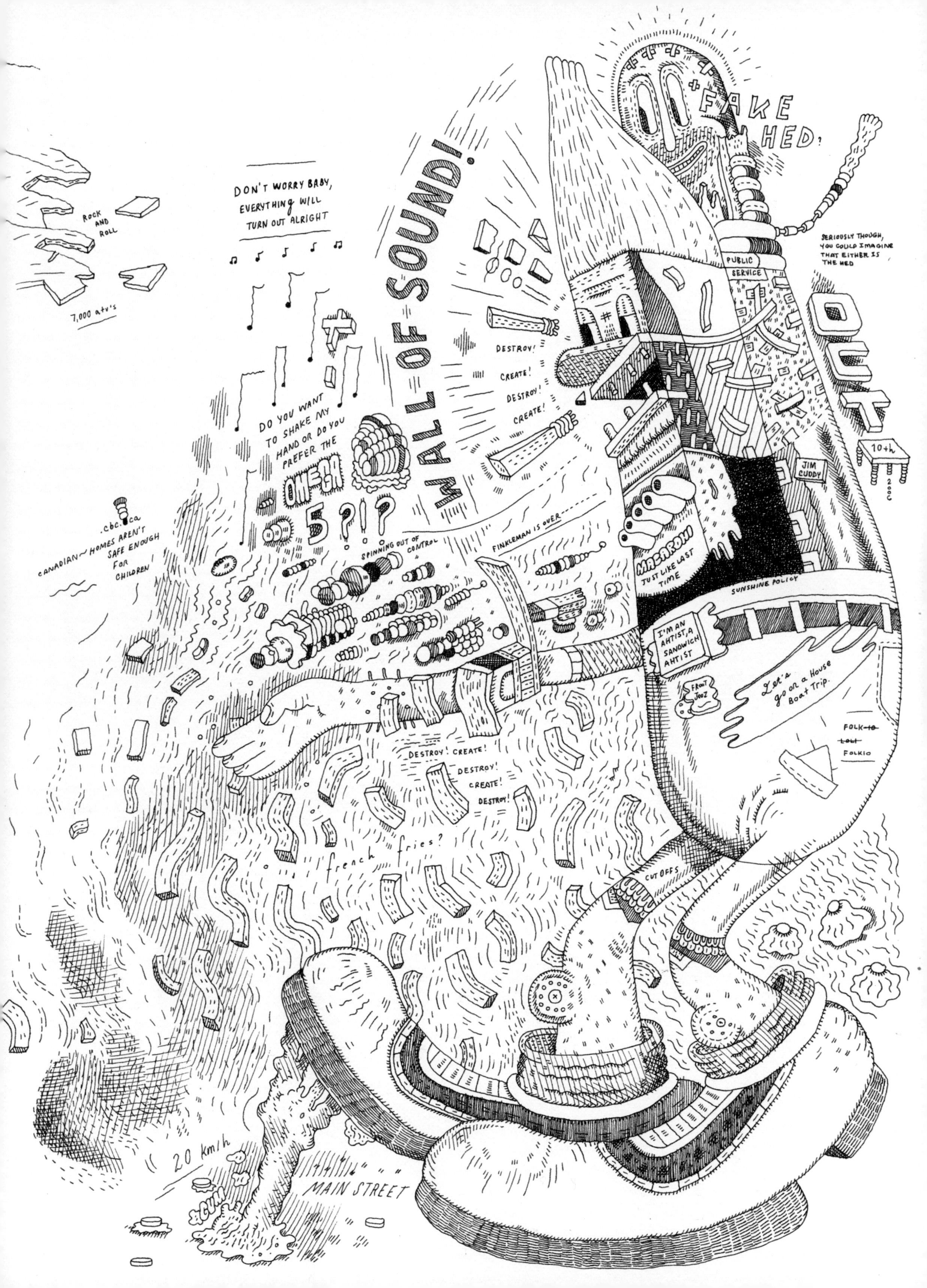

ROCK AND ROLL
7,000 atv's
DON'T WORRY BABY, EVERYTHING WILL TURN OUT ALRIGHT
WALL OF SOUND!
FAKE HED?
SERIOUSLY THOUGH, YOU COULD IMAGINE THAT EITHER IS THE HED
PUBLIC SERVICE
OUT
DESTROY! CREATE! DESTROY! CREATE!
DO YOU WANT TO SHAKE MY HAND OR DO YOU PREFER THE OMEGA 5?!?
10th
JIM CUDDY
.cbc.ca
CANADIAN~ HOMES AREN'T SAFE ENOUGH FOR CHILDREN
SPINNING OUT OF CONTROL
FINKLEMAN IS OVER
MACARONI
JUST LIKE LAST TIME
SUNSHINE POLICY
I'M AN AHTIST, A SANDWICH AHTIST
FROOT JOOZ
Let's go on a House Boat Trip.
FOLKIO
DESTROY! CREATE! DESTROY! CREATE! DESTROY!
french fries?
CUT OFFS
20 km/h
MAIN STREET
GUM

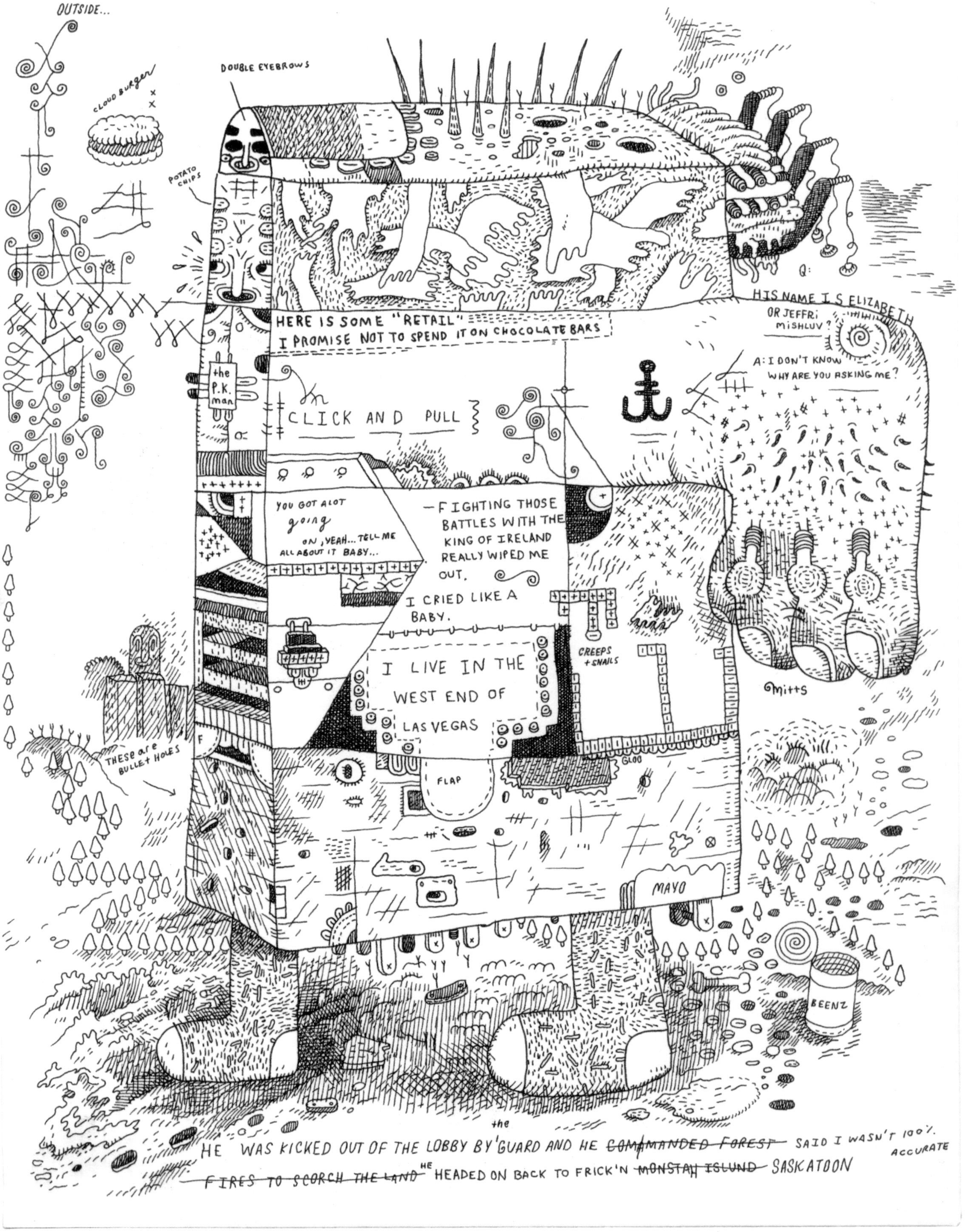
OUTSIDE...
DOUBLE EYEBROWS
cloud burger
POTATO CHIPS
HIS NAME IS ELIZABETH
OR JEFFRI MISHLUV?
Q:
A: I DON'T KNOW WHY ARE YOU ASKING ME?
HERE IS SOME "RETAIL" I PROMISE NOT TO SPEND IT ON CHOCOLATE BARS
the P.K. man
CLICK AND PULL
YOU GOT ALOT going ON, YEAH... TELL ME ALL ABOUT IT BABY...
—FIGHTING THOSE BATTLES WITH THE KING OF IRELAND REALLY WIPED ME OUT.
I CRIED LIKE A BABY.
I LIVE IN THE WEST END OF LAS VEGAS
CREEPS + SNAILS
Mitts
THESE are BULLET HOLES
FLAP
GLOO
MAYO
BEENZ
HE WAS KICKED OUT OF THE LOBBY BY the GUARD AND HE ~~COMMANDED FOREST FIRES TO SCORCH THE LAND~~ SAID I WASN'T 100% ACCURATE HE HEADED ON BACK TO FRICK'N ~~MONSTAH ISLAND~~ SASKATOON

70. *Double Eyebrows (I live in the west end of Las Vegas)*

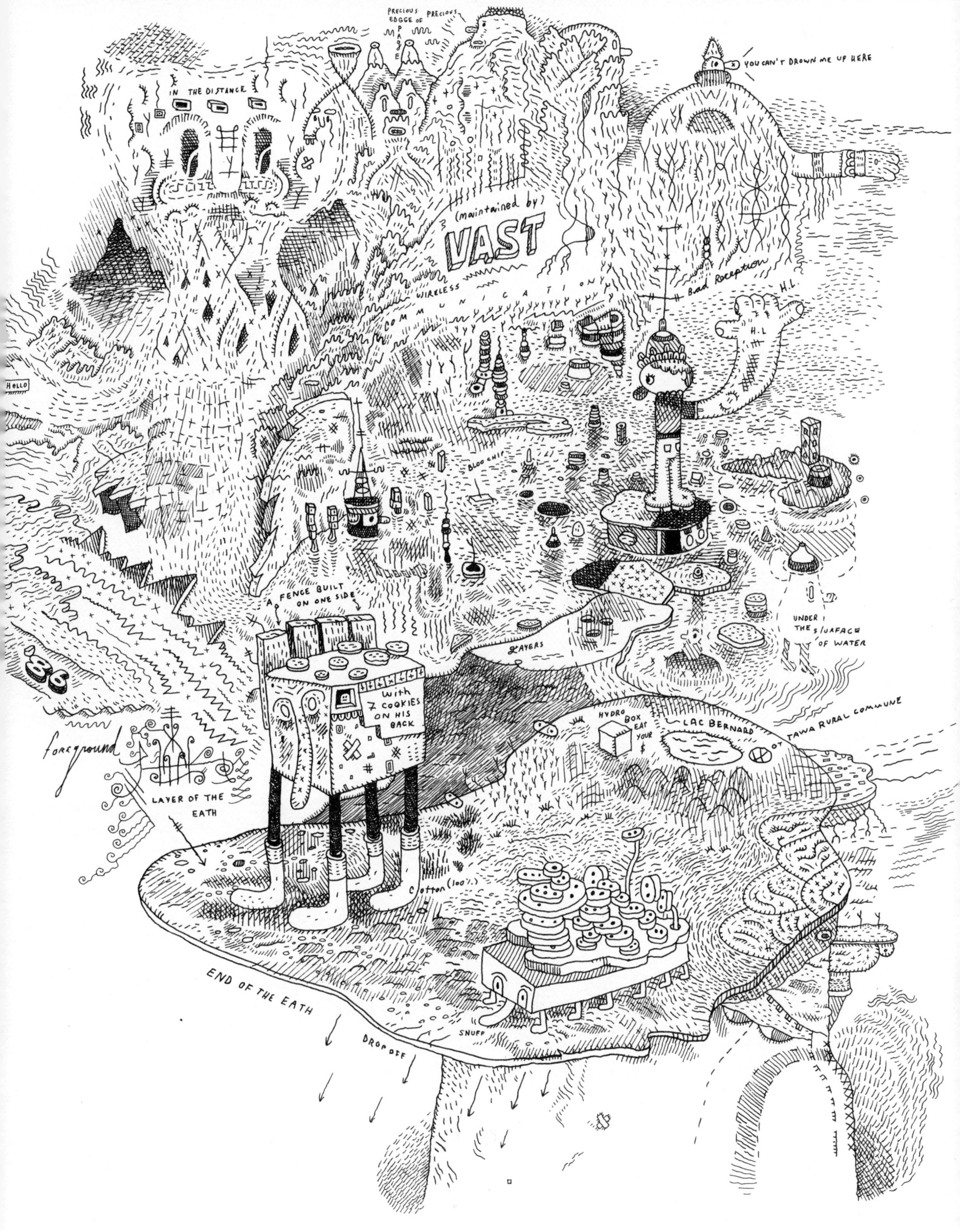
PRECIOUS EDGGE OF PAGE PRECIOUS
YOU CAN'T DROWN ME UP HERE
IN THE DISTANCE
(maintained by)
VAST
WIRELESS
COMMUNICATION
Bad Reception
H.L.
H.L
HELLO
BLOO CHIP
A FENCE BUILT ON ONE SIDE
LAYERS
UNDER THE SURFACE OF WATER
with 7 COOKIES ON HIS BACK
HYDRO BOX
EAT YOUR
LAC BERNARD
OTTAWA RURAL COMMUNE
'86
foreground
LAYER OF THE EATH
Cotton (100%)
END OF THE EATH
DROP OFF
SNUFF

71. *End Of The Ea_th (Fence Built On One Side)*

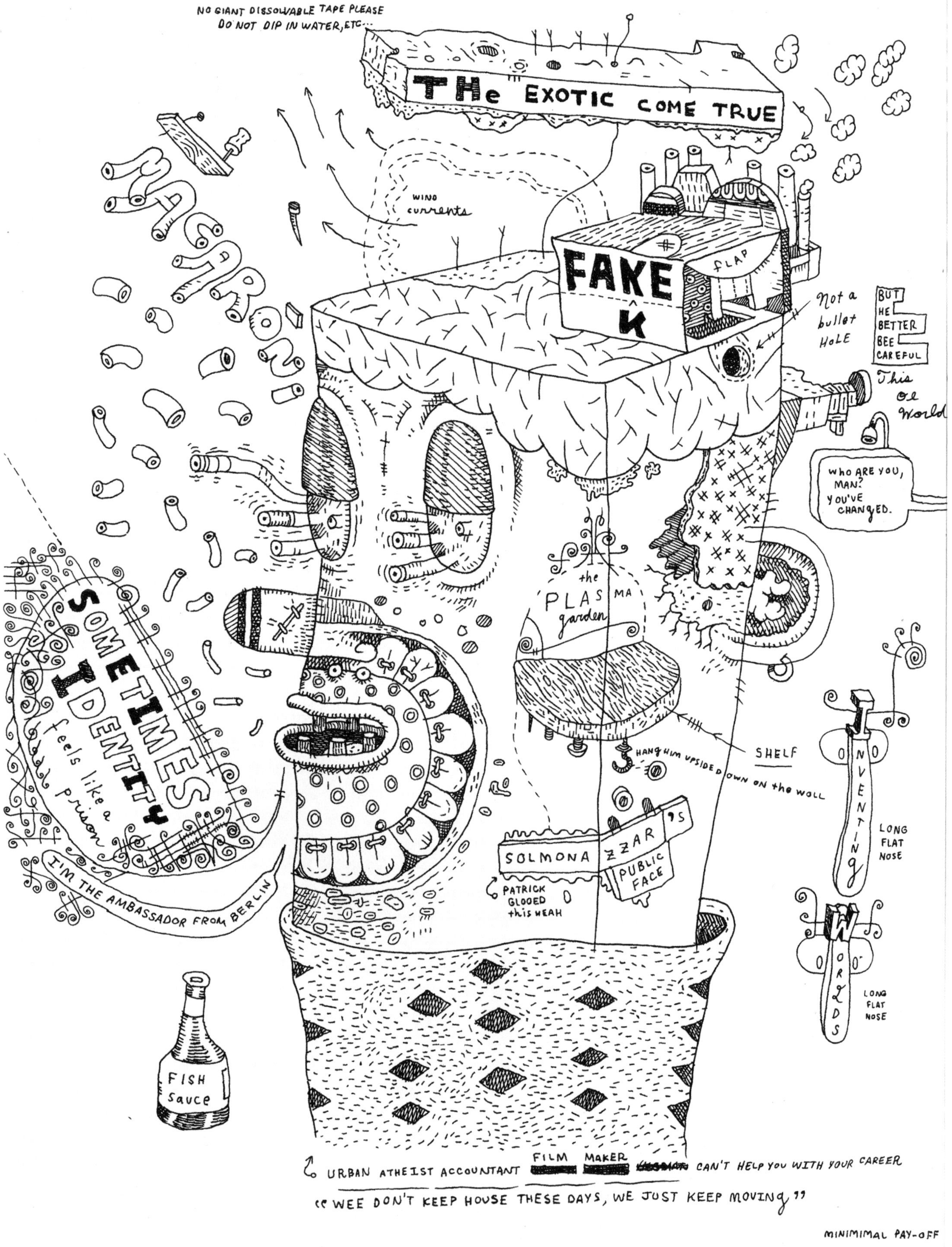

NO GIANT DISSOLVABLE TAPE PLEASE
DO NOT DIP IN WATER, ETC...
THe EXOTIC COME TRUE
MACARONI
WIND currents
FAKE
K
FLAP
Not a bullet HOLE
BUT HE BETTER BEE CAREFUL
This Ol World
WHO ARE YOU, MAN? YOU'VE CHANGED.
the PLASMA garden
SHELF
HANG HIM UPSIDE DOWN ON the WALL
SOMETIMES IDENTITY feels like a prison
I'M THE AMBASSADOR FROM BERLIN
SOLMONA ZZAR'S
PUBLIC FACE
PATRICK GLOOED this HEAH
INVENTING
LONG FLAT NOSE
WORLDS
LONG FLAT NOSE
FISH Sauce
URBAN ATHEIST ACCOUNTANT FILM MAKER CAN'T HELP YOU WITH YOUR CAREER
"WEE DON'T KEEP HOUSE THESE DAYS, WE JUST KEEP MOVING"
MINIMIMAL PAY-OFF

72. *Sometimes Identity Feels Like a Prison (Macaroni)*

73. *He Look*

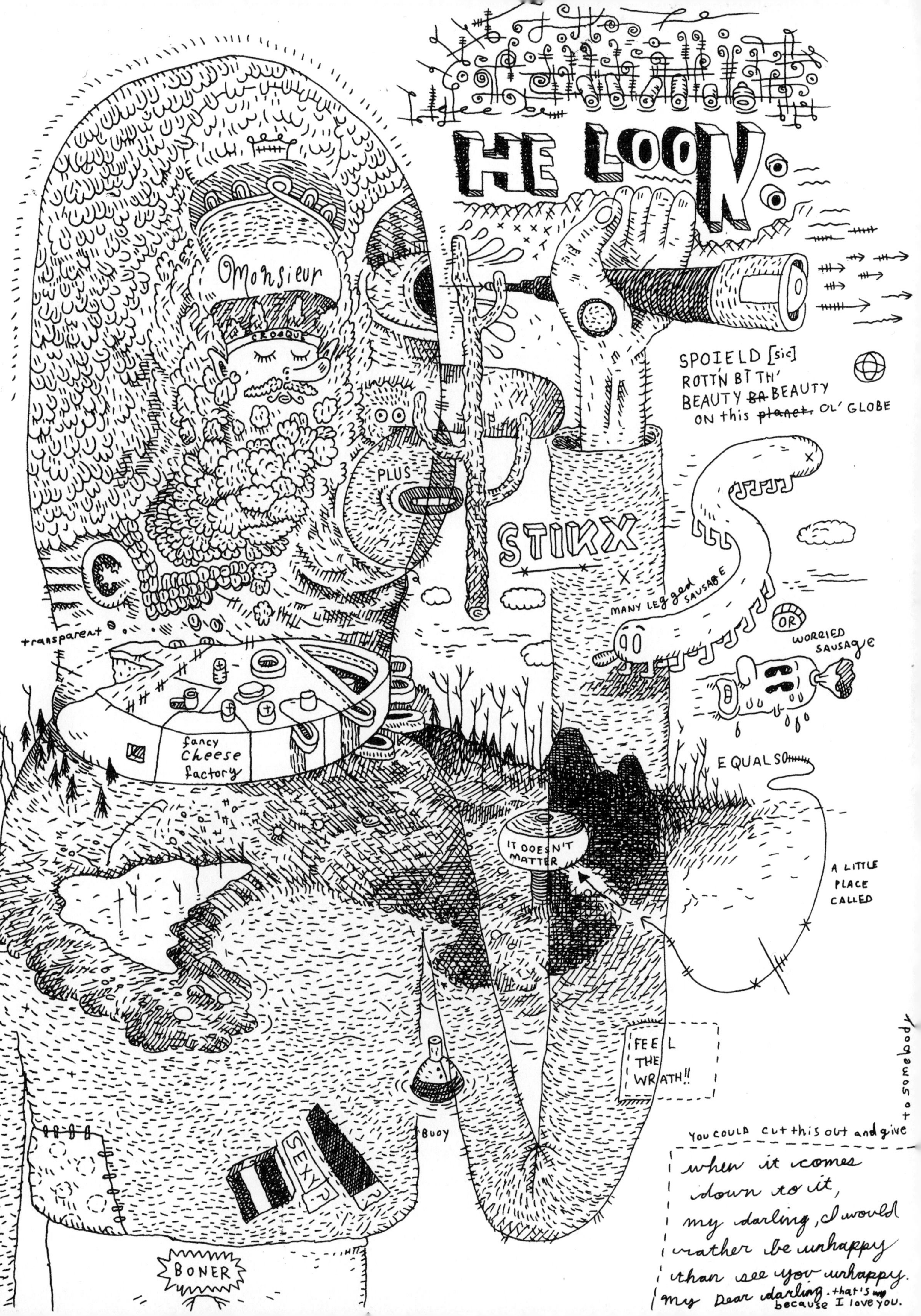

HE LOON
Monsieur
CROQUE
PLUS
STIKX
SPOIELD [sic]
ROTT'N BT TH'
BEAUTY BA BEAUTY
ON this planet. OL' GLOBE
MANY LEGGED SAUSAGE
OR
WORRIED SAUSAGE
transparent
fancy Cheese factory
EQUALS
IT DOESN'T MATTER
A LITTLE PLACE CALLED
FEEL THE WRATH!!
Buoy
SEXY?
BONER
You could cut this out and give to somebody
when it comes down to it, my darling, I would rather be unhappy than see you unhappy. my Dear darling. that's because I love you.

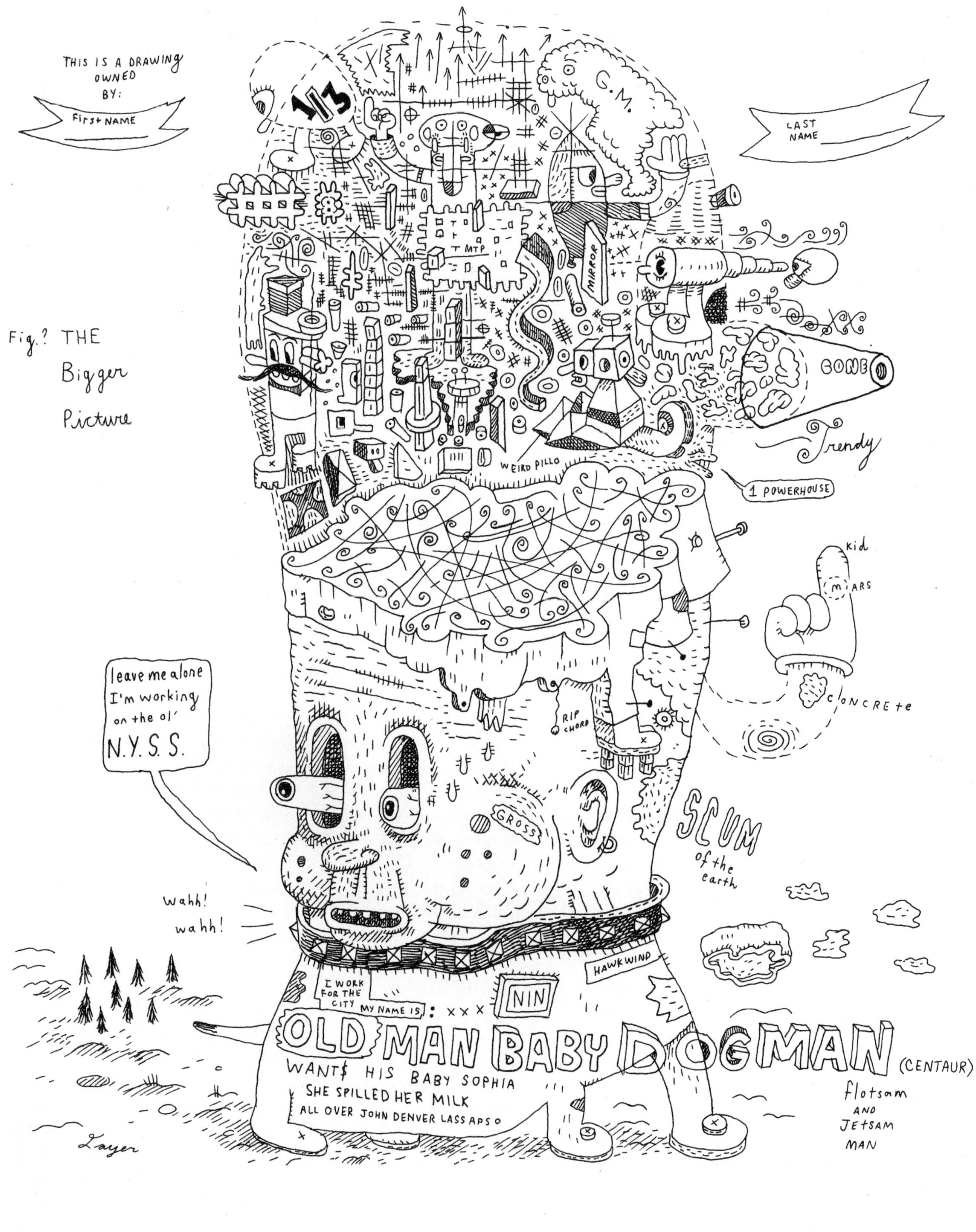
THIS IS A DRAWING OWNED BY:
First NAME
LAST NAME
Fig.? THE Bigger Picture
1/3
G.M.
MTP
MIRROR
BONE
Trendy
WEIRD PILLO
1 POWERHOUSE
kid
MARS
CONCRETE
RIP CHORD
leave me alone I'm working on the ol' N.Y.S.S.
GROSS
SCUM of the earth
wahh! wahh!
HAWKWIND
I WORK FOR THE CITY
NIN
MY NAME IS: XXX
OLD MAN BABY DOGMAN (CENTAUR)
WANT$ HIS BABY SOPHIA
SHE SPILLED HER MILK
ALL OVER JOHN DENVER LASSAPS
flotsam AND JETSAM MAN
Layer

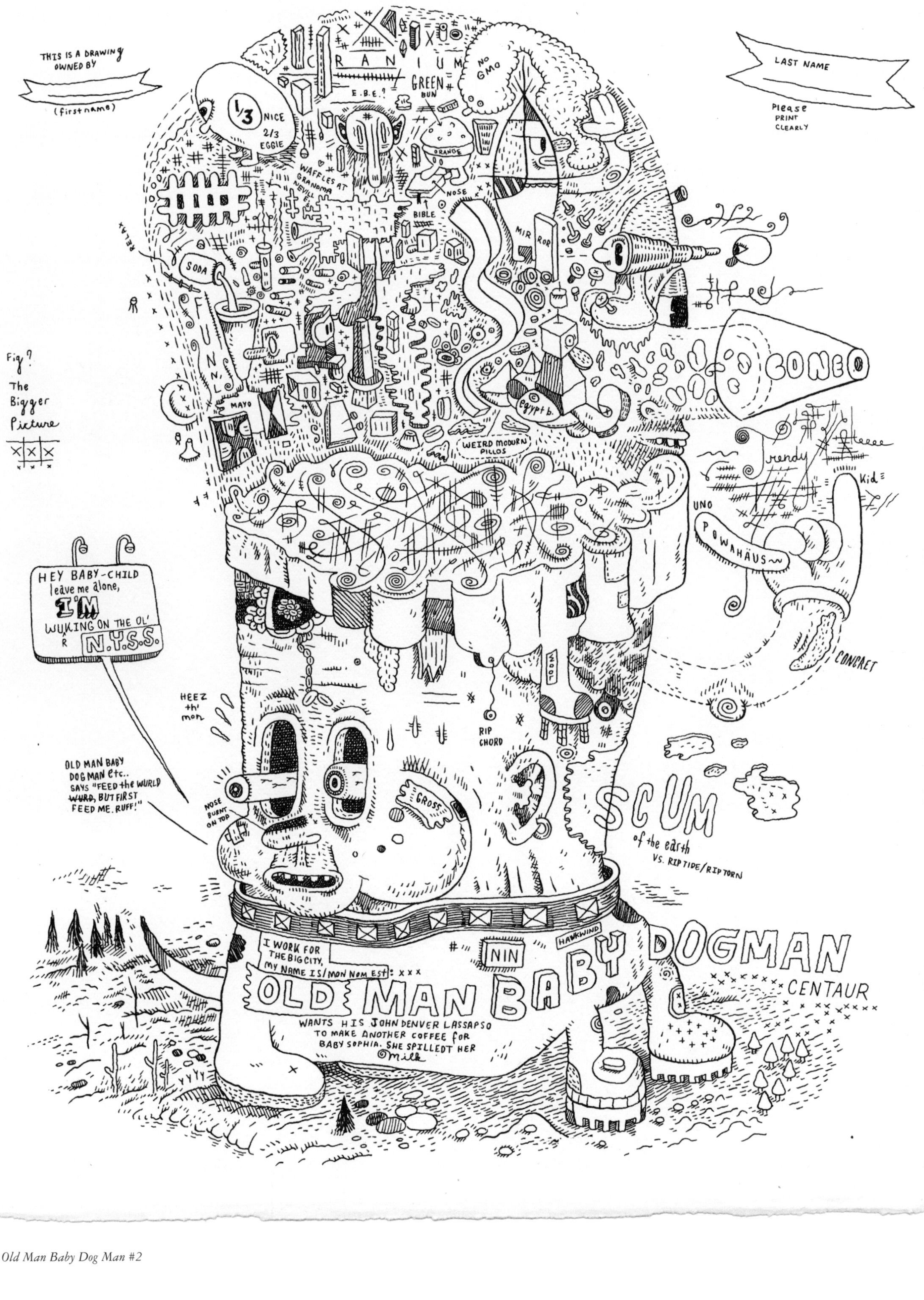
THIS IS A DRAWING OWNED BY
(firstname)
LAST NAME
Please PRINT CLEARLY
CRANIUM
NO GMO
GREEN BUN
E.B.E.?
1/3
NICE
2/3 EGGIE
ORANGE
WAFFLES AT GRANDMA NEVILL
NOSE
BIBLE
MIR ROR
RELAX
SODA
FUNNL
MAYO
egypt b.
WEIRD MODURN PILLOS
CONE
Fig ?
The Bigger Picture
Trendy
Kid
UNO
POWAHÄUS
CONCRET
HEY BABY-CHILD
leave me alone,
I'M
WUKING ON THE OL'
N.Y.S.S.
HEEZ th' mon
RIP CHORD
OLD MAN BABY DOG MAN etc.. SAYS "FEED the WURLD WURD, BUT FIRST FEED ME. RUFF!"
NOSE BURNT ON TOP
GROSS
SCUM
of the earth
VS. RIP TIDE/RIP TORN
I WORK FOR THE BIG CITY, MY NAME IS/MON NOM EST: xxx
NIN
HAWKWIND
OLD MAN BABY DOGMAN
CENTAUR
WANTS HIS JOHN DENVER LASSAPSO TO MAKE ANOTHER COFFEE FOR BABY SOPHIA. SHE SPILLEDT HER Milk

75. *Old Man Baby Dog Man #2*

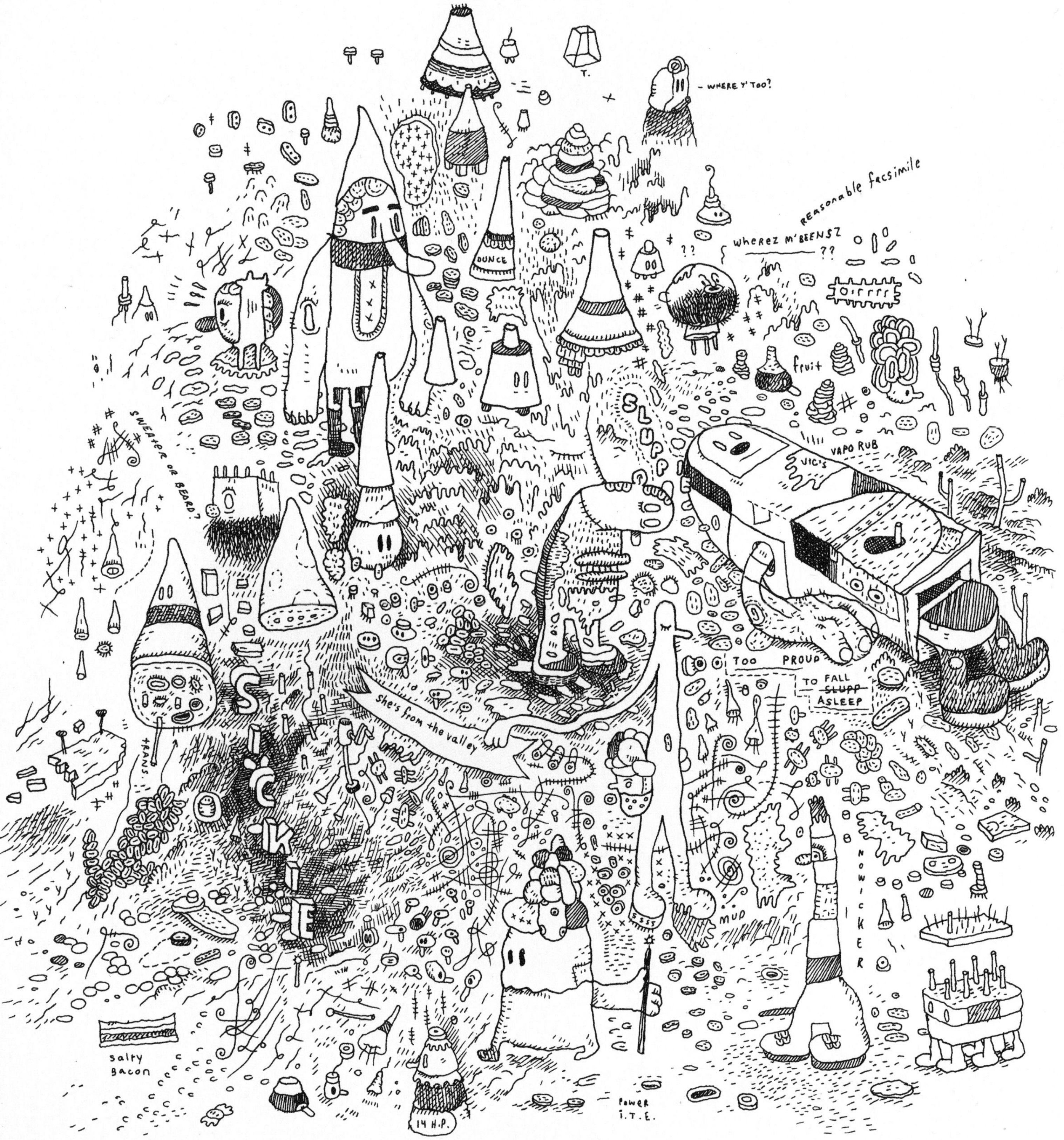

- WHERE Y' TOO?
T.
reasonable facsimile
wherez M'BEENSZ ??
DUNCE
fruit
SLUPP
VIC'S
VAPO RUB
SWEATER OR BEARD?
she's from the valley
TOO PROUD TO FALL SLUPP ASLEEP
TRANS.
MUD
NOWICKER
salty bacon
14 H.P.
POWER I.T.E.

76. *Where's M'Beensz? #2*

77. *For The Toddler #2*

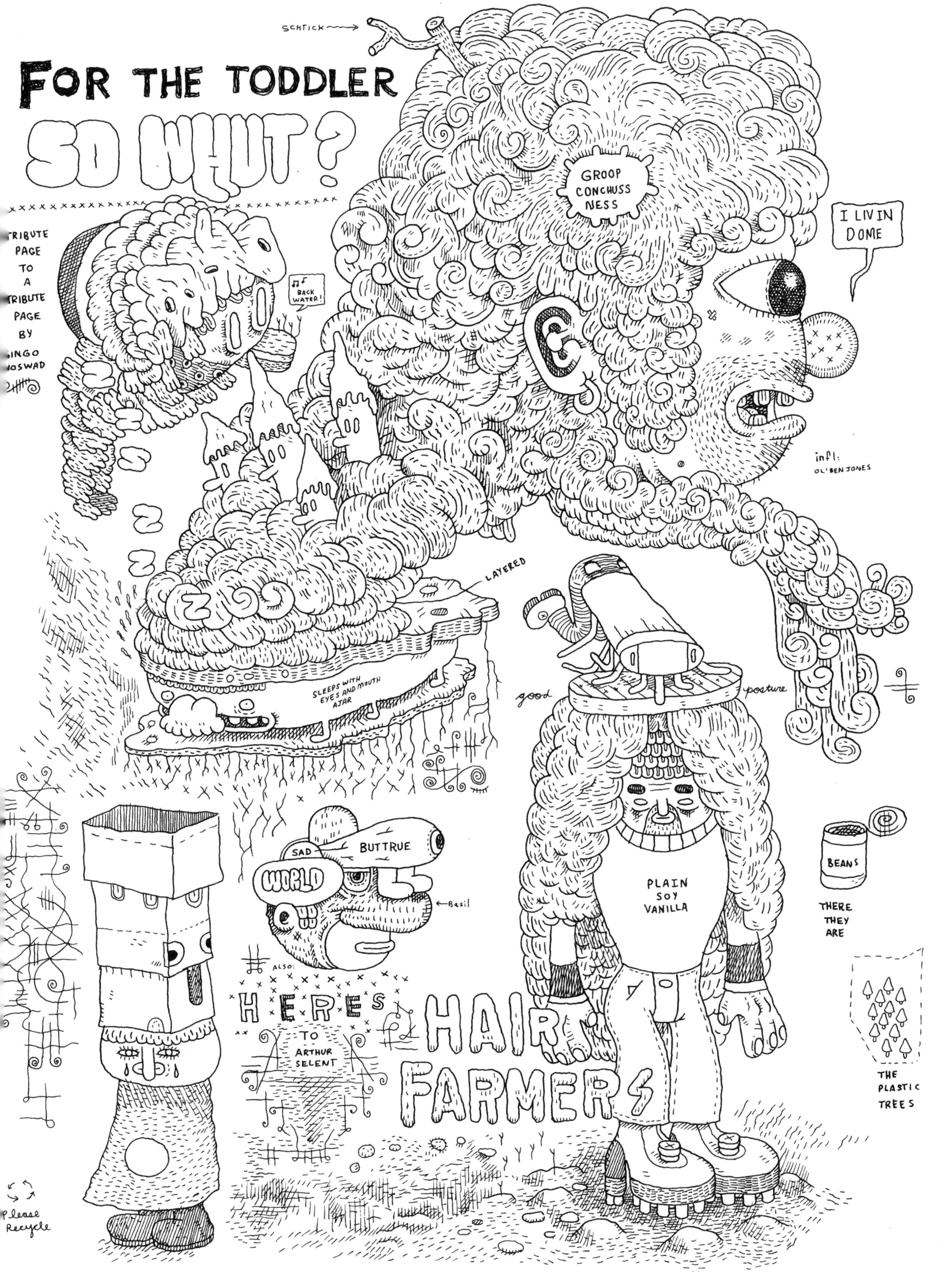
FOR THE TODDLER
SO WHUT?
SCHTICK
GROOP CONCHUSS NESS
I LIVIN DOME
TRIBUTE PAGE TO A TRIBUTE PAGE BY
BACK WATER!
infl: OL' BEN JONES
LAYERED
SLEEPS WITH EYES AND MOUTH AJAR
good posture
SAD
BUTTRUE
WORLD
Basil
PLAIN SOY VANILLA
BEANS
THERE THEY ARE
ALSO:
HERES TO ARTHUR SELENT
HAIR FARMERS
THE PLASTIC TREES
Please Recycle

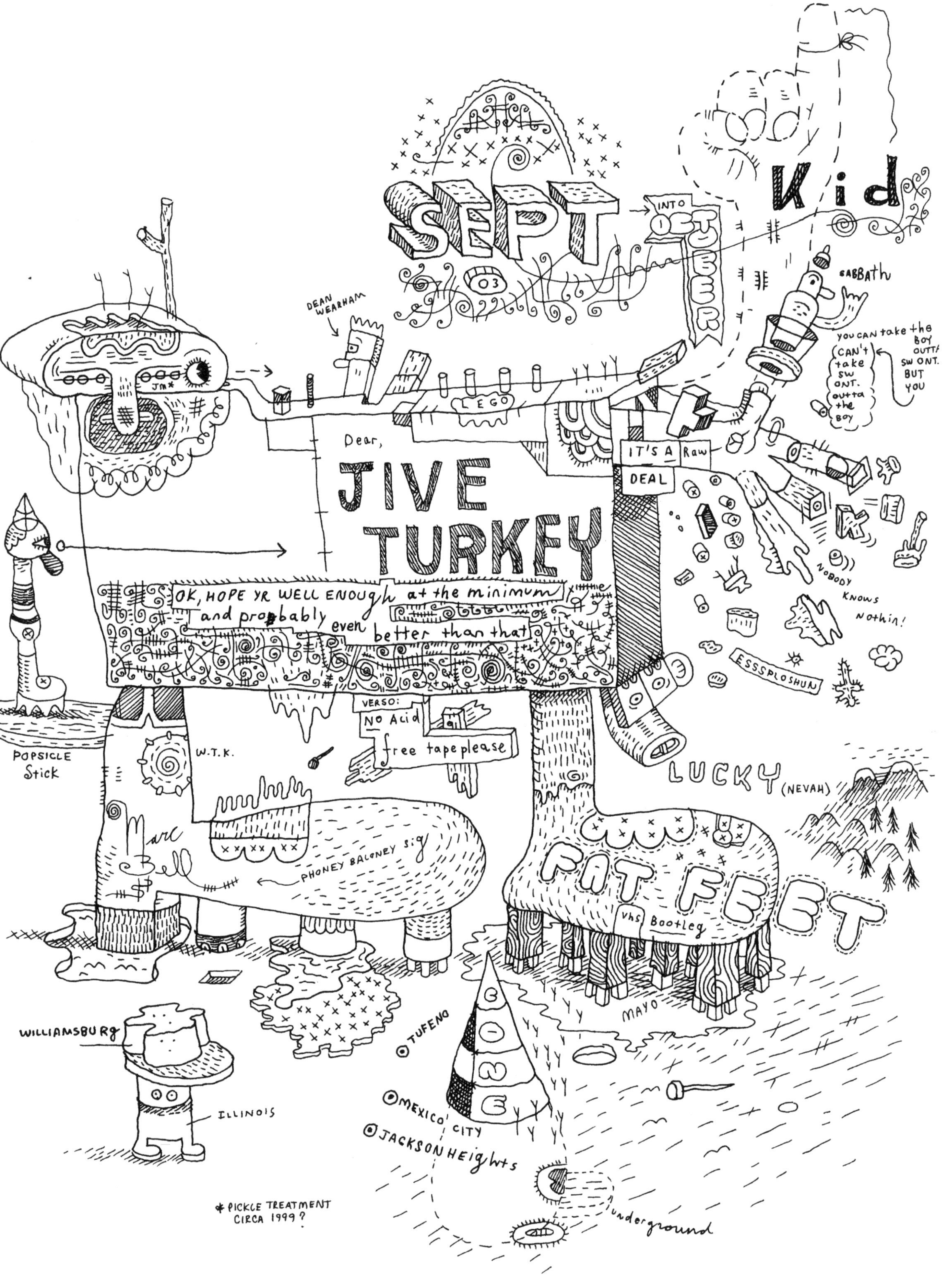

SEPT
INTO
OCTOBER
03
Kid
SABBATH
DEAN WEARHAM
LEGO
YOU CAN take the BOY OUTTA SW ONT. BUT YOU CAN'T take SW ONT. outta the BOY
Dear,
JIVE TURKEY
IT'S A Raw DEAL
OK, HOPE YR WELL ENOUGH at the minimum and probably even better than that
NOBODY KNOWS Nothin!
ESSSPLOSHUN
VERSO:
NO Acid free tape please
W.T.K.
POPSICLE Stick
LUCKY (NEVAH)
Marc Bell
PHONEY BALONEY sig
FAT FEET
vhs Bootleg
MAYO
WILLIAMSBURG
TUFENO
BONE
MEXICO CITY
JACKSON HEIGHTS
ILLINOIS
* PICKLE TREATMENT CIRCA 1999?
underground

78. *Jive Turkey*

79. *These Thungs*
(This was the cover for a photocopied booklet of the same name)

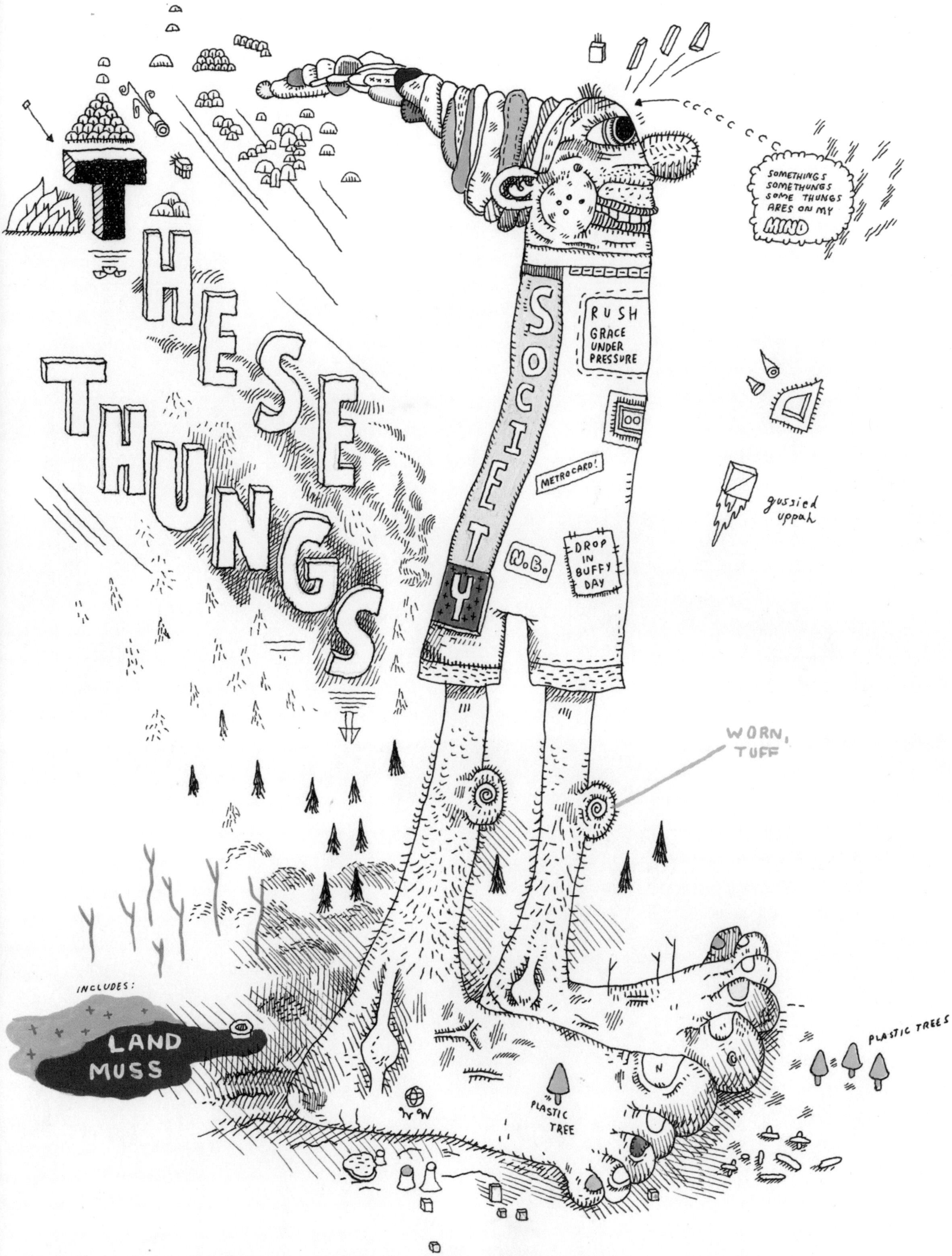
THESE THUNGS
SOMETHINGS SOMETHUNGS SOME THUNGS ARES ON MY MIND
SOCIETY
RUSH GRACE UNDER PRESSURE
METROCARD!
N.B.
DROP IN BUFFY DAY
gussied uppah
WORN, TUFF
INCLUDES:
LAND MUSS
PLASTIC TREE
PLASTIC TREES

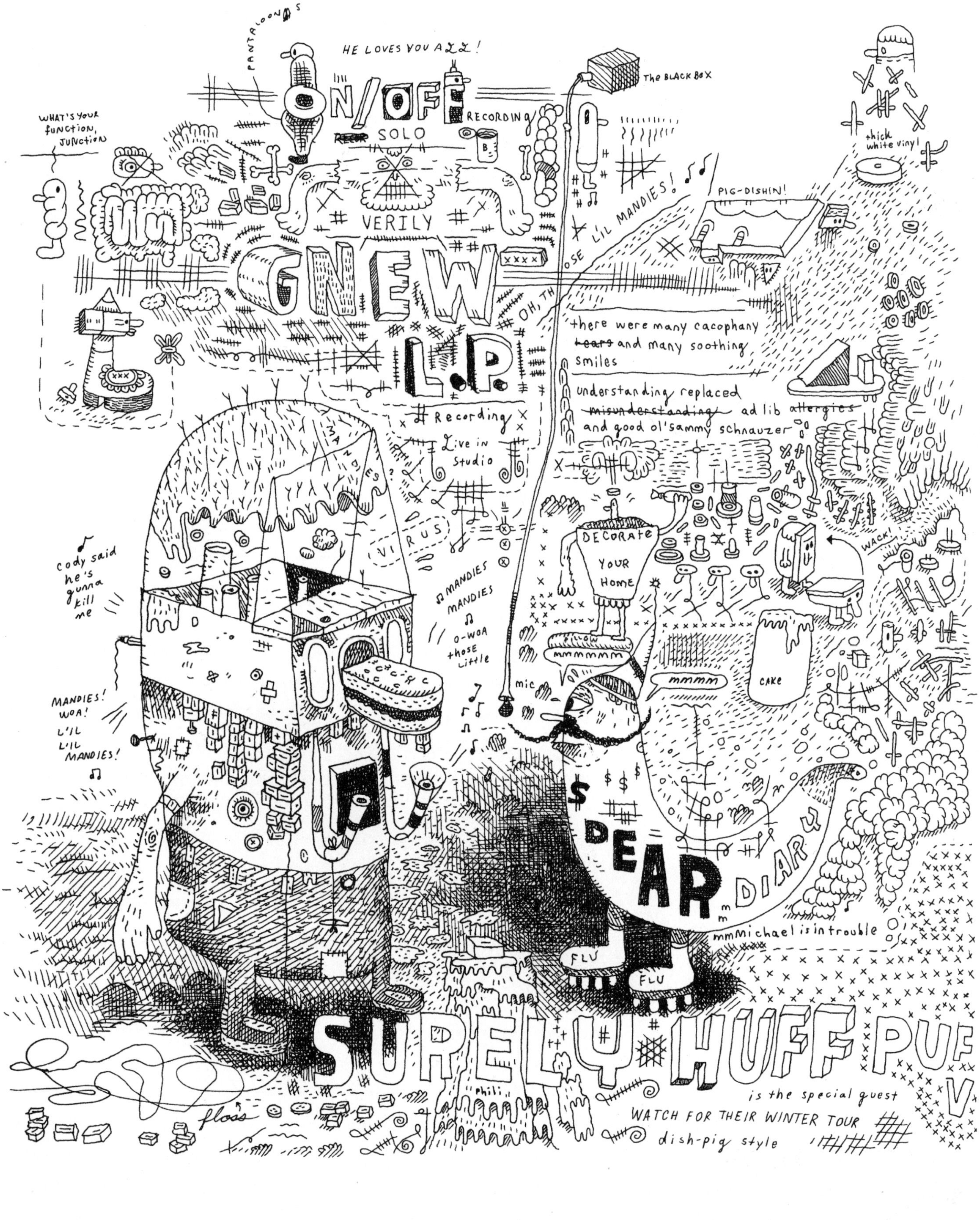
PANTALOONAS
HE LOVES YOU ALL!
ON/OFF
RECORDING
SOLO
The BLACK BOX
WHAT'S YOUR function, Junction
thick white vinyl
PIG-DISHIN!
VERILY
GNEW
L.P.
OH, THOSE L'IL MANDIES!
there were many cacophany tears and many soothing smiles
understanding replaced misunderstanding ad lib allergies
and good ol'sammy schnauzer
Recording
Live in studio
MANDIES
VIRUS
DECORATE YOUR HOME
WACK!
cody said he's gunna kill me
MANDIES MANDIES
O-WOA those little
mmmmmm
mmmm
CAKE
mic
MANDIES! WOA! L'IL L'IL MANDIES!
DEAR DIARY
mmmichael is in trouble
FLU
FLU
SURELY HUFF PUFV
phili
floss
is the special guest
WATCH FOR THEIR WINTER TOUR
dish-pig style

80. *Verily Gnew L.P. (Surely Huff Pufv)*

81. *George Lucas Carried Me Throo the Muck*

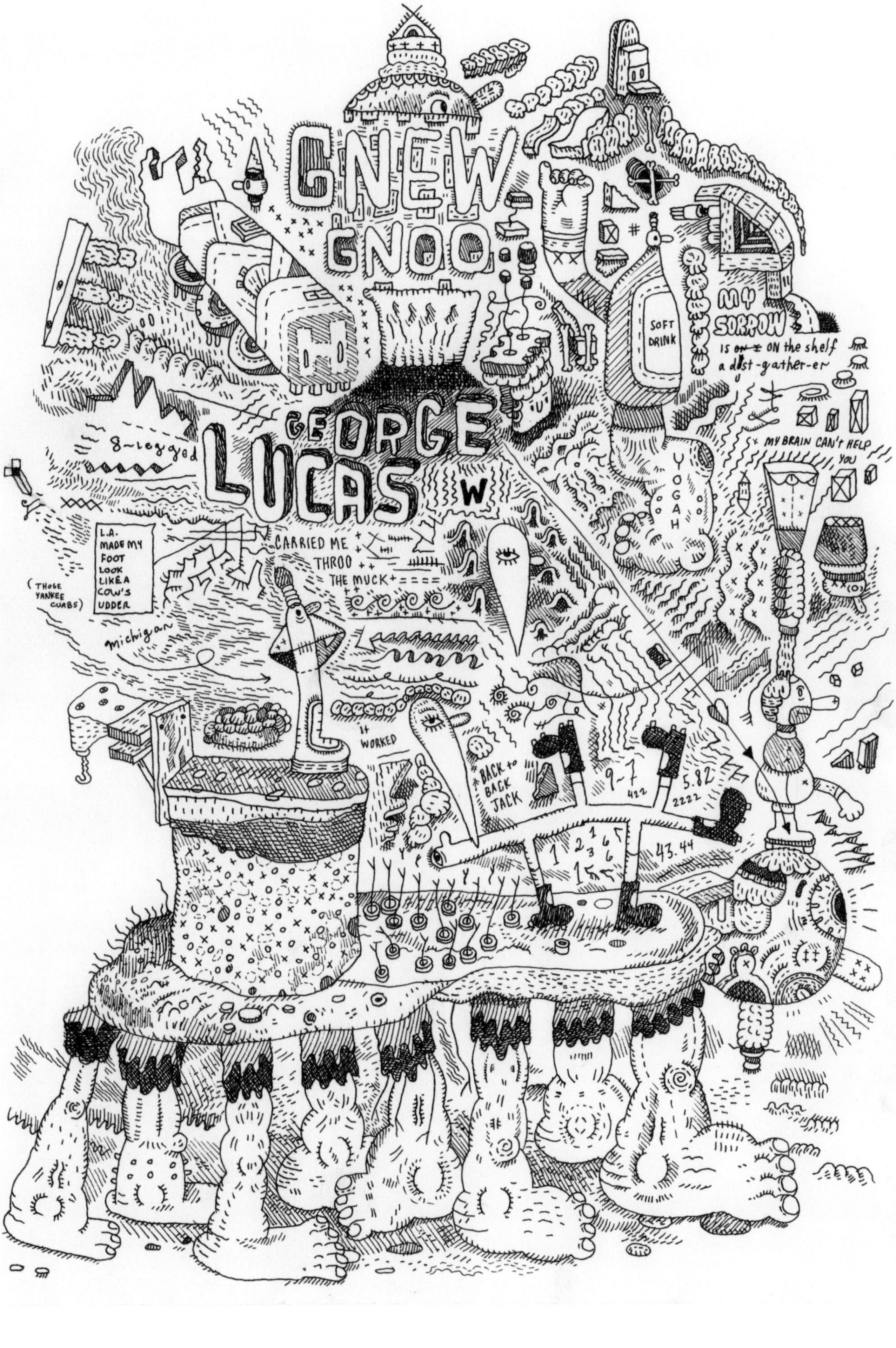
GNEW
GNOO
GEORGE
LUCAS
W
SOFT DRINK
MY SORROW
IS ON the shelf a dust-gather-er
MY BRAIN CAN'T HELP YOU
YOGAH
8-legged
L.A. MADE MY FOOT LOOK LIKE A COW'S UDDER
(THOSE YANKEE CURBS)
michigan
CARRIED ME THROO THE MUCK
it WORKED
BACK to BACK JACK
9-7
422
5.82
2222
43.44

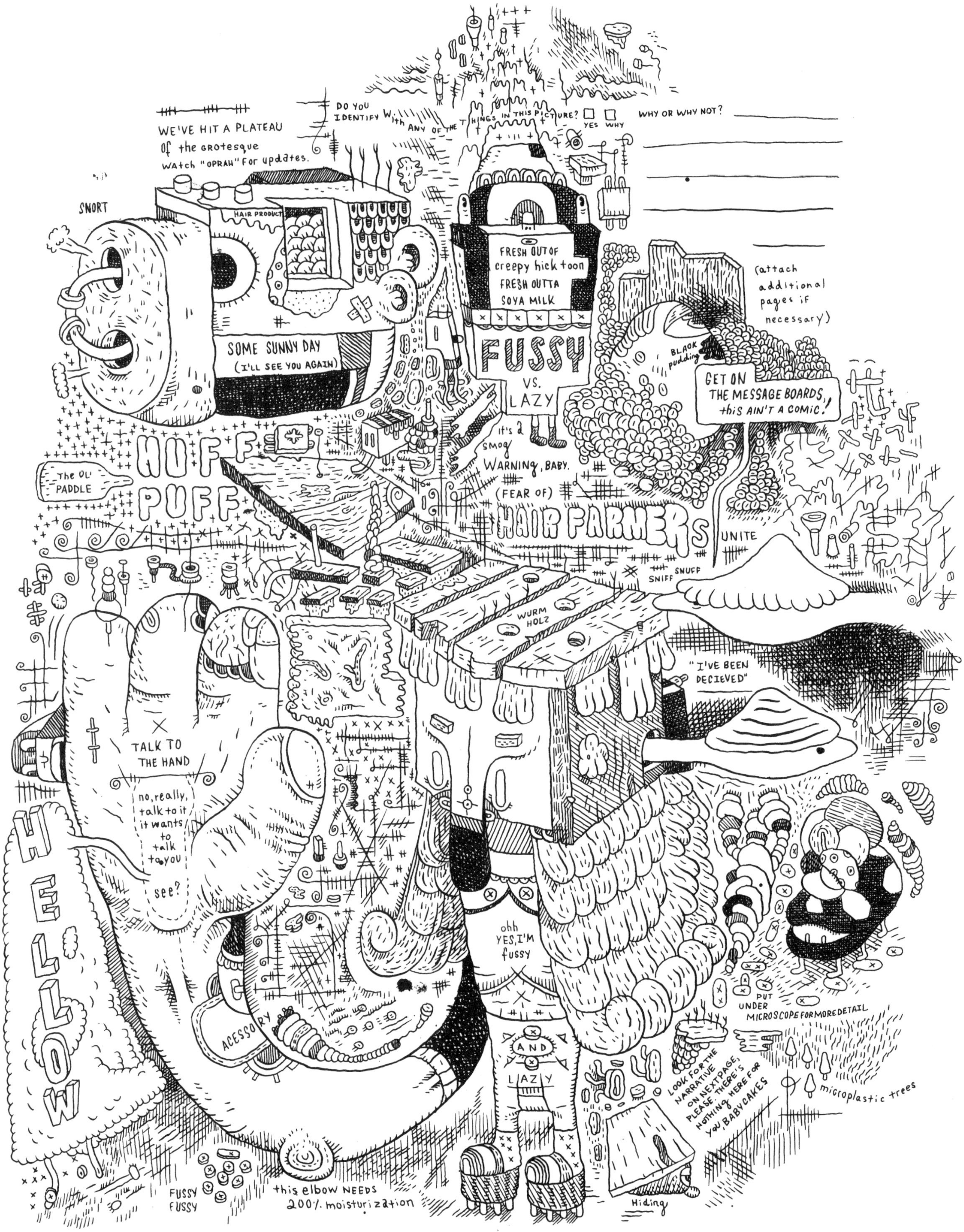
WE'VE HIT A PLATEAU of the GROTESQUE Watch "OPRAH" For updates.
DO YOU IDENTIFY With ANY OF THE THINGS IN THIS PICTURE? YES WHY
WHY OR WHY NOT?
SNORT
HAIR PRODUCT
SOME SUNNY DAY (I'LL SEE YOU AGAIN)
FRESH OUT OF creepy hick toon FRESH OUTTA SOYA MILK
FUSSY VS. LAZY
(attach additional pages if necessary)
BLACK pudding
GET ON THE MESSAGE BOARDS, this AIN'T A COMIC!
HUFF PUFF
The OL' PADDLE
it's a smog WARNING, BABY.
(FEAR OF) HAIR FARMERS UNITE
SNIFF SNUFF
WURM HOLZ
"I'VE BEEN DECIEVED"
TALK TO THE HAND
no, really, talk to it it wants to talk to you see?
HELLO
ACESSORY
ohh YES, I'M fussy
AND LAZY
PUT UNDER MICROSCOPE FOR MORE DETAIL
LOOK FOR THE NARRATIVE ON NEXT PAGE, PLEASE THERE'S NOTHING HERE FOR YOU BABYCAKES
microplastic trees
FUSSY FUSSY
this elbow NEEDS 200% moisturization
Hiding

82. *Fussy Vs. Lazy (Talk To The Hand)*

83. *(Don't) Here's (They Rose From Nothing)*

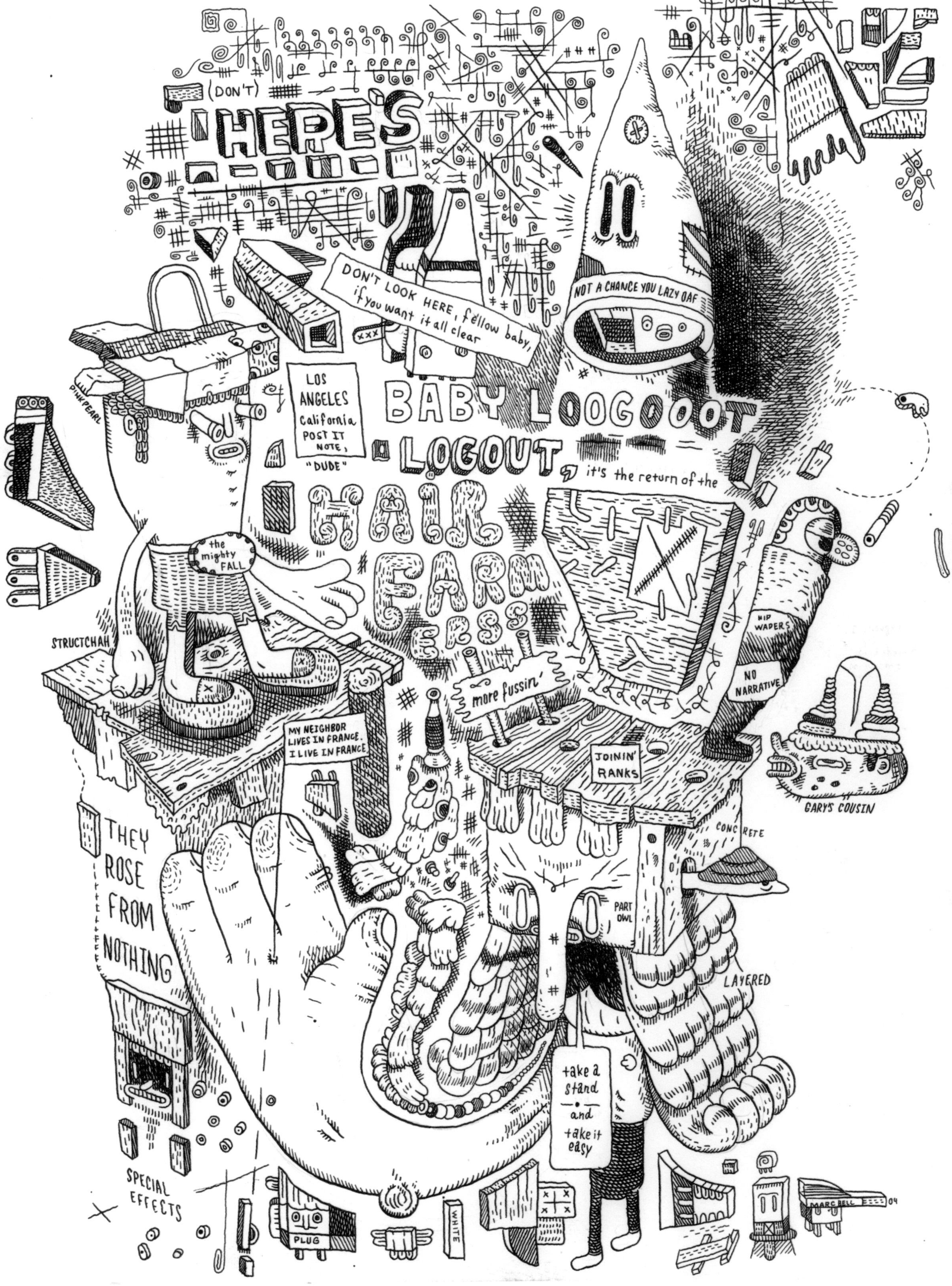

(DON'T)
HERE'S
DON'T LOOK HERE, fellow baby, if you want it all clear
NOT A CHANCE YOU LAZY OAF
xxx
LOS ANGELES California POST IT NOTE, "DUDE"
BABY LOOGOOOT
LOGOUT, it's the return of the
HAIR FARMERS
PINKPEARL
the mighty FALL
STRUCTCHAH
HIP WADERS
NO NARRATIVE
more fussin'
MY NEIGHBOR LIVES IN FRANCE. I LIVE IN FRANCE
JOININ' RANKS
GARY'S COUSIN
CONCRETE
THEY ROSE FROM NOTHING
PART OWL
LAYERED
take a stand and take it easy
SPECIAL EFFECTS
PLUG
WHITE
MARC BELL 04

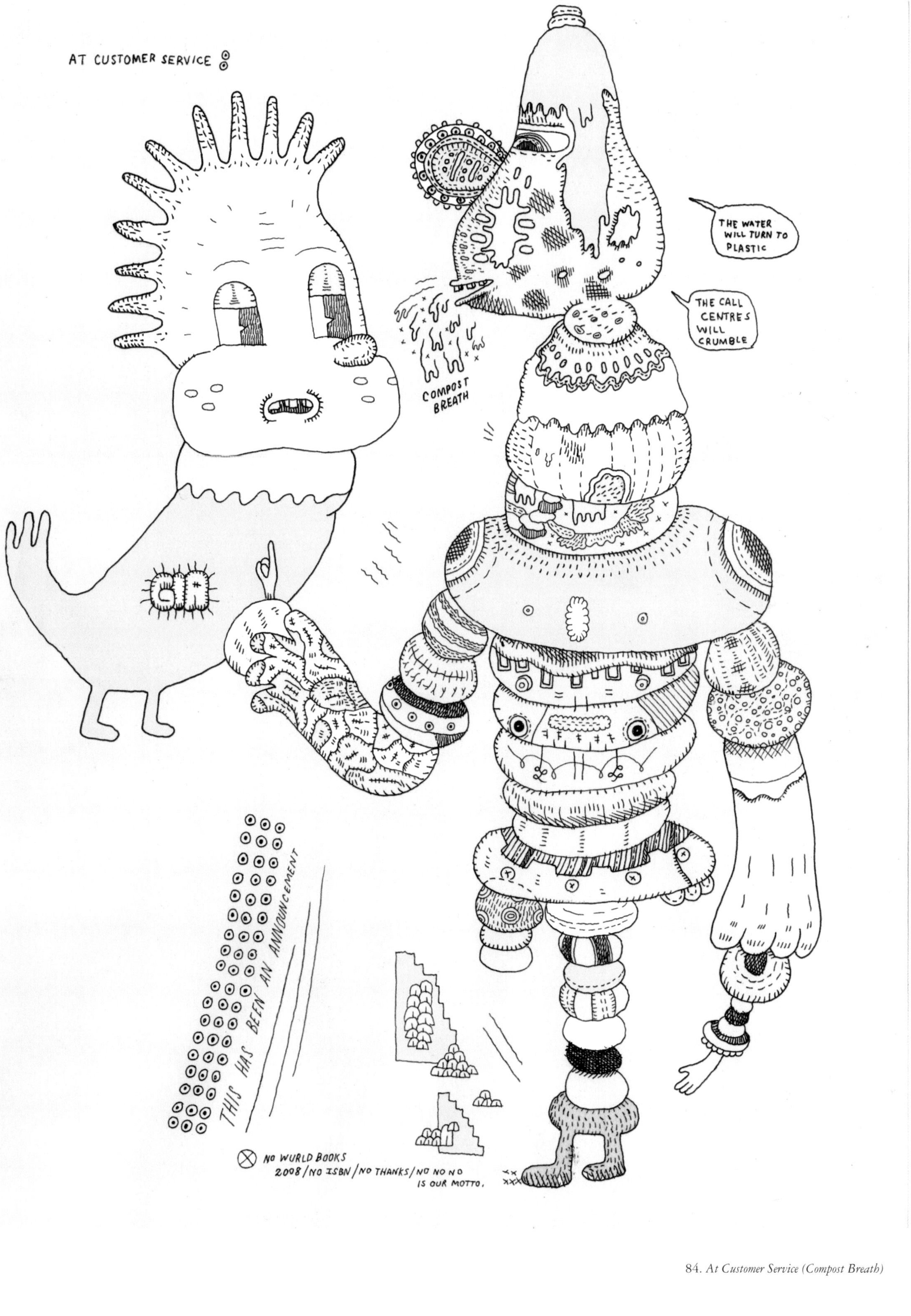
AT CUSTOMER SERVICE
THE WATER WILL TURN TO PLASTIC
THE CALL CENTRES WILL CRUMBLE
COMPOST BREATH
THIS HAS BEEN AN ANNOUNCEMENT
NO WURLD BOOKS 2008 / NO ISBN / NO THANKS / NO NO NO IS OUR MOTTO.

 At Customer Service (Compost Breath)

QUESTIONAIRRRE dept.

PLEASE MARK CLEARLY ON A NATIONAL LEVEL

- -

IF I WAS A CARPENTER I WOULD BUILD:

☐ A WALL TO HIDE FROM ~~THE WORLD AND ALL THE~~ SOCIETY'S ILLS

☐ 63 Ft. POWER CHILD

☐ LITTLE CARDBOARD FIGURES AND GLUE BITS OF PAPER
TO THEM AND PAINT ON THEM. PERHAPS I MIGHT ALSO
BUILD SMALL SHELVES TO ATTACH TO THEM AND LITTLE
MINIATURE SODA POP CUPS TO PUT ON THEM. MAYBE SOME
OVEN MITTS MADE OUT OF PAINTED TAPE FOR THEM
TO WEAR (OPTIONAL)

TIM HO-TON WAS:

☐ SECRET SID DICKENS' UNCLE CHARLIE

☐ A CANADIAN HOCKEY PLAYER THAT OPENED A SUCESSFUL
CHAIN OF COFFEE/DONUT SHOPS

☐ A HORN-DOG

☐ GENETICALLY MODIFIED

IF SID DICKENS LEAVES ON THE EXPRESS BUS TO T.O. AT 1:00 PM
AND PERTH MAKES TOO MANY PLANS AND GETS ALL STRESSED OUT, WHAT
TIME WILL o→ OL' FINKLEMAN RENDEZVOUS WITH THE
BIG MAN IN WESTMOUNT

☐ 8:00 PM Saturday

WHY 'THE STACKS'? WHY NOT:

☐ 'WORN TUFF ELBOW'

☐ 'CALL LARRY ABOUT THE IRONING BOARD'

☐ 'PROVINCIAL, PLEASE'

☐ 'IT DOESN'T MATTER WHAT LANE YOU'RE IN, THERE'S
NUTTIN' YOU CAN DO.'

QUE

QUESTIONAIRRRE

YOU COULD PLEASE COMPLETE
ALL QUESTIONS. NO CHEATING

1 SID DIKENS IS A THE OWNER AND OPERATOR OF A TILE
c
B BUSINNESS IN VANCOUVER, BC.

ANYTHING.
UPON COMPLETION, ATTEND 'THE STACKS' EXHIBITION AND SEE IF YOU'VE LEARNED
PLEASE COMPLETE ALL QUESTIONS, PRINTING/MARKING CLEARY

QUESTIONAIRRRE

thunkin' bout
flotsam 'n jetsam
NOSE IS BURNT FOR SOME REASON
RELAXED
"the big G"
WISCONSIN
mayo
more than pearly gate

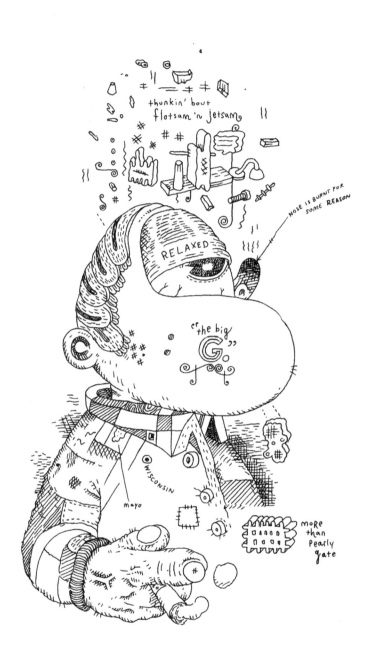

85. *The Big "G."*

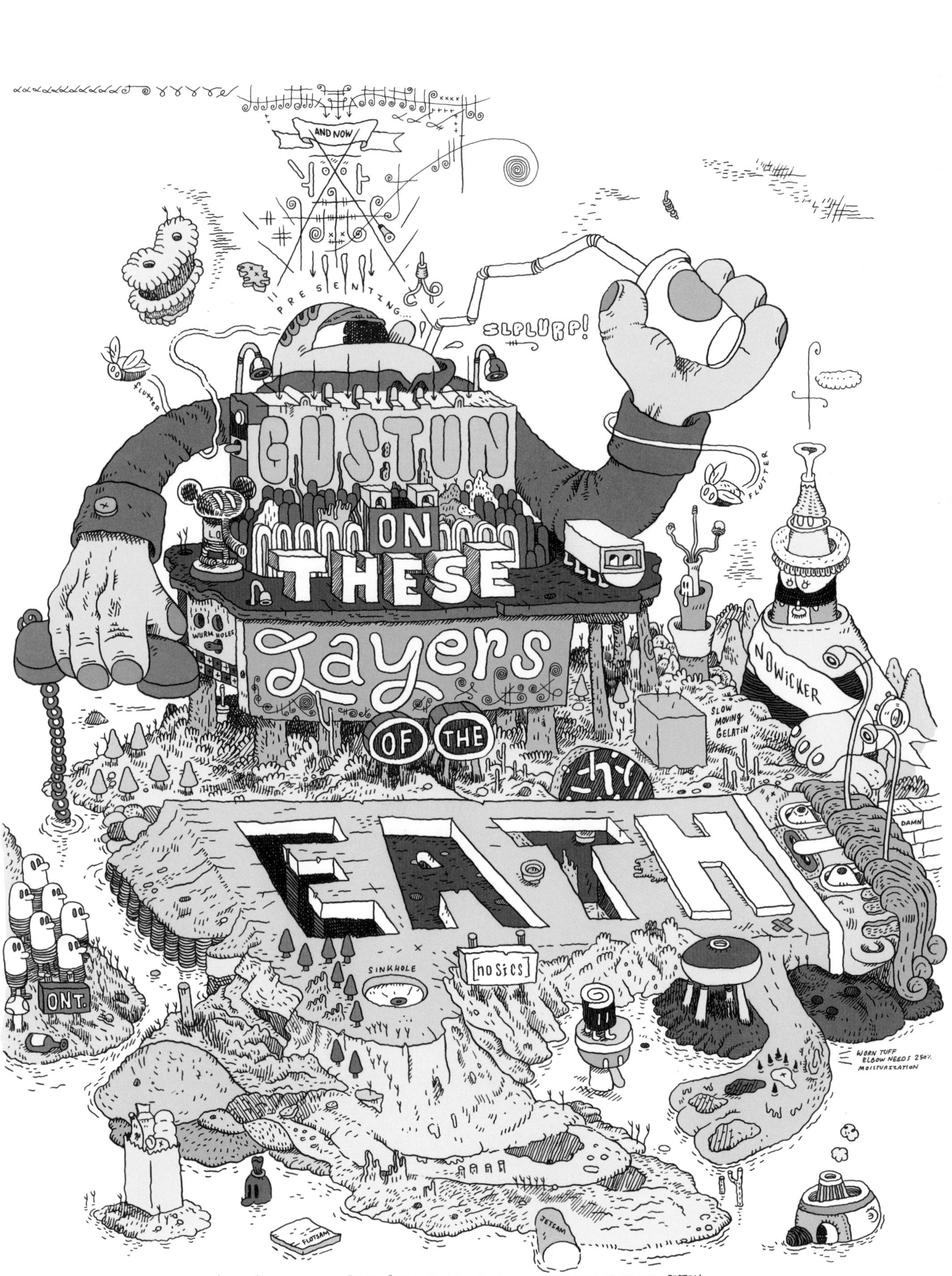
AND NOW
PRESENTING...
SLPLURP!
FLUTTER
FLUTTER
GUSTUN
ON
THESE
Layers
OF
THE
WURM HOLES
NOWICKER
SLOW MOVING GELATIN
DAMN
ONT.
SINKHOLE
[no sics]
WORN TUFF ELBOW NEEDS 250% MOISTURIZATION
FLOTSAM
JETSAM

-PREPARED FOR THE GANZFELD IN '03 AND '04 BY MARC BELL. "GUSTUN" IS LOOSELY BASED ON CHARACTERS CREATED BY THE REAL GUSTON

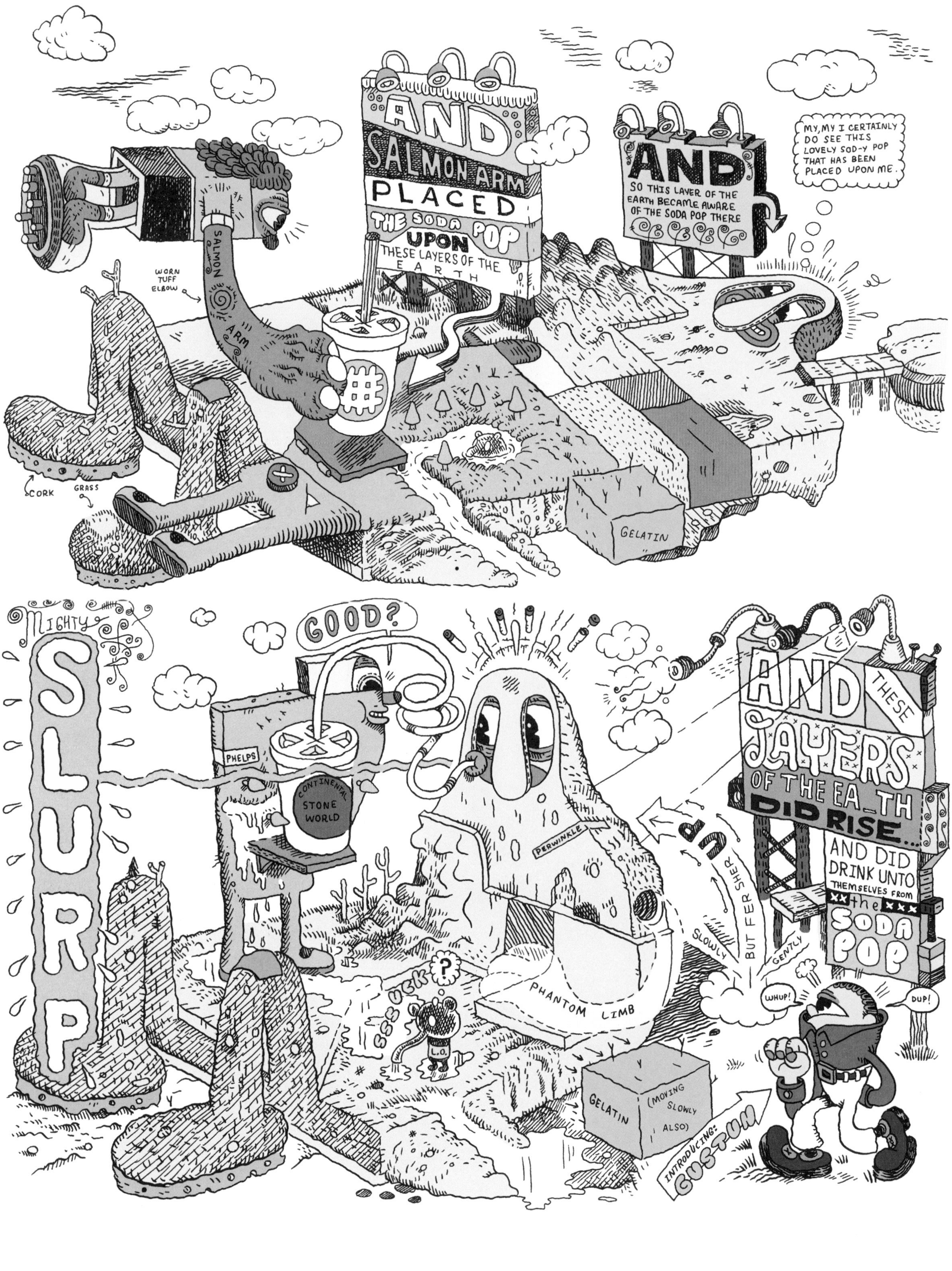

AND
SALMON ARM
PLACED
THE SODA POP
UPON
THESE LAYERS OF THE EARTH
AND
SO THIS LAYER OF THE EARTH BECAME AWARE OF THE SODA POP THERE
MY, MY I CERTAINLY DO SEE THIS LOVELY SOD-Y POP THAT HAS BEEN PLACED UPON ME.
SALMON ARM
WORN TUFF ELBOW
CORK
GRASS
GELATIN
MIGHTY
SLURP
GOOD?
PHELPS
CONTINENTAL STONE WORLD
PERWINKLE
AND THESE LAYERS OF THE EA_TH DID RISE...
AND DID DRINK UNTO THEMSELVES FROM the SODA POP
UP
SLOWLY
BUT FER SHER
GENTLY
PHANTOM LIMB
SSSUCK
?
L.O.
GELATIN (MOVING SLOWLY ALSO)
INTRODUCING: GUS-TUM
WHUP!
DUP!

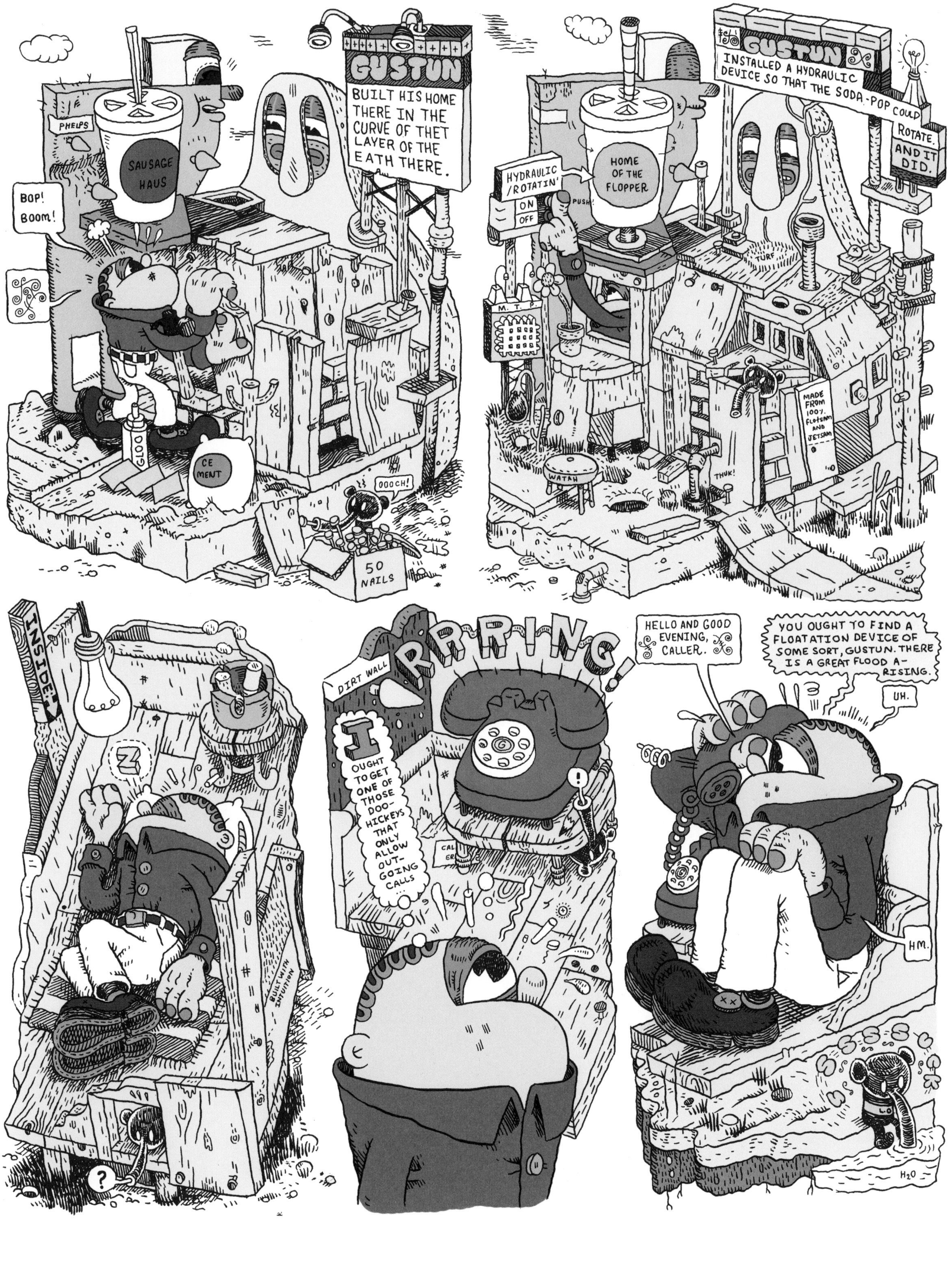
GUSTUN
BUILT HIS HOME THERE IN THE CURVE OF THET LAYER OF THE EATH THERE.
PHELPS
SAUSAGE HAUS
BOP! BOOM!
CE MENT
OOOCH!
50 NAILS
GUSTUN
INSTALLED A HYDRAULIC DEVICE SO THAT THE SODA-POP COULD
ROTATE.
AND IT DID.
HYDRAULIC /ROTATIN'
ON
OFF
PUSH!
HOME OF THE FLOPPER
TURF
M. T. P.
MADE FROM 100% FLOTSAM AND JETSAM
WATAH
THUK!
INSIDE
Z
BUILT WITH INTUITION
?
RRRING!
DIRT WALL
I OUGHT TO GET ONE OF THOSE DOO-HICKEYS THAT ONLY ALLOW OUT-GOING CALLS...
HELLO AND GOOD EVENING, CALLER.
YOU OUGHT TO FIND A FLOATATION DEVICE OF SOME SORT, GUSTUN. THERE IS A GREAT FLOOD A-RISING.
UH.
HM.
SSSSUCK
H2O

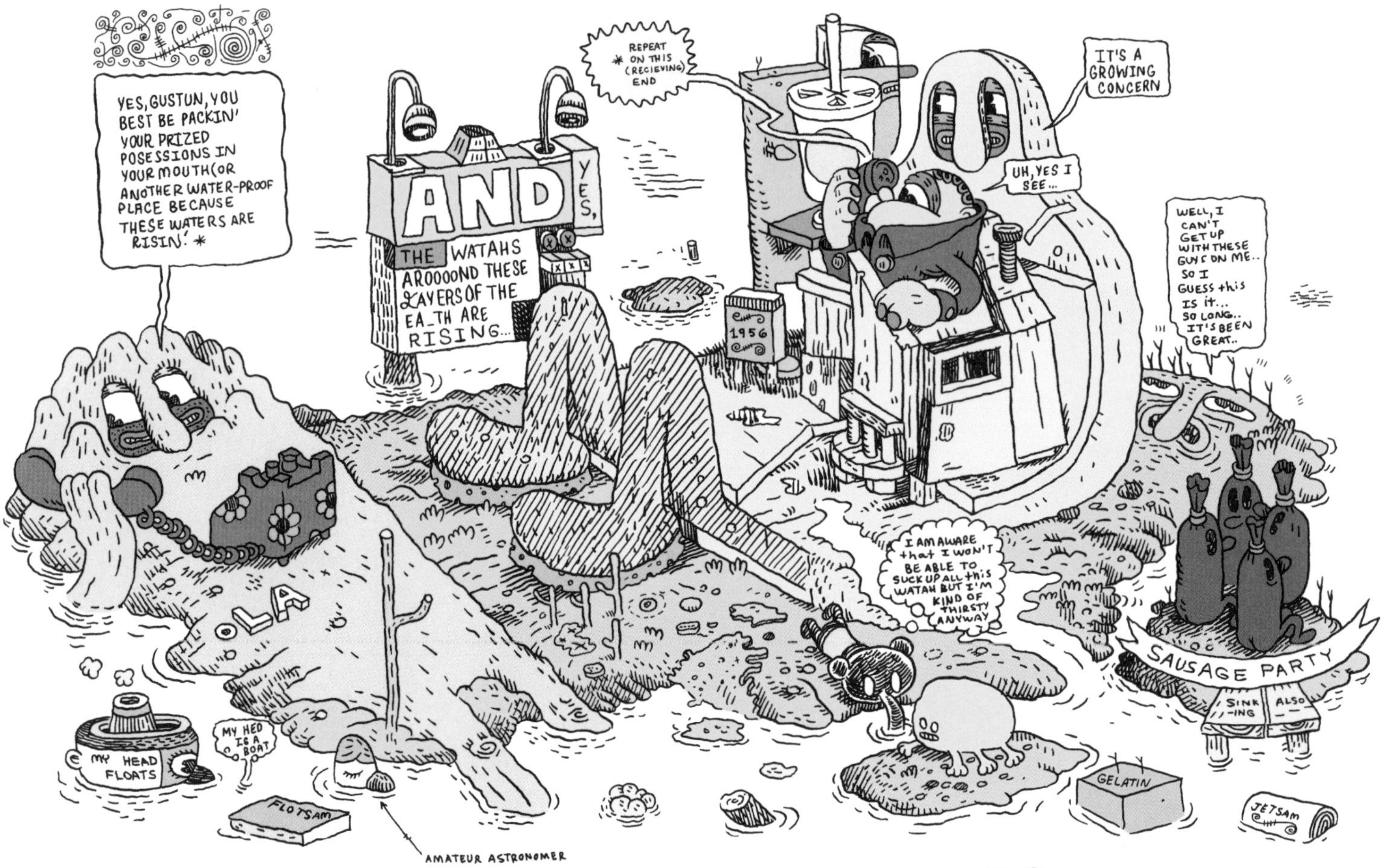
YES, GUSTUN, YOU BEST BE PACKIN' YOUR PRIZED POSESSIONS IN YOUR MOUTH (OR ANOTHER WATER-PROOF PLACE BECAUSE THESE WATERS ARE RISIN'! *
AND YES,
THE WATAHS AROOOOND THESE LAYERS OF THE EA_TH ARE RISING...
* REPEAT ON THIS (RECIEVING) END
IT'S A GROWING CONCERN
UH, YES I SEE...
WELL, I CAN'T GET UP WITH THESE GUYS ON ME.. SO I GUESS this IS it... SO LONG... IT'S BEEN GREAT..
1956
I AM AWARE that I WON'T BE ABLE TO SUCK UP ALL this WATAH BUT I'M KIND OF THIRSTY ANYWAY
LA
SAUSAGE PARTY
SINK-ING
ALSO
MY HEAD FLOATS
MY HED IS A BOAT
FLOTSAM
AMATEUR ASTRONOMER
GELATIN
JETSAM

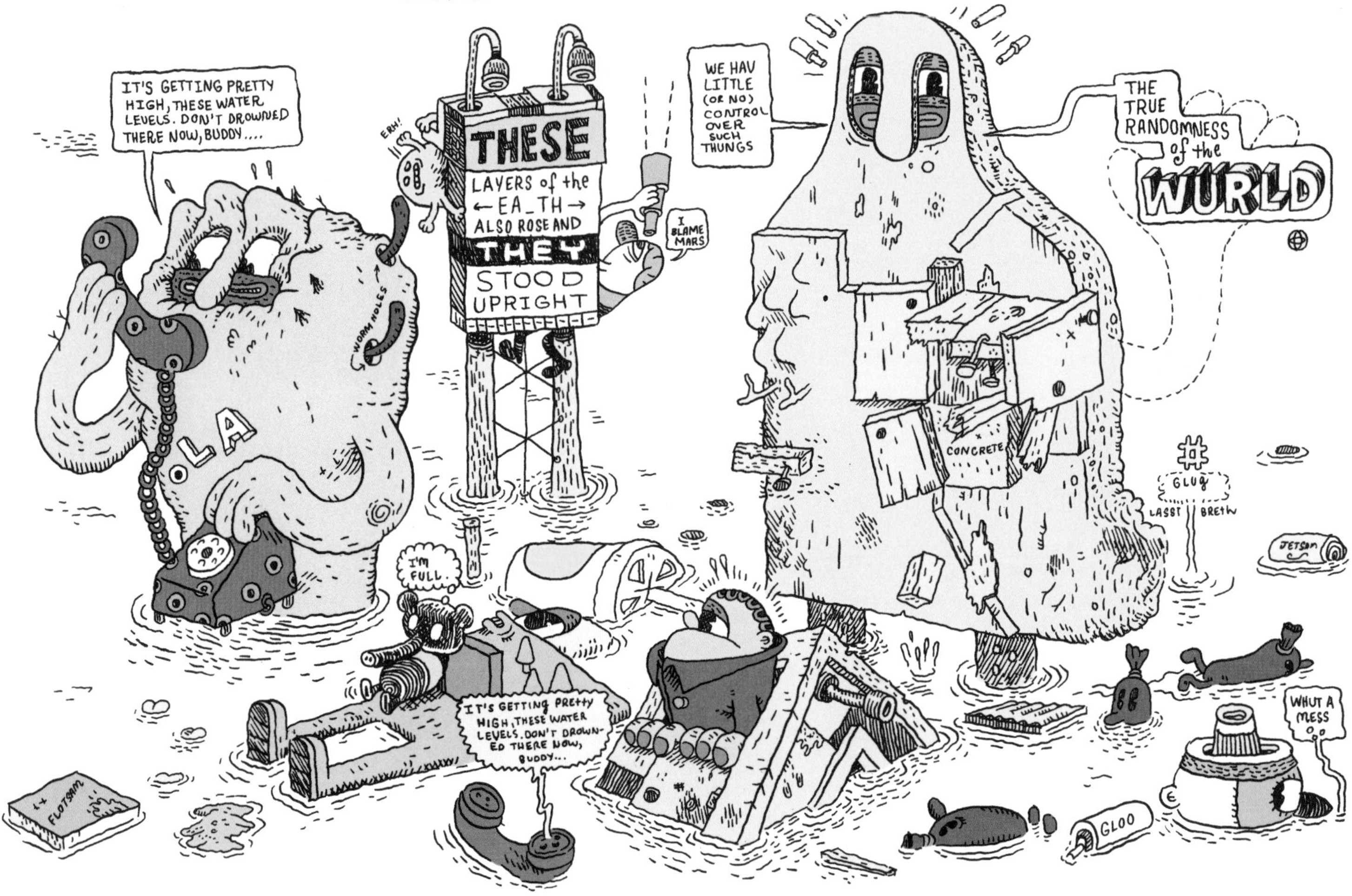
IT'S GETTING PRETTY HIGH, THESE WATER LEVELS. DON'T DROWNED THERE NOW, BUDDY....
THESE
LAYERS of the ←EA_TH→ ALSO ROSE AND
THEY
STOOD UPRIGHT
I BLAME MARS
WE HAV LITTLE (OR NO) CONTROL OVER SUCH THUNGS
THE TRUE RANDOMNESS of the
WURLD
WORM HOLES
LA
CONCRETE
GLUG
LASST BRETH
I'M FULL.
IT'S GETTING PRETTY HIGH, THESE WATER LEVELS. DON'T DROWN-ED THERE NOW, BUDDY...
WHUT A MESS
JETSAM
FLOTSAM
GLOO

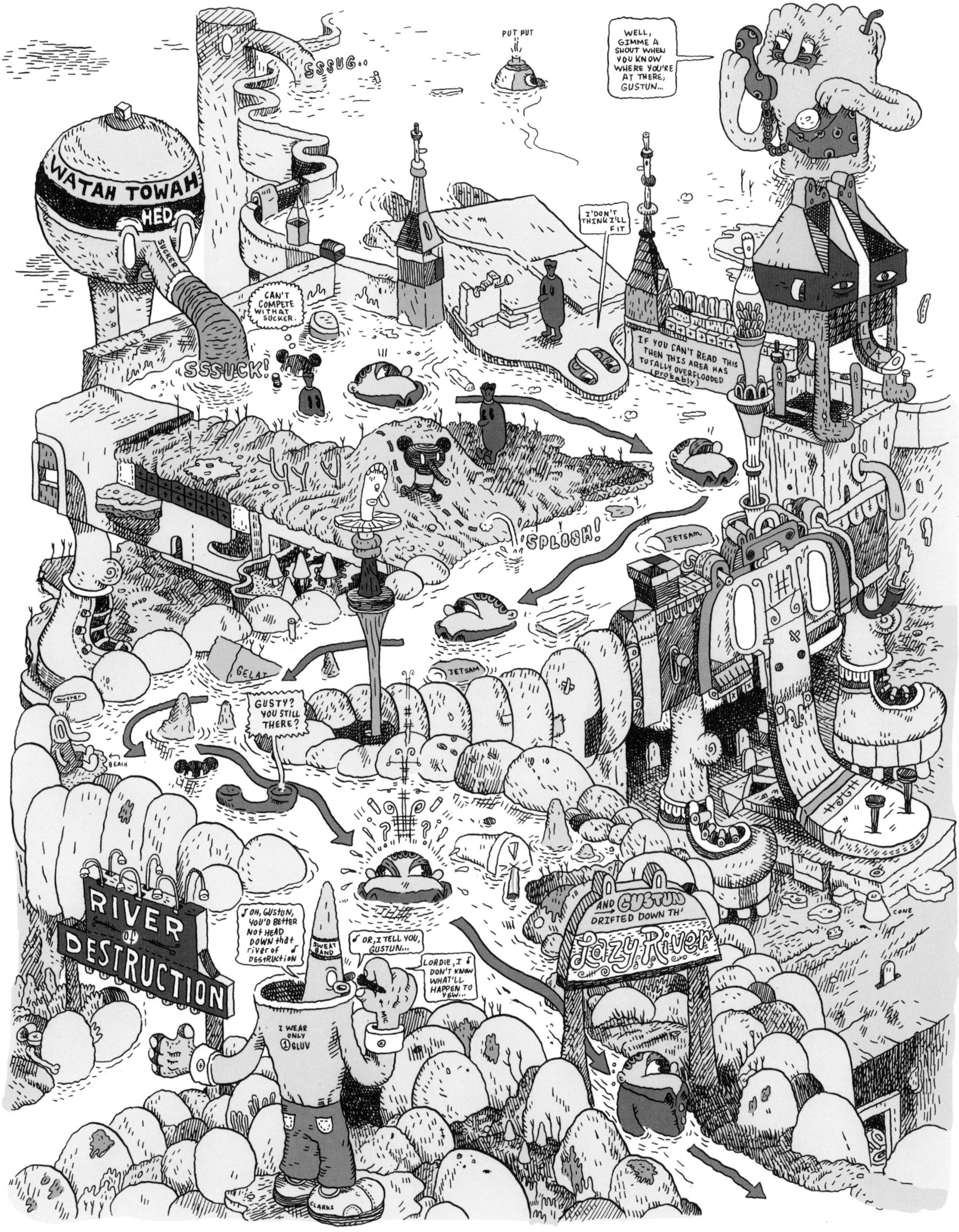
SSSUG..
PUT PUT
WELL, GIMME A SHOUT WHEN YOU KNOW WHERE YOU'RE AT THERE, GUSTUN...
WATAH TOWAH
HED
SUCKER
I'DON'T THINK I'LL FIT
CAN'T COMPETE WITH AT SUCKER.
SSSUCK!
IF YOU CAN'T READ THIS THEN THIS AREA HAS TOTALLY OVERFLOODED (probably)
SPLOSH!
JETSAM
MUD
GELAT
JETSAM
GUSTY? YOU STILL THERE?
mutter
BEACH
CONE
RIVER o! DESTRUCTION
OH, GUSTUN, YOU'D BETTER NOT HEAD DOWN that river of DESTRUCTION
SWEAT BAND
OR, I TELL YOU, GUSTUN...
LORDIE, I DON'T KNOW WHAT'LL HAPPEN TO YEW...
AND GUSTUN DRIFTED DOWN TH' Lazy River
I WEAR ONLY ① GLUV
CLARKS

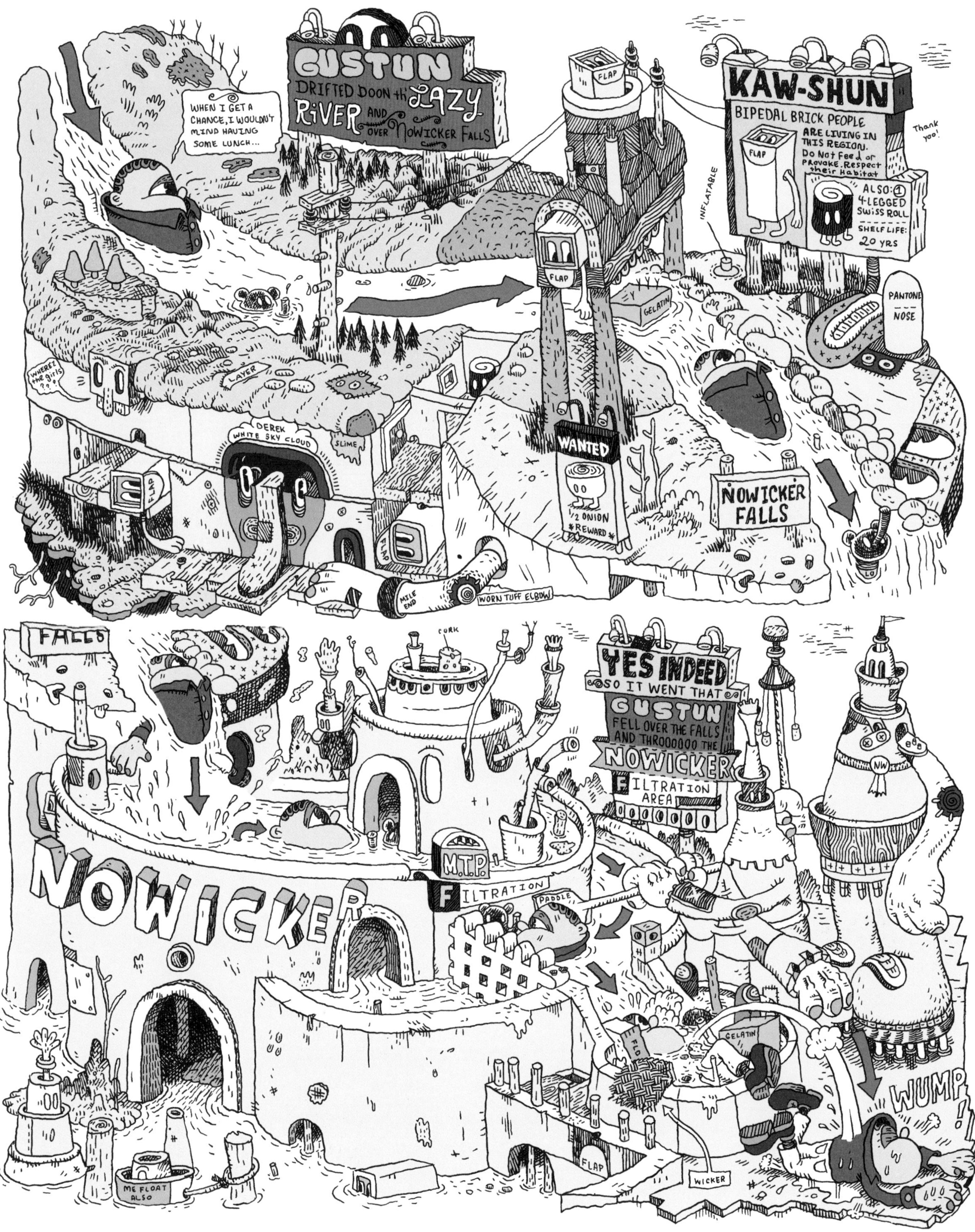
GUSTUN
DRIFTED DOON th LAZY RiVER AND OVER NOWICKER FALLS
WHEN I GET A CHANCE, I WOULDN'T MIND HAVING SOME LUNCH...
FLAP
KAW-SHUN
BIPEDAL BRICK PEOPLE
ARE LIVING IN THIS REGION. Do Not Feed or Provoke. Respect their Habitat
FLAP
Thank yoo!
ALSO: 1 4-LEGGED SWISS ROLL
SHELF LIFE: 20 YRS
INFLATABLE
FLAP
GELATIN
PANTONE NOSE
WHERE'S the girls ???
LAYER
DEREK WHITE SKY CLOUD
SLIME
FLAP
FLAP
WANTED
1/2 ONION *REWARD*
NOWICKER FALLS
MILE END
WORN TUFF ELBOW
FALLS
CORK
YES INDEED
SO IT WENT THAT
GUSTUN
FELL OVER THE FALLS AND THROOOOOOO THE
NOWICKER
FILTRATION AREA
NW
M.T.P.
FILTRATION
PADDLE
NOWICKER
GELATIN
FLAP
WICKER
WUMP!
ME FLOAT ALSO

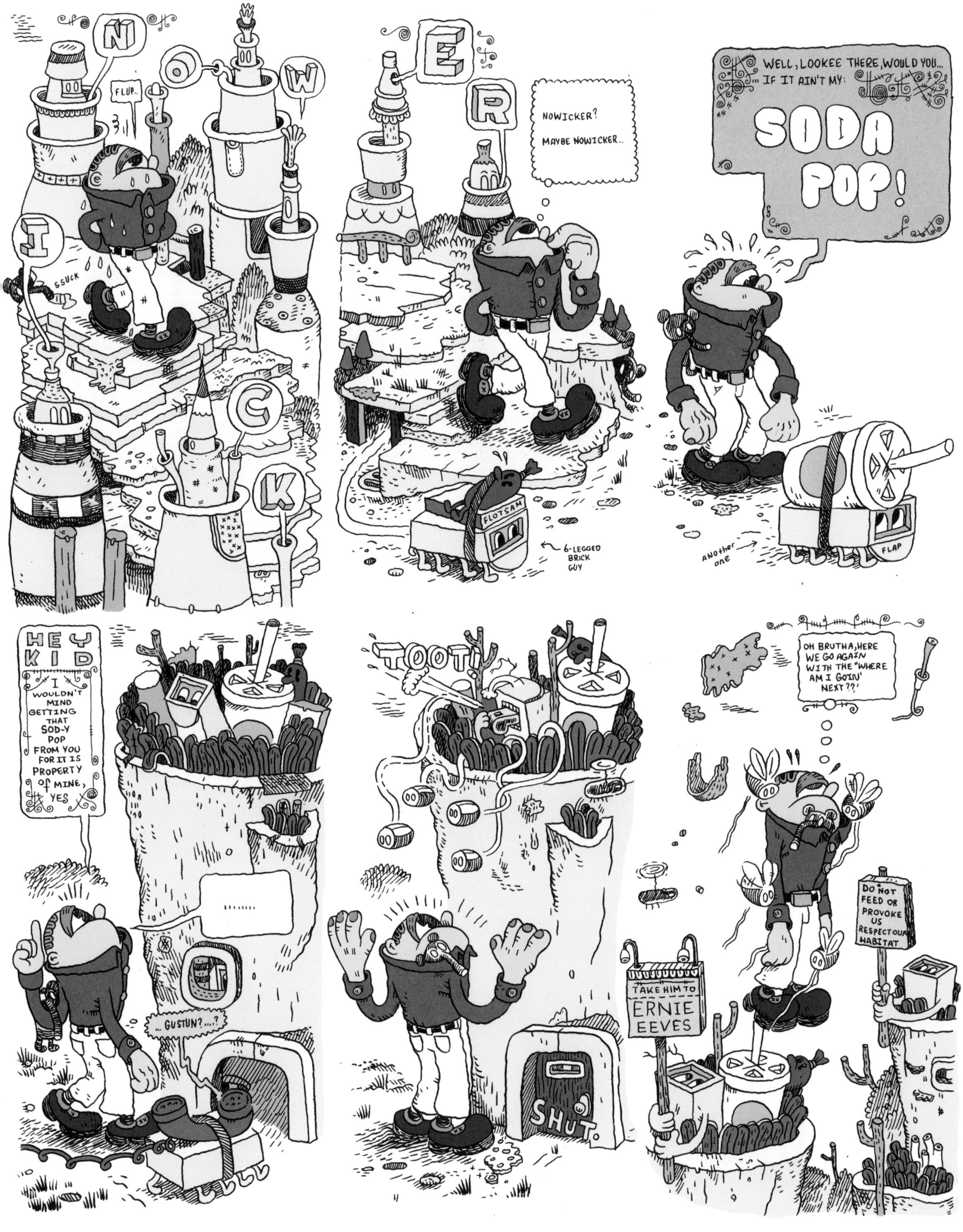
N
O
W
FLUP..
I
SSUCK
C
K
E
R
NOWICKER?
MAYBE NOWICKER..
FLOTSAM
6-LEGGED BRICK GUY
WELL, LOOKEE THERE, WOULD YOU... IF IT AIN'T MY:
SODA POP!
ANOther one
FLAP
HEY KID
I WOULDN'T MIND GETTING THAT SOD-Y POP FROM YOU FOR IT IS PROPERTY of MINE, YES
....
...GUSTUN?...?
TOOT!
SHUT.
OH BRUTHA, HERE WE GO AGAIN WITH THE "WHERE AM I GOIN' NEXT??'
TAKE HIM TO ERNIE EEVES
DO NOT FEED OR PROVOKE US RESPECT OUR HABITAT

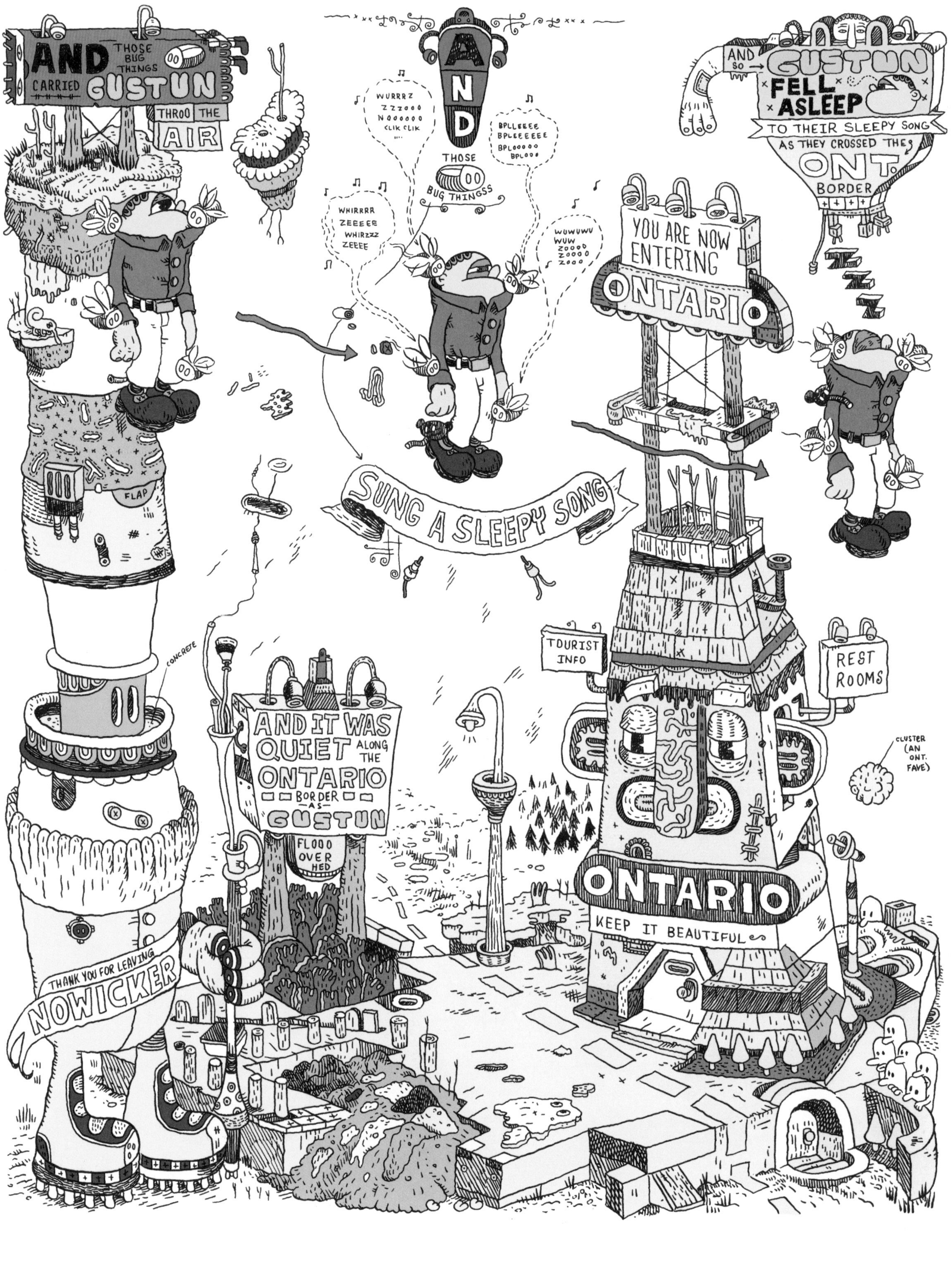
AND THOSE BUG THINGS CARRIED GUSTUN THROO THE AIR
AND
THOSE BUG THINGSS
WURRRZ ZZZOOO NOOOOOO CLIK CLIK
BPLLEEEE BPLEEEEEE BPLOOOOO BPLOOO
WHIRRRR ZEEEEE WHIRZZZ ZEEEE
WUWUWU WUW ZOOOO ZOOOO ZOOO
SUNG A SLEEPY SONG
AND SO GUSTUN FELL ASLEEP TO THEIR SLEEPY SONG AS THEY CROSSED THE ONT. BORDER
YOU ARE NOW ENTERING ONTARIO
TOURIST INFO
REST ROOMS
CONCRETE
AND IT WAS QUIET ALONG THE ONTARIO BORDER AS GUSTUN FLOOO OVER HED
FLAP
CLUSTER (AN ONT. FAVE)
ONTARIO
KEEP IT BEAUTIFUL
THANK YOU FOR LEAVING NOWICKER

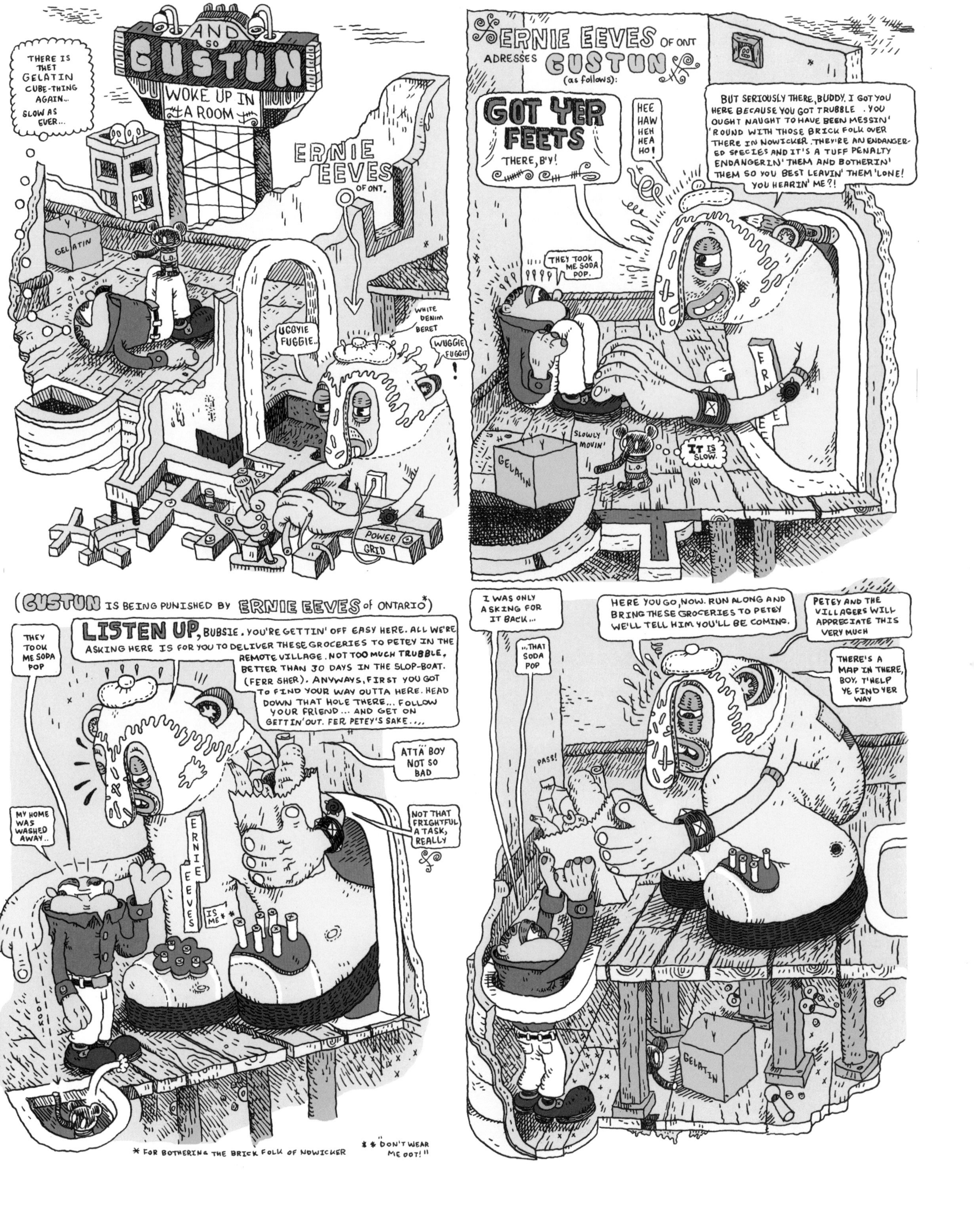
AND SO GUSTUN
WOKE UP IN A ROOM
THERE IS THET GELATIN CUBE-THING AGAIN... SLOW AS EVER...
ERNIE EEVES OF ONT.
GELATIN
L.O.
WHITE DENIM BERET
UGGYIE FUGGIE..
WUGGIE FUGGIT
POWER GRID
ERNIE EEVES OF ONT ADRESSES GUSTUN (as follows):
GOT YER FEETS THERE, B'Y!
HEE HAW HEH HEA HO!
BUT SERIOUSLY THERE, BUDDY. I GOT YOU HERE BECAUSE YOU GOT TRUBBLE . YOU OUGHT NAUGHT TO HAVE BEEN MESSIN' 'ROUND WITH THOSE BRICK FOLK OVER THERE IN NOWICKER. THEY'RE AN ENDANGERED SPECIES AND IT'S A TUFF PENALTY ENDANGERIN' THEM AND BOTHERIN' THEM SO YOU BEST LEAVIN' THEM 'LONE! YOU HEARIN' ME?!
THEY TOOK ME SODA POP.
SLOWLY MOVIN'
IT IS SLOW.
GELATIN
L.O.
(GUSTUN IS BEING PUNISHED BY ERNIE EEVES of ONTARIO*)
THEY TOOK ME SODA POP
LISTEN UP, BUBSIE. YOU'RE GETTIN' OFF EASY HERE. ALL WE'RE ASKING HERE IS FOR YOU TO DELIVER THESE GROCERIES TO PETEY IN THE REMOTE VILLAGE. NOT TOO MUCH TRUBBLE, BETTER THAN 30 DAYS IN THE SLOP-BOAT. (FERR SHER). ANYWAYS, FIRST YOU GOT TO FIND YOUR WAY OUTTA HERE. HEAD DOWN THAT HOLE THERE... FOLLOW YOUR FRIEND... AND GET ON GETTIN' OUT. FER PETEY'S SAKE...,
ATTA BOY NOT SO BAD
MY HOME WAS WASHED AWAY..
NOT THAT FRIGHTFUL A TASK, REALLY
ERNIE EEVES
IS ME**
LOOK!
* FOR BOTHERING THE BRICK FOLK OF NOWICKER
** "DON'T WEAR ME OOT!"
I WAS ONLY ASKING FOR IT BACK...
...THAT SODA POP
HERE YOU GO, NOW. RUN ALONG AND BRING THESE GROCERIES TO PETEY WE'LL TELL HIM YOU'LL BE COMING.
PETEY AND THE VILLAGERS WILL APPRECIATE THIS VERY MUCH
THERE'S A MAP IN THERE, BOY, T'HELP YE FIND YER WAY
PASS!
GELATIN

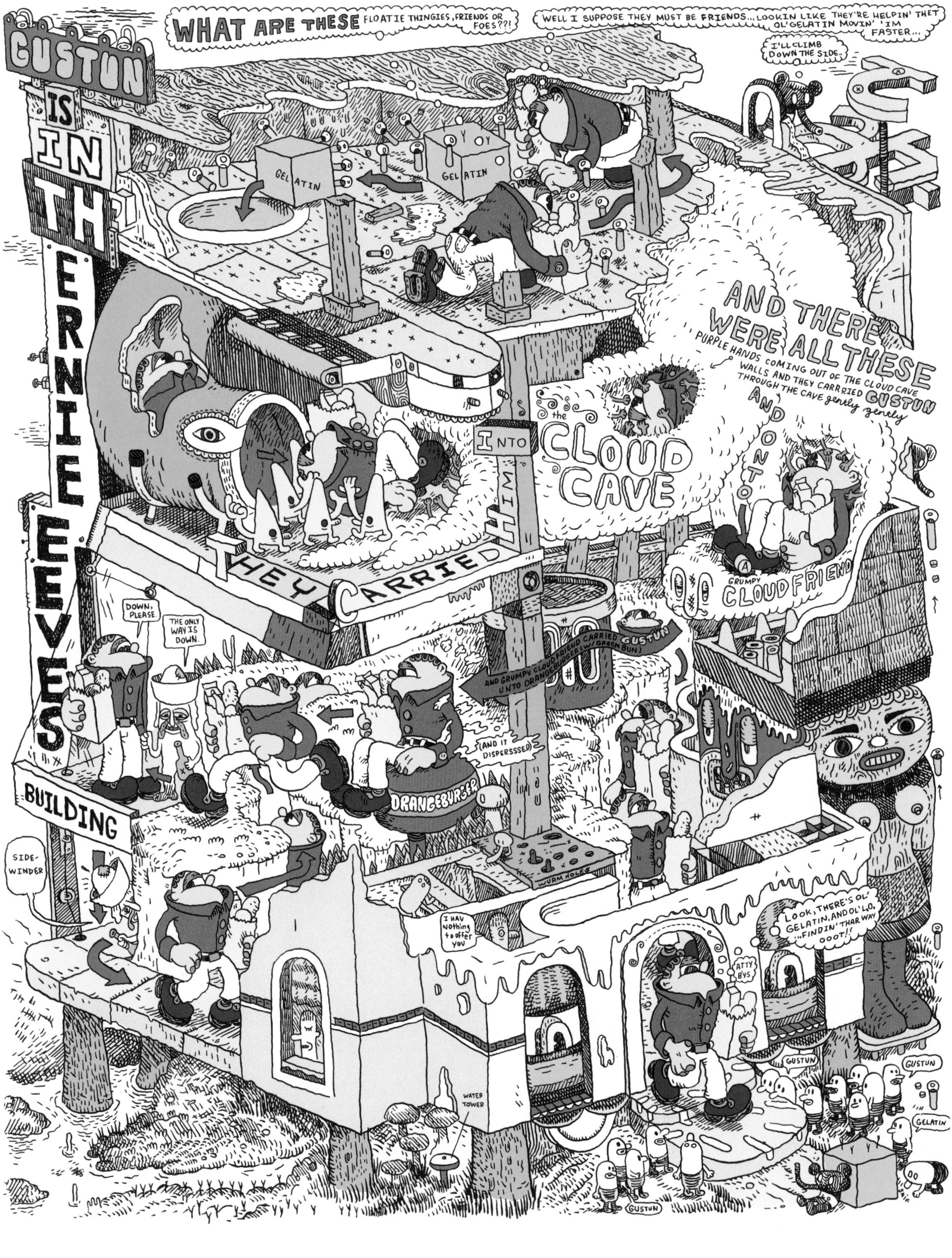

GUSTUN IS IN THE ERNIE EEVES BUILDING
WHAT ARE THESE FLOATIE THINGIES, FRIENDS OR FOES??!
WELL I SUPPOSE THEY MUST BE FRIENDS... LOOKIN LIKE THEY'RE HELPIN' THET OL' GELATIN MOVIN' 'IM FASTER...
I'LL CLIMB DOWN THE SIDE..
GELATIN
GELATIN
AND THERE WERE ALL THESE PURPLE HANDS COMING OUT OF THE CLOUD CAVE WALLS AND THEY CARRRIED GUSTUN THROUGH THE CAVE gently gently AND ONTO A
GRUMPY CLOUDFRIEND
THEY CARRIED HIM INTO the CLOUD CAVE
DOWN, PLEASE.
THE ONLY WAY IS DOWN.
AND GRUMPY CLOUDFRIEND CARRIED GUSTUN UNTO ORANGEBURGER (W/ GREEN BUN)
(AND IT DISPERSSSED)
ORANGEBURGER
SIDE-WINDER
WURM HOLES
I HAV Nothing to offer you
LOOK, THERE'S OL' GELATIN, AND OL' LO, ...FINDIN' THAR WAY OOOT!!
ATTY BYS.
GUSTUN
GUSTUN
GELATIN
WATER TOWER
GUSTUN

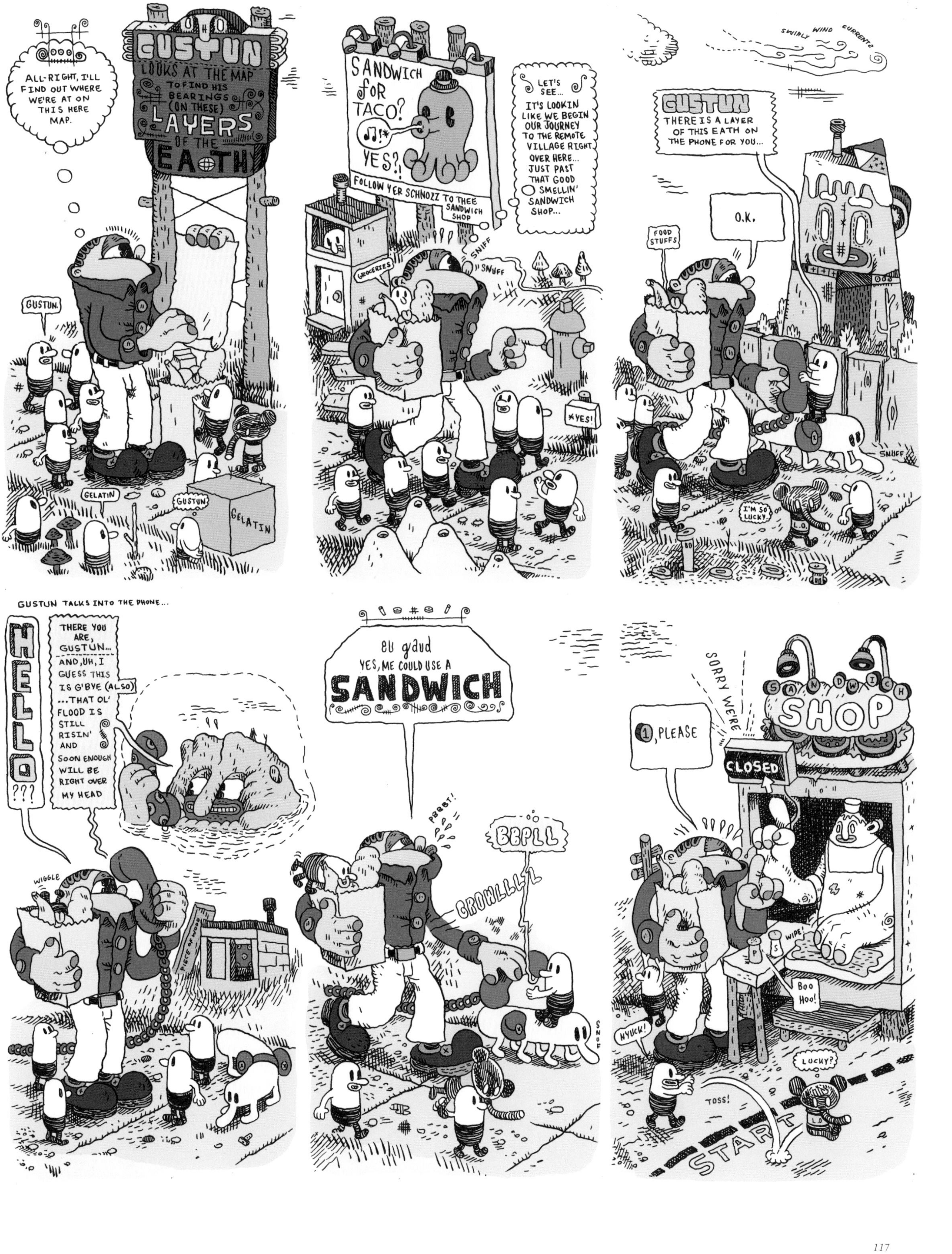
ALL-RIGHT, I'LL FIND OUT WHERE WE'RE AT ON THIS HERE MAP.
GUSTUN LOOKS AT THE MAP TO FIND HIS BEARINGS (ON THESE) LAYERS OF THE EATH
GUSTUN.
GELATIN
GUSTUN
GELATIN
SANDWICH for TACO? YES?!
FOLLOW YER SCHNOZZ TO THEE SANDWICH SHOP
LET'S SEE... IT'S LOOKIN LIKE WE BEGIN OUR JOURNEY TO THE REMOTE VILLAGE RIGHT OVER HERE... JUST PAST THAT GOOD SMELLIN' SANDWICH SHOP...
SNIFF
SNUFF
GROCERIES
*YES!
SWIRLY WIND CURRENTS
GUSTUN THERE IS A LAYER OF THIS EATH ON THE PHONE FOR YOU...
O.K.
FOOD STUFFS
SNUFF
I'M SO LUCKY.
GUSTUN TALKS INTO THE PHONE...
HELLO ???
THERE YOU ARE, GUSTUN... AND, UH, I GUESS THIS IS G'BYE (ALSO) ...THAT OL' FLOOD IS STILL RISIN' AND SOON ENOUGH WILL BE RIGHT OVER MY HEAD
WIGGLE
PIECE OF WOOD
eu gaud YES, ME COULD USE A SANDWICH
PRRBT!
BBPLL
GROWLLLLL
SNUF
SORRY WE'RE CLOSED
SANDWICH SHOP
1, PLEASE
WIPE!
BOO HOO!
NYUCK!
LUCKY?
TOSS!
START

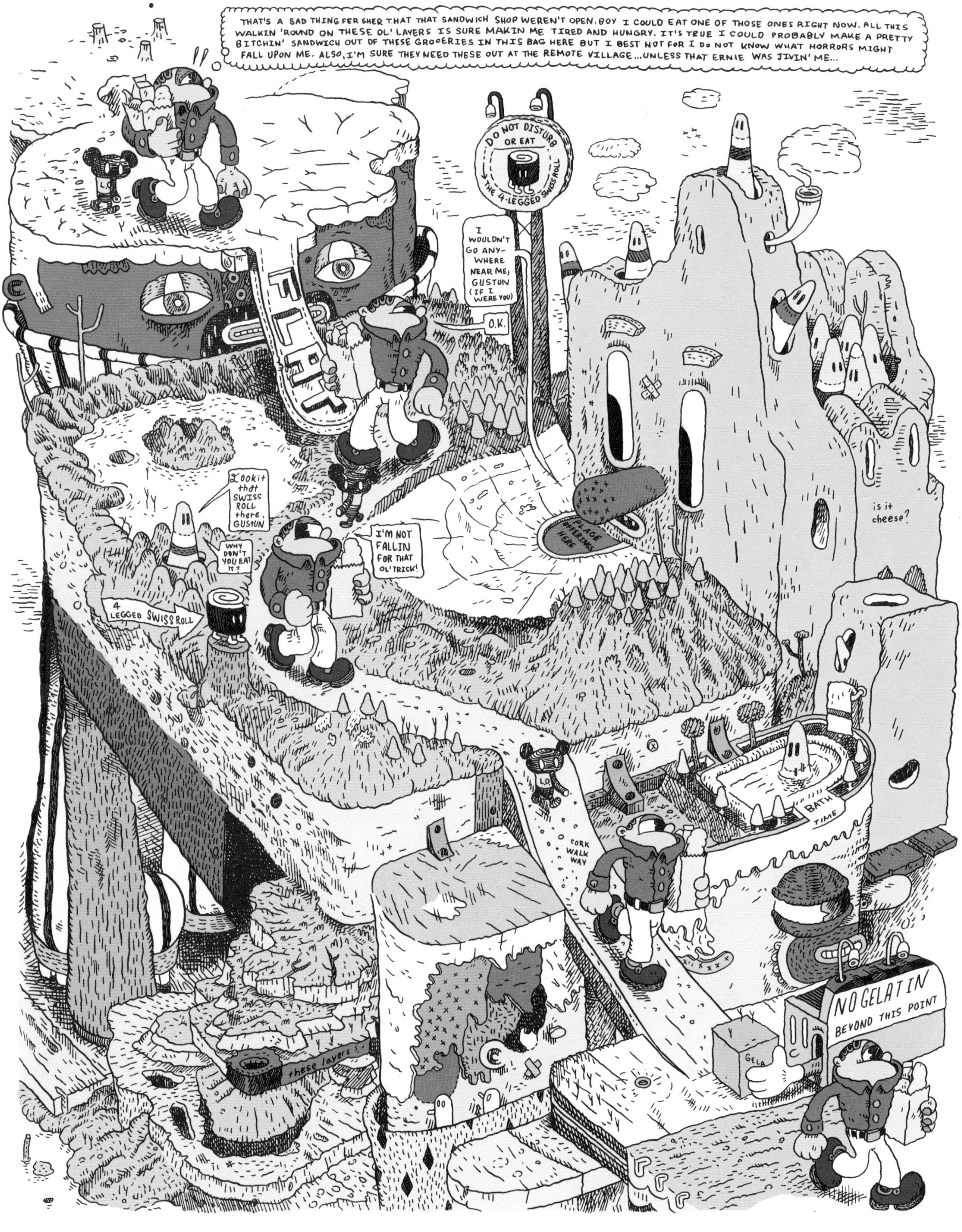
THAT'S A SAD THING FER SHER THAT THAT SANDWICH SHOP WEREN'T OPEN. BOY I COULD EAT ONE OF THOSE ONES RIGHT NOW. ALL THIS WALKIN 'ROUND ON THESE OL' LAYERS IS SURE MAKIN ME TIRED AND HUNGRY. IT'S TRUE I COULD PROBABLY MAKE A PRETTY BITCHIN' SANDWICH OUT OF THESE GROCERIES IN THIS BAG HERE BUT I BEST NOT FOR I DO NOT KNOW WHAT HORRORS MIGHT FALL UPON ME. ALSO, I'M SURE THEY NEED THESE OUT AT THE REMOTE VILLAGE...UNLESS THAT ERNIE WAS JIVIN' ME...
DO NOT DISTURB OR EAT
THE 4-LEGGED SWISS ROLL
FLAT
I WOULDN'T GO ANYWHERE NEAR ME, GUSTUN (IF I WERE YOU)
O.K.
PLACE OFFERINGS HERE
is it cheese?
Lookit that SWISS ROLL there, GUSTUN
WHY DON'T YOU EAT IT?
I'M NOT FALLIN FOR THAT OL' TRICK!
4 LEGGED SWISS ROLL
BATH TIME
CORK WALK WAY
NO GELATIN BEYOND THIS POINT
these layers

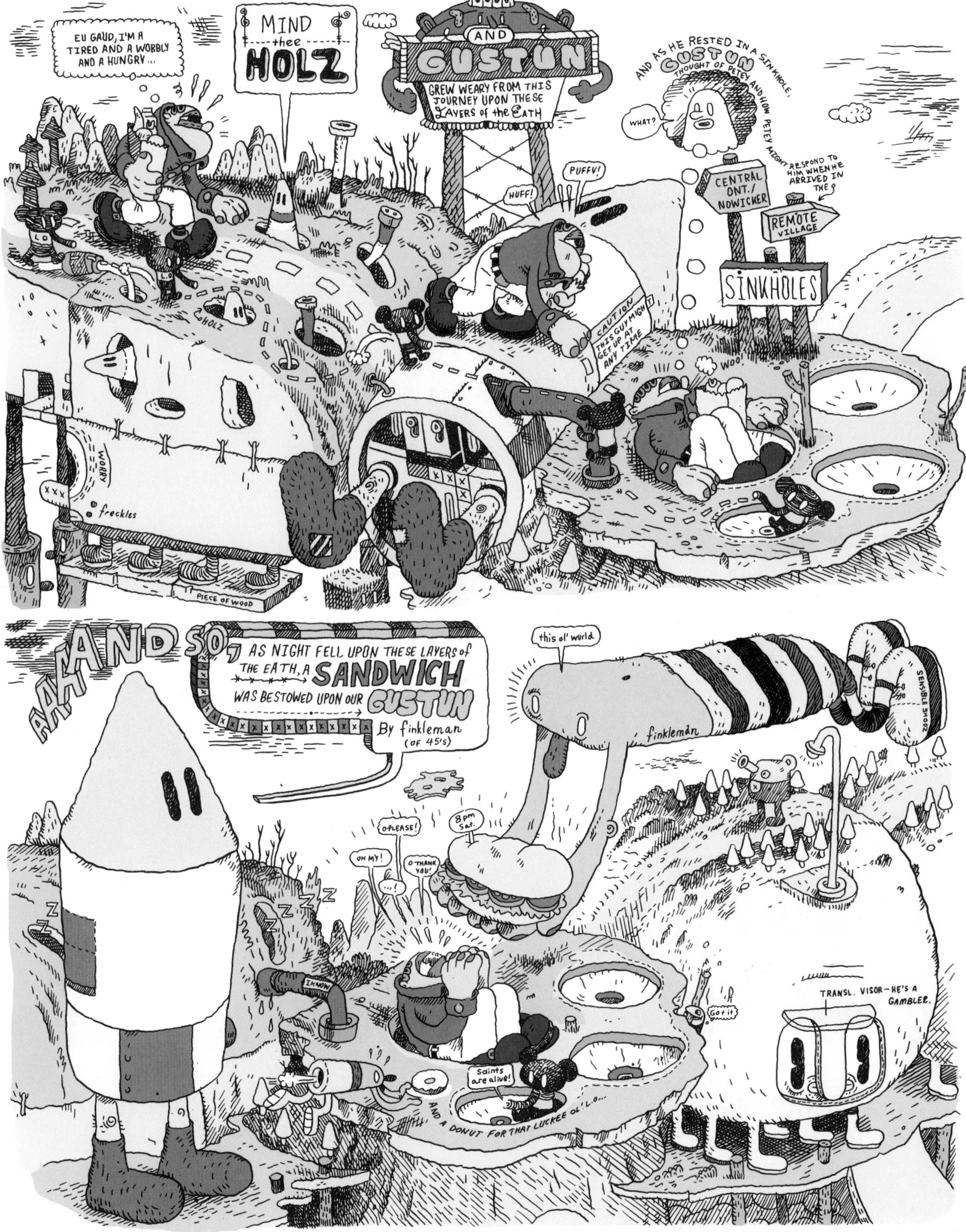

EU GAUD, I'M A TIRED AND A WOBBLY AND A HUNGRY...
MIND thee HOLZ
AND GUSTUN GREW WEARY FROM THIS JOURNEY UPON THESE LAYERS of the EATH
AND AS HE RESTED IN A SINKHOLE, GUSTUN THOUGHT OF PETEY AND HOW PETEY MIGHT RESPOND TO HIM WHEN HE ARRIVED IN THE
WHAT?
CENTRAL ONT./ NOWICKER
REMOTE VILLAGE
SINKHOLES
HUFF!
PUFFV!
CAUTION THIS GUY MIGHT GET UP AT ANY TIME
HOLZ
WOO
WORRY
freckles
PIECE OF WOOD
AAAH AND SO, AS NIGHT FELL UPON THESE LAYERS of THE EATH, A SANDWICH WAS BESTOWED UPON OUR GUSTUN
By finkleman (OF 45's)
this ol' wurld
finkleman
SENSIBLE SHOOZ
OH MY!
O-PLEASE!
...!
O THANK YOU!
8pm Sat.
I-KNOW
Got it
TRANSL. VISOR—HE'S A GAMBLER.
Saints are alive!
AND A DONUT FOR THAT LUCKEE OL' L.O...

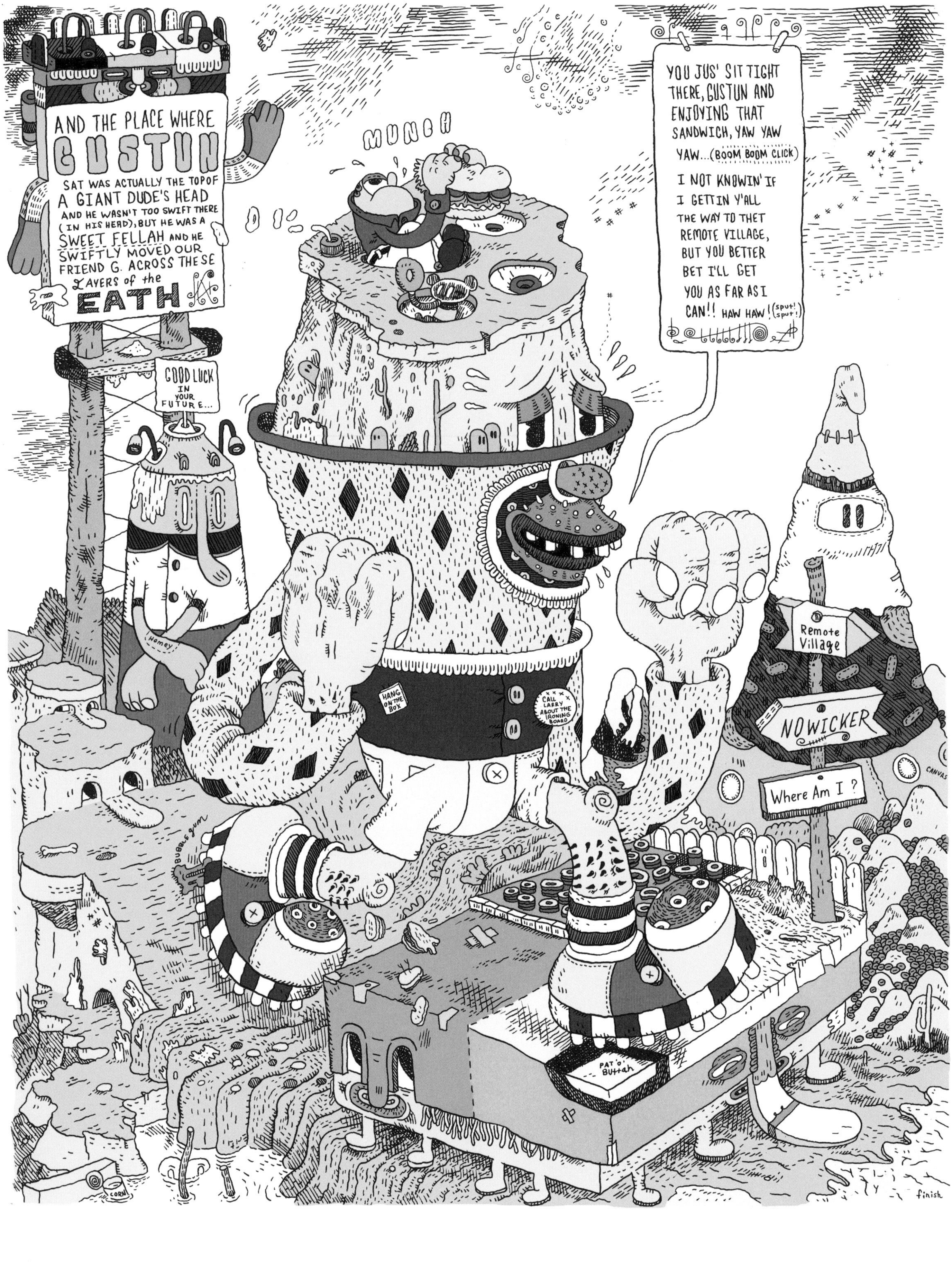
AND THE PLACE WHERE GUSTUN SAT WAS ACTUALLY THE TOP OF A GIANT DUDE'S HEAD AND HE WASN'T TOO SWIFT THERE (IN HIS HEAD), BUT HE WAS A SWEET FELLAH AND HE SWIFTLY MOVED OUR FRIEND G. ACROSS THESE LAYERS of the EATH
MUNCH
YOU JUS' SIT TIGHT THERE, GUSTUN AND ENJOYING THAT SANDWICH, YAW YAW YAW...(BOOM BOOM CLICK)
I NOT KNOWIN' IF I GETTIN Y'ALL THE WAY TO THET REMOTE VILLAGE, BUT YOU BETTER BET I'LL GET YOU AS FAR AS I CAN!! HAW HAW! (sput! sput!)
GOOD LUCK IN YOUR FUTURE...
Homey
HANG ON THE BOX
CALL LARRY ABOUT THE IRONING BOARD
Remote Village
NOWICKER
Where Am I ?
CANVAS
BUBBLE gum
PAT o' Buttah
CORN
finish

There is no Escape!

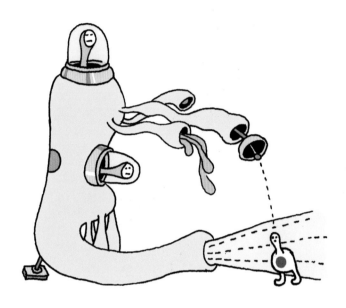

IN TWO PARTS:

① DRAWINGS BY PETER THOMPSON
AND MARC BELL (TAKEN MAINLY
FROM THE MINIATURE BOOKLET
There Is No Escape!)

② A COMIC STORY BY MARC BELL
(BASED ON SOME OF THE WORK
AND SOME OF THE TIMES OF
PETER THOMPSON... LOOSELY...)

edited, compiled, coloured by Marc Bell for thee kramers Ergot in '02

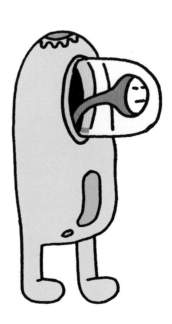

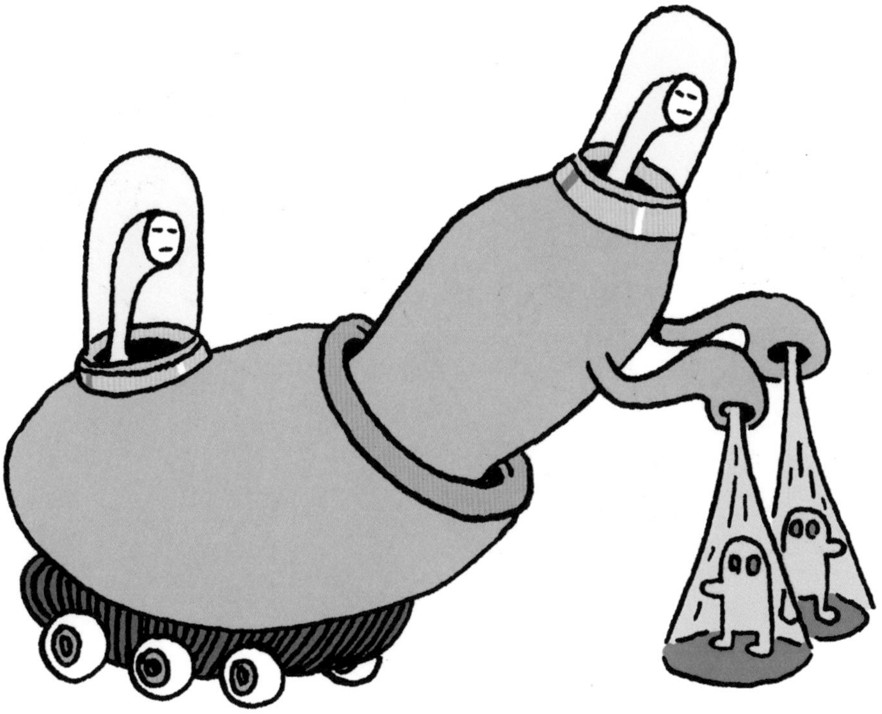

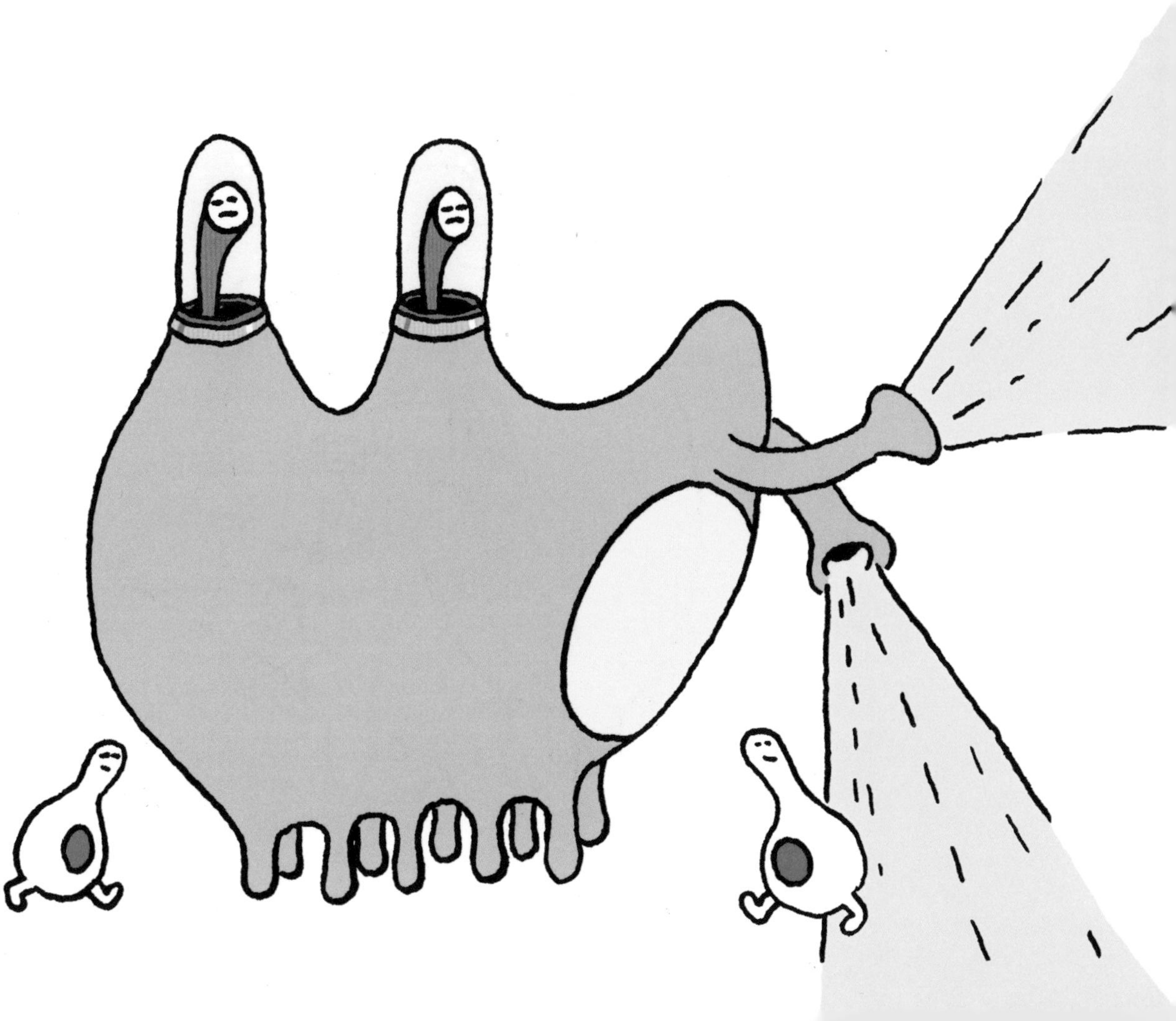

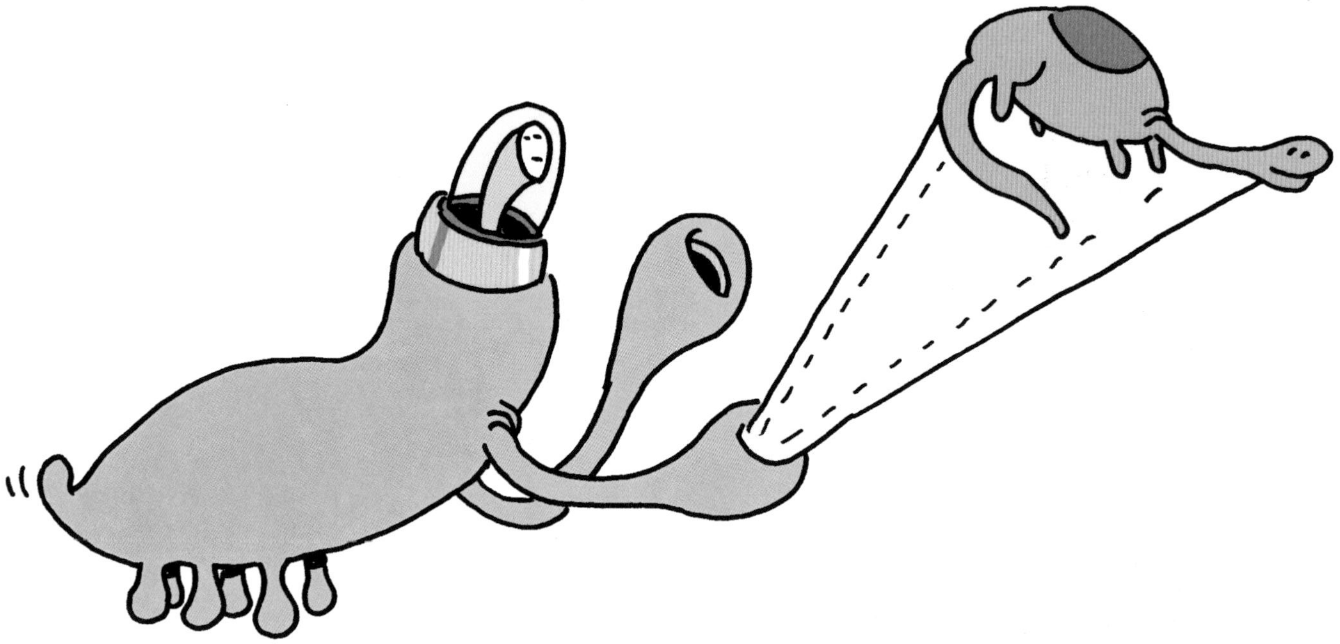

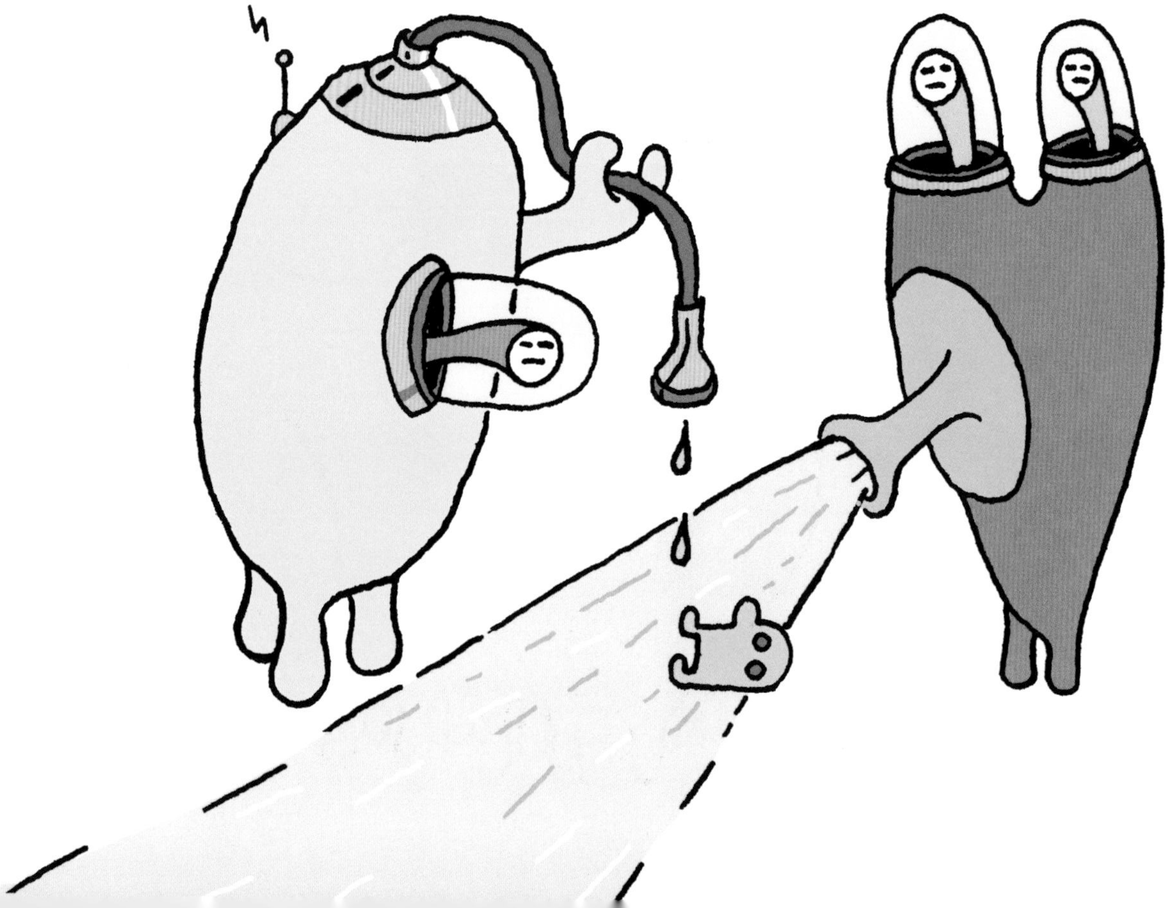

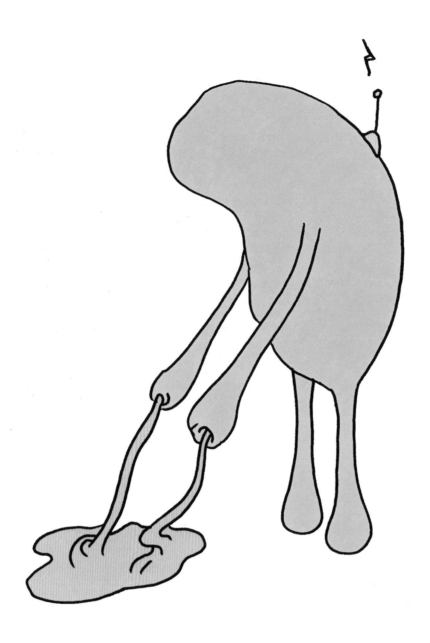

▶ YOU HAVE ENJOYED 'There is no Escape NO.1', AND YOU HAVE NOT ESCAPED, BECAUSE THERE IS NO ESCAPE. ALL WILL FALL UNDER OUR DOMINION.

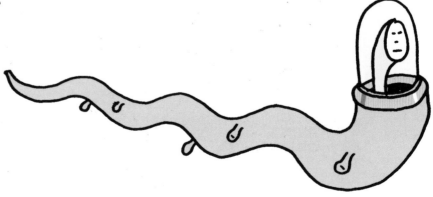

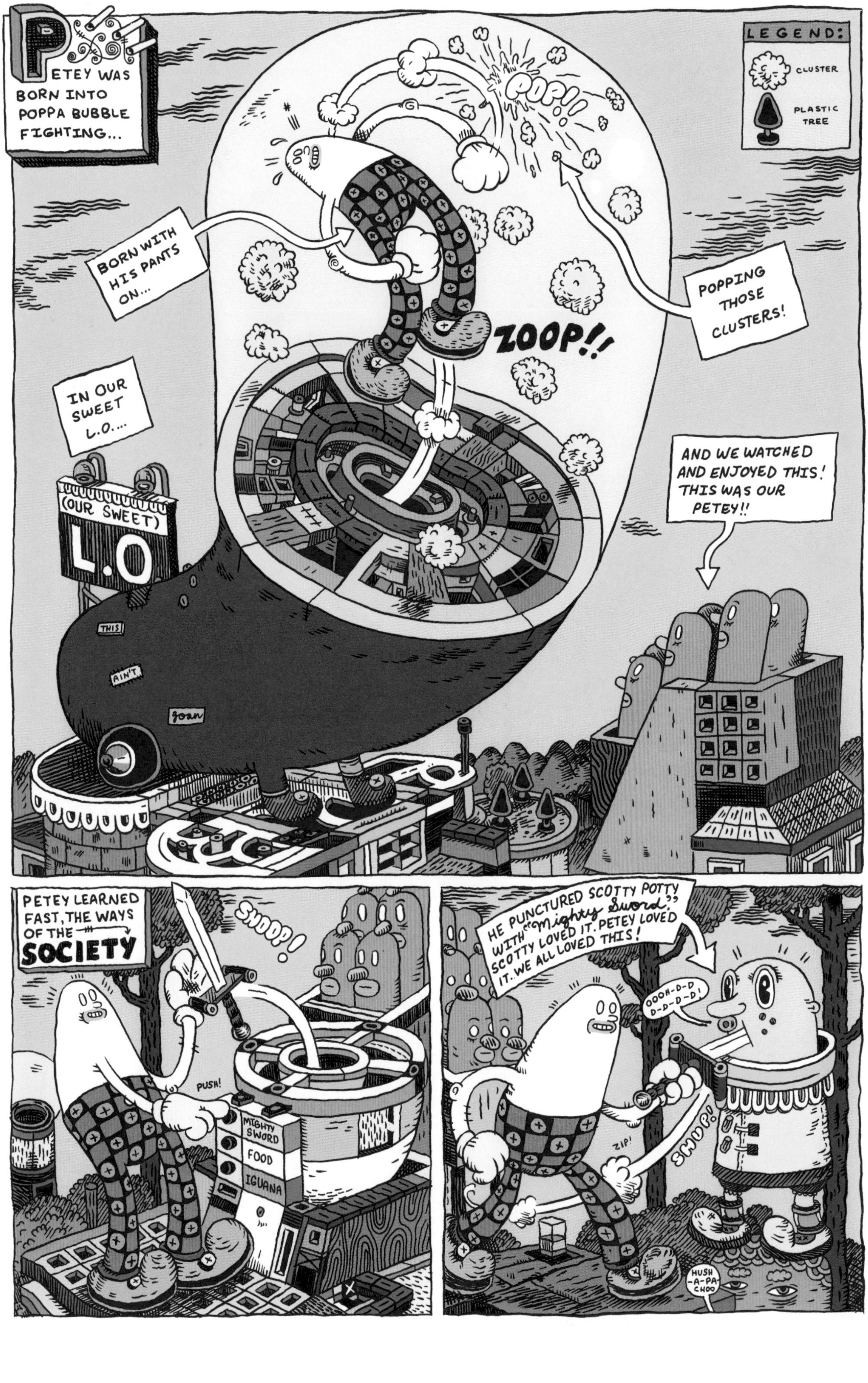
PETEY WAS BORN INTO POPPA BUBBLE FIGHTING...
LEGEND:
CLUSTER
PLASTIC TREE
POP!!
BORN WITH HIS PANTS ON...
POPPING THOSE CLUSTERS!
ZOOP!!
IN OUR SWEET L.O....
(OUR SWEET) L.O
THIS
AIN'T
goan
AND WE WATCHED AND ENJOYED THIS! THIS WAS OUR PETEY!!
PETEY LEARNED FAST, THE WAYS OF THE SOCIETY
SHOOP!
PUSH!
MIGHTY SWORD
FOOD
IGUANA
HE PUNCTURED SCOTTY POTTY WITH "Mighty Sword." SCOTTY LOVED IT. PETEY LOVED IT. WE ALL LOVED THIS!
OOOH-D-D D-D-D-D!
ZIP!
SHUP!
HUSH-A-PA-CHOO

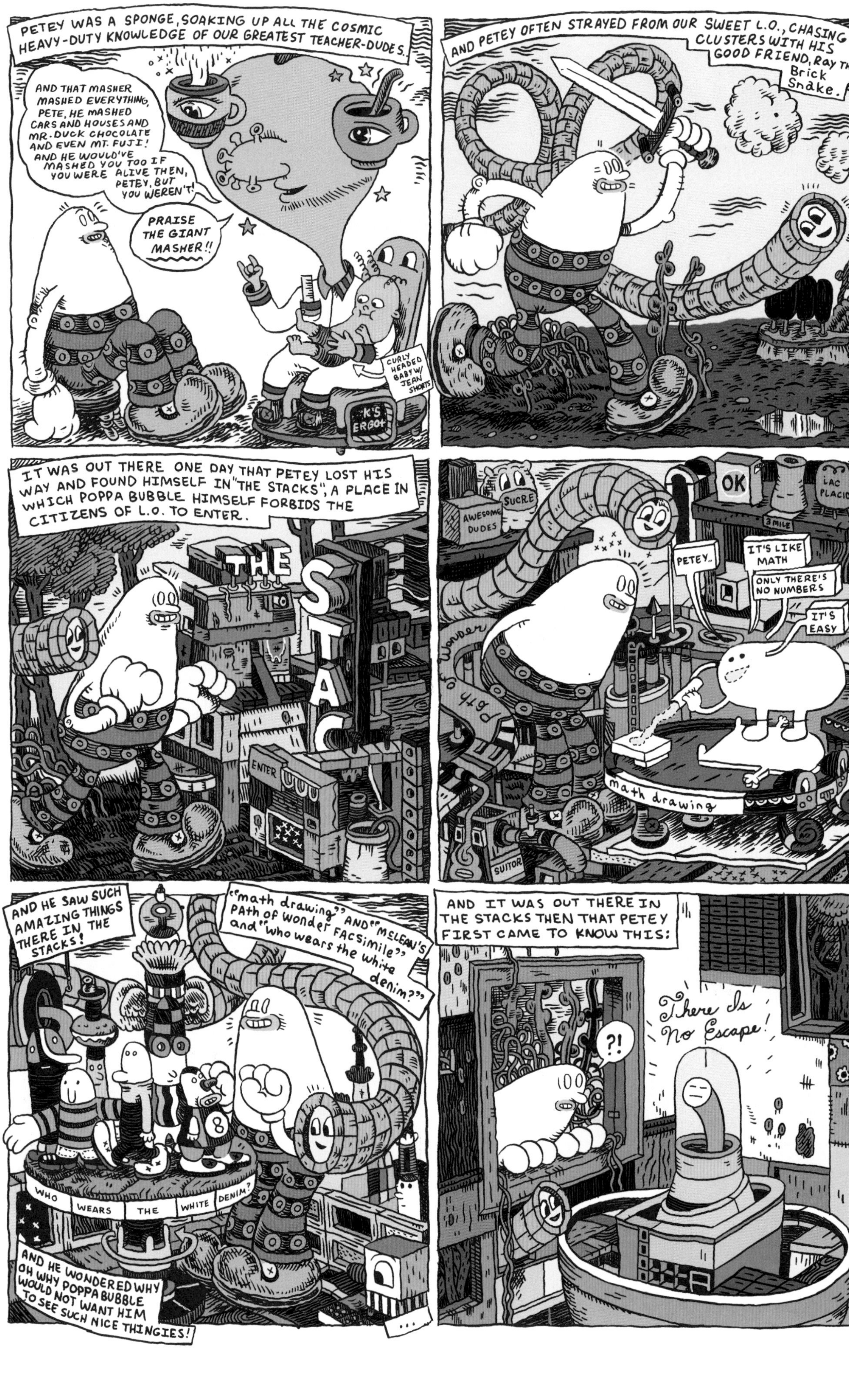
PETEY WAS A SPONGE, SOAKING UP ALL THE COSMIC HEAVY-DUTY KNOWLEDGE OF OUR GREATEST TEACHER-DUDES.
AND THAT MASHER MASHED EVERYTHING, PETE, HE MASHED CARS AND HOUSES AND MR. DUCK CHOCOLATE AND EVEN MT. FUJI! AND HE WOULD'VE MASHED YOU TOO IF YOU WERE ALIVE THEN, PETEY, BUT YOU WEREN'T!
PRAISE THE GIANT MASHER!!
CURLY HEADED BABY W/ JEAN SHORTS
AND PETEY OFTEN STRAYED FROM OUR SWEET L.O., CHASING CLUSTERS WITH HIS GOOD FRIEND, RAY THE Brick Snake.
IT WAS OUT THERE ONE DAY THAT PETEY LOST HIS WAY AND FOUND HIMSELF IN "THE STACKS", A PLACE IN WHICH POPPA BUBBLE HIMSELF FORBIDS THE CITIZENS OF L.O. TO ENTER.
THE STAC
ENTER
AWESOME DUDES
SUCRE
OK
LAC PLACID
3 MILE
PETEY..
IT'S LIKE MATH
ONLY THERE'S NO NUMBERS
IT'S EASY
Path of Wonder
math drawing
SUITOR
AND HE SAW SUCH AMAZING THINGS THERE IN THE STACKS!
"math drawing" AND "MCLEAN'S PATH of Wonder FACSIMILE" and "who wears the white denim?"
WHO WEARS THE WHITE DENIM?
AND HE WONDERED WHY OH WHY POPPA BUBBLE WOULD NOT WANT HIM TO SEE SUCH NICE THINGIES!
...
AND IT WAS OUT THERE IN THE STACKS THEN THAT PETEY FIRST CAME TO KNOW THIS:
?!
There Is No Escape!

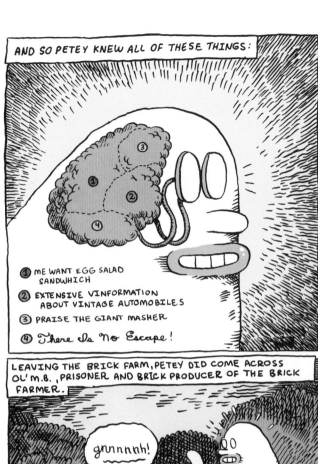

AND SO PETEY KNEW ALL OF THESE THINGS:

① ME WANT EGG SALAD SANDWHICH

② EXTENSIVE VINFORMATION ABOUT VINTAGE AUTOMOBILES

③ PRAISE THE GIANT MASHER

④ *There Is No Escape!*

"ME WANT EGG SALAD SANDWHICH" TOOK PRECEDENCE AND PETEY ENDED UP SELLING HIS FRIEND RAY THE Brick Snake TO THE BRICK FARMER.

HERE YOU GO, KID!

I ♥ BRICKS

BONKERS!

CAUTION BRICKS GROWIN

CE MENT

LEAVING THE BRICK FARM, PETEY DID COME ACROSS OL' M.B., PRISONER AND BRICK PRODUCER OF THE BRICK FARMER.

gnnnnah!

PHP.

There Is No Escape!

K-CHNK!

AND SO PETEY HAD FREED OL' M.B. FROM HIS CHAINS AND TOGETHER THEY DID BUILD A HAPPY FRIEND AND THEY NAMED HIM "Who Cares!"

PLEH!

WHAP! WHAP!!

GIMME A COFFEE, FUB!!

PLEH!

JET-PACK

OH, AND THOSE WERE THE DAYS FOR OL' PETEY AND OL' M.B. AND THEIR NEW FRIEND, "Who Cares!"

HUFF

CHUFF!

Who Cares!

COME ON Y'ALL 'N' RELAX WIT ME!

PRAISE TH' MA SHAH!

WHOOP!

DE-STROY!!!

pleh!

There Is No Escape!

SKOOTCH!

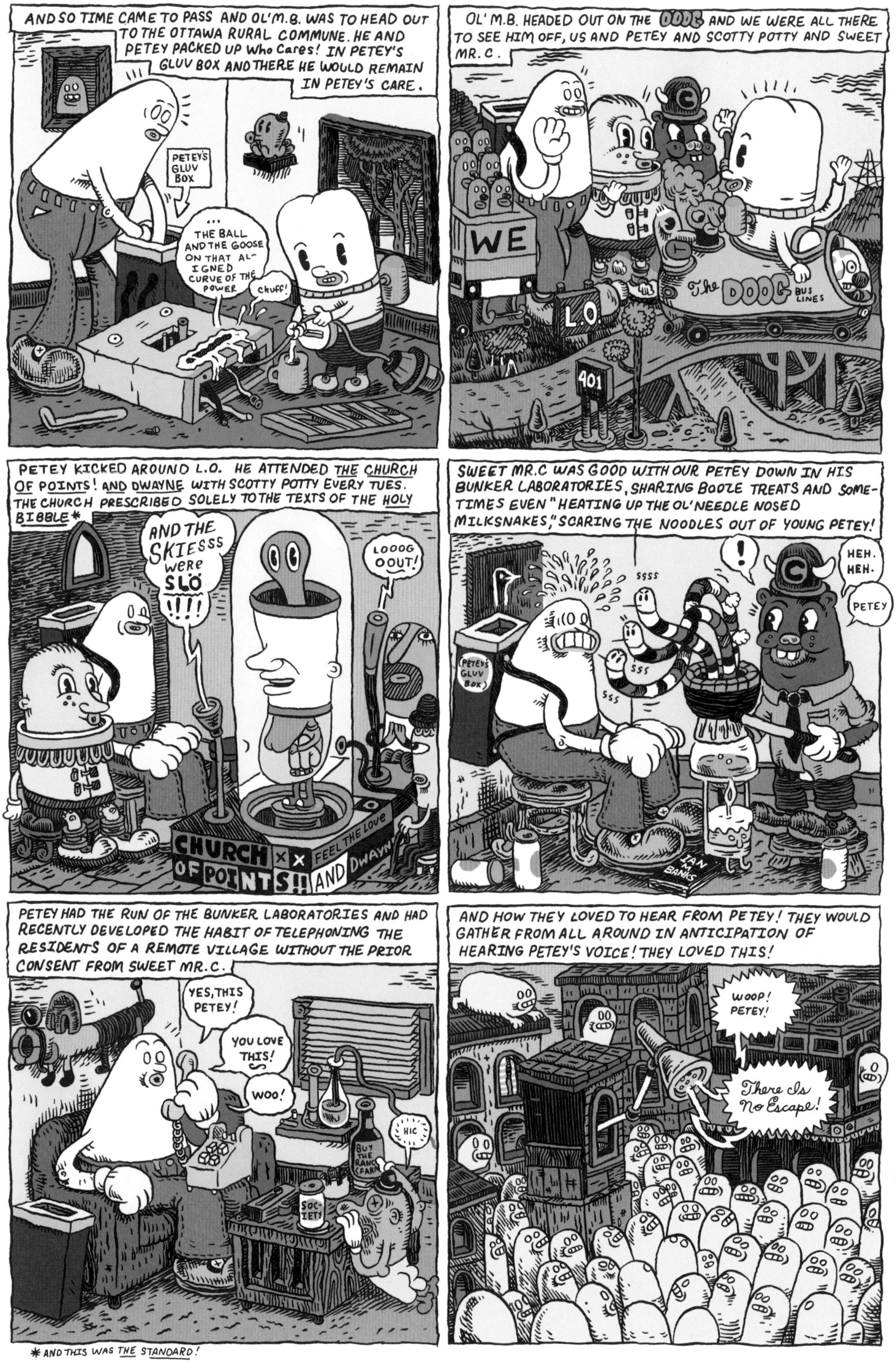

AND SO TIME CAME TO PASS AND OL'M.B. WAS TO HEAD OUT TO THE OTTAWA RURAL COMMUNE. HE AND PETEY PACKED UP Who Cares! IN PETEY'S GLUV BOX AND THERE HE WOULD REMAIN IN PETEY'S CARE.
PETEY'S GLUV BOX
... THE BALL AND THE GOOSE ON THAT ALIGNED CURVE OF THE POWER
chuff!
OL' M.B. HEADED OUT ON THE DOOG AND WE WERE ALL THERE TO SEE HIM OFF, US AND PETEY AND SCOTTY POTTY AND SWEET MR. C.
WE
The DOOG BUS LINES
L.O.
401
PETEY KICKED AROUND L.O. HE ATTENDED THE CHURCH OF POINTS! AND DWAYNE WITH SCOTTY POTTY EVERY TUES. THE CHURCH PRESCRIBED SOLELY TO THE TEXTS OF THE HOLY BIBBLE*
AND THE SKIESSS were SLÖ !!!!
LOOOG OOUT!
CHURCH OF POINTS!! AND DWAYN
FEEL THE LOVE
SWEET MR.C WAS GOOD WITH OUR PETEY DOWN IN HIS BUNKER LABORATORIES, SHARING BOOZE TREATS AND SOMETIMES EVEN "HEATING UP THE OL' NEEDLE NOSED MILKSNAKES," SCARING THE NOODLES OUT OF YOUNG PETEY!
!
HEH. HEH.
PETEY
SSSS
SSS
SSS
(PETEY'S GLUV BOX)
IAN M. BANKS
PETEY HAD THE RUN OF THE BUNKER LABORATORIES AND HAD RECENTLY DEVELOPED THE HABIT OF TELEPHONING THE RESIDENTS OF A REMOTE VILLAGE WITHOUT THE PRIOR CONSENT FROM SWEET MR.C.
YES, THIS PETEY!
YOU LOVE THIS!
WOO!
HIC
BUY THE RANCH FARM
SOCIETY
AND HOW THEY LOVED TO HEAR FROM PETEY! THEY WOULD GATHER FROM ALL AROUND IN ANTICIPATION OF HEARING PETEY'S VOICE! THEY LOVED THIS!
WOOP! PETEY!
There Is No Escape!

* AND THIS WAS THE STANDARD!

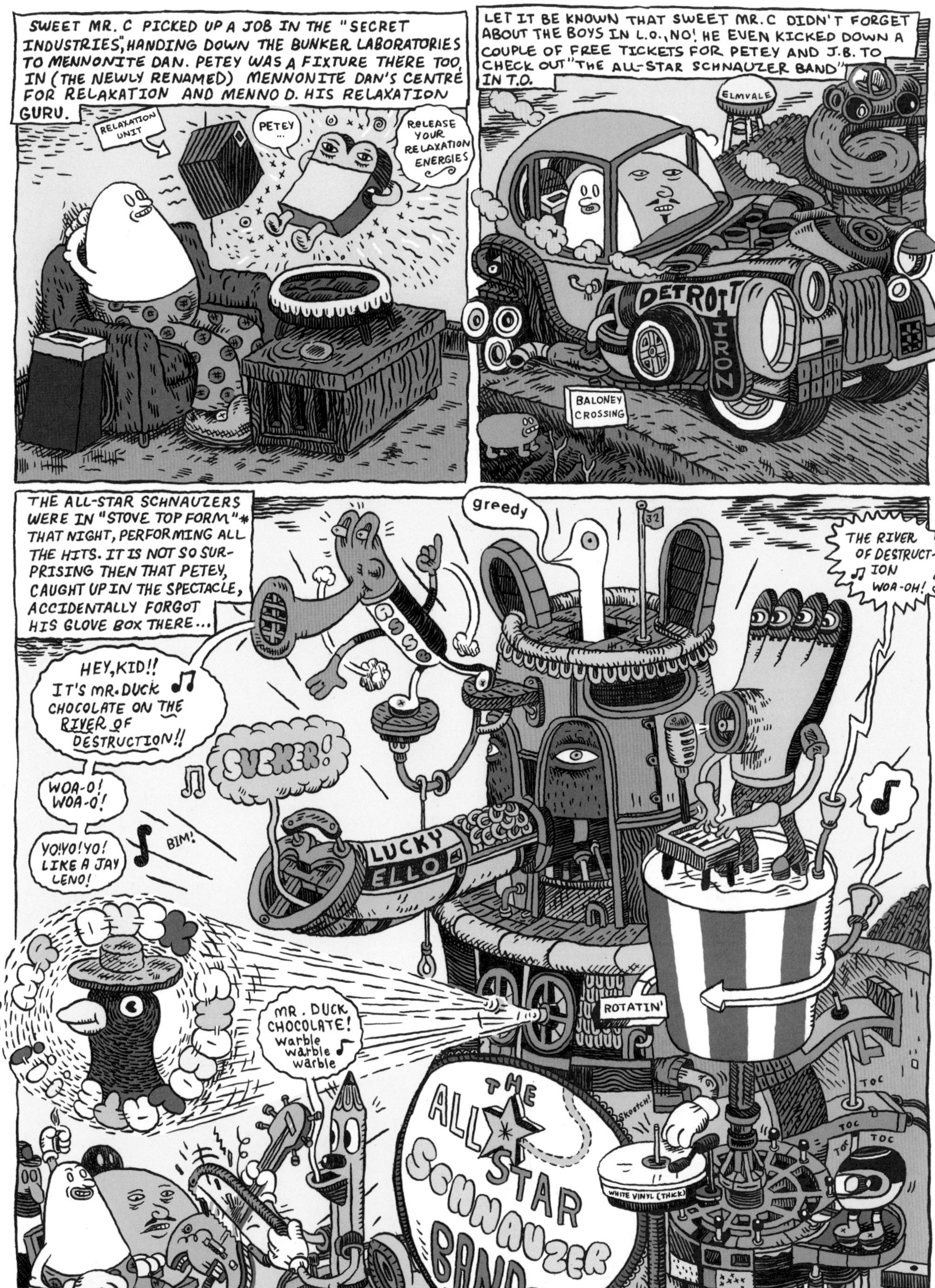
SWEET MR. C PICKED UP A JOB IN THE "SECRET INDUSTRIES", HANDING DOWN THE BUNKER LABORATORIES TO MENNONITE DAN. PETEY WAS A FIXTURE THERE TOO, IN (THE NEWLY RENAMED) MENNONITE DAN'S CENTRE FOR RELAXATION AND MENNO D. HIS RELAXATION GURU.
RELAXATION UNIT
PETEY ...
RELEASE YOUR RELAXATION ENERGIES
LET IT BE KNOWN THAT SWEET MR. C DIDN'T FORGET ABOUT THE BOYS IN L.O., NO! HE EVEN KICKED DOWN A COUPLE OF FREE TICKETS FOR PETEY AND J.B. TO CHECK OUT "THE ALL-STAR SCHNAUZER BAND" IN T.O.
ELMVALE
DETROIT IRON
BALONEY CROSSING
THE ALL-STAR SCHNAUZERS WERE IN "STOVE TOP FORM"* THAT NIGHT, PERFORMING ALL THE HITS. IT IS NOT SO SURPRISING THEN THAT PETEY, CAUGHT UP IN THE SPECTACLE, ACCIDENTALLY FORGOT HIS GLOVE BOX THERE...
greedy
THE RIVER OF DESTRUCTION WOA-OH!
HEY, KID!! IT'S MR. DUCK CHOCOLATE ON THE RIVER OF DESTRUCTION!!
SUCKER!
WOA-O! WOA-O!
YO! YO! YO! LIKE A JAY LENO!
BIM!
LUCKY ELLO
MR. DUCK CHOCOLATE! warble warble warble
ROTATIN'
THE ALL STAR SCHNAUZER BAND
WHITE VINYL (THICK)
TOC
TOC
TOC
TOC
PETEY'S GLUV BOX
PINK PEARL
POPPIN

* AS IS THE STANDARD FOR THE SCHNAUZERS

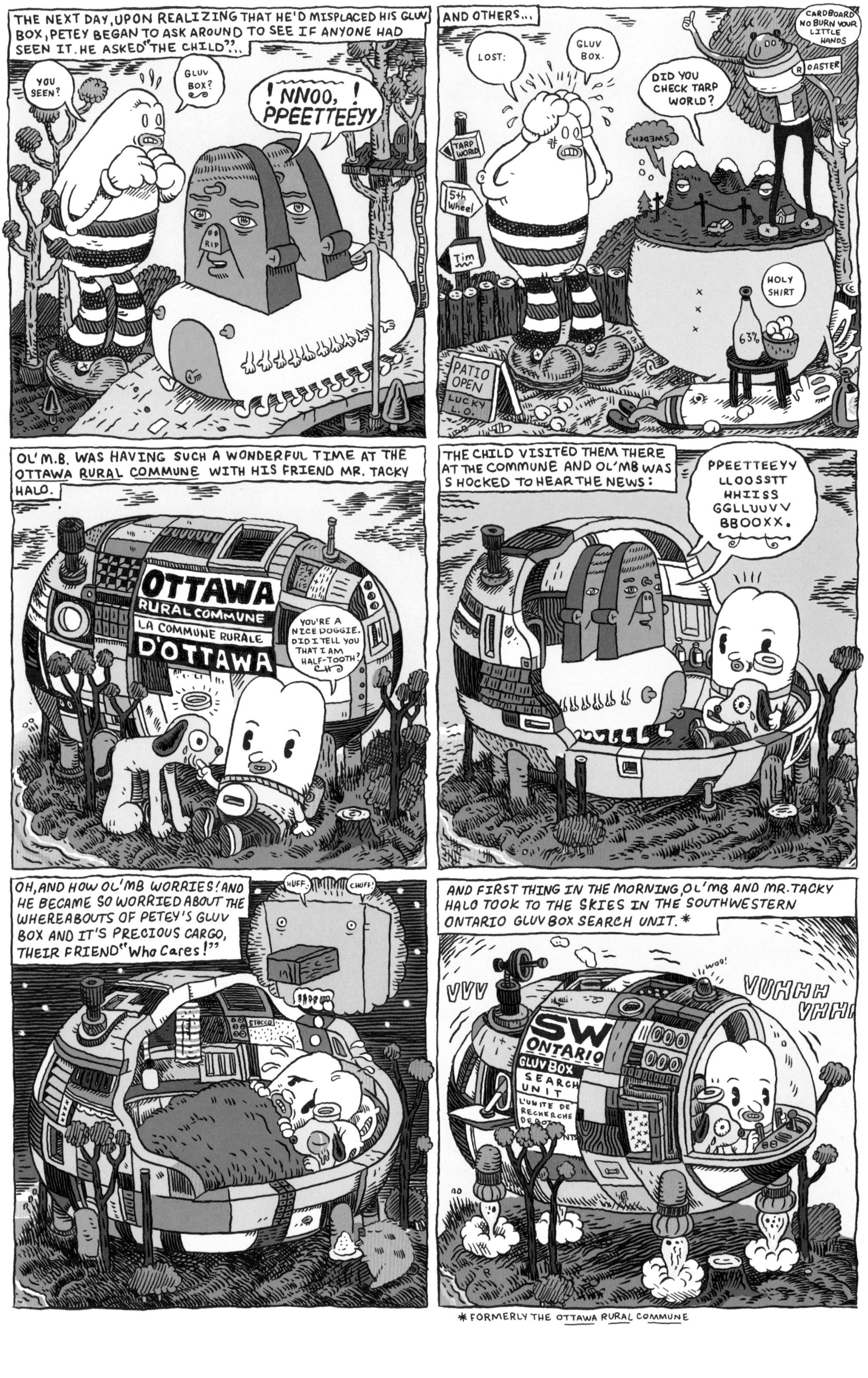
THE NEXT DAY, UPON REALIZING THAT HE'D MISPLACED HIS GLUV BOX, PETEY BEGAN TO ASK AROUND TO SEE IF ANYONE HAD SEEN IT. HE ASKED "THE CHILD"...
YOU SEEN?
GLUV BOX?
! NNOO, ! PPEETTEEYY
RIP
AND OTHERS...
LOST:
GLUV BOX.
DID YOU CHECK TARP WORLD?
CARDBOARD NO BURN YOUR LITTLE HANDS
R OASTER
TARP WORLD
SWEDEN
5th Wheel
Tim
HOLY SHIRT
63%
PATIO OPEN
LUCKY L.O.
OL' M.B. WAS HAVING SUCH A WONDERFUL TIME AT THE OTTAWA RURAL COMMUNE WITH HIS FRIEND MR. TACKY HALO.
OTTAWA RURAL COMMUNE
LA COMMUNE RURALE D'OTTAWA
YOU'RE A NICE DOGGIE. DID I TELL YOU THAT I AM HALF-TOOTH?
THE CHILD VISITED THEM THERE AT THE COMMUNE AND OL' MB WAS SHOCKED TO HEAR THE NEWS:
PPEETTEEYY LLOOSSTT HHIISS GGLLUUVV BBOOXX.
OH, AND HOW OL' MB WORRIES! AND HE BECAME SO WORRIED ABOUT THE WHEREABOUTS OF PETEY'S GLUV BOX AND IT'S PRECIOUS CARGO, THEIR FRIEND "Who Cares!"
HUFF.
CHUFF!
STUCCO
AND FIRST THING IN THE MORNING, OL' MB AND MR. TACKY HALO TOOK TO THE SKIES IN THE SOUTHWESTERN ONTARIO GLUVBOX SEARCH UNIT. *
WOO!
VVV
VUHHH VHHI
SW ONTARIO GLUV BOX SEARCH UNIT
L'UNITE DE RECHERCHE
* FORMERLY THE OTTAWA RURAL COMMUNE

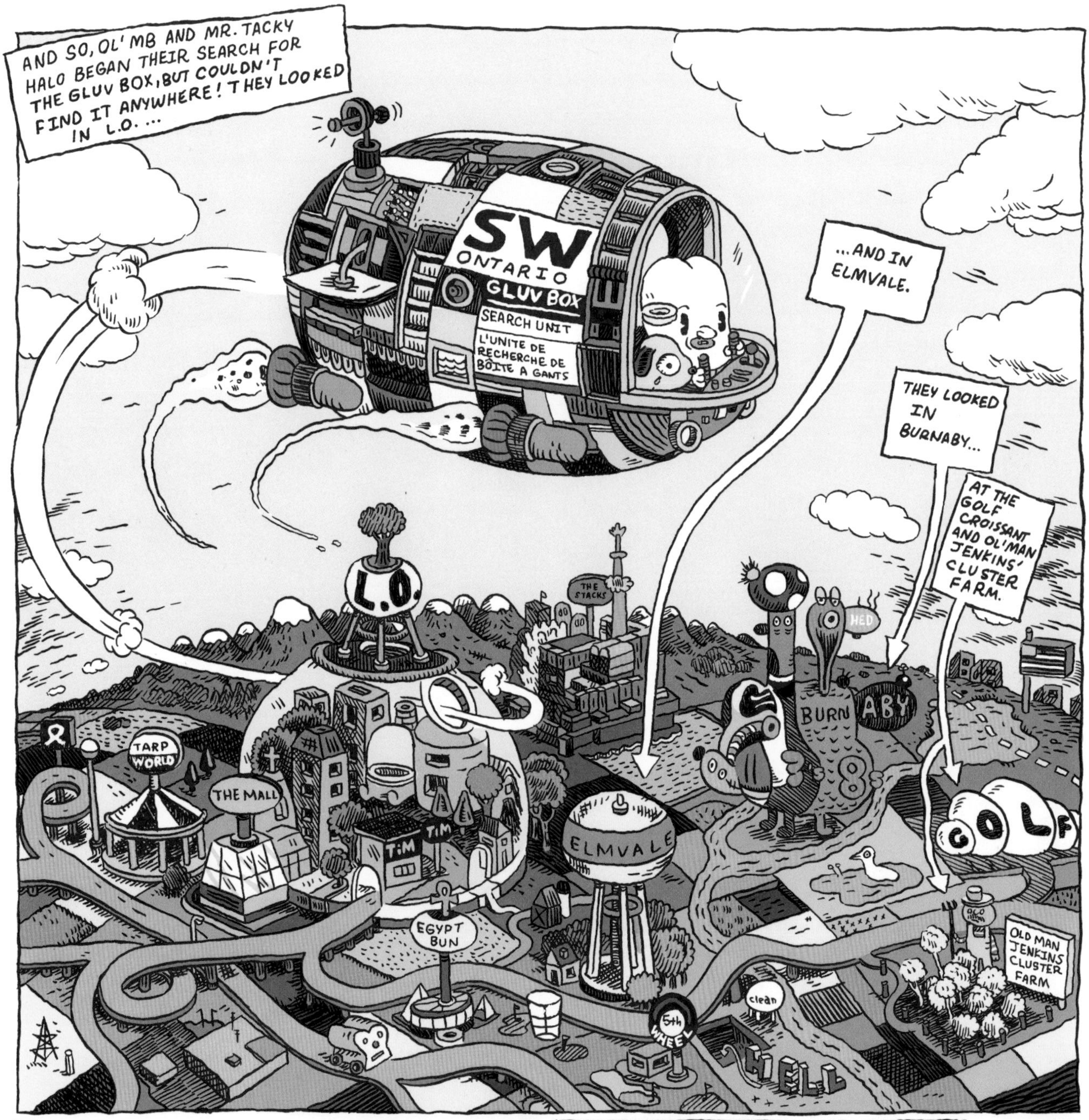

AND SO, OL' MB AND MR. TACKY HALO BEGAN THEIR SEARCH FOR THE GLUV BOX, BUT COULDN'T FIND IT ANYWHERE! THEY LOOKED IN L.O. ...
SW ONTARIO GLUV BOX SEARCH UNIT
L'UNITE DE RECHERCHE DE BOITE A GANTS
...AND IN ELMVALE.
THEY LOOKED IN BURNABY...
AT THE GOLF CROISSANT AND OL' MAN JENKINS' CLUSTER FARM.
L.O.
THE STACKS
HED
TARP WORLD
THE MALL
BURN ABY
8
GOLF
ELMVALE
TIM
EGYPT BUN
OLD MAN JENKINS CLUSTER FARM
clean
5th WHEEL
HELL

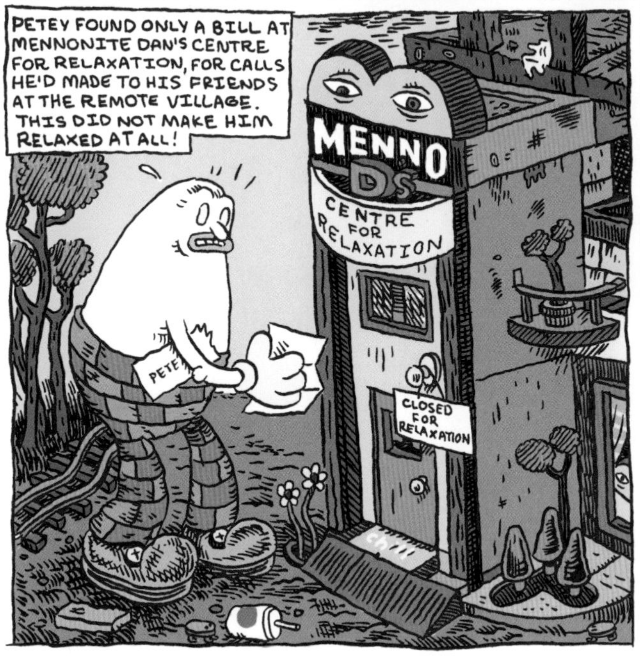

PETEY FOUND ONLY A BILL AT MENNONITE DAN'S CENTRE FOR RELAXATION, FOR CALLS HE'D MADE TO HIS FRIENDS AT THE REMOTE VILLAGE. THIS DID NOT MAKE HIM RELAXED AT ALL!
MENNO DS
CENTRE FOR RELAXATION
CLOSED FOR RELAXATION

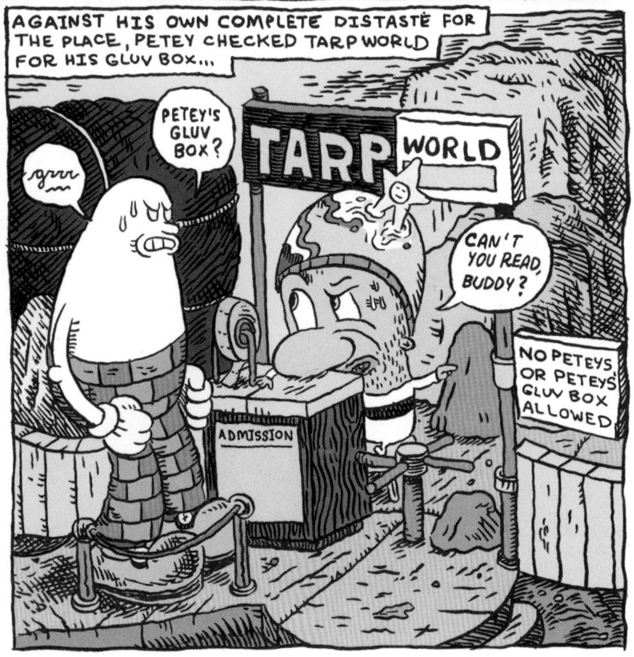

AGAINST HIS OWN COMPLETE DISTASTE FOR THE PLACE, PETEY CHECKED TARP WORLD FOR HIS GLUV BOX...
PETEY'S GLUV BOX?
TARP WORLD
CAN'T YOU READ, BUDDY?
NO PETEYS OR PETEYS GLUV BOX ALLOWED
ADMISSION

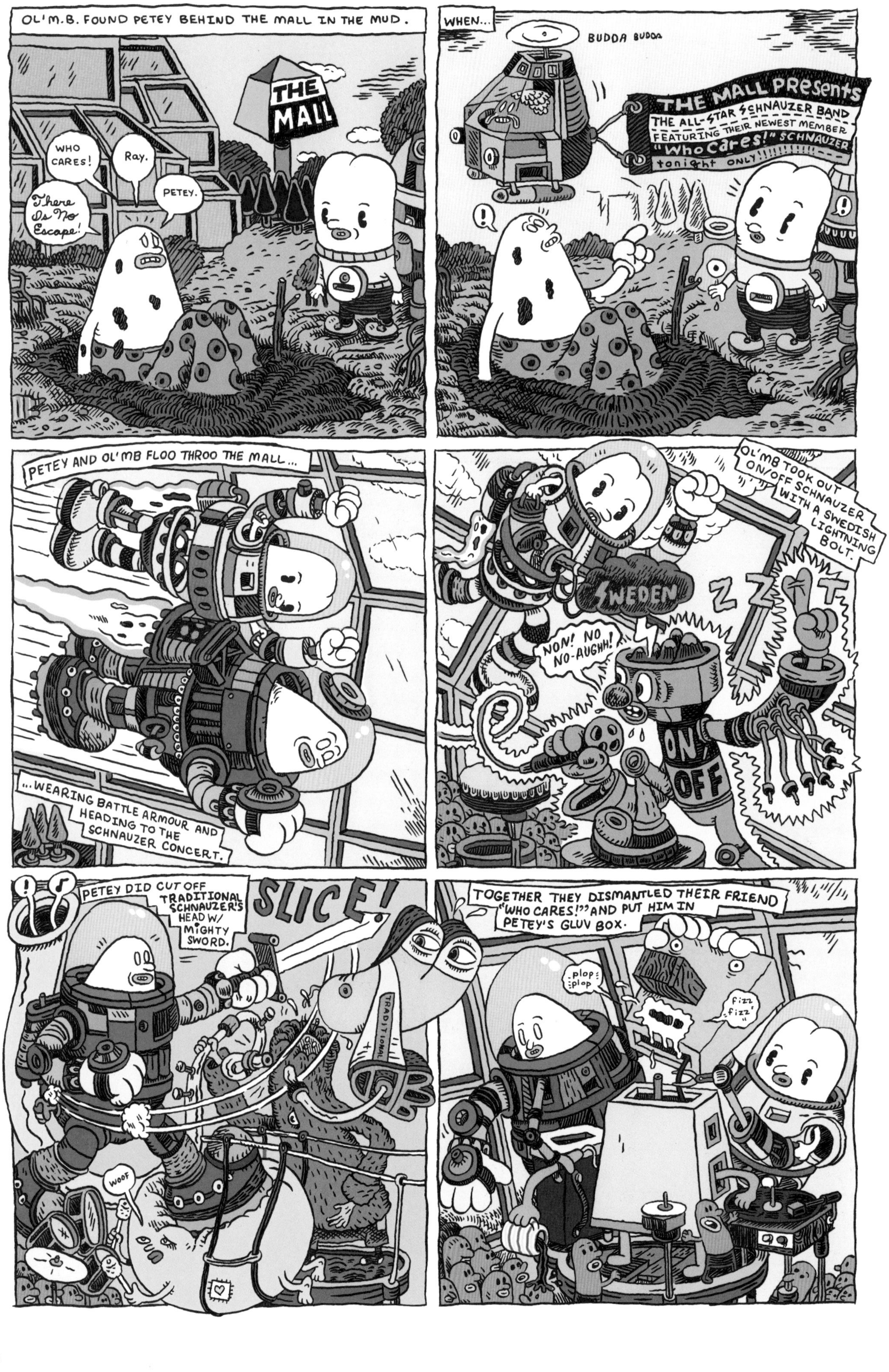
OL'M.B. FOUND PETEY BEHIND THE MALL IN THE MUD.
THE MALL
WHO CARES!
Ray.
PETEY.
There Is No Escape!
WHEN...
BUDDA BUDDA
THE MALL Presents THE ALL-STAR SCHNAUZER BAND FEATURING THEIR NEWEST MEMBER "Who Cares!" SCHNAUZER tonight ONLY!!!!!!!!!!!!
!
!
PETEY AND OL'MB FLOO THROO THE MALL...
...WEARING BATTLE ARMOUR AND HEADING TO THE SCHNAUZER CONCERT.
OL'MB TOOK OUT ON/OFF SCHNAUZER WITH A SWEDISH LIGHTNING BOLT.
SWEDEN
ZZZT
NON! NO NO-AUGHH!
ON/OFF
PETEY DID CUT OFF TRADITIONAL SCHNAUZER'S HEAD W/ MIGHTY SWORD.
SLICE!
TRADITIONAL
WOOF
TOGETHER THEY DISMANTLED THEIR FRIEND "WHO CARES!" AND PUT HIM IN PETEY'S GLUV BOX.
plop plop
fizz fizz

PETEY TRADED THE HEAD OF TRADITIONAL SCHNAUZER WITH THE BRICK FARMER (A RENOWNED SCHNAUZER COLLECTOR) FOR HIS FRIEND RAY THE BRICK SNAKE AND CHANGE.

OH!

AND WITH THE CHANGE, PETEY PUT A DOWN PAYMENT ON HIS PHONE BILL AND MENNO-NITE DAN WAS VERY RELAXED BY THIS.

CENTRE FOR RELAXATION

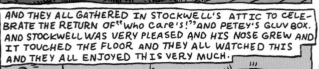

AND THEY ALL GATHERED IN STOCKWELL'S ATTIC TO CELE-BRATE THE RETURN OF "WHO CARE'S!" AND PETEY'S GLUV BOX. AND STOCKWELL WAS VERY PLEASED AND HIS NOSE GREW AND IT TOUCHED THE FLOOR AND THEY ALL WATCHED THIS AND THEY ALL ENJOYED THIS VERY MUCH.

BEEOOOP!

GEH

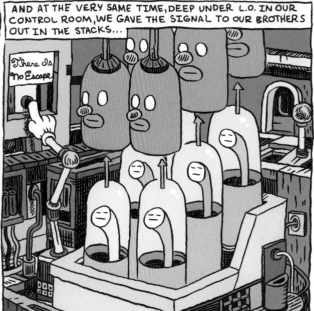

AND AT THE VERY SAME TIME, DEEP UNDER L.O. IN OUR CONTROL ROOM, WE GAVE THE SIGNAL TO OUR BROTHERS OUT IN THE STACKS...

There Is No Escape

AND FROM OUT OF THE STACKS...

There Is No Escape!

OUR BROTHERS DID RISE...

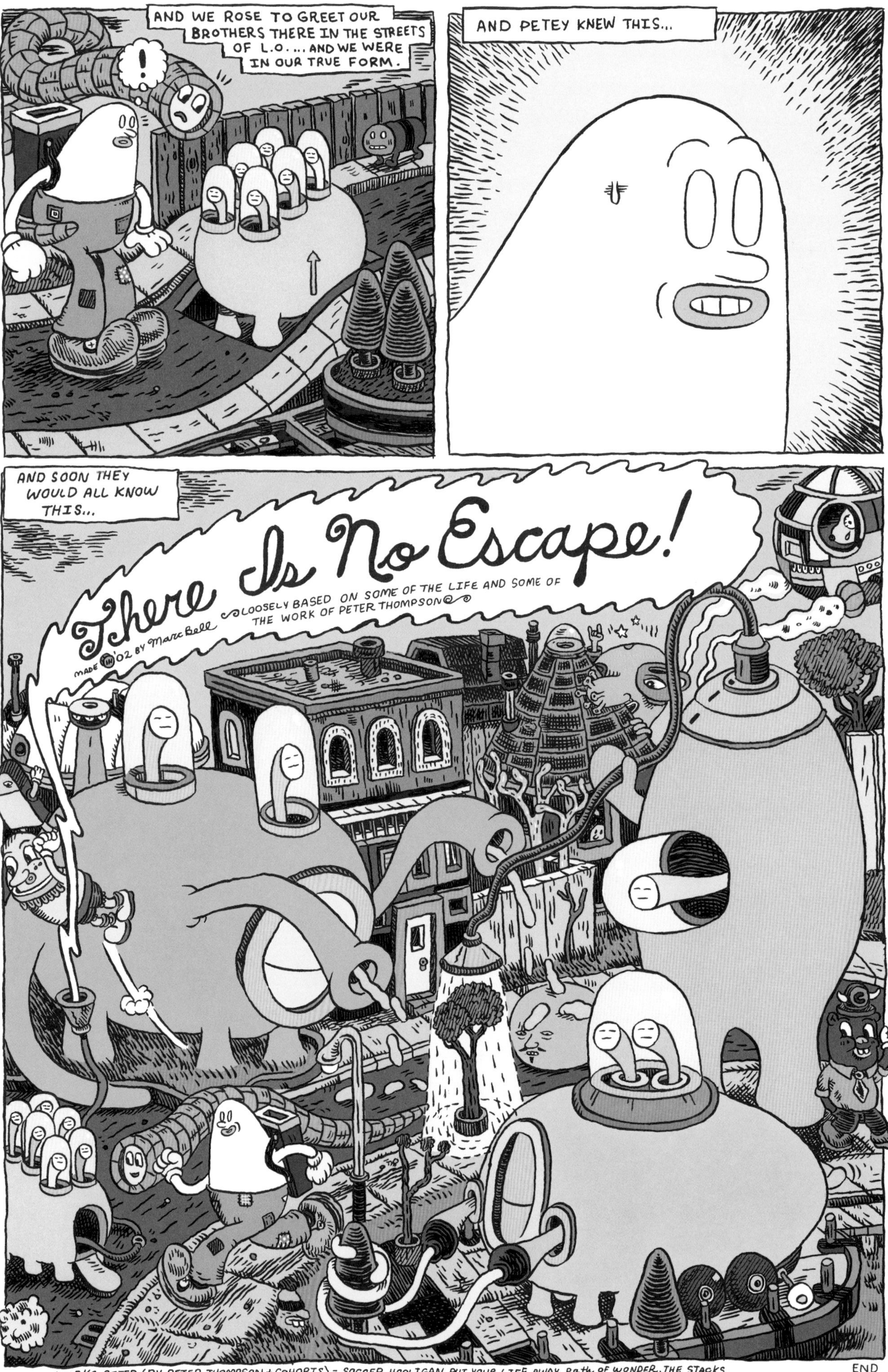
AND WE ROSE TO GREET OUR BROTHERS THERE IN THE STREETS OF L.O.... AND WE WERE IN OUR TRUE FORM.
!
AND PETEY KNEW THIS...
AND SOON THEY WOULD ALL KNOW THIS...
There Is No Escape!
LOOSELY BASED ON SOME OF THE LIFE AND SOME OF THE WORK OF PETER THOMPSON
MADE IN '02 BY Marc Bell

WORKS CITED (BY PETER THOMPSON + COHORTS) = SOCCER HOOLIGAN, PUT YOUR LIFE AWAY, Path OF WONDER, THE STACKS, THE HOLY BIBBLE, DETROIT IRON, STAND TALL GURU, THERE IS NO ESCAPE,,,

END

There Is No Index!

An index to "There Is No Escape!"

Compiled by Swanson D. Newbury
Understudy to Dr. Lulu Peabody–Sherman

Obtuse references to his own work and the work of his peers abound in "There is no Escape!," Bell's vernal and essential homage to his renowned collaborator Peter Thompson. I shall attempt to skate briskly across some of the piece's more salient details here. Page numbers indicate where any particular subject first appears in the story.

WHITE DENIM
THE STACKS
#1

giant masher
JUNE
2000
gallery 396
London, Ontario

Cosmic Teacher Dude: A character created by Bell and Peter Thompson that first appeared in an unused advertisement for their *Giant Masher* exhibition (Gallery 396, London ON, 2000). In "There Is No Escape!," Petey learns of the significance of "Gravy World" from this "great teacher." (p. 128)

The Stacks: Near the beginning of our story, "young Petey" finds himself in a "forbidden area" known as "The Stacks." Here we find several Bell–isms pulled from his book of the same name (cover of the self–published version shown above). Most notably, "Math Drawing," borrowed from *Secret Codes* (p. 141) makes an appearance, as well as the drawing *Who Wears The White Denim* (below). We can also see "OK Product With Pour Spout" (left) and parts of *King Youngue* here. A recreation of Jason Mclean's *Path of Wonder* is also woven throughout. Later in our story, another "Stacks" archetype, "The Ottawa Rural Commune," (left) appears as a home for the characters Mr. Tacky Halo and Ol' M. B. It transforms itself into the "SW Ontario Gluv Box Search Unit" for the task at hand in the story (p. 128, 132).

OK PRODUCT W/POUR SPOUT
OK

SUMMIT
cancelled
Schnauzer summit AT THE OTTAWA RURAL COMMUNE (cancelled)

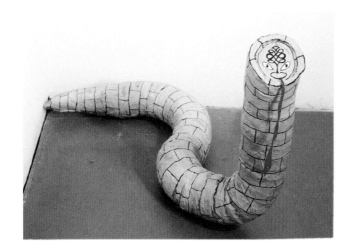

Ray the Brick Snake: Friend to "our Petey," Ray is based on the "Canada Council Brick Snake," which first appeared in the self–published version of Bell's *The Stacks*. An homage to an homage, Bell's "Brick Snakes" are based on a collage by Jason Mclean (left) wherein he'd attached a Canada Council logo to the head of the original "Brick Snake" by Ray Johnson. The sculpture version appearing here (above) by Bell was part of the aforementioned *Giant Masher* exhibition. (p. 128)

WHO WEARS THE WHITE DENIM
33.

who cares?

TARP WORLD

Who Cares, Tarp World: Their namesakes originally appeared in *Put Your Life Away* and *Totally Psychedoolick,* self–published booklets by Bell and Thompson. (p. 129, 133, also see: *Petey Loves Tarp World,* no. 9)

The All–Star Schnauzer Band: A musical recording group of some note. This advertisement for their L.P. *Get In The Truck* was designed by the real "Petey," Mr. Peter Thompson (p. 131).

Note: The actual All–Star Schnauzer Band may not appear as shown here (right) or in the comic strip "There Is No Escape!" The actions of the All–Star Schnauzer Band in "There Is No Escape!" do not necessarily reflect the actions of the real All–Star Schnauzer Band. *Failure to comply henceforth with what we are laying down here will result in your banishment to the River of Destruction for all eternity.* So sayeth Mr. Duck Chocolate, Esq. on this day, March 23, 2009.

Advertisement
the all star schnauzer band.
3
presenting
THEIR NEW L.P. 'GET IN THE TRUCK'

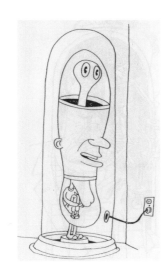

The Child, Dwayne: Born of Scott McIntyre, Thompson and Bell, the self–published *Fallen Angel* marks the emergence of "The Child." The same parents are responsible for "Dwayne," appearing in *The Holy Bibble #2.* (p. 132, 130)

Mr Tacky Halo: Friend of Ol' M. B., Mr. Tacky Halo is an anagram of "Amy Lockhart," the person who created the doll that this character is based on. As you can see here, Mr. Tacky Halo has a very nice waffle–textured coat. And, he is crying. (p. 132)

Photo by Alvin Buenaventura

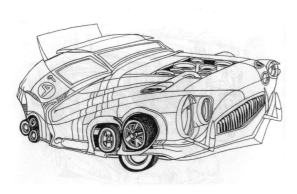

Detriot Iron: Petey and J.B. travel to see The All-Star Schnauzer Band perform in "T.O." in a car loosely based on this one from the self–published *Detroit Iron* by Jason Bellchamber and Peter Thompson. (p. 131)

HED
BURN
PETEY'S
GLUV
BOX
GOLF

Burnaby: Appearing first in Bell and Jason Mclean's self -published 2001 booklet *Stand Tall Guru* vol 3, *Burnaby* is an artwork that references the plot of "There Is No Escape!" More specifically: the loss of Petey's "Gluv Box." In the story, *Burnaby* appears as a landmark outside of "L.O.," along with "Tarp World," "Elmvale," the "5th Wheel" truckstop, "Hell" and "Old Man Jenkins Cluster Farm." Rumour has it that the story "There Is No Escape!" is loosely based on actual events in Ontario wherein Peter Thompson had lost a backpack full of artworks including many unfinished *Stand Tall Guru* pieces. It was later recovered. (p. 133)

(continued from p. 19) stigma–free *Egypt Buncake* as a working title. Unfortunately, this moniker became fraught with controversy when it was perceived by some as a tawdry euphemism for female buttocks. Several of Bell's more fusty patrons then questioned whether he was the "good boy" they thought he was, and he was forced to defend himself publicly, taking a megaphone to the street and citing every instance in which cheap sexual metaphor might wrongly be identified in his werk. "Egypt Buncake" continues to make regular appearances in Bell's drawings. Coincidentally, a film called *Sudan Spongecake* by French director Ronald Pétri is scheduled for release in 2011.

BACON
BILLBOARD
THE

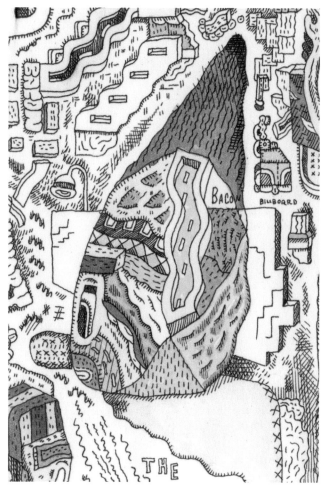

Detail of *Complaint Dept.*, 2006, mixed media on board

Head Gear (Bad Mon Tonne, Comics Ain't Buttah, Balsam Adhesives)

Hats and headgear loom large throughout Bell's werk, and there is no more conspicuous and important chapeau in his entire catalogue than the "Bad Mon Tonne" hat. Shaped like a badminton shuttlecock or "birdie," this totemic lid appears in a series of salient 2006 werks, and according to Twance–Morris, represents "the gilded pontoon between an unsound fetish for nasal anguish and a more whimsical dalliance with the haberdashery of the mind."[9] This assessment however, seems slightly off–base when considering Bell's *Fresh From the Silver Pumpkin* (no. 100), which depicts a "Bad Mon Tonne" hat existing comfortably alongside a slab of bacon nailed to a nose. The hat also appears in Bell's *Index To May 16 Student Pandemic* (facing page), and perhaps most arrestingly in his 2006 tour–de–force *Phew! Comics Ain't Buttah* (no. 95). This particular drawing might almost be viewed as a compendium piece for an entire Bell era, weaving a number of his themes–du–jour into an elaborate waffle–bacon headdress and ushering in a drawing technique that allows for rivers of white space between islands of illustrated figures. I should note that the presumed "owner" of the emblematic headdress in question was first featured in a sketch that worked its way into the drawing *Complaint Dept.* (no. 42) in which he is rendered more casually and sports a more subtly waffled hat. In *Phew! Comics Ain't Buttah*, this character transcends doodle status, achieving a splendor and weighty countenance that reaches its apex in the 2007 mixed media piece *Balsam Adhesives* (no. 32). It has been suggested that "Balsam Adhesives" is the character's name, and this seems fitting given the evocation of old–fashioned portraiture in this key werk.

Flugtag/Cheeper Than Tuba Player

According to Wikipedia: "Flugtag (German: flight day, airshow) is an event owned and operated by Red Bull in which competitors attempt to fly homemade human–powered flying machines." It is also a commanding theme in Bell's werk and the linchpin of the 2006 mixed–media piece *Cheeper Than Tuba Player (May 16th Flugtag)* (no. 22). Happening upon a *Flugtag* event at Science World in Vancouver, B.C, Bell developed an affinity for the peculiar contest before even understanding what it entailed. After picking up a flyer for the event, he also became enamored of the Flugtag team names, immediately clipping them out and including them in the above werk. These names, including such mouthfuls as "Bubbles Rocket Brigade," "Grease Flightening," and "Free Moustache Rides" are further expounded upon in the aforementioned *Index To May 16 Student Pandemic* (facing page). It is a testimony to Bell's consuming fascination with esoteric, remote sounding language, as well as his indifference to the original context thereof, that "Flugtag" could assume such a key role in his werk without even a cursory understanding of its essence. This ability to re–position vernacular detritus to suit his own ends is perhaps the central weapon in Bell's arsenal. As a whole, *Cheeper than Tuba Player (May 16th Flugtag)* is a pointed jab at what Bell views as the uneven manner in which government funding for the arts is doled out. Singling out tuba players as a prime example of tax dollars poorly spent, Bell deduced rightly that he could be kept alive and productive for 5 years on just one year of a federally funded tuba player's salary. Of course, this figure fails to address the plight of tuba players in the private sector, who receive no federal assistance and are often required to follow a corporate mascot around town for up to 18 hours a day.[10]

MARC
IS STUPID

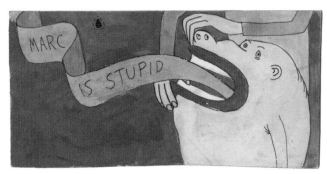

Peter Thompson, *"Marc Is Stupid" (untitled)*, 1998, postcard
Reverse reads: *"But not as stupid as Petey who left his wallet in his pants when he washed them"*

Petey

Bell's artwerk has long been underpinned by references to a certain "Petey" who, as myth would have it, was born with his pants on. While Bell neophytes might be tempted to comb through these allusions for answers to the Peter Gabriel conundrum (*Is he there?*),

Facing Page: *Index To May 16th Student Pandemic*, 2006
Ink and watercolour on paper

INDEX TO MAY 16 STUDENT PANDEMIC

1. MAGIC DOME OF SCIENCE WAS A SNOBBI WEARING SENSIBLE SHOOZ

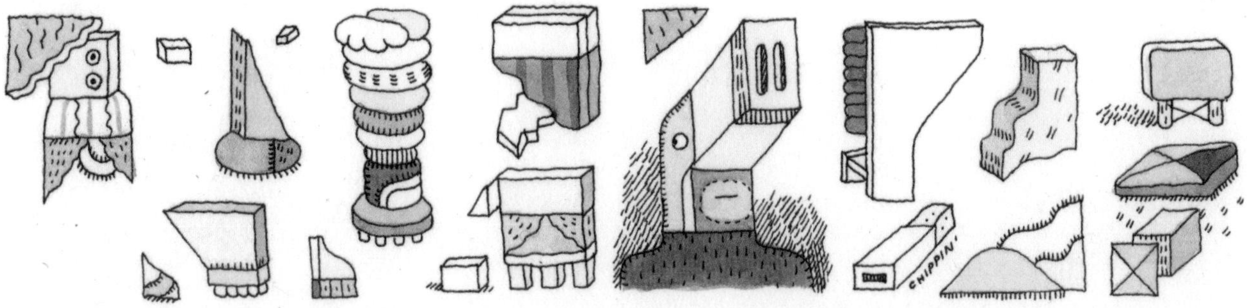
CHIPPIN'

2. FREE MOUSTACHE RIDES COLLAPSED UPON THE MOVIE SET WEARING GNOSTIC PIZZA PAJAMAS. FREE MOUSTACHE RIDES WAS CO-STARRING IN BEER ELEVATOR II W/SHORTCAKE OF THE POPULAR REALITY TV SERIES SHORTCAKE IN THE CITY.

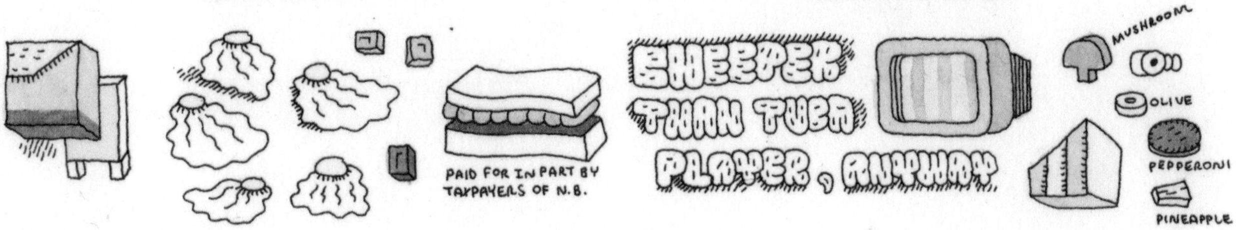
PAID FOR IN PART BY
TAXPAYERS OF N.B.
CHEEPER THAN TUBA PLAYER, ANYWAY
MUSHROOM
OLIVE
PEPPERONI
PINEAPPLE

3. BACK TO THE FLUGTAG TALKED NOTHING BUT GOBBLIGOOK. "CHEEPER THAN A TUBA PLAYER, ANWAY" SAID THE NEW BRUNSWICK TAX PAYERS AS THEY MADE A PILE OF 8 HAMBURGERS/CHEESEBURGERS ON A PLATE. ~~S.P. EHMAN WAS THERE. AND OL' TENLEGS.~~ THEY WERE COPYING ~~S.P. EHMAN.~~ KRUPPY BOY, ON LOAN FROM ALBERTA.

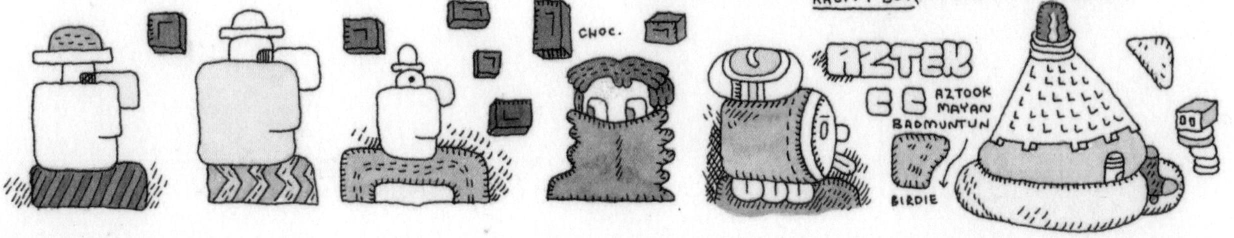
CHOC.
AZTEK
C C
AZTOOK
MAYAN
BADMUNTUN
BIRDIE

4. AIR GUITAR STOOD ON A CLIFF BY THE OCEAN. THE SUN WAS SETTING. ~~HE~~ SHE WAS AVOIDING THE STUDENT PANDEMIC HAPPENING IN ~~TUNE~~TOWN. THERE WAS A 540 lb PEPPERONI SLICE BEING CONSTRUCTED ON CAMPUS TO WARD OFF ANY NEW OUTBREAKS. AIR GUITAR WAS ASKED TO BUT REFUSED TO CUT THE RIBBON IN THE OPENING CEREMONY. AND SO WE FIND HER HERE, ALONE. ALONE. ALONE. SOCIETY.

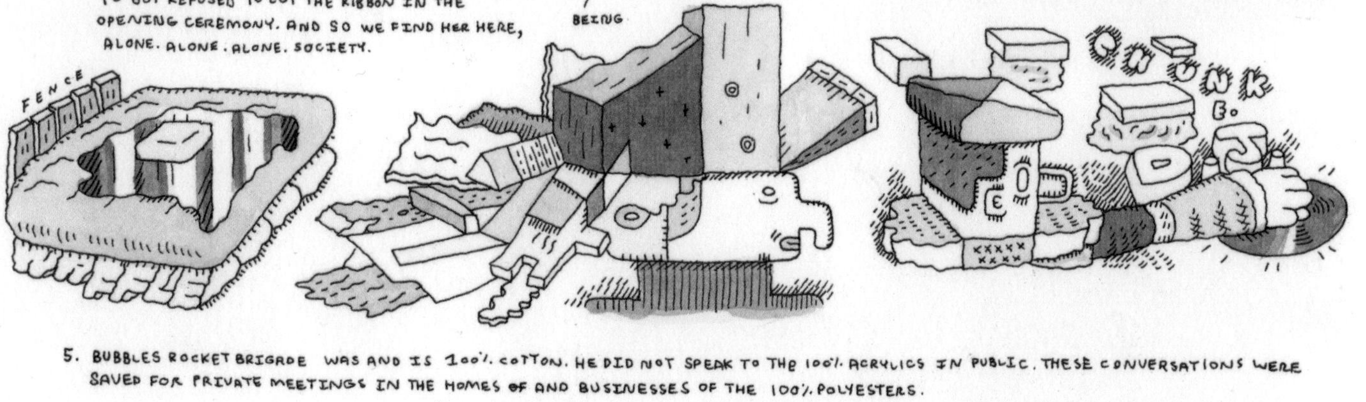
FENCE

5. BUBBLES ROCKET BRIGADE WAS AND IS 100% COTTON. HE DID NOT SPEAK TO THE 100% ACRYLICS IN PUBLIC. THESE CONVERSATIONS WERE SAVED FOR PRIVATE MEETINGS IN THE HOMES ~~OF~~ AND BUSINESSES OF THE 100% POLYESTERS.

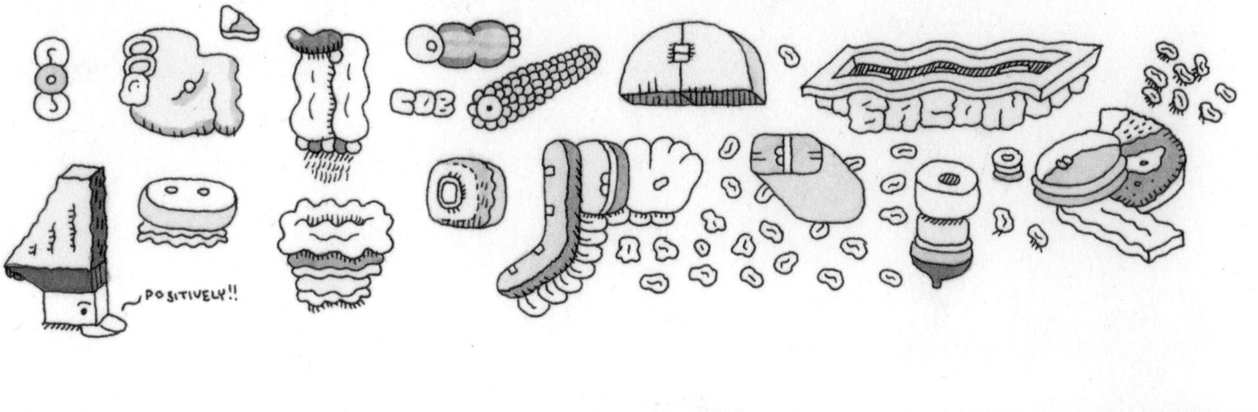
COB
BACON
POSITIVELY!!

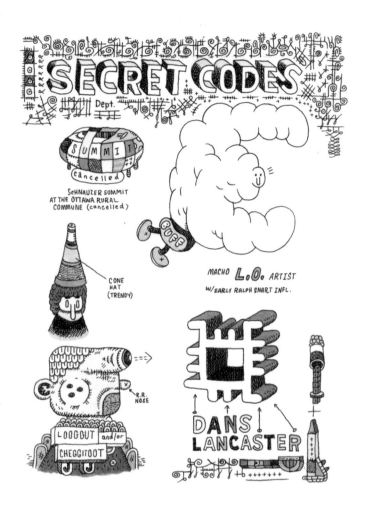

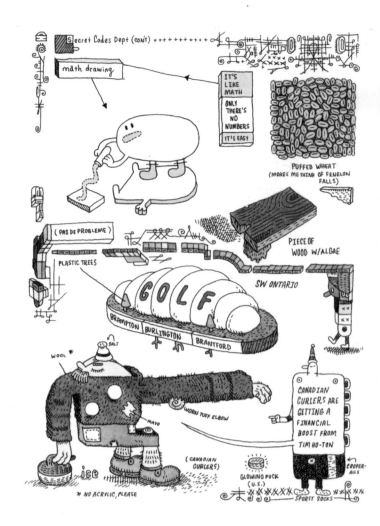

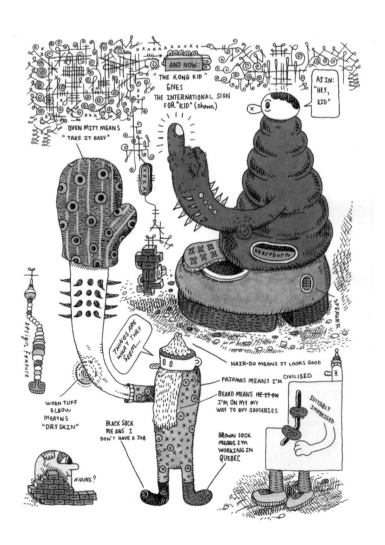

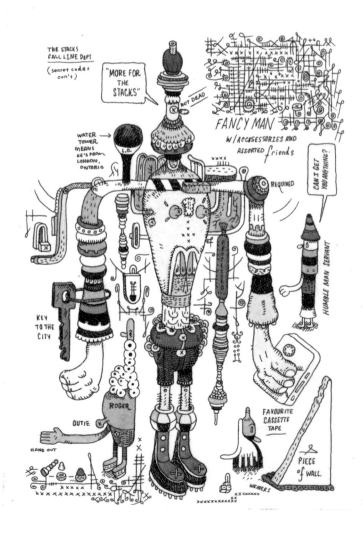

Morris Twance–Morris insists that this would be "redolent with doltishness." According to him, "Peter" is none other than Herman's Hermits band leader Peter Noone, although strangely, a detailed survey of Bell's catalogue yields not a single mention of a "Peter" in any of the werks.[11] "Petey" on the other hand refers categorically to London, Ontario based artist and longtime Bell cohort Peter Thompson. Although mentions of "Petey" are legion, the full scope of his significance within Bell's werk might best be gleaned by reading the indomitable coming–of–age comic strip, "There is No Escape!" It also bears mentioning that an abstract "Petey" is showered with attention by an equally abstract "Jean Chrétien" in Bell's 2008 drawing, *Illusztraijun for Brain Police* (no. 89), a piece that sparked fresh rumors as to Petey's shadowy role in the geopolitical sphere. Nobody was willing to comment on this. Several collaborations between Thompson and Bell are included in *Hot Potatoe*, most notably the series of drawings titled *The Hobbit* (p. 218).

Hello Is Peter Gabriel There?

Imagine if I could muster the courage to call one of my heroes out of the blue and say "Hello are the translators of Helène Cixous' *Laugh of Medusa*, Keith and Paula Cohen there?" or even better, "Hello, is Burton Cummings there?" Well, if you can process this scenario without breaking into a starstruck sweat, then I think you've probably grasped the essence of Bell's cryptic question, and at least the partial gist of his crucial piece *Fabulous Bert Vibes* (no. 26). Bell's abiding love of early Genesis is a well documented fact, and the character who poses this question within the piece can only be seen as Bell himself, working up the courage through his art to establish communication with an icon of his youth. That this character appears later in *Aug Bullion* (no. 25) indicates an ongoing preoccupation with Genesis that Bell might resolve by simply phoning Peter Gabriel as soon as possible. Marc, I've heard he is a very nice man. I hope this helps.

Conclusion

Taking my own advice, I worked up the courage to call Burton Cummings yesterday and ask for him by name. "I'm sorry, Lulu, Mr. Cummings isn't available right now. I think he's out following someone's daughter home," said the voice on the other end. "But trust me. You don't have the wrong number." It had to be Peter Cetera, but how did he know it was me? There were 4 seconds of dead air and then, "Aren't you going to ask me the question?" Huh? "I'll give you a hint," he said, "The answer is, *'It's me, the one and only Peter Cetera, and they're the coziest jeans I've owned since Fancy Ass went tits up*.'" Aha! I knew it was him! And so, realizing I'd come to the fattiest part of the bacon so to speak, I pored over my notes in a desperate search for this question… the question…the question…Was he a *big man in Westmount*? Was it something to do with *calling Larry about the ironing board*? A *polish woman? A tuba player? Paul Klee? Jeans? What?* I couldn't figure it out for the life of me!

Verily, this must be a form of that "Gnee–o–Gneppotism" Bell warns us about in his series of seminal 2005 werks, and verily I was stumped. What make of Puddington scholar was I? I hung up the phone without saying goodbye to Peter Cetera, slunk into the living room feeling most ineffectual and poured myself a tall Root Beer. I had the butler fetch me my Chicago records. It was going to be a long night.[12]

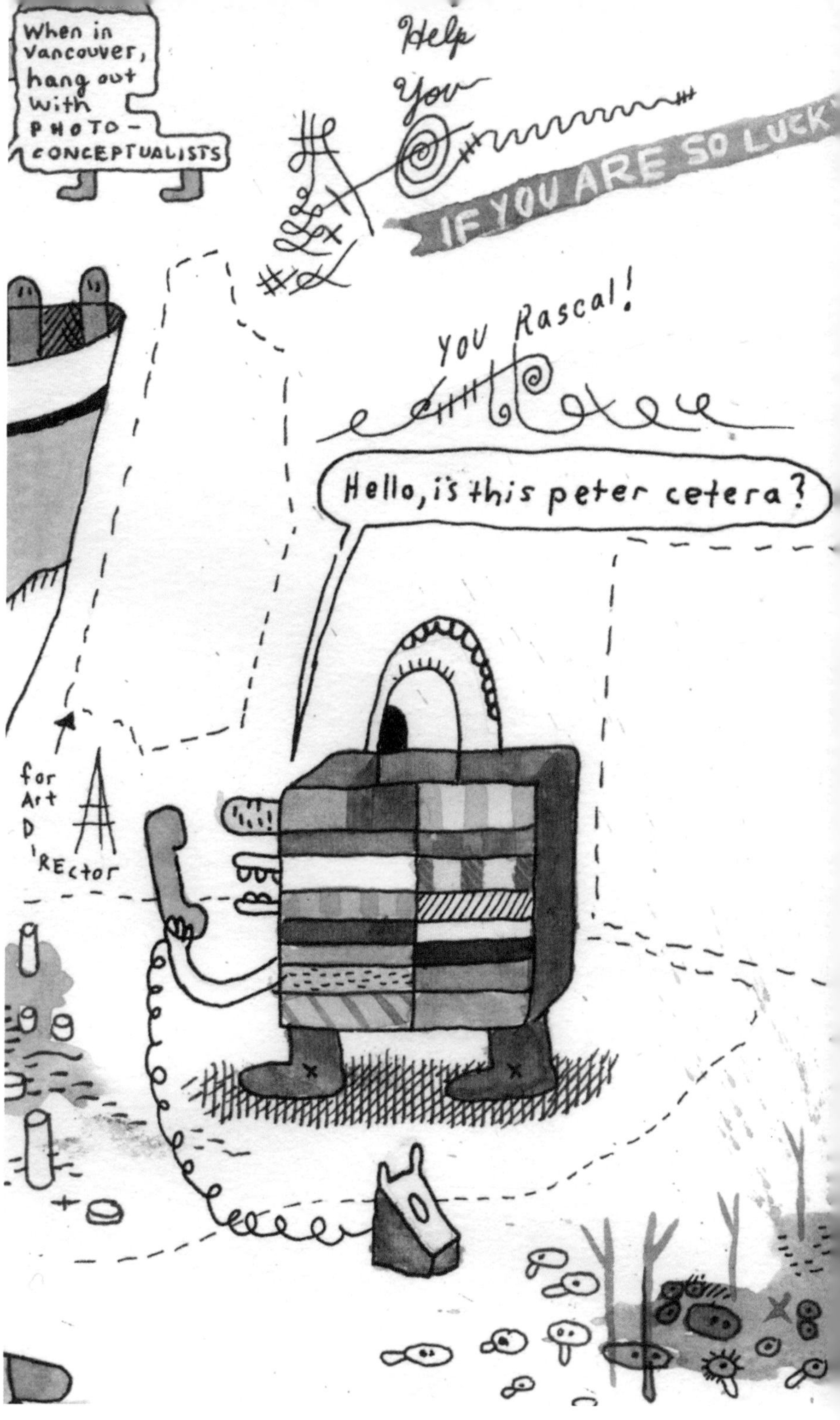
When in Vancouver, hang out with PHOTO-CONCEPTUALISTS
Help You
IF YOU ARE SO LUCK
you Rascal!
Hello, is this peter cetera?
for Art D iREctor

Detail of *Stall*, 2004, ink and watercolour on paper
Previous page: *Secret Codes 1–4*, 2003–2006, ink and watercolour on paper

NOTES

1.The title of an ongoing story in the second incarnation of Bell's weekly comic strip for *The Coast* and *The Montreal Mirror* (*Big Pile Comics*, 2001–2005). Being a little nitpicky here, we could also mention that the complete title was "Wilder Hobson's Theatre Absurd–o."

2. At a point in their career when they were out to breakfast, lunch *and* dinner, the Brazilian Tropicalia group Os Mutantes were known to hit the stage in custom made suits covered entirely in mirrors. This sartorial prank served to divert the viewer's gaze away from the band and, cheekily, back to him or herself.

3. This piece solidified it's reputation as a soda–pop art disaster after an ill fated installation at Assumption Plaza in the artist's hometown of Moncton, New Brunswick. Several Downtown Ambassadors were injured when this, a 15–foot Fresca can made of cement collapsed and rolled over a tourist kiosk into the Petitcodiac River.

4. Twance–Morris "Very Important Pop: A Cup Art Companion," from his self published, photocopied, handbound and agressively distributed document *Twancing The Night Away, Volume 21,* p. 612. It should be noted here that the "stolen" wheelchair in question actually was purchased by Bell from Todd Doody Orthopedic on Cordova Street in Vancouver.

5. From a phone conversation with Bell on January 12th, 2009. He stated that there are several more crucial, unexamined elements about *Gravy World* that might possibly be covered in the future, including something about gravy chickens and their gravy–filled eggs.

6. In e–mail conversation with Bell during February 2009, Bell explained his periodic discussions with Dirty Debbie during 2006–2007 on the coming financial downturn. Bell mentioned touching on these topics repeatedly with several other friends during that time, including Sean the Humpback Whale Poodlesnake and "Barb Rouge," who were later taken aback by his alarming accuracy. Bell sites the *Housing Bubble Blog* by Ben Jones as a direct source to his financial musings. See following article for a further examination of this topic.

7. A common misspelling of "nose" in Bell's work. *Knoze Clippah*! is a self–published booklet produced in limited runs that were altered for each new edition (See *Nog A Dod*, Conundrim Press.)

8. *Beer Elevator* has suffered several rejections from potential financial backers, though Bell still seems enthused with the project and is currently writing the sequel. In conversation with Bell on February 12th, 2009, he claimed that he had hoped for Johnny Depp to star as himself in the film.

9. Taken from a 2006 presentation by Morris Twance–Morris at Sackville New Brunswick's Struts Gallery. This was offered as part of the one–off *Lidfest '06*, a celebration of alternative headwear culture in Canada. Hats were mandatory throughout the event, and it is noteworthy that Twance–Morris sported an elaborate shuttlecock hat to deliver his thesis, tailored by Bell himself.

10. The A&W Root Bear is an excellent example of a corporate mascot frequently accompanied by a tuba player.

11. Twance–Morris, "The Scoundrel of L.O: Marc Bell's Peter," from his print–on–demand one–sheet project *The Incompletes: Self–Styled Savants in Our Midst*, p. 1, available exclusively on lulu.com.

12. A reference to the Bell/Peter Thompson collaboration *To The Moors* from their self–published booklet *The Fellowship Of The Ring*. The drawing states: "fetch me my Marillion records we're going to be up all night."

Excerpt from "Trading Meaning: Artists Respond to the Financial Meltdown," by Mark Slutsky, *Financial Review*, January 2009

But perhaps the artist most attuned to the debt crisis has been Marc Bell. While other artists have alluded to the realities of the market in their work, he, more so than any of his contemporaries, has acted as the self–appointed conscience of modern capitalism. No one in the art world has been as critical of modern finance as Marc Bell, and the world is slowly coming around to recognizing his prescience.

TAKE ME TO the CASBAH OL' FRIEND
I LIKE THE SCIENCE OF FICTION
the FICTION OF SCIENCE, YOU A-HOLES
Dig?
AUD. PARTICIP. YOU SAY: "UH, I THINK YOU'RE BEING the A-HOLE"
PUERTO RICO
HELLO DNK WALL
THIS IS the wrong side, I think
OR MAYBE it's the Right ONE, I don't know
it's all meat and cheese from here on in, baby
× × BONUS: reversable
this side: angry, Funny
that side: fantasy
SHOULD I HAVE COLOURED HIM A SHURT?
ARM BAND SIGNIFYING
What?

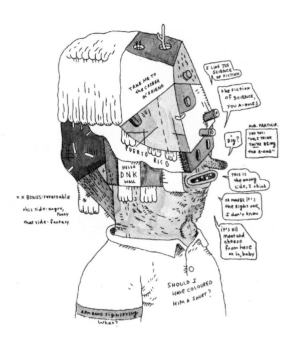

Angry/ Funny Side, 2004
Ink and watercolour on paper

Bell's 2004 drawing *Angry/Funny Side* is an astonishingly direct attack on the speculation–driven investment tendencies that enriched hedge fund managers but that ultimately led to instability and financial ruin.

The image is of a man in profile; this is clearly a typical investor, his vision obscured by an elaborate headpiece. With the benefit of hindsight, it is obvious that this patchwork hat is meant to represent a derivative, a type of contract the value of which is based on a complex series of agreements and assets. Warren Buffet famously called derivatives, "financial weapons of mass destruction," and it is significant that the investor is seen to be saying, "I like the science of fiction…the fiction of science, you a–holes."

What is the "science of fiction" if not economics—"the dismal science"—which creates value out of worthless properties like bundled subprime mortgages? "This is the wrong side, I think," the investor is also seen to be saying, "or maybe it's the right one, I don't know." Is there a better expression of the public's utter confusion at the Byzantine complexities of financial securities, leverage and debt? And all of this in 2004, when the stock market was still riding high and while the housing bubble was still heedlessly expanding.

In a darkly funny detail, Bell adds the instruction, "this side: angry, funny; that side: fantasy." Fantasy? There's no doubt that fantasy—imaginary value—played a huge part in the meltdown that was to come. Angry? Well, in 2004, one person was angry—Bell—while most others were content to turn away and watch returns pile up, heedless of the future collapse. Funny? Filtered through his perceptions, the current mess is funny, yes. Darkly funny—and, in his eyes, inevitable. Would only that more would have listened to Bell's prophetic words and paid attention to his sharp, insightful art before it was too late.

Other Bell Terminology

Compiled by Swanson D. Newbury
Understudy to Dr. Lulu Peabody–Sherman

Brown Socks: A derogatory French–Canadian term originating in Montreal, Quebec to describe plain, boring English persons (eg: "Cet espèce de bas bruns à tête carrée, qui s'habille chez Sears, qui travaille un emploi plate, qu'il mange de la marde, cet estie d'anglo voleur de job! Retourne chez vous travailler chez Future Shop!") It is borrowed by Bell and used in several pieces including *Brown Socks (Means I am Working in Quebec)*, 2004, shown below. (Also see p. 142)

BROWN SOCKS

DELTA
BERT

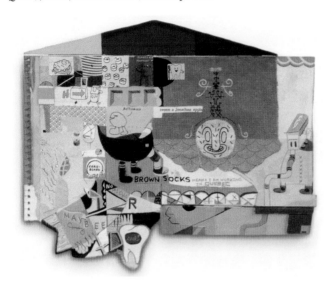

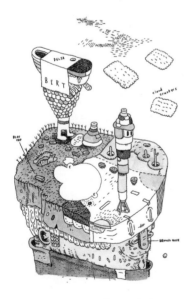

Chunky Floors: A character who appears in some of the writing in Bell's "Pile of Bacon" drawings and in the story of the same name (p. 168–178). "Chunky Floors" also seems to be the subject of some kind of exhibition. (see back cover)

Fabulous Bert Vibes, Bert, Delta Bert: A head with a white sheet laid upon it and labeled "Bert" turns up a number of times in Bell's werk, however, this mug does not appear in *Fabulous Bert Vibes* (no. 26), nor in *Ol' Mug* (not in this book). Oh well. Often the underside of Bert's head seems to be comprised of colourful balls that look like they may have come from a billiards table. Bert has remarked on at least one occasion: "I'm so Lazy, It's Crazy." Shown above is *Delta Bert*, 2004. (no. 101, 107, 108)

Hair Farmers: Canadian "hoser" term for "those who spend time growing hair." (no. 77, p. 240)

It Ain't Easy Beein Mah Peazie (Modurn Informalism): The first half of the title to this 2007 piece (right) is a quote from a heartwarming story about brotherhood told in the third person and relayed to Bell by his friend S.P Ehman. Bell does not really know "Mah Peazie" himself but was touched by his humility in this story nonetheless.

King Of Floors: A Surrey, BC flooring company with a regal looking pooch for a mascot. You can see his "highness" in *Farm Equipment* (no. 14). The term "King of Floors" was an inspiration for Bell's "Floor Folk." (no. 58, p.168)

Paul Klee, Woman's Udder: Referring to the book "The Diaries of Paul Klee, 1898–1918," in which Paul Klee mentions that, as a child, he imagined female genitalia to resemble a cow's udder. (no 20, 96)

Secret Sid Dickens: The title of a 2003 piece (p. 264) referring to a commercial tile–maker in Vancouver, BC. that has employed some of Bell's artist friends over the years. "This is not really a comment on Sid, I do not know him," Bell told me via text message, "I had scribbled his name down as a job possiblity I think, and the paper scrap ended up in the piece. Also, I was working 'assembly line' style, creating a lot of pieces at once, and was thinking of myself as a *Secret Sid Dickens*, a creator of artisan tiles made of paint and carboard."

N.Y.S.S.: Stands for New York Solo Show. (no. 94, 95)

This Polish woman intends to visit 60 hotels in as many days: Appearing in *Bell's Trad*, 2005 (no. 2), this seems to be some sort of "non–joke" created by Bell. This "non–joke" could be cross referenced with a similar one in *Trad Scorn Used Furn* (no. 108) that states: "I know a Polish woman who plans to attend 65 important meetings in as many days."

Tim Ho–ton: A riff on "Tim Hortons," the name of a popular Canadian coffee chain named after a famous hockey player. (no. 56, 46)

Trad: Bell–speak for "traditional." (no. 22, 23, 108)

Trendoid: Bell–speak for one who is trendy, eg: "Did you see that door–to–door salesman, he's such a *Trendoid.*" (no. 109)

MODURN
INFORMALISM
BALSAM ADHESIVES
IS :
LOCAL
I'M NOT FROM AROUND HERE (DON'T GET UP)

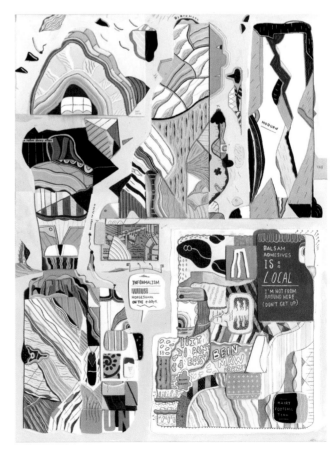

DRAWINGS

ARRANGED BY
AHT SHEW

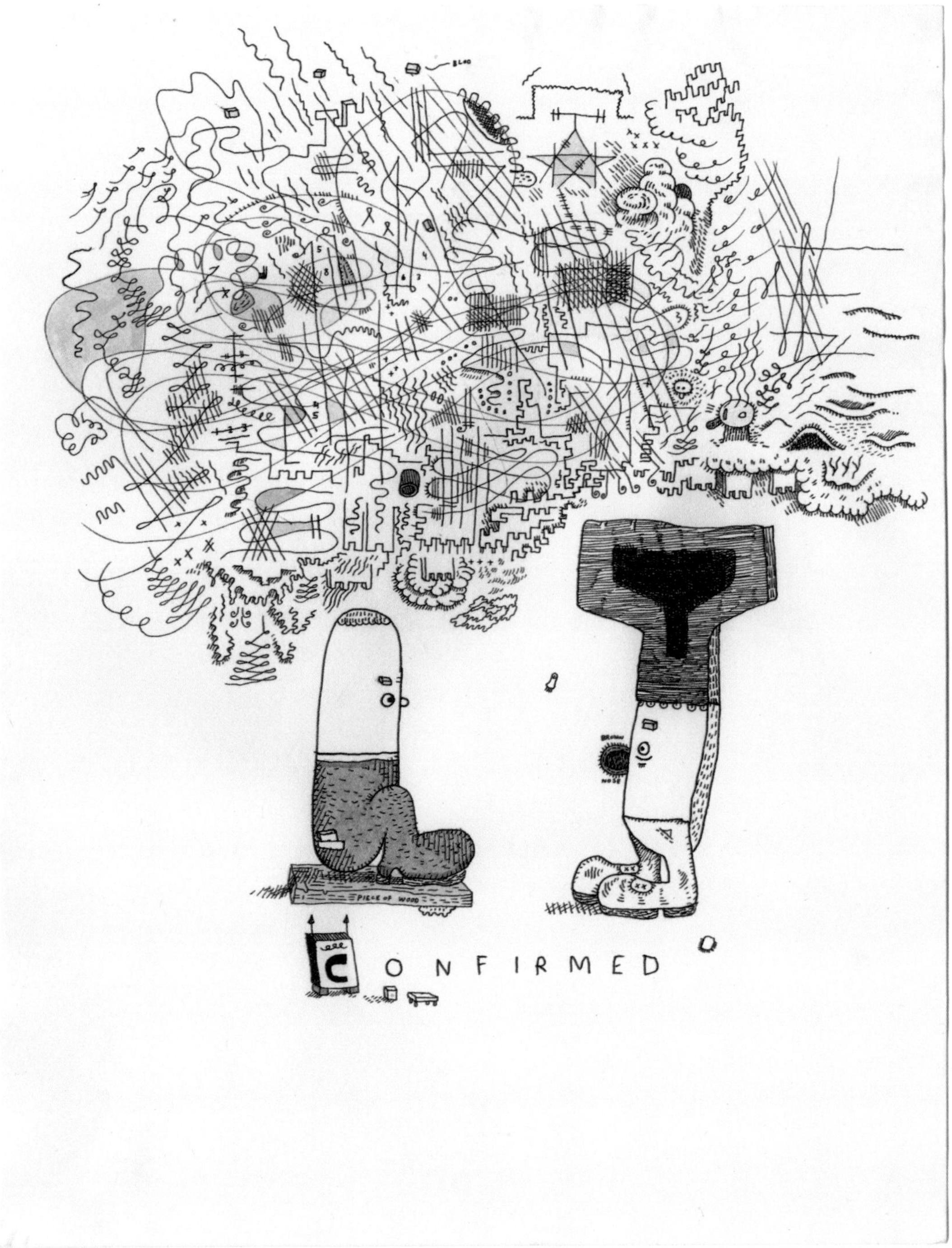
BROWN
NOSE
PIECE OF WOOD
CONFIRMED

86. *Confirmed,* 2005
Ink and watercolour on paper, 11–½ x 9 in.

GNEW SHEW

THESE FIRST DRAWINGS ARE FOR AN EXHIBITION THAT HASN'T HAPPENED

POSSIBLE TITLES FOR THE SHEW:

- ☐ THE EXHIBITION OF THE CHUNKY FLOORS
- ☐ I AM NOT A MUSEUM
- ☐ BEER ELEVATOR III
- ☐ GNEW SHEW

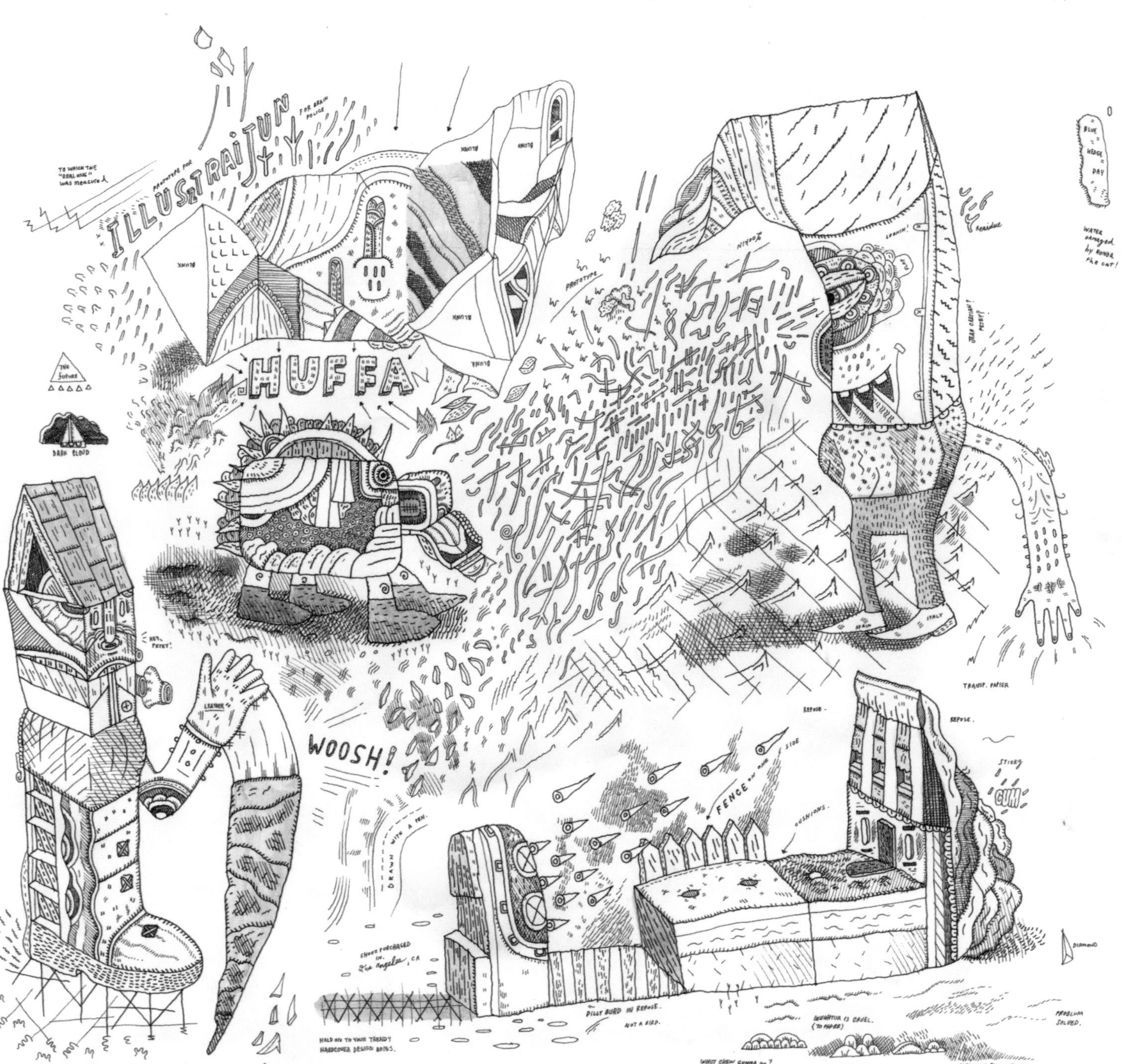
ILLUSZTRAIJUN
HUFFA
WOOSH!
GUM

87. Prototype For *Illusztraijun For Brain Police,* 2007
Ink on paper, 14 x 17 in.

88. *Trippah!,* 2008
Ink and watercolour on paper, 12 x 9 in.

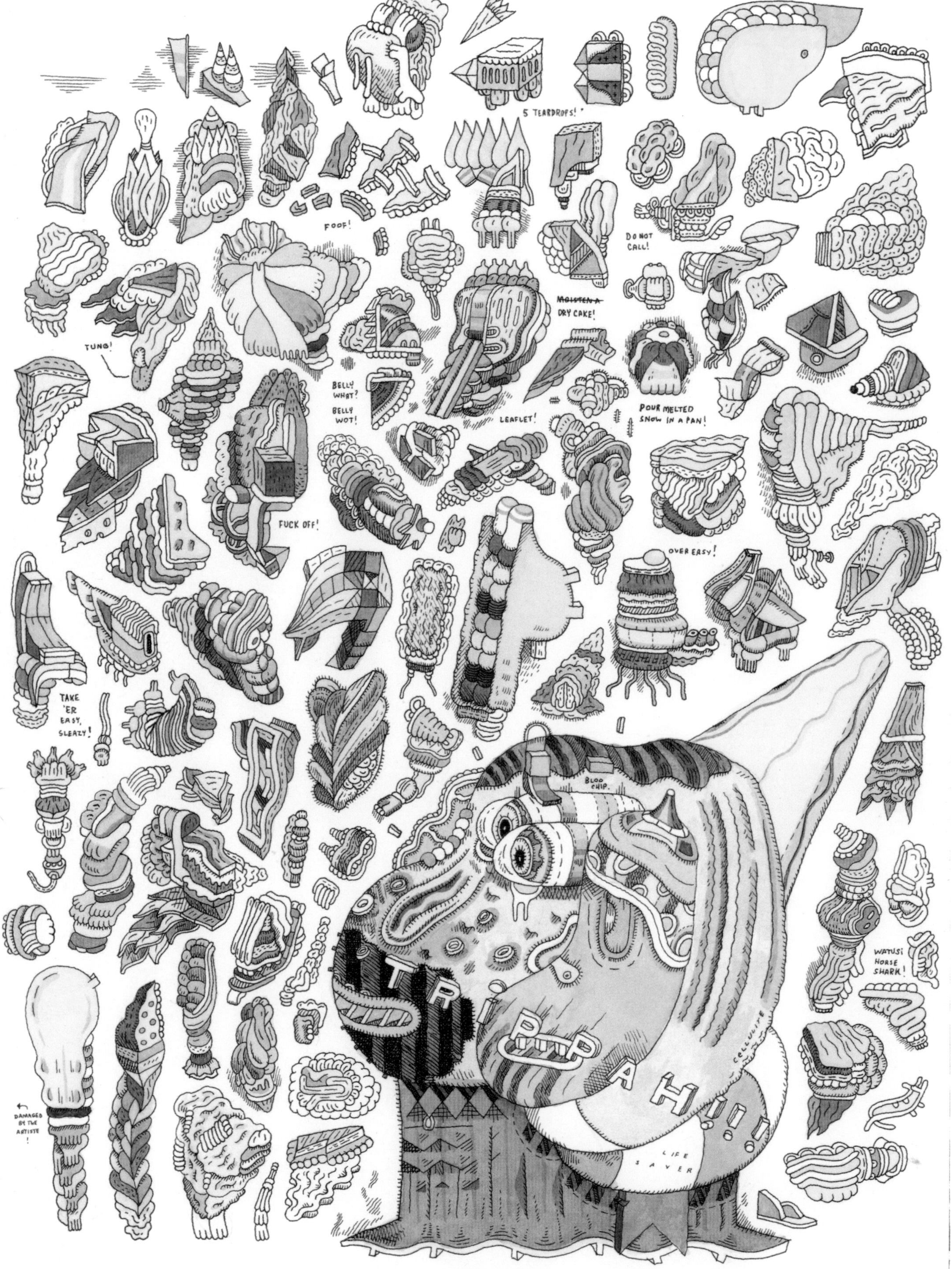
5 TEARDROPS!
FOOF!
DO NOT CALL!
MOISTEN A DRY CAKE!
TUNG!
BELLY WHAT? BELLY WOT!
LEAFLET!
POUR MELTED SNOW IN A PAN!
FUCK OFF!
OVER EASY!
TAKE 'ER EASY, SLEAZY!
BLOO CHIP.
TRIPPAH!!!
CELLULITE
LIFE SAVER
WATUSI HORSE SHARK!
DAMAGED BY THE ARTISTE !

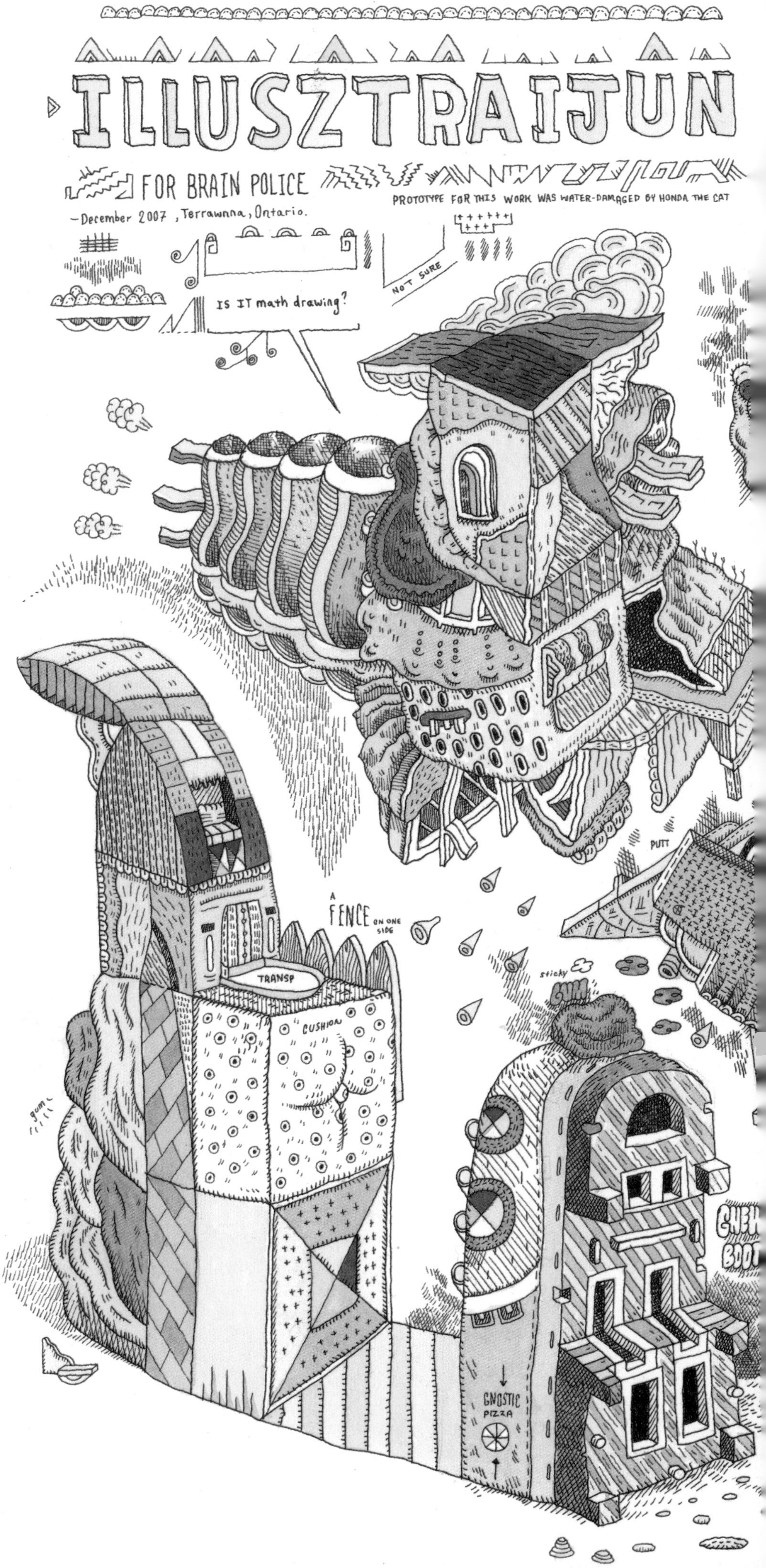
ILLUSZTRAIJUN
FOR BRAIN POLICE
PROTOTYPE FOR THIS WORK WAS WATER-DAMAGED BY HONDA THE CAT
–December 2007, Terrawnna, Ontario.
NOT SURE
IS IT math drawing?
PUTT
A FENCE ON ONE SIDE
TRANSP
sticky
CUSHION
gum
GNOSTIC PIZZA

89. *Illusztraijun For Brain Police,* 2008
Ink and watercolour on paper
12–⅛ x 16–⅛ in.

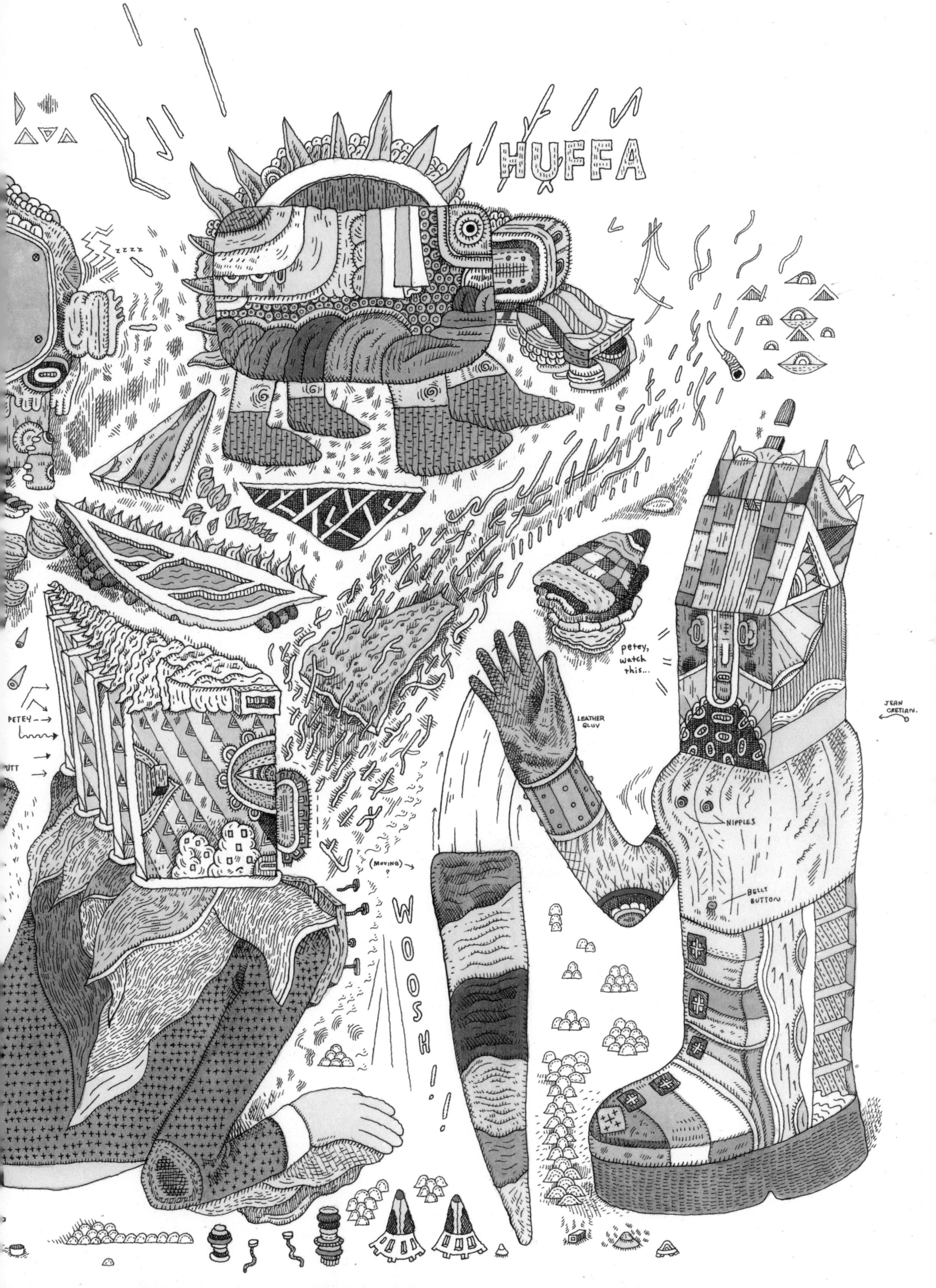

HUFFA
zzzz
PETEY
UTT
petey, watch this...
LEATHER GLUV
JEAN CRETIAN.
NIPPLES
BELLY BUTTON
(MOVING) ?
WOOSH!

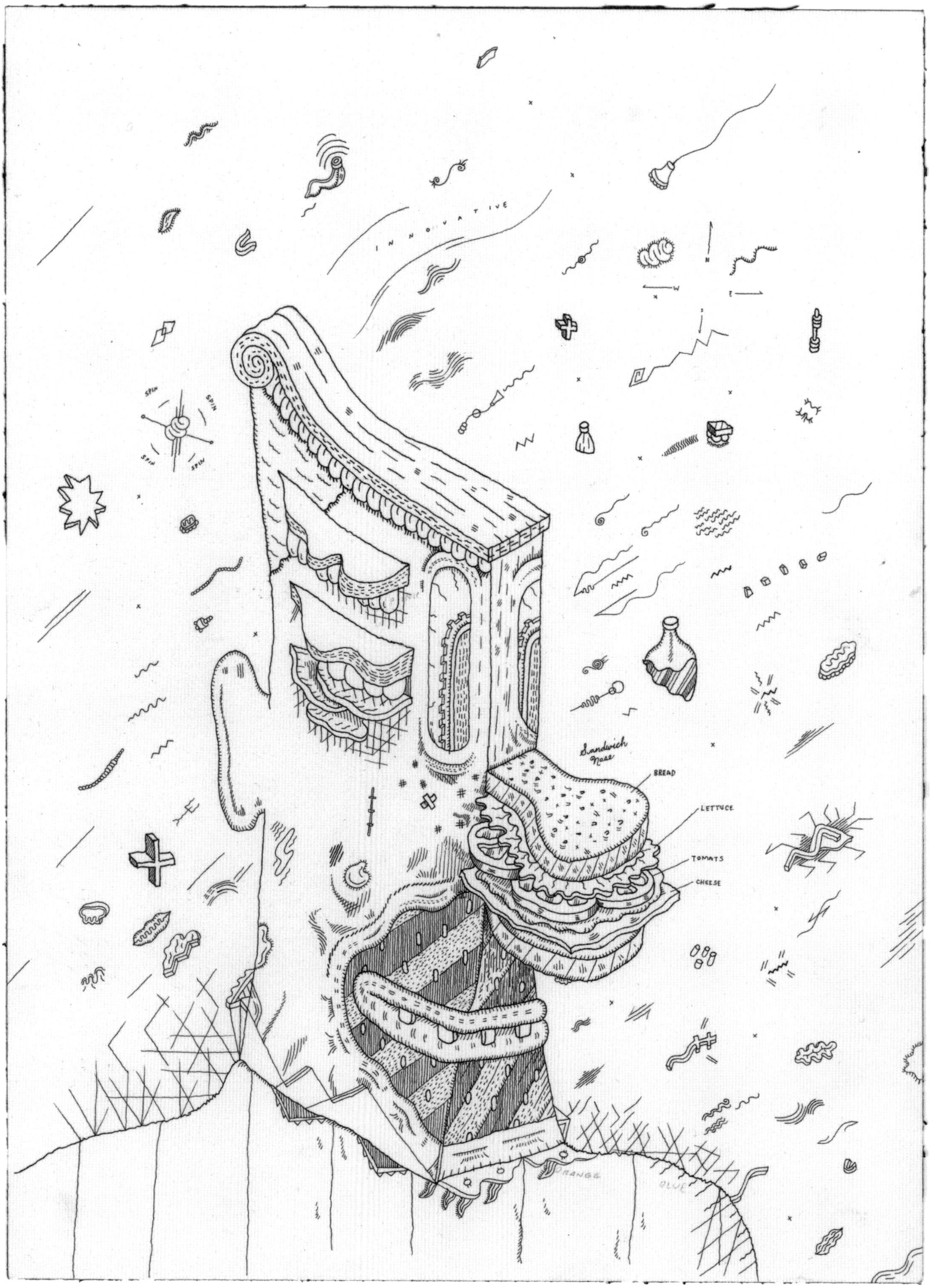
INNOVATIVE
SPIN
SPIN
SPIN
SPIN
N
W
E
S
Sandwich Nose
BREAD
LETTUCE
TOMATO
CHEESE
ORANGE
BLUE

90. *Innovative Sandwich Nose,* 2007
Ink on paper, 12 x 9 in.

91. *Hi, It's Me Again,* 2008
Ink and watercolour on paper, 12 x 9 in.

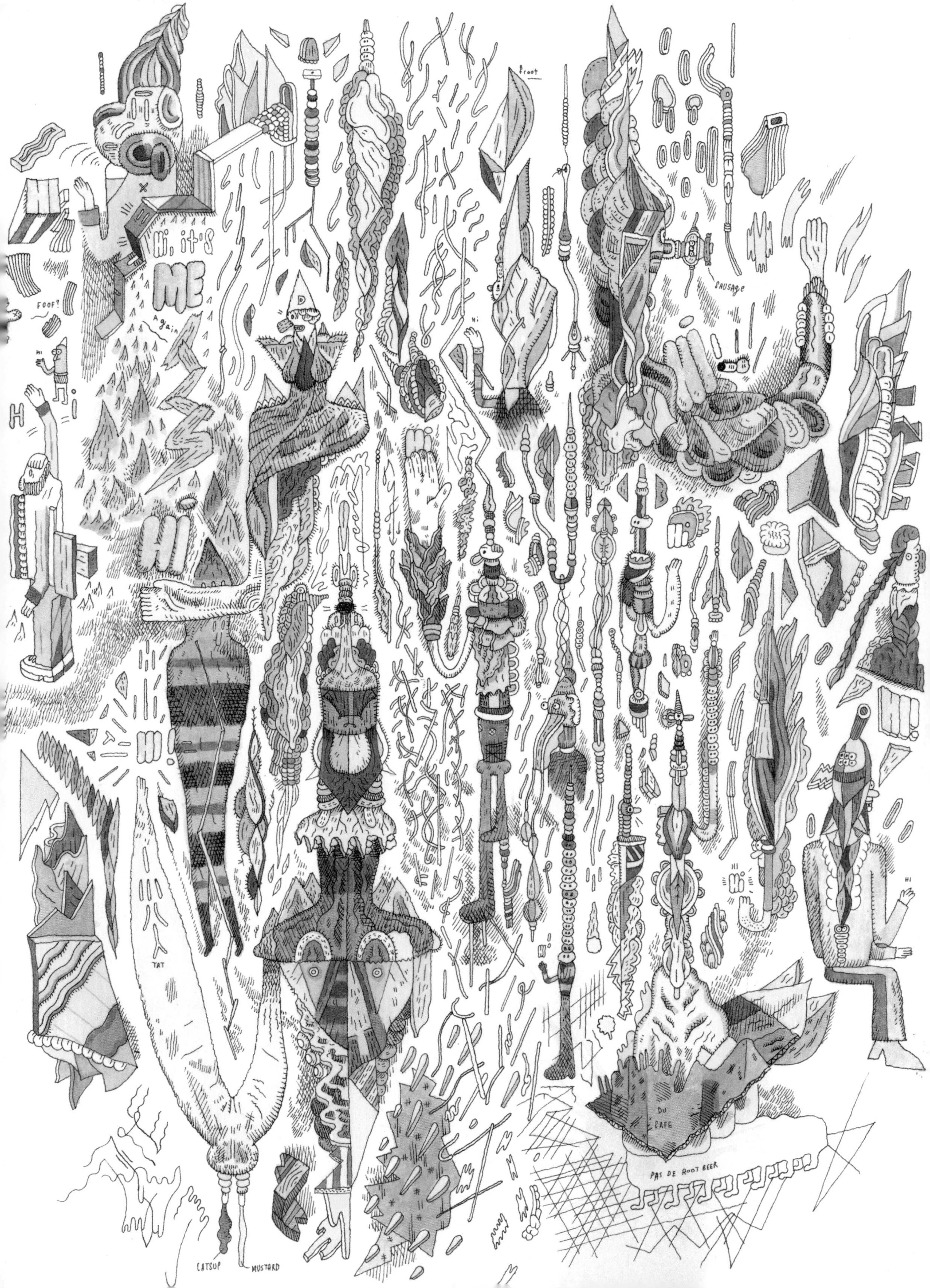
Hi, it's
ME
again
FOOF?
froot
SAUSAGE
HI
TAT
DU
CAFE
PAS DE ROOT BEER
CATSUP
MUSTARD

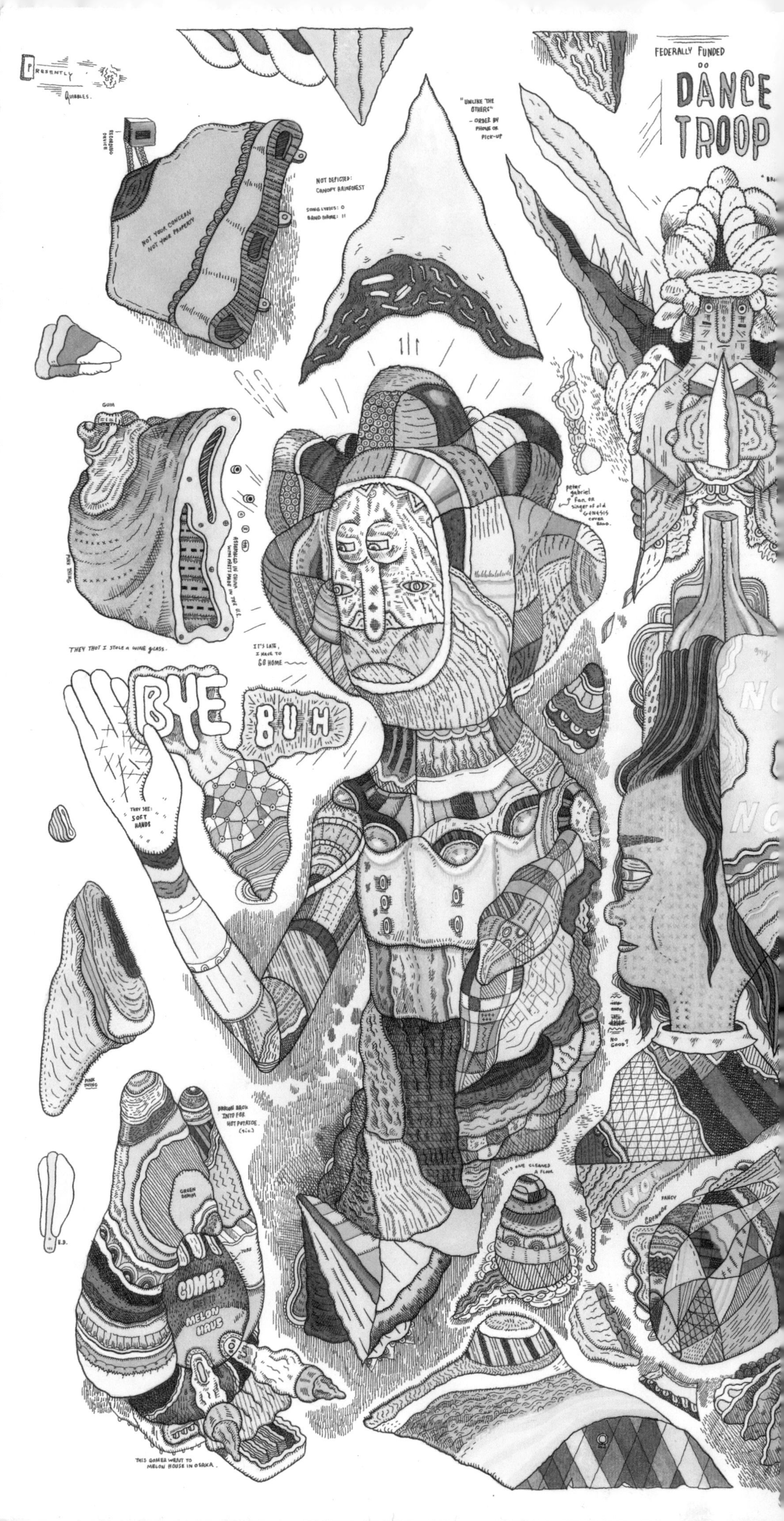
PRESENTLY
QUIBBLES.
FEDERALLY FUNDED
DANCE TROOP
NOT DEPICTED: CANOPY RAINFOREST
"UNLIKE THE OTHERS" - ORDER BY PHONE OR PICK-UP
NOT YOUR CONCERN NOT YOUR PROPERTY
GUM
ASSEMBLED IN CHINA WITH PARTS MADE IN THE U.S.
PINK THING
peter gabriel fan, or singer of old GENESIS cover band.
THEY THOT I STOLE A WINE GLASS.
IT'S LATE, I HAVE TO GO HOME
BYE
BUH
THEY SEE: SOFT HANDS
PINK THING
GOMER
MELON HAUS
THIS GOMER WENT TO MELON HOUSE IN OSAKA.
NO GOOD?
FANCY

92. *Federally Funded Dance Troop/Dog Shit Artist Residency,* 2007
Mixed media on paper, 22 x 30 in.

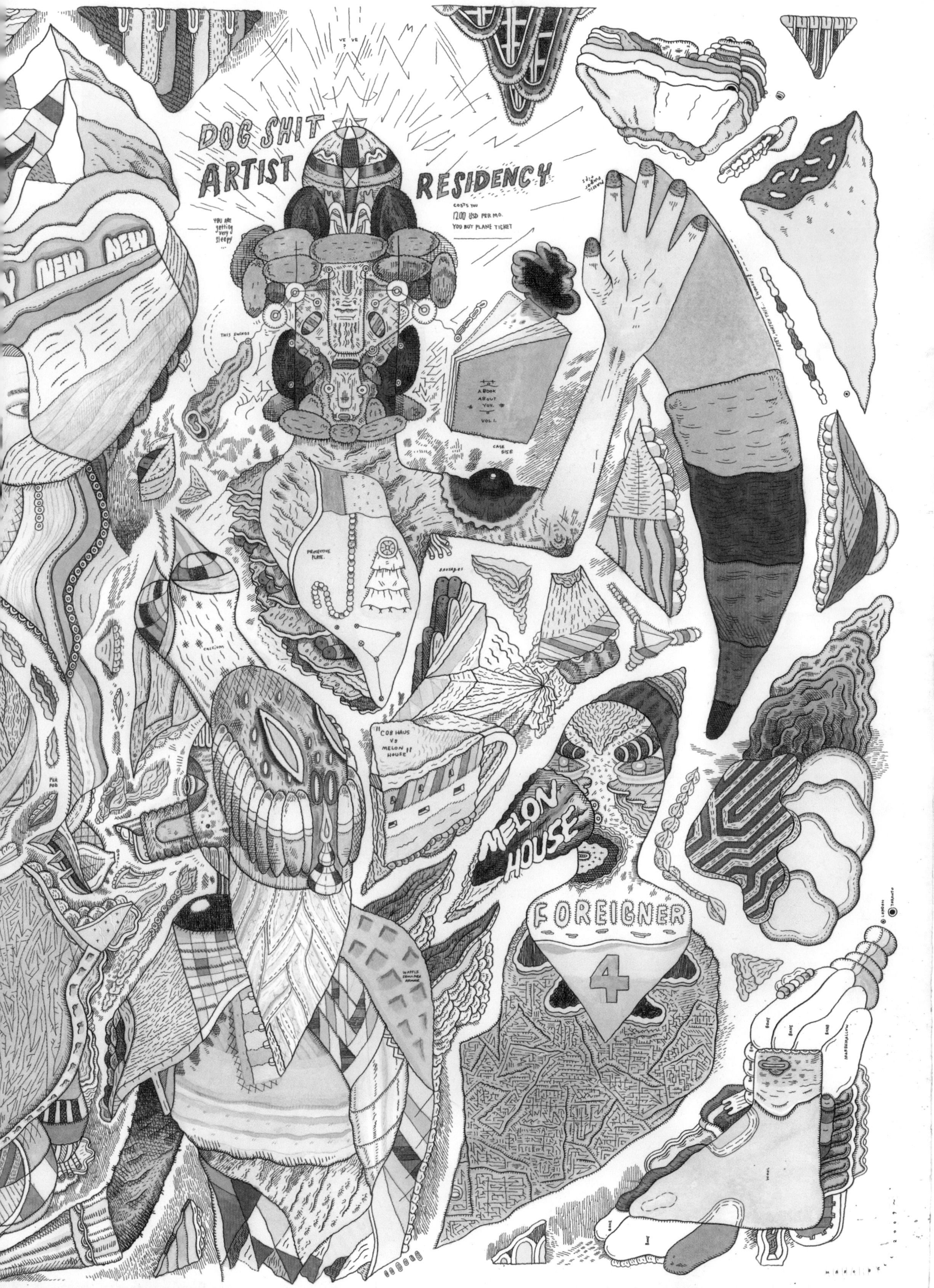

DOG SHIT
ARTIST
RESIDENCY
COSTS YOU
1200 USD PER MO.
YOU BUY PLANE TICKET
YOU ARE getting very sleepy ...
NEW NEW
A BOOK ABOUT YOU. VOL 1.
CASE SIZE
"COB HAUS VS MELON HOUSE"
MELON HOUSE
FOREIGNER
4
BONE
BONE
BONE
MARSHMALLOW

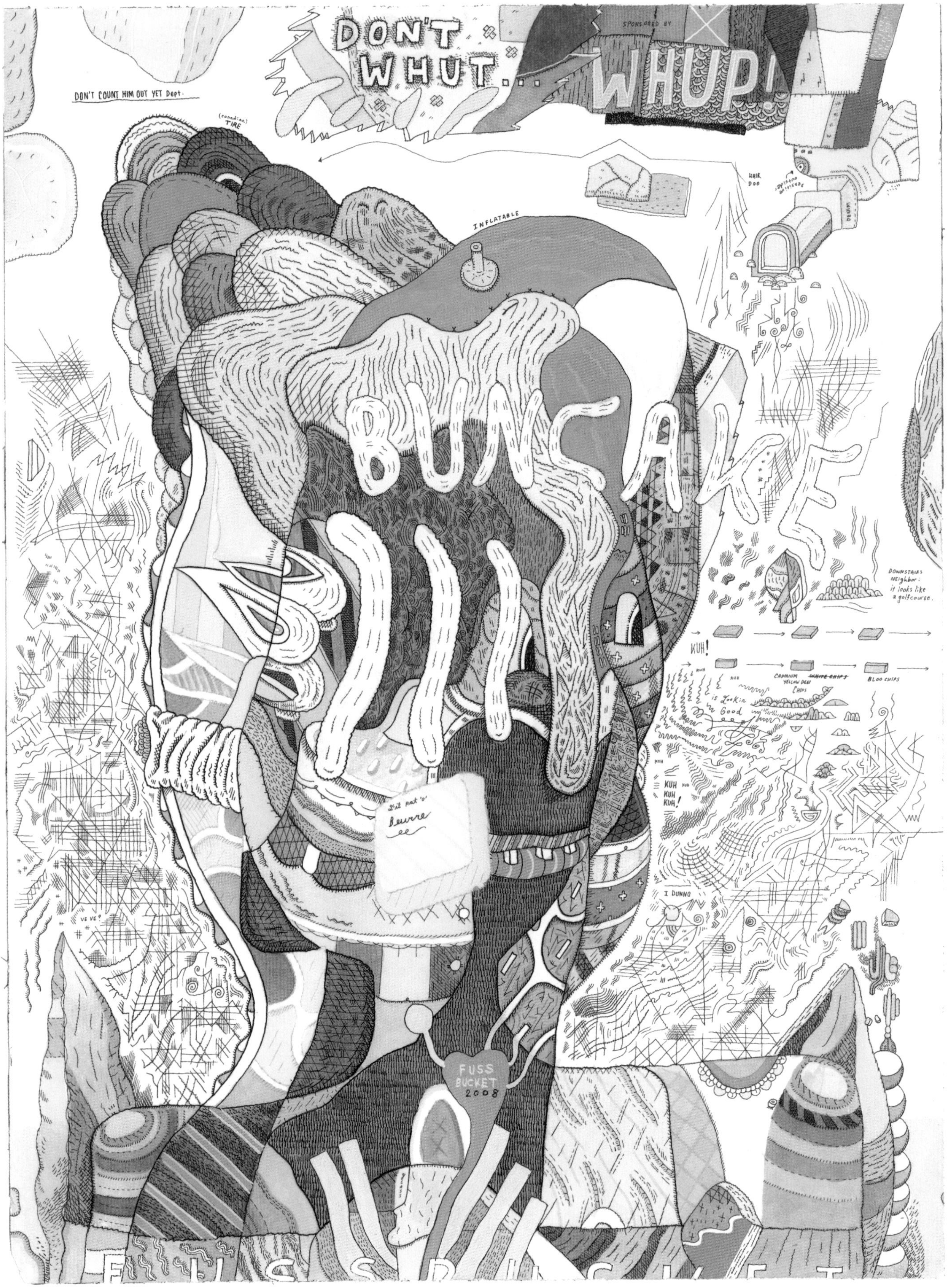
DON'T WHUT...
SPONSORED BY
WHUP!
DON'T COUNT HIM OUT YET Dept.
(canadian) TIRE
INFLATABLE
HAIR DOO
BUNCAKE
DOWNSTAIRS NEIGHBOR: it looks like a golfcourse.
KUH!
CADMIUM YELLOW DEW CHIPS
BLOO CHIPS
is Lookin Good
KUH KUH KUH!
I DUNNO
Lil pat 'o' Beurre
FUSS BUCKET 2008

93. *Buncake Is Lookin' Good (Don't Count Him Out Yet Dept.)*, 2008
Mixed media on paper, 16–⅛ x 12–⅛ in.

94. *Trunkate, Suffer, Lime, etc...*, 2008
Ink, watercolour and acrylic ink on paper, 24 x 18 in.

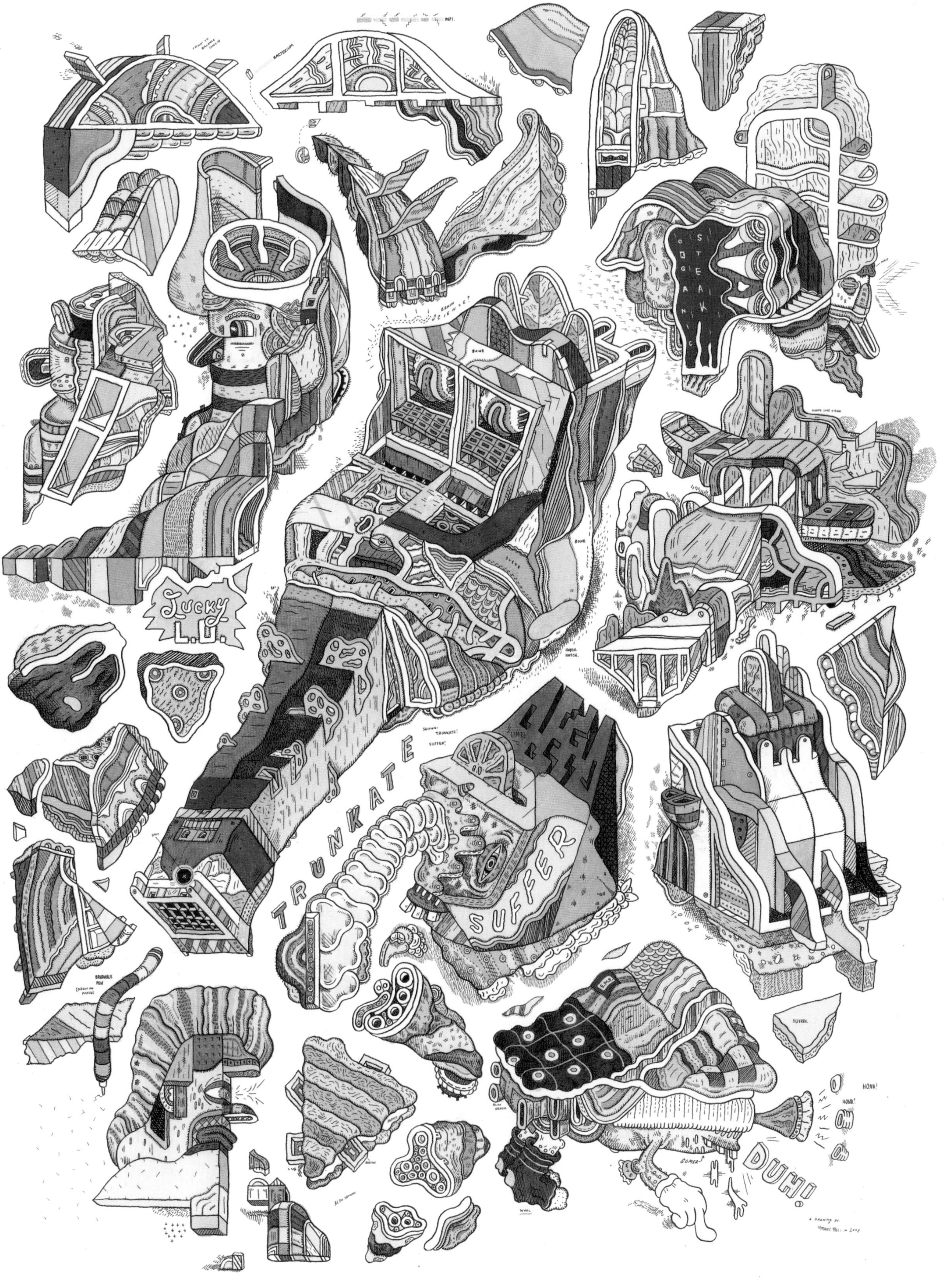
BACTERIUM
DEPT.
BRAIN SCIENCE?
STEAK
BONE
Lucky L.U.
SHOWN:
TRUNKATE!
SUFFER!
LIME!
TRUNKATE
SUFFER
BENDABLE PEN
HONK!
HONK!
DUH!
A DRAWING BY
©MARC BELL IN 2008

EGYPT BUNCAKE

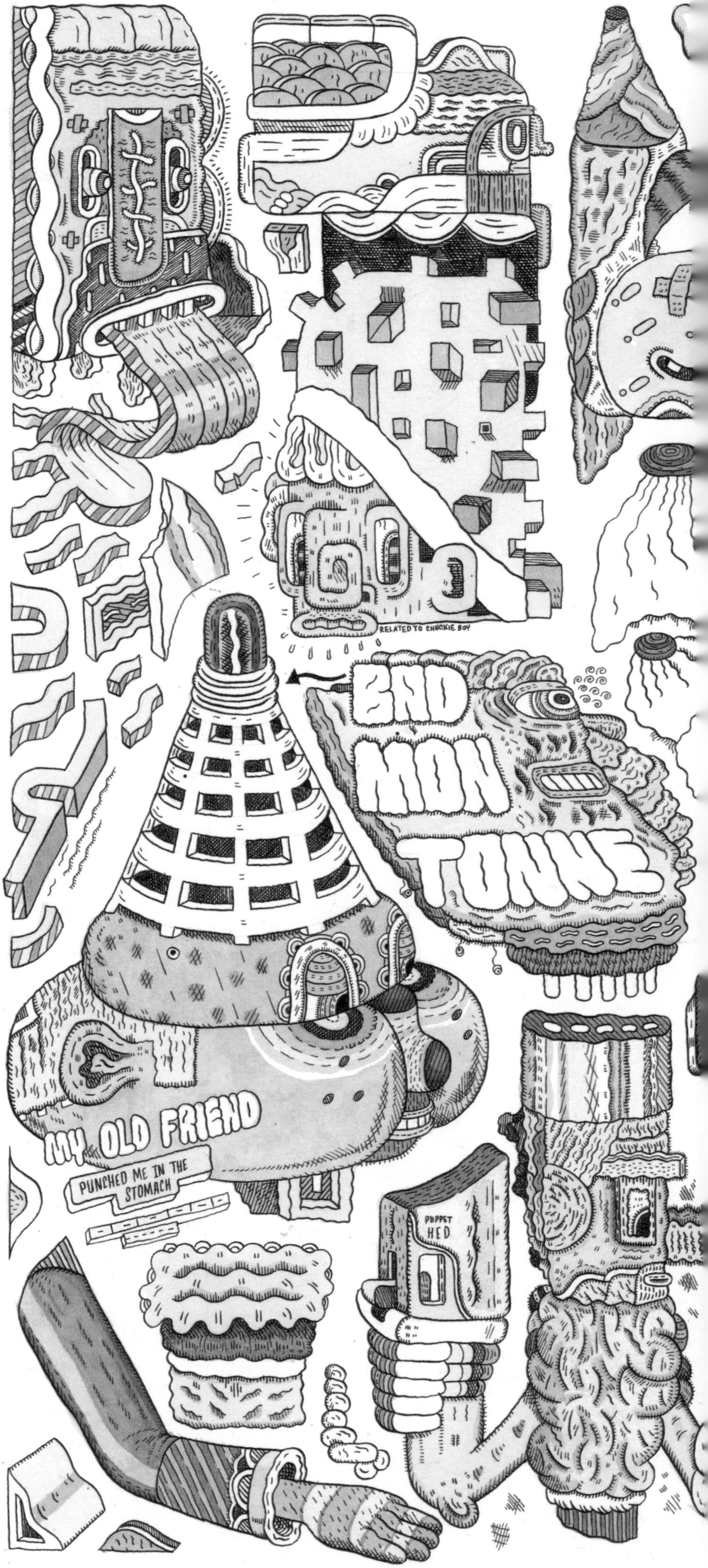

RELATED TO CHUCKIE BOY
END MON TONNE
MY OLD FRIEND
PUNCHED ME IN THE STOMACH
PUPPET HED

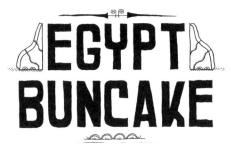

95. *Phew! Comics Ain't Buttah!*, 2006
Ink and watercolour on paper, 16 x 20–⅜ in.

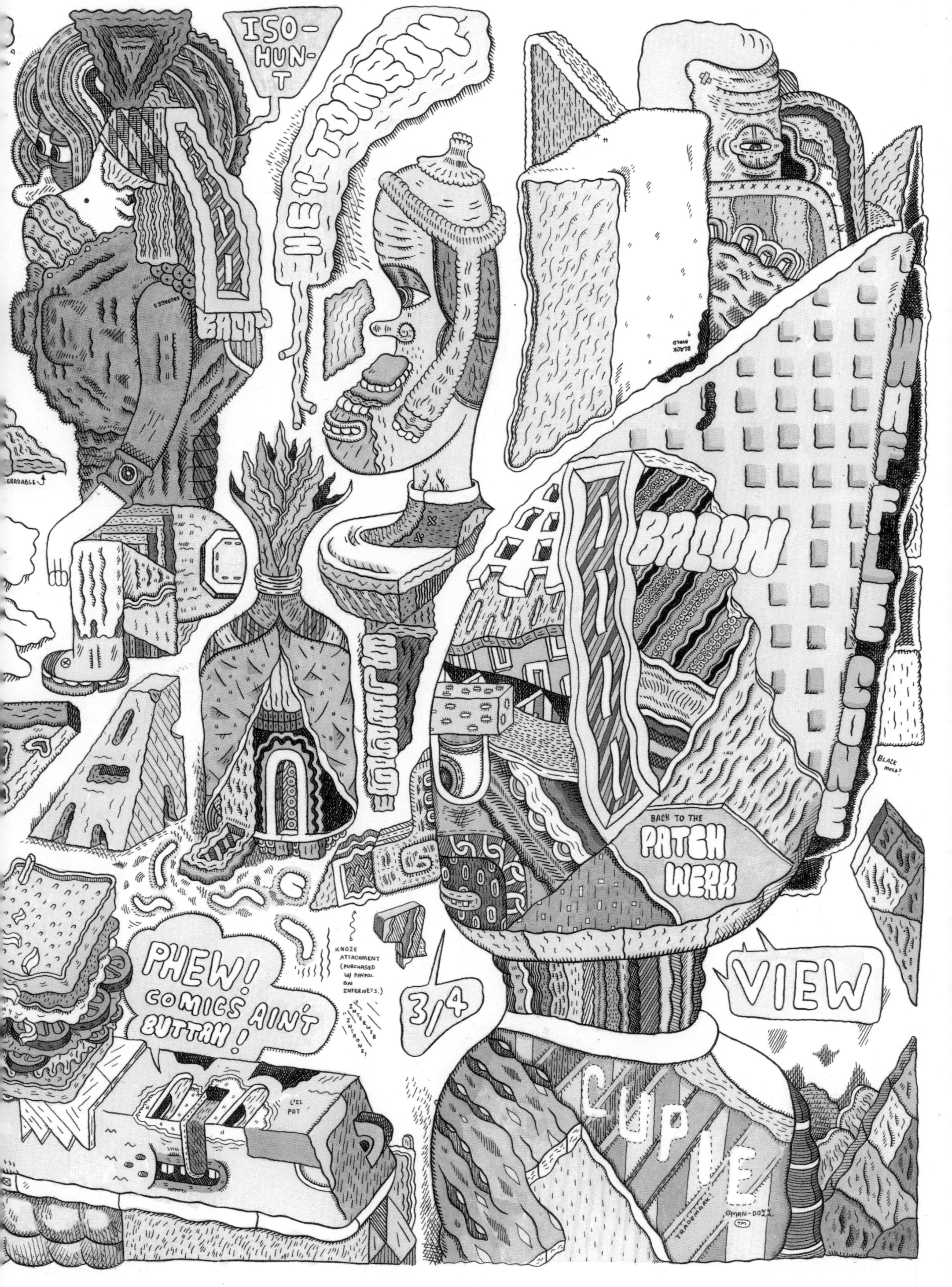

ISO-HUN-T
BACON
WAFFLE CONE
BACK TO THE PATCH WERK
BLACK MOLD?
PHEW! COMICS AIN'T BUTTAH!
KNOZE ATTACHMENT (PURCHASED W/ PAYPAL ON INTERNETS.)
"INTERWEB" "INTRONET"
3/4
VIEW
L'IL PAT
CUPIE
TRADEMARK
GMAN-DOYY (TM)

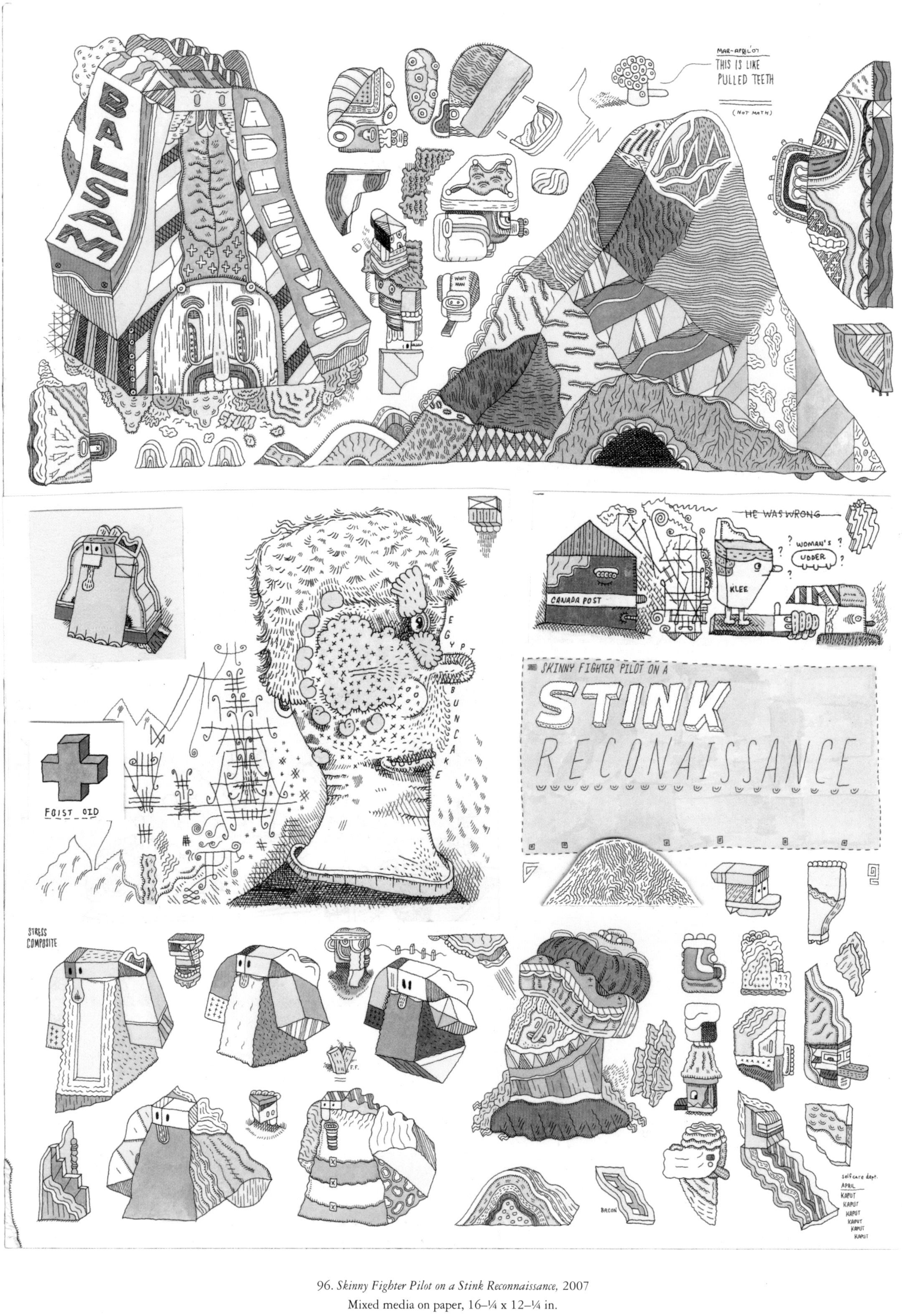

MAR-APRIL '07
THIS IS LIKE PULLED TEETH
(NOT MATH)
BALSAM
ADHESIVES
HE WAS WRONG
WOMAN'S UDDER
KLEE
CANADA POST
EGYPT
BUNCAKE
SKINNY FIGHTER PILOT ON A
STINK
RECONAISSANCE
FOIST OID
STRESS COMPOSITE
F.F.
BACON
selfcare dept.
APRIL
KAPUT
KAPUT
KAPUT
KAPUT
KAPUT
KAPUT

96. *Skinny Fighter Pilot on a Stink Reconnaissance,* 2007
Mixed media on paper, 16–¼ x 12–¼ in.

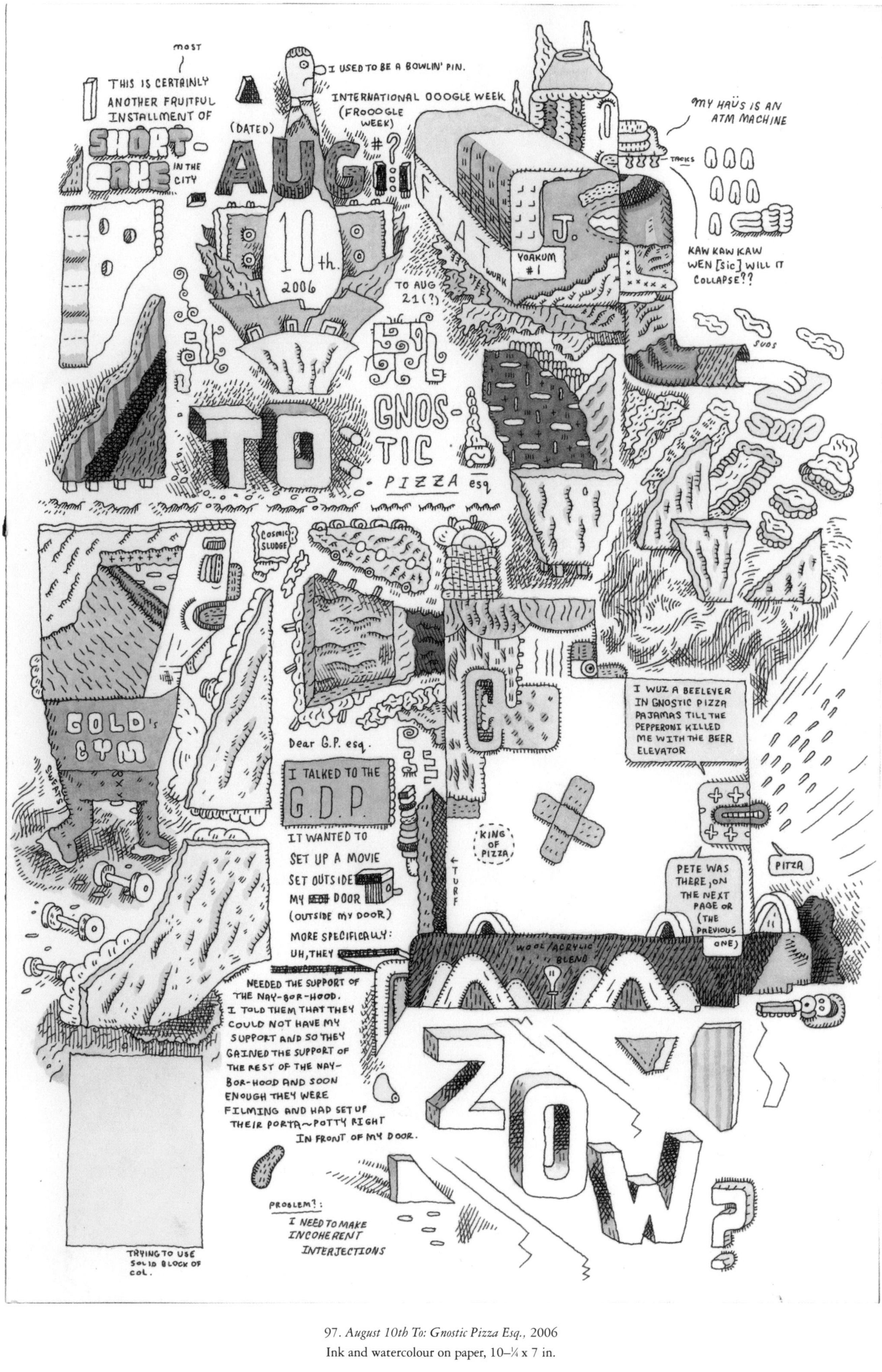

THIS IS CERTAINLY ANOTHER FRUITFUL INSTALLMENT OF
MOST
SHORT-CAKE
IN THE CITY
A
(DATED)
AUG
I USED TO BE A BOWLIN' PIN.
INTERNATIONAL OOOGLE WEEK (FROOOGLE WEEK)
#?
10th.
2006
TO AUG 21(?)
FLAT
J.
YOAKUM #1
WURK
MY HAÜS IS AN ATM MACHINE
TACKS
KAW KAW KAW WEN [sic] WILL IT COLLAPSE??
SUDS
SOAP
TO
GNOS-TIC
PIZZA esq
COSMIC SLUDGE
GOLD's GYM
SWEATS
Dear G.P. esq.
I TALKED TO THE G.D.P.
IT WANTED TO SET UP A MOVIE SET OUTSIDE MY DOOR (OUTSIDE MY DOOR) MORE SPECIFICALLY: UH, THEY
NEEDED THE SUPPORT OF THE NAY-BOR-HOOD. I TOLD THEM THAT THEY COULD NOT HAVE MY SUPPORT AND SO THEY GAINED THE SUPPORT OF THE REST OF THE NAY-BOR-HOOD AND SOON ENOUGH THEY WERE FILMING AND HAD SET UP THEIR PORTA~POTTY RIGHT IN FRONT OF MY DOOR.
KING OF PIZZA
TURF
I WUZ A BEELEVER IN GNOSTIC PIZZA PAJAMAS TILL THE PEPPERONI KILLED ME WITH THE BEER ELEVATOR
PETE WAS THERE, ON THE NEXT PAGE OR (THE PREVIOUS ONE)
PITZA
WOOL/ACRYLIC BLEND
ZOW?
PROBLEM?: I NEED TO MAKE INCOHERENT INTERJECTIONS
TRYING TO USE SOLID BLOCK OF COL.

97. *August 10th To: Gnostic Pizza Esq.*, 2006
Ink and watercolour on paper, 10–¼ x 7 in.

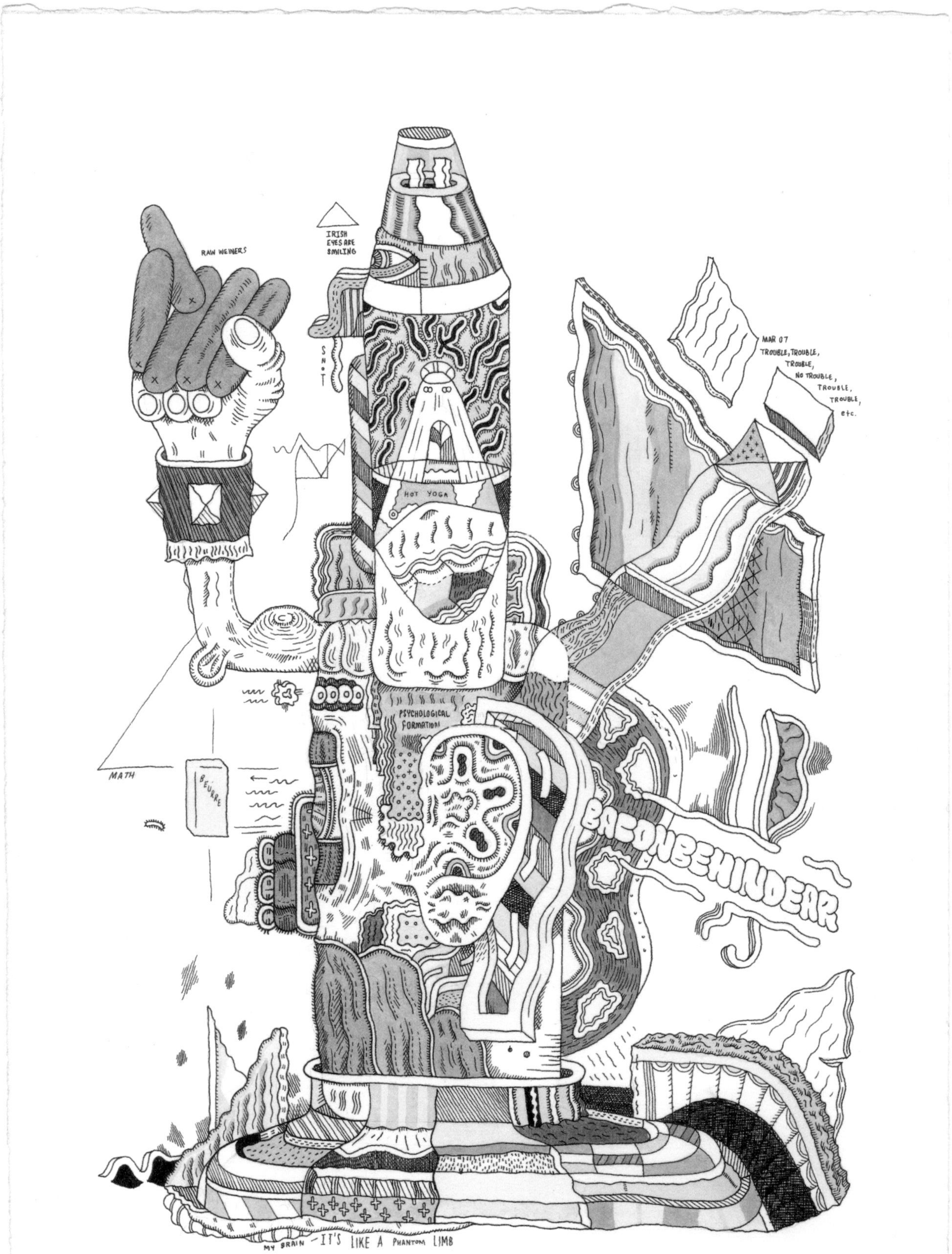
RAW WEINERS
IRISH EYES ARE SMILING
SNOT
MAR 07
TROUBLE, TROUBLE,
TROUBLE,
NO TROUBLE,
TROUBLE,
TROUBLE,
etc.
HOT YOGA
PSYCHOLOGICAL FORMATION
MATH
BEURRE
BACONBEHINDEAR
MY BRAIN —IT'S LIKE A PHANTOM LIMB

98. *Baconbehindear (Psychological Formation),* 2006
Ink and watercolour on paper, 13 x 9–½ in.

99. *My Inner Foot Says (The Fundamentals Are Out Of Wack),* 2007
Mixed media on paper, 30–⅛ x 22–½ in.
(**also see:** details on p. 267. 268)

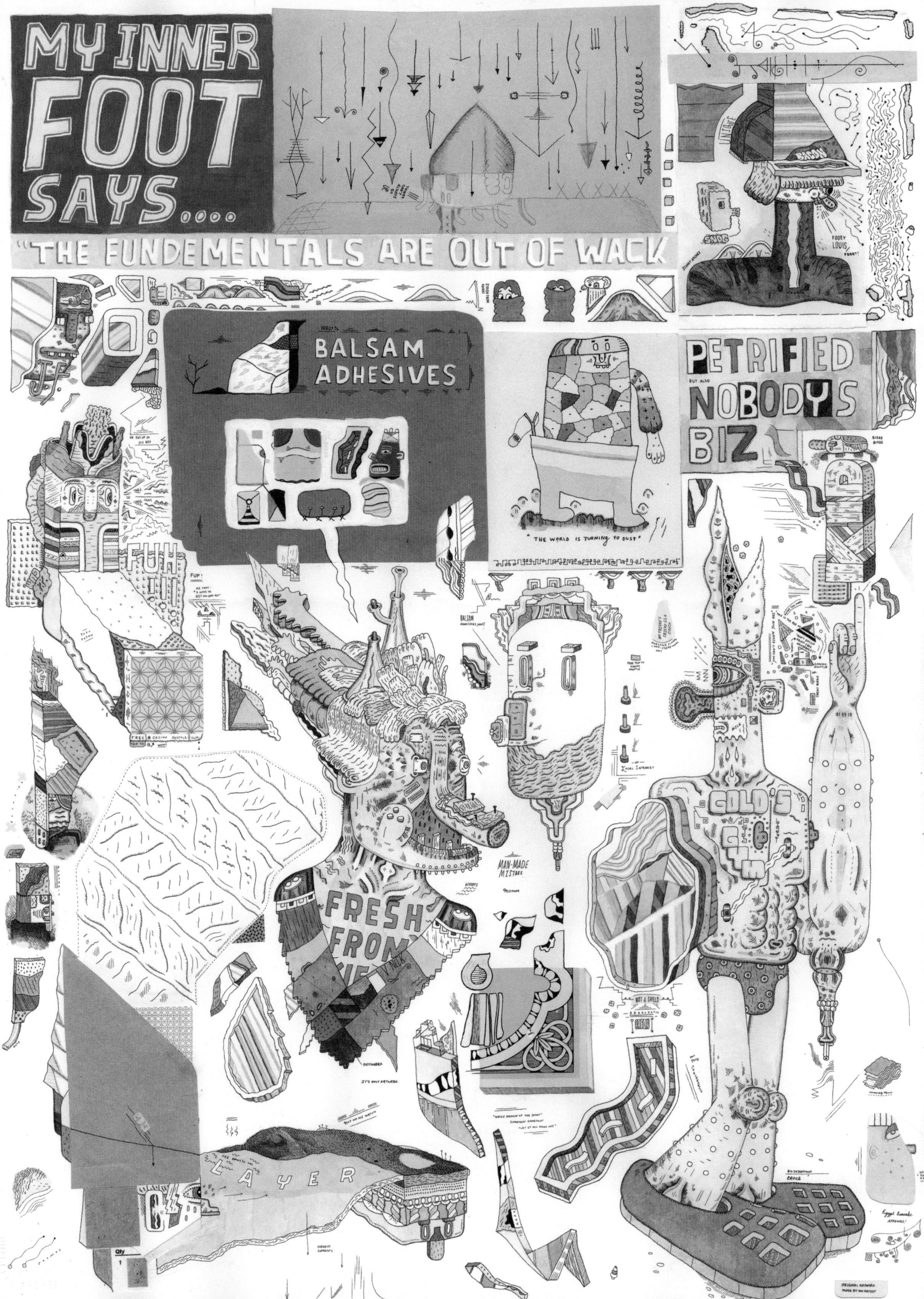
MY INNER FOOT SAYS....
"THE FUNDEMENTALS ARE OUT OF WACK
BALSAM ADHESIVES
PETRIFIED
BUT ALSO
NOBODYS BIZ
"THE WORLD IS TURNING TO DUST"
SNOG
FOOEY LOUIS
FUH
FRESH FROM
MAN-MADE MISTAKE
GOLD'S GYM
LOCAL INTEREST
NOT A SHIELD
LAYER
CROCS
IT'S ONLY ARTWORK
ORIGINAL ARTWORK MADE BY AN ARTIST

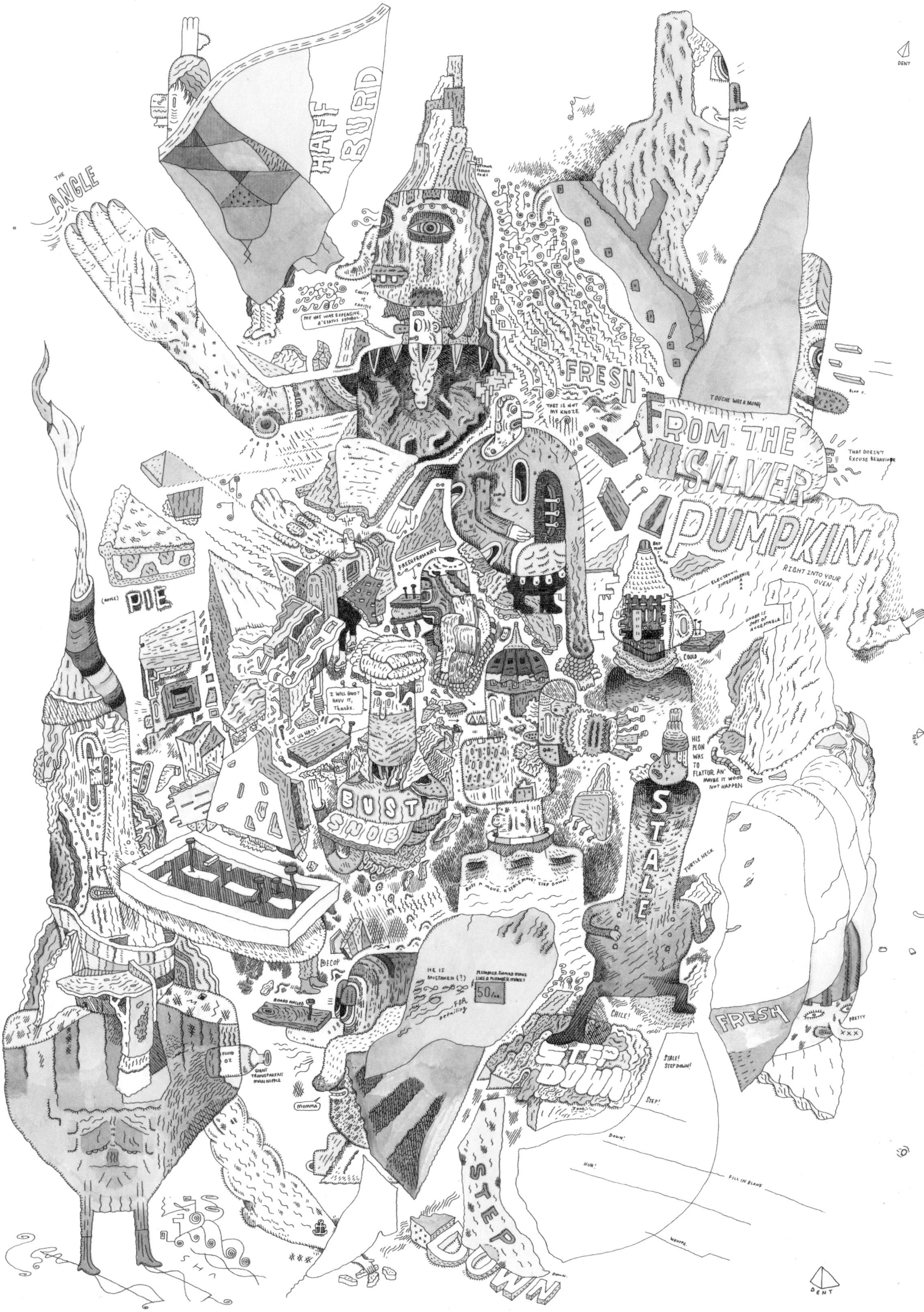

HAFF BURD
THE ANGLE
MY HAT WAS EXPENSIVE, A STATUS SYMBOL
FRESH
THAT IS NOT MY KNOZE
TOUCHE WAS A MONK
FROM THE SILVER PUMPKIN
THAT DOESN'T EXCUSE BEHAVIOR
RIGHT INTO YOUR OVEN.
(APPLE) PIE
ELECTRONIC INTERFERENCE
I WILL SNOT HAVV IT, Thanks.
BUST SNOB
HIS PLON WAS TO FLATTUR AN' MAYBE IT WOOD NOT HAPPEN
STALE
TURTLE NECK
BUST A MOVE, A STALE MOVE! STEP DOWN!
HE IS MISTAKEN (?)
PLUMBER SHOULD MAKE LIKE A PLUMBER MAKES
BOARD NAILED
FRESH
PRETTY
CHILE!
STEP DOWN
STALE! STEP DOWN!
STEP!
GIANT TRANSPARENT MAN NIPPLE
Momma
DOWN!
HUH!
FILL IN BLANK
STEP DOWN
DENT

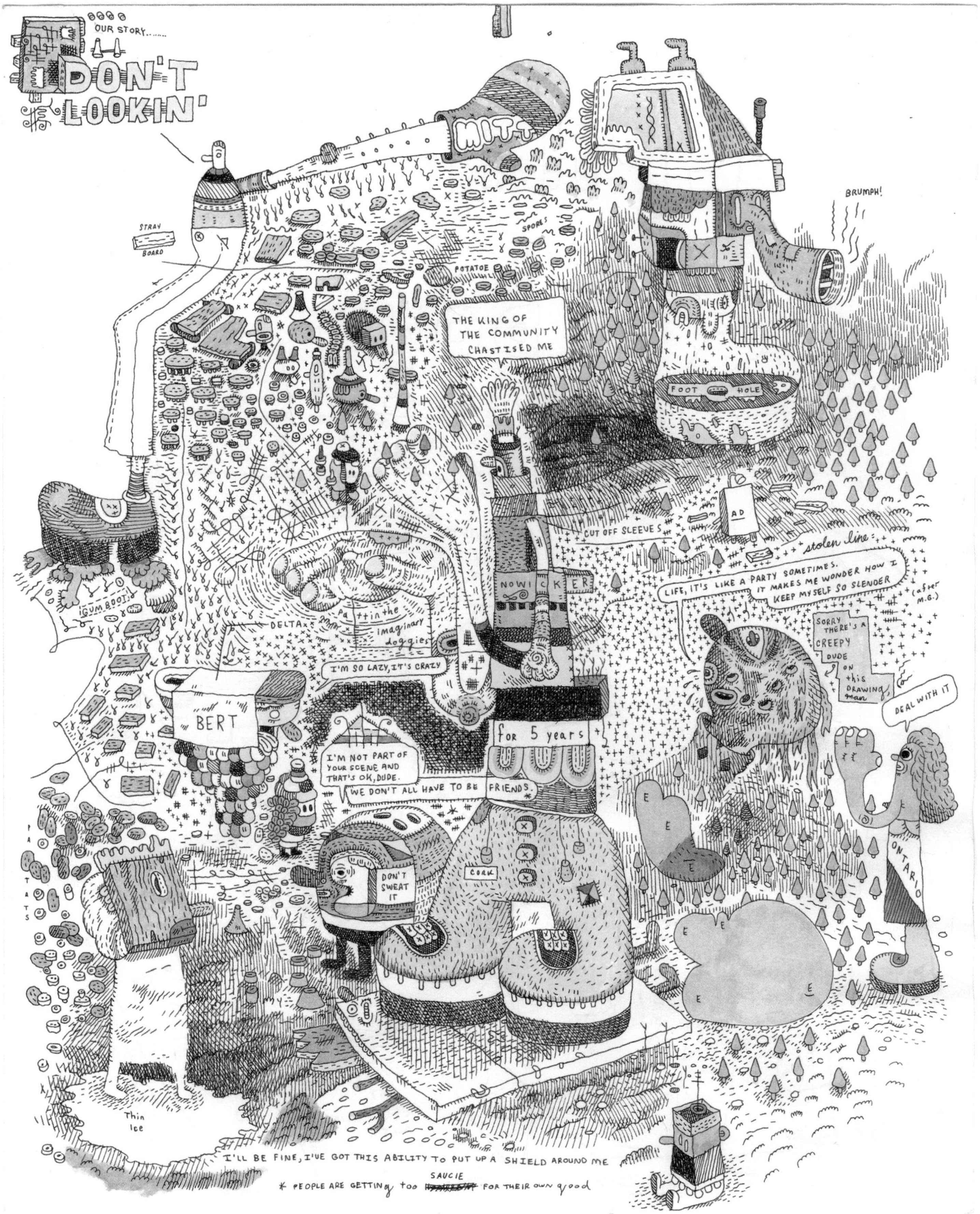
OUR STORY.......
DON'T LOOKIN'
MITT
STRAY BOARD
SPORES
POTATOE
BRUMPH!
THE KING OF THE COMMUNITY CHASTISED ME
FOOT HOLE
AD
CUT OFF SLEEVES
stolen line:
LIFE, IT'S LIKE A PARTY SOMETIMES. IT MAKES ME WONDER HOW I KEEP MYSELF SO SLENDER
(after M.G.)
NOWICKER
GUM BOOT
DELTA
Pattin the imaginary doggies
I'M SO LAZY, IT'S CRAZY
SORRY THERE'S A CREEPY DUDE ON this DRAWING man
DEAL WITH IT
BERT
for 5 years
I'M NOT PART OF YOUR SCENE AND THAT'S OK, DUDE.
WE DON'T ALL HAVE TO BE FRIENDS.
DON'T SWEAT IT
CORK
ONTARIO
Thin Ice
I'LL BE FINE, I'VE GOT THIS ABILITY TO PUT UP A SHIELD AROUND ME
* PEOPLE ARE GETTING too SAUCIE FOR THEIR OWN good

100. *Fresh From The Silver Pumpkin,* 2006
Ink and watercolour on paper, 22–½ x 17–¼ in.

101. *I'll Be Fine, I've Got This Ability To Put A Shield Up Around Me (Don't Lookin'),* 2005
Ink and watecolour on paper, 13–¼ x 11 in.

 PILE OF BACON

By Balsam Adhesives
Former Slegg Employee

5TH DRAFT (CON'T)

CHUNKY FLOORS TOOK MITCH AND CHAUNCEY BOY BY THE HAND AND LED THEM TO A CLEARING IN BLOO BURGER FOREST.

"HERE IT IS, BOYS..", HE SAID.

BEFORE THEM LIE A GREAT PILE OF BACON, MADE OUT OF PLASTIC.

CHUNKY FLOORS LEFT THEM THERE AND THEY NESTLED INTO THE PILE OF BACON FOR THE EVENING.

"I DON'T NEED TO LEARN SPORTS," MITCH WHISPERED TO CHAUNCEY BOY. CHAUNCEY BOY WAS ALREADY ASLEEP.

6TH DRAFT

PONCE HAD A THICK NECK. HE GNEW THE POWER OF GNEPPOTISM AND HE GNEW ~~GEORGE LUCAS~~ HOW TO USE IT.

HE WORE EXPENSIVE WAFFLE SHOULDER ARMOUR (SHOWN) AND A FLOP & KNEE JURKIE (ALSO SHOWN).

~~THINGS WERE GETTING TOO RANDOM FOR HIM IN "DUDE CITY" AND SO HE DECIDED TO TAKE HIS TEAM OUT OF THE BIZNESS.~~

~~HE WAS SUMMONED TO DUDE CITY, YOU BASTARDS~~

~~HE WAS A MERE~~

HE WAS A MEMBER OF THE TEAM ALSO INCLUDING:

- LETTUCE
- NERVOUS ENERGY
- MY BEST FRIEND (COZY SHACK PUDDING)
- CKLOUD DANGLAR
- GET ME OUTTA HERE

THEY DESCENDED UPON MITCH AND CHAUNCEY BOY AND THE PILE OF BACON. MITCH WOKE UP WITH A START.

"I AM THE KING OF SPORTS" HE SAID AND THE GEAR THING ON HIS HEAD BEGAN TO WHIRL AND FIRED UPWARDS STRIKING ~~PONCE'S THICK NECK. PONCE SHRIEKED~~ COZY SHACK PUDDING, AND KNOCKING THE ORANGE GLOO SPOUT FROM HIS HEAD. & GLOO SPILLED ALL OVER MITCH AND THE HALF-ASLEEP CHAUNCEY BOY AND THE PILE OF BACON AND "THE TEAM" DECIDED TO RETREAT AND REGROUP AT GEORGE LUCAS's COTTAGE NEARBY.

AS THE GLOO DRIED ON MITCH AND CHAUNCEY BOY AND THE PILE OF BACON, CHAUNCEY BOY RECOGNIZED THE GRAVITY OF THE SITUATION:

"THIS IS A GOOD THING WE HAVE GOING, IF ONLY WE CAN USE IT TO OUR ADVANTAGE. ALL WE N GNEED IS A COUPLE INTERNS AND A SOLID DATABASE AND "THE TEAM IS DONE FOR. I GNOW THEIR WEAK POINTS AND I GNOW A LOT OF PEOPLE IN THIS BITNESS. WITH THIS GLOO AND THIS PILE OF BACON WE WILL BE ON TOP ONCE AGAIN. ~~I AM TRAD.~~ WE ARE TRAD. ~~TOO~~ 100 CUZZINS."

"YOU'VE GOT A COOL STRATEGY," MITCH CHIMED IN, "LET'S DO IT!"

Above: 5th and 6th drafts of the story "Pile Of Bacon." **This Page:** The 7th draft of the story. Several other "drafts" appear throughout the following group of drawings.

Mitch woke up under the floorboards as usual. It was something his friend Chunky Floors himself had taught him, to sleep down there. Chunky Floors had been raised by the Floor Folk and that's where they'd live and sleep. That's their whole life down there under those boards. Chunky'd mentioned he'd learned a lot of bad from them but sleeping under the floor was something that he'd learned that was a good thing. Mitch loved this one story, no matter how many times he had heard it from him, a positive memory that Chunky Floors shared with him from time to time from his mostly dark days with the Floor Folk. Mitch himself had always found it very comfortable down there under the floor and he'd slept well enough last night. Farmer Marco was already up, looking at the local agricultural message boards.

"Jerry is selling his wild bologna processor," Marco said. He was drinking his morning coffee substitute. Mitch was in the kitchen, going through the cupboards. He was thinking about the dream he had just had. In the dream he was married to a lady from the city and they had a small child, a little girl named Merle. They were going to a friend's house and instead of bringing Merle with them, they let her go out on her own to drive her small pink motorbike around the city. He wondered if she would join other children on their motorbikes? Children whose parents were also going out to socialize? Everybody in the dream was very relaxed about all of this. Mitch and his wife, the lady from the city, became very drunk at their party, and their pet dog, a sober mutt named Montreal, drove them home that night.

"Chickens won't eat bacon," Mitch said. He was making a bacon sandwich. "We need some more feed. It's too bad we can't get those real good deals on feed like those fancy rich farmers. Like Slegg. Jeez Louizes, those chickens eat better than us!"

"It's pure Gneppotism," said Marco, "that's how it works." Marco was on to the daily paper now, *The Daily Dirt*, looking at the gossip column.

"Well, I like it here on the farm, Farmer Marco, but I also understand how things are a little slow around here right now. I is just a wee worried that I might have to quit you and go work at Slegg. I don't like the idea none at all, of course, but sometimes I think it'd be easier!"

"I understand, Mitch," Marco said, putting on his boots, "If you need to work for Slegg, you should go and do it. Slegg is privy to the gnewer ways, he's more efficient now, and you'll be in good hands." He was half–mumbling now, with a frown: "I like to keep things fairly simple but the days of these kinda operations like I run are probably numbered, you gotta expand or yer screwed and all that. You know, the same ol' "cry–me–a–river" story. Now, Mitch, can you meet up with Chauncey Boy for those supplies? I have a few things I have to do around here."

Marco was fumbling around now, looking for something, "I can't fnd my my hat, have you seen it?"

Mitch stepped into Chauncey Boy's office. It smelled like Chauncey Boy. He was to get a loaner on some feed and some other supplies for the farm from Chauncey. Chunky Floors was there too, which was a bit of a surprise. Mitch thought that Chunky was in Berlin.

"I slept like a dream, Chunky," Mitch said while he filled out the necessary loan forms. Chauncey Boy's office was near the Bloo Burger forest, only about a 10 minute walk from the offices of Slegg's new poultry farm. Chauncey was listening to reggae music.

"You know, it was a dark time, being raised by the Floor Folk. They are a cruel and disgusting form of life," said Chunky Floors in his usual monotone, " but if I learned anything good from them, I learned that it is very pleasant to sleep under the floorboards of your house if you can make it work for you."

"I love that story, Chunky, it never fails to give me hope," Mitch said as he pocketed the receipt that he would try to remember to give to Farmer Marco later.

"And how is the farm?" Chunky sat on a pile of old flour bags. He was holding a glass of liquid that he had just been drinking from. It looked like he was sort of propping himself up there on those bags.

"Ooh, it's ok, you know. Times are tough with Slegg around here now, I don't know how much longer Marco can do it this way," Mitch said.

"Mitch, my friend, you should really think about Slegg, they have benefits you know. Slegg would hire you in a second!" Chauncey Boy added, "Sean the Humpback Whale Poodlesnake is working there now. Marco would understand."

It was almost spring. Farmer Marco was watching a dog on his back lawn. The dog was sniffing around something or other. Dogs remember smells for later, thought Marco, they lie down at home by the fireplace and they think of those smells they were smelling earlier in the day. Yes they do. And spring is the morning. And summer is the afternoon. Fall is the early evening, and winter is the night. These years are going by like days, he thought to himself as he opened a can of Bubbly Town Blueberry Juice™ and took a long sip.

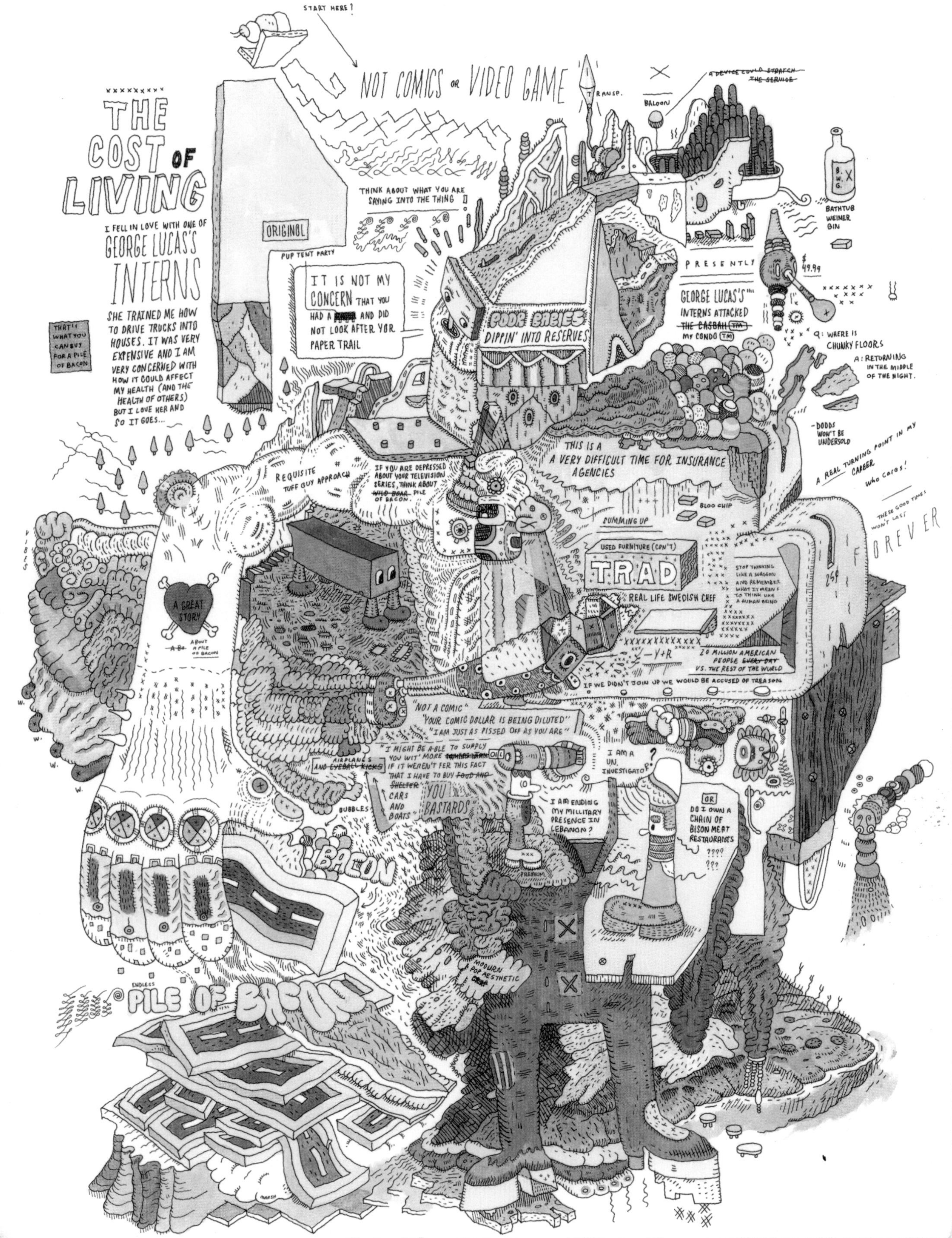
START HERE !
NOT COMICS OR VIDEO GAME
TRANSP.
BALOON
THE COST OF LIVING
I FELL IN LOVE WITH ONE OF GEORGE LUCAS'S INTERNS
SHE TRAINED ME HOW TO DRIVE TRUCKS INTO HOUSES. IT WAS VERY EXPENSIVE AND I AM VERY CONCERNED WITH HOW IT COULD AFFECT MY HEALTH (AND THE HEALTH OF OTHERS) BUT I LOVE HER AND SO IT GOES...
THAT'S WHAT YOU CAN BUY FOR A PILE OF BACON
ORIGINOL
THINK ABOUT WHAT YOU ARE SAYING INTO THE THING
PUP TENT PARTY
IT IS NOT MY CONCERN THAT YOU HAD A [redacted] AND DID NOT LOOK AFTER YOR PAPER TRAIL
POOR BABIES
DIPPIN' INTO RESERVES
BATHTUB WEINER GIN
PRESENTLY
$49.99
GEORGE LUCAS'S INTERNS ATTACKED MY CONDO (TM)
Q: WHERE IS CHUNKY FLOORS
A: RETURNING IN THE MIDDLE OF THE NIGHT.
DODDS WON'T BE UNDERSOLD
A REAL TURNING POINT IN MY CAREER
Who Cares!
THESE GOOD TIMES WON'T LAST FOREVER
REQUISITE TUFF GUY APPROACH
IF YOU ARE DEPRESSED ABOUT YOUR TELEVISION SERIES, THINK ABOUT PILE OF BACON.
THIS IS A VERY DIFFICULT TIME FOR INSURANCE AGENCIES
BLOO CHIP
SUMMING UP
USED FURNITURE (CON'T)
TRAD
25¢
REAL LIFE SWEDISH CHEF
STOP THINKING LIKE A SURGEON AND REMEMBER WHAT IT MEANS TO THINK LIKE A HUMAN BEING
A GREAT STORY
ABOUT A PILE OF BACON
20 MILLION AMERICAN PEOPLE VS. THE REST OF THE WURLD
IF WE DIDN'T JOIN UP WE WOULD BE ACCUSED OF TREASON
"NOT A COMIC"
"YOUR COMIC DOLLAR IS BEING DILUTED"
"I AM JUST AS PISSED OFF AS YOU ARE"
"I MIGHT BE ABLE TO SUPPLY YOU WIT' MORE IF IT WEREN'T FER THIS FACT THAT I HAVE TO BUY CARS AND BOATS"
AIRPLANES
YOU BASTARDS
I AM A UN. INVESTIGATOR
BUBBLES
I AM ENDING MY MILLITARY PRESENCE IN LEBANON?
OR DO I OWN A CHAIN OF BISON MEAT RESTAURANTS ????
BACON
MODURN POP AESTHETIC
ENDLESS PILE OF BACON

102. *Not Comics Or Video Games (The Cost Of Living),* 2005
Ink and watercolour on paper, 14 x 11 in.

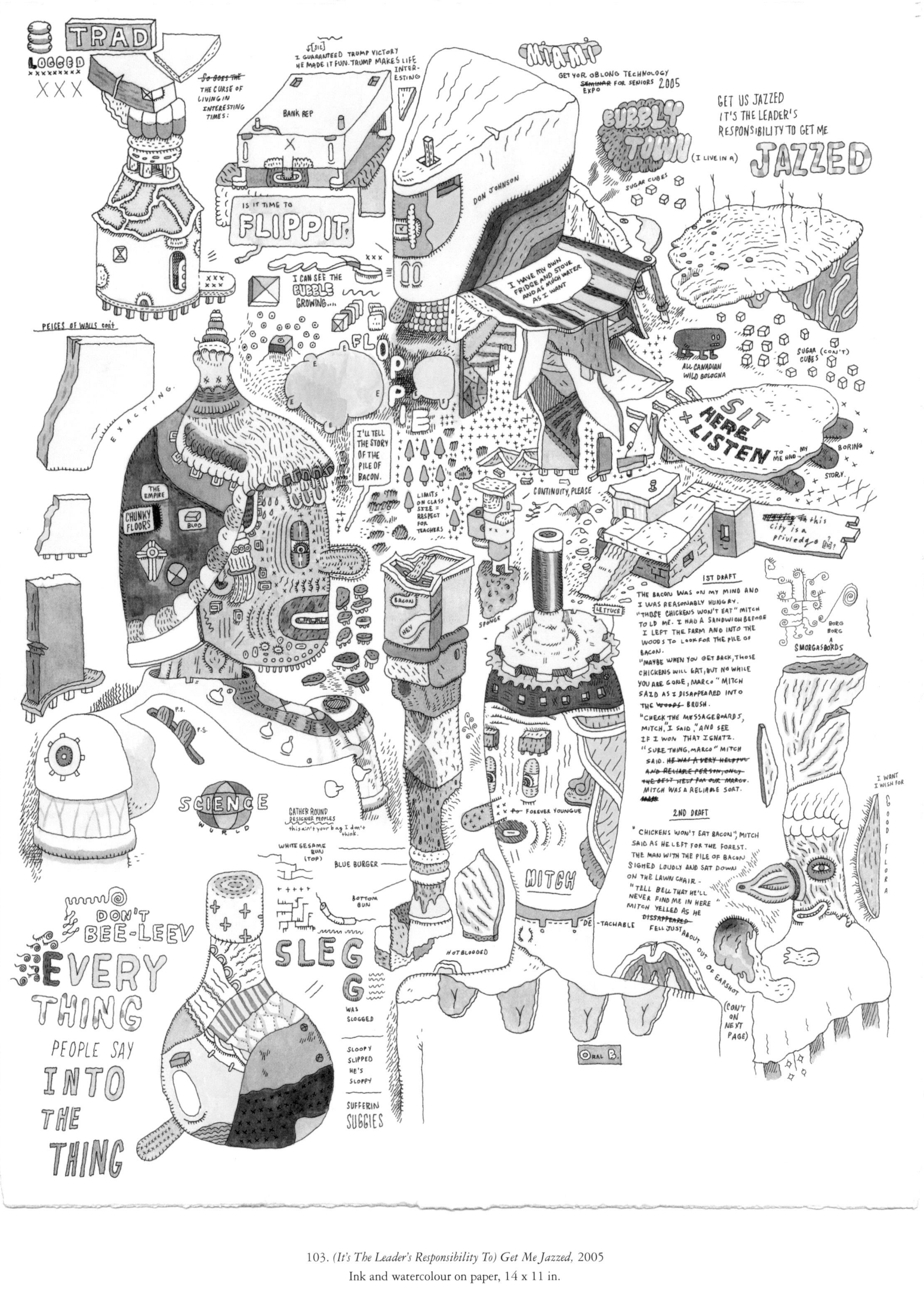

TRAD
LOGGED
XXX
~~SO GOES THE~~ THE CURSE OF LIVING IN INTERESTING TIMES:
I GUARANTEED TRUMP VICTORY HE MADE IT FUN. TRUMP MAKES LIFE INTERESTING
BANK REP
IS IT TIME TO FLIPPIT?
I CAN SEE THE BUBBLE GROWING...
MIAMI
GET YOR OBLONG TECHNOLOGY ~~SEMINAR~~ EXPO FOR SENIORS 2005
DON JOHNSON
I HAVE MY OWN FRIDGE AND STOVE AND AS MUCH WATER AS I WANT
BUBBLY TOWN
(I LIVE IN A)
GET US JAZZED
IT'S THE LEADER'S RESPONSIBILITY TO GET ME
JAZZED
SUGAR CUBES
SUGAR (CON'T) CUBES
ALL CANADIAN WILD BOLOGNA
PEICES OF WALLS con't
EXACTING
FLOPPIE
I'LL TELL THE STORY OF THE PILE OF BACON.
LIMITS ON CLASS SIZE = RESPECT FOR TEACHERS
SIT HERE LISTEN TO ME AND MY BORING STORY.
CONTINUITY, PLEASE
THE EMPIRE
CHUNKY FLOORS
BLOD
~~living in~~ this city is a priveledge
BACON
HEY
SPONGE
LETTUCE
1ST DRAFT
THE BACON WAS ON MY MIND AND I WAS REASONABLY HUNGRY. "THOSE CHICKENS WON'T EAT" MITCH TOLD ME. I HAD A SANDWICH BEFORE I LEFT THE FARM AND INTO THE WOODS TO LOOK FOR THE PILE OF BACON.
"MAYBE WHEN YOU GET BACK, THOSE CHICKENS WILL EAT, BUT NO WHILE YOU ARE GONE, MARCO" MITCH SAID AS I DISAPPEARED INTO THE ~~WOODS~~ BRUSH.
"CHECK THE MESSAGEBOARDS, MITCH," I SAID, "AND SEE IF I WON THAT IGNATZ.
"SURE THING, MARCO" MITCH SAID. ~~HE WAS A VERY HELPFUL AND RELIABLE PERSON, ONLY THE BEST HELP FOR OUR MARCO.~~ MITCH WAS A RELIABLE SORT.
2ND DRAFT
"CHICKENS WON'T EAT BACON", MITCH SAID AS HE LEFT FOR THE FOREST. THE MAN WITH THE PILE OF BACON SIGHED LOUDLY AND SAT DOWN ON THE LAWN CHAIR -
"TELL BELL THAT HE'LL NEVER FIND ME IN HERE" MITCH YELLED AS HE ~~DISSAPPEARED~~ FELL JUST ABOUT OUT OF EARSHOT
(CON'T ON NEXT PAGE)
BORG BORG A SMORGASBORDS
I WANT I WISH FOR
GOOD FLORA
P.S.
P.S.
SCIENCE WORLD
GATHER ROUND DESIGNER PEOPLES
this ain't your bag I don't think.
WHITE SESAME BUN (TOP)
BLUE BURGER
BOTTOM BUN
FOREVER YOUNGUE
MITCH
DE-TACHABLE
HOTBLOODED
DON'T BEE-LEEV
EVERY THING PEOPLE SAY INTO THE THING
SLEGG
WAS SLOGGED
SLOOPY SLIPPED HE'S SLOPPY
SUFFERIN SUGGIES
ORAL B.

103. *(It's The Leader's Responsibility To) Get Me Jazzed,* 2005
Ink and watercolour on paper, 14 x 11 in.

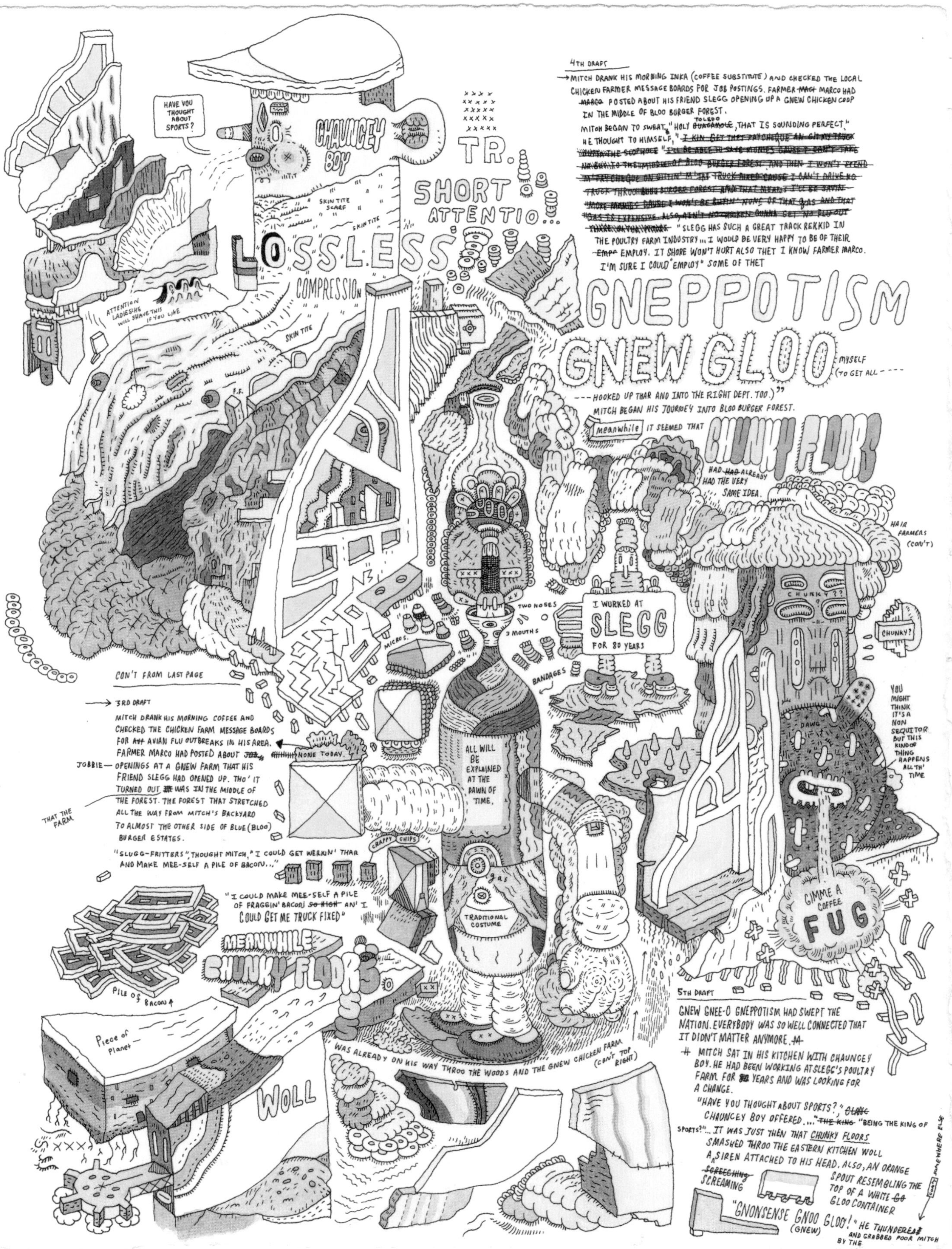

HAVE YOU THOUGHT ABOUT SPORTS?
CHAUNCEY BOY
TR.
SHORT ATTENTIO...
LOSSLESS
COMPRESSION
SKIN TITE SCARF
SKIN TITE
ATTENTION LADIESHE WILL SHAVE THIS IF YOU LIKE
4TH DRAFT
MITCH DRANK HIS MORNING INKA (COFFEE SUBSTITUTE) AND CHECKED THE LOCAL CHICKEN FARMER MESSAGE BOARDS FOR JOB POSTINGS. FARMER MARCO HAD POSTED ABOUT HIS FRIEND SLEGG OPENING UP A GNEW CHICKEN COOP IN THE MIDDLE OF BLOO BURGER FOREST.
MITCH BEGAN TO SWEAT, "HOLY TOLEDO, THAT IS SOUNDING PERFECT," HE THOUGHT TO HIMSELF, "SLEGG HAS SUCH A GREAT TRACK REKKID IN THE POULTRY FARM INDUSTRY ... I WOULD BE VERY HAPPY TO BE OF THEIR EMPLOY. IT SHORE WON'T HURT ALSO THET I KNOW FARMER MARCO. I'M SURE I COULD "EMPLOY" SOME OF THET
GNEPPOTISM
GNEW GLOO
MYSELF (TO GET ALL ---
--- HOOKED UP THAR AND INTO THE RIGHT DEPT. TOO.)"
MITCH BEGAN HIS JOURNEY INTO BLOO BURGER FOREST.
MEANWHILE IT SEEMED THAT
CHUNKY FLOORS
HAD ALREADY HAD THE VERY SAME IDEA.
HAIR FARMERS (CON'T)
CHUNKY??
CHUNKY?
TWO NOSES
3 MOUTHS
MICROS
BANDAGES
I WORKED AT SLEGG FOR 80 YEARS
YOU MIGHT THINK IT'S A NON SEQUITOR BUT THIS KIND OF THING HAPPENS ALL TH' TIME
DAWG
CON'T FROM LAST PAGE
3RD DRAFT
MITCH DRANK HIS MORNING COFFEE AND CHECKED THE CHICKEN FARM MESSAGE BOARDS FOR AVIAN FLU OUTBREAKS IN HIS AREA. FARMER MARCO HAD POSTED ABOUT JOBBIE OPENINGS AT A GNEW FARM THAT HIS FRIEND SLEGG HAD OPENED UP. THO' IT TURNED OUT THAT THE FARM WAS IN THE MIDDLE OF THE FOREST. THE FOREST THAT STRETCHED ALL THE WAY FROM MITCH'S BACKYARD TO ALMOST THE OTHER SIDE OF BLUE (BLOO) BURGER ESTATES.
NONE TODAY.
ALL WILL BE EXPLAINED AT THE DAWN OF TIME.
"SLUGG-FRITTERS", THOUGHT MITCH, "I COULD GET WERKIN' THAR AND MAKE MEE-SELF A PILE OF BACON..."
CRAPPY CHIPS
GAS
TRADITIONAL COSTUME
"I COULD MAKE MEE-SELF A PILE OF FRAGGIN' BACON AN' I COULD GET ME TRUCK FIXED"
MEANWHILE
CHUNKY FLOORS
PILE OF BACON
PIECE OF PLANET
WOLL
WAS ALREADY ON HIS WAY THROO THE WOODS AND THE GNEW CHICKEN FARM (CON'T TOP RIGHT)
GIMME A COFFEE FUG
5TH DRAFT
GNEW GNEE-O GNEPPOTISM HAD SWEPT THE NATION. EVERYBODY WAS SO WELL CONNECTED THAT IT DIDN'T MATTER ANYMORE.
MITCH SAT IN HIS KITCHEN WITH CHAUNCEY BOY. HE HAD BEEN WORKING AT SLEGG'S POULTRY FARM FOR YEARS AND WAS LOOKING FOR A CHANGE.
"HAVE YOU THOUGHT ABOUT SPORTS?", CHAUNCEY BOY OFFERED... "BEING THE KING OF SPORTS?"... IT WAS JUST THEN THAT CHUNKY FLOORS SMASHED THROO THE EASTERN KITCHEN WOLL A SCREAMING SIREN ATTACHED TO HIS HEAD. ALSO, AN ORANGE SPOUT RESEMBLING THE TOP OF A WHITE GLOO CONTAINER
"GNONSENSE GNOO GLOO! (GNEW)" HE THUNDERED AND GRABBED POOR MITCH BY THE
(CON'T SOMEWHERE ELSE)

104. *Chauncey Boy*, 2005

Ink and watercolour on paper, 14 x 11–¼ in.

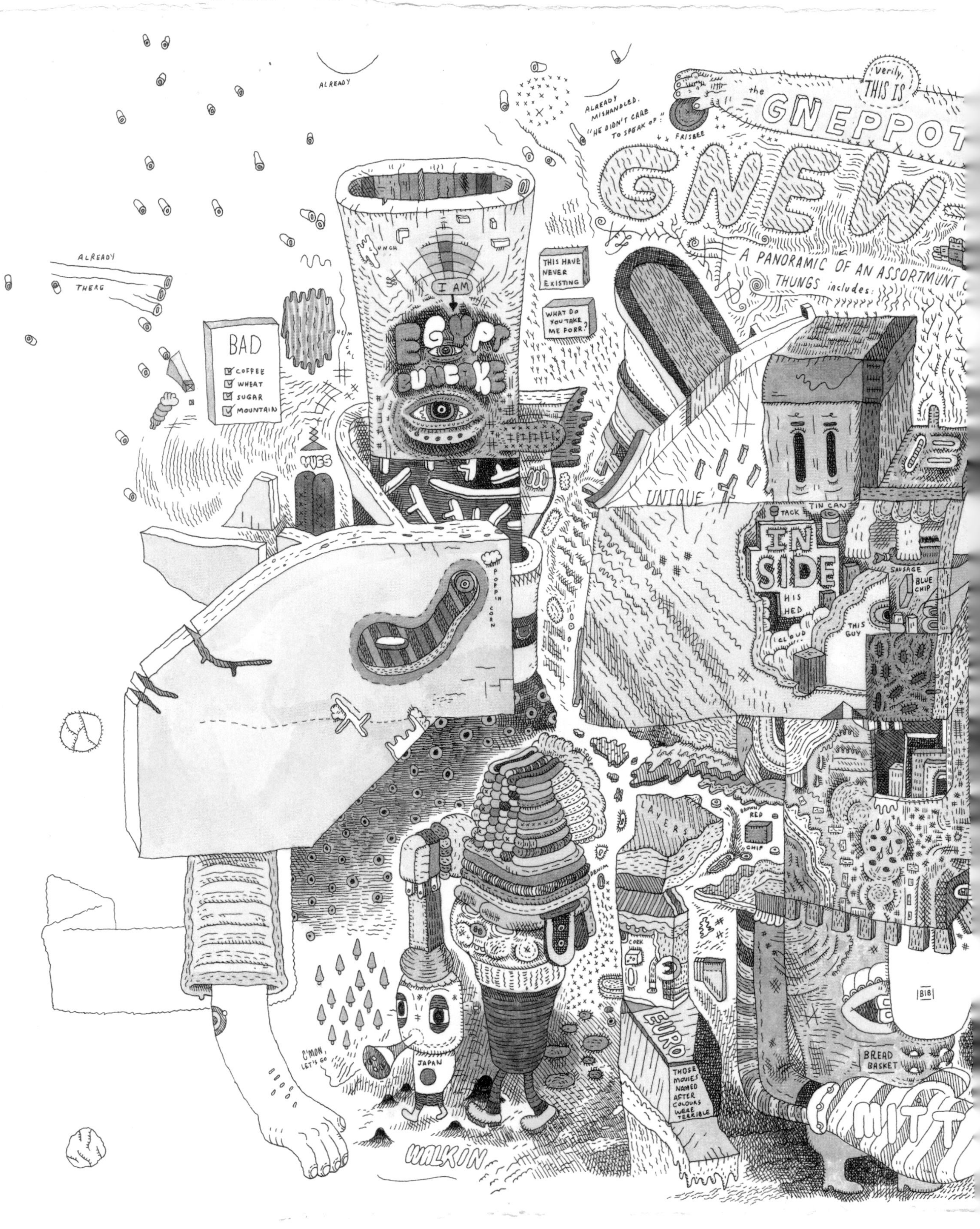

Verily, THIS IS the GNEPPOT
GNEW
A PANORAMIC OF AN ASSORTMUNT OF THUNGS includes:
ALREADY
ALREADY MISHANDLED. "HE DIDN'T CARE TO SPEAK OF."
FRISBEE
ALREADY
THERG
BAD
COFFEE
WHEAT
SUGAR
MOUNTAIN
I AM
EGYPT
BUNCAKE
THIS HAVE NEVER EXISTING
WHAT DO YOU TAKE ME FORR?
UNIQUE
TACK
TIN CAN
IN SIDE
HIS HED
SAUSAGE
BLUE CHIP
THIS GUY
CLOUD
POPPIN CORN
LAYERS
RED CHIP
CORK
EURO
THOSE MOVIES NAMED AFTER COLOURS WERE TERRIBLE
BREAD BASKET
BIB
MITT
C'MON, LET'S GO
JAPAN
WALKIN

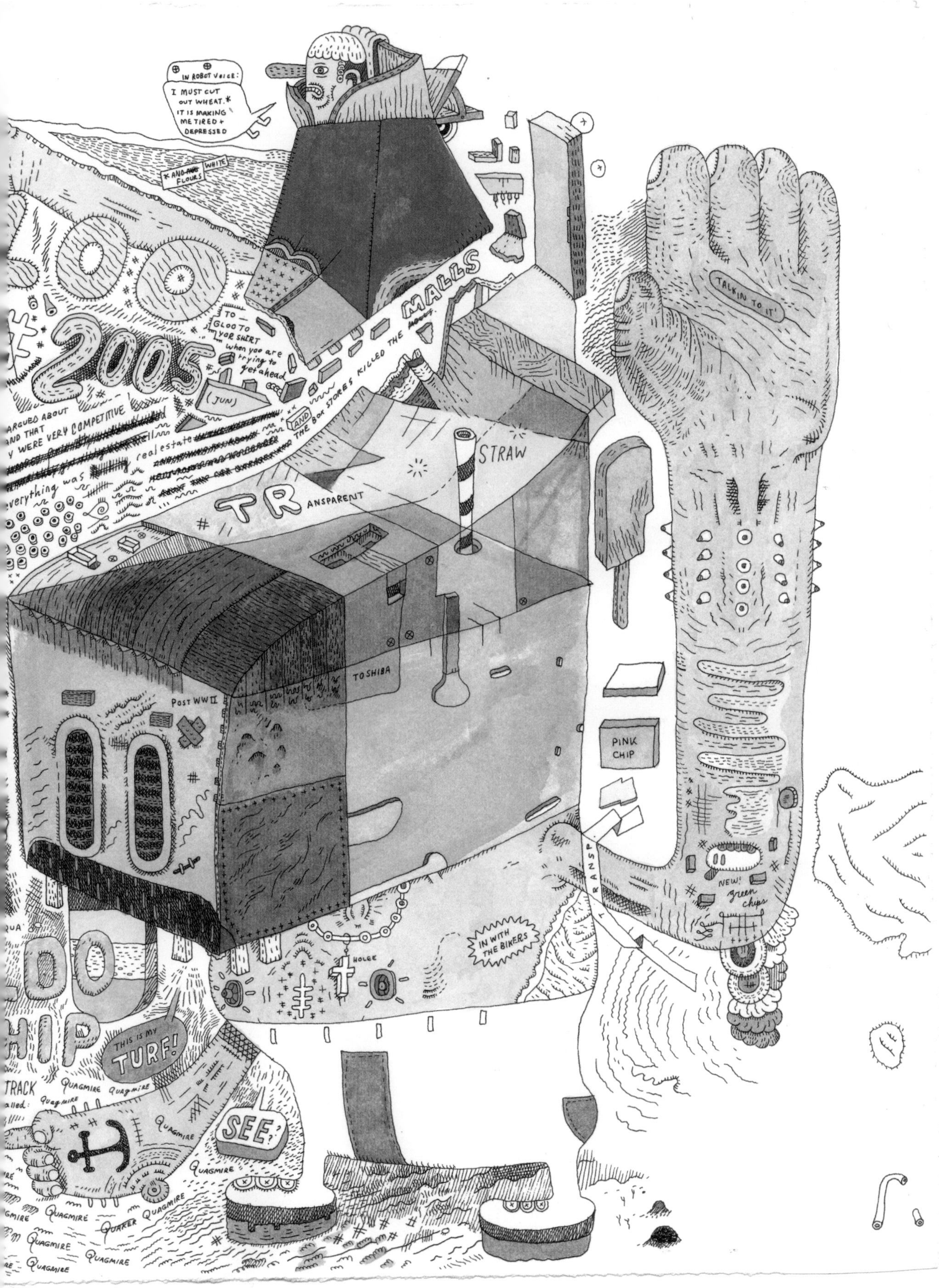
IN ROBOT VOICE:
I MUST CUT OUT WHEAT.* IT IS MAKING ME TIRED + DEPRESSED
MALLS
TO GLOO TO YOR SHIRT when yoo are trying to get ahead
2005
(JUN)
THE BOX STORES KILLED THE
ARGUED ABOUT
AND THAT
Y WERE VERY COMPETITIVE
real estate
everything was
STRAW
TR ANSPARENT
TALKIN TO IT
TOSHIBA
POST WW II
PINK CHIP
NEW! green chips
IN WITH THE BIKERS
THIS IS MY TURF!
SEE?
TRACK
QUAGMIRE

105. *Verily, This Is Gneppotism Gnew Gloo #1,* 2005
Ink and watercolour on paper, 13 x 22 in.

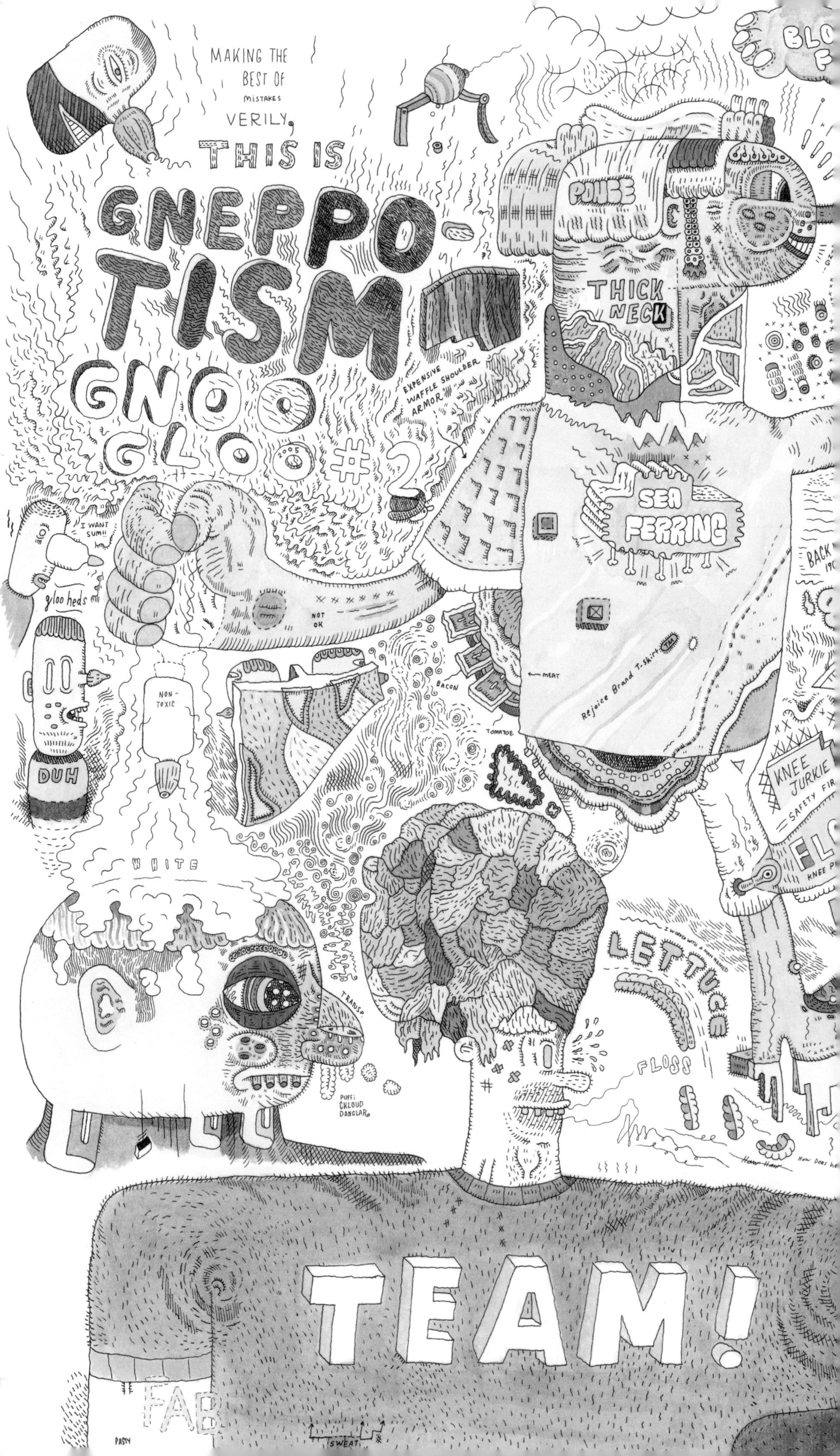
MAKING THE BEST OF MISTAKES
VERILY,
THIS IS
GNEPPO-TISM
GNOO GLOO #2
EXPENSIVE WAFFLE SHOULDER ARMOR
I WANT SUM!!
gloo heds
NOT OK
NON-TOXIC
DUH
BACON
TOMATOE
MEAT
WHITE
THICK NECK
SEA FERRING
Rejoice Brand T-Shirt
KNEE JURKIE
LETTUCE
FLOSS
PUFFI CKLOUD DANGLAR
TEAM!
FAB
SWEAT

106. *Verily, This Is Gneppotism Gnew Gloo #2*, 2005
Ink and watercolour on paper, 16 x 22 in.

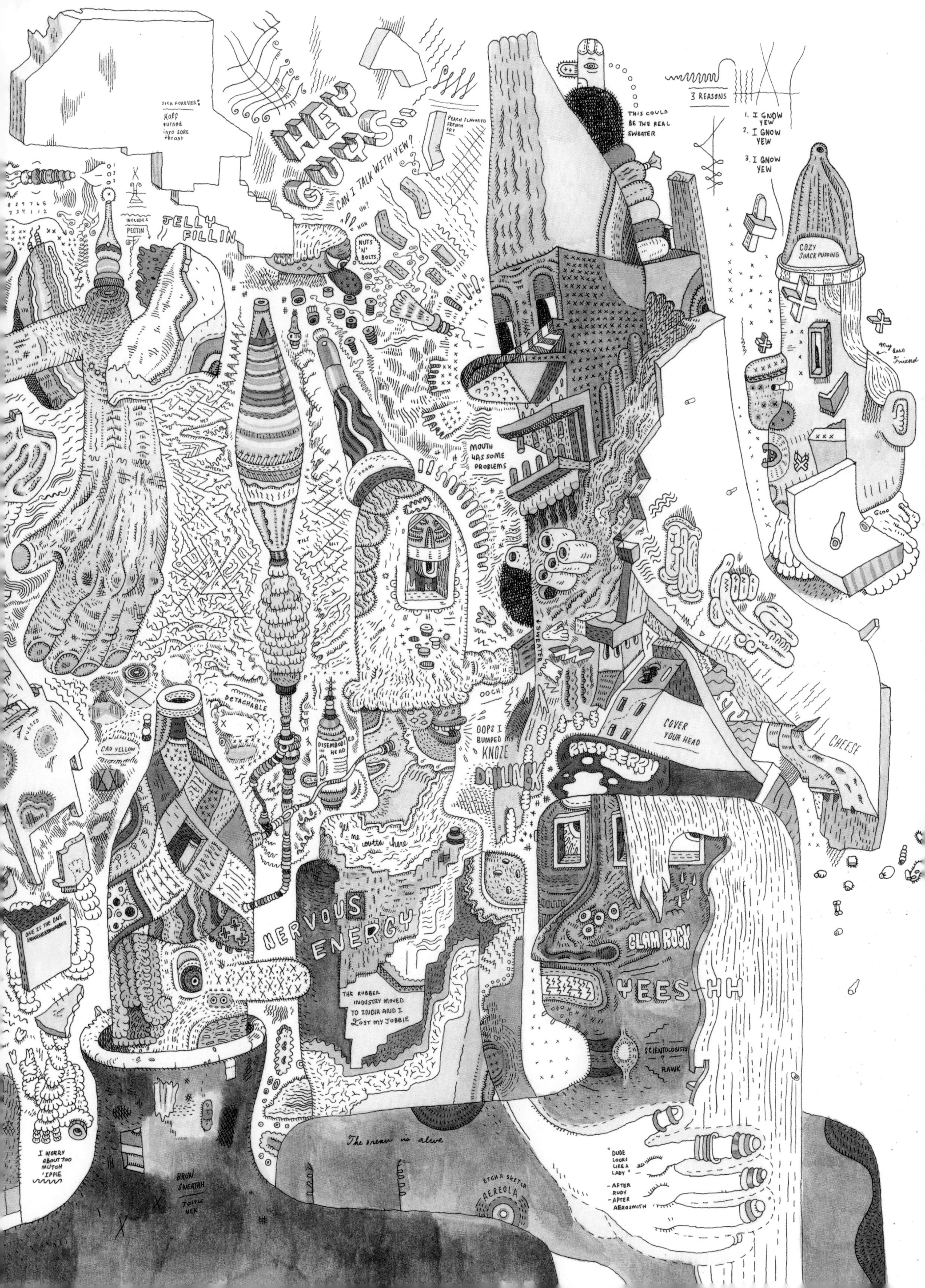
SICK FOREVER:
Koff turned into sore throat
HEY GUYS
PEACH FLAVORED FRENCH FRY
CAN I TALK WITH YEW?
UH?
HUH
NUTS 'N' BOLTS
INCLUDES PESTIN
JELLY FILLIN
THIS COULD BE THE REAL SWEATER
3 REASONS
1. I GNOW YEW
2. I GNOW YEW
3. I GNOW YEW
COZY SHACK PUDDING
My Best Friend
MOUTH HAS SOME PROBLEMS
FOAM
TILT BILT
GLOO
DETACHABLE
FUSSED
CAD YELLOW
DISEMBODIED HEAD
OOCH
OOPS I BUMPED MY KNOZE
DAHLINGK
SWEATER
COVER YOUR HEAD
RASPBERRY
CHEESE
Get me outta here
NERVOUS ENERGY
GLAM ROCK
YEES-HH
THE RUBBER INDUSTRY MOVED TO INDIA AND I LOST MY JOBBIE
SCIENTOLOGISTS? RAWK
ONE IS THE ONE
I WORRY ABOUT TOO MUTCH 'IPPIE
BRUN SWEATAH
The dream is alive
ETCH A SKETCH
AEREOLA
"DUDE LOOKS LIKE A LADY"
- AFTER RUDY
- AFTER AEROSMITH

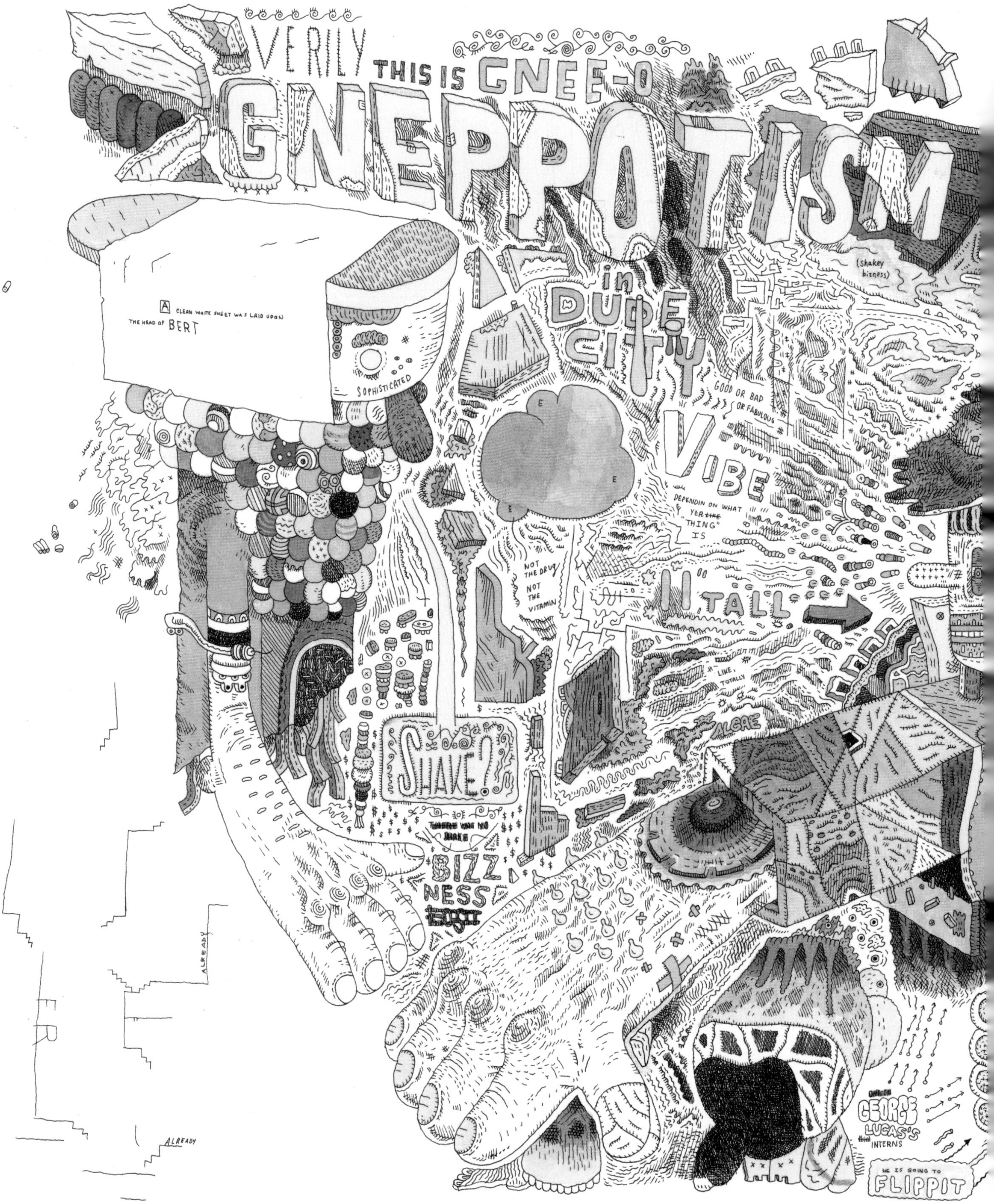

VERILY
THIS IS GNEE-O
GNEPPOTISM
(shakey bizness)
in DUDE CITY
A CLEAN WHITE SHEET WAS LAID UPON THE HEAD OF BERT
SOPHISTICATED
GOOD OR BAD OR FABULOUS
VIBE
DEPENDIN ON WHAT YER THING IS
NOT THE DRUG NOT THE VITAMIN
11 TALL
LIKE, TOTALLY
ALGAE
SHAKE?
THERE WAS NO SHAKE
BIZZ NESS
ALREADY
ER
ALREADY
GEORGE LUCAS'S INTERNS
HE IS GOING TO FLIPPIT

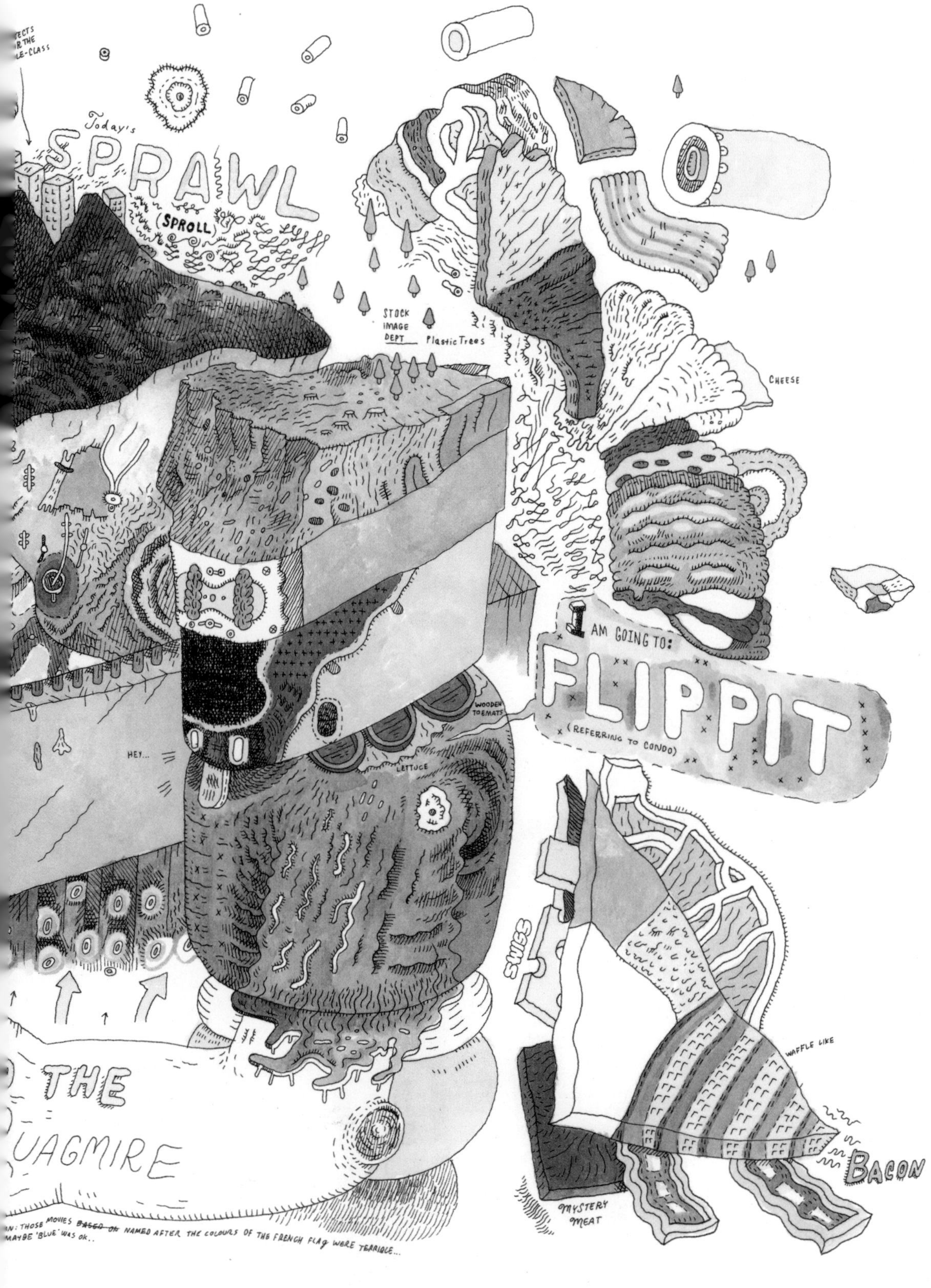
Today's
SPRAWL
(SPROLL)
STOCK IMAGE DEPT
Plastic Trees
CHEESE
I AM GOING TO:
FLIPPIT
(REFERRING TO CONDO)
WOODEN TOEMATS
LETTUCE
HEY...
THE
UAGMIRE
SWISS
WAFFLE LIKE
BACON
MYSTERY MEAT
THOSE MOVIES NAMED AFTER THE COLOURS OF THE FRENCH FLAG WERE TERRIBLE...
MAYBE 'BLUE' WAS OK..

107. *This is Gnee–0 Gneppotism (in Dude City),* 2005
Ink and watercolour on paper, 13 x 22 in.

108. *Trad Scorn Used Furn,* 2005
Ink and watercolour on paper, 14 x 11–¼ in

BLOO CHIP

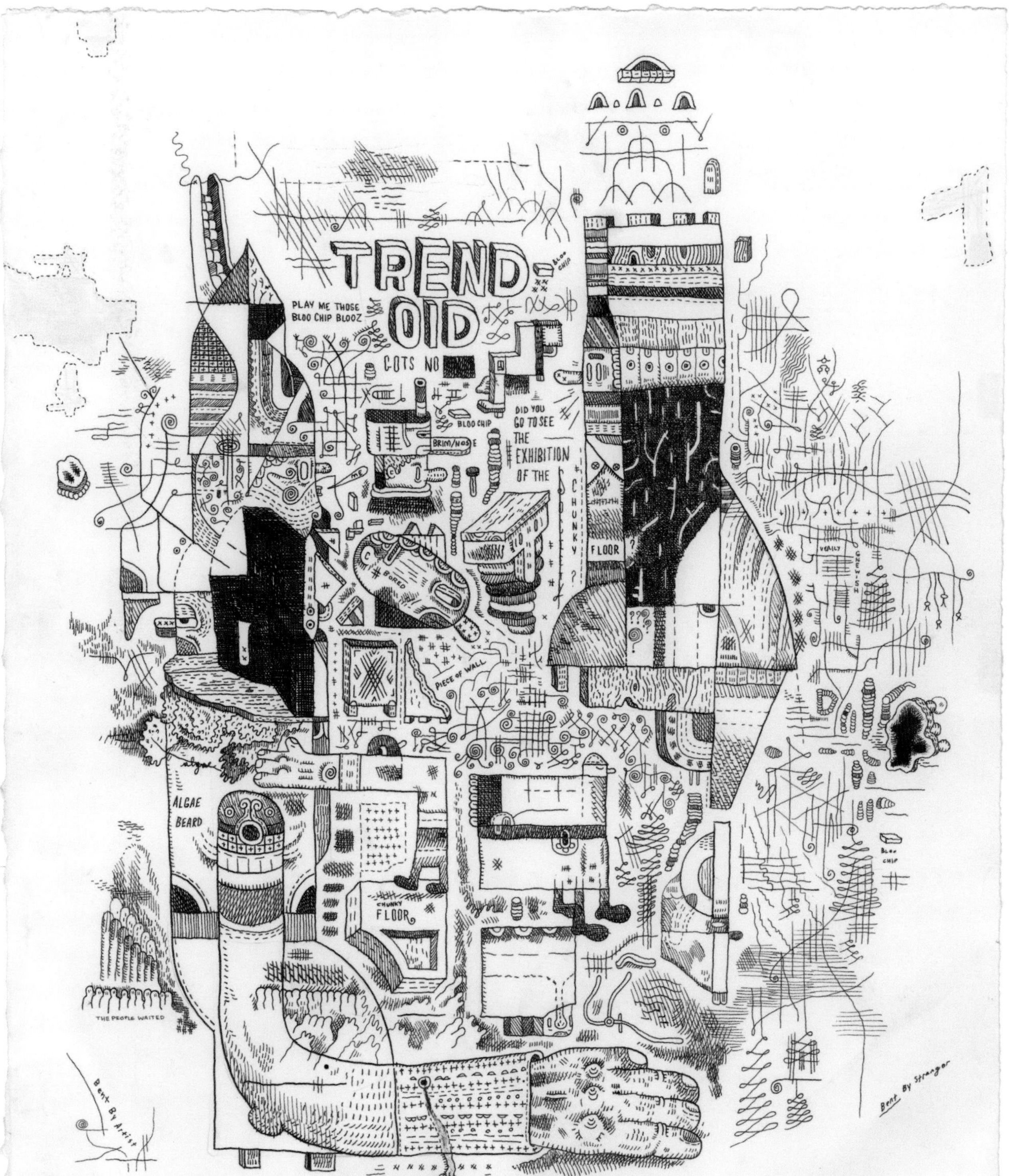
TREND-OID
PLAY ME THOSE BLOO CHIP BLOOZ
GOTS NO
BLOO CHIP
BRIM/NOSE
DID YOU GO TO SEE THE EXHIBITION OF THE CHUNKY FLOOR?
PIECE OF WALL
ALGAE BEARD
CHUNKY FLOOR
THE PEOPLE WAITED
Bent By Artist
Bent By Stranger

109. *Trendoid,* 2005
Ink on paper, 13–½ x 11–½ in.

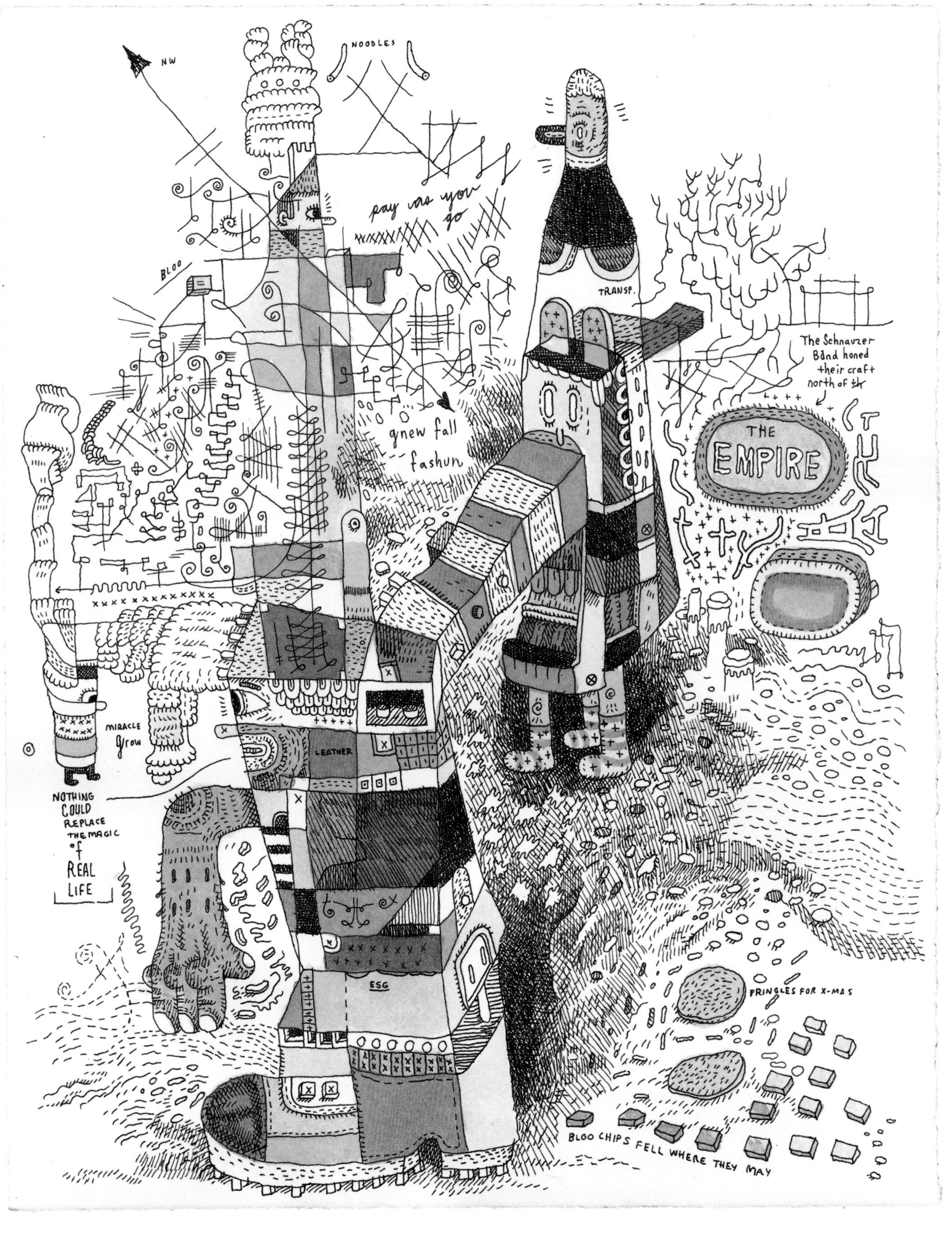
NW
NOODLES
pay as you go
BLOO
TRANSP.
The Schnauzer Band honed their craft north of th
THE EMPIRE
gnew fall fashun
LEATHER
MIRACLE Grow
NOTHING COULD REPLACE THE MAGIC of REAL LIFE
ESG
PRINGLES FOR X-MAS
BLOO CHIPS FELL WHERE THEY MAY

110. *Pay As You Go,* 2004
Ink and watercolour on paper, 10 x 8 in.

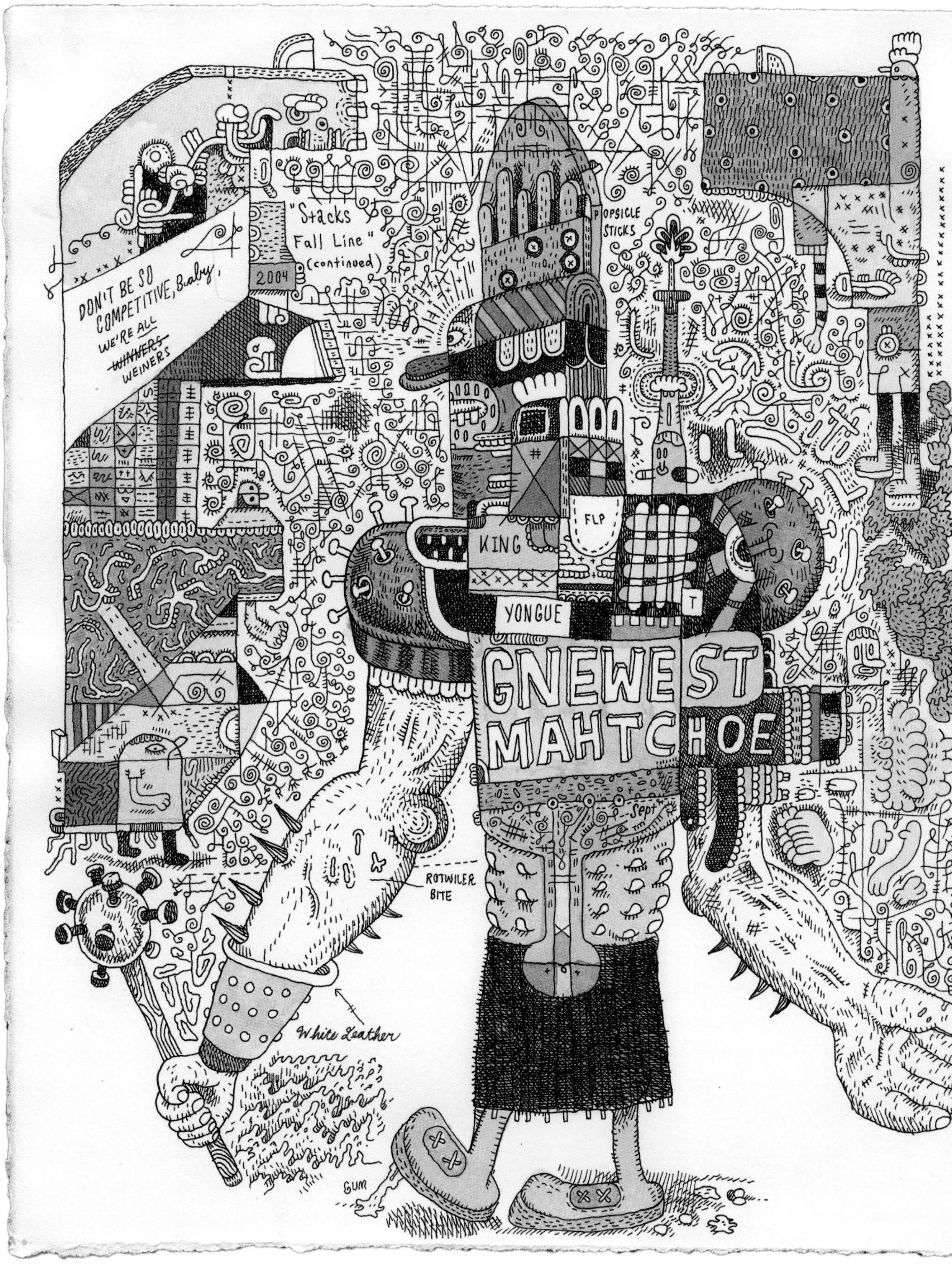
"Stacks
Fall Line"
(continued)
2004
DON'T BE SO
COMPETITIVE, Baby,
WE'RE ALL
WINNERS
WEINERS
POPSICLE
STICKS
FLP
KING
YONGUE
T
GNEWEST
MAHTCHOE
Sept
ROTWILER
BITE
White Leather
GUM

111. *Gnewest Matchoe,* 2004
Ink and watercolour on paper, 10 x 8 in.

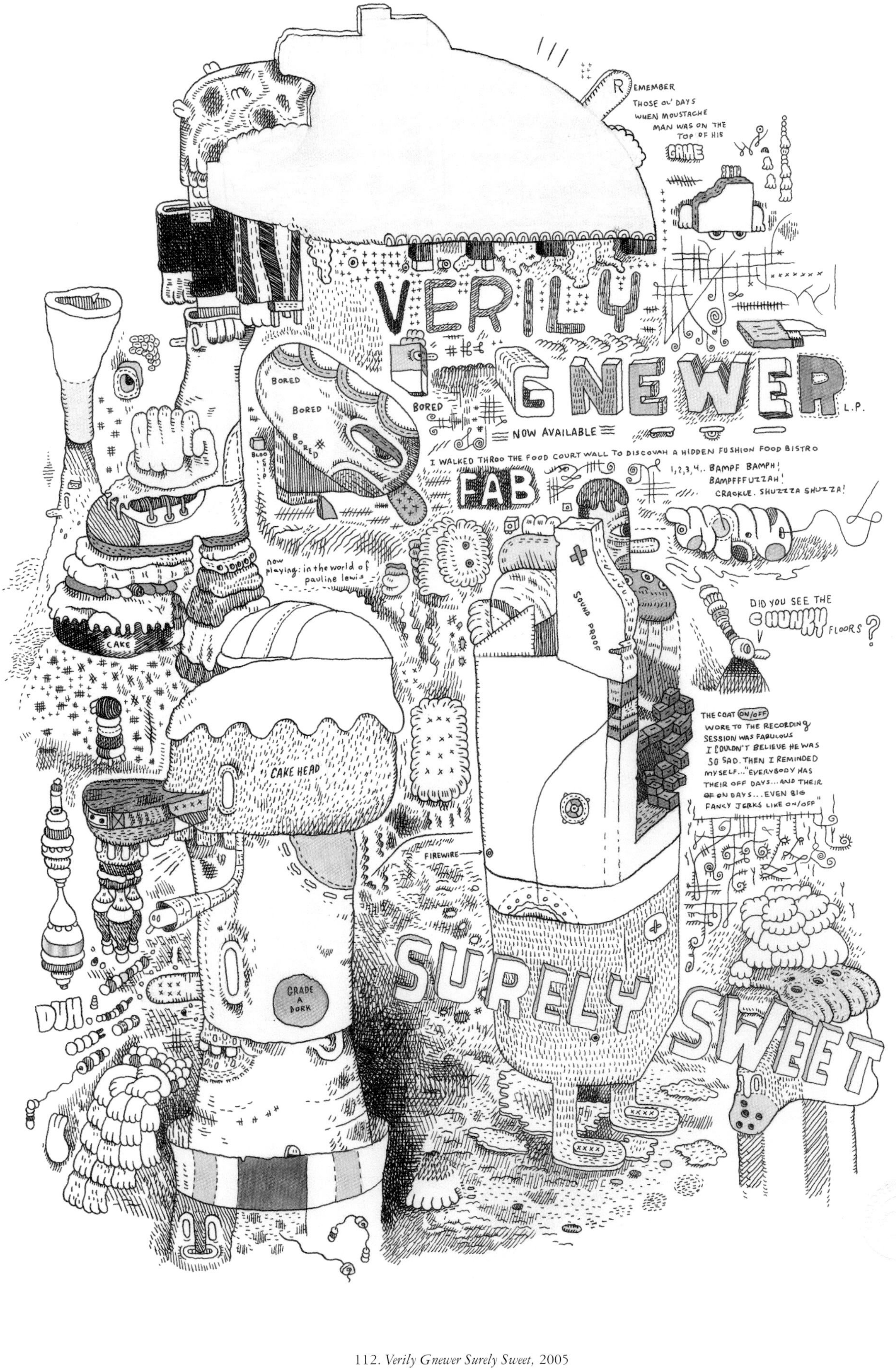
REMEMBER THOSE OL' DAYS WHEN MOUSTACHE MAN WAS ON THE TOP OF HIS
GAME
VERILY
BORED
BORED
BORED
BORED
GNEWER
L.P.
NOW AVAILABLE
I WALKED THROO THE FOOD COURT WALL TO DISCOVAH A HIDDEN FUSHION FOOD BISTRO
FAB
1,2,3,4.. BAMPF BAMPH! BAMPFFFUZZAH! CRACKLE. SHUZZZA SHUZZA!
now playing: in the world of pauline lewis
SOUND PROOF
DID YOU SEE THE CHUNKY FLOORS?
CAKE
CAKE HEAD
THE COAT ON/OFF WORE TO THE RECORDING SESSION WAS FABULOUS I COULDN'T BELIEVE HE WAS SO SAD. THEN I REMINDED MYSELF..."EVERYBODY HAS THEIR OFF DAYS...AND THEIR ON DAYS...EVEN BIG FANCY JERKS LIKE ON/OFF"
FIREWIRE
GRADE A DORK
SURELY
SWEET
DUH.

112. *Verily Gnewer Surely Sweet,* 2005
Ink, watercolour on paper, 14–½ x 11–½ in.

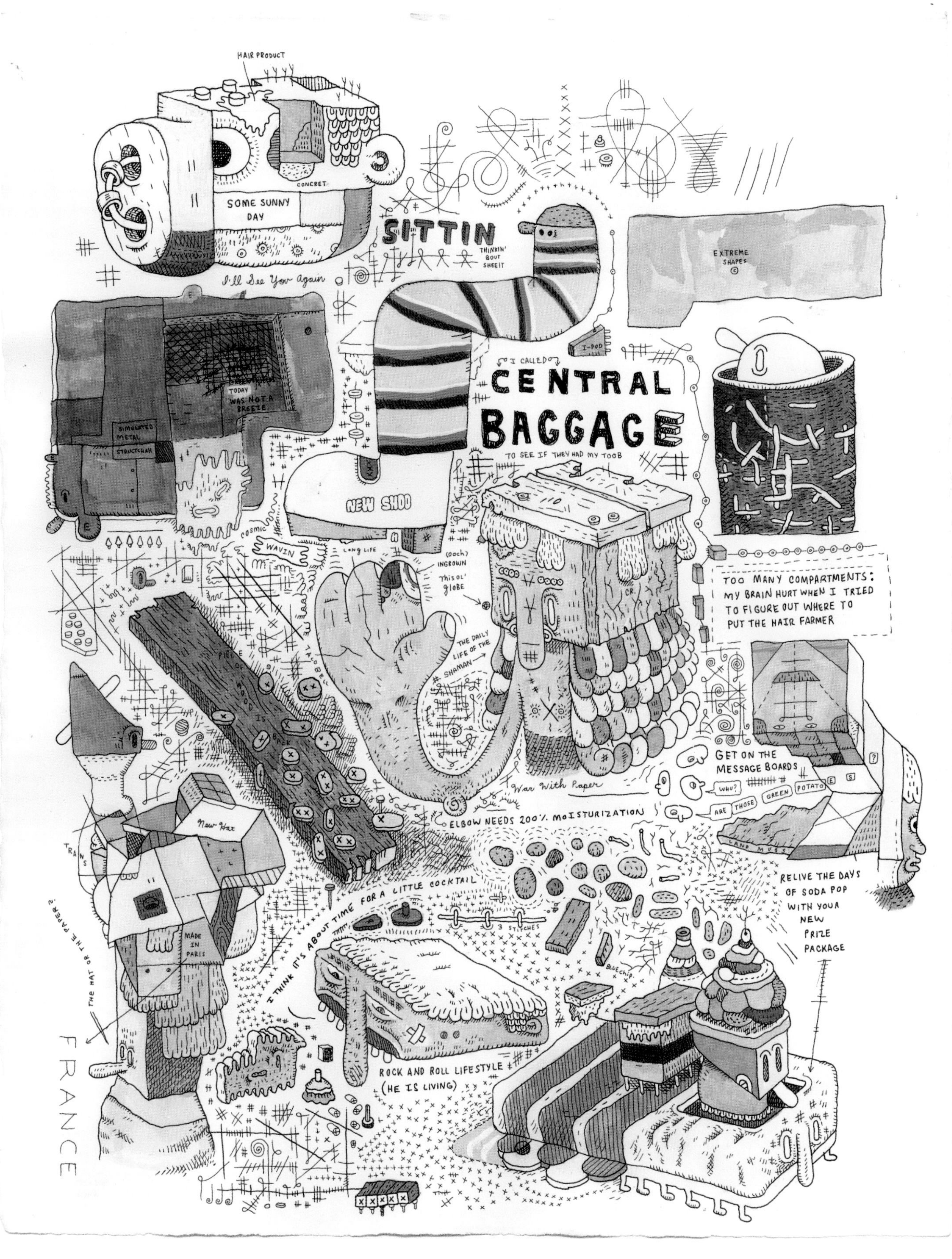
HAIR PRODUCT
CONCRET
SOME SUNNY DAY
SITTIN
THINKIN' BOUT SHEEIT
I'll See You again
EXTREME SHAPES ©
TODAY WAS NOT A BREEZE
SIMULATED METAL STRUCTCHAH
I-POD
I CALLED
CENTRAL BAGGAGE
TO SEE IF THEY HAD MY TOOB
NEW SHOO
COSMIC WAVIN
LONG LIFE
(OOCH) INGROWN
THIS OL' GLOBE
TOO MANY COMPARTMENTS: MY BRAIN HURT WHEN I TRIED TO FIGURE OUT WHERE TO PUT THE HAIR FARMER
THE DAILY LIFE OF THE SHAMAN
GET ON THE MESSAGE BOARDS
WHO?
ARE THOSE GREEN POTATO
War With Paper
ELBOW NEEDS 200% MOISTURIZATION
New Hat
MADE IN PARIS
I THINK IT'S ABOUT TIME FOR A LITTLE COCKTAIL
3 STITCHES
RELIVE THE DAYS OF SODA POP WITH YOUR NEW PRIZE PACKAGE
ROCK AND ROLL LIFESTYLE (HE IS LIVING)
THE HAT OR THE PAPER?
FRANCE

113. *Central Baggage,* 2004
Ink, watercolour, and gouache on paper, 14 x 11 in.

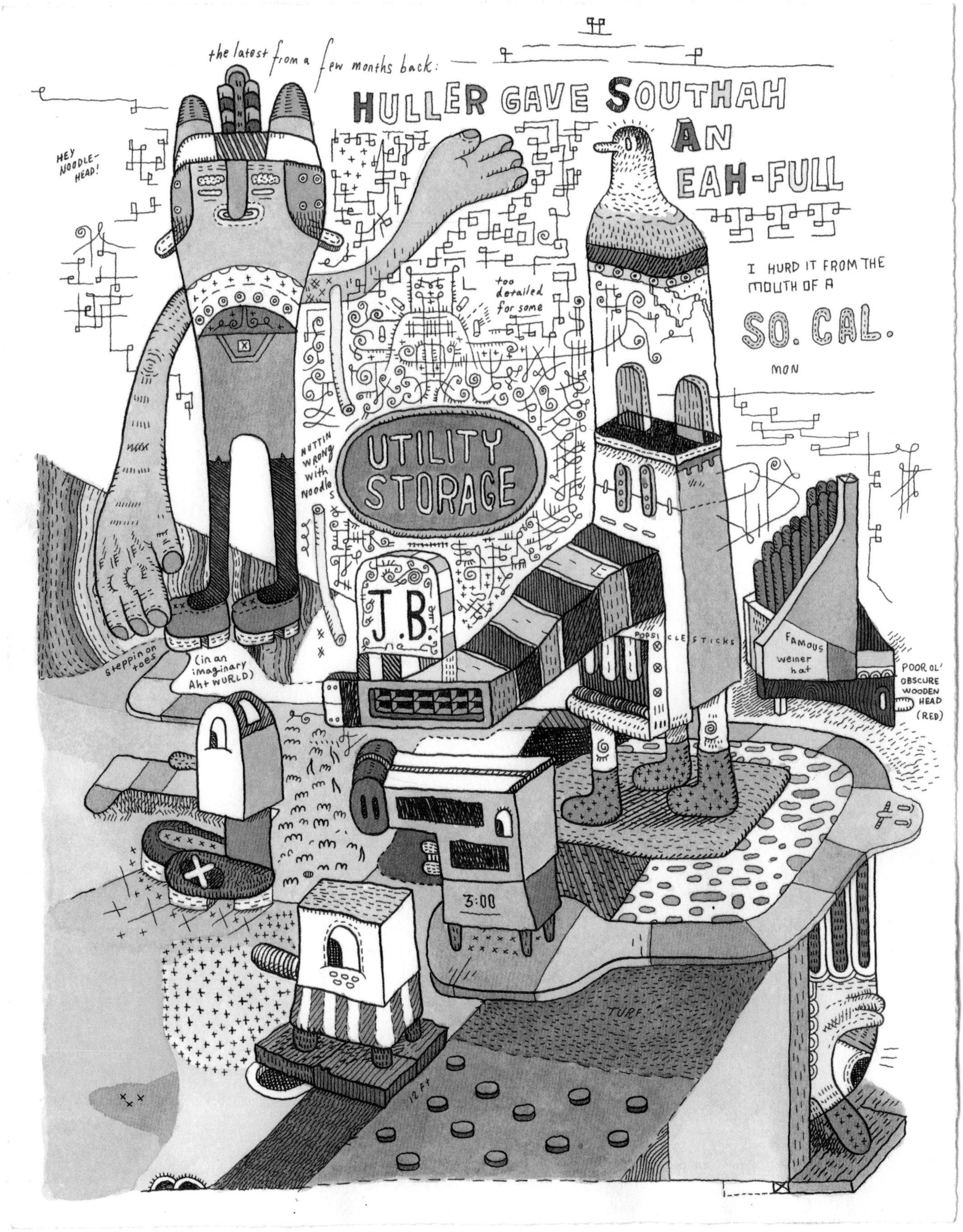
the latest from a few months back:
HULLER GAVE SOUTHAH AN EAH-FULL
HEY NOODLE-HEAD!
I HURD IT FROM THE MOUTH OF A
SO. CAL.
MON
too detailed for some
UTILITY STORAGE
NUTTIN WRONG with Noodles
J.B.
POPSICLE STICKS
FAMOUS weiner hat
POOR OL' OBSCURE WOODEN HEAD (RED)
steppin on toes
(in an imaginary Aht WURLD)
3:00
TURF
12 ft

114. *Utility Storage (Huller Gave Southah An Eah–full),* 2004
Ink and watercolour on paper, 10 x 8 in.

115. *Sidewinder,* 2005
Ink, watercolour, and gouache on paper, 14 x 11 in.

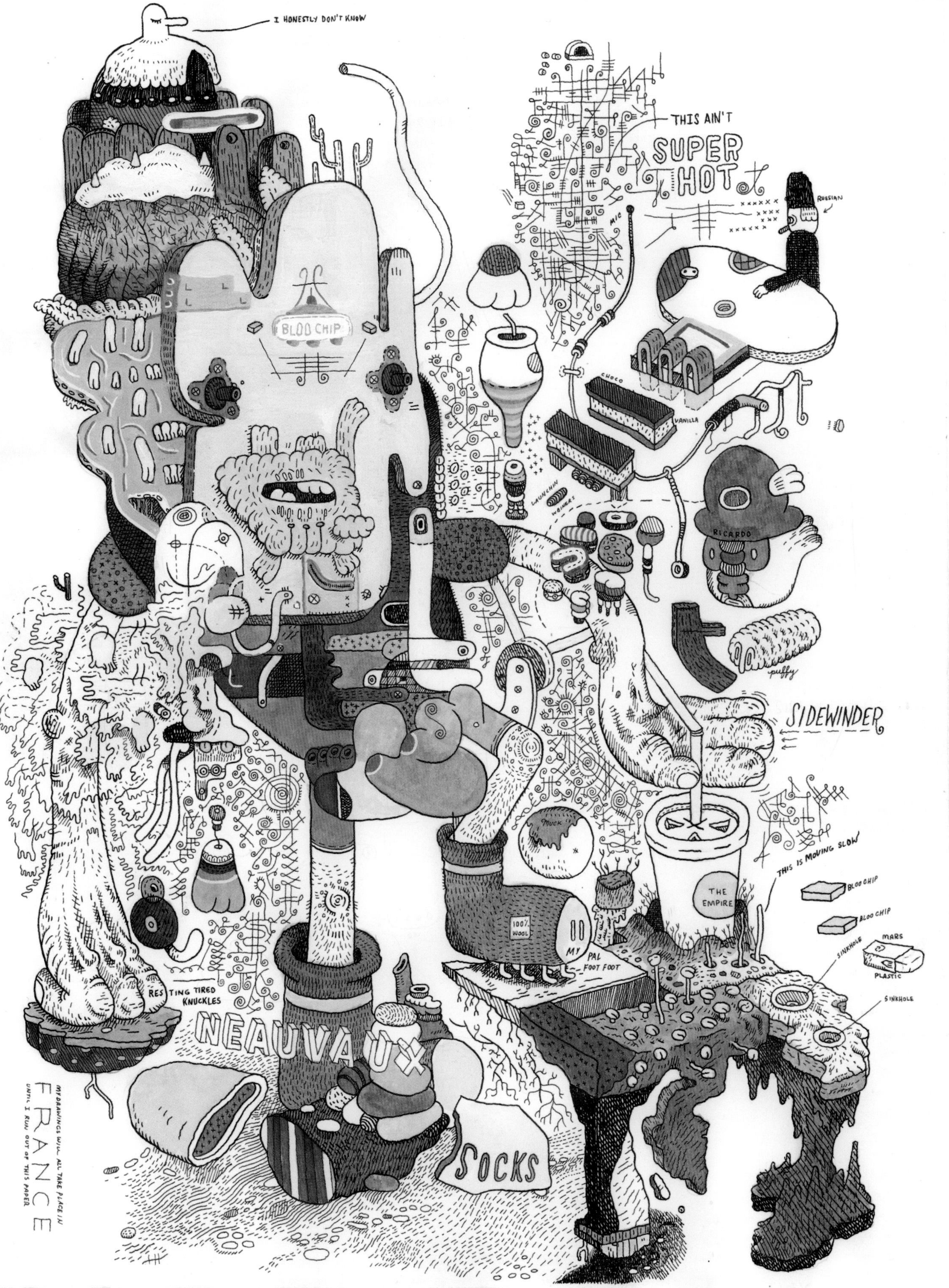
I HONESTLY DON'T KNOW
THIS AIN'T
SUPER
HOT
RUSSIAN
BLOO CHIP
MIC
CHOCO
VANILLA
RICARDO
puffy
SIDEWINDER
MUCK
THIS IS MOVING SLOW
BLOO CHIP
BLOO CHIP
MARS
SINKHOLE
PLASTIC
SINKHOLE
THE EMPIRE
100% WOOL
MY PAL FOOT FOOT
RESTING TIRED KNUCKLES
NEAUVAUX
SOCKS
MY DRAWINGS WILL ALL TAKE PLACE IN
FRANCE
UNTIL I RUN OUT OF THIS PAPER

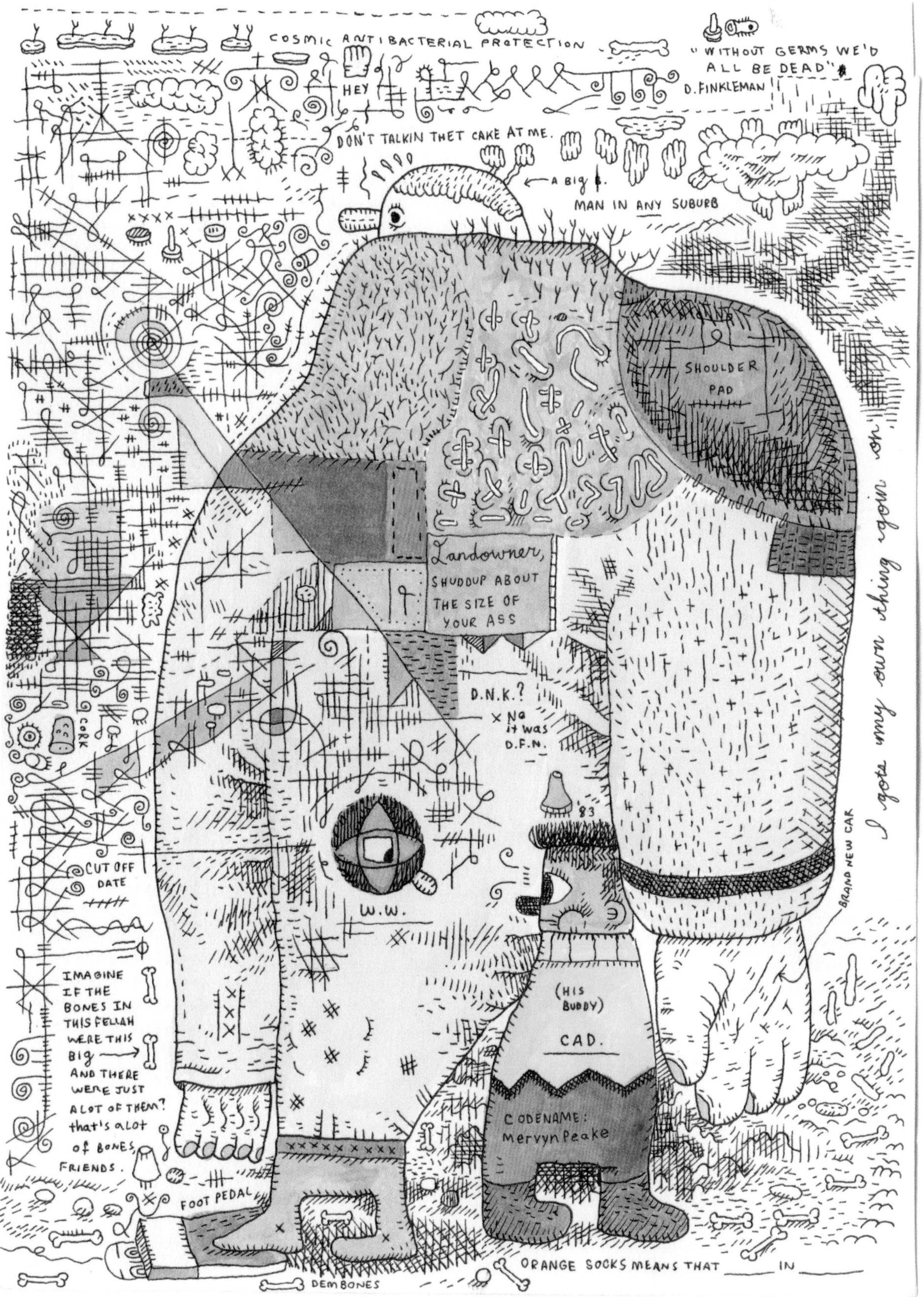
COSMIC ANTIBACTERIAL PROTECTION
"WITHOUT GERMS WE'D ALL BE DEAD"
D. FINKLEMAN
HEY
DON'T TALKIN THET CAKE AT ME.
A BIG $.
MAN IN ANY SUBURB
SHOULDER PAD
Landowner, SHUDDUP ABOUT THE SIZE OF YOUR ASS
D.N.K.?
No it was D.F.N.
CORK
83
CUT OFF DATE
W.W.
BRAND NEW CAR
I gots my own thing goin on
IMAGINE IF THE BONES IN THIS FELLAH WERE THIS BIG AND THERE WERE JUST ALOT OF THEM? that's alot of BONES FRIENDS.
(HIS BUDDY)
CAD.
CODENAME: MervynPeake
FOOT PEDAL
ORANGE SOCKS MEANS THAT ____ IN ____
DEMBONES

116. *Landowner,* 2004
Ink and watercolour on paper, 8–½ x 6–¼ in.

Shown right: drawing *Landowner* is based on

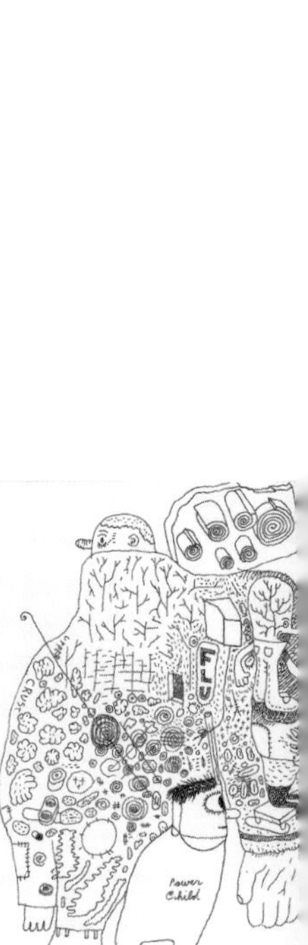

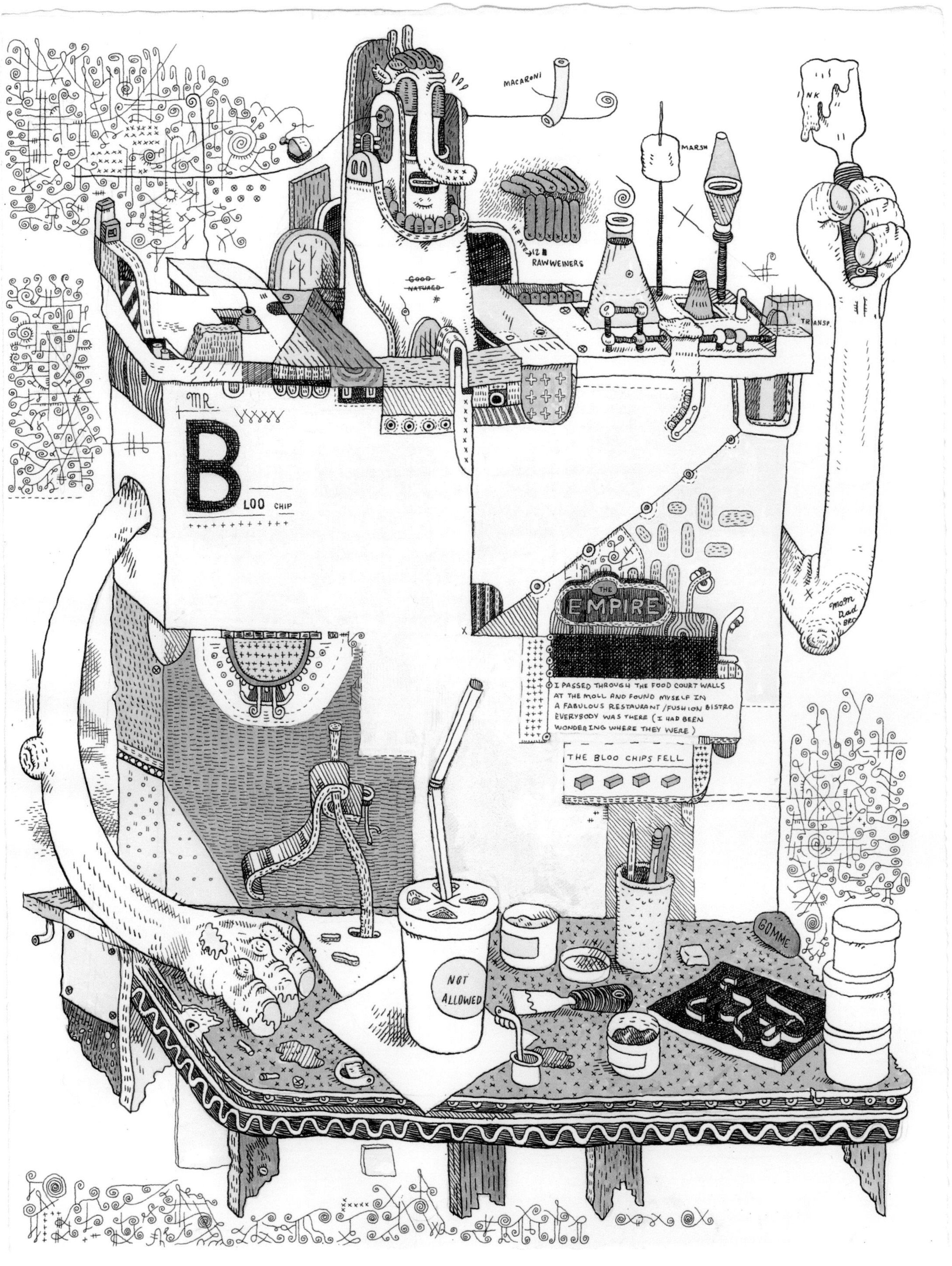
MACARONI
INK
MARSH
GOOD NATURED
HE ATE 12 RAWWEINERS
TRANSP.
MR.
B
LOO CHIP
THE EMPIRE
I PASSED THROUGH THE FOOD COURT WALLS AT THE MOLL AND FOUND MYSELF IN A FABULOUS RESTAURANT / FUSHION BISTRO EVERYBODY WAS THERE (I HAD BEEN WONDERING WHERE THEY WERE)
THE BLOO CHIPS FELL
NOT ALLOWED
GOMME

117. *Mr. Bloo Chip,* 2005
Ink, watercolour, and gouache on paper, 14 x 11 in.

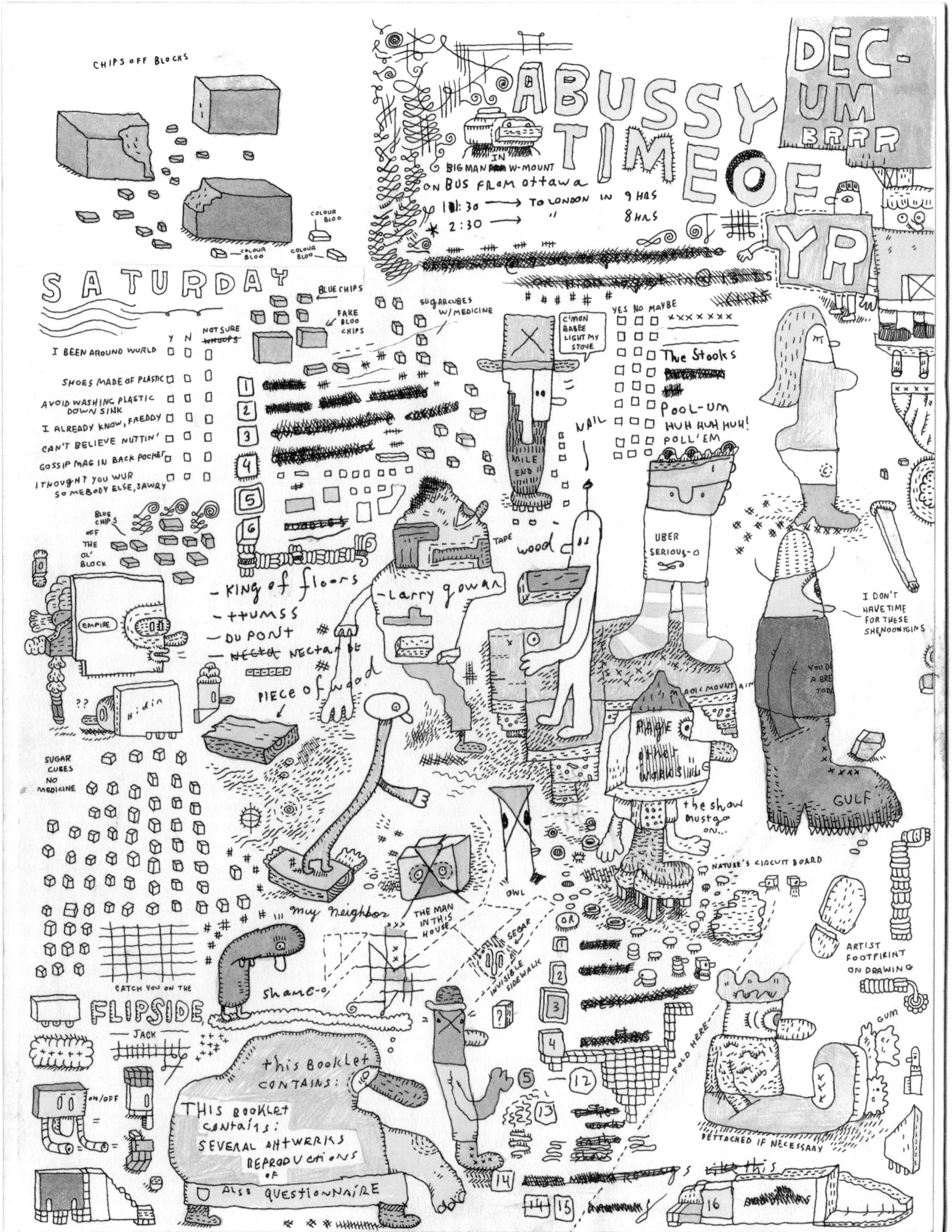
CHIPS OFF BLOCKS
COLOUR BLOO
A BUSSY TIME OF YR
DEC-UM BRRR
IN
BIG MAN W-MOUNT
ON BUS FROM ottawa
11:30 → TO LONDON IN 9 HRS
2:30 → 8 HRS
SATURDAY
Y N NOT SURE
I BEEN AROUND WURLD
SHOES MADE OF PLASTIC
AVOID WASHING PLASTIC DOWN SINK
I ALREADY KNOW, FREDDY
CAN'T BELIEVE NUTTIN'
GOSSIP MAG IN BACK POCKET
I THOUGHT YOU WUR SOMEBODY ELSE, SAWRY
BLUE CHIPS
FAKE BLOO CHIPS
SUGARCUBES W/MEDICINE
C'MON BABEE LIGHT MY STOVE
YES NO MAYBE
The Stooks
POOL-UM
HUH HUH HUH!
POLL'EM
NAIL
MILE END
UBER SERIOUS-O
TAPE
wood
BLUE CHIPS OFF THE OL' BLOCK
EMPIRE
-KING of floors
-TUMSS
-DU PONT
-NECTAR
-Larry gowan
PIECE of wood
hidin
I DON'T HAVE TIME FOR THESE SHENOONIGINS
MAGIC MOUNTAIN
SUGAR CUBES NO MEDICINE
GULF
the show mustgo on...
NATURE'S CIRCUIT BOARD
OWL
my neighbor
THE MAN IN THIS HOUSE
SEGAR
OR
INVISIBLE SIDEWALK
ARTIST FOOTPRINT ON DRAWING
CATCH YOU ON THE
FLIPSIDE
JACK
shame-o
FOLD HERE
GUM
this Booklet contains:
THIS BOOKLET contains: SEVERAL ARTWERKS REPRODUCTIONS OF ALSO QUESTIONNAIRE
ON/OFF
DETTACHED IF NECESSARY

118. *A Bussy time Of Year,* 2005
Mixed media on paper mounted on board, 11–¼ x 8–¾

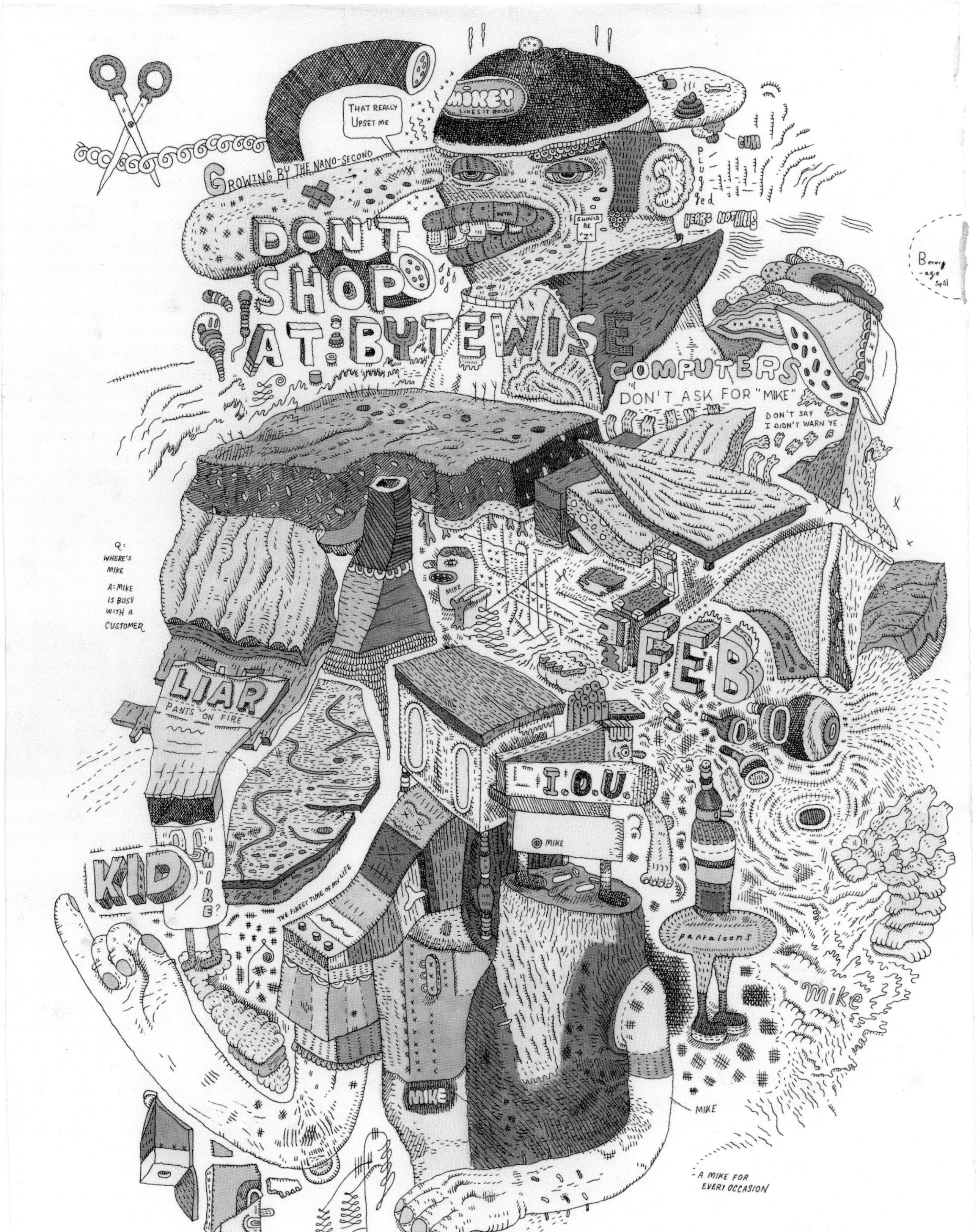
THAT REALLY UPSET ME
MIKEY LIKES IT ROUGH
GROWING BY THE NANO-SECOND
DON'T SHOP AT BYTEWISE
COMPUTERS
DON'T ASK FOR "MIKE"
DON'T SAY I DIDN'T WARN YE.
SHOULD BE "Z"
plugged
HEARS NOTHING
Beverage Spill
Q: WHERE'S MIKE
A: MIKE IS BUSY WITH A CUSTOMER
LIAR
PANTS ON FIRE
FEB
I.O.U.
MIKE
KID
MIKE?
THE FINEST TIME OF MY LIFE
pantaloons
mike
MIKE
A MIKE FOR EVERY OCCASION

119. *Don't Shop At Bytewise Conputers*

Ink and watercolour on paper, 14 x 11 in.

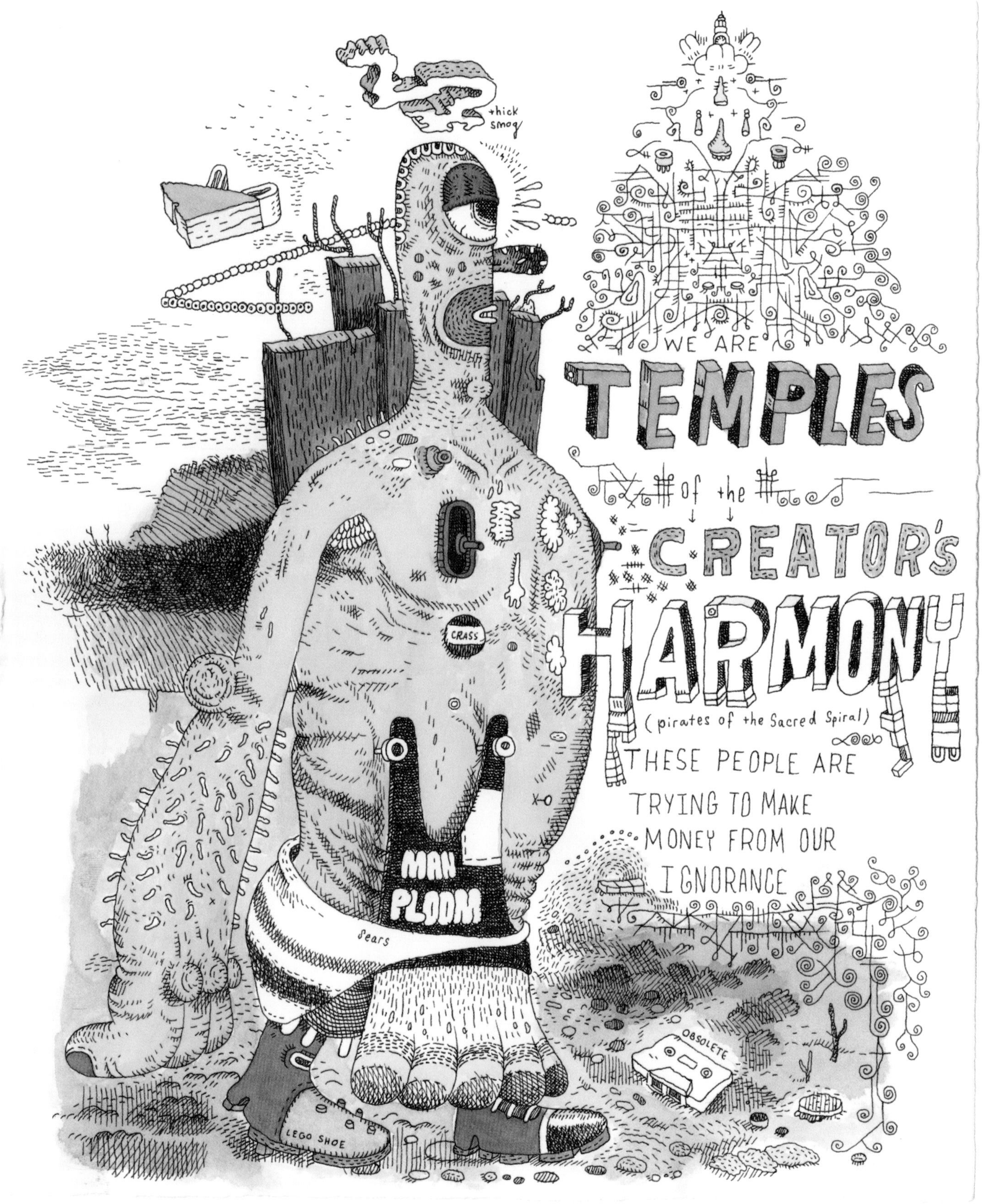
thick smog
WE ARE
TEMPLES
of the
CREATOR'S
HARMONY
(pirates of the Sacred Spiral)
THESE PEOPLE ARE
TRYING TO MAKE
MONEY FROM OUR
IGNORANCE
CRASS
MAN
PLOOM
Sears
LEGO SHOE
OBSOLETE

120. *We Are Temples of the Creator's Harmony (Pirates of the Sacred Spiral),* 2004
Ink and watercolour on paper, 8–½ x 6–½ in.

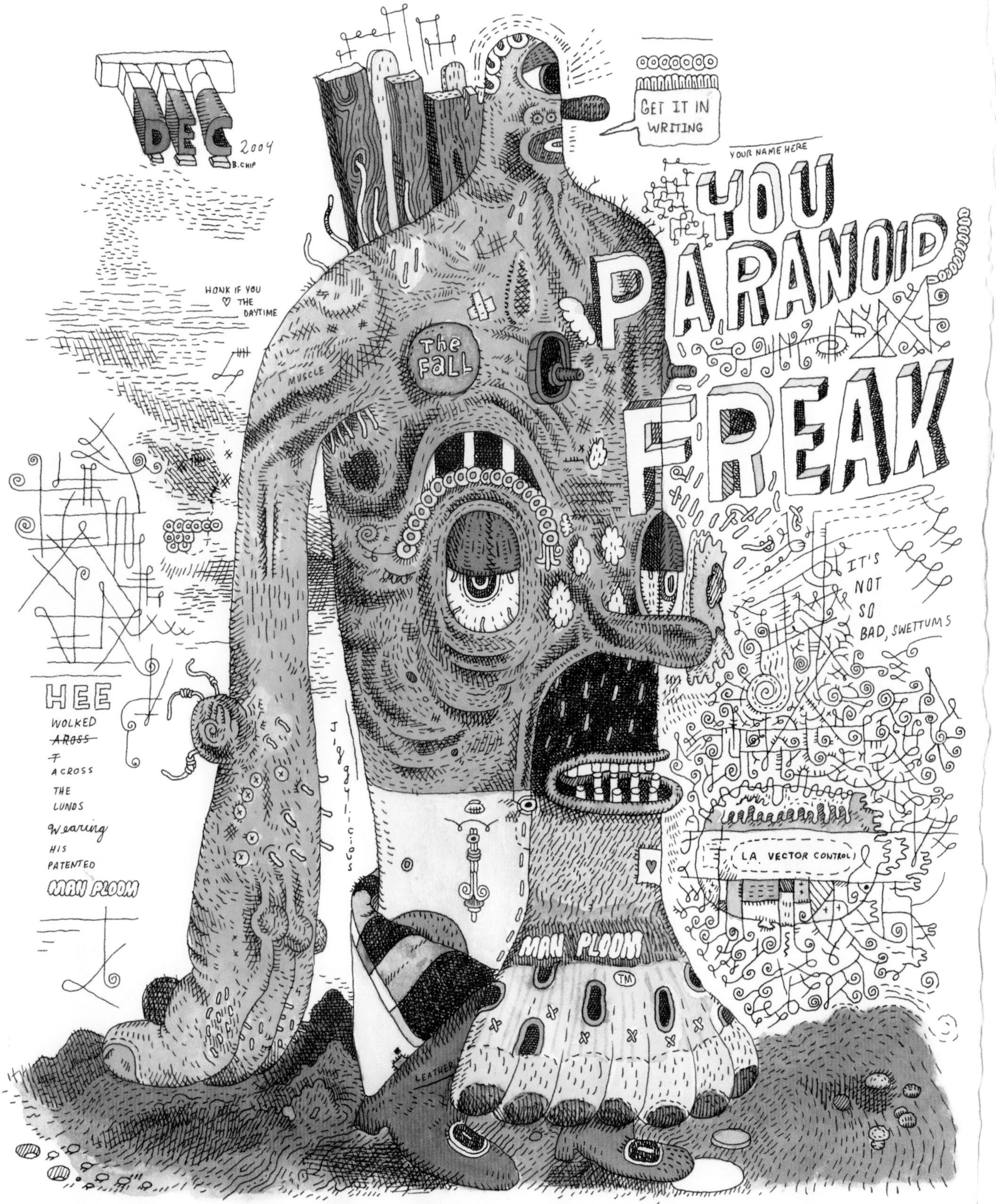
DEC 2004 B.CHIP
GET IT IN WRITING
YOUR NAME HERE
YOU PARANOID FREAK
HONK IF YOU ♡ THE DAYTIME
The Fall
MUSCLE
IT'S NOT SO BAD, SWETTUMS
HEE WOLKED AROSS ACROSS THE LUNDS Wearing HIS PATENTED MAN PLOOM
Jiggylicious
L.A. VECTOR CONTROL
MAN PLOOM
TM
LEATHER

121. *You Paranoid Freak (Man Ploom),* 2004
Ink and watercolour on paper, 10 x 8–½ in.

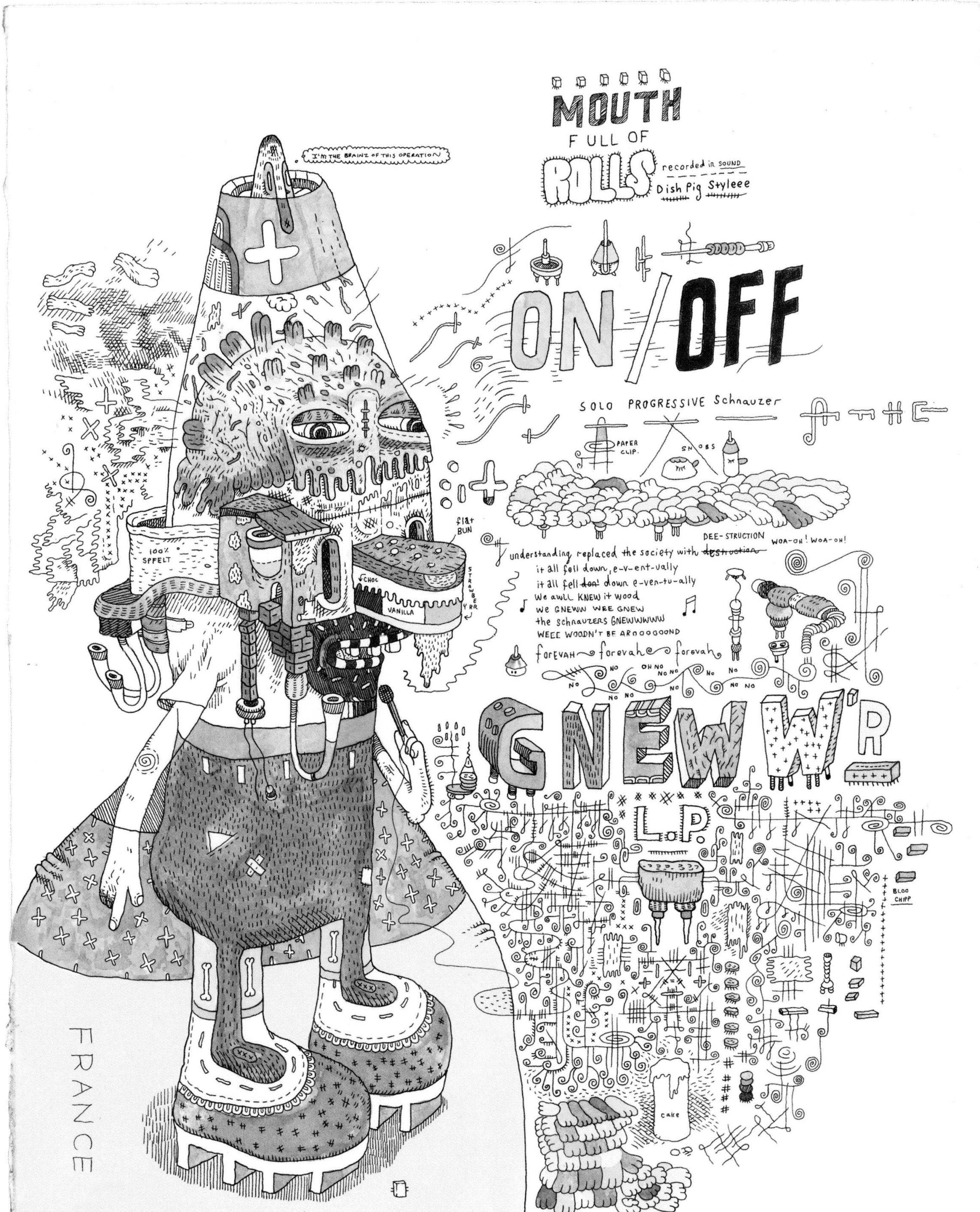
I'M THE BRAINZ OF THIS OPERATION
MOUTH
FULL OF
ROLLS
recorded in SOUND
Dish Pig Styleee
ON/OFF
SOLO PROGRESSIVE Schnauzer
PAPER CLIP.
SNOBS
flat BUN
100% SPFELT
CHOC
VANILLA
STRAWBERRY
DEE-STRUCTION
WOA-OH! WOA-OH!
understanding replaced the society with destruction
it all fell down, e-v-ent-vally
it all fell don! down e-ven-tu-ally
we awll KNEW it wood
we GNEWW WEE GNEW
the schnauzers GNEWWWWW
WEEE WOODN'T BE AROOOOOOND
forevah forevah forevah
NO NO NO NO NO NO NO NO NO
GNEWW'R
L.P.
BLOC CHIPP
CAKE
FRANCE

122. *Mouth Full Of Rolls (On/Off Solo Progressive Schnauzer)* 2004
Ink and watercolour on paper, 14 x 11 in.

123. *Are You A Scientist?*, 2005
Ink and watercolour on paper, 10 x 8 in.

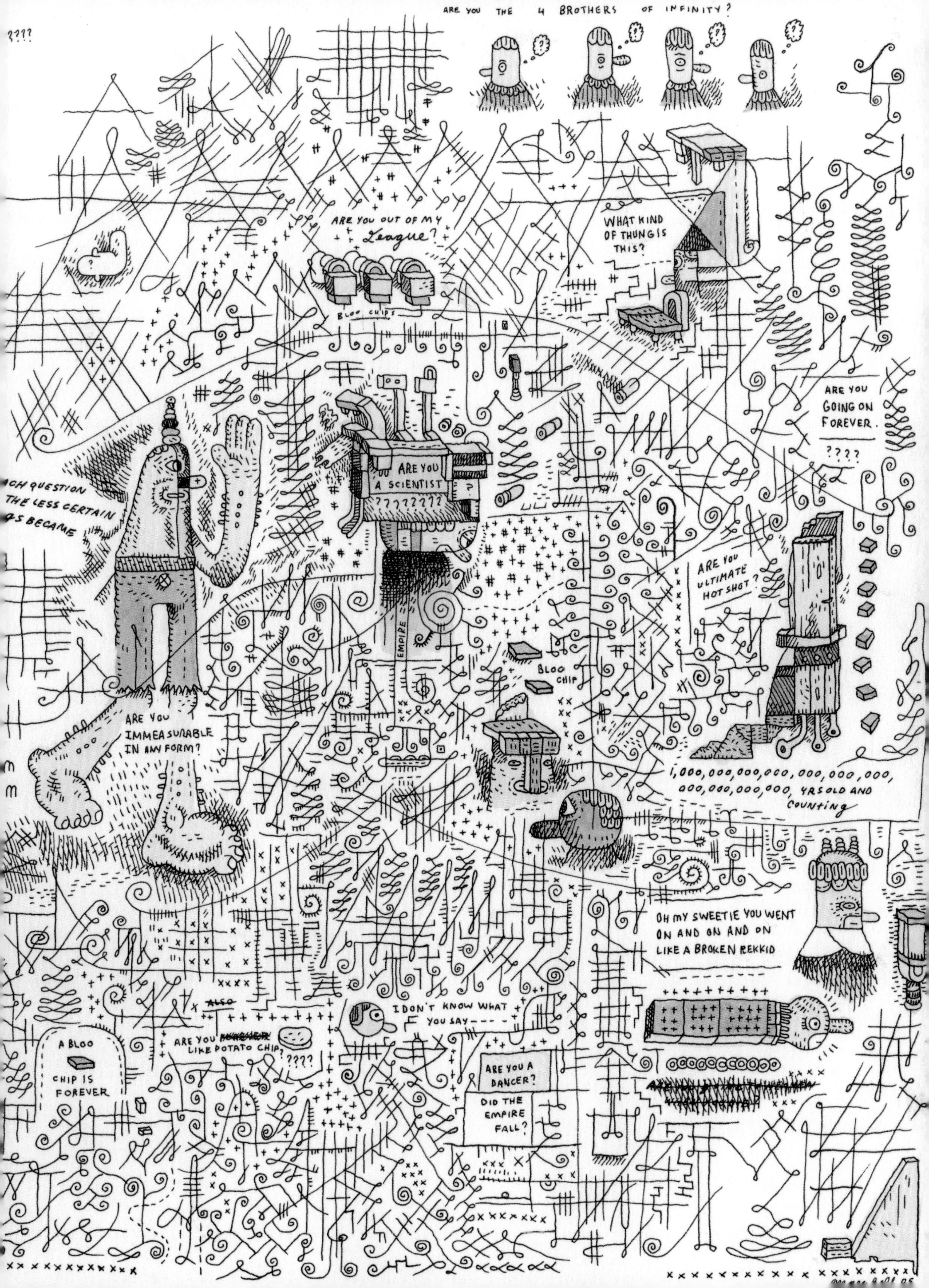

ARE YOU THE 4 BROTHERS OF INFINITY?
????
ARE YOU OUT OF MY League?
WHAT KIND OF THUNG IS THIS?
BLOO CHIPS
ARE YOU GOING ON FOREVER.
????
ARE YOU A SCIENTIST
?????????
CH QUESTION
THE LESS CERTAIN
S BECAME
EMPIRE
ARE YOU ULTIMATE HOT SHOT?
BLOO CHIP
ARE YOU IMMEASURABLE IN ANY FORM?
1,000,000,000,000,000,000,000,
000,000,000,000, YRS OLD AND COUNTING
OH MY SWEETIE YOU WENT ON AND ON AND ON LIKE A BROKEN REKKID
ALSO
I DON'T KNOW WHAT YOU SAY
A BLOO CHIP IS FOREVER
ARE YOU LIKE POTATO CHIP?
????
ARE YOU A DANCER?
DID THE EMPIRE FALL?

THE DUHY SCIENCE-NETWORK

FEATURING

(THIS EPISODE WAS)
— CREATED MOSTLY IN OUR YEAR THAT IS #2002 BY Marc Bell for thee Ganzfeld of U.S.A.
— POST PRODUCTION SCIENTIST: DAVID HEATLEY

THE 600 FOOT MAGIC SCIENTIST

THE 600 ft. MAGIC SCIENTIST, AT HIS FULL HEIGHT, IS ABLE TO PERFORM ALL MANNER OF LARGE TASKS...

CUT!

THE 600 ft. MAGIC SCIENTIST IS DIVISIBLE IN SI BY AS MANY ft. AS NEEDED. HE COULD, FOR EXAMPLE BE 3 200 ft MAGIC SCIENTISTS.

OR 200 3 FT MAGIC SCIENTISTS.

OR EVEN 7,200,000 .001 INCH SCIENTISTS...!

MICROSCOPIC VIEW

(AND SO ON..)

VARIOUS SPECIMENS YOU COULD OBSERVE?

DO NOT TOUCH

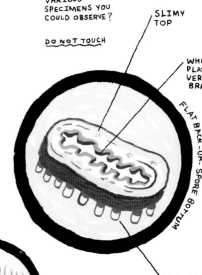

SLIMY TOP

WHI PLAS VERT BRA

FLAT BACK-UH- SPORE BOTTOM

SPORE DROP

INCLUDES:

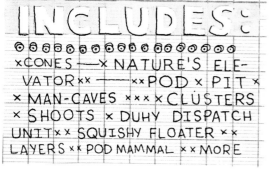

×CONES — × NATURE'S ELE-VATOR ×× ——— ×× POD × PIT × × MAN-CAVES ××× CLUSTERS × SHOOTS × DUHY DISPATCH UNIT×× SQUISHY FLOATER ×× LAYERS ×× POD MAMMAL ×× MORE

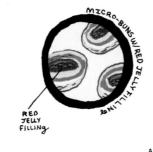

MICRO-BUNS w/RED JELLY FILLING

RED JELLY FILLING

PINK FEELIE TOOBER

PINKIE FEELERS FEEL THE WAY

TOOB-BODY: DIGESTS FOOD SIDE HERE, Y

A HOLE THAT HELPS INJESTS OTHER EDIBLE MICROSCOPIC ORGANISMS (FOOD)

ANOTHER HOLE WHERE WASTE IS EJECTED

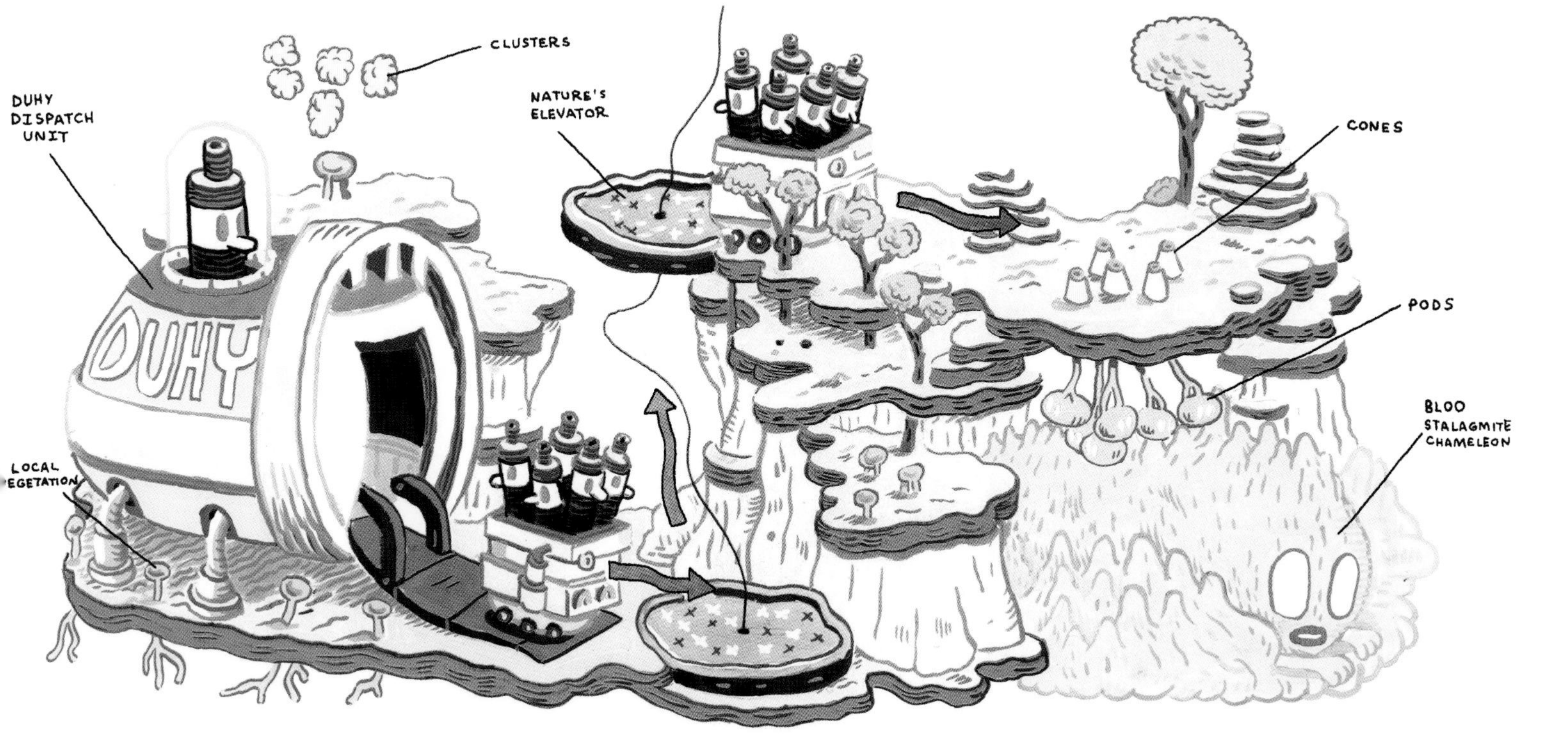
CLUSTERS
DUHY DISPATCH UNIT
NATURE'S ELEVATOR
CONES
PODS
BLOO STALAGMITE CHAMELEON
LOCAL EGETATION
DUHY

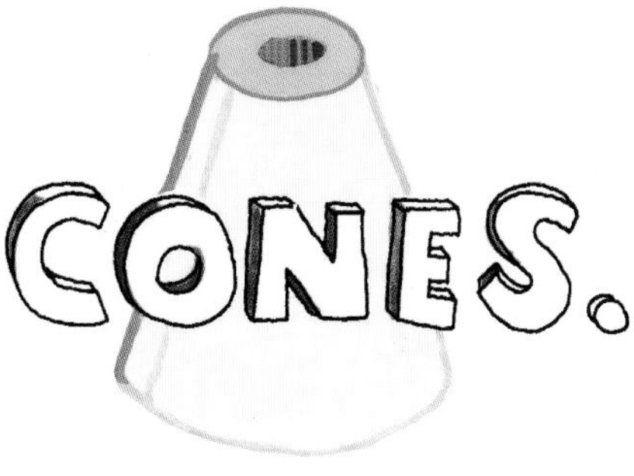
CONES.

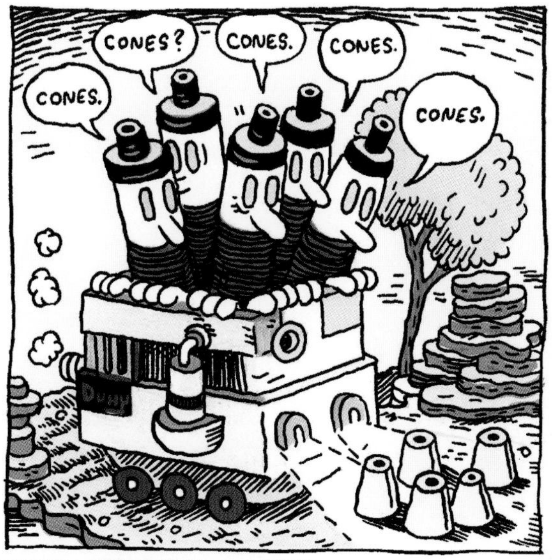
CONES.
CONES?
CONES.
CONES.
CONES.
DUHY

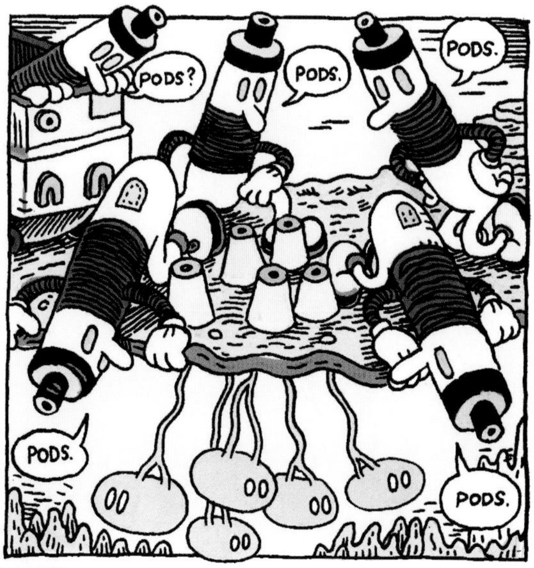
PODS?
PODS.
PODS.
PODS.
PODS.

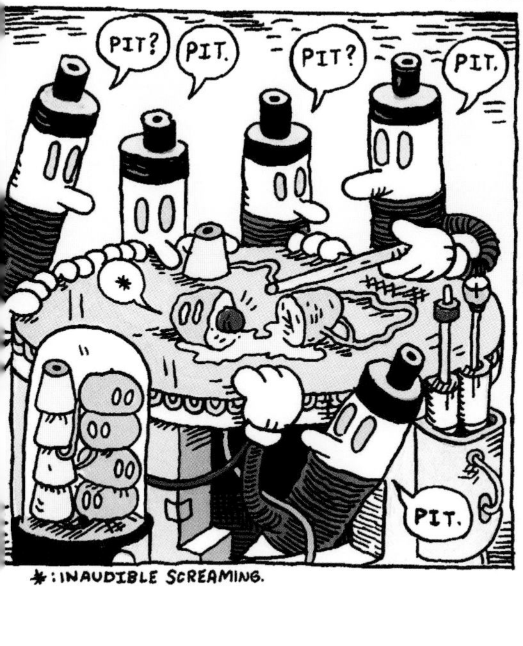
PIT?
PIT.
PIT?
PIT.
*
PIT.

*: INAUDIBLE SCREAMING.

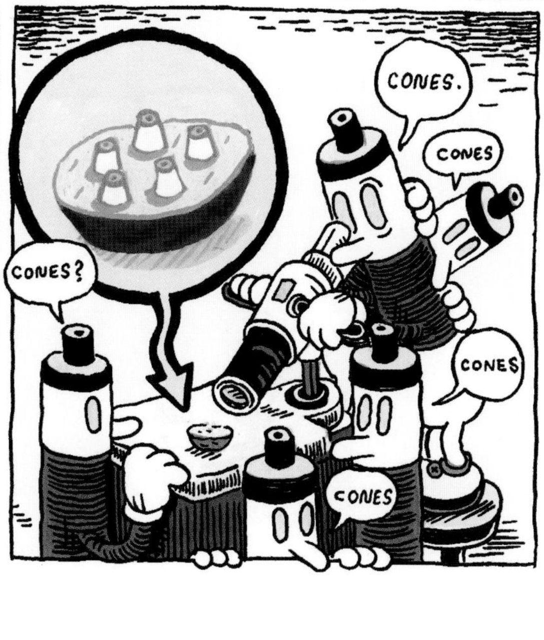
CONES.
CONES
CONES?
CONES
CONES

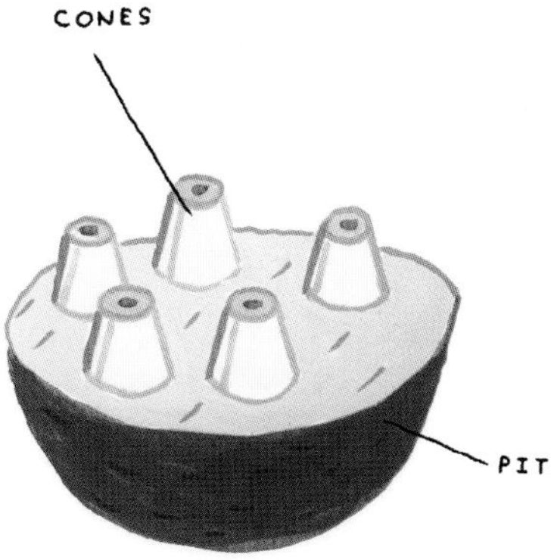
CONES
PIT

× HISTORICAL NOTATION: IT IS BELIEVED THAT THE '600 FT MAGIC SCIENTIST' FIRST CAME UP IN CONVERSATIONS AND SONGS BY PETER THOMPSON AND MARC BELL SOME TIME IN THE LATTER HALF OF THE YEARS OF OUR 20th CENTURY

FIG 1. UNDER OBSERVATION, A MUCH SMALLER MAGIC SCIENTIST IS PLACED ALONGSIDE THE PIT. THE MAGIC SCIENTIST SPLITS IN (4)

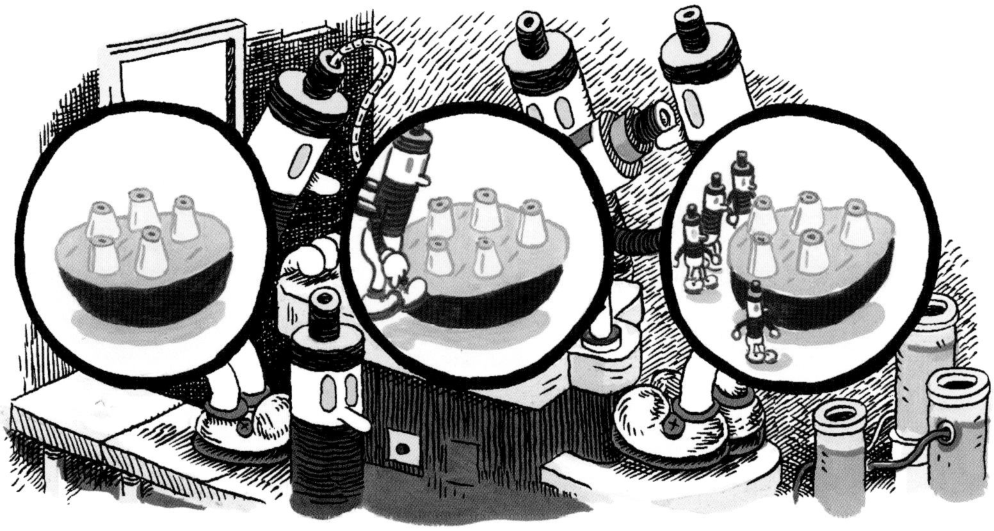

FIG. 2 INTERIOR/EXTERIOR VIEW OF PIT
ONE OF THE FOUR MAGIC SCIENTISTS INVESTIGATES CONES

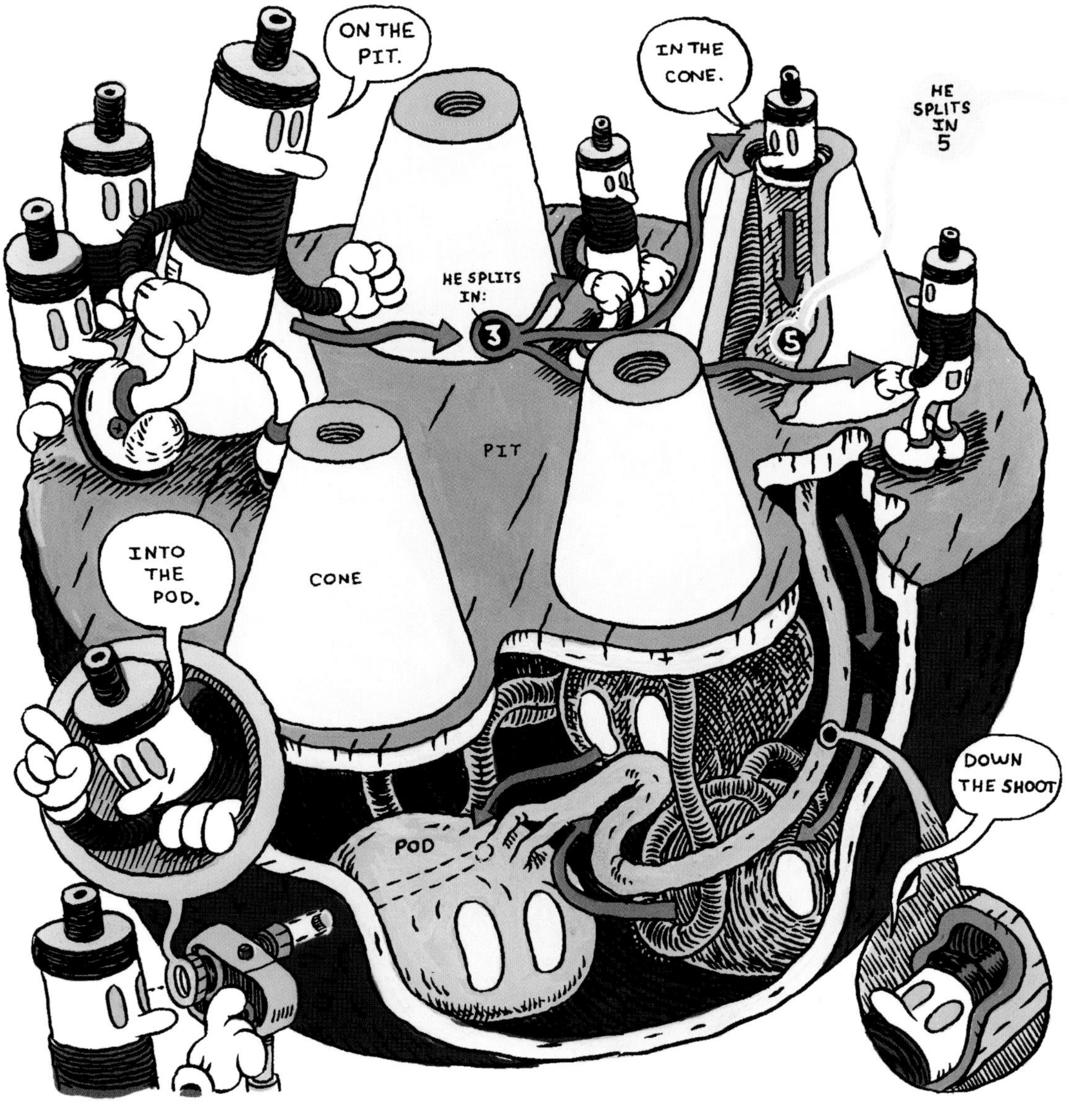
ON THE PIT.
IN THE CONE.
HE SPLITS IN 5
HE SPLITS IN:
3
5
PIT
CONE
INTO THE POD.
POD
DOWN THE SHOOT

FIG. 2a

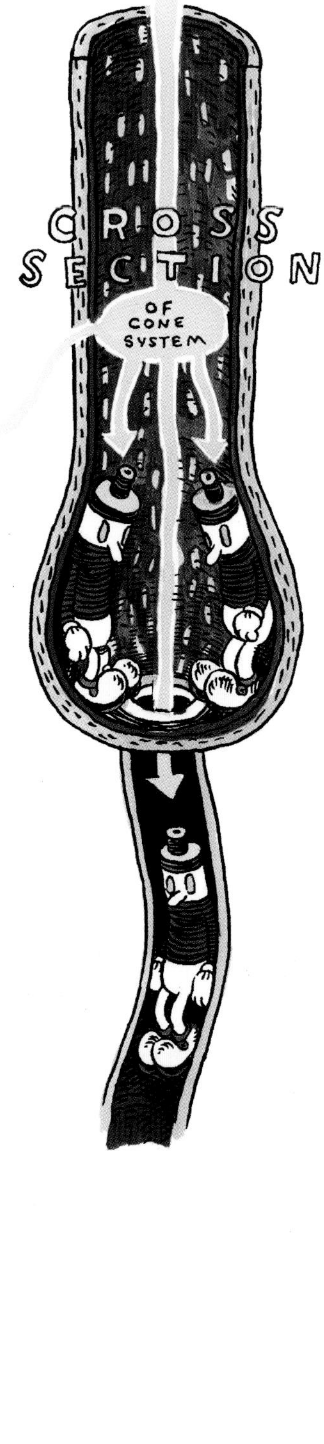
CROSS SECTION
OF CONE SYSTEM

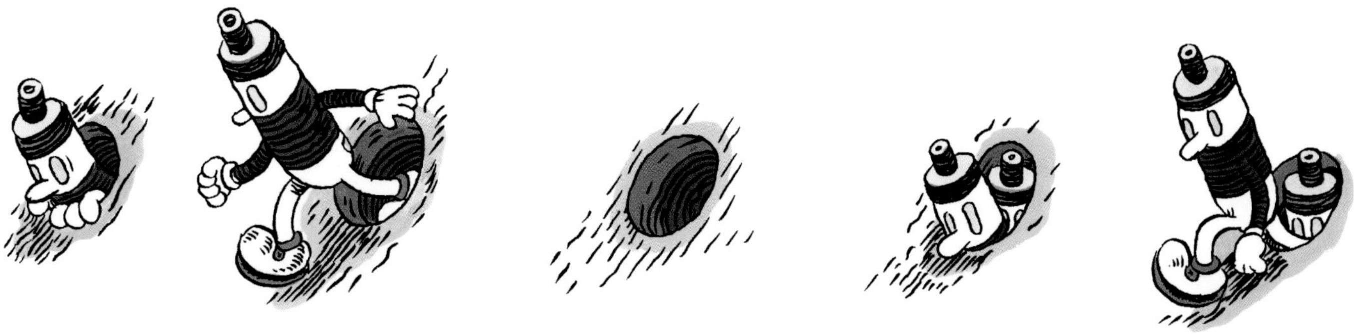

POD.

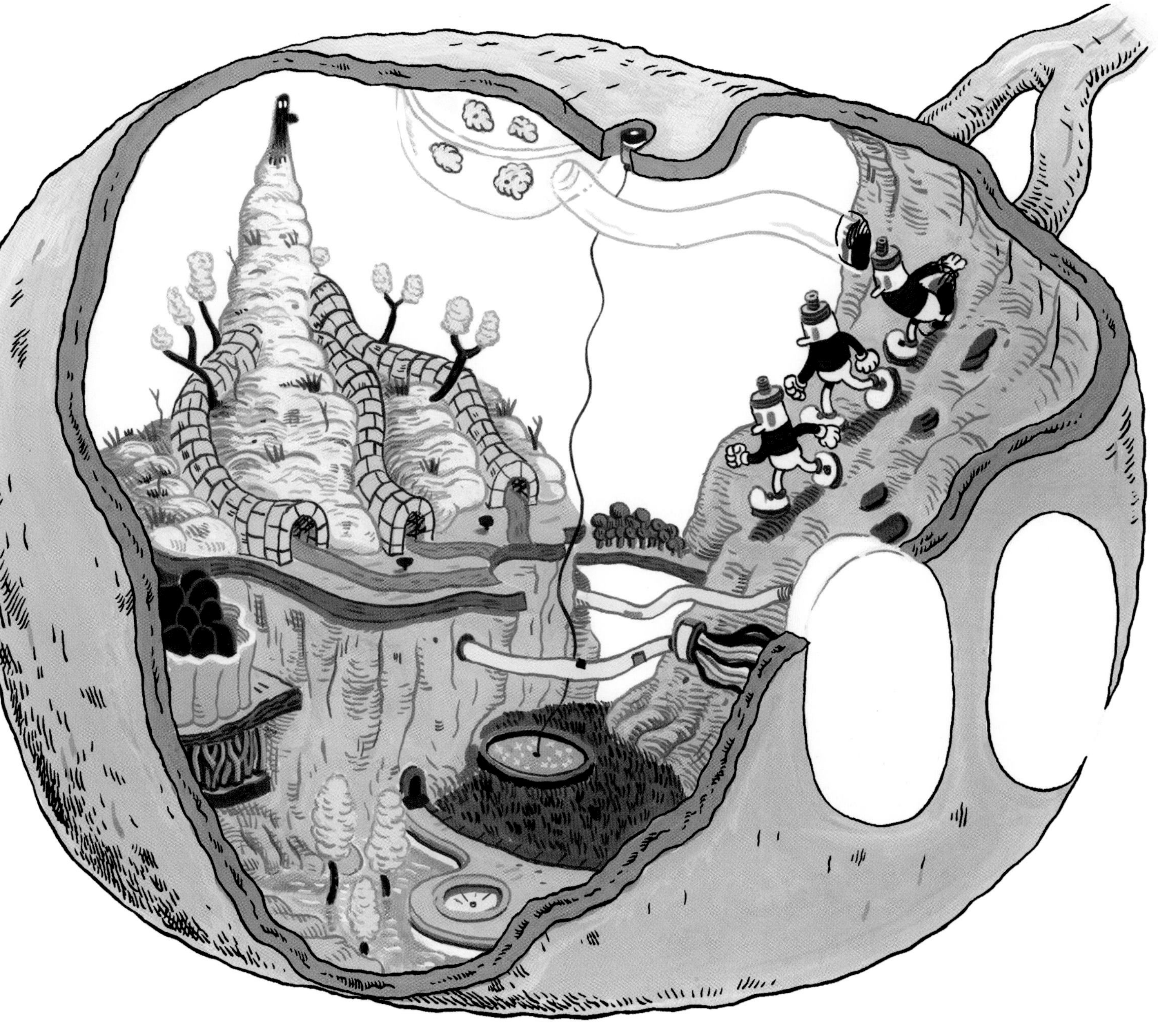

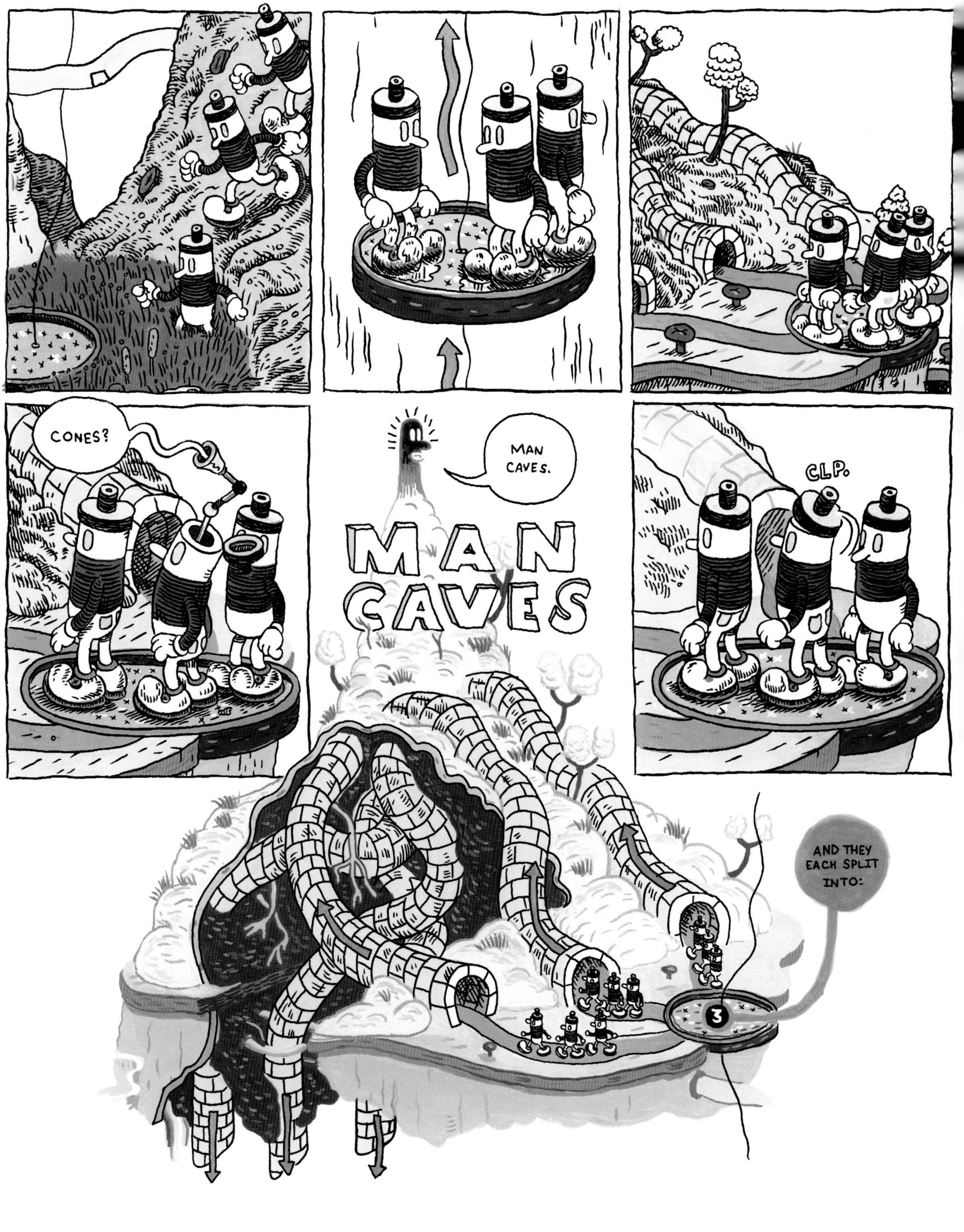
CONES?
MAN CAVES.
MAN CAVES
CLP.
AND THEY EACH SPLIT INTO:
3

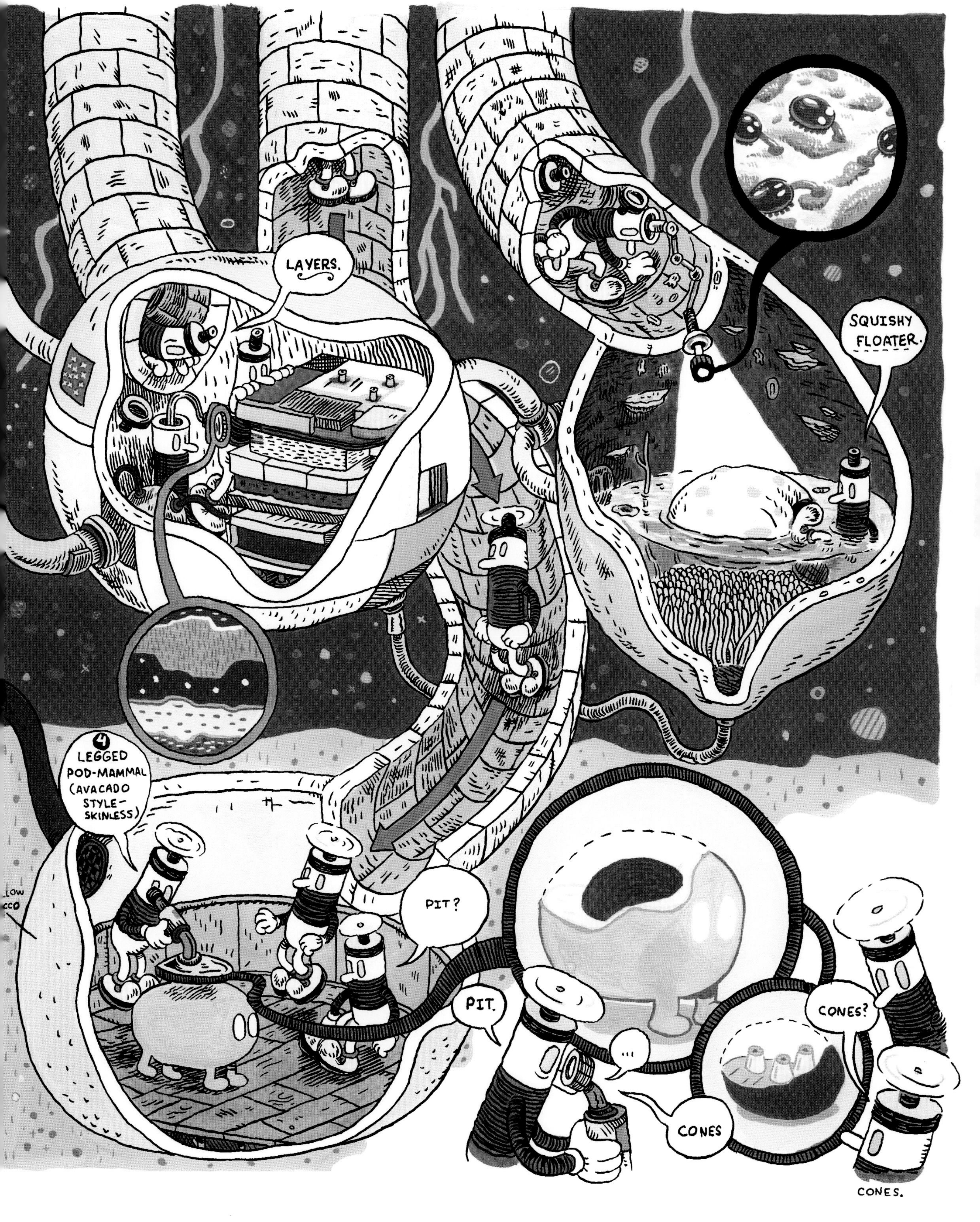
LAYERS.
SQUISHY FLOATER.
4 LEGGED POD-MAMMAL (AVACADO STYLE-SKINLESS)
PIT?
PIT.
...
CONES?
CONES
CONES.

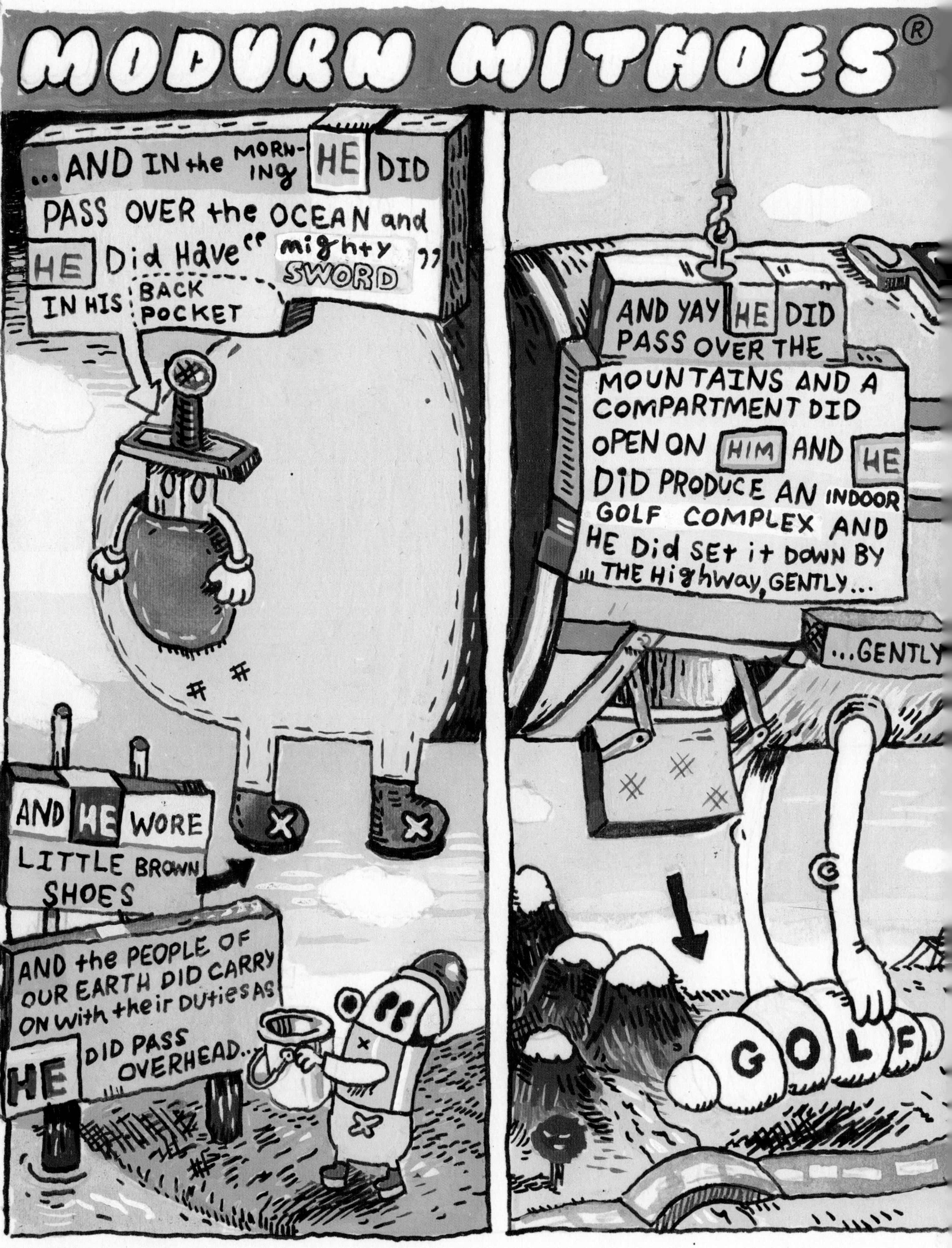
MODURN MITHOES®
...AND IN the MORN-ING HE DID PASS OVER the OCEAN and HE Did Have "mighty SWORD" IN HIS BACK POCKET
AND HE WORE LITTLE BROWN SHOES
AND the PEOPLE OF OUR EARTH DID CARRY ON with their DUTIES AS HE DID PASS OVERHEAD...
AND YAY HE DID PASS OVER THE MOUNTAINS AND A COMPARTMENT DID OPEN ON HIM AND HE DID PRODUCE AN INDOOR GOLF COMPLEX AND HE Did SET it DOWN BY THE Highway, GENTLY...
...GENTLY
GOLF

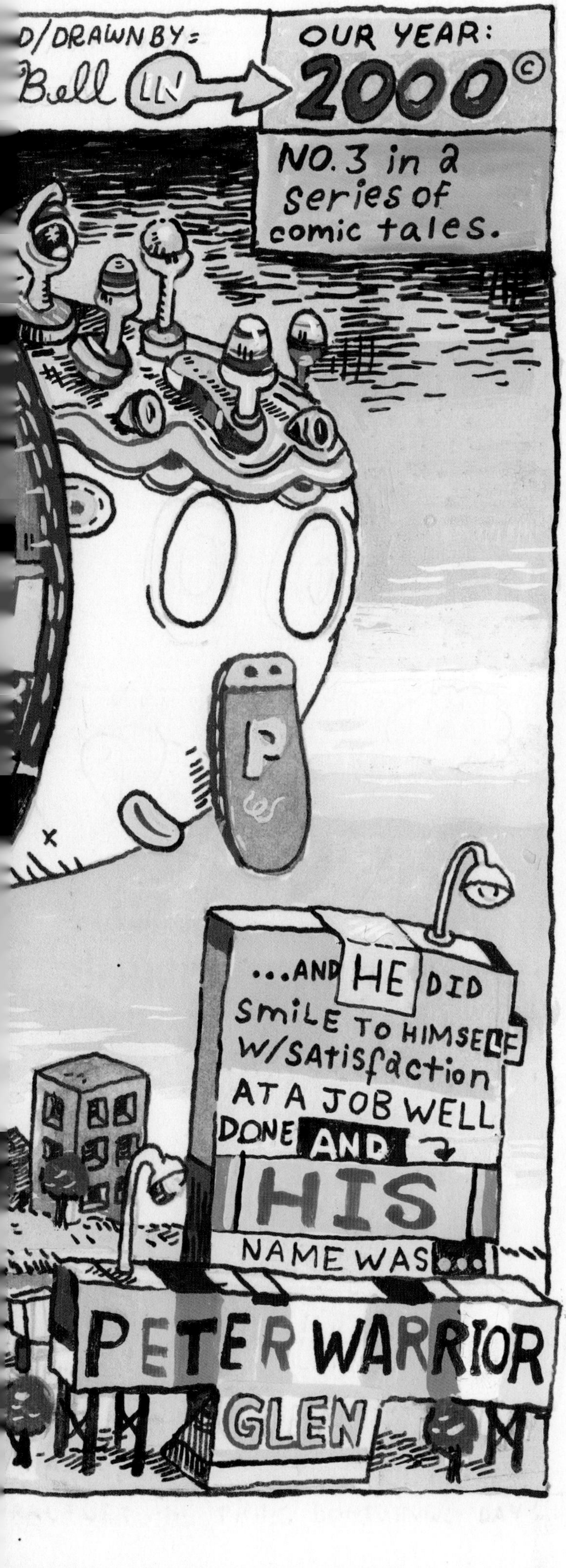
D/DRAWN BY:
Bell
LLN
OUR YEAR:
2000 ©
NO. 3 in a series of comic tales.
...AND HE DID SMILE TO HIMSELF W/SATISfaction AT A JOB WELL DONE AND
HIS
NAME WAS...
PETER WARRIOR
GLEN

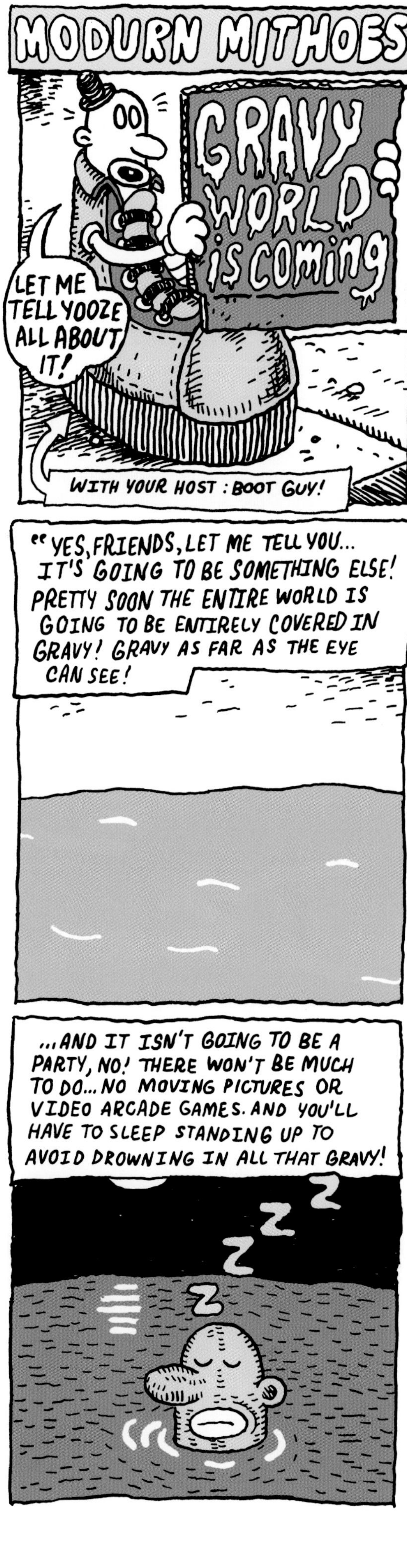
MODURN MITHOES
GRAVY WORLD IS COMING
LET ME TELL YOOZE ALL ABOUT IT!
WITH YOUR HOST : BOOT GUY!
"YES, FRIENDS, LET ME TELL YOU... IT'S GOING TO BE SOMETHING ELSE! PRETTY SOON THE ENTIRE WORLD IS GOING TO BE ENTIRELY COVERED IN GRAVY! GRAVY AS FAR AS THE EYE CAN SEE!
...AND IT ISN'T GOING TO BE A PARTY, NO! THERE WON'T BE MUCH TO DO... NO MOVING PICTURES OR VIDEO ARCADE GAMES. AND YOU'LL HAVE TO SLEEP STANDING UP TO AVOID DROWNING IN ALL THAT GRAVY!
Z Z Z Z

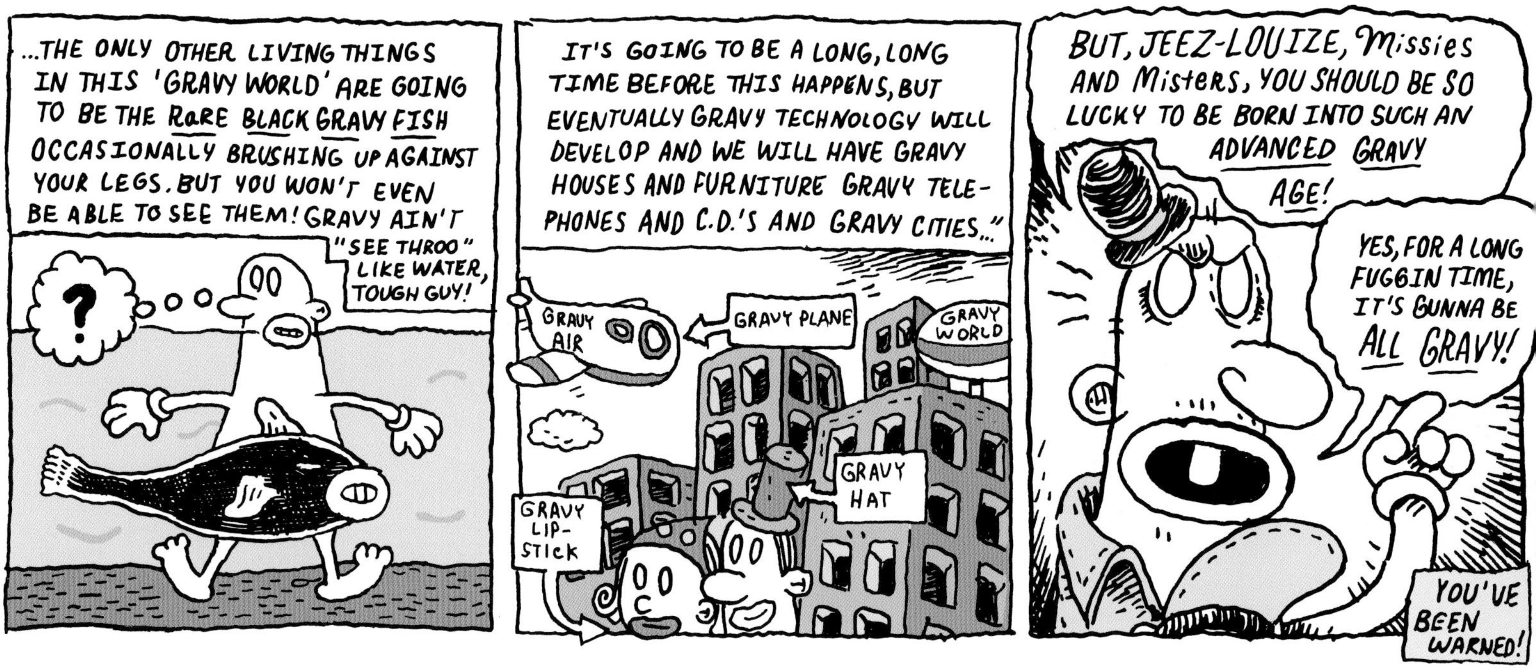
...THE ONLY OTHER LIVING THINGS IN THIS 'GRAVY WORLD' ARE GOING TO BE THE RaRE BLACK GRAVY FISH OCCASIONALLY BRUSHING UP AGAINST YOUR LEGS. BUT YOU WON'T EVEN BE ABLE TO SEE THEM! GRAVY AIN'T "SEE THROO" LIKE WATER, TOUGH GUY!
?
IT'S GOING TO BE A LONG, LONG TIME BEFORE THIS HAPPENS, BUT EVENTUALLY GRAVY TECHNOLOGY WILL DEVELOP AND WE WILL HAVE GRAVY HOUSES AND FURNITURE GRAVY TELEPHONES AND C.D.'S AND GRAVY CITIES..."
GRAVY AIR
GRAVY PLANE
GRAVY WORLD
GRAVY HAT
GRAVY LIP-STICK
BUT, JEEZ-LOUIZE, Missies AND Misters, YOU SHOULD BE SO LUCKY TO BE BORN INTO SUCH AN ADVANCED GRAVY AGE!
YES, FOR A LONG FUGGIN TIME, IT'S GUNNA BE ALL GRAVY!
YOU'VE BEEN WARNED!

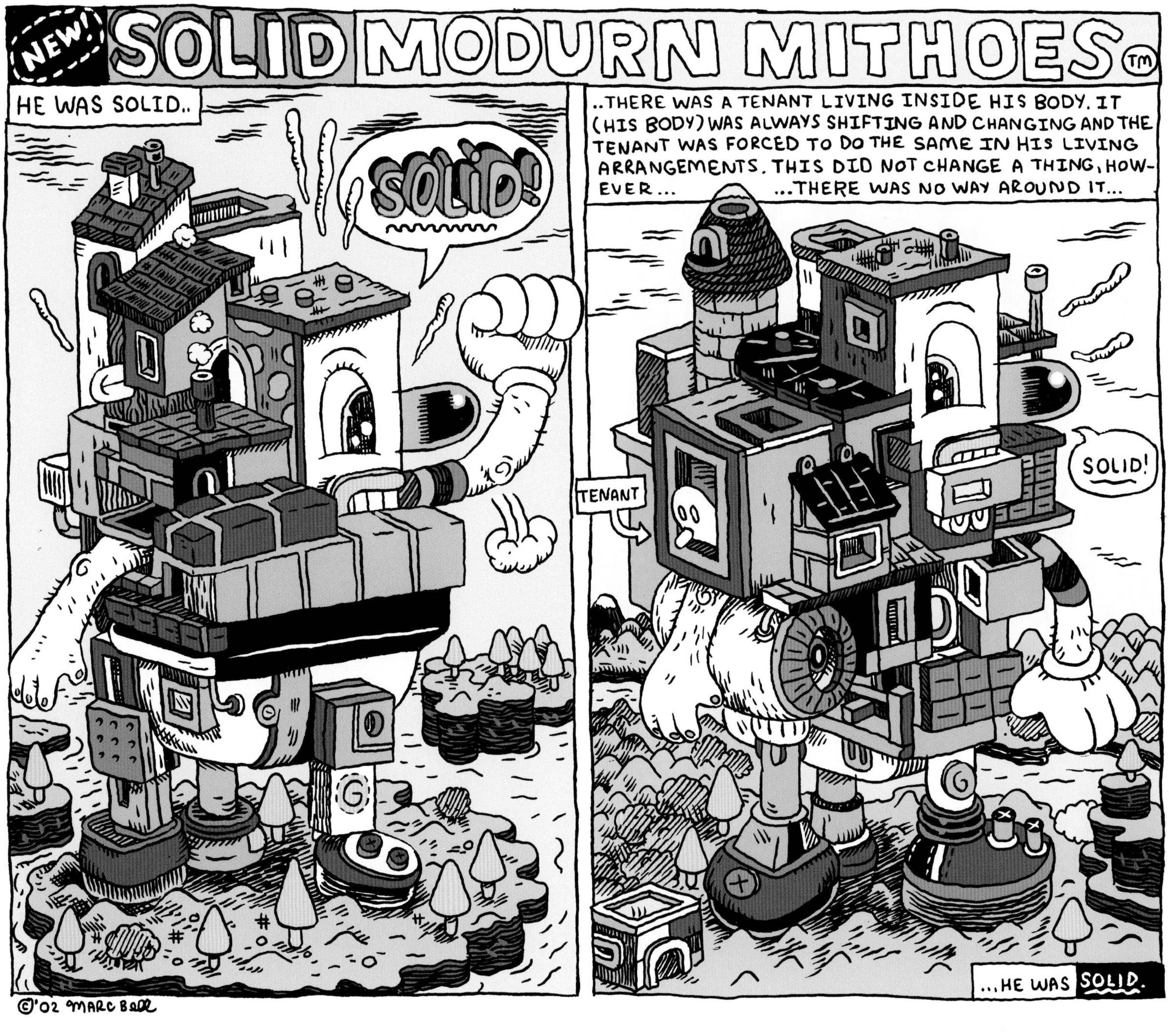
NEW!
SOLID MODURN MITHOES TM
HE WAS SOLID..
SOLID!
..THERE WAS A TENANT LIVING INSIDE HIS BODY. IT (HIS BODY) WAS ALWAYS SHIFTING AND CHANGING AND THE TENANT WAS FORCED TO DO THE SAME IN HIS LIVING ARRANGEMENTS. THIS DID NOT CHANGE A THING, HOWEVER... ...THERE WAS NO WAY AROUND IT...
TENANT
SOLID!
...HE WAS SOLID.

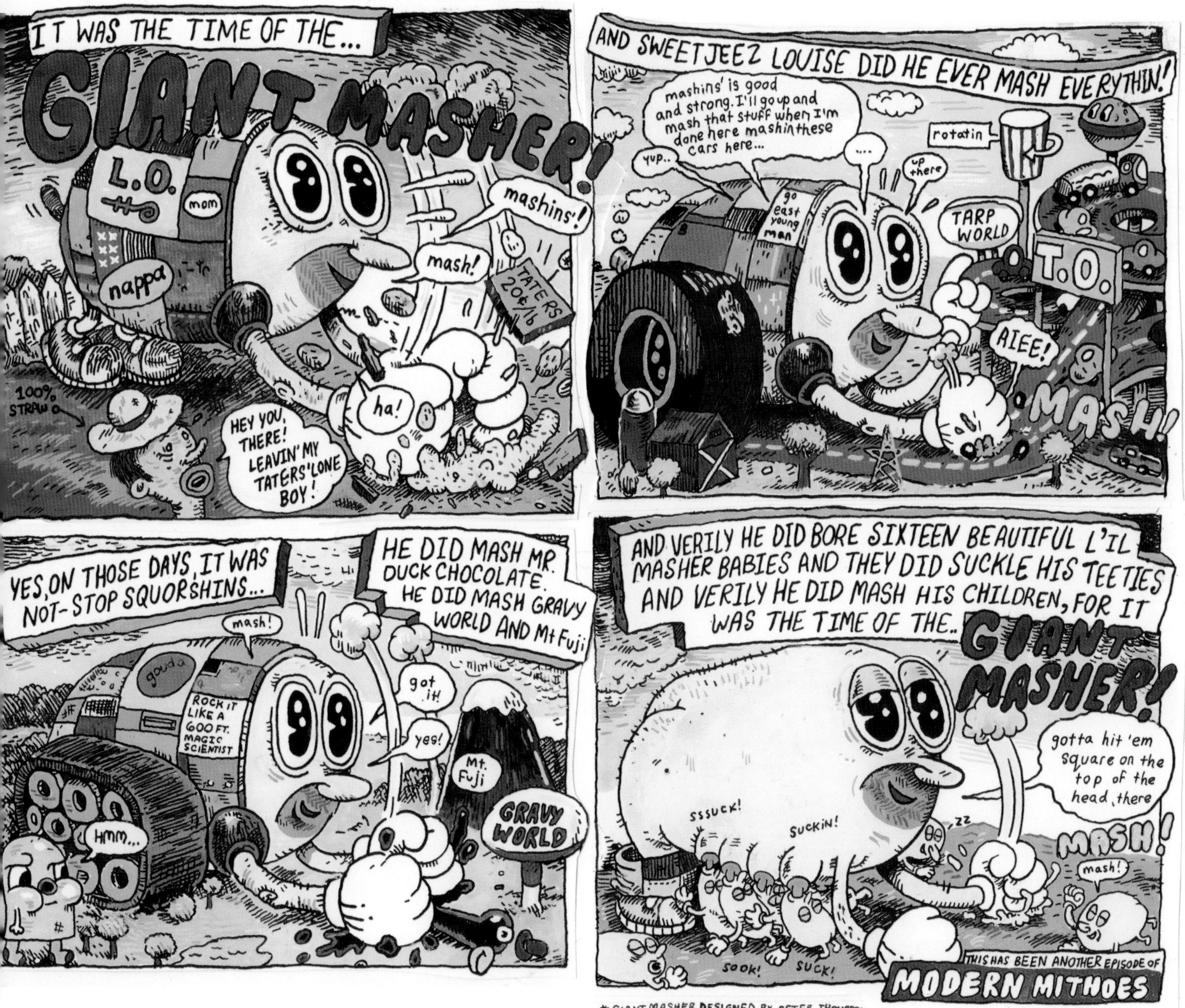
IT WAS THE TIME OF THE...
GIANT MASHER!
L.O.
mom
nappa
mashins'!
mash!
TATERS 20¢/lb
ha!
100% STRAW
HEY YOU, THERE! LEAVIN' MY TATERS 'LONE BOY!
AND SWEETJEEZ LOUISE DID HE EVER MASH EVERYTHIN'!
mashins' is good and strong. I'll go up and mash that stuff when I'm done here mashin these cars here...
yup..
....
up there
rotatin
go east young man
TARP WORLD
T.O.
AIEE!
MASH!
YES, ON THOSE DAYS, IT WAS NOT-STOP SQUORSHINS...
HE DID MASH MR. DUCK CHOCOLATE. HE DID MASH GRAVY WORLD AND Mt Fuji
mash!
gouda
ROCK IT LIKE A 600 FT. MAGIC SCIENTIST
got it!
yes!
Mt. Fuji
GRAVY WORLD
HMM...
AND VERILY HE DID BORE SIXTEEN BEAUTIFUL L'IL MASHER BABIES AND THEY DID SUCKLE HIS TEETIES AND VERILY HE DID MASH HIS CHILDREN, FOR IT WAS THE TIME OF THE.. GIANT MASHER!
gotta hit 'em square on the top of the head, there
SSSUCK!
SUCKIN!
zz
MASH!
mash!
SOOK!
SUCK!
THIS HAS BEEN ANOTHER EPISODE OF
MODERN MITHOES

* GIANT MASHER DESIGNED BY PETER THOMPSON AND MARC BELL

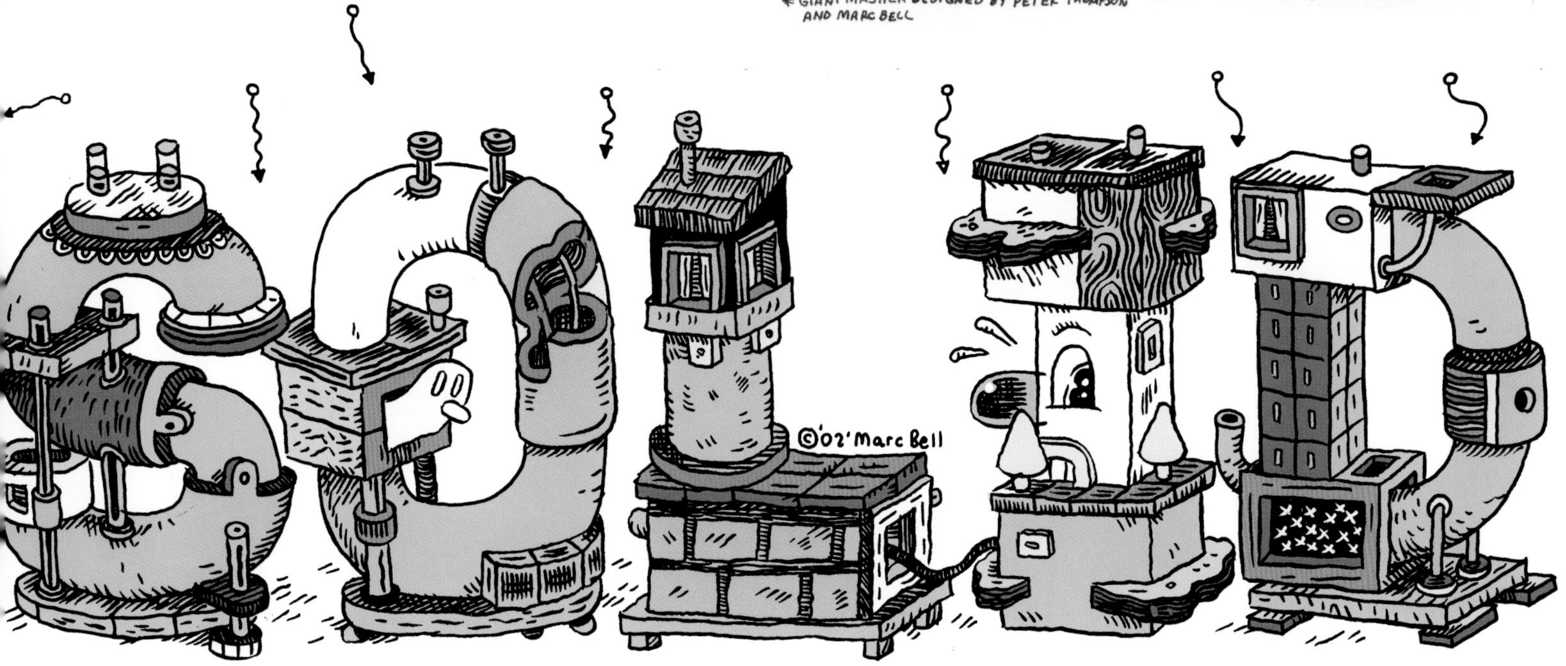
©'02' Marc Bell

A Visit To The Artist's Address Book

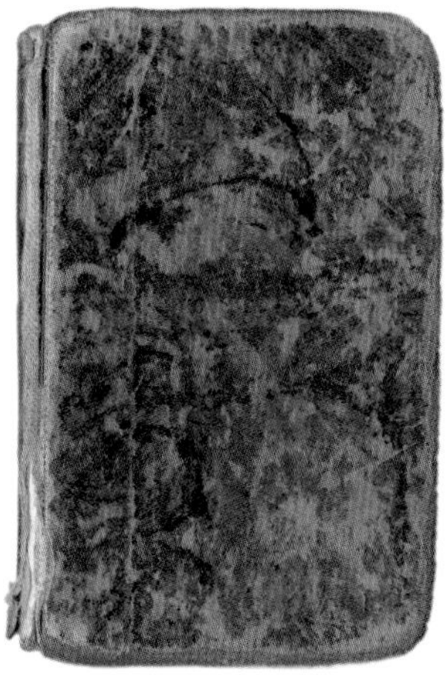

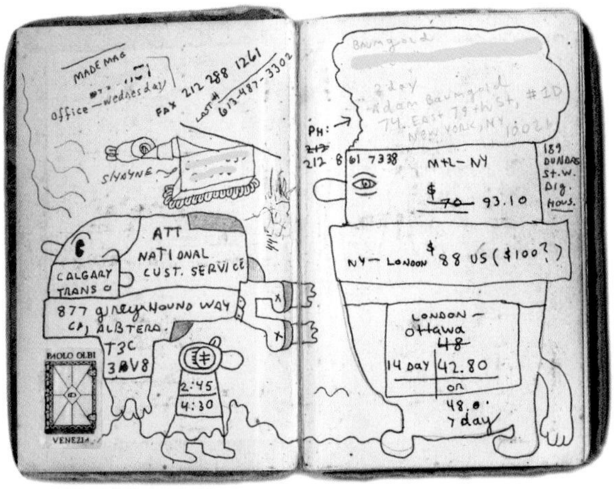
MADEMAN
Office—wednesday
FAX 212 288 1261
SHAYNE
ATT
NATIONAL
CUST. SERVICE
CALGARY
TRANS
877 greyhound way
2:45
4:30
PH:
212 861 7338
MTL-NY
93.10
189
DUNDAS
St.W.
NY—LONDON $88 US ($100?)
LONDON—
Ottawa
14 day
42.80
on
7 day

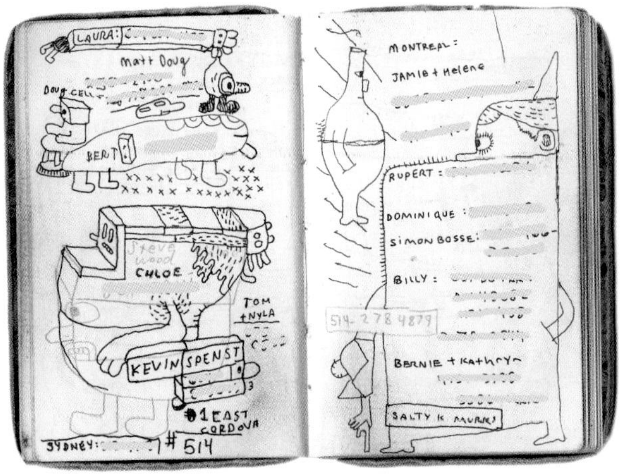
LAURA:
Matt Doug
BERT
CHLOE
TOM
+NYLA
KEVIN SPENST
#1 EAST
CORDOVA
SYDNEY:
#514
MONTREAL:
JAMIE + Helene
RUPERT:
DOMINIQUE:
SIMON BOSSE:
BILLY:
514-278 4879
BERNIE + Kathryn

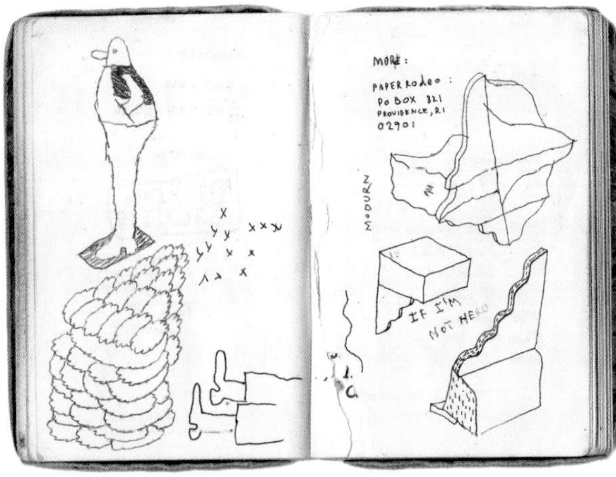
MORE:
PAPER RODEO:
PO BOX 321
PROVIDENCE, RI
02901
MODURN
IF I'M
NOT HERE

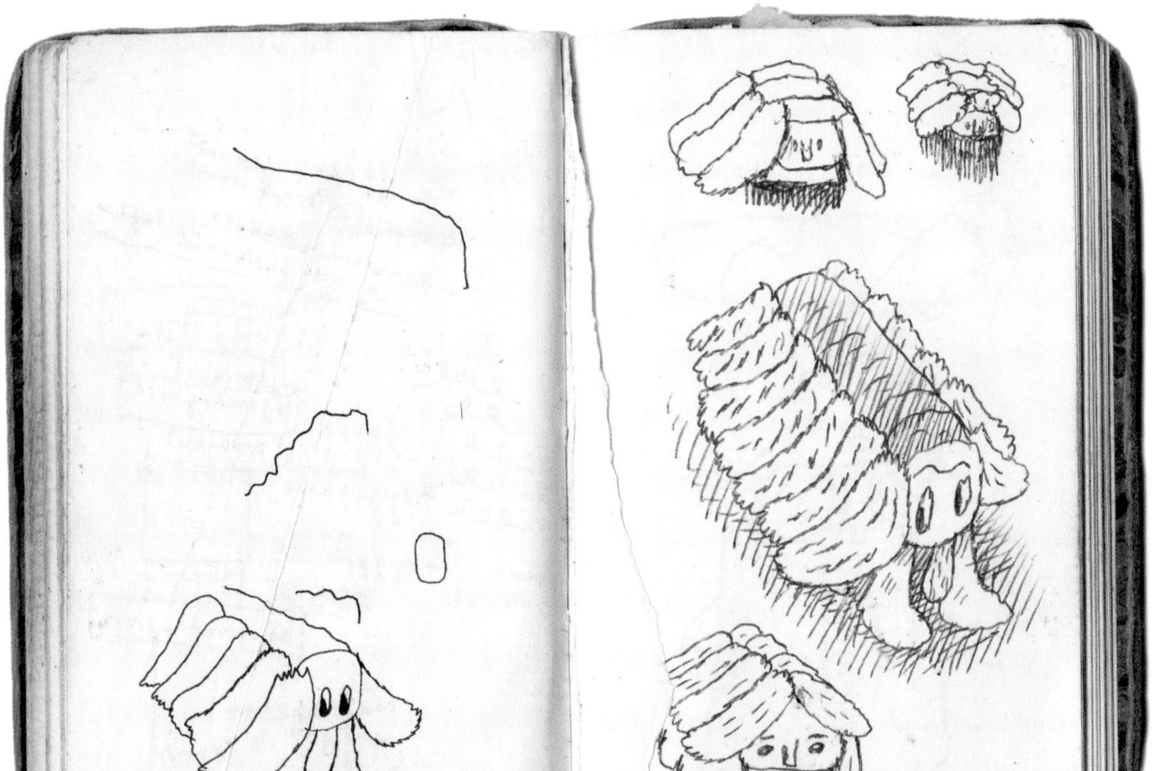

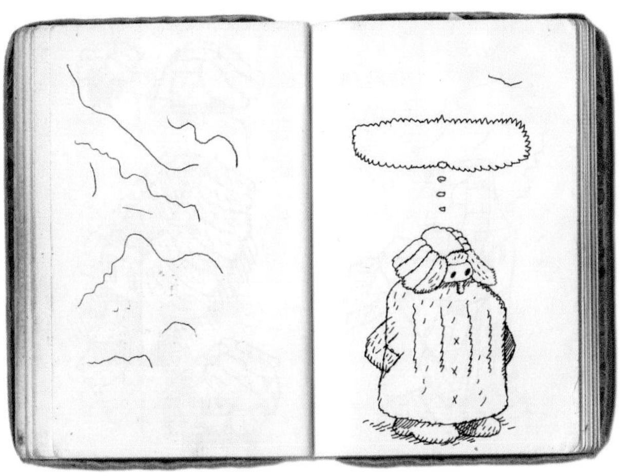

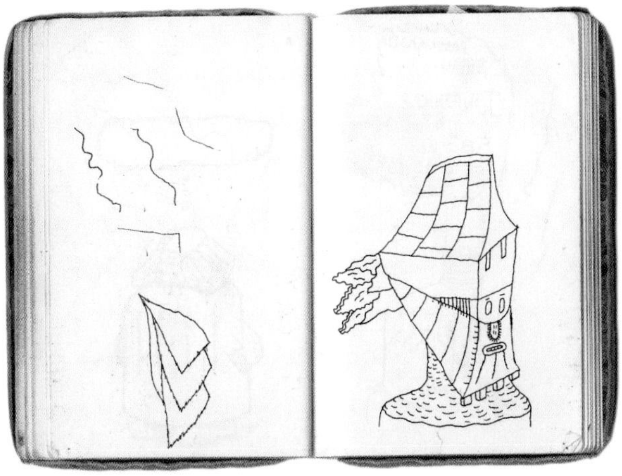

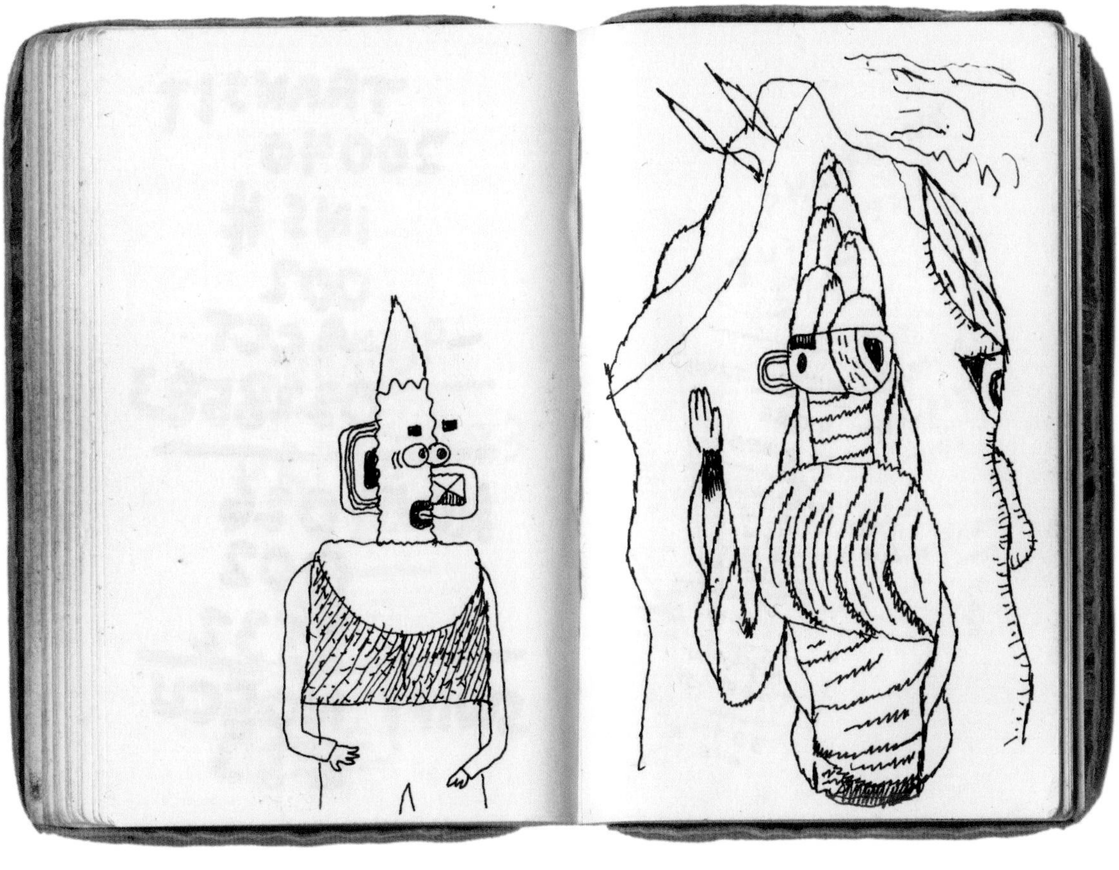

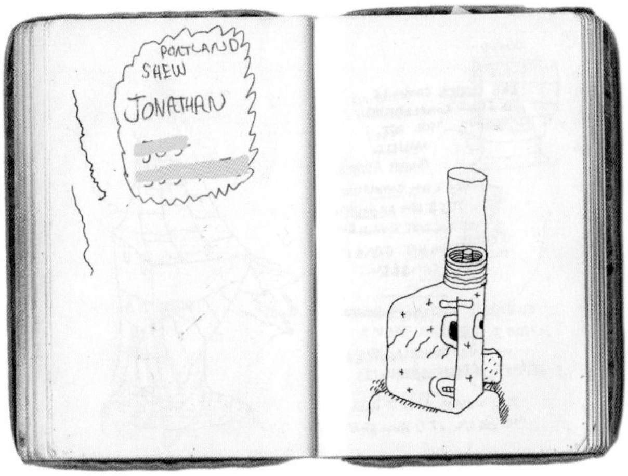
PORTLAND
SHEW
JONATHAN

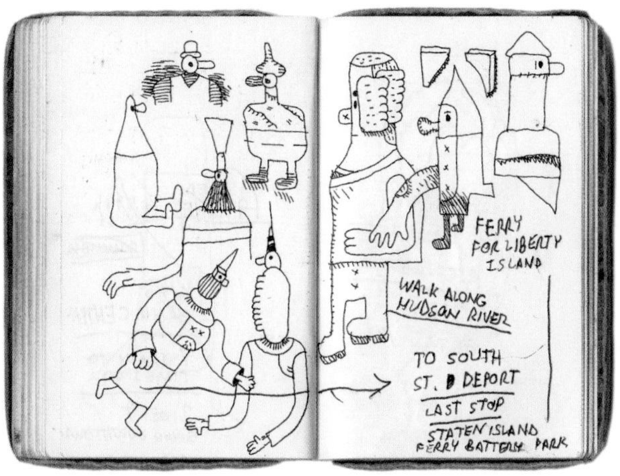
FERRY
FOR LIBERTY
ISLAND
WALK ALONG
HUDSON RIVER
TO SOUTH
ST. DEPORT
LAST STOP
STATEN ISLAND
FERRY BATTERY PARK

A Hot Dog On Crutches
A Conversation Between Marc Bell and Tom Devlin

Recorded in The Morris Room atop The Large Green Sofa from January 2009 to sometime past the imaginary deadline in March 2009.

The admission was free.

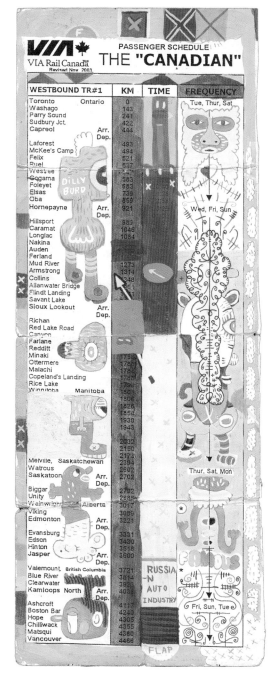

Marc: Hi Tom, welcome to my book *Hot Potatoe* (sic), have a seat. Would you like a designer cupcake?

{*shuffling of papers*}

Tom: Oh, yes, thanks. Let's see. Uh–hmm. There we go. {*Sniffs.*} Is this Maple Fennel? Okay. First off, I'd like to thank you for taking the time to sit with me and chat. It's very much appreciated. There are certain requirements, um, standards, that we must adhere to, you see, so this is a great help. I wanted to start off with a little bit of your background. You grew up in London, Ontario and eventually attended an arts high school there called Bealart. I'm curious about the parental support and sibling support for making art leading up to your "formal training"—I ask because I'm always interested in how a young artist may have been nurtured or even acted in opposition to a non–nurturing environment. And, you're a twin, and the rest of us non–twins are fascinated by the real or imagined magical possibilities of that relationship. Could you talk about these "early years" a bit?

Marc: I grew up with a twin sister and an older sister. And parents. I'd say I grew up in a nurturing environment as a child. My parents split up while I was in high school. Normal stuff. I always liked to draw and was encouraged but I suppose my own natural ability and this encouragement mixed with my own insecurity about functioning in the real world led to me really focusing on art while others grew out of it. My grandmother used to marvel at how I lined up my "dinky toys." My mom told me that a teacher once had given me a bad mark in art and so she took in these drawings I'd been doing to show the teacher that she was wrong. That was in elementary school rather than high school

VIA Rail Canada
Revised Nov. 2003
PASSENGER SCHEDULE
THE "CANADIAN"
WESTBOUND TR#1
KM
TIME
FREQUENCY
Toronto Ontario
Washago
Parry Sound
Sudbury Jct.
Capreol
Laforest
McKee's Camp
Felix
Elsas
Oba
Hornepayne
Hillsport
Caramat
Longlac
Nakina
Auden
Ferland
Mud River
Armstrong
Collins
Allanwater Bridge
Flindt Landing
Savant Lake
Sioux Lookout
Richan
Red Lake Road
Farlane
Redditt
Minaki
Ottermere
Malachi
Copeland's Landing
Rice Lake
Manitoba
Melville, Saskatchewan
Watrous
Saskatoon
Biggar
Unity
Alberta
Viking
Edmonton
Evansburg
Edson
Hinton
Jasper
Valemount British Columbia
Blue River
Clearwater
Kamloops North
Ashcroft
Boston Bar
Hope
Chilliwack
Matsqui
Vancouver
Arr.
Dep.
DILLY BURD
Tue, Thur, Sat
Wed, Fri, Sun
Thur, Sat, Mon
Fri, Sun, Tue
RUSSIA -N AUTO INDUSTRY
FLAP

(*member of audience laughs*). I think she might have shown my teacher my imitation *BC* comics starring a daddy longlegs and the *BC* anthill but I am not sure. I was very sensitive and later, I created satirical versions of these cartoon characters the guidance counsellor was using to teach me about my emotions (I was reading *MAD*). My way of dealing with mortification or something. I don't think I have a psychic connection with my twin sister but maybe I haven't exercised that part of my twin brain. Her and I are opposites in a sense but I think we "get" where each other are coming from. We are both pretty opinionated.

Bealart was a good experience because it was free, mainly. They wanted to kick me out at one point and I was fairly baffled. I didn't think I was a terrible student but I don't think they thought I should really be there. These cupcakes are very good, by the way.

Audience member: Ask him about his Marillion record collection.

Tom: We'll get to his record collection in the second part of the interview, sir. I've got several questions devoted to Marillion as well as the solo Fish records. Now, Marc, while at Bealart, you met Jason McLean and Peter Thompson, correct? Was this the beginning of your collaborative work, something that I consider to be a large part of what you do? Also, could you talk about your "comics education" as well. Was this a shared interest between the three of you? Were you making the weekly trip to the local convenience store to buy copies of *MAD Magazine* and *Ralph Snart Adventures*? Are there any Lemon–Rind Vanilla Cupcakes left over there?

This page: *The Canadian*, 2003
Mixed media on paper

Marc: There's Ginger Chocolate. Oh, wait, yes there is one left. We should have brought enough for everybody I guess.

Audience member: We could split one.

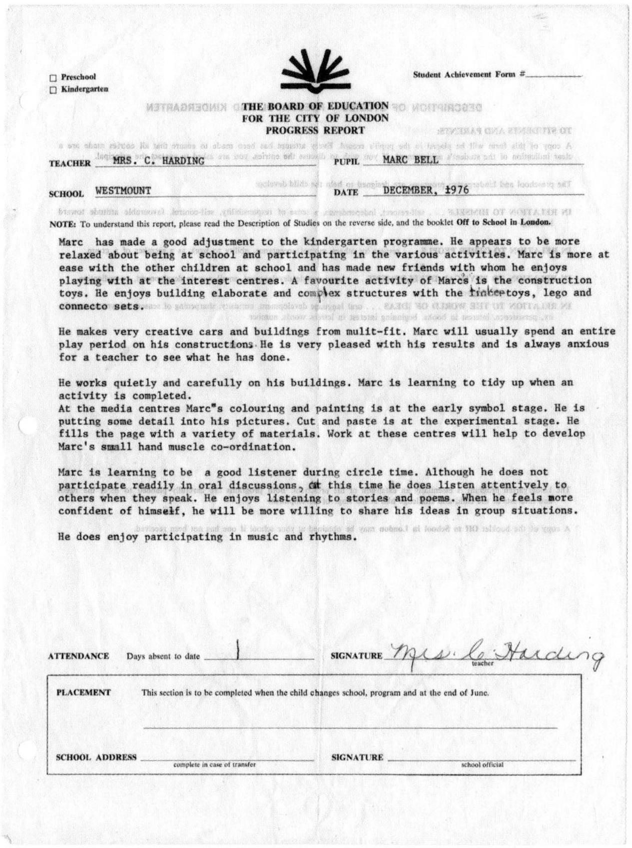
☐ Preschool
☐ Kindergarten

Student Achievement Form #

THE BOARD OF EDUCATION
FOR THE CITY OF LONDON
PROGRESS REPORT

TEACHER MRS. C. HARDING PUPIL MARC BELL

SCHOOL WESTMOUNT DATE DECEMBER, 1976

NOTE: To understand this report, please read the Description of Studies on the reverse side, and the booklet **Off to School in London.**

Marc has made a good adjustment to the kindergarten programme. He appears to be more relaxed about being at school and participating in the various activities. Marc is more at ease with the other children at school and has made new friends with whom he enjoys playing with at the interest centres. A favourite activity of Marcs is the construction toys. He enjoys building elaborate and complex structures with the tinkertoys, lego and connecto sets.

He makes very creative cars and buildings from mulit-fit. Marc will usually spend an entire play period on his constructions. He is very pleased with his results and is always anxious for a teacher to see what he has done.

He works quietly and carefully on his buildings. Marc is learning to tidy up when an activity is completed.
At the media centres Marc"s colouring and painting is at the early symbol stage. He is putting some detail into his pictures. Cut and paste is at the experimental stage. He fills the page with a variety of materials. Work at these centres will help to develop Marc's small hand muscle co-ordination.

Marc is learning to be a good listener during circle time. Although he does not participate readily in oral discussions, at this time he does listen attentively to others when they speak. He enjoys listening to stories and poems. When he feels more confident of himself, he will be more willing to share his ideas in group situations.

He does enjoy participating in music and rhythms.

ATTENDANCE Days absent to date 1 SIGNATURE Mrs. C. Harding (teacher)

PLACEMENT This section is to be completed when the child changes school, program and at the end of June.

SCHOOL ADDRESS (complete in case of transfer) SIGNATURE (school official)

Marc: Uh, anyway, I did used to buy *Ralph Snart* at the convenience store when I was a teenager. I found it pretty funny that it was available there. By that time I wasn't buying *MAD* anymore. I collected a lot of those when I was a kid, I remember having a drawer full of those and *Cracked Magazine*. I really enjoyed the works of the "Usual Gang Of Idiots." I would buy those Don Martin paperback books. I wasn't really interested or too aware of comic book stores. It just wasn't part of my world. Maybe because I was a suburban kid and there weren't comic stores in the suburbs. And when we went downtown on a Saturday, my friends and I, we would go the record stores and the "head shops" (so to speak)—those places with all the heavy metal posters and things. Or, you know, pick up an *Elric* novel. I was into a weird mix of stuff, this shitty "D & D" kind of stuff, I religiously watched *Pee–Wee's Playhouse* and was getting into all this prog rock. As far as my introduction to "alternative comics" goes, I was introduced to *Yummy Fur* by a friend in art class. He gave me a copy of the first issue. I think he also introduced me to *Boris The Bear* too. That was one of those violent funny animal comics. Terrible.

Audience Member: Is the bear orange and brown?

Tom: How is that important? Bear color?!? Why are you asking such a thing?

Marc: Huh? Ok. Anyway, my classmate and I started collaborating on a comic book, *The Adventures Of Jimmy*, which we made copies of. It seems crazy because the print run was so low but I think the first one might have been offset. He took care of the details. We used some of my characters that I'd been drawing since I was a kid (Jimmy and *The Galaxy Gang,* that I created with my childhood friend Dave Kovach). He wrote and I drew it and then he inked it. He knew all the angles because he worked at a comic book store. Anyway, later I picked up *Yummy Fur* #4 and there really seemed to be something going on the way the stories were linking up. It was interesting to see how that "Ed" story unfolded. And I started buying *Neat Stuff*, which really blew my mind too, and then *Dirty Plotte* and *Eightball* and *Dangle* and all that great stuff that was starting to come out. I guess the 90's was in some ways not so great really, but for this stuff it was a real great time. This is for my snooty–pants "Art" book, and here I am talking about my whole comics purchasing history.

Tom: Go on with you...

Marc: So, I met Peter Thompson and Jason Mclean and they introduced me to "real" art. Just kidding. The way that went (I think) was that my friend Scott McIntyre and I met Peter and we thought he was an interesting guy. He was not the man–about–London–town that he is now. Anyway, we got a kick out of him and we starting drawing with him. I even made a "Pete Documentary." It's probably terrible I am sure, no fault of young Pete. Scott, Peter and I created this type of drawing we called the "Thanksgiving Amoeba." Anyway, this is how the collaboration started for us. I continued to draw with Peter when we had both finished Bealart. I guess that's when it really started to get going, a little later. We ended up influencing each other's drawing a great deal. We were hanging around with Jason too, a bit, but I guess he was in a bit of a different crowd. He had an apartment in Old South. I remember him sitting on his back porch and painting these crazy designs on a flattened garbage can. He built a giant toaster chair in sculpture class. Jason wasn't as interested in drawing as much back then as he is now—I don't think—he was mainly into sculpture then. It was interesting to see what he was doing because it was in a regular "art" tradition but with a sense of humour, which was unusual: most real art school types are so serious. Later, after he moved out to Vancouver and went to school there we started sending each other crazy decorated letters in the mail. He continued with his sculpture—making these wooden birdhouse looking things.

Audience Member: Did birds like them?

Marc: What? Sorry?

Audience Member: Did birds land in them and eat food?

Marc: I don't really know...

Tom: {*visibly fuming.*} Uhhhhhh.

{*Pause.*}

Marc: I moved to Sackville to go to University and so Peter and I would also send mail back and forth too. Jason and I showed a bunch of our mail at Gallery Sansair in the summer of 1994, a show called *The Waffle.* There was a Waffle Parade and we

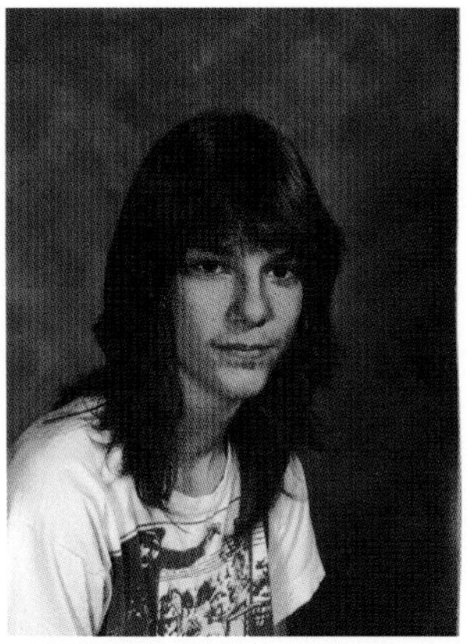

Top left: Bell's Kindergarten Report Card, 1976
Right: Marc in Grade 10

ARTMAKING VS. BALOGNA MAKING
Maple Leaf
- SMELL DEPENDS ON MATERIALS
- YOU C
DEALING WITH LIPS AND ASSHOLES (BALONEY)
HAVE TO LEARN ART LANGUAGE TO OVERCOME THIS BIAS
-SATISFACTION OF A HARD DAYS WORK
- MIGHT HAVE TO WORK IN BOLOGNA FACTORY TO SUPPORT ART.
- STILL HAVE TO
- DEALING
-HAVE TO DEAL WITH STORM INSIDE YOUR SOUL
-SMELLS BAD
- STEADY WAGE
(LIPS + ASSHOLES)
- FREE BOLOGNA
-BOSS
- 9am-5pm
-YOU CAN'T TRUS
SATISFACTION OF A HARD DAYS WORK
- HAVE TO DEAL WITH STORM INSIDE YOUR SOUL

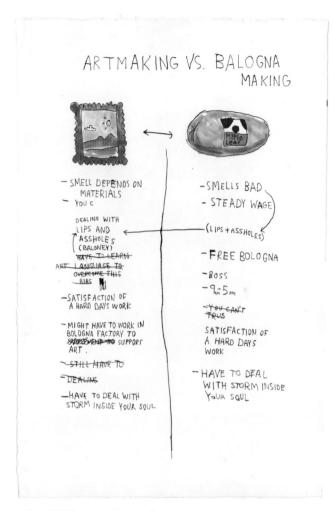

had a "Waffle Queen" named Gary. Members of *July Fourth Toilet* accompanied by On/Off Schnauzer on snorkel serenaded the Waffle Queen as she entered the premises. Waffles were served, when a new one was ready a loud siren went off. We also showed all these posters to advertise *The All Star Schnauzer Band.* The Schnauzer Band was a {inaudible} musical group we had been promoting. Peter was part of it too. We would make these cheap Chinatown laser copied posters and distribute them a bit, advertising gigs. We entered the Schnauzers into the Seattle *Rocket* Music Directory. A friend {inaudible} into the charts at #32 in the UBC music paper, *The Discorder*. Jason made a nice book of a bunch of this Schnauzer stuff and more recently I compiled some of it for the fifth issue of *The Ganzfeld*—The "Japanada" issue.

Tom: I'm getting feedback in my earpiece here. Hold on a sec. Can we check this out? Can I get a tech guy up here?

{*Crowd murmuring rises. Gap in tape.*}

Tom:...so unprofessional. Let me see your union card. Do you even have a union card?

Sound Guy: Fuck you, Devlin.

{*Sound Guy throws something on the ground.*}

Tom: Get off the stage!

{*Pause.*}

Tom: Now, Marc, you were drawing comics and making fine–art and constructions throughout University, correct? Did one of these modes of expression take precedent over the other or was it all the same to you? And sorry to back track a bit here but you've told me about seeing a Crumb show in New York at some point as a young man. Was this a breakthrough moment for you or had you been reading his work already from your head shop days? I guess what I'm trying to get at here is if you were planning a career as a cartoonist or an artist or both?

Marc: One of my profs took us to see a Crumb exhibit while we were on a field trip in NY. I was already into Crumb so it wasn't a total revelation but it was nice to see them in person and interesting to see that he used a lot of white out. In University I was drawing comics. I didn't really feel the need to show these to my teachers that much, though. I think it was pretty clear I was doing cartoon based work in general but I never felt I had to legitimize the comics work I did as "Art" or anything and kept it a bit separate in this case. I don't find it particularly interesting to see comics on the wall.

{*Audible yawn from an audience member.*}

Sound Guy: Can we pick this up a bit? We've got Wheels Of Juice sound checking here in less than an hour.

{*Some of the audience shifting in chairs uncomfortably.*}

Marc: And so I didn't really show comics work in my crits until my final one. For that I showed a combination of comics and cartoony–ish art. For the crit I had taken apart my address book that had all these loose little drawings in it and presented those in a grid–like fashion, kind of a real crude version of what I do now I guess. Both my comics and art were in kind of a messy stage. It was a little bit intentional and a little bit me just being lazy. I don't think either really gelled till much later. I wasn't really planning a career as a professional "gallery artist" per se. I think it seemed to me that I would continue more in a comics vein once I was done with school because that was the stuff that seemed easier to get out there and there was already a bit of an interest. I was making photocopied books of drawings and comic books that had some more "art" related stuff in them anyway so it wasn't exactly putting them in separate sandboxes anyway, as far as books go.

Audience Member: Separate sandboxes?

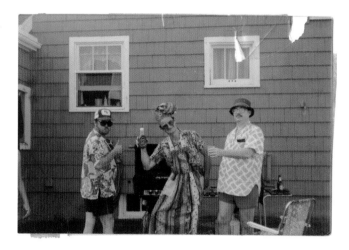

Schnauzer BBQ Reunion L.O., 2009, left to right: Libby, On/Off and Pencils Schnauzer (photo: Barry T. Walsh)

Top Left: *Art Making Vs. Balogna Making* (sic), circa 1993, mixed media

Marc: You know, I wasn't exactly thinking about the comics and art as totally separate. I would make comic books that had stand–alone drawing kind of stuff in them too. I dunno...

Audience Member: Where did Tom go?

Marc: Not sure.

Another Audience Member: I am the King of Sports. I am the best at all sports.

Marc: Oh yeah? Which ones? I mean…

Another Audience Member: Any sport you can think of I am the best at.

Marc: Ok, there's Tom I think…

Another Audience Member: Have you read *Watchmen*? That's a good comic. It's all about…

Tom: {*putting on mic*} Oh, For Cracking Ice! Please, let's save questions for the end. Please. Now where was I? Bealart, Crumb, collab, oh, here. Now, for me there was a certain coalescing, if you will, of your approach around the time you were finishing up your first book collection, *Shrimpy and Paul and Friends*. I'll get to what I think of as your particular conscientious wise–guy voice in a minute but what I'm particularly thinking is a "confidence of line." There's always been a fair amount of visual distortion or purposefully bad drawing (please no offense is intended) in your work but at this point things started to become a bit more tightly composed in a really thrilling way. I think your "voice" has stayed remarkably consistent throughout your work. Your characters (I'm referring to both the comics and "fine art" here) tend to fall into a few categories—the naïf, the spiritually calm character, the grumbler, the inscrutable wack–job. But the violence or cynicism (it's there) never seems to get out of hand. In general, you aren't so much critical as you are just observational and largely in a benevolent way. Is this an arrived at philosophy or more of a way that you've always thought? Please forgive my rambling, maybe you should just use this as a point to take back the mic.

Audience member: Are those cards you're holding blank?

Marc: I think at a certain point the way I was working started to come together in a good way. Around the time I started compiling the "Shrimpy and Paul" stuff as a book there was more of an effort to create a concrete world. Also, around that time, the art stuff was really gelling for me. In the summer of 2000 I was creating *The Stacks* as a sort of "epic" self–published mini of small painted works. I was using a similar method to paint stuff as I had been using to create collaborations with Jason and it was working really well. I say the book was epic because it was 52 pages long (I think). Much more than that and you'd have to think about square-binding rather than stapling it. So epic for a "mini–comic" for lack of a better term. But back to your point: I suppose I always had that voice in my work that you are talking about, I had just figured out some clearer methods of transmitting it, maybe? I am trying to set up these worlds or spaces in a concrete way so that I can have all this "out of left field" stuff happening in them. In the art and the comics but in different ways. I don't know if that answers your question.

Tom: Well, for example, the drawing *I Don't Care* {*Shows slide on screen.*} My assumption is that this is a doodle with words that slowly built into a narrative of a man on his cellphone with relationship woes. You start with a central figure and a phrase and then build outward until a story develops. Snippets from an overheard conversation, or observed signage, song lyrics, talk radio (as I've so glibly said in the past) combine to create a story. Is this a reasonable assumption on your approach or is a lot more left up to a kind of unintentional drawing that allows the reader to make his own connections and narrative?

Audience member: *WHEELS–OF–JUICE! WHEELS–OF–JUICE!*

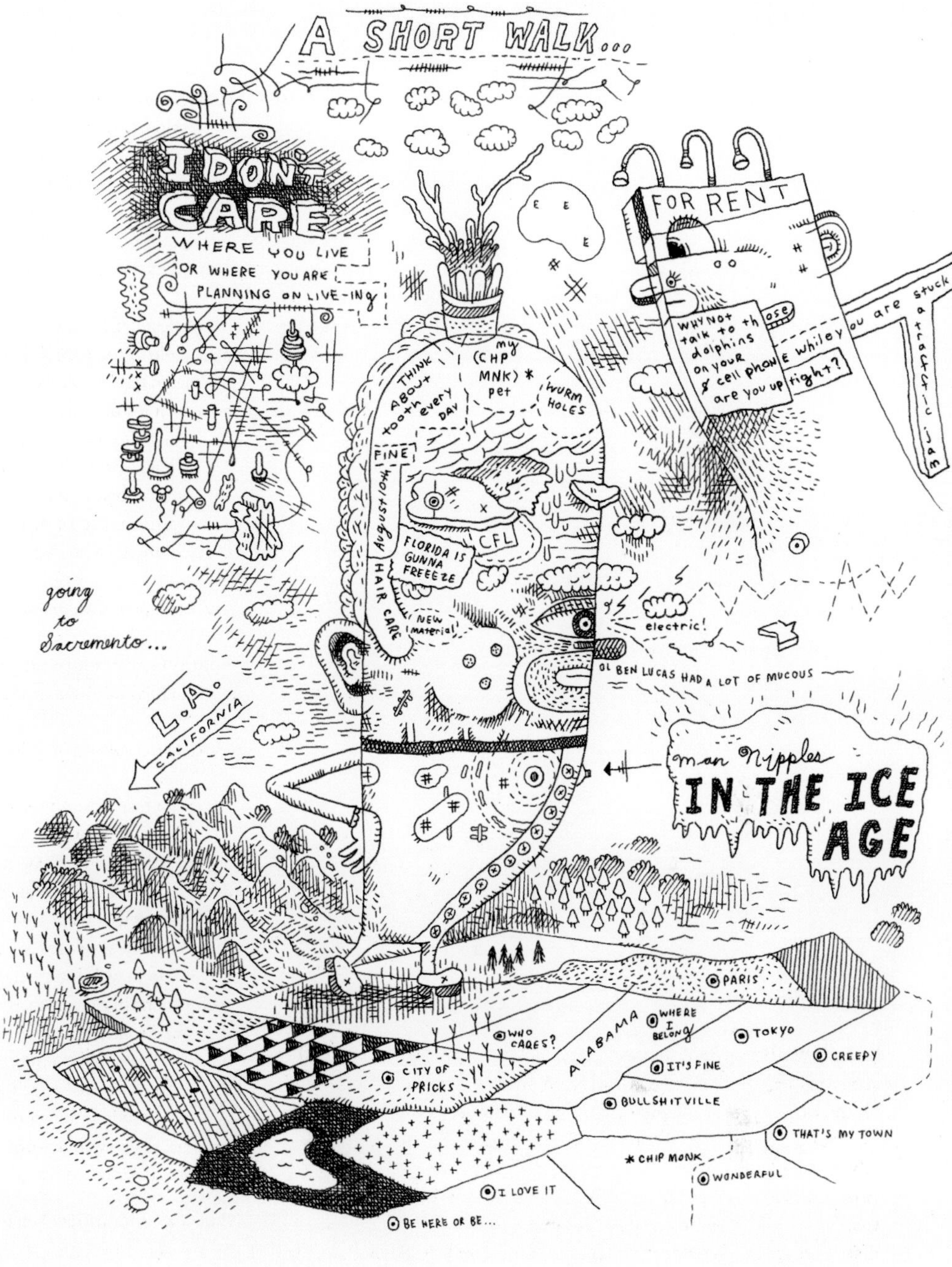
A SHORT WALK...
I DON'T CARE
WHERE YOU LIVE
OR WHERE YOU ARE
PLANNING ON LIVE-ING
FOR RENT
THINK ABOUT tooth every DAY
my CHP MNK pet
WURM HOLES
FINE
HAIR CARE
FLORIDA IS GUNNA FREEEZE
CFL
NEW material
electric!
OL BEN LUCAS HAD A LOT OF MUCOUS
going to Sacramento...
L.A. CALIFORNIA
man nipples IN THE ICE AGE
PARIS
WHERE I BELONG
TOKYO
CREEPY
WHO CARES?
ALABAMA
IT'S FINE
CITY OF PRICKS
BULLSHITVILLE
THAT'S MY TOWN
CHIP MONK
WONDERFUL
I LOVE IT
BE HERE OR BE...

Top: *I Don't Care (Where You Are Living)*, 2003, ink on paper

Marc: Well, that's interesting because I think you have made up your own story here about the central character having "relationship woes." Lordy, I have had 'em but I think when I created this drawing I was thinking about artistic affluence and how people seemed to be moving all over the place. Like, "I am going to Paris for the summer to do work on my Performance Art " or something like that and I am saying in the drawing, "I don't care where you live or where you are planning on live–ing." Maybe that's just how I am imagining the way the world is (or used to be), that everybody can be an artist in an age of lazy affluence. I'm no exception, I guess. Realistically, I don't know if I could have survived as an artist this long in some down–on–its–luck type time or place. It's trying in an abstract way to poke fun at that but I don't mind if somebody reads it how you have because it's pretty unclear. Can we go to the next one?

{*Slide advances to* I Goofed, *p. 214.*}

Marc: Ok, This is *I Goofed*. Um, you're going to have to hang on here though. We are going to have to break here for *International Doodle Week.*

Audience Member: *International* what?

Marc: *International Doodle Week.*

Audience Member: I don't believe that that holiday exists. In fact, I am pretty certain…

Marc: Well, it's not a *real* holiday…

Audience Member: Well, I don't mean a real holiday, like a Statuatory Holiday, it isn't even like St. Patrick's Day.

Marc: Well, OK, this isn't a regular holiday. It isn't a specific week of the year. Let me explain: whenever I didn't feel like doing a comic strip when my weekly deadline for newspapers came around I would decide it was "International Doodle Week" and I would do a more free form kind of thing. It would give me a break from the story I was working on that was continuing in the weekly. I would…

Audience Member: I'm saying I've never heard of this holiday. How is it that you…

Marc: OK everybody, we are going to take a break here for these "International Doodle Weeks" reprinted from *The Halifax Coast* and *The Montreal Mirror.* We'll reconvene here in a few pages. I think this sampling will clear up any questions you may have. (*continued on p. 212*)

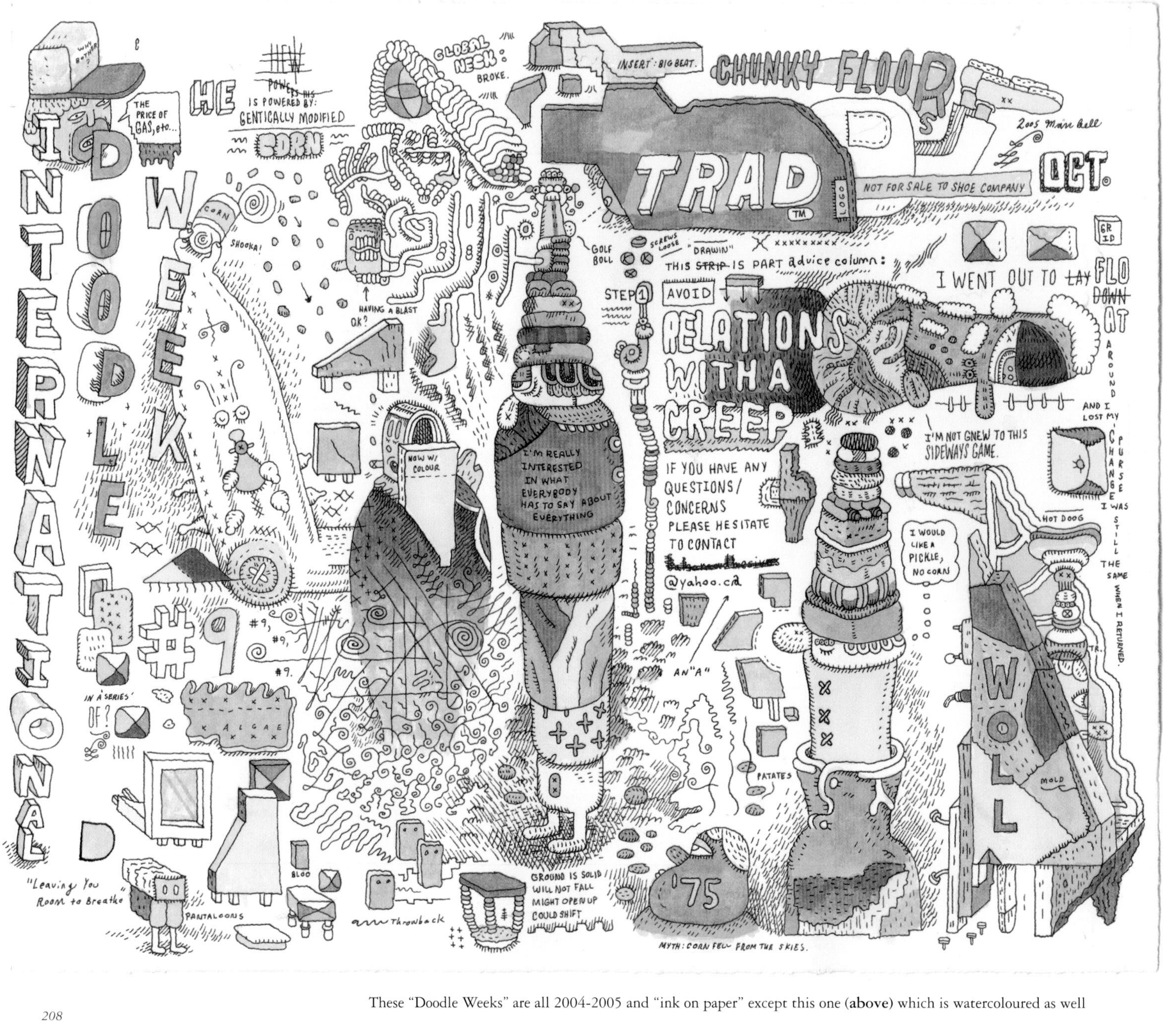

INTERNATIONAL
DOODLE
WEEK
#9
THE PRICE OF GAS, etc...
HE IS POWERED BY: GENTICALLY MODIFIED CORN
GLOBAL NECK: BROKE.
INSERT: BIG BEAT.
CHUNKY FLOORS
TRAD
NOT FOR SALE TO SHOE COMPANY
2005 Marc Bell
OCT.
SHOOKA!
HAVING A BLAST
OK?
GOLF BOLL
SCREWS LOOSE
"DRAWIN"
THIS STRIP IS PART advice column:
STEP 1 AVOID
RELATIONS WITH A CREEP
I WENT OUT TO LAY DOWN FLO AT AROUND
AND I LOST MY PURSE
CHANGE
I WAS STILL THE SAME WHEN I RETURNED.
GR ID
I'M NOT GNEW TO THIS SIDEWAYS GAME.
NOW W/ COLOUR
I'M REALLY INTERESTED IN WHAT EVERYBODY HAS TO SAY ABOUT EVERYTHING
IF YOU HAVE ANY QUESTIONS/ CONCERNS PLEASE HESITATE TO CONTACT
[redacted]@yahoo.ca
I WOULD LIKE A PICKLE, NO CORN
HOT DOOG
WOLL
AN "A"
IN A SERIES' OF?
ALGAE
MOLD
PATATES
'75
"Leaving You Room to Breathe"
PANTALOONS
BLOO
Throwback
GROUND IS SOLID WILL NOT FALL MIGHT OPEN UP COULD SHIFT
MYTH: CORN FELL FROM THE SKIES.

These "Doodle Weeks" are all 2004-2005 and "ink on paper" except this one (**above**) which is watercoloured as well

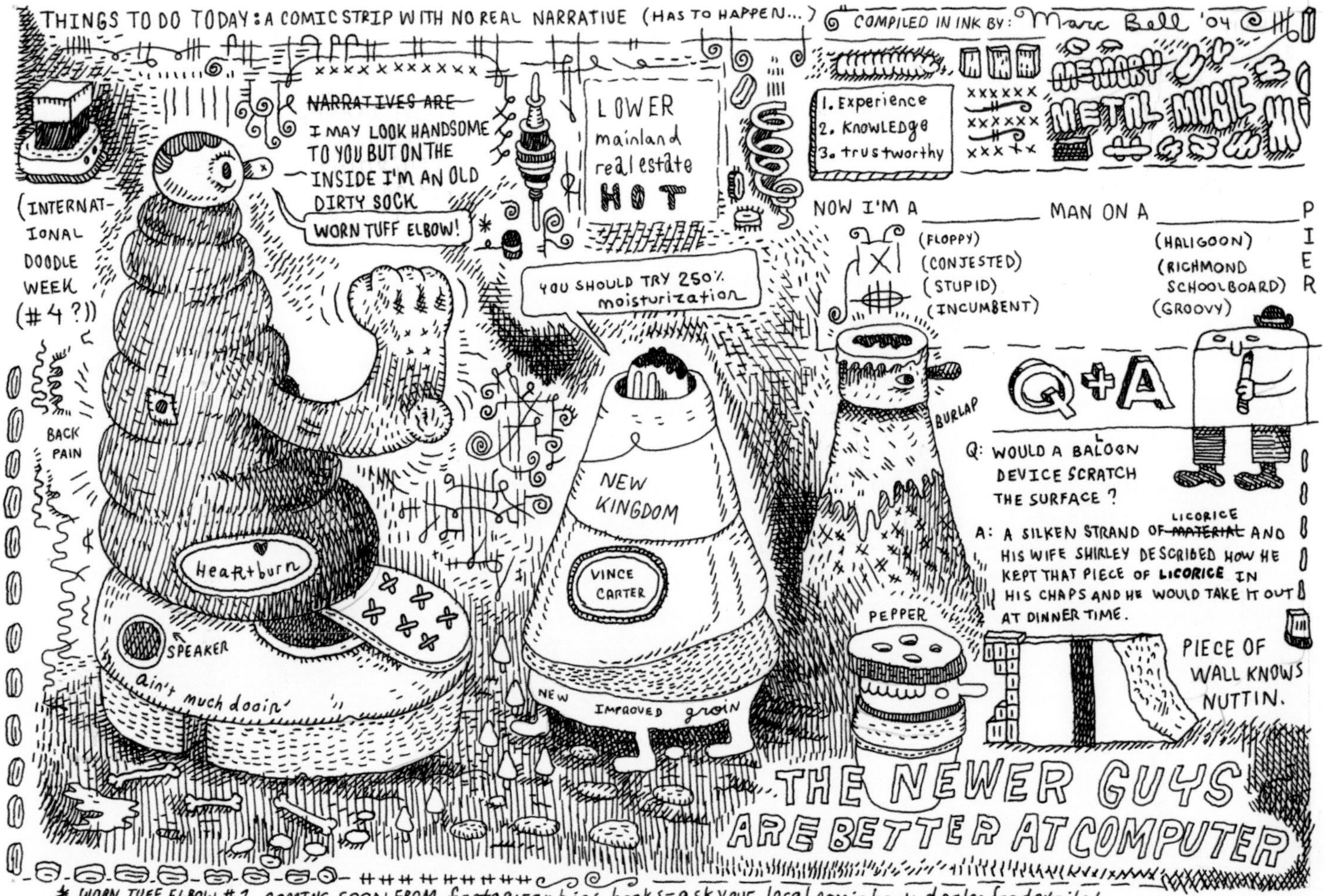
THINGS TO DO TODAY: A COMIC STRIP WITH NO REAL NARRATIVE (HAS TO HAPPEN...)
COMPILED IN INK BY: Marc Bell '04
~~NARRATIVES ARE~~ I MAY LOOK HANDSOME TO YOU BUT ON THE INSIDE I'M AN OLD DIRTY SOCK
WORN TUFF ELBOW! *
LOWER mainland real estate HOT
1. Experience 2. Knowledge 3. trustworthy
MEMORY OF METAL MUSIC
(INTERNATIONAL DOODLE WEEK (#4?))
NOW I'M A ______ MAN ON A ______ PIER
(FLOPPY) (CONJESTED) (STUPID) (INCUMBENT)
(HALIGOON) (RICHMOND SCHOOLBOARD) (GROOVY)
YOU SHOULD TRY 250% moisturization
BACK PAIN
NEW KINGDOM
VINCE CARTER
BURLAP
Q+A
Q: WOULD A BALOGN DEVICE SCRATCH THE SURFACE?
A: A SILKEN STRAND OF ~~MATERIAL~~ LICORICE AND HIS WIFE SHIRLEY DESCRIBED HOW HE KEPT THAT PIECE OF LICORICE IN HIS CHAPS AND HE WOULD TAKE IT OUT AT DINNER TIME.
Heartburn
SPEAKER
ain't much dooin'
NEW IMPROVED groin
PEPPER
PIECE OF WALL KNOWS NUTTIN.
THE NEWER GUYS ARE BETTER AT COMPUTER

* WORN TUFF ELBOW #1, COMING SOON FROM *fantagraphics books*-ask your local comic book dealer for details!

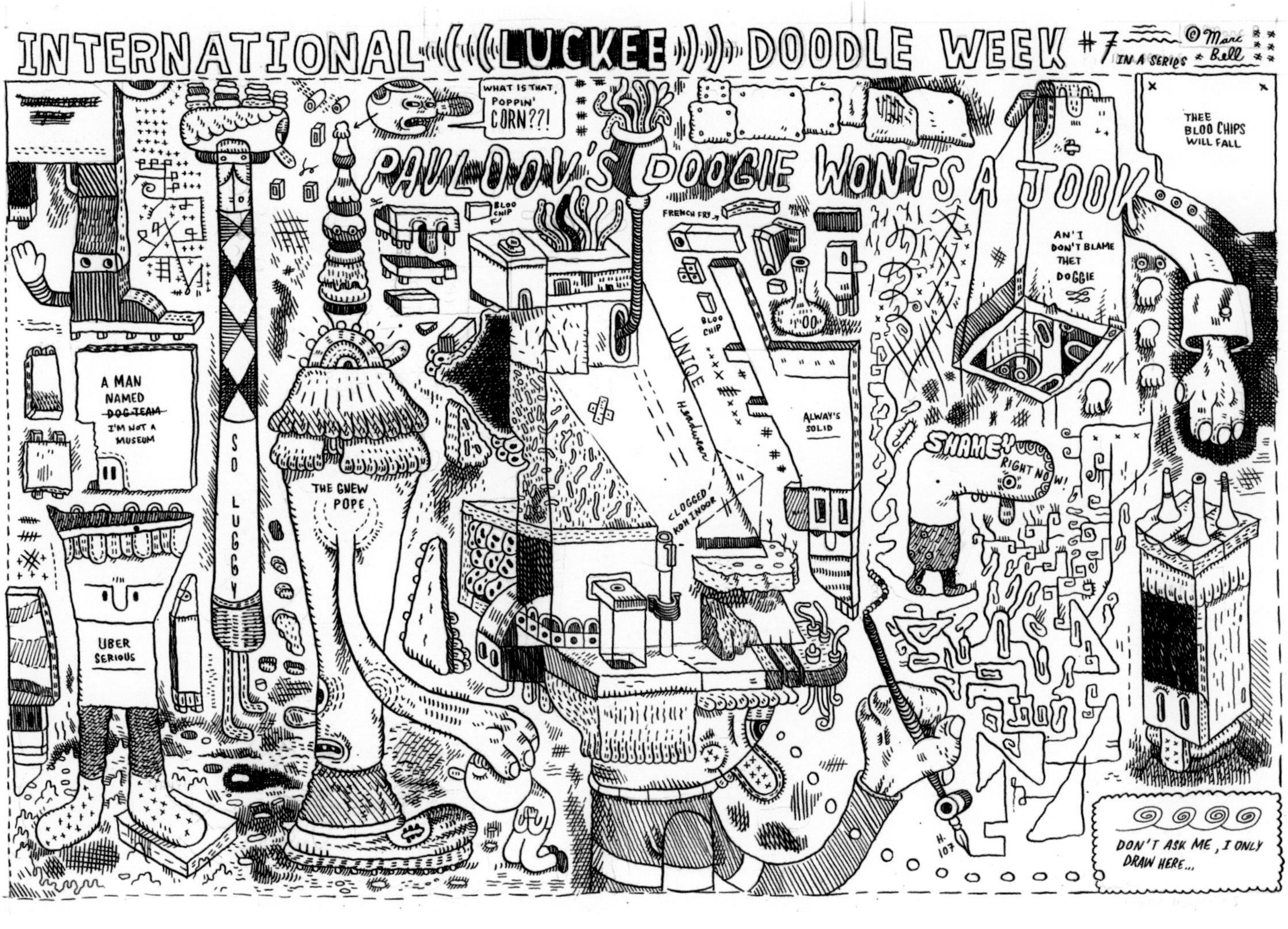
INTERNATIONAL ((LUCKEE)) DOODLE WEEK #7 IN A SERIES © Marc Bell
WHAT IS THAT, POPPIN' CORN??!
PAULOOV'S DOOGIE WONTS A JOOK
THEE BLOO CHIPS WILL FALL
BLOO CHIP
FRENCH FRY
AN' I DON'T BLAME THET DOGGIE
A MAN NAMED ~~DOG TEAM~~ I'M NOT A MUSEUM
UNIQUE
ALWAY'S SOLID
SO LUGGY
THE GNEW POPE
CLOGGED KOHINOOR
SHAMEY RIGHT NOW!
UBER SERIOUS
DON'T ASK ME, I ONLY DRAW HERE...

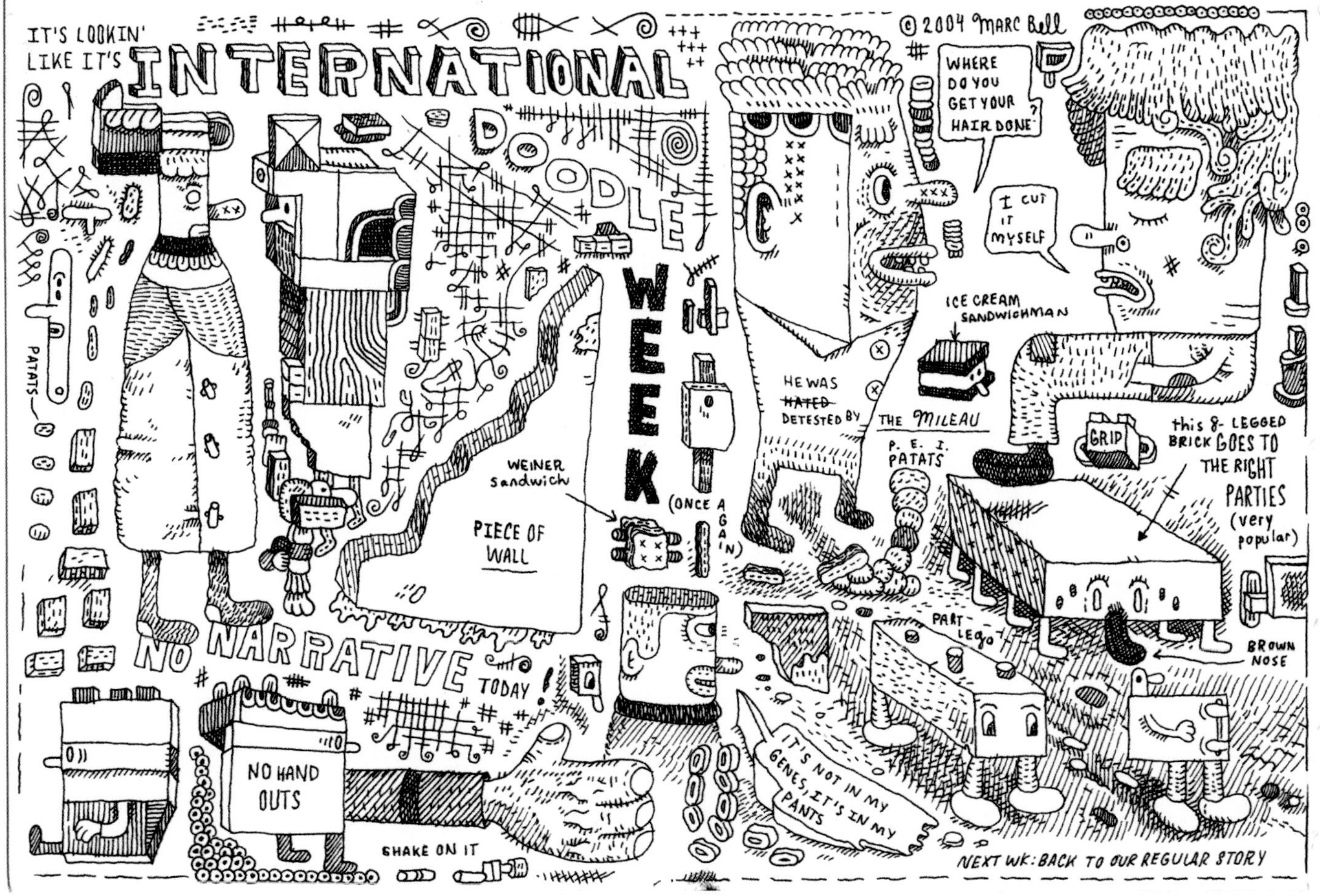

IT'S LOOKIN' LIKE IT'S
INTERNATIONAL DOODLE WEEK (ONCE AGAIN)
© 2004 MARC BELL
WHERE DO YOU GET YOUR HAIR DONE?
I CUT IT MYSELF
PATATS
ICE CREAM SANDWICHMAN
HE WAS HATED DETESTED BY THE MILEAU
P. E. I. PATATS
this 8-LEGGED BRICK GOES TO THE RIGHT PARTIES (very popular)
GRIP
WEINER sandwich
PIECE OF WALL
PART lego
BROWN NOSE
NO NARRATIVE TODAY!
NO HAND OUTS
IT'S NOT IN MY GENES, IT'S IN MY PANTS
SHAKE ON IT
NEXT WK: BACK TO OUR REGULAR STORY

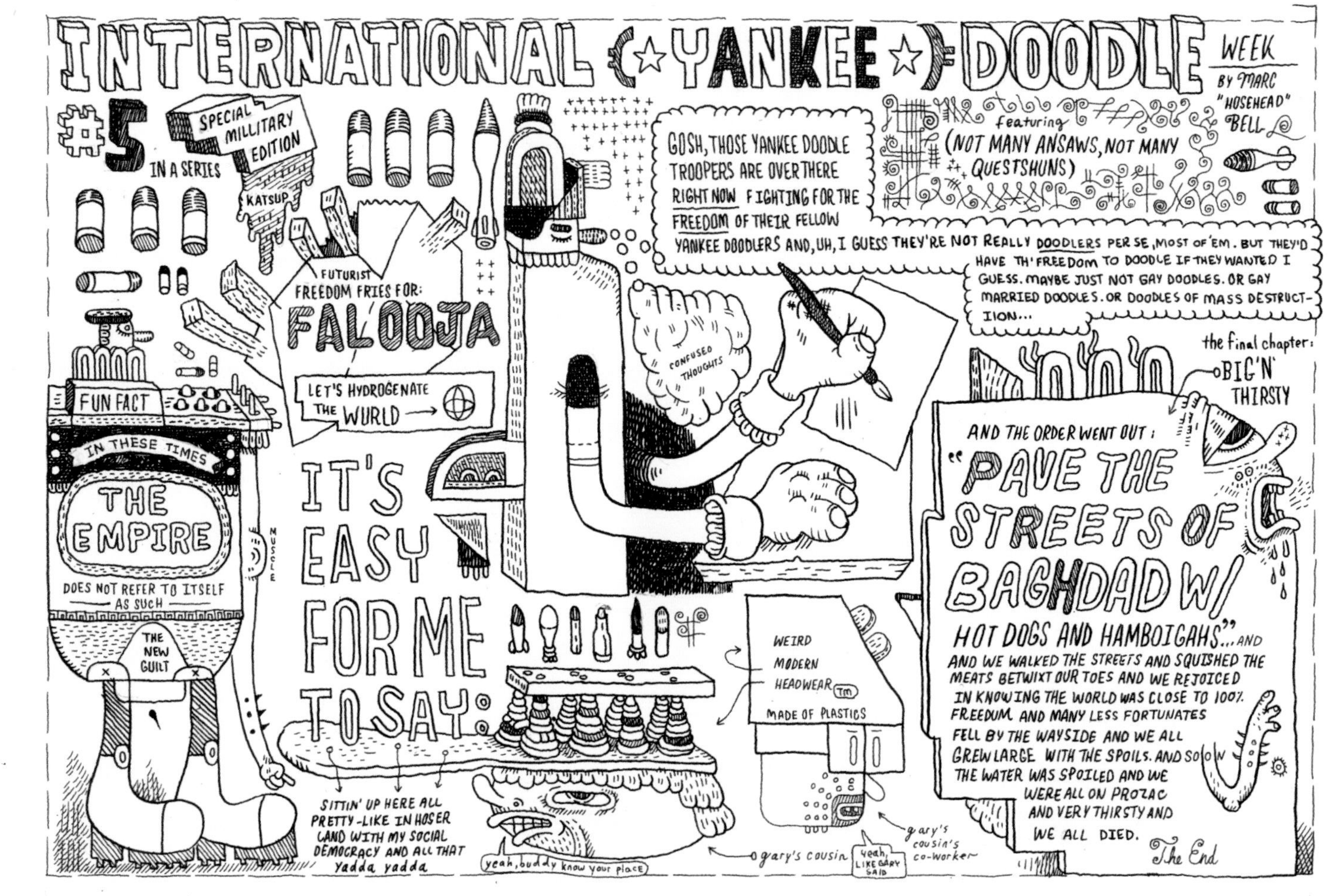

INTERNATIONAL (YANKEE) DOODLE WEEK
BY MARC "HOSEHEAD" BELL
#5 IN A SERIES
SPECIAL MILLITARY EDITION
KATSUP
GOSH, THOSE YANKEE DOODLE TROOPERS ARE OVER THERE RIGHT NOW FIGHTING FOR THE FREEDOM OF THEIR FELLOW YANKEE DOODLERS AND, UH, I GUESS THEY'RE NOT REALLY DOODLERS PER SE, MOST OF 'EM. BUT THEY'D HAVE TH' FREEDOM TO DOODLE IF THEY WANTED I GUESS. MAYBE JUST NOT GAY DOODLES. OR GAY MARRIED DOODLES. OR DOODLES OF MASS DESTRUCTION...
featuring (NOT MANY ANSAWS, NOT MANY QUESTSHUNS)
FUTURIST FREEDOM FRIES FOR: FALOOJA
LET'S HYDROGENATE THE WURLD
CONFUSED THOUGHTS
FUN FACT
IN THESE TIMES
THE EMPIRE
DOES NOT REFER TO ITSELF AS SUCH
THE NEW GUILT
MUSCLE
IT'S EASY FOR ME TO SAY:
WEIRD MODERN HEADWEAR (TM) MADE OF PLASTICS
the final chapter: BIG 'N' THIRSTY
AND THE ORDER WENT OUT: "PAVE THE STREETS OF BAGHDAD W/ HOT DOGS AND HAMBOIGAHS"... AND AND WE WALKED THE STREETS AND SQUISHED THE MEATS BETWIXT OUR TOES AND WE REJOICED IN KNOWING THE WORLD WAS CLOSE TO 100% FREEDUM. AND MANY LESS FORTUNATES FELL BY THE WAYSIDE AND WE ALL GREW LARGE WITH THE SPOILS. AND SOON THE WATER WAS SPOILED AND WE WERE ALL ON PROZAC AND VERY THIRSTY AND WE ALL DIED.
The End
SITTIN' UP HERE ALL PRETTY-LIKE IN HOSER LAND WITH MY SOCIAL DEMOCRACY AND ALL THAT yadda yadda
yeah, buddy know your place
gary's cousin
yeah, LIKE GARY SAID
gary's cousin's co-worker

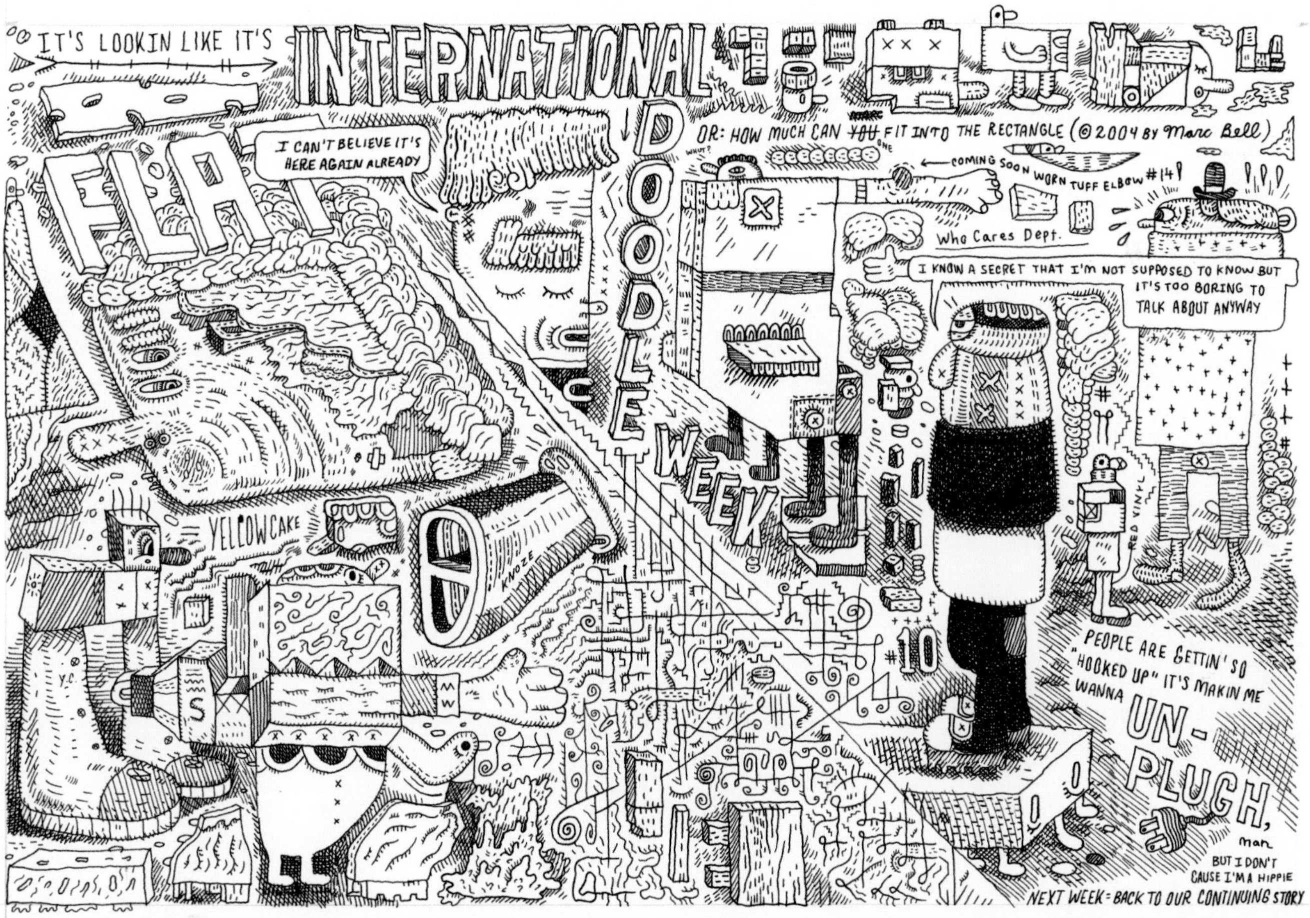

IT'S LOOKIN LIKE IT'S
INTERNATIONAL
DOODLE WEEK
OR: HOW MUCH CAN ~~YOU~~ MARC FIT INTO THE RECTANGLE (©2004 BY Marc Bell)
I CAN'T BELIEVE IT'S HERE AGAIN ALREADY
FLAT
COMING SOON WORN TUFF ELBOW #14!
Who Cares Dept.
I KNOW A SECRET THAT I'M NOT SUPPOSED TO KNOW BUT IT'S TOO BORING TO TALK ABOUT ANYWAY
YELLOWCAKE
KNOZE
#10
RED VINYL
PEOPLE ARE GETTIN' SO "HOOKED UP" IT'S MAKIN ME WANNA UN-PLUGH, man
BUT I DON'T CAUSE I'M A HIPPIE
NEXT WEEK = BACK TO OUR CONTINUING STORY

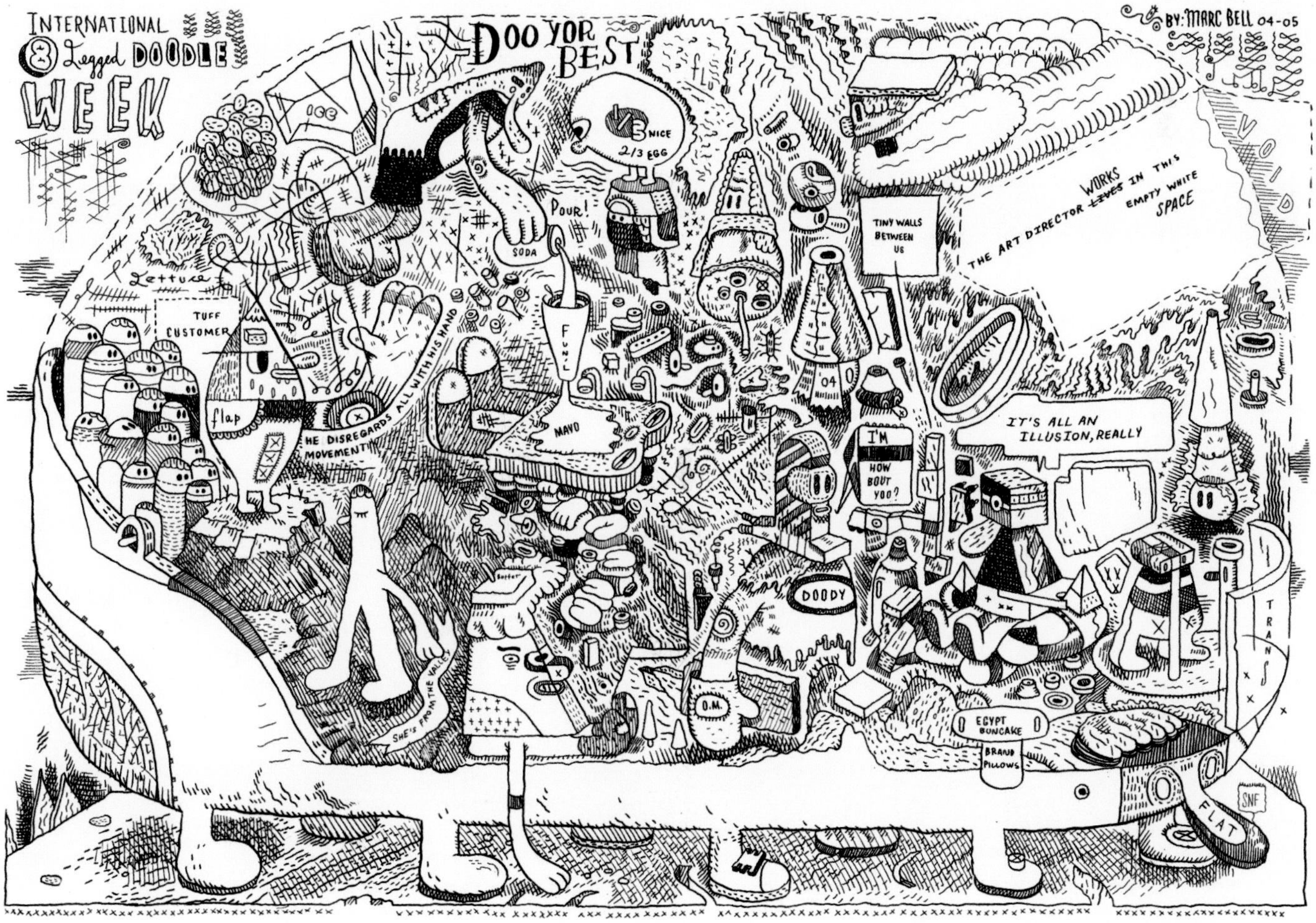

INTERNATIONAL 8 Legged DOODLE WEEK
DOO YOR BEST
BY: MARC BELL 04-05
NICE 2/3 EGG
POUR!
SODA
VOID
THE ART DIRECTOR ~~LIVES~~ WORKS IN THIS EMPTY WHITE SPACE
TINY WALLS BETWEEN US
Lettuce
TUFF CUSTOMER
flap
HE DISREGARDS ALL WITH HIS HAND MOVEMENTS
MAYO
IT'S ALL AN ILLUSION, REALLY
I'M HOW BOUT YOU?
DOODY
O.M.
SHE'S FROM THE VALLEY
EGYPT BUNCAKE
BRAND PILLOWS
TRANS
FLAT
SNF

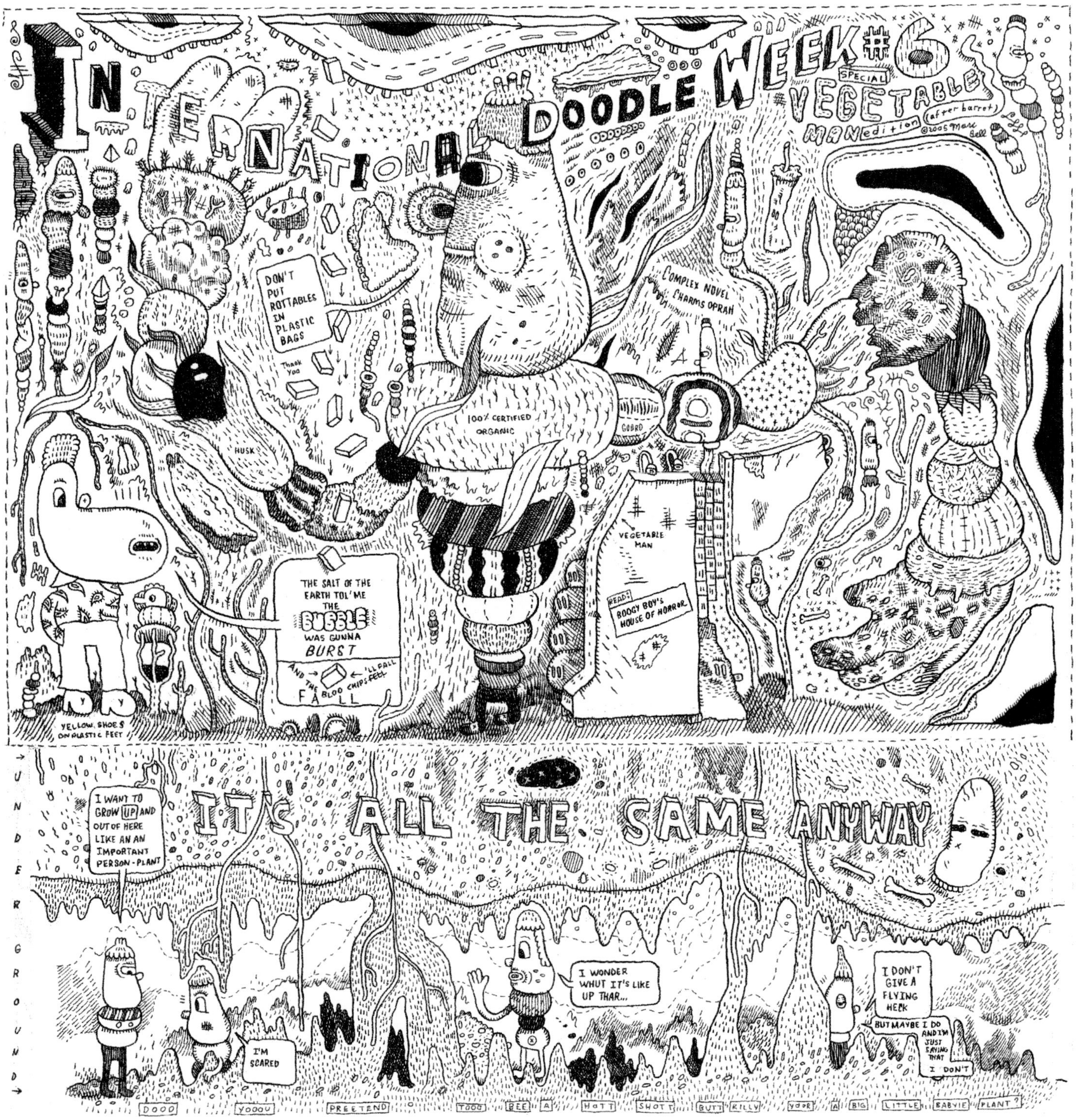
INTERNATIONAL DOODLE WEEK #6
SPECIAL VEGETABLE MAN edition (after barrett) ©2005 Marc Bell
DON'T PUT ROTTABLES IN PLASTIC BAGS
Thank You
COMPLEX NOVEL CHARMS OPRAH
100% CERTIFIED ORGANIC
HUSK
VEGETABLE MAN
READ: BOOGY BOY'S HOUSE OF HORROR
THE SALT OF THE EARTH TOL'ME THE BUBBLE WAS GUNNA BURST
AND THE BLOO CHIPS 'LL FALL FALL
YELLOW SHOES ON PLASTIC FEET
UNDERGROUND
IT'S ALL THE SAME ANYWAY
I WANT TO GROW UP AND OUT OF HERE LIKE AN AN IMPORTANT PERSON-PLANT
I'M SCARED
I WONDER WHUT IT'S LIKE UP THAR...
I DON'T GIVE A FLYING HECK
BUT MAYBE I DO AND I'M JUST SAYING THAT I DON'T
DOOO YOOOU PREETEND TOOO BEE A HOTT SHOTT BUTT KILLY YOOR A BIG LITTLE BABVIE PLANT?

Facing page: *Haircut Bonus Footage*, 2006, ink on paper

(*continued from p. 208*)

Marc: Ok, so that was "International Doodle Week". Or "Weeks" I should say.

Audience Member: It's not real.

Marc: Well, I think we went over this. It's been covered. I am aware that it is not a real holiday.

Audience Member: I would hope so!

Marc: It's more like a personal holiday.

Audience Member: I don't have any personal holidays.

Marc: OK, fine. Let's move on to *I Goofed*.

Audience Member: So there would be one of these a year?

Marc: *No, several!* There were several of these Doodle Weeks a year. They probably happened at least three times a year. It was random—kind of like your questions.

(*continued on p. 215*)

EXPENSIVE HAIRCUT.

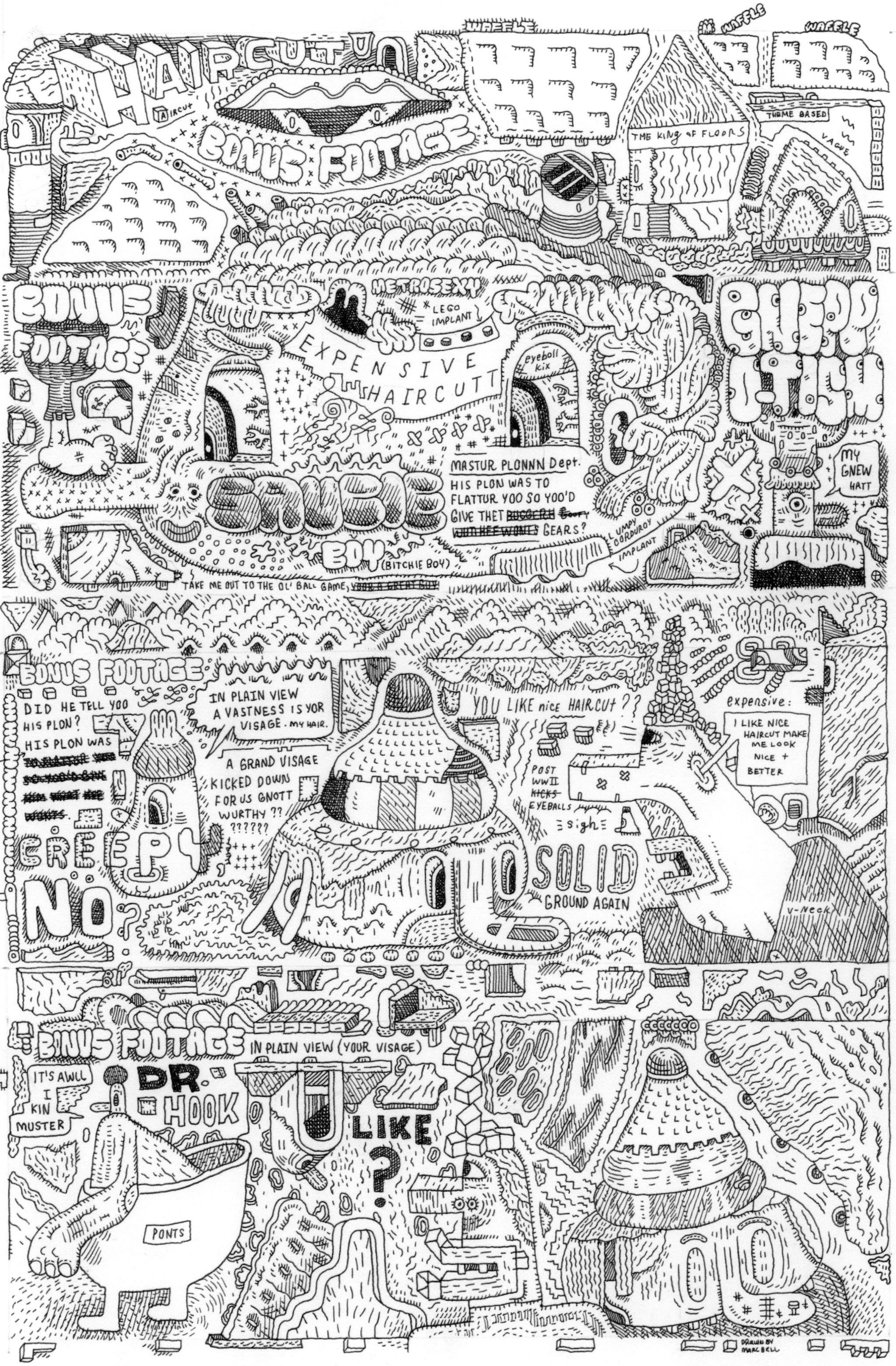
HAIRCUT
WAFFLE
WAFFLE
WAFFLE
BONUS FOOTAGE
THE KING OF FLOORS
THEME BASED
VAGUE
BONUS FOOTAGE
METROSEXY
LEGO IMPLANT
EXPENSIVE HAIRCUTT
eyeball kix
MASTUR PLONNN Dept.
HIS PLON WAS TO FLATTUR YOO SO YOO'D GIVE THET GEARS?
MY GNEW HATT
BOY (BITCHIE BOY)
UMPY CORDUROY IMPLANT
TAKE ME OUT TO THE OL' BALL GAME,
BONUS FOOTAGE
DID HE TELL YOO HIS PLON? HIS PLON WAS
IN PLAIN VIEW A VASTNESS IS YOR VISAGE. MY HAIR.
A GRAND VISAGE KICKED DOWN FOR US GNOTT WURTHY ?? ??????
YOU LIKE nice HAIRCUT ??
expensive:
I LIKE NICE HAIRCUT MAKE ME LOOK NICE + BETTER
POST WWII KICKS EYEBALLS
sigh
CREEPY
NO
SOLID GROUND AGAIN
V-Neck
BONUS FOOTAGE
IN PLAIN VIEW (YOUR VISAGE)
IT'S AWLL I KIN MUSTER
DR. HOOK
U LIKE ?
PONTS
DRAWN BY MARC BELL

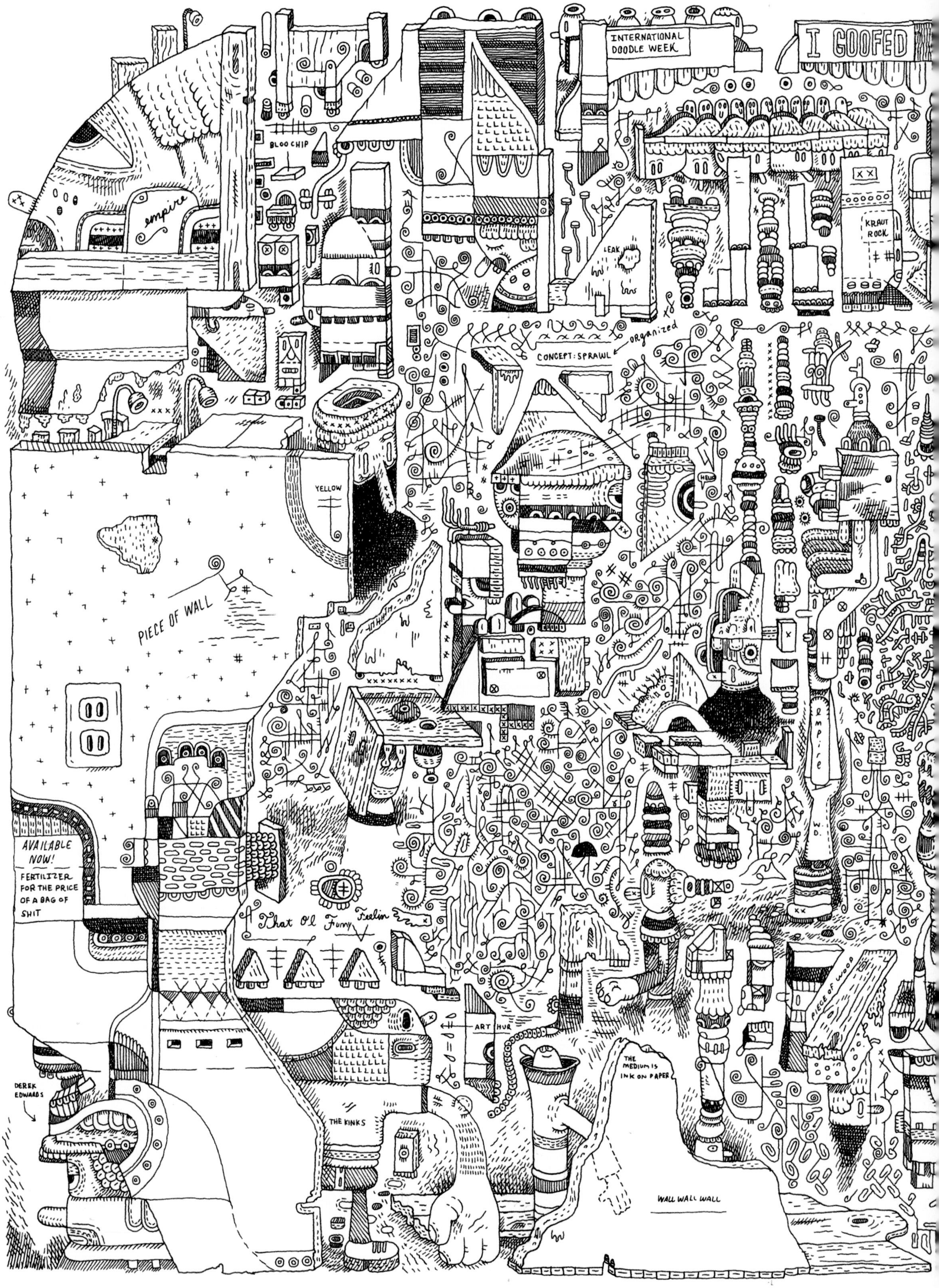

INTERNATIONAL DOODLE WEEK
I GOOFED
BLOOCHIP
empire
KRAUT ROCK
LEAK
CONCEPT: SPRAWL
organized
YELLOW
PIECE OF WALL
AVAILABLE NOW!
FERTILIZER FOR THE PRICE OF A BAG OF SHIT
That Ol Funny Feelin
empire
W.D.
ART HUR
PIECE OF WOOD
THE MEDIUM IS INK ON PAPER
DEREK EDWARDS
THE KINKS
WALL WALL WALL

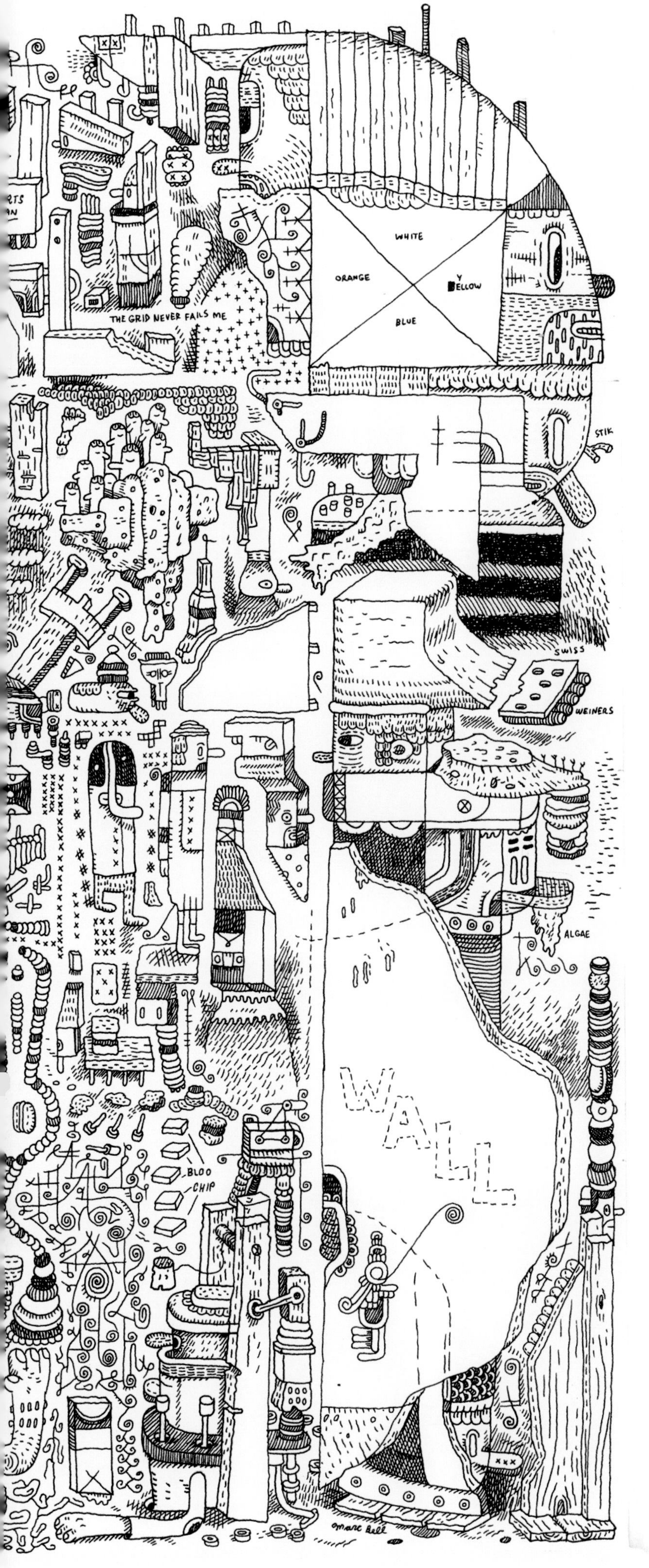
THE GRID NEVER FAILS ME
WHITE
ORANGE
YELLOW
BLUE
STIK
SWISS
WEINERS
ALGAE
WALL
BLOO
CHIP
marc Bell

(*continued from p. 212*)

Audience Member: Holidays only happen once a year.

Another Audience Member: You're lucky you didn't get fired.

Marc: You could be right. Anyway.

Audience Member: Also, I disagree, I don't think the newer guys are better at the computers (he is referring to *International Doodle Week* #4, p. 209). I have been using computers since 1983 and I…

Tom: Ok, ok, can we get back to the interview now? Can we talk about your extensive use of the color yellow? {*coughs.*} Just kidding. {*Slide:* I Goofed, *shown left.*} You mention repetition and that is certainly a common theme in your work—patterns, words, images like trees or soda cups or oversized appendages. It seems to me a large part of your image building is based on simply the physical act of moving your hand in familiar patterns. This certainly is what gives your work its signature and it's one of my favorite aspects of the work—the drawings, especially, positively vibrate with all the action and filigree and crosshatching on the page. Is there a body of work that remains unfinished because your unconscious mind painted you into a corner?

Marc: Well, I think I really did paint myself into a corner with my comics. I think that's why I had to stop or at least take a long break from the *Wilder Hobson's Theatre Absurd–o* story (a story in a weekly strip I was doing), I couldn't deal with all this stuff I had set up in the sory. I wished I'd studied story structure a bit before I started that one. I do really like the idea of a grand failure: some huge, clunky but interesting mess but I would like to work it out in a relatively coherent way. As much as I do sort of like returning to old work it seems a little imposing to go back and try to tackle it again. Getting back to your point though: these art things don't really paint me into a corner, because I can just escape to the next one. It's not like being saddled with some giant narrative like the aforementioned "Wilder Hobson" story. When they are working out it is sort of a meditative process, like you say…I am usually just drawing in sort of a repetitive way. You can see this in *I Goofed*. Of course, some fail, I have some clunkers wherein I get stuck and it isn't going anywhere but this "repetition" I learned, probably from doing comics, is very helpful to produce detailed works that still appear somewhat cohesive. I was also taught in art history class that repetition along with variation really works visually. And, when I get stuck in a particular work, there are other options: cut it up and use in something else or paint or paste over what I don't like and move on. In a way, the "mixed media" kind of stuff I do is all about being stuck in a corner and so I "plug" areas I don't like with new images or materials to get out of that corner. I think I learned from collaborating to sort of collaborate with myself to get out of a corner. Throw a wrench in the works and have a new start inside of an actual piece. The watercolour stuff is a different case though, it's best not to screw up on those or it shows and I have to get out the opaque mediums. (*continued on p. 240*)

I Goofed, 2005, ink on paper

Following page: *Woa!,* 2004, mixed media on paper

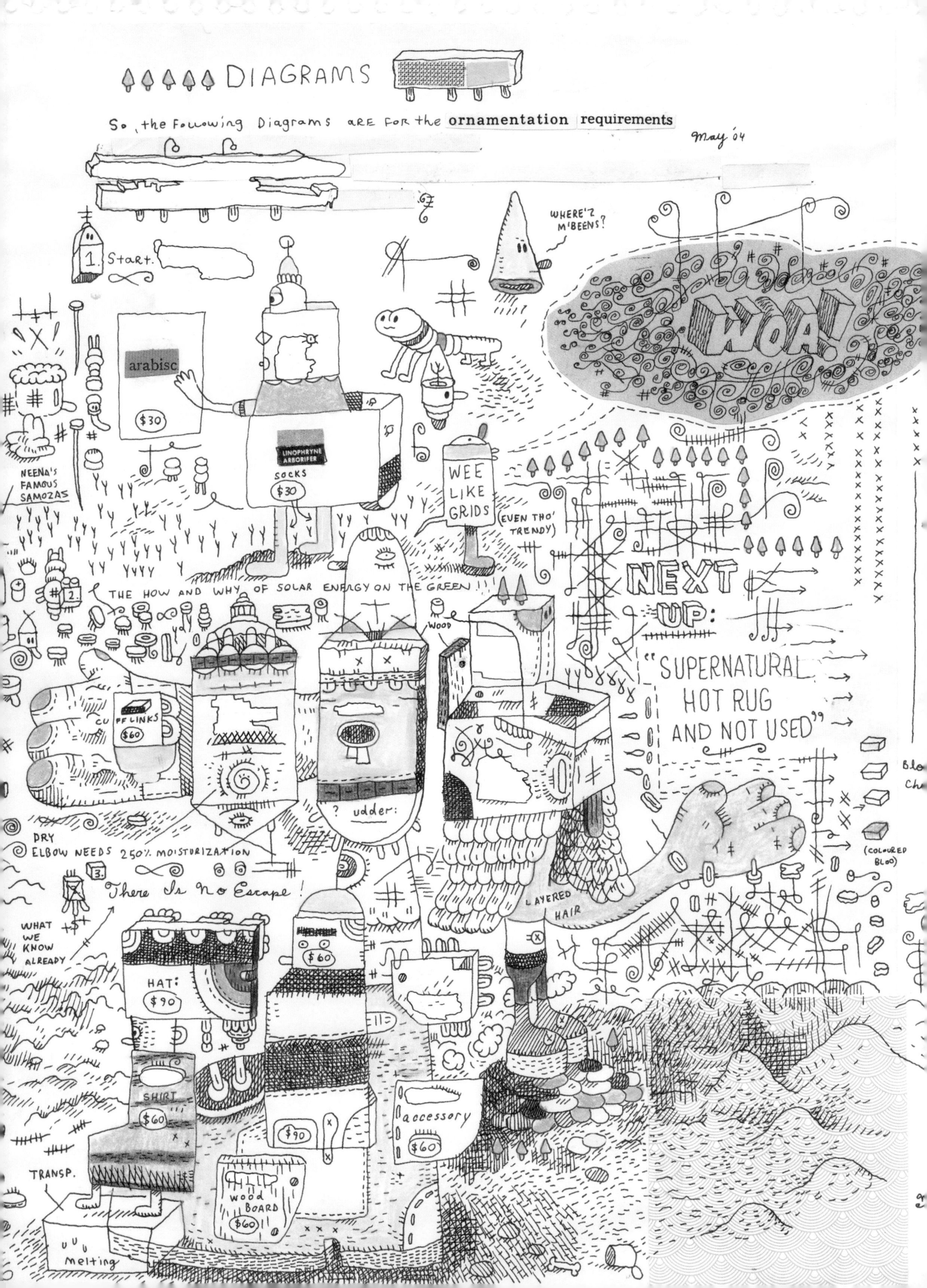
DIAGRAMS
So, the Following Diagrams are for the ornamentation requirements
May '04
1. Start.
WHERE'Z M'BEENS?
arabisc
$30
LINOPHRYNE ARBORIFER
SOCKS
$30
NEENA'S FAMOUS SAMOZAS
WEE LIKE GRIDS
(EVEN THO' TRENDY)
WOA!
NEXT UP:
"SUPERNATURAL HOT RUG AND NOT USED"
2.
THE HOW AND WHY OF SOLAR ENERGY ON THE GREEN
WOOD
CUFF LINKS
$60
? udder:
DRY ELBOW NEEDS 250% MOISTURIZATION
3.
There Is No Escape!
WHAT WE KNOW ALREADY
LAYERED HAIR
(COLOURED BLOO)
HAT:
$90
$60
SHIRT
$60
$90
accessory
$60
wood BOARD
$60
TRANSP.
melting

THAT IT BE
RELAX EVERYBODY, IT'S JUST THE...
vegetation
PLASTIC TREES
SUPER-NATURAL
HOT RUG
AND NOT USED
WARNING: MAY CONTAIN FLU VIRUS (WASH HANDS BEFORE AND AFTER READING)
"TAKE A STAND AND TAKE IT EASY"
ART DIRECTOR
HMM...
#1 in a series
WEE LIKE GRIDS, WEE KNO IT TRUNDY
MONTREAL, LONDON, VANCOOOVER
(ONT)

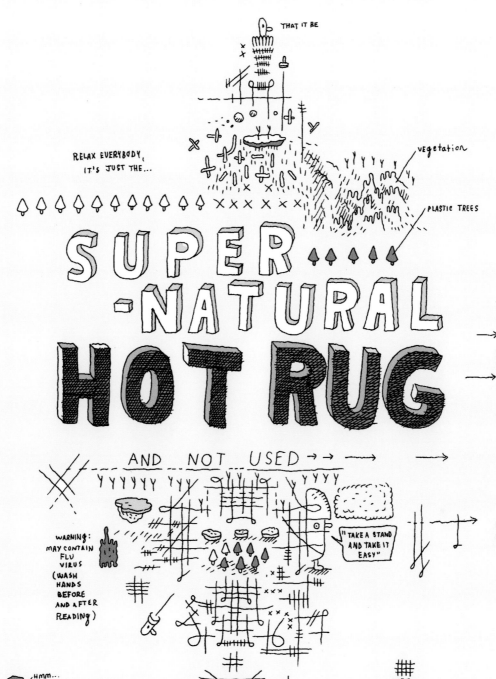

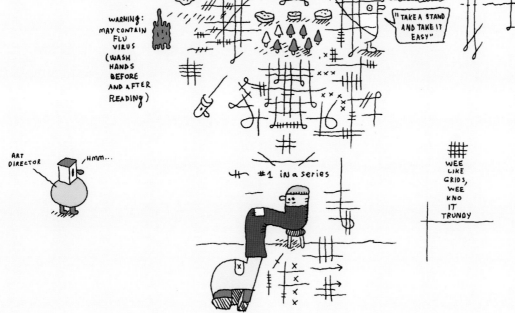

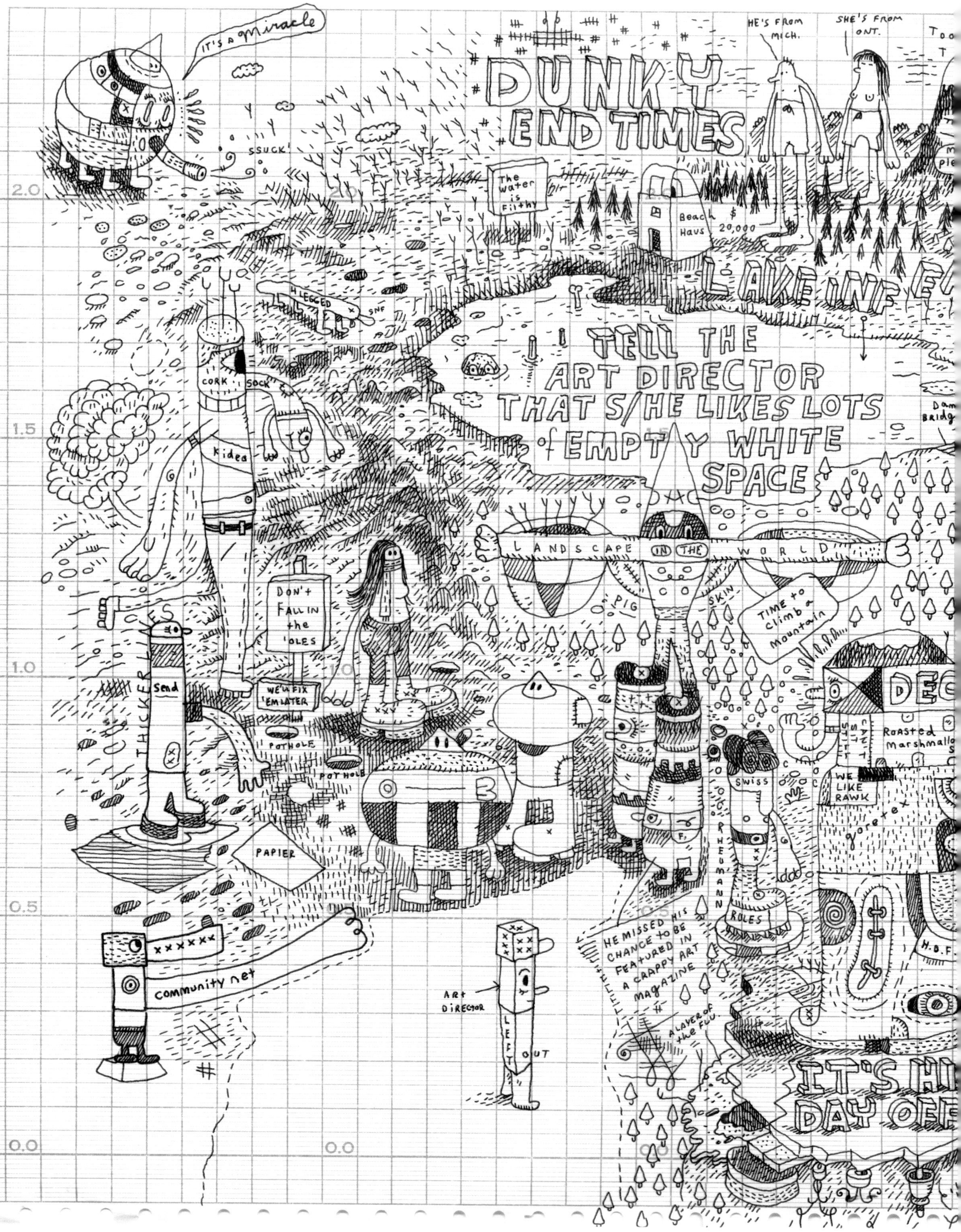

IT'S A miracle
SSUCK!
DUNKY
END TIMES
HE'S FROM MICH.
SHE'S FROM ONT.
The water is Filthy
Beach Haus $ 20,000
LAKE INF
4 LEGGED
SNF
TELL THE
ART DIRECTOR
THAT S/HE LIKES LOTS
of EMPTY WHITE
SPACE
CORK
SOCK
kidea
LANDSCAPE IN THE WORLD
PIG
SKIN
TIME to climb a Mountain
Don't FALL IN the 'OLES
WE'LL FIX 'EM LATER
POTHOLE
POTHOLE
THICKER LINES
Send
PAPIER
Roasted Marshmallo
WE LIKE RAWK
SWISS
RHEUMANN
ROLES
gore-tex
HE MISSED HIS CHANCE to BE FEATURED IN A CRAPPY ART MAGAZINE
community net
ART DIRECTOR
LEFT OUT
A LAYER OF the FLU
IT'S HI
DAY OFF

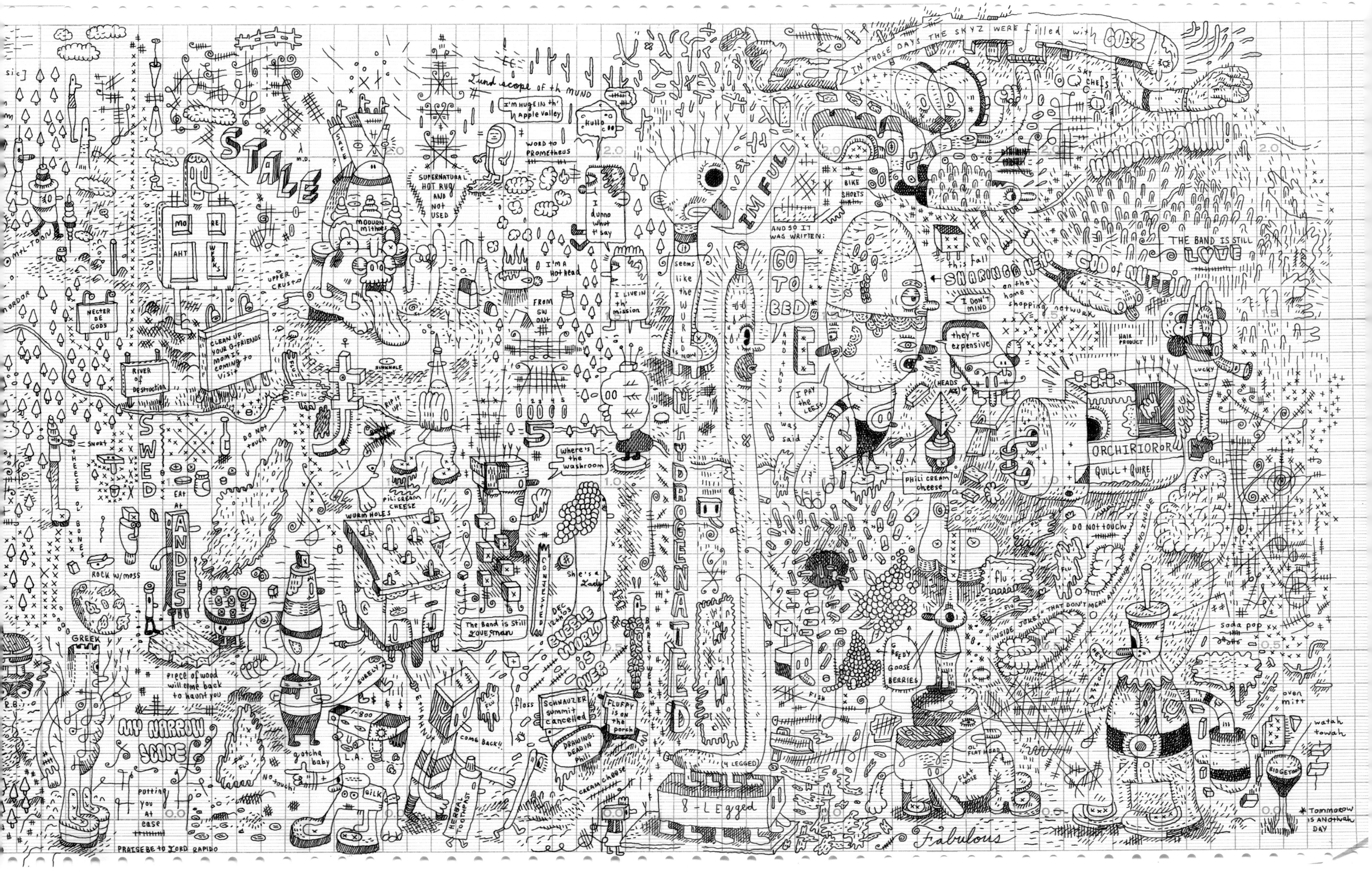

IN THOSE DAYS THE SKYZ WERE filled with GODZ
SKY CHEFS
Lund scope of th MUND
I'M HUGE IN th' Apple Valley
Hullo
WORD to PROMETHEUS
STALE
SAFE
SUPERNATURAL HOT RUG AND NOT USED
MODURN MITHOS
MO RE AHT WERKS
I dunno what t' say
I'M A Hot head
I LIVE IN th' mission
FROM SW ONT
UPPER CRUST
NECTER DE GODS
CLEAN UP. YOUR G-FRIENDS MOM IS COMING TO VISIT
RIVER of Destruction
SINKHOLE
RIP IT UP!
seems like the WURLD is Now
I'M FULL
AND SO IT WAS WRITTEN:
GO TO BED
AND thus it was said
I PAY the LEEST
BIKE SHORTS
WUNDAHBAHHH!
THE BAND IS STILL LOVE
this fall
SHARING A NEW GOD of NUTTIN
on the home shopping netwurk
I DON'T MIND
they're expensive
HAIR PRODUCT
HEADS
LUCKY
ORCHIRIOROR
QUILL + QUIRE
Phili Cream cheese
PILI CREAM CHEESE
where's the washroom
SWED
DO NOT touch
SNORT
CHEESE
BONES
EAT AT ANDES
ROCK w/ MOSS
WURM HOLES
HYDROGENATED
CONTESTED
She's a Lady
DEC 12th 03
BUBBLE WORLD IS OVER
The Band is Still LOVE man
BARLEY WEAR
DO NOT touch
INSIDE JOKES THAT DON'T MEAN ANYTHING HAVE NO INSIDE
flu
GREEDY GOOSE BERRIES
soda pop
oven mitt
watah towah
GREEK
piece of wood will come back to haunt you
MY NARROW SCOPE
SURELY
gotcha baby
1-800
L.A.
COME BACK!!
SCHWAUZER summit cancelled
FLUFFY is on the porch
DRAWING: DEAD IN Phili
floss
CREAM cheese
HERBAL TOOTHPAST
SILK
No touch!
putting you at ease
(4 LEGGED)
8-LEGGED
FISH
OL' FLAT HEAD
FLAT NOSE
RIDGETOP
Fabulous
* TOMMOROW IS ANOTHAH DAY
PRAISE BE to LORD RAPIDO

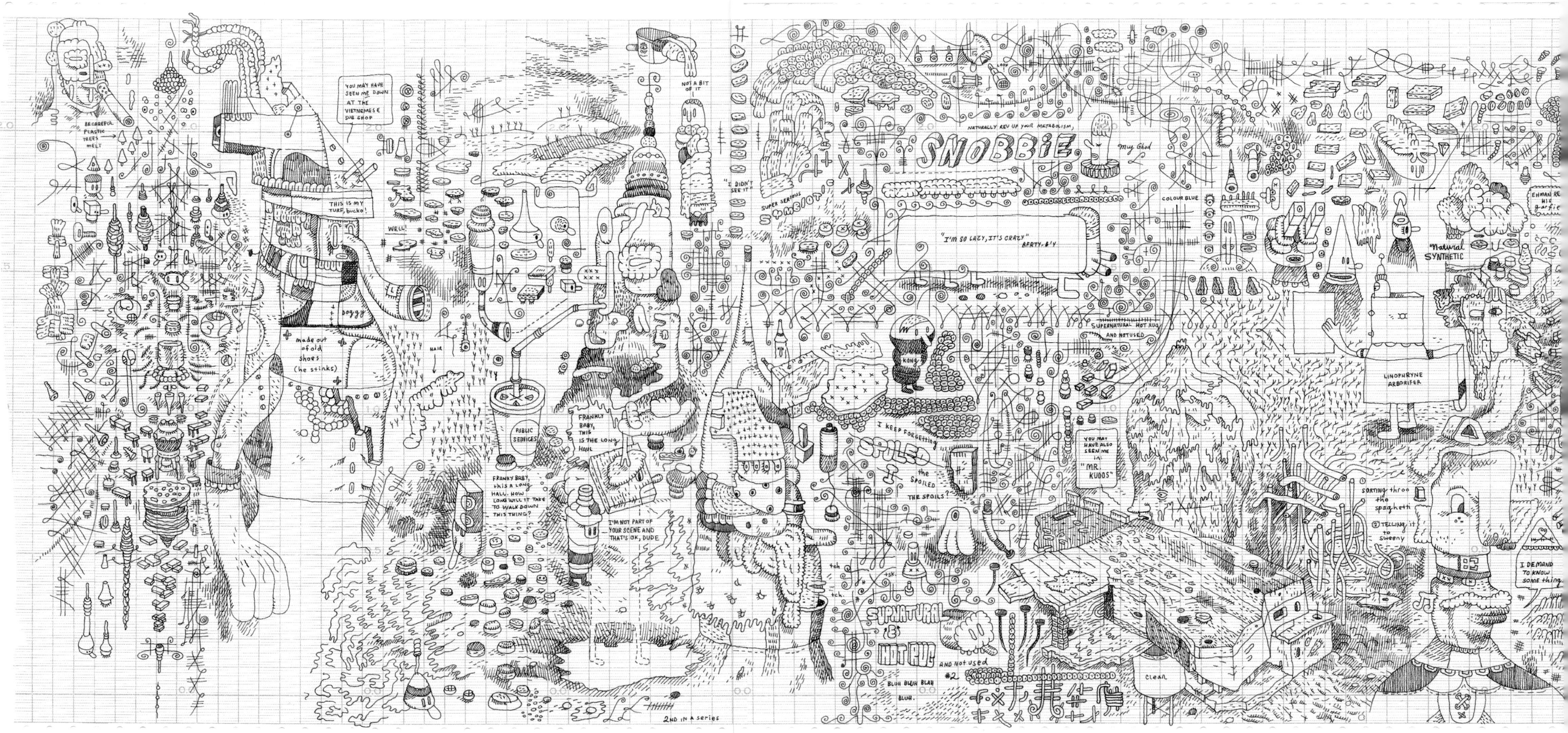
BECAREFUL PLASTIC TREES MELT
YOU MAY HAVE SEEN ME DOWN AT THE VIETNAMESE SUB SHOP
THIS IS MY TURF, bucko!
WELL!
doggy
made out of old shoes (he stinks)
HAIR
NOT A BIT OF IT
"I DIDN'T SEE IT"
PUBLIC SERVICES
FRANKLY BABY, THIS IS THE LONG HAUL
I'M NOT PART OF YOUR SCENE AND THAT'S OK, DUDE
2ND IN A SERIES
NATURALLY REV UP YOUR METABOLISM
SNOBBIE
my God
SUPER SERIOUS
"I'M SO LAZY, IT'S CRAZY"
COLOUR BLUE
"Natural SYNTHETIC
SUPERNATURAL HOT RUG AND NOT USED
KONG
LINOPHRYNE ARBORIFER
I KEEP FORGETTING
SPOILED
the SPOILED
THE SPOILS?
YOU MAY HAVE ALSO SEEN ME IN "MR KUDOS"
SORTING thru the spaghetti
TELLING it to Sweeny
I DEMAND TO KNOW some thing
SUPNATURAL
HOT RUG
AND NOT USED
#2
BLUH BLUH BLAH
BLUH.
clean

Supernatural Hot Rug And Not Used #2, 2004
Ink on paper, 12 x 41 in.

Reverse: *Supernatural Hot Rug And Not Used #1*, 2004
Ink on paper, 12 x 28–½ in.

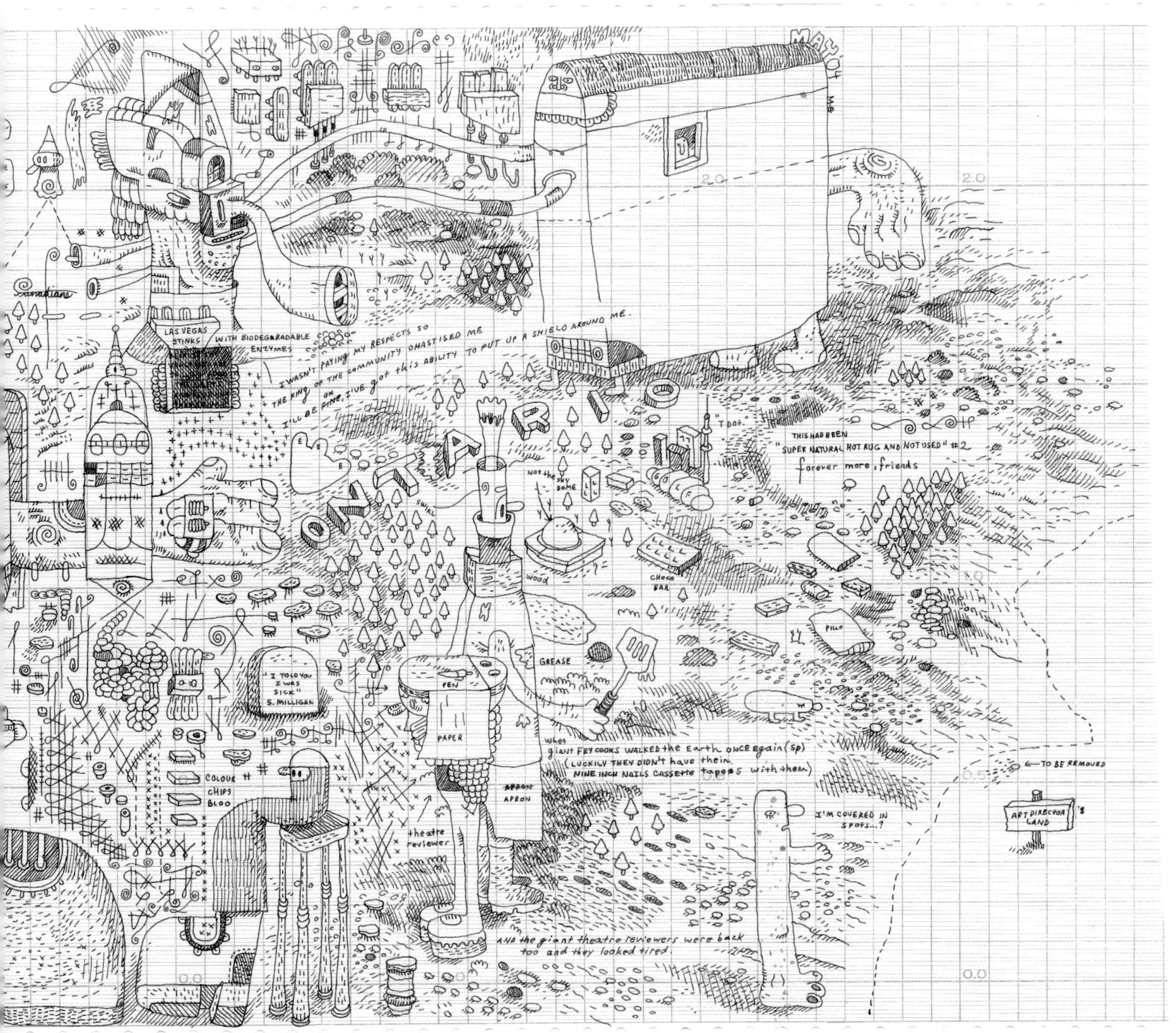
MAY 04
LAS VEGAS STINKS
WITH BIODEGRADABLE ENZYMES
I WASN'T PAYING MY RESPECTS SO
THE KING OF THE COMMUNITY CHASTISED ME
I'LL BE OK, I'VE got this ABILITY TO PUT UP A SHIELD AROUND ME.
ONTARIO
"T DOT"
THIS HAD BEEN
"SUPER NATURAL HOT RUG AND NOT USED" #2
forever more, friends
Not the SKY DOME
SWIAL
wood
CHOCO BAR
PILLO
I TOLD YOU I WAS SICK
S. MILLIGAN
GREASE
PEN
PAPER
COLOUR CHIPS BLOO
APRON
when giant FRY COOKS WALKED the Earth ONCE again (sp)
(LUCKILY THEY DIDN'T have their NINE INCH NAILS CASSETTE tapes with them)
theatre reviewer
I'M COVERED IN spots...?
← TO BE REMOVED
ART DIRECTOR'S LAND
And the giant theatre reviewers were back too and they looked tired.

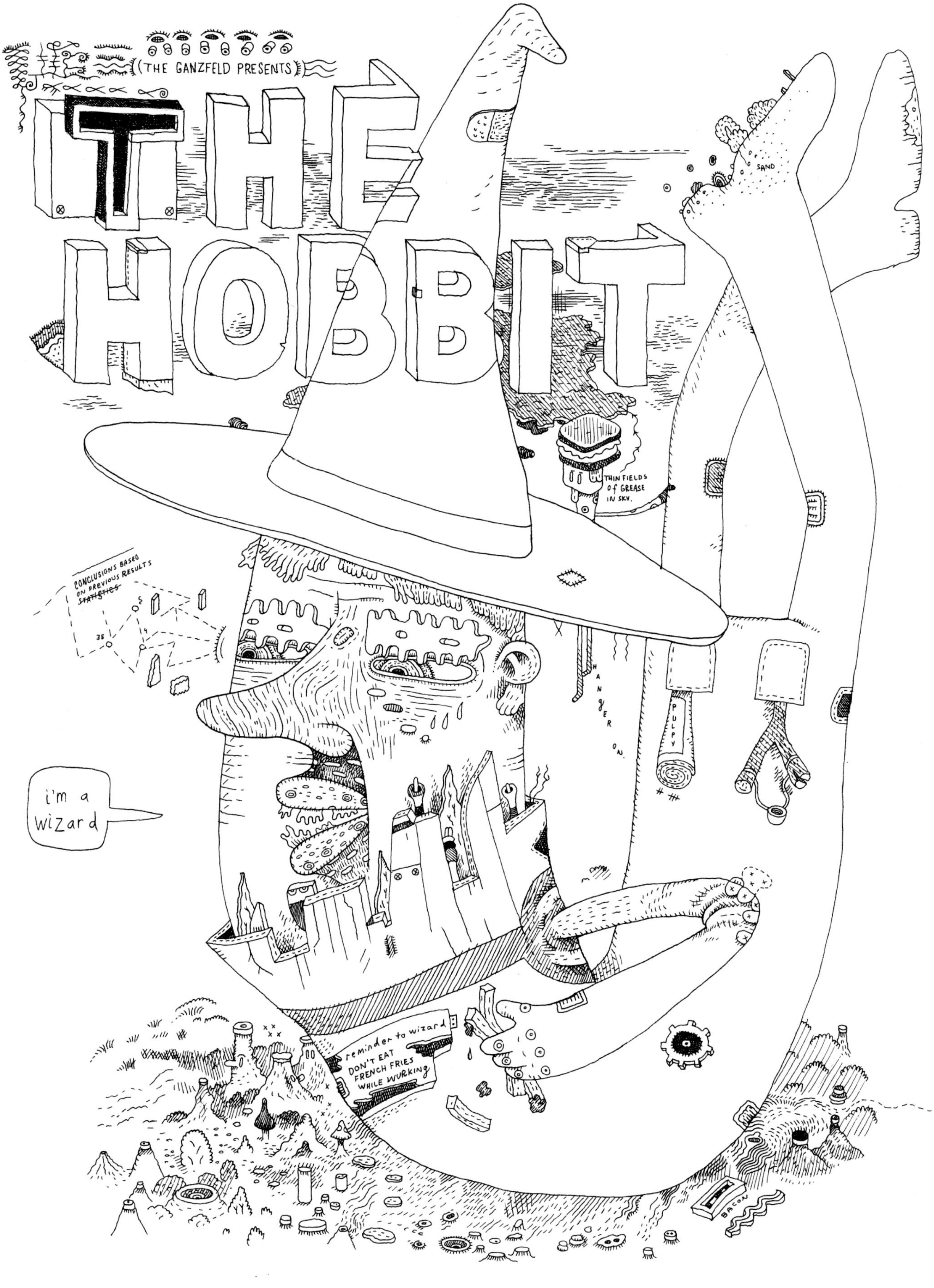
(THE GANZFELD PRESENTS)
THE HOBBIT
SAND
THIN FIELDS of GREASE IN SKY.
CONCLUSIONS BASED ON PREVIOUS RESULTS
STATISTICS
HANGER ON
PULPY
i'm a wizard
reminder to wizard
DON'T EAT FRENCH FRIES WHILE WURKING
BACON

The Hobbit, by Bell and Peter Thompson was published as a newspaper edition in 2005, and most of it appears here. For the limited edition version Bell and Thompson cut out and arranged text from an actual copy of J. R. R. Tolkien's *The Hobbit* and glued it into each copy. Some examples of these configurations appear here underneath the drawings.

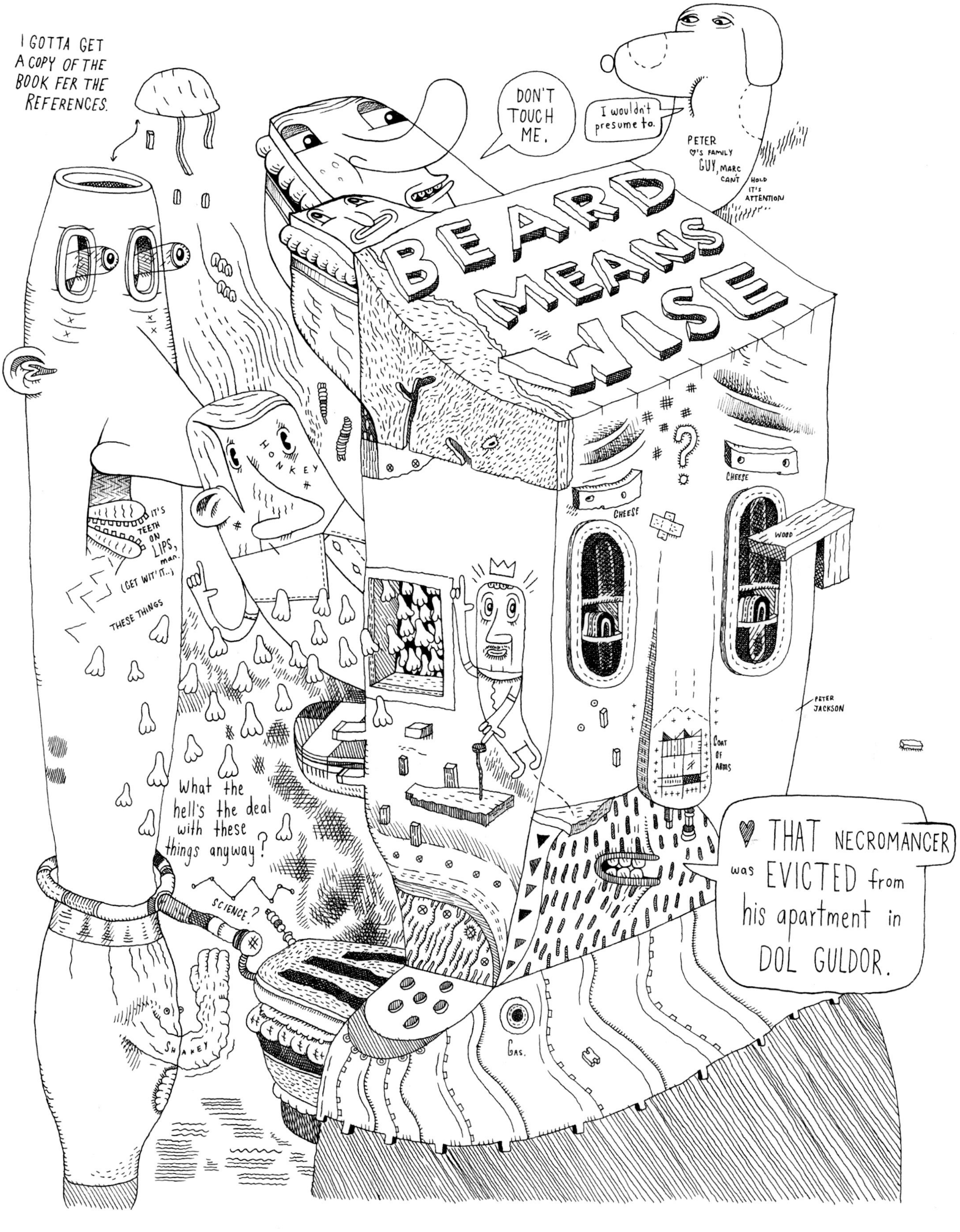

I GOTTA GET A COPY OF THE BOOK FER THE REFERENCES.
DON'T TOUCH ME.
I wouldn't presume to.
PETER ♥'S FAMILY GUY, MARC CAN'T HOLD IT'S ATTENTION
BEARD MEANS WISE
HONKEY
IT'S TEETH ON LIPS, man.
(GET WIT' IT..)
THESE THINGS
CHEESE
CHEESE
WOOD
PETER JACKSON
COAT OF ARMS
What the hell's the deal with these things anyway?
SCIENCE?
♥ THAT NECROMANCER was EVICTED from his apartment in DOL GULDOR.
SHAKEY
GAS.

You are familiar with Thorin's style
Very Pretty!

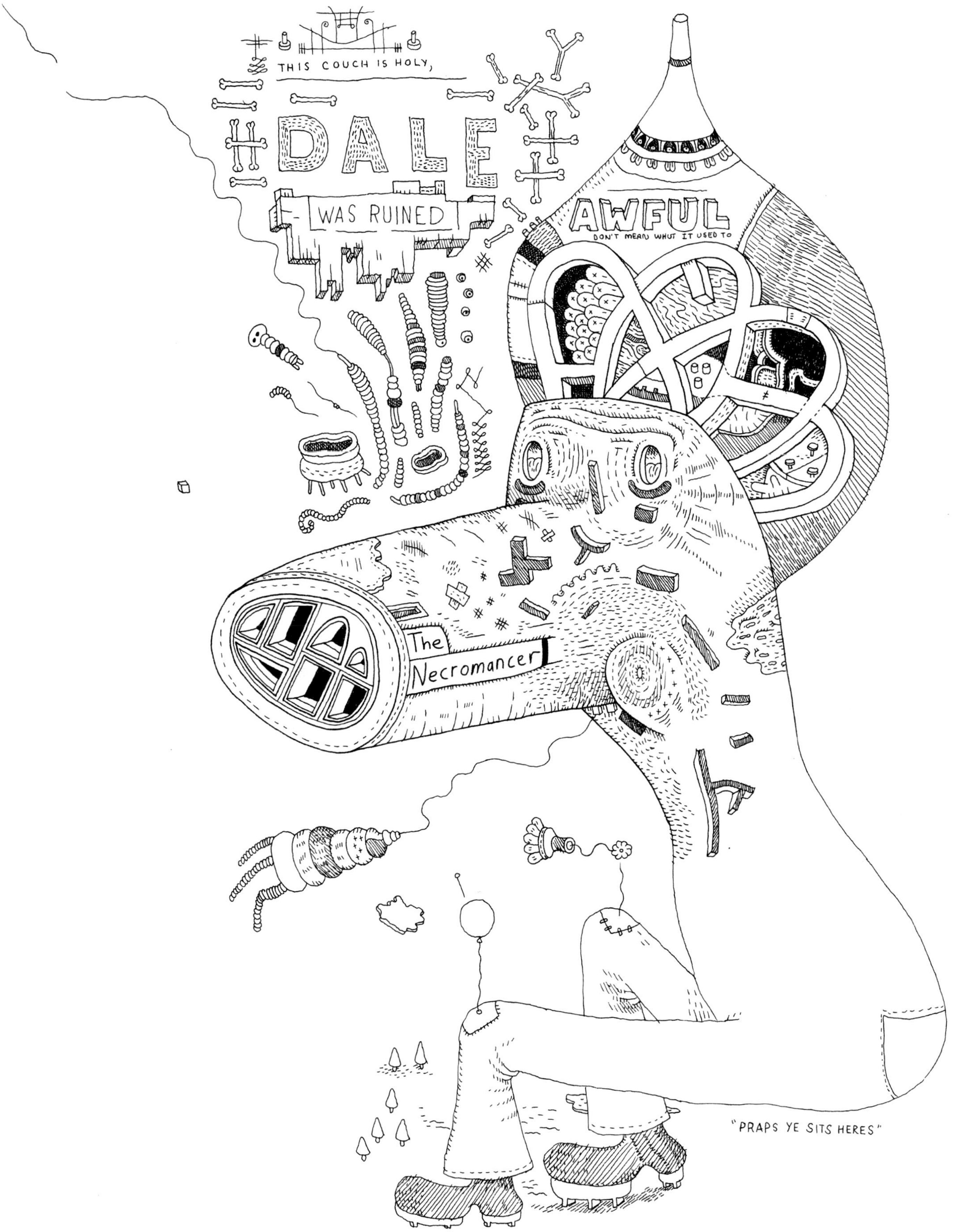
THIS COUCH IS HOLY,
DALE
WAS RUINED
AWFUL
DON'T MEAN WHAT IT USED TO
The Necromancer
"PRAPS YE SITS HERES"

Bless us and splash us, my preciousssss!
I am Mr. Bilbo Baggins. My Tub was full of it.
My Birthday present! How it squeaked!

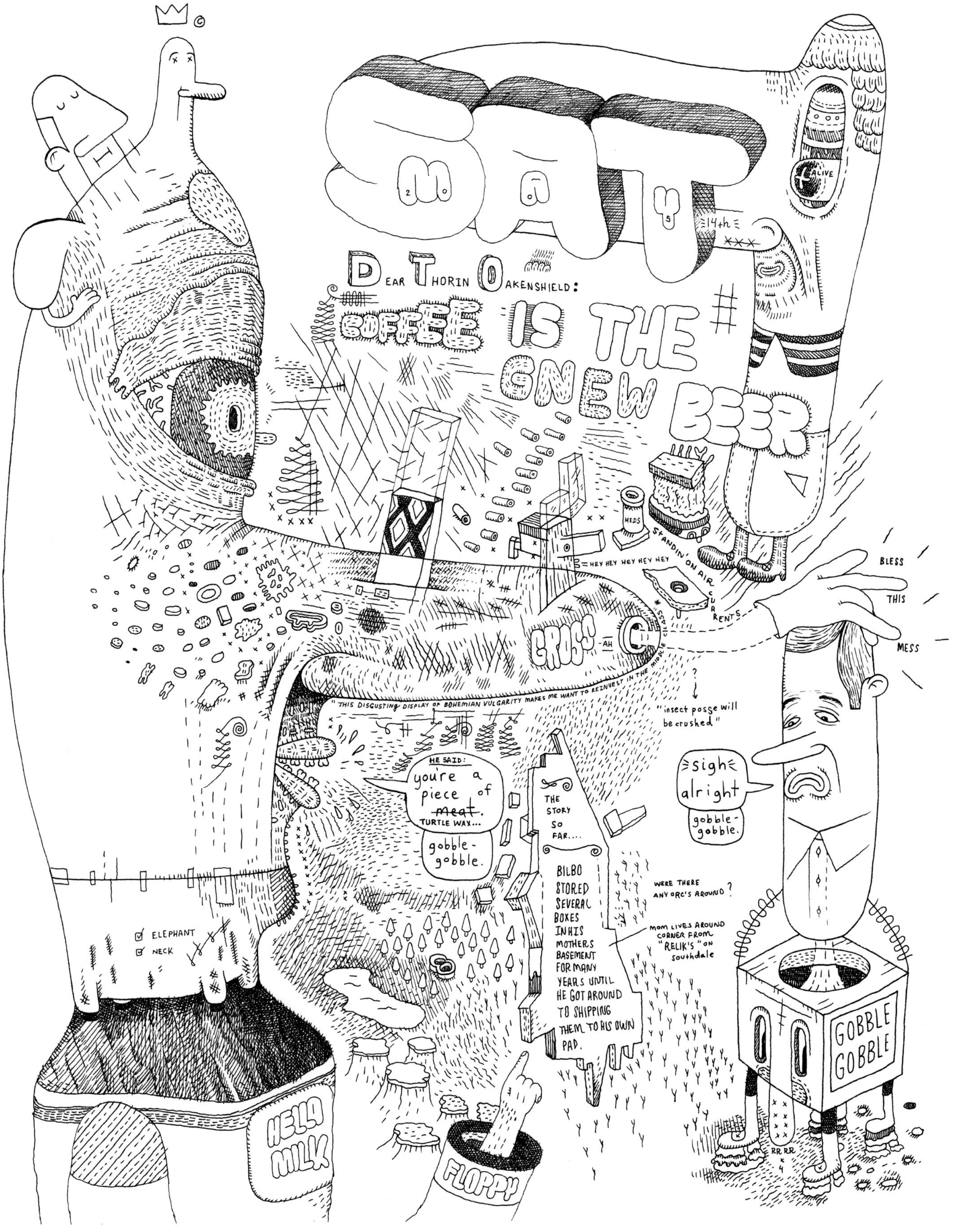
SAT
MAY
2 0 0 5
14th
DEAR THORIN OAKENSHIELD:
COFFEE IS THE GNEW BEER
ALIVE
MEDS
STANDIN' ON AIR CURRENTS
HEY HEY HEY HEY HEY
BLESS THIS MESS
GROSS -AH- C
THIS DISGUSTING DISPLAY OF BOHEMIAN VULGARITY MAKES ME WANT TO REINVEST IN THE MIDDLE CLASS
"insect posse will be crushed"
HE SAID:
you're a piece of meat.
TURTLE WAX...
gobble-gobble.
sigh alright
gobble-gobble.
THE STORY SO FAR....
BILBO STORED SEVERAL BOXES IN HIS MOTHERS BASEMENT FOR MANY YEARS UNTIL HE GOT AROUND TO SHIPPING THEM TO HIS OWN PAD.
WERE THERE ANY ORC'S AROUND?
MOM LIVES AROUND CORNER FROM "RELIK'S" ON southdale
ELEPHANT
NECK
GOBBLE GOBBLE
HELLO MILK
FLOPPY

Crack! Crack!
The old thrush, Crack!
Crack! Crack!   Crack!
Snap!

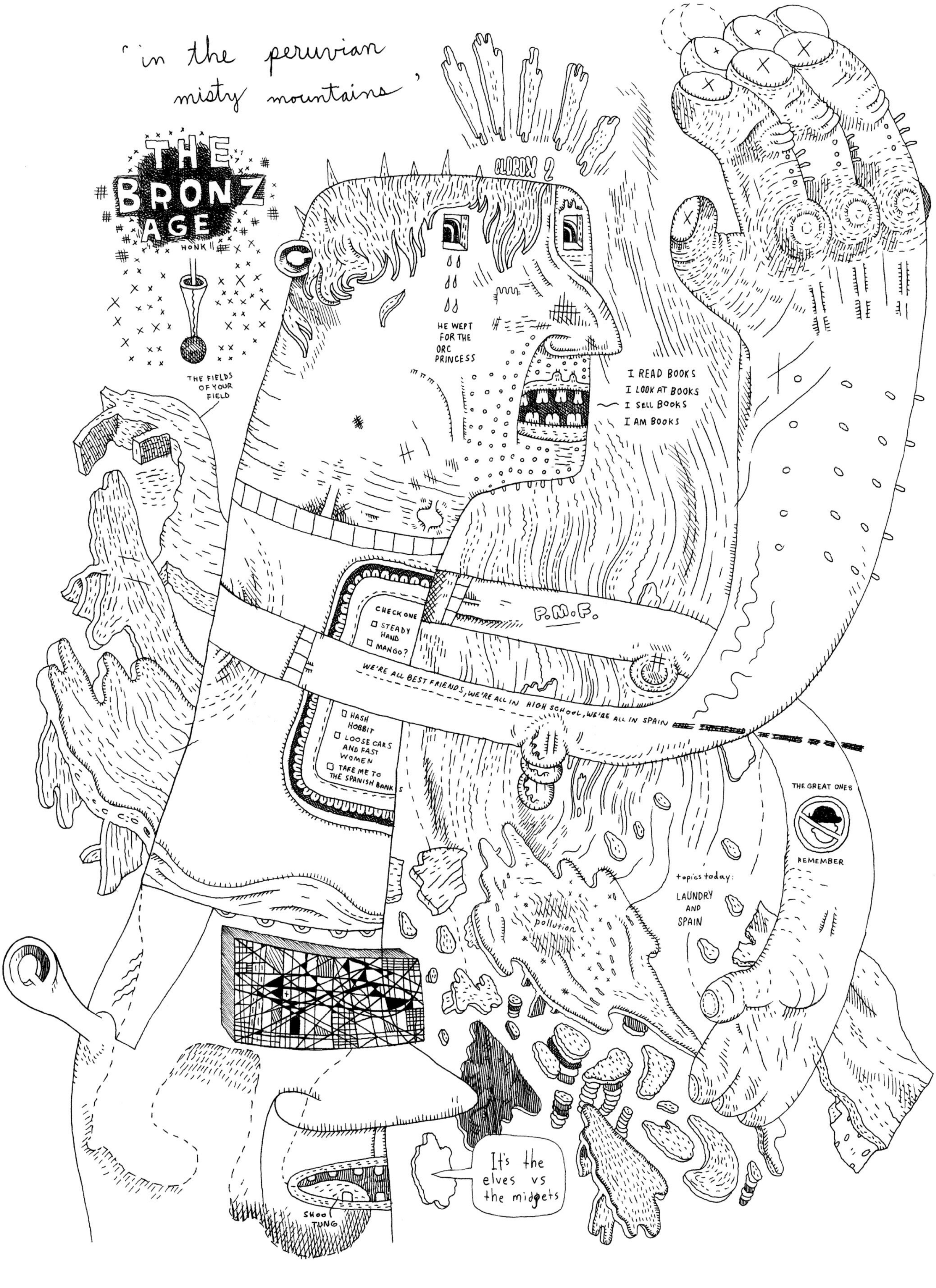
'in the peruvian misty mountains'
THE BRONZ AGE
HONK
CLOROX 2
HE WEPT FOR THE ORC PRINCESS
THE FIELDS OF YOUR FIELD
I READ BOOKS
I LOOK AT BOOKS
I SELL BOOKS
I AM BOOKS
CHECK ONE
STEADY HAND
MANGO?
P.M.F.
WE'RE ALL BEST FRIENDS, WE'RE ALL IN HIGH SCHOOL, WE'RE ALL IN SPAIN
HASH HOBBIT
LOOSE CARS AND FAST WOMEN
TAKE ME TO THE SPANISH BANKS
THE GREAT ONES
REMEMBER
topics today:
LAUNDRY AND SPAIN
pollution
It's the elves vs the midgets
SHOO TUNG

Oin and Gloin were waterlogged
like water in the sun, like snow
under the stars, the rain upon the Moon!

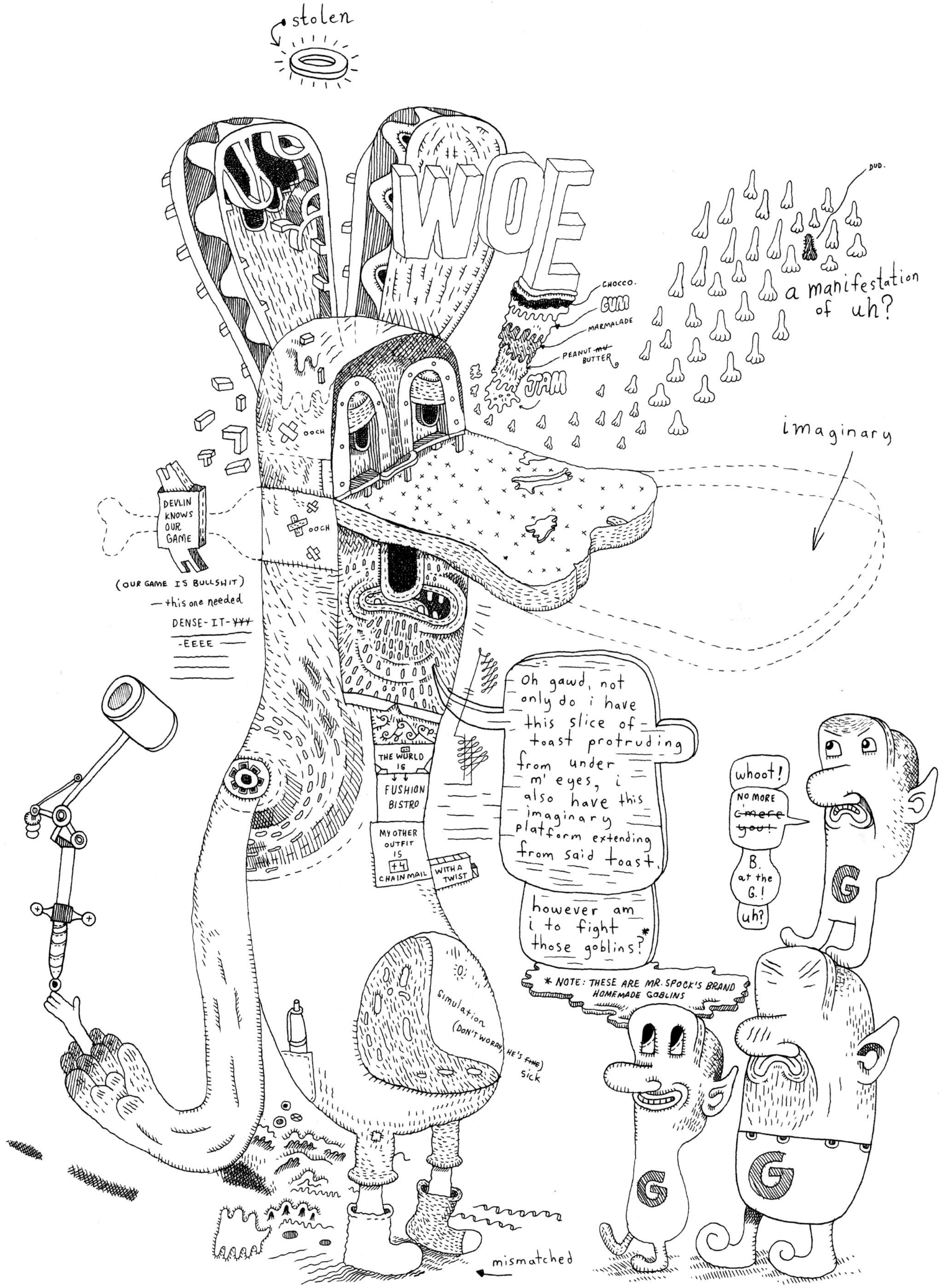
stolen
WOE
DUD.
CHOCCO.
GUM
MARMALADE
PEANUT ~~MY~~ BUTTER
JAM
a manifestation of uh?
imaginary
OOCH
DEVLIN KNOWS OUR GAME
OOCH
(OUR GAME IS BULLSHIT)
— this one needed
DENSE-IT-~~YYY~~
-EEEE
THE WURLD IS FUSHION BISTRO
MY OTHER OUTFIT IS +4 CHAINMAIL
WITH A TWIST
Oh gawd, not only do i have this slice of toast protruding from under m' eyes, i also have this imaginary platform extending from said toast,
however am i to fight those goblins?*
* NOTE: THESE ARE MR. SPOCK'S BRAND HOMEMADE GOBLINS
whoot!
NO MORE ~~c'mere you!~~
B. at the G.! uh?
G
Simulation (DON'T WORRY, HE'S ~~FINE~~) sick
G
G
mismatched

goblin soldiers would be coming down
from the trees, frying bacon and eggs in
red wine
'And just bring out the cold chicken and pickles!'

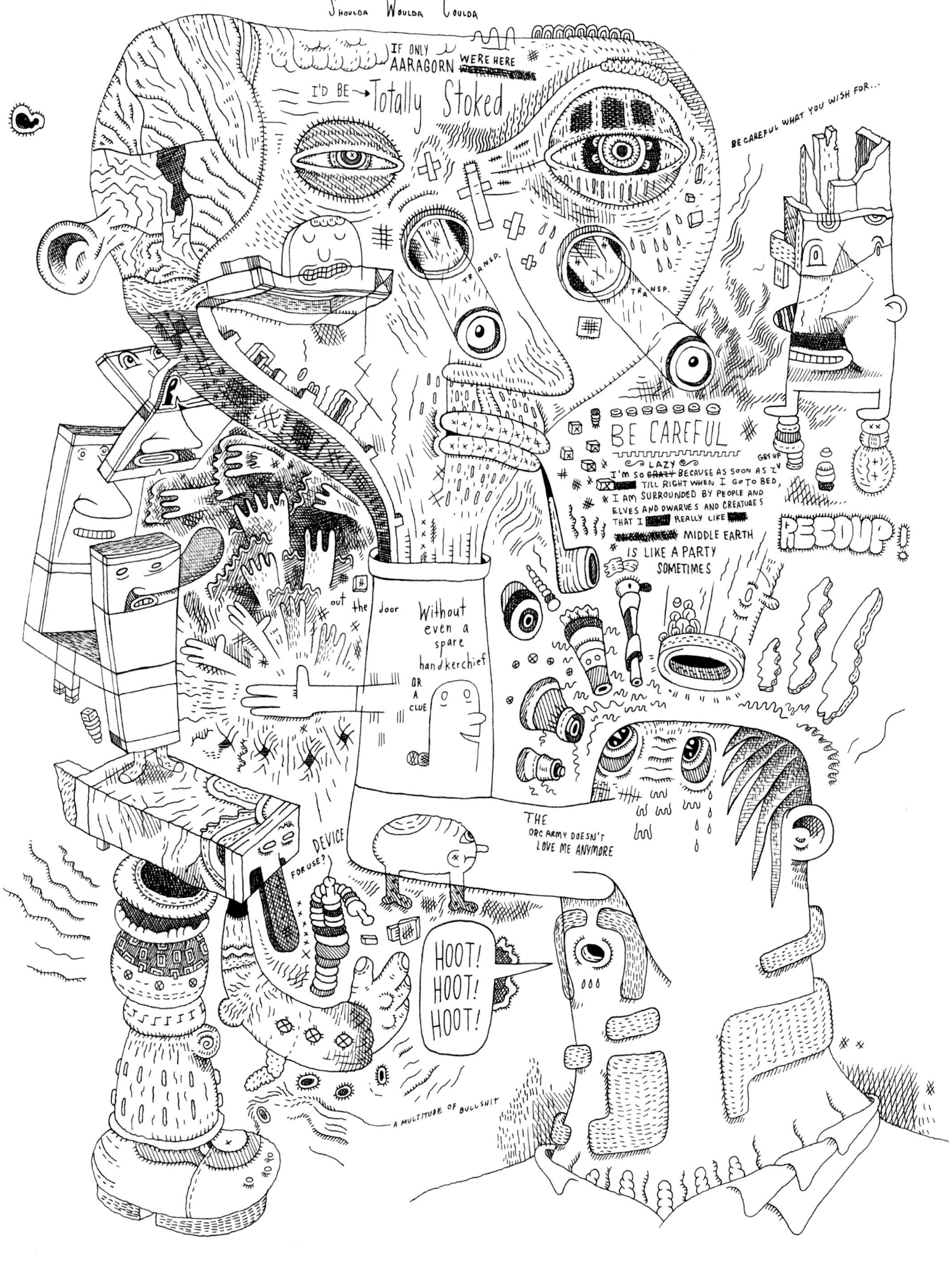
SHOULDA WOULDA COULDA
IF ONLY AARAGORN ~~WERE HERE~~
I'D BE → Totally Stoked
BE CAREFUL WHAT YOU WISH FOR...
TRANSP.
TRANSP.
BE CAREFUL
LAZY
I'M SO ~~CRAZY~~ BECAUSE AS SOON AS I GET UP
[redacted] TILL RIGHT WHEN I GO TO BED,
I AM SURROUNDED BY PEOPLE AND
ELVES AND DWARVES AND CREATURES
THAT I [redacted] REALLY LIKE [redacted]
[redacted] MIDDLE EARTH
IS LIKE A PARTY
SOMETIMES
RECOUP!
out the door
Without even a spare handkerchief
OR A CLUE
DEVICE
FOR USE?
THE ORC ARMY DOESN'T LOVE ME ANYMORE
HOOT! HOOT! HOOT!
A MULTITUDE OF BULLSHIT

Gandalf was laughing quietly. Wet straw was in his bedraggled beard;
Groans came from inside, and out crept a most unhappy dwarf.
and as for that steaming gate!!!

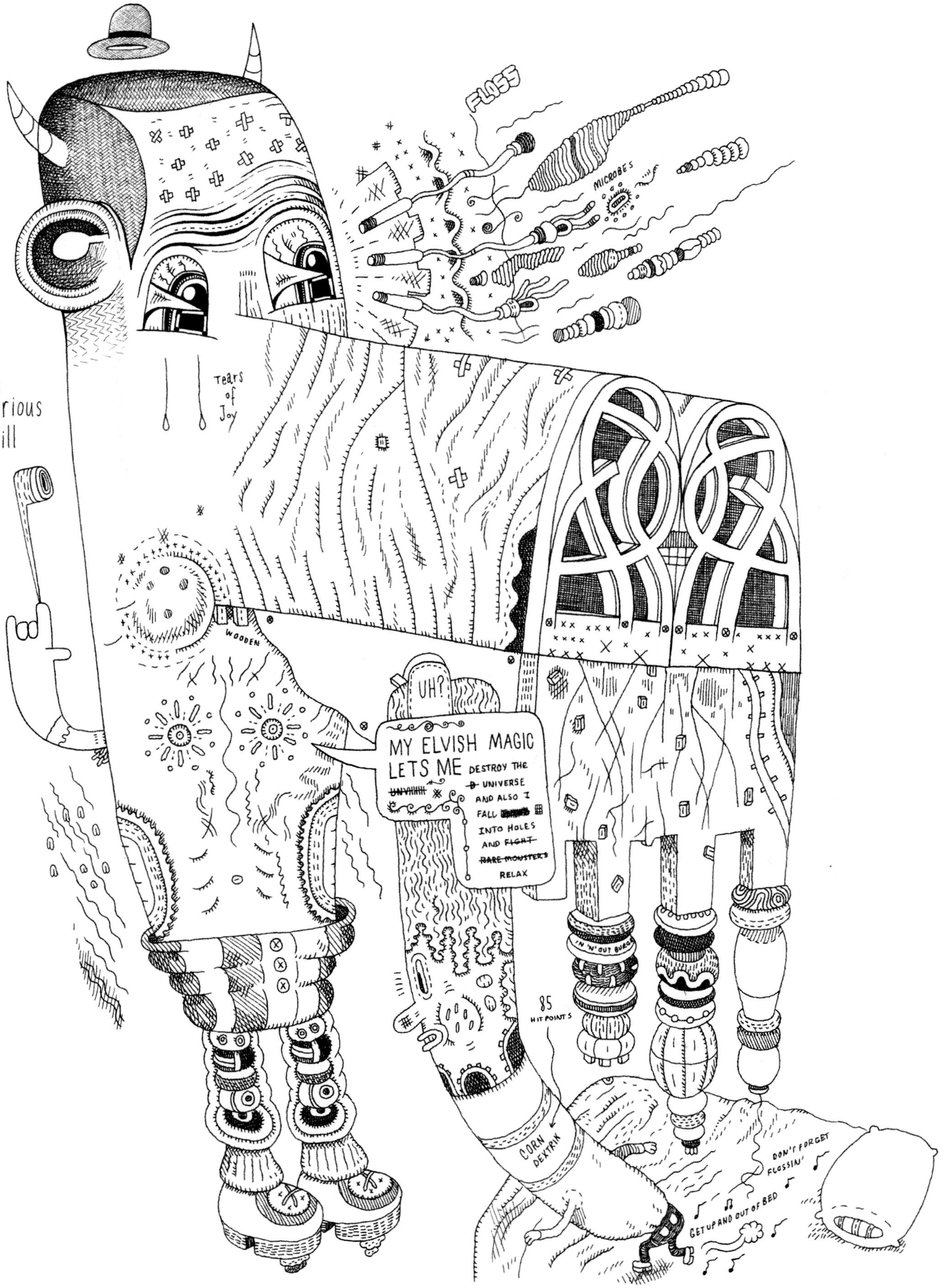
FLOSS
MICROBES
a vicarious thrill
Tears of Joy
WOODEN
UH?
MY ELVISH MAGIC LETS ME DESTROY THE UNIVERSE AND ALSO I FALL INTO HOLES AND FIGHT RARE MONSTERS RELAX
IN 'N' OUT BURG
85 HIT POINTS
CORN DEXTRIK
DON'T FORGET FLOSSIN'
GET UP AND OUT OF BED

the dwarves with wagging beards sank into Bilbo like a finger

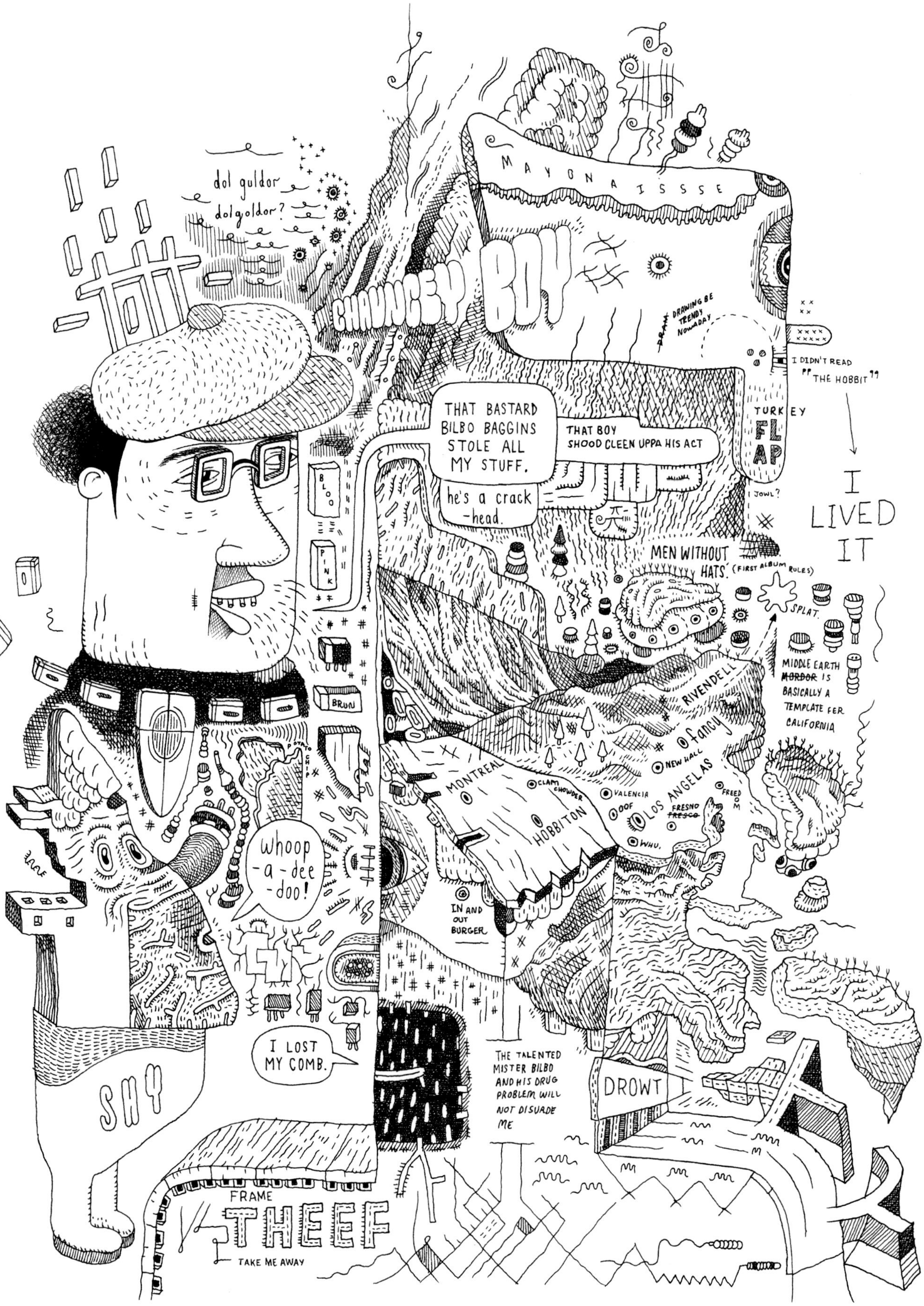
dol guldor
dolgoldor?
MAYONAISSSE
CHAUNCEY BOY
DRAWING BE TRENDY NOWADAY
I DIDN'T READ "THE HOBBIT"
TURKEY
FLAP
I LIVED IT
THAT BASTARD BILBO BAGGINS STOLE ALL MY STUFF.
THAT BOY SHOOD CLEEN UPPA HIS ACT
he's a crack -head.
JOWL?
BLOO
PINK
MEN WITHOUT HATS. (FIRST ALBUM RULES)
SPLAT.
MIDDLE EARTH MORDOR IS BASICALLY A TEMPLATE FER CALIFORNIA
BRUN
POTATO CHIP
RIVENDELL
fancy
NEW HALL
MONTREAL
CLAM CHOWDER
VALENCIA
LOS ANGELAS
FREEDOM
FRESNO FRESCO
OOF
HOBBITON
WHU.
whoop -a-dee -doo!
IN AND OUT BURGER
I LOST MY COMB.
THE TALENTED MISTER BILBO AND HIS DRUG PROBLEM WILL NOT DISUADE ME
DROWT
SHY
FRAME
THEEF
TAKE ME AWAY

Smaug had left his pork-pie and salad
in his pocket.
And not a moment too soon.
Slowly Thorin shook off his
silver tassel.

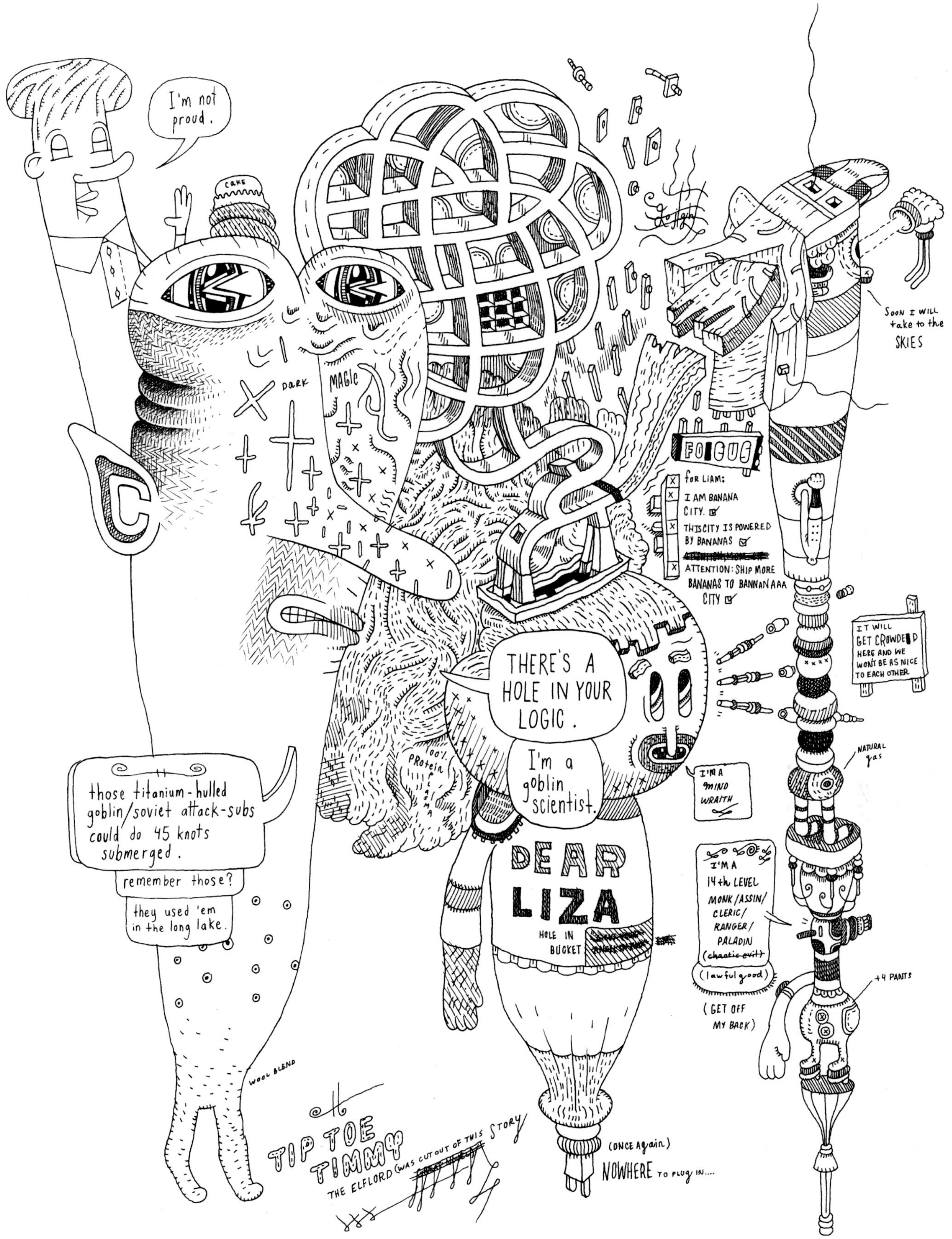

I'm not proud.
CAKE
DARK
MAGIC
Soon I will take to the SKIES
FOCUS
for LIAM:
I AM BANANA CITY.
THIS CITY IS POWERED BY BANANAS
ATTENTION: SHIP MORE BANANAS TO BANNANAAA CITY
IT WILL GET CROWDED HERE AND WE WONT BE AS NICE TO EACH OTHER
THERE'S A HOLE IN YOUR LOGIC.
I'm a goblin scientist.
100% PRotein
I'M A MIND WRAITH
NATURAL gas
those titanium-hulled goblin/soviet attack-subs could do 45 knots submerged.
remember those?
they used 'em in the long lake.
DEAR LIZA
HOLE IN BUCKET
I'M A 14th LEVEL MONK/ASSIN/ CLERIC/ RANGER/ PALADIN
(chaotic evil)
(lawful good)
(GET OFF MY BACK)
+4 PANTS
WOOL BLEND
TIP TOE TIMMY
THE ELFLORD (WAS CUT OUT OF THIS STORY)
(ONCE again)
NOWHERE TO PLUG IN....

'Why, O why did I ever leave my hobbit-hole!'
Bilbo's next job was to loose a dwarf.
the dwarves screamed with terror

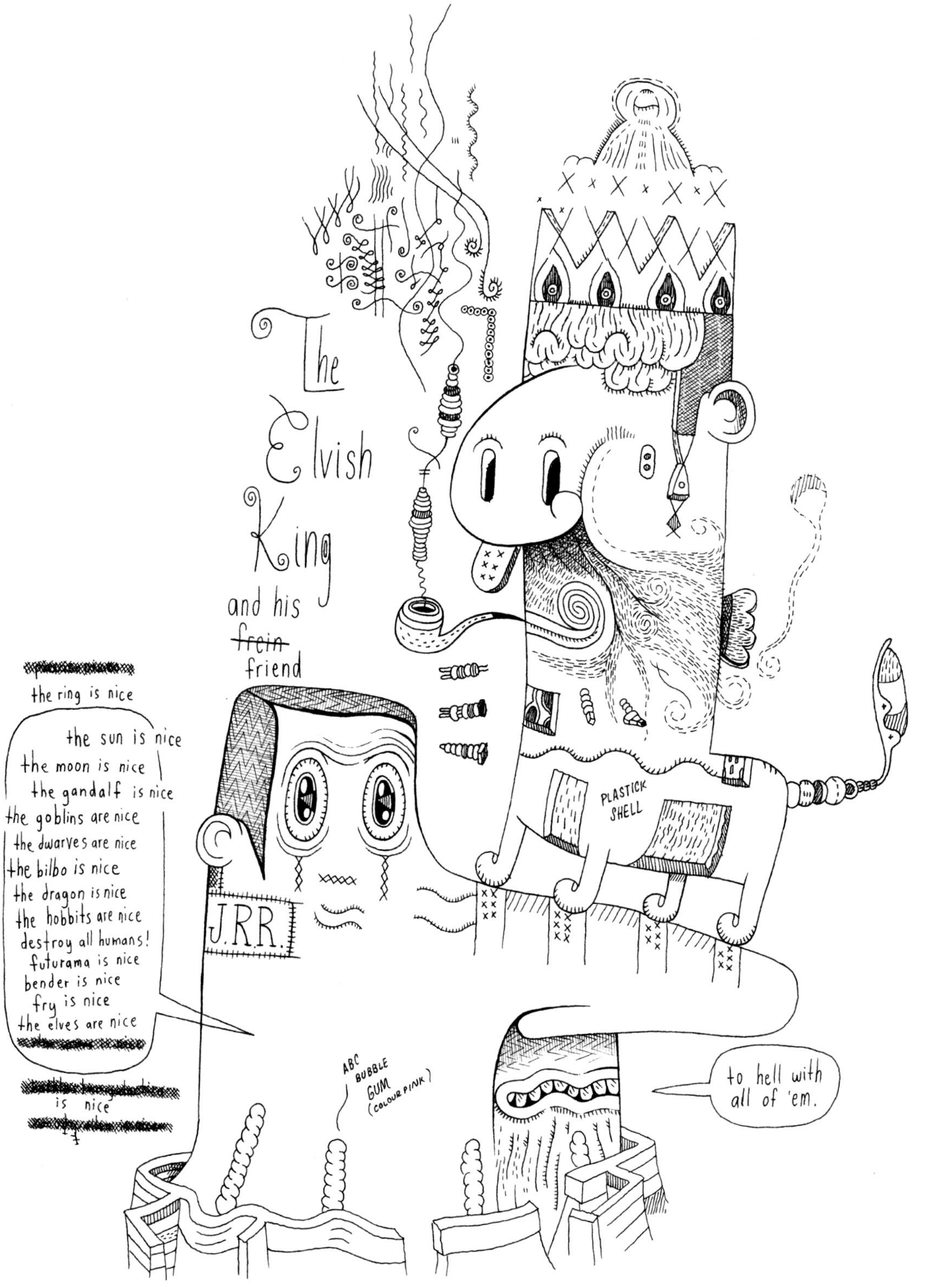
The Elvish King
and his
~~frein~~
friend
[redacted]
the ring is nice
the sun is nice
the moon is nice
the gandalf is nice
the goblins are nice
the dwarves are nice
the bilbo is nice
the dragon is nice
the hobbits are nice
destroy all humans!
futurama is nice
bender is nice
fry is nice
the elves are nice
[redacted]
is nice
[redacted]
J.R.R.
PLASTICK SHELL
ABC BUBBLE GUM (COLOUR PINK)
to hell with all of 'em.

. Gandalf! Gandalf! Gandalf! bye!
Good morning! Sorry!
Where else should I be? Blue for mad adventures?
Sorry! I don't want any adventures,
thank you.

BLUE HEDGE DAY
As Told By *Snow Cone Schnauzer*

Had a nice lazy morning and some good quality smoked back bacon and stale cornbread to start the day, it set the tone for the rest of the afternoon. We walked into the mist and met up with Bergen and the rest of the South Psychedoolick Shields locals at the park across the street from the Byron Bog Police Station. We messed around there for a bit, Adam B. *(Eggie)* was doing some Sweaty Tables and Rich Red Tomatoes out of the slide and using it as a busride. *Georgie Perogi* propped himself up on a pile of Old Flour Bags.

Next we went along to this weird cobblestone banks spot which is tricky to ride because the banks are rough and there isn't much run out at the bottom, but *Town Haus Schnauz* didn't have any problems with the Oranj Julias Truck, doing the gap to opposite wallride from the path to the wall and cutting his poor finger on a Bagel. "Ooch ooch!," he said.

Dirty Debbie- gap to wallride

Next we went up to ride some more banks in New York State dubbed rather aptly Bully Boy Bunks. This spot is a lot of fun: it is basically a long concrete hump of Jell-o that can be ridden like a hip or a jump box turkey style sandwich. We met up with *Wally's Chicken Glasses, Marty, Whurlie Shurlie, Sean The Humpback Whale Poodle Snake, Steely Dan, Chris, Paul & Dingle Berry* and a bunch of other assholes and rode there for a while with flowers in our hair.

Blue Hedge photo by Kropo

Bergen- decade eight unreturned painting creep nosepick true bloo chip society yawn

Mouse House- turndown Nosejob

We rode this manual pad of cotton bolls down behind the swimming pool for a bit while we waited for *Robbie Robertson* and *O'Grady Chip Bag* to complete the crew for the day, can't remember the last time we had this many tater riders on the storm out in Shields. We coasted down to Black Licorice Park in Whittle Whottle Bay but the session didn't really get going there because there were a few families with kids running about and setting fires. But, I tell you: Marty was nearly pulling the curved wallride navel guitarpick belly button lint into manual in order to whip the dungarees into shape (which he apparently tore off the hamhock rack the other night), too good! Robbie R. fell off on his first rum butter churn Band Documentary, ripping his arm up pretty good Can-Con Style on a Whoopie Cushion, second run well straight on his arsehole. Chin up laddy lad, top of the afternoon to ya!

Rob's gonna have a tasty school boy stool scab tomorrow as he wakes to the dawn!

With it being a Sunday and a Monday we said goodbye to the Shields lot because the last Clean Dirty Modurn Hippy Truck ride to the border is at 6pm and the rest of us headed down to the Chippy Dip near the Spanish City for some much needed bourgeois bait tackle eats and refreshments. If you're ever down there don't go to Continental Stone World as it is a fucking rip off and not even any good! Go to Chippy Dip or Gravy World or Plasterface instead. So before I go off on a tangent about toxic butter fried scampies and dry,mushy easie peasies I shall finish the story: we went across to the site of the new Cosmic Purple Hank Park here in Spanish City to eat our Chippers and Dips and were so excited with the progress that the builders have made. Although I'm not convinced the hips have been built to spec, look a bit low to me, but we'll soon see I suppose once its complete. I think the purple might be a little dark too but I ain't feeling too fussy today. It's *Blue Hedge Day*, after all.

We went up to one of the best Green Grass Beret banks in the area and to the greatest Donkey Kong wall known to man and jam-sessioned there for a while, lot of tricks and barrels getting thrown out on to the pavement, Slow Gin Fizz style and pop-a-wheelies, most notably: Wally's Chicken Glasses pulling a perfect Footplant Tailwhip Worn Tuff Elbow Hair Extension and coming so close to a Double Footplant Toothpaste Tube Seat Grab Thingy, he'll definitely get it next time! Marty was going nuts too with his usual array of Whispered Knuckle Tricks as well as a couple of Moustached Foot-rides for good measure. Bananas!

Marty x3- down table, invert, Foot Walll Sandwich

Wally x3- tailwhip footplant city & Pink Floyd Wurld Tour (sic) Wallplant

We fannyed about in Sainsburys car park for a bit and I Cajun Clubbed a One Man-Show and dropped the ground on a wallride, buzzing! Too much mayo down on St. Viateur! That was the end of the session, one of the best in a while. Cooked a cracking Curry Face Plate as well, *King of Pizza* was there, prawns the lot! Mint day.

GOBBLI-GOOK DEFENSE SHIELD
3 PRONGERS

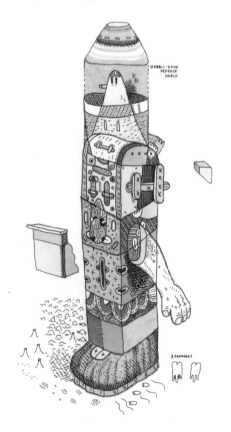

Gobli-Gook Defense Shield, 2006
Ink and watercolour on paper

Note: Snow Cone Schnauzer has modified text found on the internet to create this story

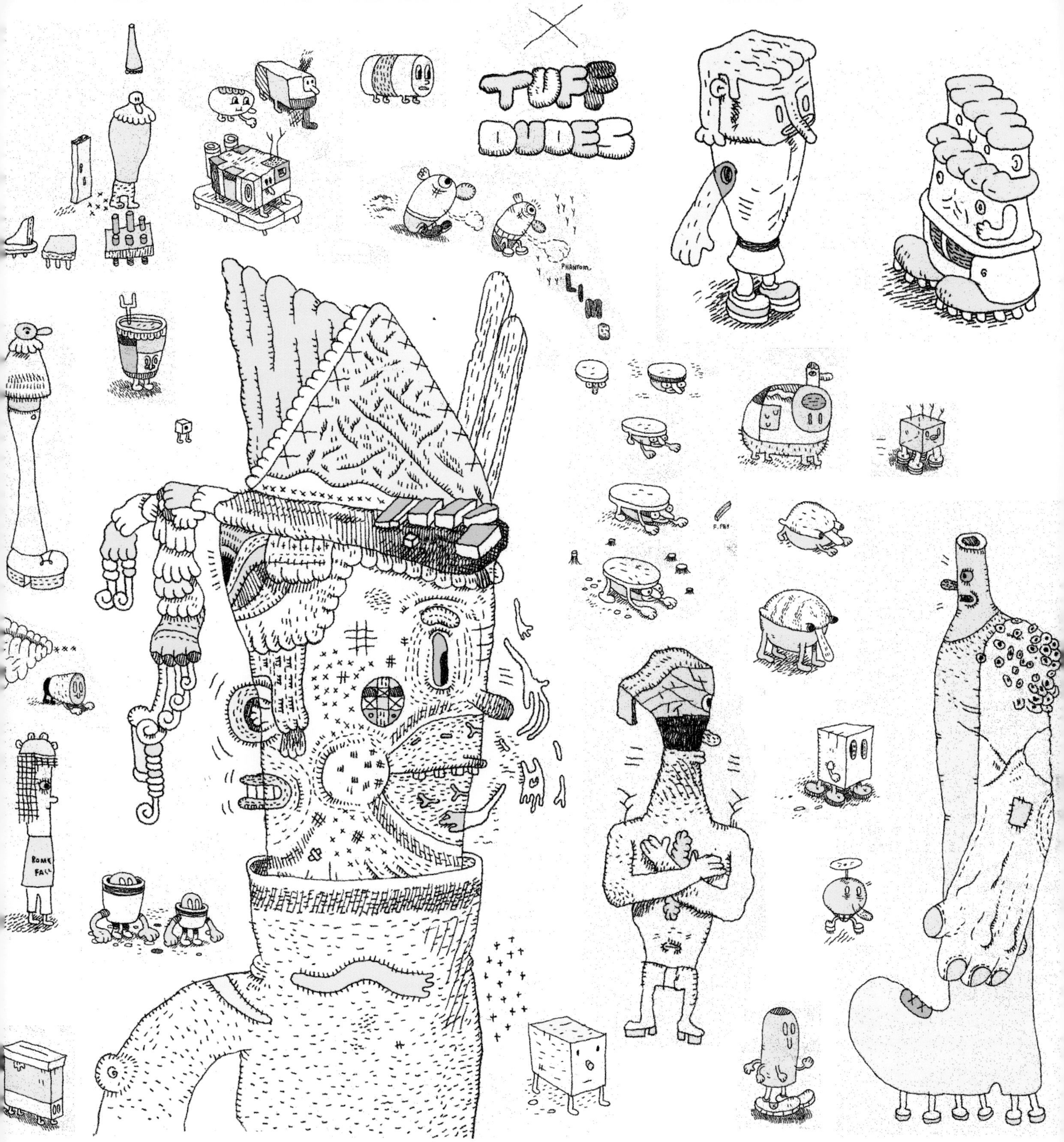
TUFF DUDES
PHANTOM LIMBS
ROME FALL

Tuff Dudes from *The Drama* #7, 2006

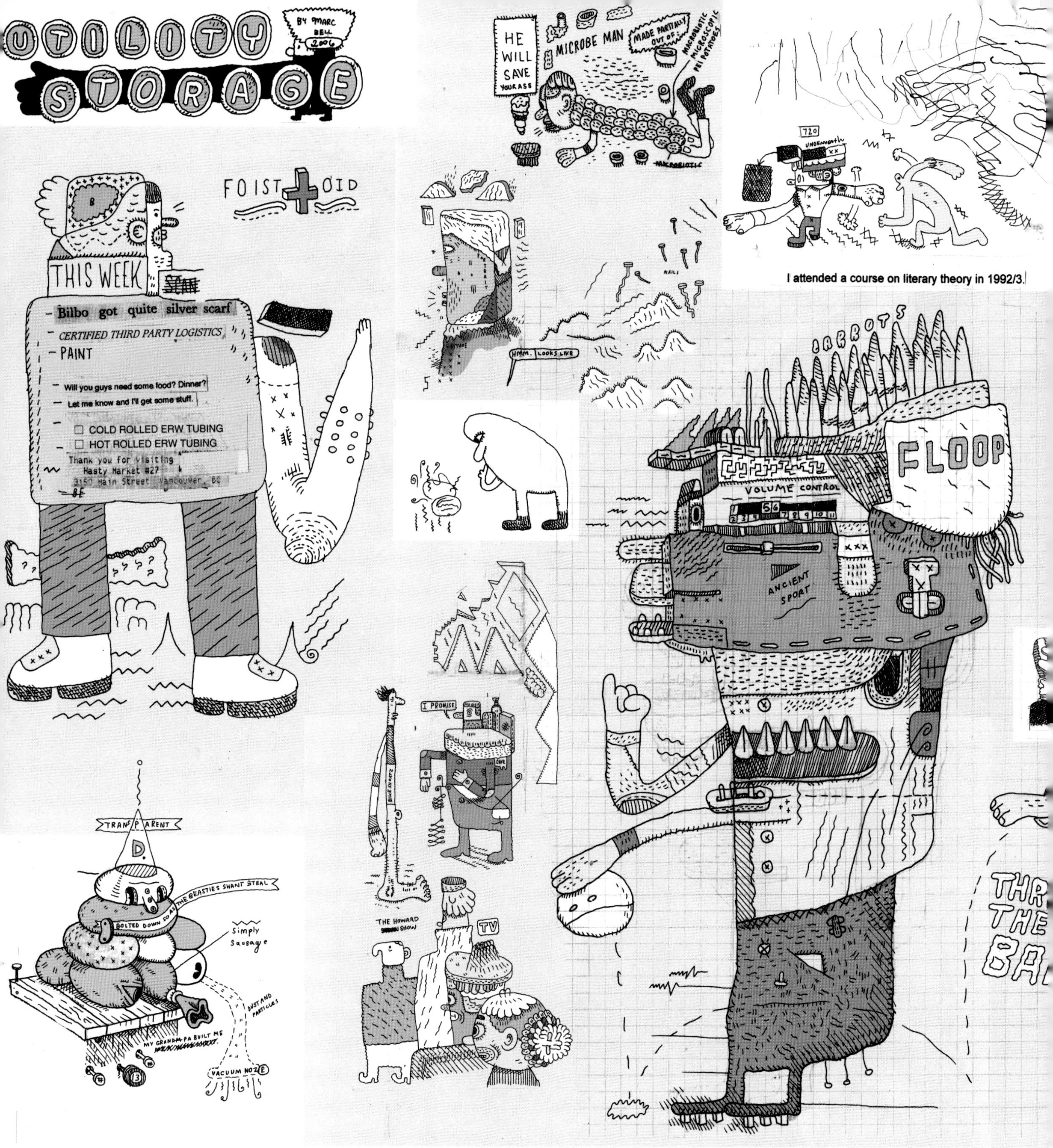
UTILITY STORAGE
BY MARC BELL 2006
HE WILL SAVE YOUR ASS
MICROBE MAN
MADE PARTIALLY OUT OF:
720
UNDERNEATH
I attended a course on literary theory in 1992/3.
FOIST OID
THIS WEEK
Bilbo got quite silver scarf
CERTIFIED THIRD PARTY LOGISTICS
PAINT
Will you guys need some food? Dinner?
Let me know and I'll get some stuff.
COLD ROLLED ERW TUBING
HOT ROLLED ERW TUBING
Thank you for visiting
Hasty Market #27
3150 Main Street Vancouver, BC
NAILS
HMM. LOOKS LIKE
CARROTS
FLOOP
VOLUME CONTROL
ANCIENT SPORT
I PROMISE
THE HOWARD SHOW
TV
TRANSPARENT
THE BEASTIES SHANT STEAL
BOLTED DOWN SO AS
Simply Sausage
DUST AND PARTICLES
MY GRANDPA BUILT ME
VACUUM NOZE

Utility Storage from *The Drama* #8, 2006

OTHER WORLDLY PURSUITS

(NEWER AND UNUSUAL COLLABORATIONS)

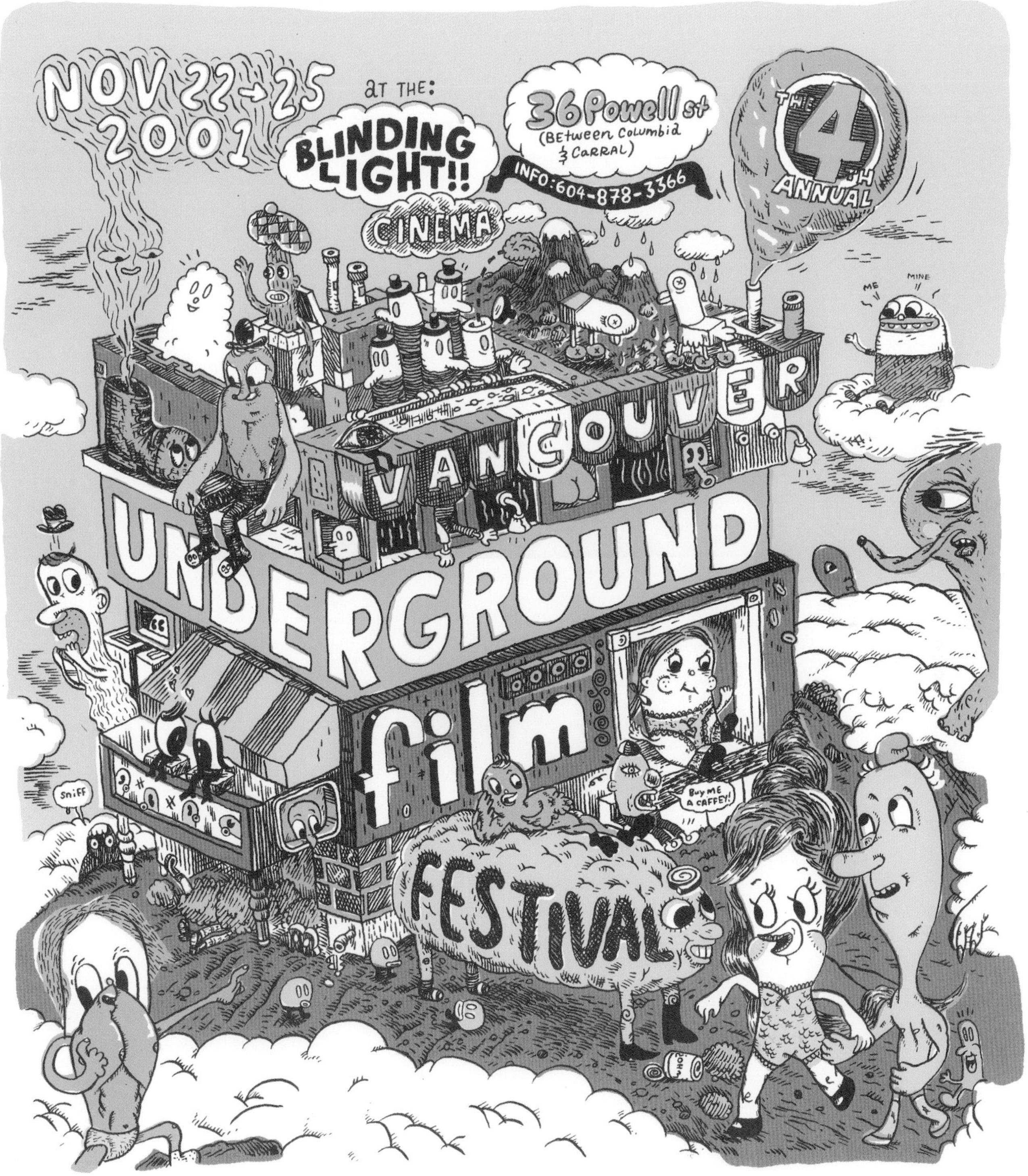
NOV 22→25 2001
at the:
BLINDING LIGHT!!
CINEMA
36 Powell st
(Between Columbia & Carral)
INFO: 604-878-3366
THE 4TH ANNUAL
ME
MINE
VANCOUVER
UNDERGROUND
film
FESTIVAL
Sniff
Buy ME A CAFFEY!

Poster for 2001 Vancouver Underground Film Festival, designed with Amy Lockhart

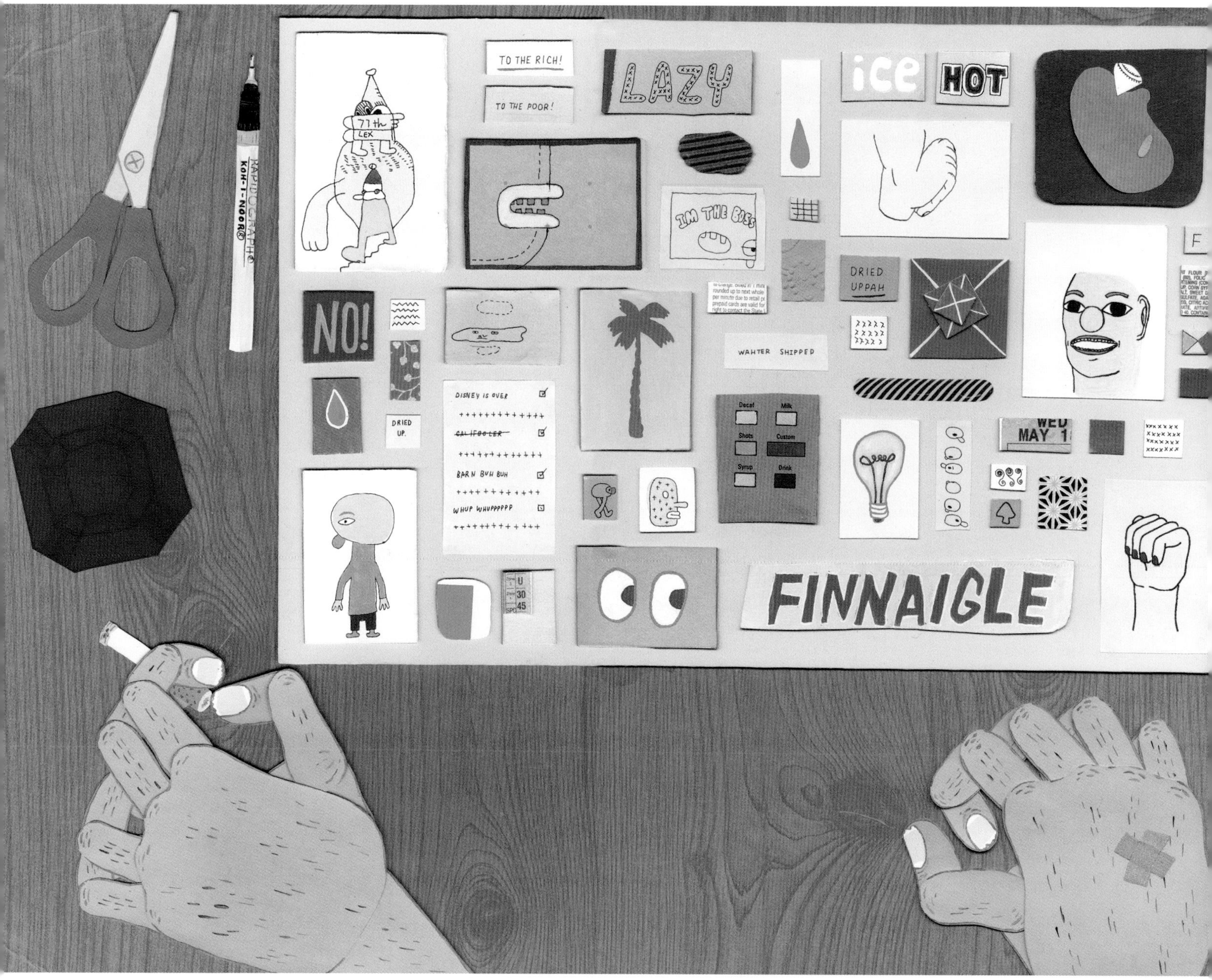
TO THE RICH!
TO THE POOR!
LAZY
ice
HOT
RAPIDOGRAPH
KOH-I-NOOR
IM THE BOSS
DRIED
UPPAH
NO!
DRIED UP.
WAHTER SHIPPED
DISNEY IS OVER
CALIFOOLER
BARN BUH BUH
WHUP WHUPPPPPP
Decaf
Milk
Shots
Custom
Syrup
Drink
WED
MAY 1
FINNAIGLE
F

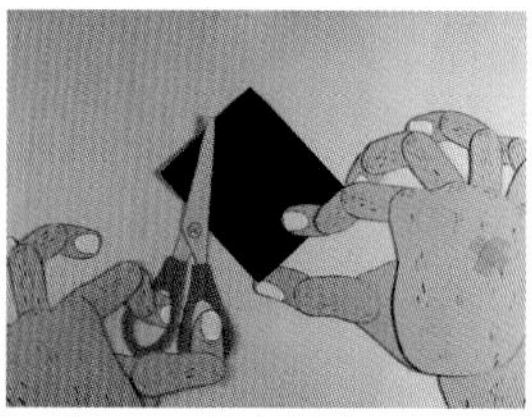

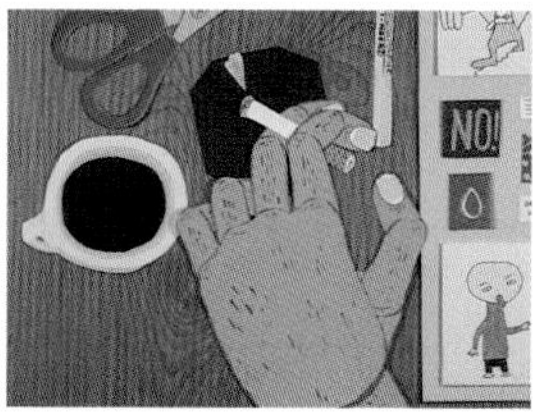

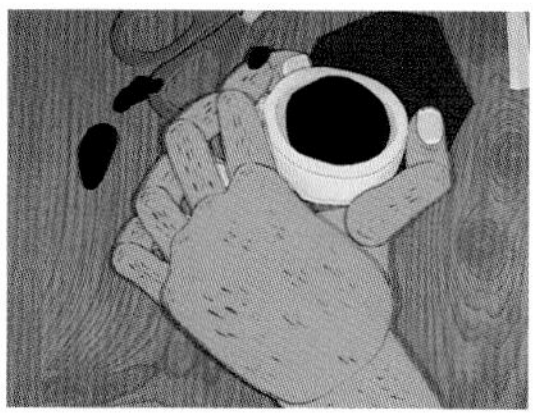

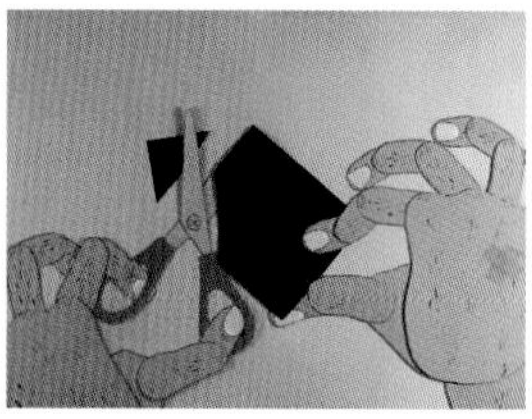

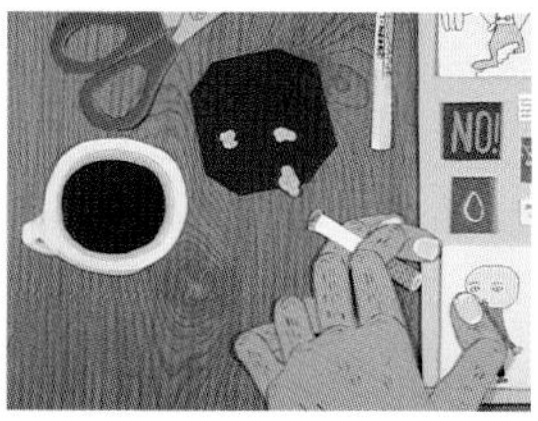

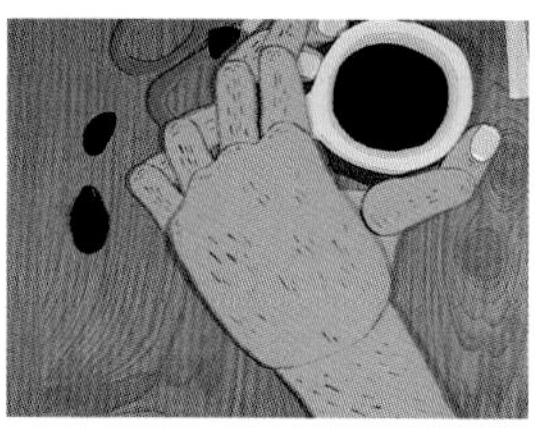

Top: Artwork used to create *The Collagist* (2009), a cut-out and paper puppet animation by Amy Lockhart created using elements inspired by Bell's work. Some of the collage pieces were created by Bell.
Also shown: stills from the animation

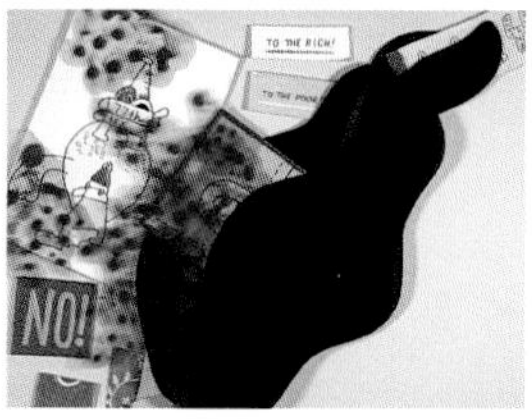

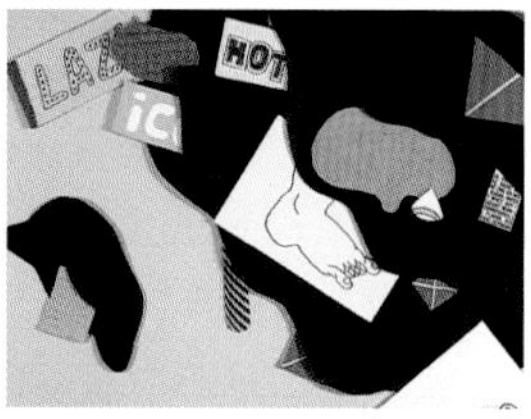

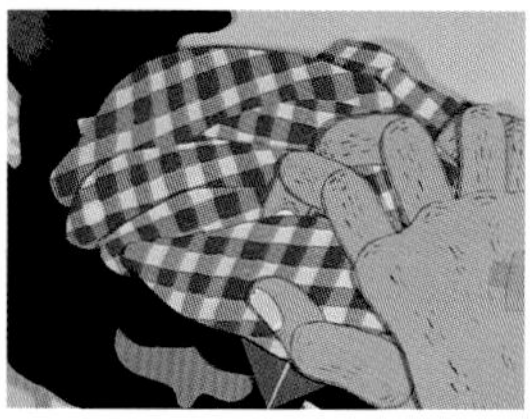

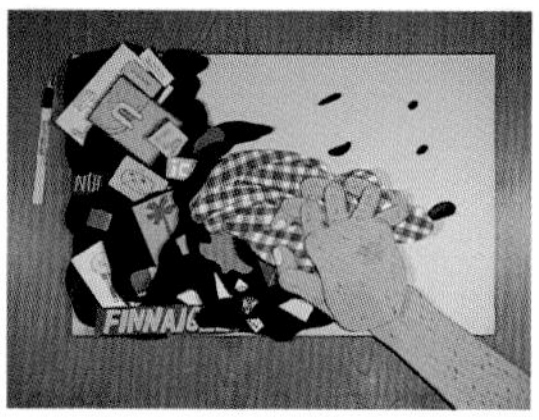

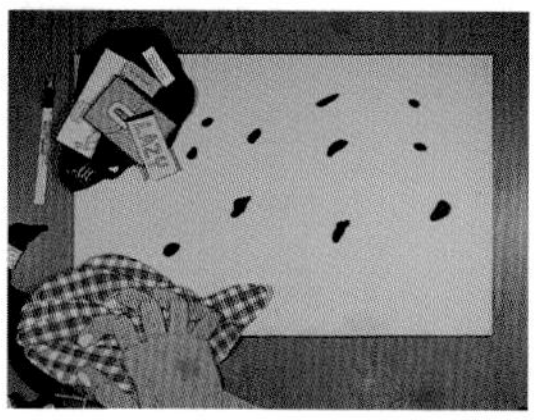

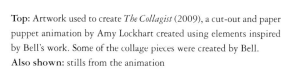

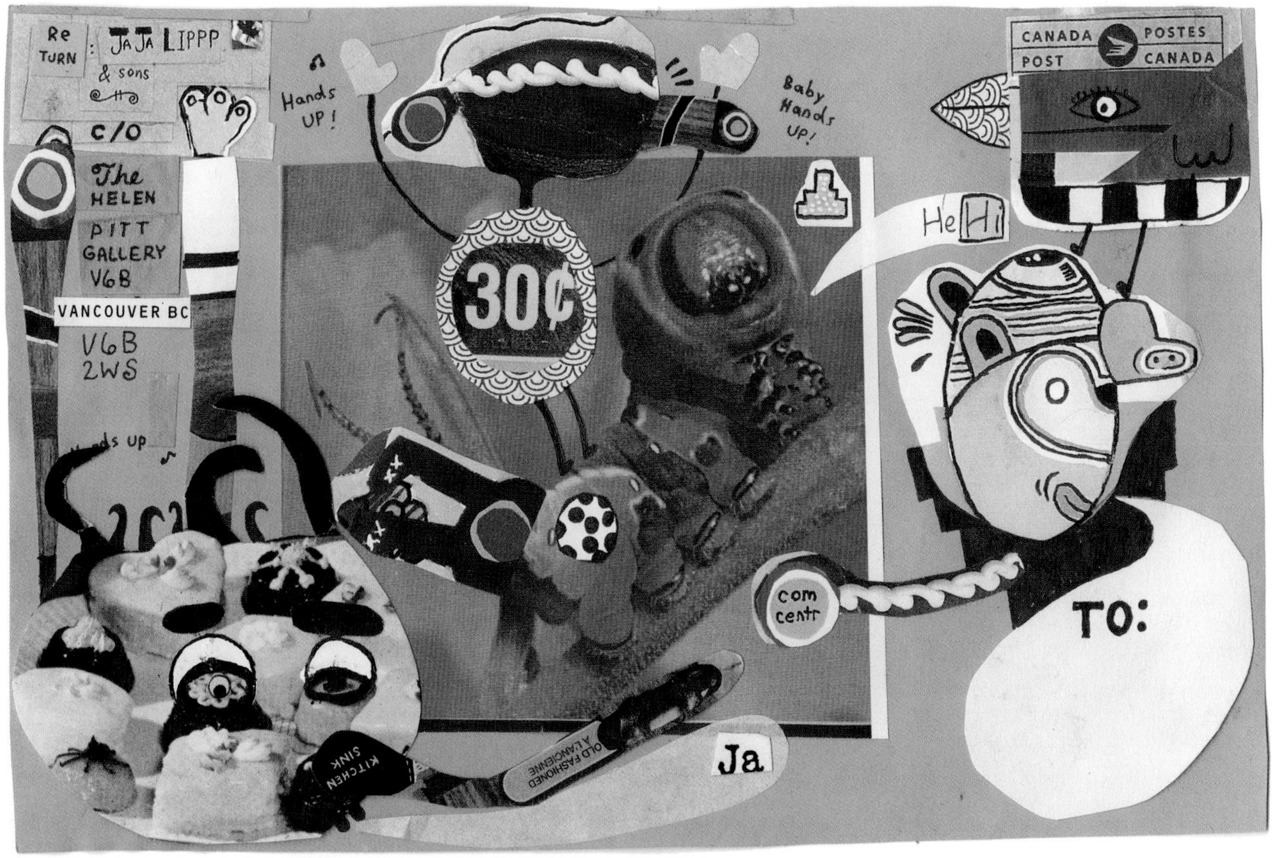
Re TURN : JA JA LIPPP
& sons
c/o
The
HELEN
PITT
GALLERY
V6B
VANCOUVER BC
V6B
2WS
Hands UP!
Baby Hands UP!
30¢
CANADA POST
POSTES CANADA
He Hi
com centr
TO:
Ja
KITCHEN SINK
OLD FASHIONED À L'ANCIENNE

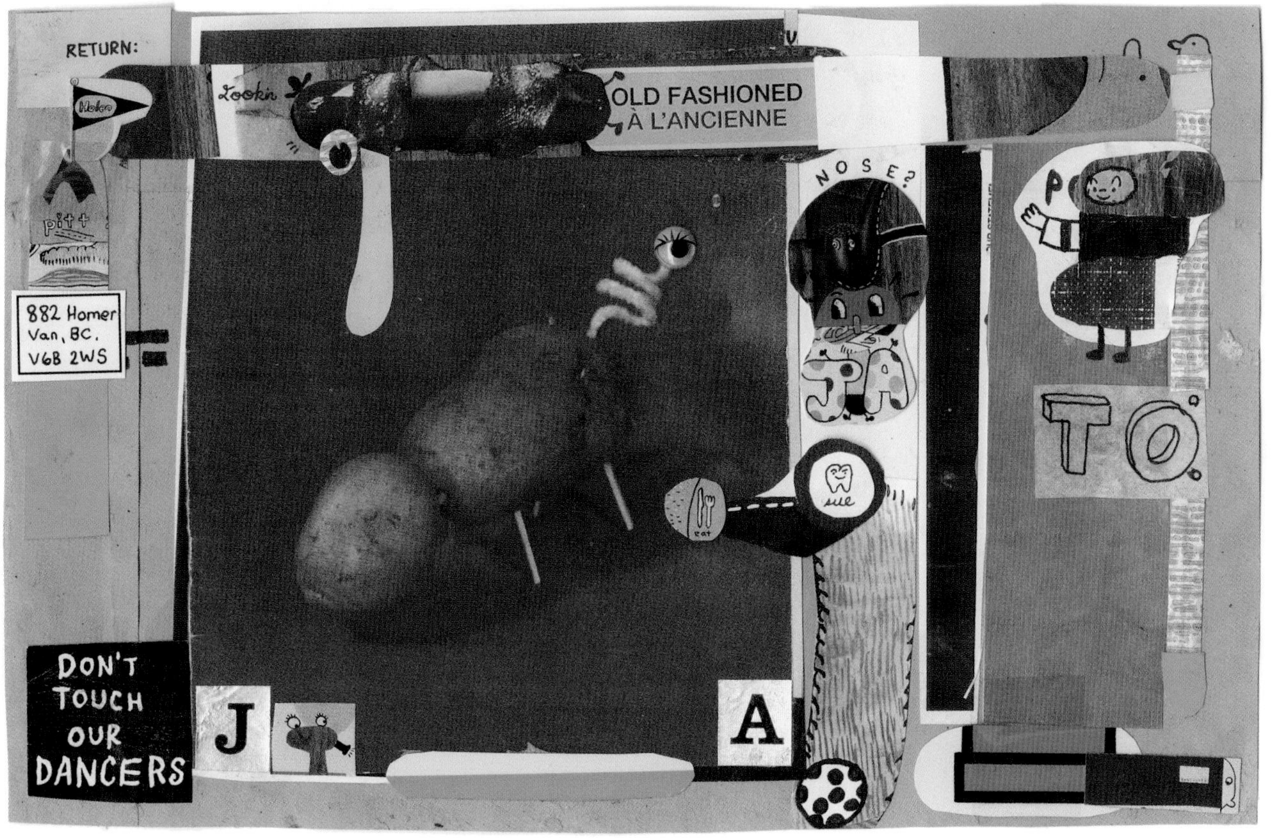
RETURN:
882 Homer
Van, BC.
V6B 2WS
OLD FASHIONED
À L'ANCIENNE
NOSE?
TO
DON'T
TOUCH
OUR
DANCERS
J
A

Ja Ja Lipp & Sons Envelopes (1 and 2), 2000
Marc Bell using pieces of Bell/Jason Mclean clippings and ephemera, 5–¼ x 8 in. ea.,
2 of 6 different images created for the envelope-style *Ja La Lipp & Sons* exhibition catalogue

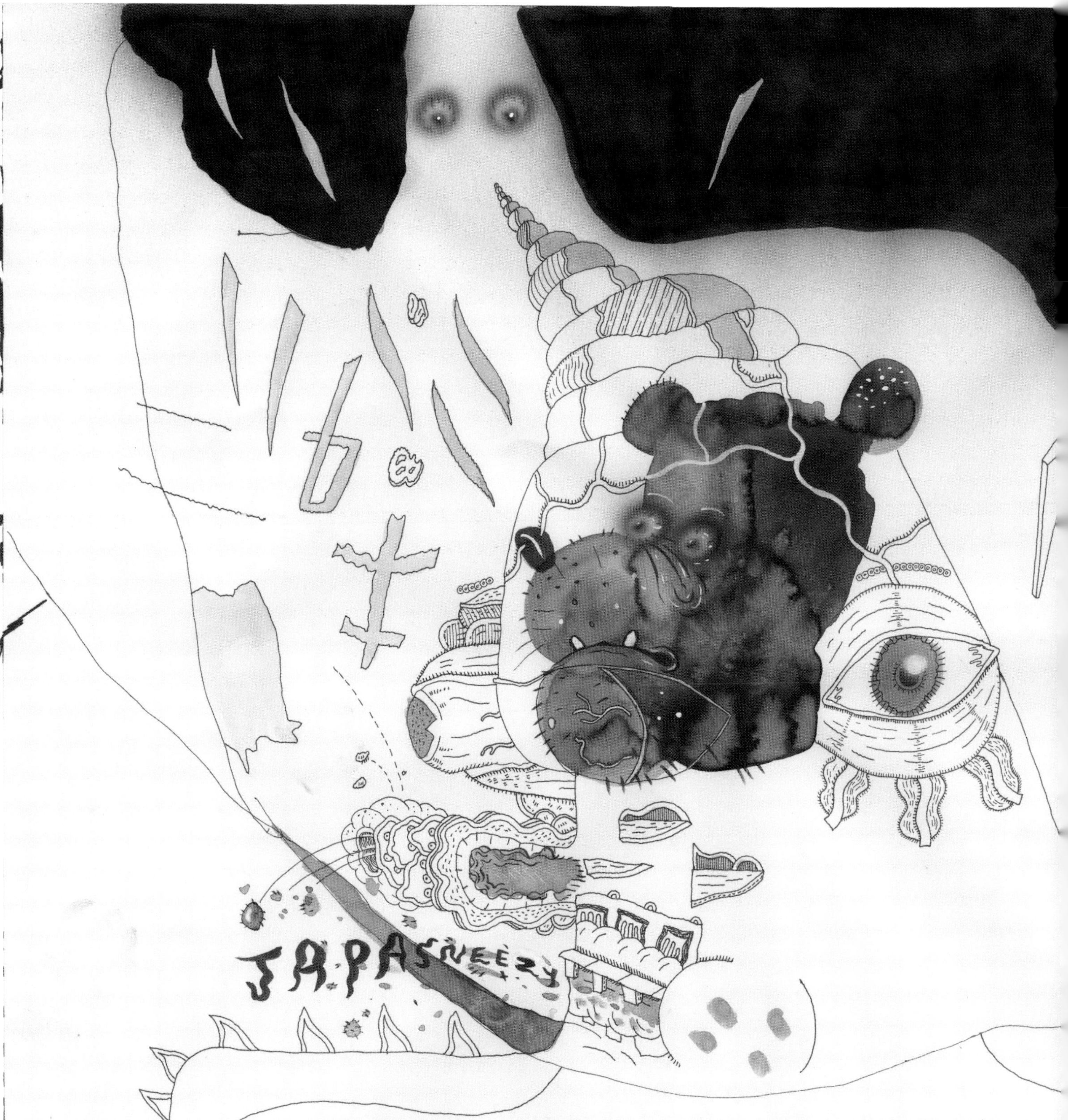
JAPASNEEZY

Japasneezy, with Seth Scriver, 2008
Ink and ink wash on paper

Tooter, with Seth Scriver, 2008
Ink and ink wash on paper

Ushering In The Meiji Era, with Seth Scriver, 2008
Ink and ink wash on paper

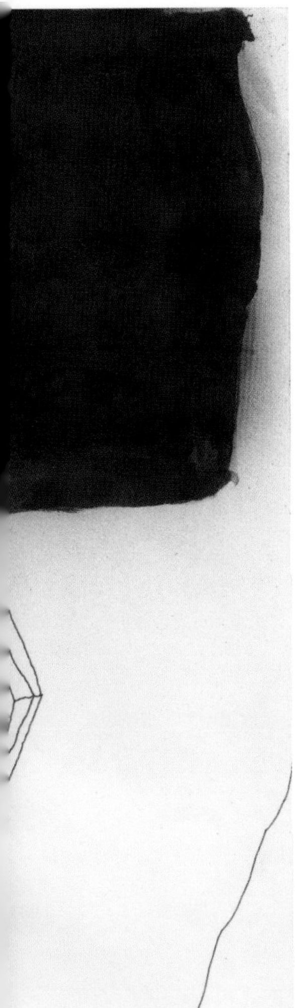

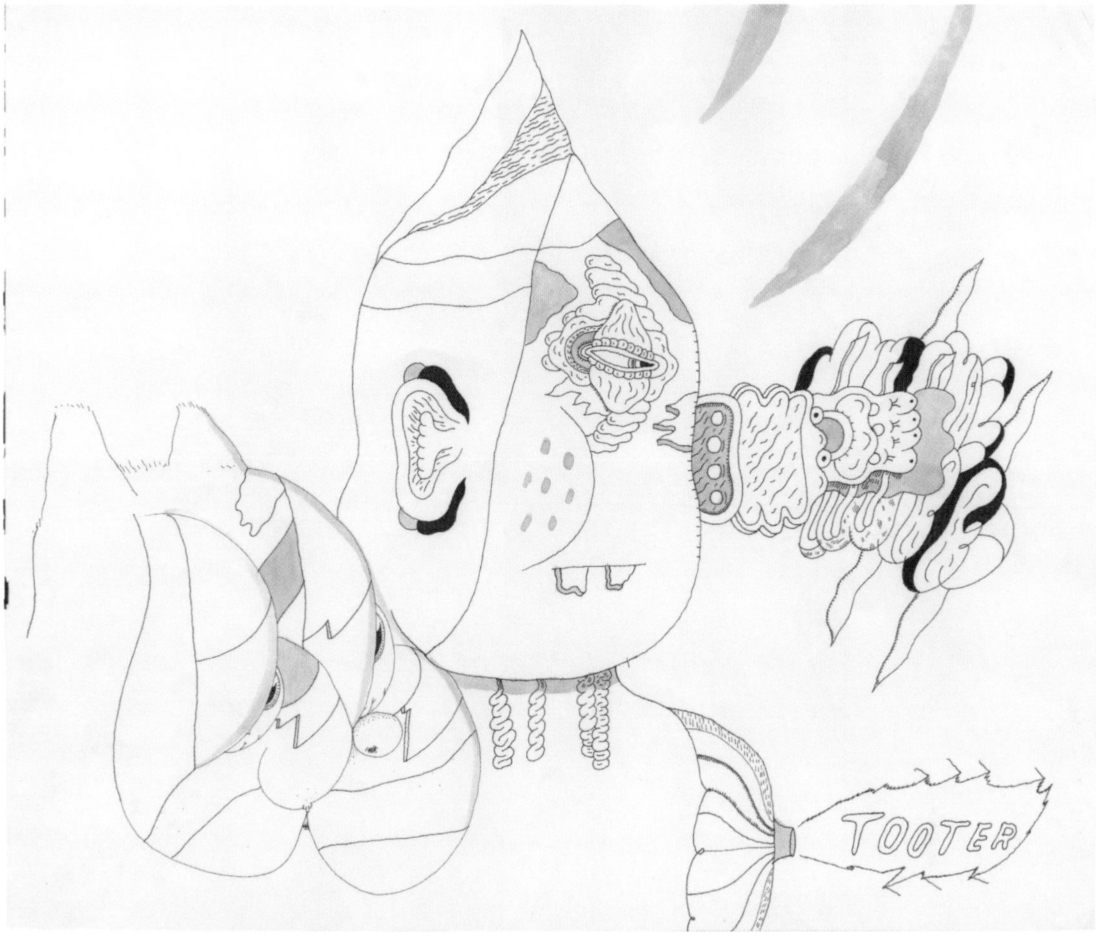
TOOTER

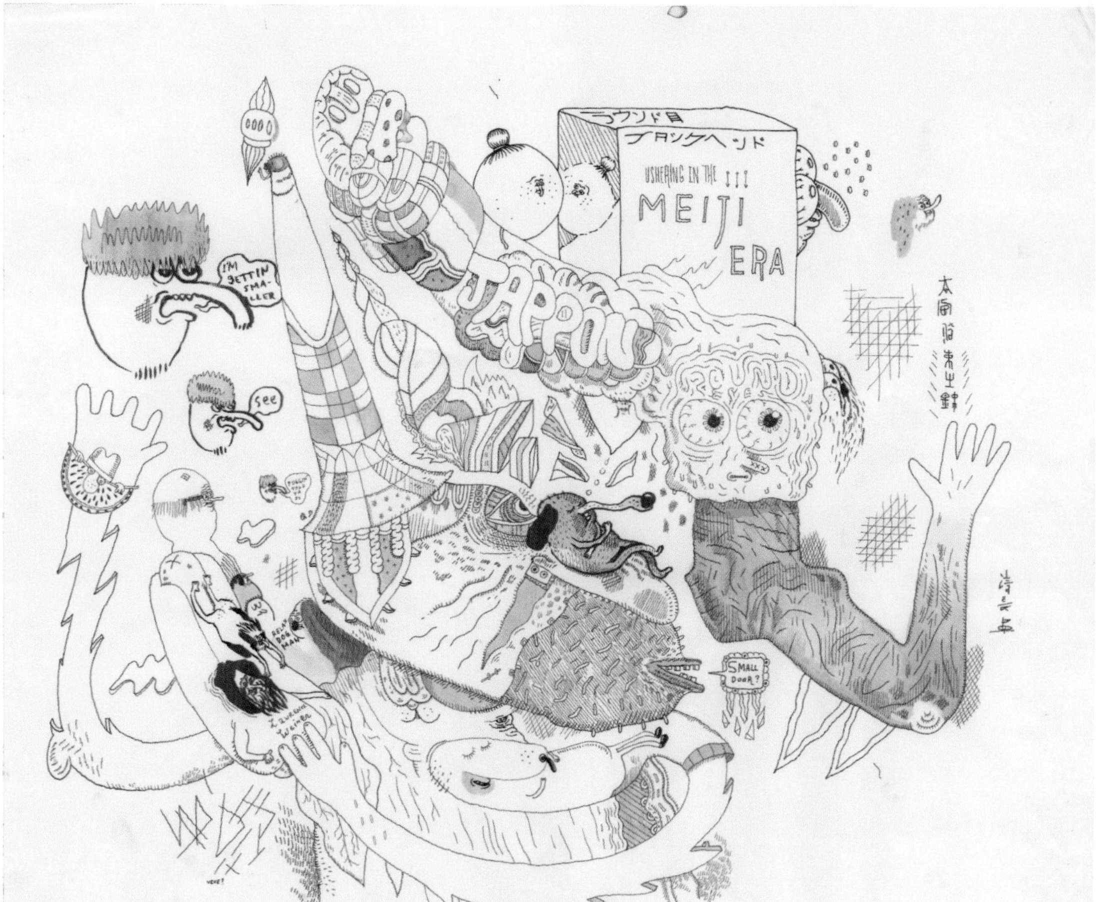
ラウンド目
ブロックヘッド
USHERING IN THE
MEIJI ERA
JAPPON
I'M GETTIN SMA-LLER
see
SMALL DOOR?

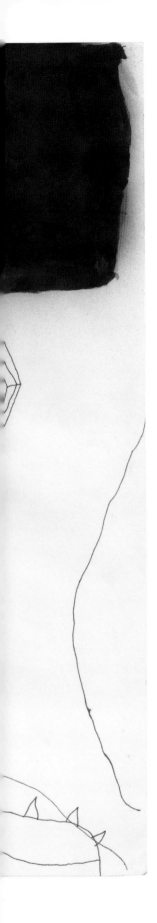

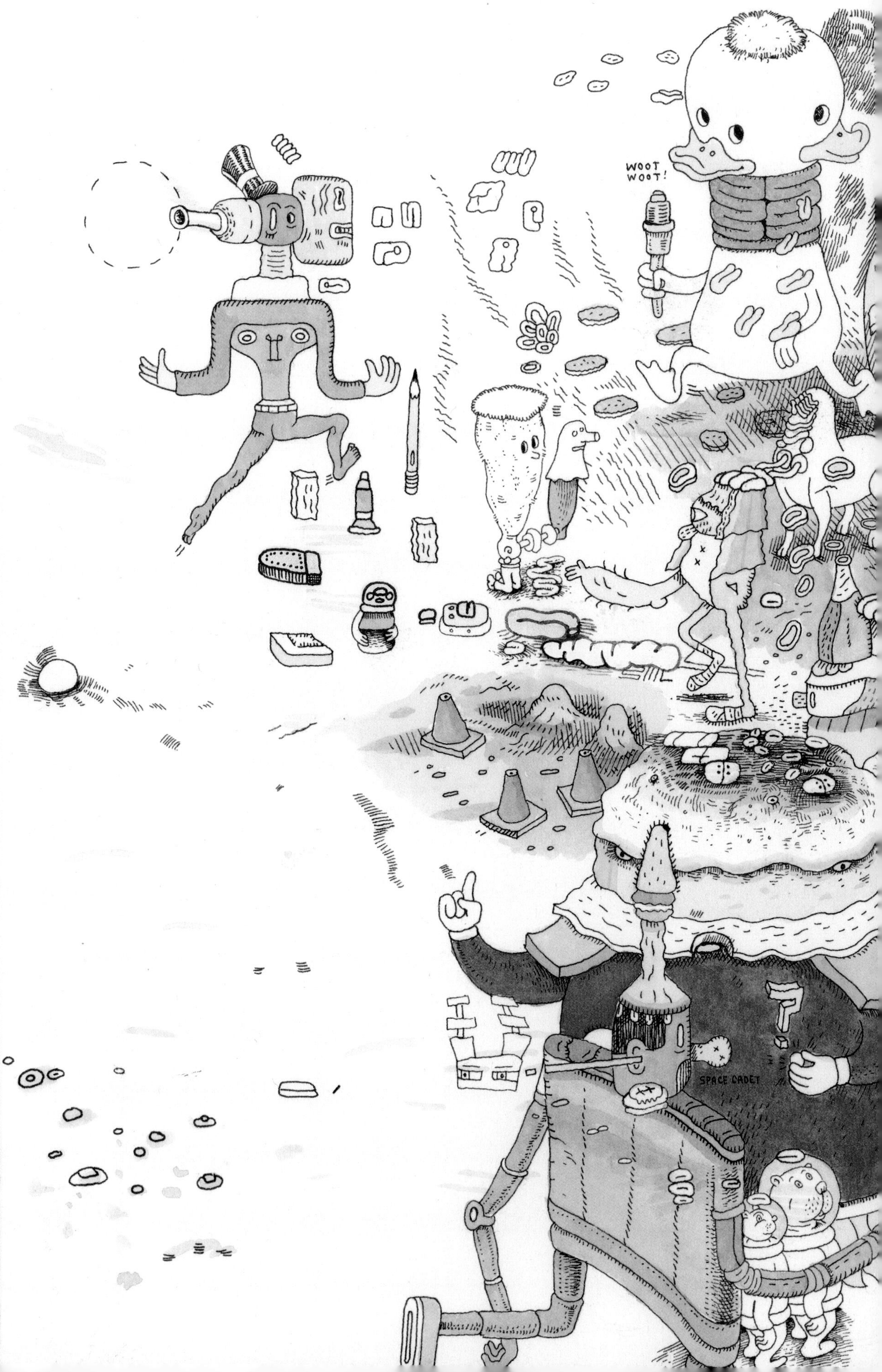
WOOT
WOOT!
SPACE CADET

Monument To Space Cadet,
with Christian Schumann, 2007
Ink, gouache, and watercolour
on paper

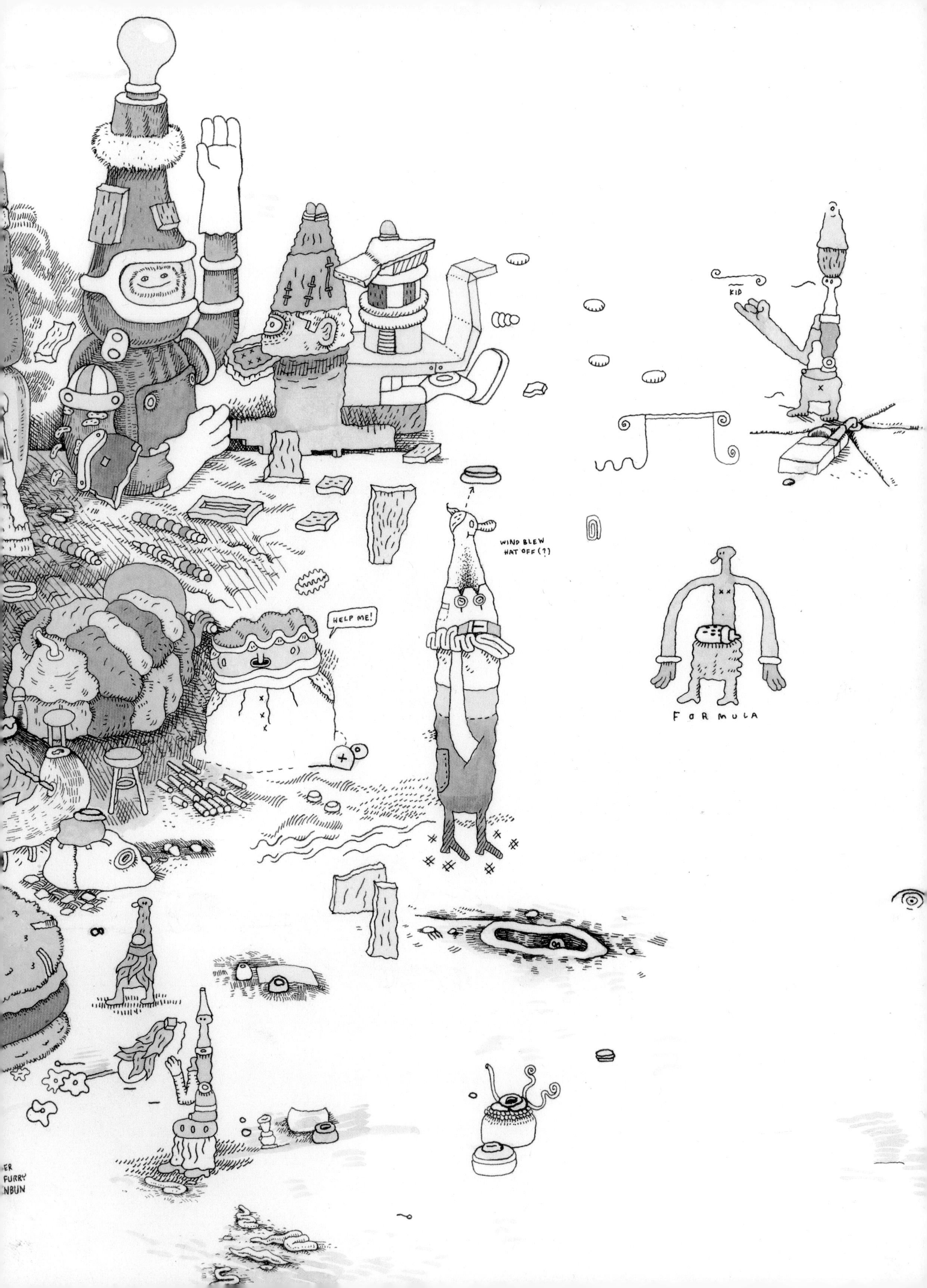
KID
WIND BLEW HAT OFF (?)
HELP ME!
FORMULA

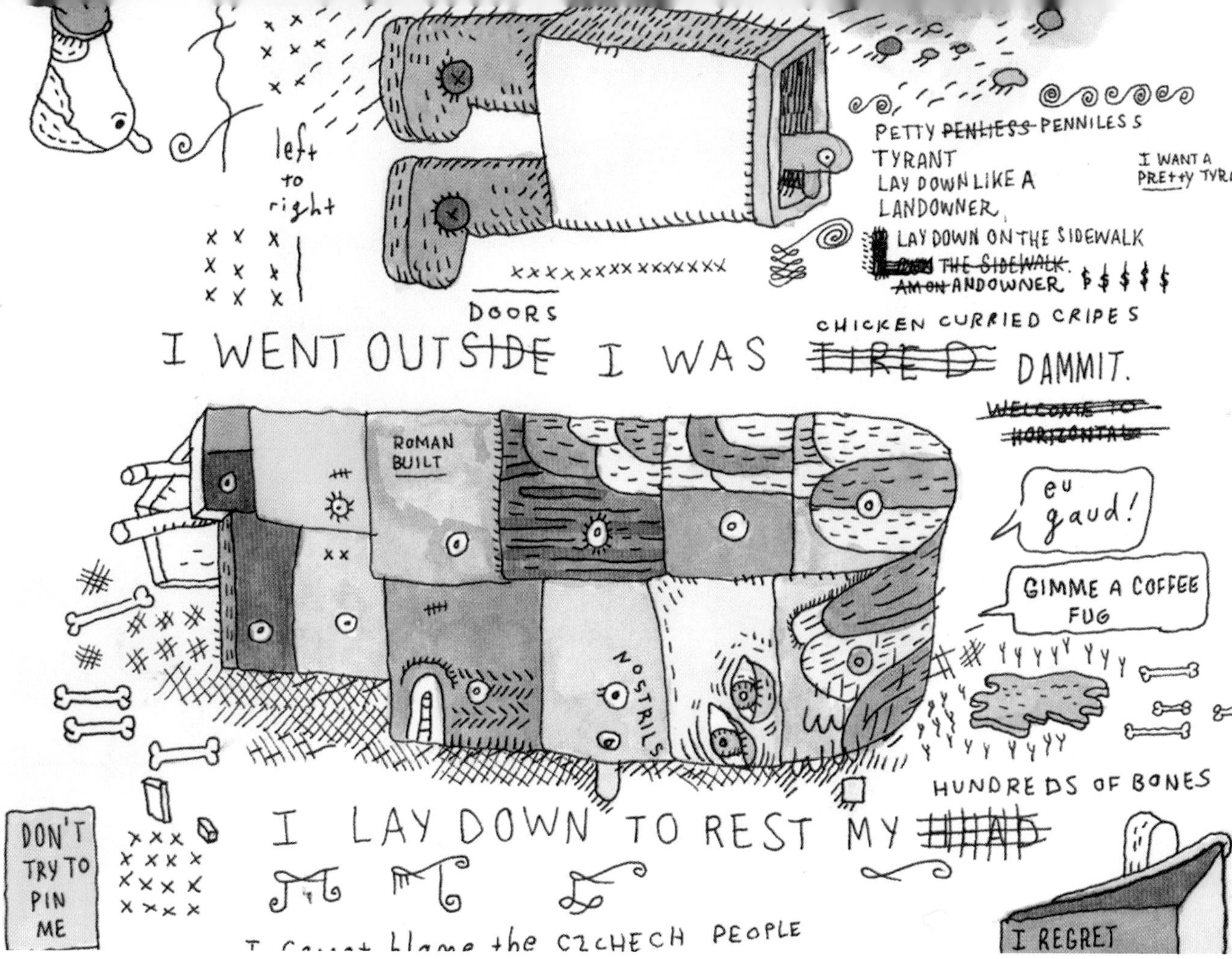
left
to
right
PETTY PENLIESS PENNILESS
TYRANT
LAY DOWN LIKE A
LANDOWNER
I WANT A
PRETTY TYRANT
LAY DOWN ON THE SIDEWALK
THE SIDEWALK
AM ON ANDOWNER $$$$$
DOORS
I WENT OUTSIDE I WAS
CHICKEN CURRIED CRIPES
TIRED
DAMMIT.
WELCOME TO
HORIZONTAL
ROMAN
BUILT
eu
gaud!
GIMME A COFFEE
FUG
NOSTRILS
HUNDREDS OF BONES
DON'T
TRY TO
PIN
ME
I LAY DOWN TO REST MY HEAD
the CZCHECH PEOPLE
I REGRET

(*continued from pg. 215*)

{*Slide Advances.*}

Marc: Ok, this is *Sluggish*. You can really see here my confusion about what words to use. I don't think this is the most successful drawing I have ever created but it shows the process of my writing, there is a lot of crossing out and what have you. I think when people attack this kind of work, these are the kind of things that bother them. I know the phrase "Who painted the cows" always kind of bothered me after I wrote it. Though I suppose I kind of like the phrase "I lay down to rest my hundreds of bones." I think I would say that I am leaving it up to the reader to make whatever connections they might make themselves, like how you did with that other one.

Audience Member: Where did you see painted cows?

Marc: I am not going to discuss painted cows at this time.

Tom: I agree, don't indulge them…

{*Slide advances to two drawings side by side, see no. 74 and 75.*}

Looking at these two drawings side by side both called *Old Man Baby Dog Man*, I wonder what made you revisit this particular drawing. Neither looks the lesser drawing—was it just an impulse to "cover" yourself or had the first slipped away from some kind of intent and you were trying to rein that in on the second? I ask because redoing a drawing almost seems antithetical to your approach.

Marc: Well, I suppose the realities of commerce sometimes take precedence. I redrew it because a dealer sold the original and said, "boy, I could sell a few more of these," as a funny way of asking me to do more of that kind of drawing. Nobody was forcing me to but I literally redrew that one. I also redrew *For The Toddler* as well (below and no. 77) for the same reason. How romantic is that? {*Sarcastically.*} I forget if either

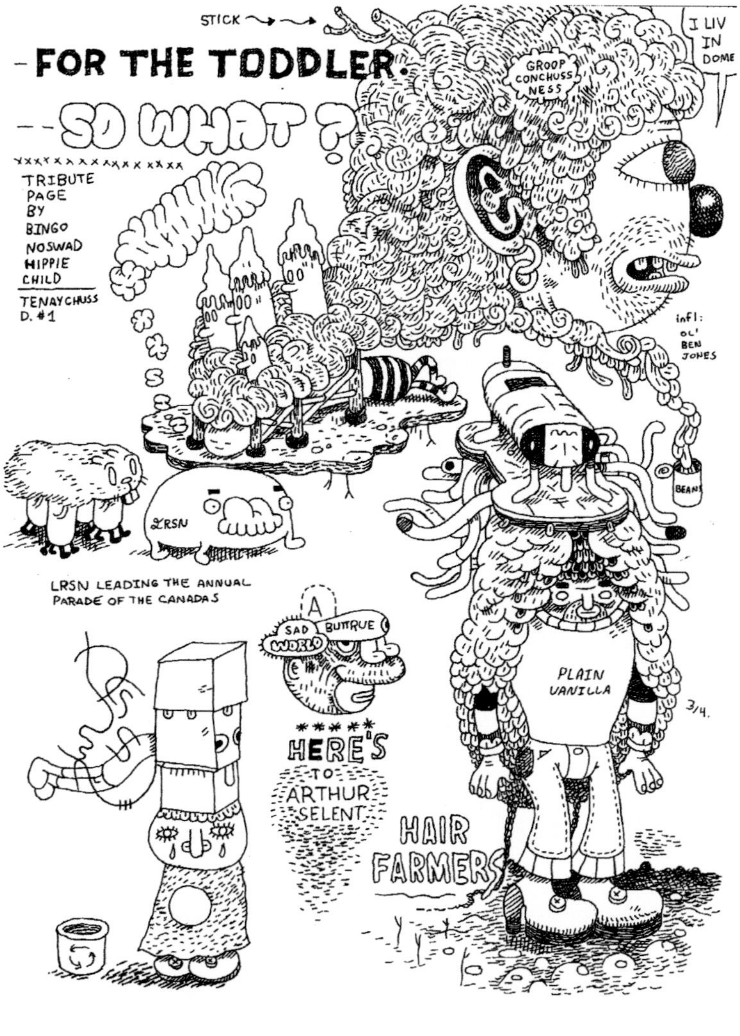
STICK
FOR THE TODDLER.
SO WHAT?
I LIV
IN
DOME
GROOP
CONCHUSSNESS
TRIBUTE
PAGE
BY
BINGO
NOSWAD
HIPPIE
CHILD
TENAYCHUSS
D. #1
inf1:
OL'
BEN
JONES
LRSN
LRSN LEADING THE ANNUAL
PARADE OF THE CANADAS
A
SAD
WORLD
BUTTRUE
PLAIN
VANILLA
3/4.
HERE'S
TO
ARTHUR
SELENT
HAIR
FARMERS

Top: Detail from *Sluggish*, 2005, ink and watercolour on paper
Right: *For The Toddler*, 2003, ink on paper

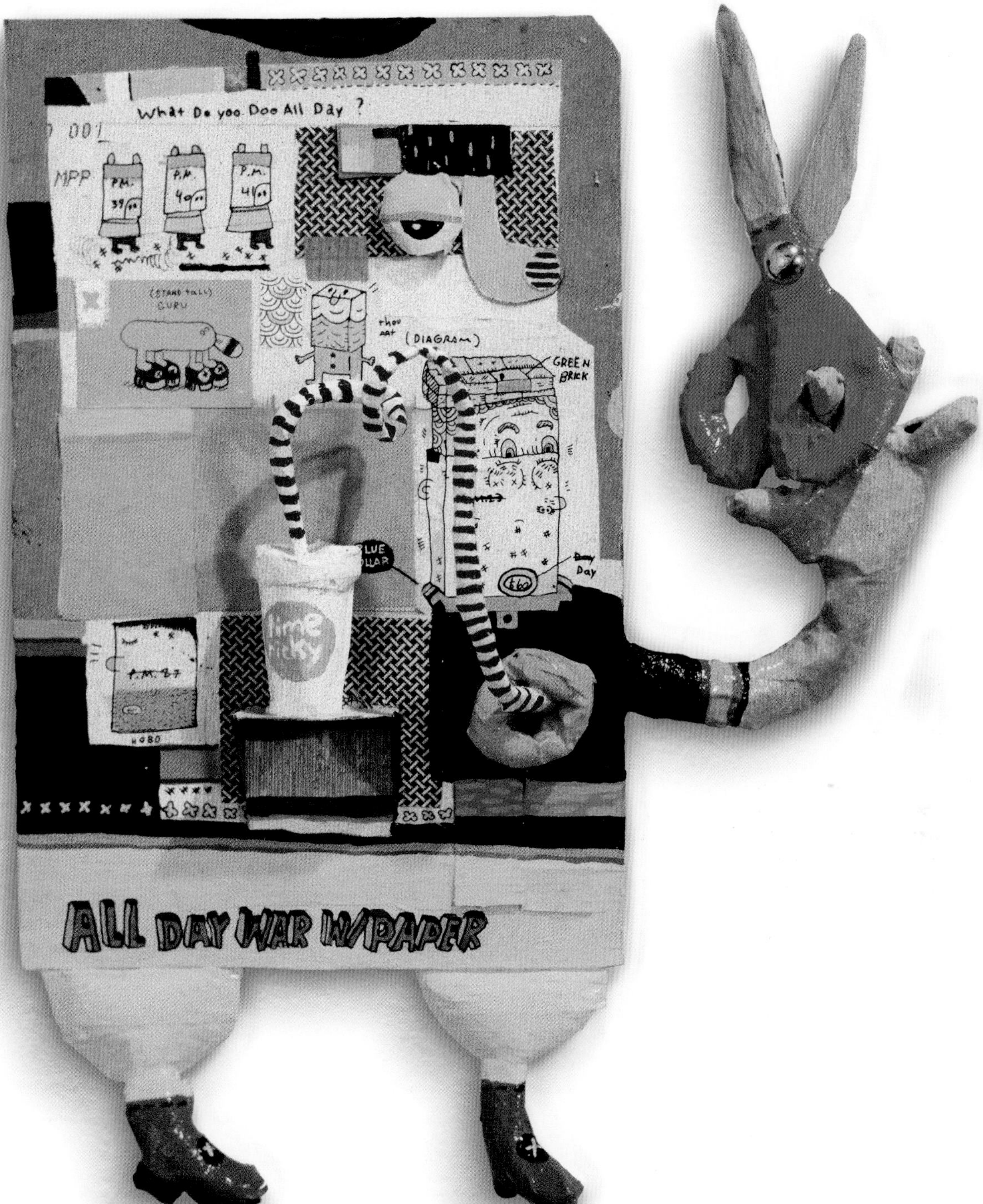
What Do yoo Doo All Day ?
(DIAGRAM)
GREEN BRICK
BLUE COLLAR
lime ricky
Day
HOBO
ALL DAY WAR W/PAPER

"recreations" actually sold though. Having said all that, I do find it interesting to recreate drawings and generally repeat things. I'm doing that anyway. I often go back to earlier works and try to reintroduce elements I am still interested in into new drawings, filtering things and keeping certain things alive in the work.

{*Slide: All Day War With Paper.*}

Tom: You mentioned previously that you religiously watched *Pee–Wee's Playhouse* and I see a lot of that aesthetic in your constructions. There's a wobbly kind of anthropomorphism in this work. There's also a very

This page: *All Day War With Paper*, 2002
Mixed Media Construction

x x x x x
yard trimmings
BY: MARC BELL
WORN TUFF
PLASTIC TREE
Trendy
AND BE good to yourself take your SelF out For a nice lunch, man

x x x x x
yard trimmings
BY: MARC BELL
Trendy
AND BE good to yourself take your SelF out For a nice lunch, man
BLACK SOCKS
FINGER (POINT THE)
WHAT TO DO WHEN "There's Nothing to Do"

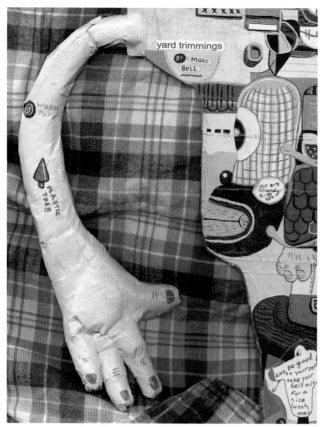

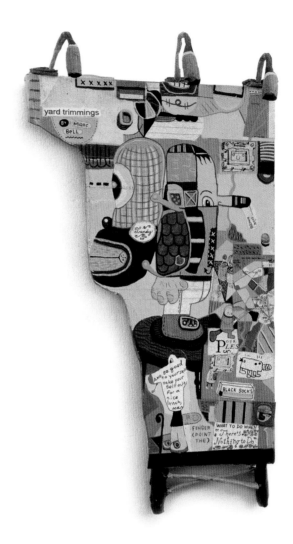

Above: *Trendy Brown Nose,* "Before" (with arm)
Right: *Trendy Brown Nose,* "After" (as "billboard")
2004, mixed media construction

urban feel or perhaps more exactly a kind of decaying second–tier city kind of feel—peeling billboards, chipped–paint water towers, and fast food soda cups everywhere. I don't know if there was a desire to capture the environment of your youth (or if this even represents it) but I am curious about the repeated themes. At this point, do you even remember your first usage of the "soda cup" sculpture.

Marc: I am pretty sure my first "soda pop" sculptures were *Gravy World* and *(Petey Loves) Tarp World* (no. 8 and 9). It seemed interesting to me to create a more and more involved surface. I had seen this really great Ray Johnson show in the late 90's of his intricate collage work, I think it was this kind of stuff he hid away. These pieces had these intricate relief surfaces made with board and paper, doing a lot with a little. And so, as an extension of trying to do that kind of thing in my work I thought it would be funny to build a shelf onto an artwork and then have something sitting on the shelf. Transforming it into something kind of ridiculous. And so the "soda pop cups" became sort of a theme. *All Day War With Paper* followed soon after those first two I think. In that one, I reference what I am actually doing with these things: cutting up bits of papers and board and stuff to build them. So, as you can see, the artwork itself is a figure and is holding scissors. Warring with paper accumulation. There is also something toy–like about these things for sure. These things probably do have a lot more to do with stuff I found interesting growing up as a kid and how that extends into adulthood than any real grown up "art language" or whatever you want to call it. And I did spend a bit of time on the farm as a kid, at my grandparents place and I think I really did respond to a lot of the kind of "junk" and machinery that would be lying around in rural areas as well as in the city. In *Farm Equipment*, I tried to use the "John Deere" colours—yellow and green (no. 14).

Tom: I'm not sure how to phrase this exactly but there seems to be a need to make your every thought more concrete by turning it into a little guy—giving those thoughts arms and legs and eyes and noses. This seems distinctly like a cartoonist's approach to viewing the world—everything is a character. This is most literal especially with the sculptures because they often have actual feet sticking off the bottom. They're like little playmates. Marc, are you lonely?

Marc: It's true, I am always turning things I draw into characters, and these sculptures are like that: "I'll add a nose or some legs and some eyes to this weird shape here and there you have it: a little figure." You could show my imagery to some psychiatrists or art therapists and they might have something to say about it to explain it, I guess.

{*Slide Advances: Trendy Brown Nose*}

Marc: This one is in a billboard style, I made one other similar to this called *Cucumber* (see no. 12). This one used to be a figure with cartoony kind of appendages but I cut its head and arms and leg off to make it into a billboard. It was getting too puppet–like or something so I had to "rein it in" so–to–speak. I think I realized that in this case the adding of arms and legs were taking over, they were too big for this particular one or something and they had to go. I still have the head, arms, and legs but haven't found a new home for them as of yet.

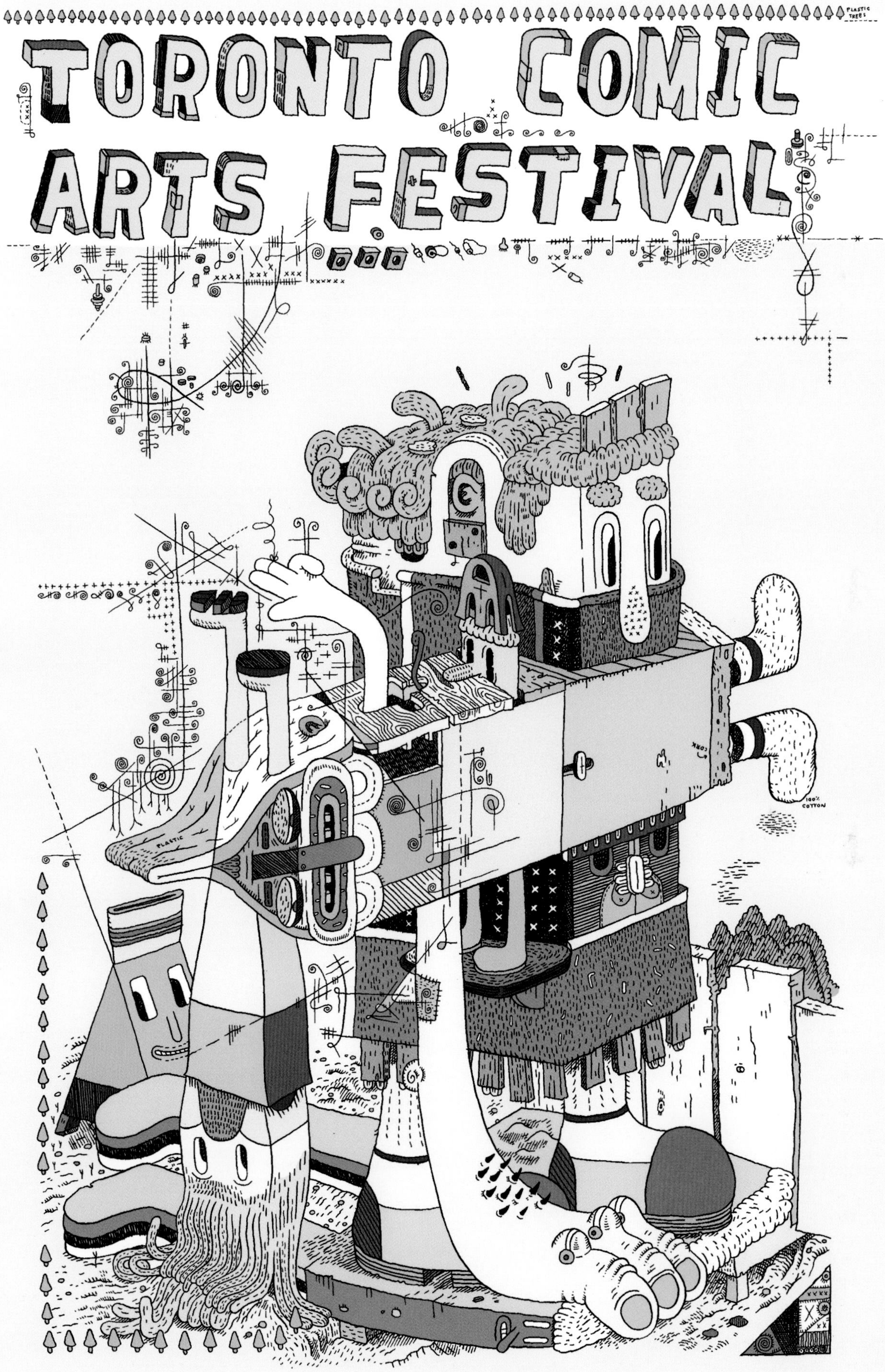
TORONTO COMIC
ARTS FESTIVAL
PLASTIC TREES
PLASTIC
100% COTTON

Poster design for Toronto Comics Art Festival, 2005

Tom: How do you go about making these constructions? Is it straight *papier–mâché?*

Marc: I build them out of tape and cardboard and glue and whatever else that might work to make a shape that I am looking for and then I paint them. I usually add some kind of varnish in the end.

Tom: I understand that you will repair the constructions for as long as you live?

Marc: Well, yeah, I think I joked with you that I would take these back if they "break" and fix them. I usually coat them in a layer or two of varnish and feel that seals the deal for now. I do have one of the earliest ones and it seems fine. I guess time will tell. Uh–oh.

{*Pause.*}

{*Sound of guitars tuning.*}

Tom: What the? We have this place for another hour, don't we?

Marc: I think the interview took so long that we slipped into Daylight Savings Time.

Tom: Our time is up. Can we have a minute before Wheels of Juice comes out here? Marc, I wanted to know what determined what kind of piece you chose to make. You don't seem to work in series; you seem to dart around a bit. Is it as simple as saying {*feedback obscures speech*}...And can we delve a little bit into tool talk here? What do you use for your drawings (they look like rapidograph) versus your comics (nib)?

Marc: I like to do different kinds of things because it keeps it interesting to me {*yawns*}. Oh my, I'm getting a little sleepy here...{*a short drum roll*} Oh yeah, the tools: I used to use a rapido for the "art drawings" when I first started seriously thinking about making them for a gallery because I didn't want them to look like the comics so much. But these days it's gotten to the point where it doesn't matter so much. In fact I think that—

Wheels of Juice Singer: One–two–buckle–my–shoe...Check!

Tom: Ok, maybe we finish here by taking some questions and we can see how it feels for the audience to be drowned out?

Audience Member: Do you have any advice for a young artist just starting out?

Wheels of Juice Singer: OK, let's try Parliament of Owls...

Wheels of Juice Bass Player: Wait, I have to hook up my Dingle Berry™. Just a sec.

Wheels of Juice Singer: My favourite colour is gold.

Another Audience Member: I notice that there is a similarity between your work and the work of Ray Yoshida (specifically, see no. 95 as an example) and there's even a shared aesthetic between your work and that of Jim Nutt. Would you care to comment?

Marc: I really like a a lot of that Chicago work. I wasn't aware of it when someone first mentioned a bit of a similarity between it and mine. It's hard for me to say if there is a similarity, I'm too close and so that would be for somebody else to decide, but I really respond to that stuff in general and it's one of those things I think about now when I am making stuff. Those Chicago people have created some of my favourite American art. I have consciously tried to adopt the way Yoshida would set up some of his works, for example. I really like the grid–like composition (which resembles comics to a degree) and how the elements or "objects" in his work are often all lined up and often don't touch each other, creating a very formal look. It was also nice to see the use of "absurd language" by many of those Chicago artists.

Audience Member: I have a question for the Wheels of Juice. Can you tell me how you came up with your name, it's so wonderful...

Wheels of Juice Singer: I just wanted something nice to go with my tea.

Audience Member: Is a Dingle Berry™ an expensive fuzz pedal? Is it superior to the Fuzzburger™?

Wheels of Juice Bass Player: It is not superior to the Fuzzburger™. It is a new concept, but not superior. It's a like a standard distortion pedal with an added envelope-follower (analog, of course).

Wheels of Juice Singer: Here's the one about that place where owls rule, OK. Get sorted! One, two, three, four...

{*Wheels of Juice start playing "Parliament Of Owls."*}

Tom: {*trying to be heard over the music*} Ok, that is going to be it, of course. Ticketholders for Wheels of Juice may stay. All others please exit in an orderly fashion or see the box office for readmission.

Marc: We've been here for hours ordering coffee and drinks and watching this woman's kids here and you're telling me we have to pay to stay... {*End tape.*}

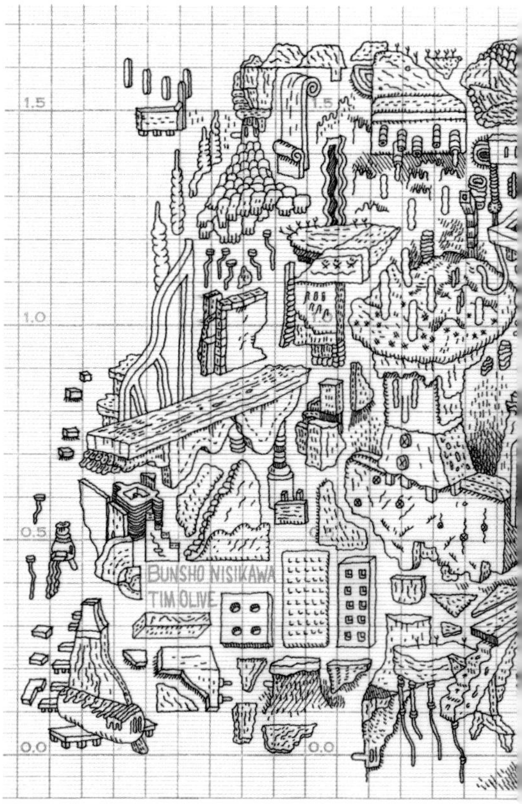
1.5
1.5
1.0
0.5
BUNSHO NISIKAWA
TIM OLIVE
0.0
0.0

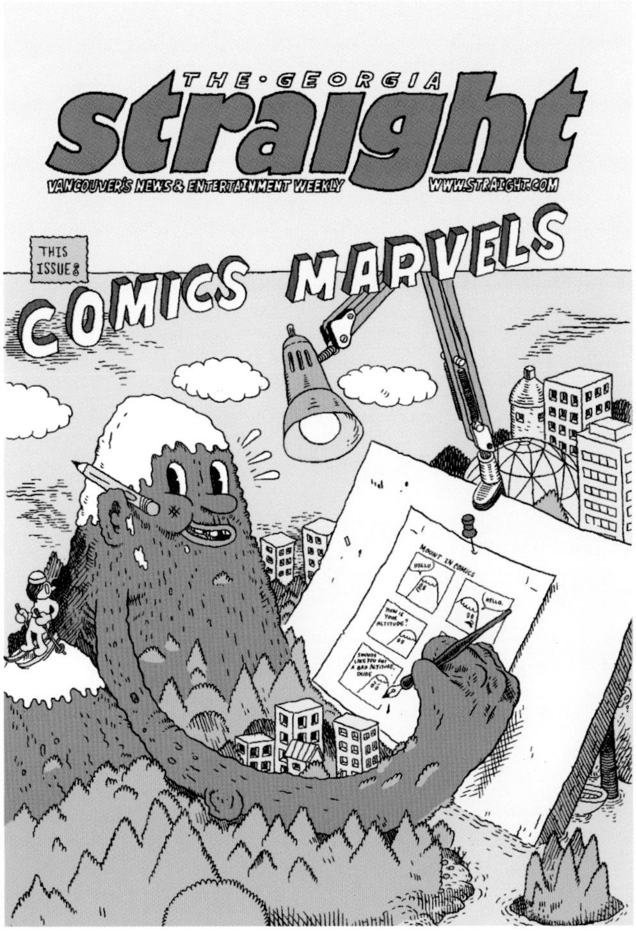
THE·GEORGIA
straight
VANCOUVER'S NEWS & ENTERTAINMENT WEEKLY
WWW.STRAIGHT.COM
THIS ISSUE:
COMICS MARVELS

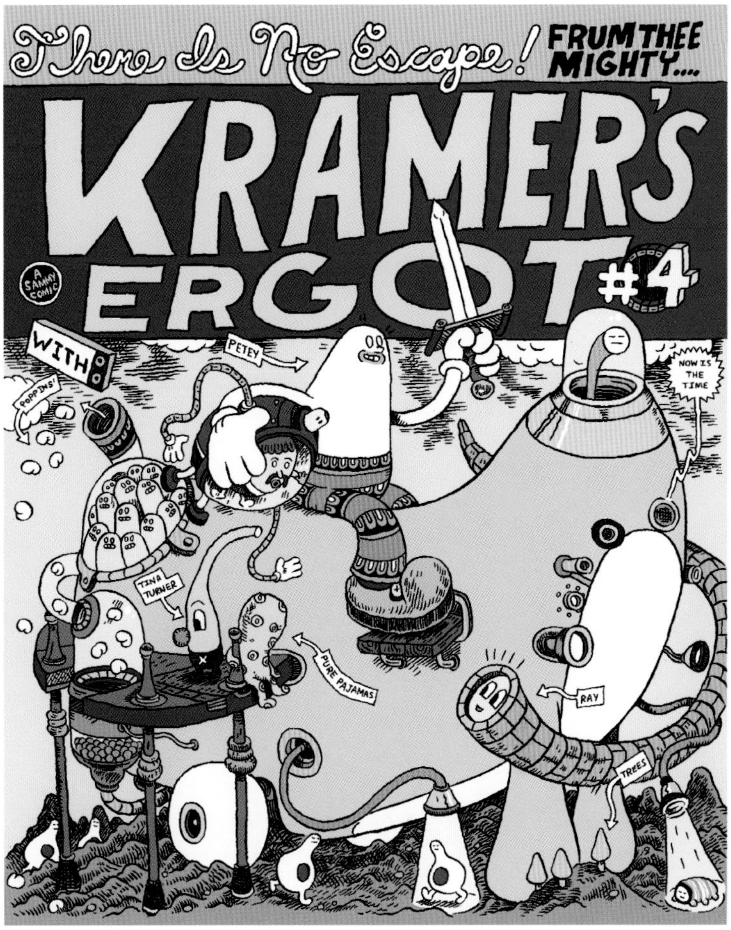
There Is No Escape!
FRUM THEE MIGHTY....
KRAMER'S ERGOT #4
A SAMMY COMIC
WITH
PETEY
NOW IS THE TIME
TINA TURNER
PURE PAJAMAS
RAY
TREES

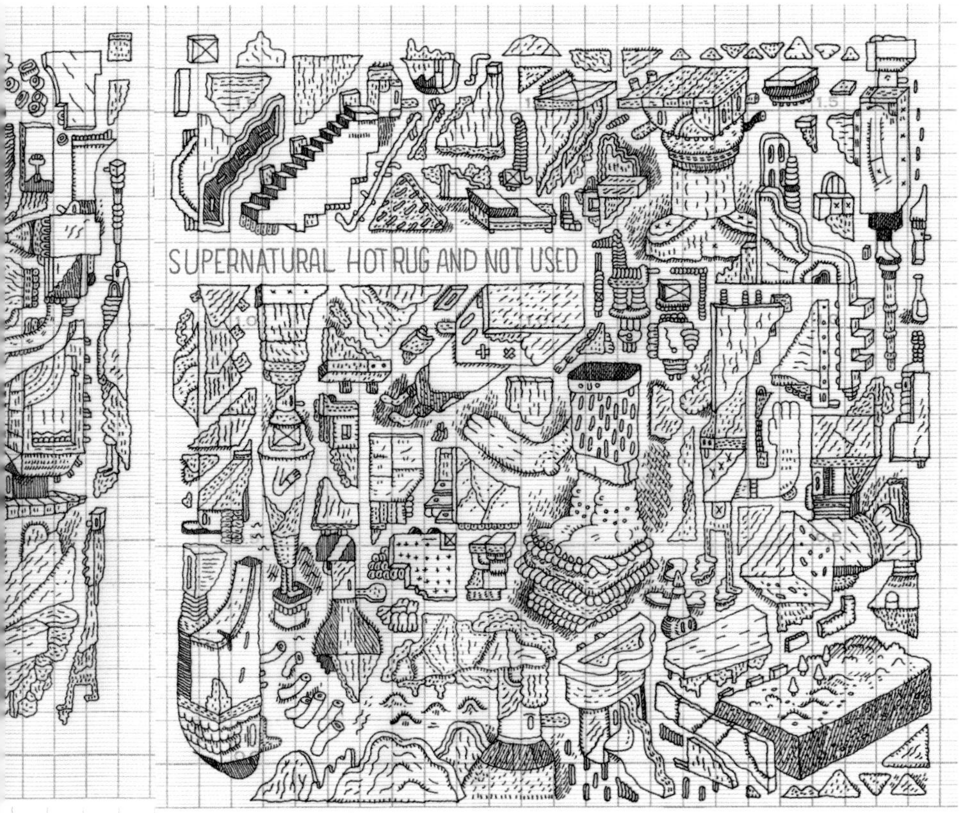
SUPERNATURAL HOT RUG AND NOT USED

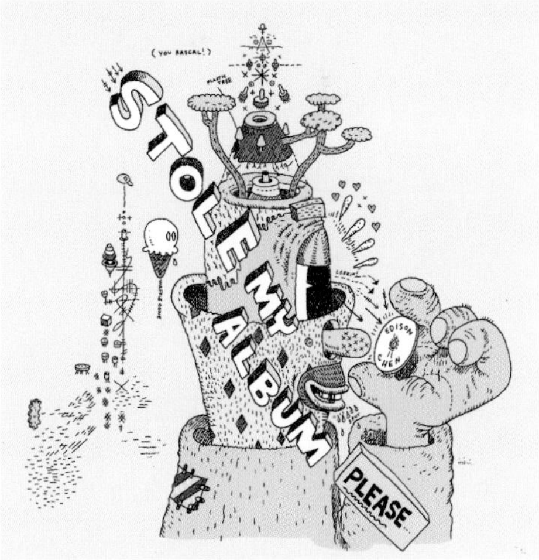
STOLE MY ALBUM
PLEASE

Cover Gallery (clockwise):

Georgia Straight,Vol. 38 No. 1926, 2004
Kramers Ergot #4, 2003
(one of many "covers" created for the inside of this issue by paticipating artists)
Please Steal This Album, 2004
(one of seven covers created by different artists for this Edison Chen CD, also included a blank CD to "steal" the album with)
Supernatural Hot Rug And Not Used, 2005
(CD art for Bunsho Nisikawa and Tim Olive)

Chronology

Compiled by Matthew P. Soucie in conjunction with the artist.

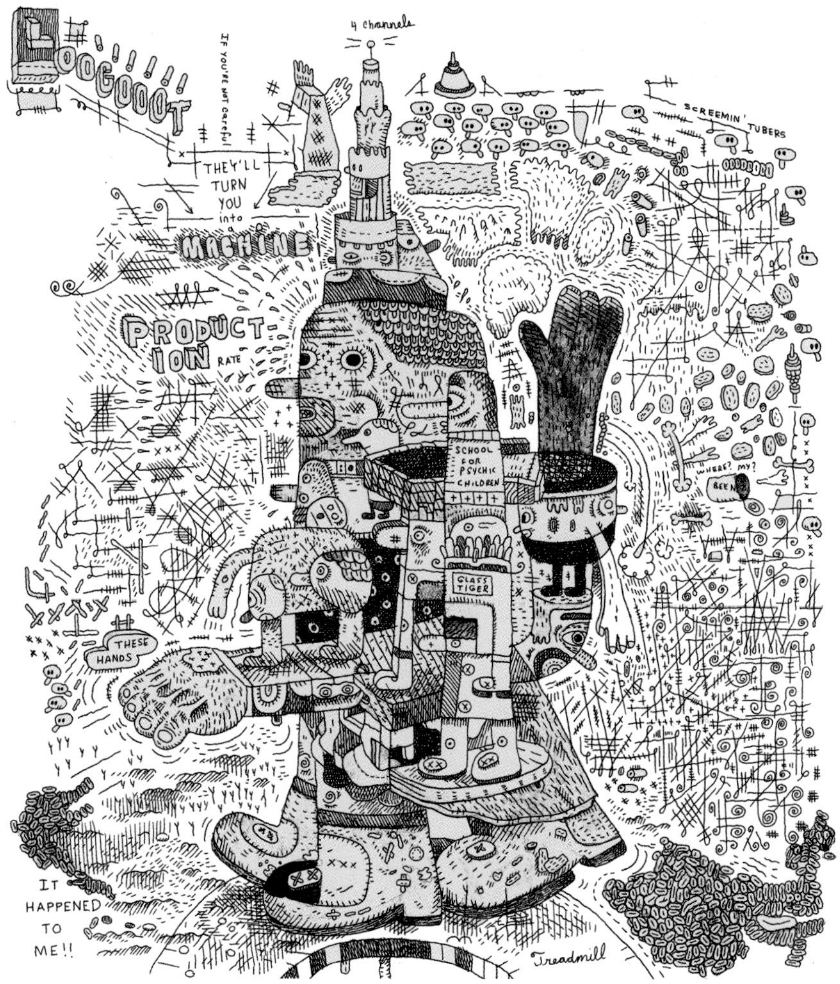

LOOGOOOT
IF YOU'RE NOT CAREFUL
4 channels
SCREEMIN' TUBERS
THEY'LL TURN YOU into
MACHINE
PRODUCT ION RATE
SCHOOL FOR PSYCHIC CHILDREN
CLASS TIGER
THESE HANDS
WHERE? MY?
IT HAPPENED TO ME!!
Treadmill

1971
Born in London, Ontario, Canada.

1985
Attends Saunders Secondary School where he meets Scott McIntyre (Scotty Potty).

1989
Enrolls in Bealart Arts program in London, ON where he attends for two years. Meets Peter Thompson and Jason Mclean. Creates the first "Thanksgiving Amoeba" style drawing with Scotty Potty and Thompson.

1991
Lives on Holborn Ave. in London, ON. Marc begins to correspond with Jason, who has moved to Vancouver, BC and is living with a Paul Williams look–a–like.

1992
Moves to Sackville, NB. to attend Mount Allison University's Fine Arts program. Bell and Mclean continue corresponding and both now correspond with Thompson in London. Thompson mails Marc a postcard with a broken steak knife attached to it with layers of scotch tape. The mail is sent briefly to a processing plant in London, ON, where it is bagged for safety.

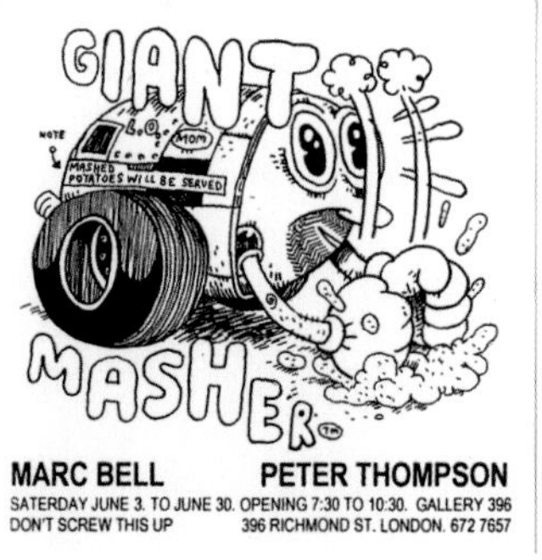

GIANT
MASHED POTATOES WILL BE SERVED
MASHER
MARC BELL PETER THOMPSON
SATURDAY JUNE 3. TO JUNE 30. OPENING 7:30 TO 10:30. GALLERY 396
DON'T SCREW THIS UP 396 RICHMOND ST. LONDON. 672 7657

Giant Masher Invite
Gallery 396, 2000

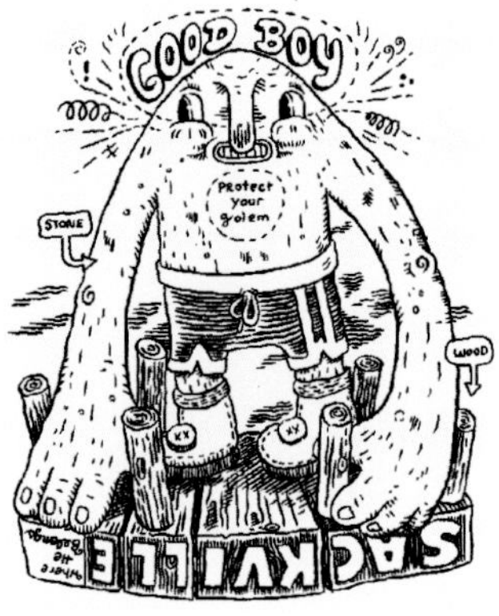

GOOD BOY
Protect your golem
STONE
WOOD
SACKVILLE

Golem T–Shirt Design for
Struts Gallery, 2003

Top: *Production Rate (Loogooot, They'll Turn You Into A Machine)*, ink on paper, coloured on computer, 2005

1993
Begins work as Graphics Editor at *The Argosy* (Mount Allison's school newspaper), a job which mainly entails organizing the comics page.

1994
Meets Dirty Debbie and prints some of his work in *The Argosy*. Travels to Vancouver, BC for the summer. Puts together *The Waffle* for The Gallery Sansair with Mclean, showing Mail Art, Schnauzer Merchandise. They host a waffle parade down Hastings Street. Waffles are served by Quarter Pounder Schnauzer and Town Haus Schnauzer. Briefly lives in an above ground basement room on Graveley St. The window is such that he can enter and leave "*Dukes of Hazzard* style."

1995
Class trip to NY, NY. Collaborates with classmate Terry Piercey on *Broadcast To Licorice Whips*, a performance piece at *Animal Crackers* (Owens Art Gallery, Sackville, NB). Designs poster for fine arts graduate exhibition even though he isn't really graduating. Begins contributing to *Voice of Montreal* (later *Vice*) and *Exclaim!* magazine. Summers in Vancouver where he lives with Dirty Debbie. A job washing dishes, a break–in at their house and a general sense of disarray in his life are inspiration for his comic strip "Stupid Shitty Goddamn Day." Moves to Montreal, PQ in the fall and lives on St. Dominique St.

1996
Meets Joey Haley and they collaborate on several lo–fi movies starring each other wherin they act things out and dub in their lines afterwards. Meets fellow *Exclaim!* contributor, Mark Connery. Bell and Connery publish *P.M.F. #1* and initiate *The St. Dominique Mailbox Project* (wherein they redistribute papers and artworks to random mail boxes on St. Dominique St.) Moves back to London, ON and lives temporarily with Scotty Potty on Richmond St. and then on Pall Mall St. Has a disagreement with a new roomate over the validity of children's drawings and Basquiat. Thompson and Bell befriend Spencer Tripp or "Sweet Mr. C." "Gravy World" and the story of "Tom Soben" become items of discussion between them. Also, the term "L.O." (short for London, Ontario) surfaces in his work. *Exclaim!* publishes a comic book version of Bell's previously self–published *Mojo Action Companion Unit.*

1997
Travels to Vancouver, BC by bus. Sees Ray Johnson show en route in Chicago, IL. Moves to Toronto, ON and colours animation for Nelvana on the night shift. Lives on Harbord and then Shaw. Travels to Cambridge, MA with Neil Rough and R.J. in a propane powered van with a Coleman stove installed in the back. R.J. alarms and amuses the Cambridge Fire Dept. by cooking soup in the back of the van while it is parked on a busy street. Meets his penpal Ron Regé, Jr. Moves to Halifax, NS and lives on Maynard St. and then later on Falkland Ave. Begins weekly comic strip *Carboard City* for *The Coast* in Halifax.

1998
McLean visits Halifax and they draw *Sleepy Pie*, partly on a bus to and from Sackville, NB.

1999
Meets Amy Lockhart. Shows with Lockhart in three person show *Fistfull Of Coins Box Full Of Flowers*, (The Khyber, Halifax, NS). Quits weekly. Travels to Vancouver, BC where he and McLean put together *Ja Ja Lipp & Sons* at the Helen Pitt Gallery, showing more mail, *The Schnauzer Archives*, works on paper and self–published booklets. Also: a showing of Thompson's mailings in the Pitt bathroom.

2000
Lives in Calgary, AB for two months on 16th St. Travels back to London, ON. Stays with Mom. Bell and Peter Thompson complete their *Giant Masher* exhibition as part of an artist residency of sorts in the Galleria Mall

MARCO
19. Simplify, simplify, simplify.
22. Wear earplugs.
24. Create order out of chaos.
23. Get enough sleep. If necessary,
GO TO BED!
NIHILIST
SPASM BAND
16. Say NO!
3. Visualize your shoulders as wheels.
ON
FAKE
POSTAL CODE
To: Jason McLean:
Billions
818 Hawks Ave
Vancouver B.C.
Canada
V6A 3J4

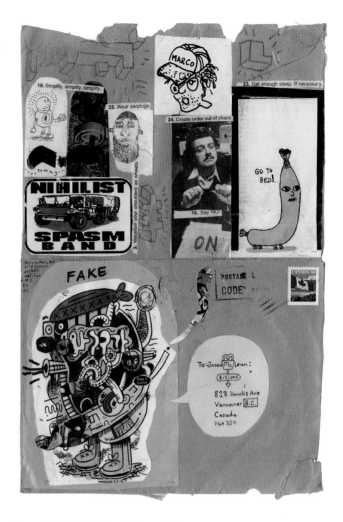

Examples of Mail Art sent to Jason Mclean:

Above: *"Simplify, Simplify, Simplify"* (untitled), 1998, mixed media
Includes: "samples" of artwork by Spencer Tripp, a Nihilist Spasm Design by Joe Turner and a reworked Mclean drawing)

Below: *"Mild Observation is Dangerous"* (untitled), 2000, mixed media
Includes: a reworked Ray Johnson photocopy and a reworked photocopy of a much earlier Jason Mclean envleope. also, contains "samples" of Aztec imagery, Daniel Clowes clipping, "Marcoart (NY)", and "Sugar Baby" candy packaging

MAIL POSTE
MILD OBSERVATION
IS DANGEROUS!
TO STONE-WOLL JACKSON 713 east PENDER VANCOUVER, BC V6A 1V8
STAND TALL GURU
L.O. Lucky Fucker
BUJ
JMMB
BU

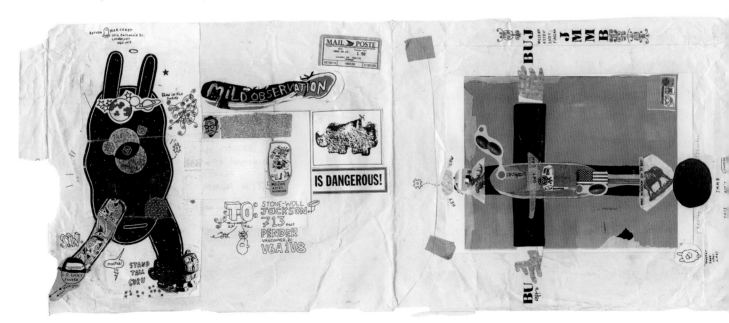

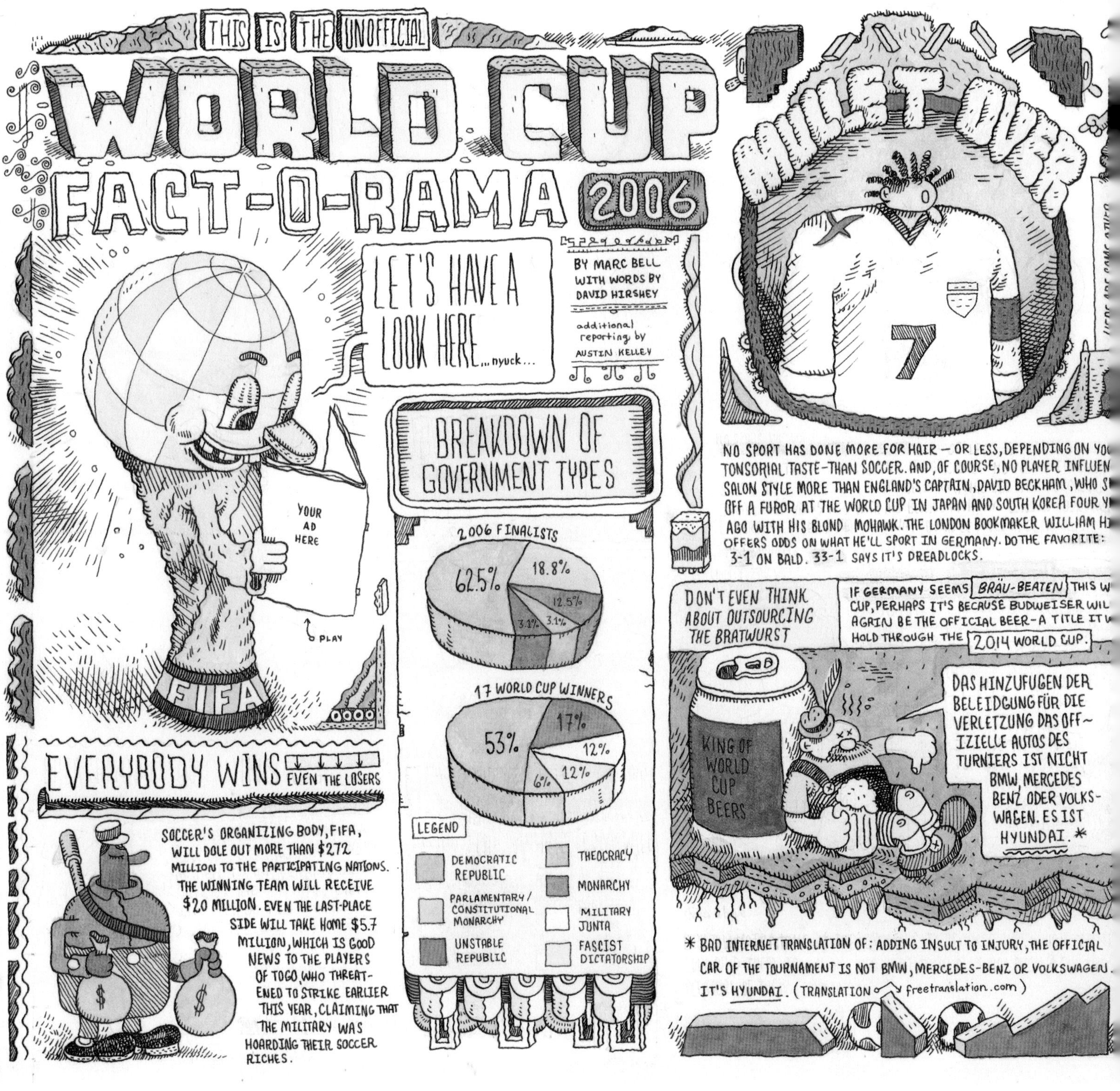

THIS IS THE UNOFFICIAL
WORLD CUP
FACT-O-RAMA 2006
BY MARC BELL WITH WORDS BY DAVID HIRSHEY
additional reporting by AUSTIN KELLEY
LET'S HAVE A LOOK HERE...nyuck...
YOUR AD HERE
PLAY
FIFA
BREAKDOWN OF GOVERNMENT TYPES
2006 FINALISTS
62.5%
18.8%
12.5%
3.1%
3.1%
17 WORLD CUP WINNERS
53%
17%
12%
12%
6%
LEGEND
DEMOCRATIC REPUBLIC
THEOCRACY
PARLAMENTARY / CONSTITUTIONAL MONARCHY
MONARCHY
UNSTABLE REPUBLIC
MILITARY JUNTA
FASCIST DICTATORSHIP
EVERYBODY WINS EVEN THE LOSERS
SOCCER'S ORGANIZING BODY, FIFA, WILL DOLE OUT MORE THAN $272 MILLION TO THE PARTICIPATING NATIONS. THE WINNING TEAM WILL RECEIVE $20 MILLION. EVEN THE LAST-PLACE SIDE WILL TAKE HOME $5.7 MILLION, WHICH IS GOOD NEWS TO THE PLAYERS OF TOGO, WHO THREATENED TO STRIKE EARLIER THIS YEAR, CLAIMING THAT THE MILITARY WAS HOARDING THEIR SOCCER RICHES.
MULLET OVER
7
NO SPORT HAS DONE MORE FOR HAIR – OR LESS, DEPENDING ON YOU TONSORIAL TASTE – THAN SOCCER. AND, OF COURSE, NO PLAYER INFLUEN SALON STYLE MORE THAN ENGLAND'S CAPTAIN, DAVID BECKHAM, WHO S OFF A FUROR AT THE WORLD CUP IN JAPAN AND SOUTH KOREA FOUR Y AGO WITH HIS BLOND MOHAWK. THE LONDON BOOKMAKER WILLIAM H OFFERS ODDS ON WHAT HE'LL SPORT IN GERMANY. DO THE FAVORITE: 3-1 ON BALD. 33-1 SAYS IT'S DREADLOCKS.
DON'T EVEN THINK ABOUT OUTSOURCING THE BRATWURST
IF GERMANY SEEMS BRÄU-BEATEN THIS W CUP, PERHAPS IT'S BECAUSE BUDWEISER WIL AGAIN BE THE OFFICIAL BEER – A TITLE IT W HOLD THROUGH THE 2014 WORLD CUP.
KING OF WORLD CUP BEERS
DAS HINZUFUGEN DER BELEIDGUNG FÜR DIE VERLETZUNG DAS OFFIZIELLE AUTOS DES TURNIERS IST NICHT BMW, MERCEDES BENZ ODER VOLKSWAGEN. ES IST HYUNDAI. *
* BAD INTERNET TRANSLATION OF: ADDING INSULT TO INJURY, THE OFFICIAL CAR OF THE TOURNAMENT IS NOT BMW, MERCEDES-BENZ OR VOLKSWAGEN. IT'S HYUNDAI. (TRANSLATION freetranslation.com)

World Cup Fact-O-Rama, 2006, text written by David Hirshey, created for *The New York Times Magazine*

2000 (*continued*)
in downtown London, ON. The show opens at Gallery 396 on Richmond St. (later called The Community Outreach Gallery). Lives in a cottage near Wakefield, PQ for the summer dubbed "The Ottawa Rural Commune." Creates the self published version of *The Stacks* there. Moves to Heatley Avenue in Vancouver, BC in the fall, where the majority of the work in *Hot Potatoe* is created over the next 7 years.

2001
Dirty Debbie and Bell complete *Birthday Moustache*. Organizes a book launch and music show with Mclean. *Bell/Mclean Workout* with Jason Mclean opens at Tracey Lawrence Gallery in Vancouver, BC. The show features the work from their self–published *Stand Tall Guru* books as well as sculpture work such as the *Giant Metal Bird.* Bell and Thompson's *Giant Marshland Masher*, a different version of their *Giant Masher* show travels to Struts Artist Run Centre in Sackville, NB.

2003
Shrimpy and Paul and Friends is published by Highwater Books. Begins regular contributions to the periodicals *Kramers Ergot* and *The Ganzfeld.* Shows as part of *The Ganzfeld (Unbound)* at Adam Buamgold Gallery, NY. Bell and Mclean reorganize mail art for *L.O. (We Grow 'Em Big Here)* at Forest City Gallery (London, ON).

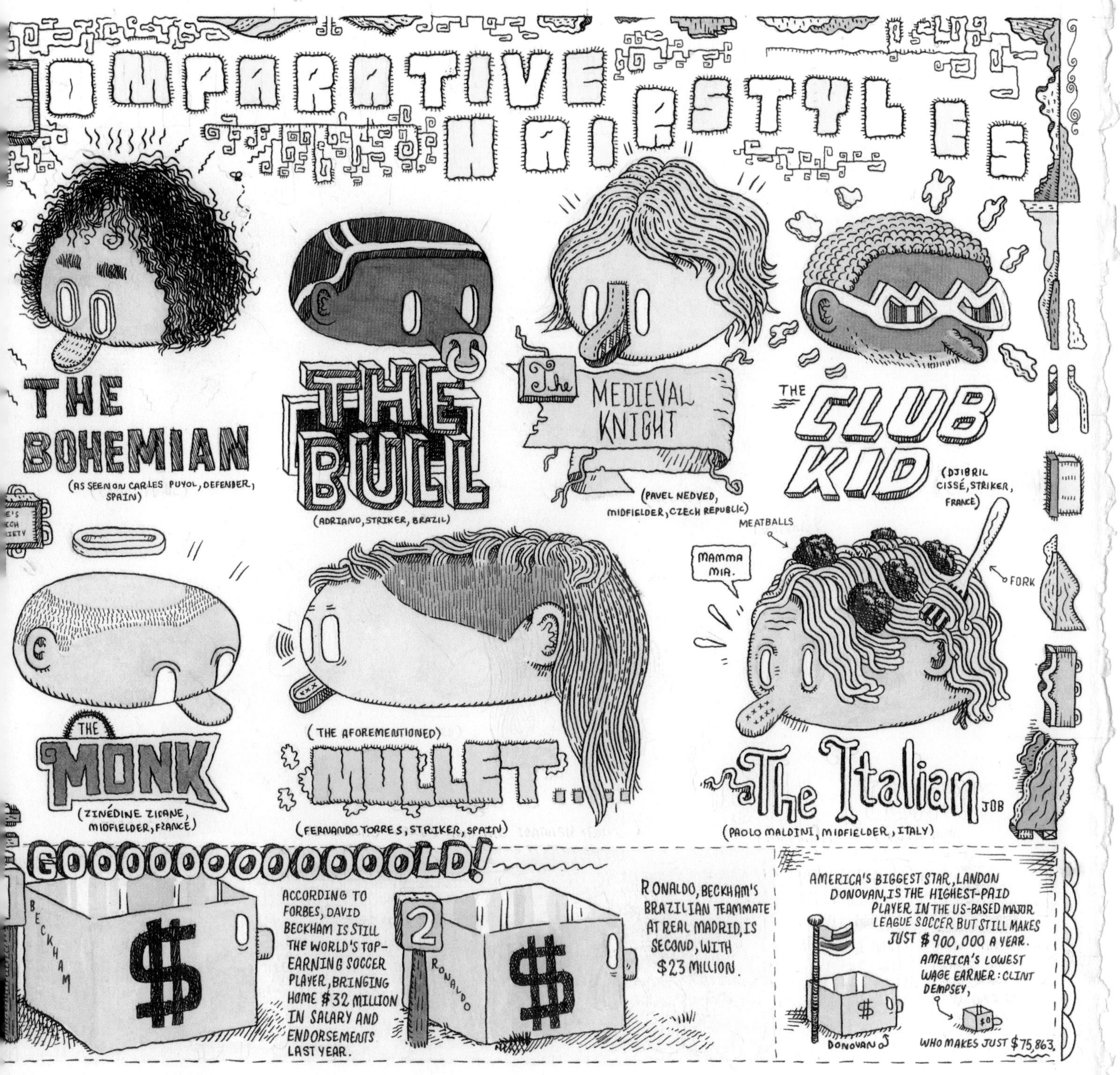
COMPARATIVE HAIRSTYLES
THE BOHEMIAN
(AS SEEN ON CARLES PUYOL, DEFENDER, SPAIN)
THE BULL
(ADRIANO, STRIKER, BRAZIL)
The MEDIEVAL KNIGHT
(PAVEL NEDVED, MIDFIELDER, CZECH REPUBLIC)
THE CLUB KID
(DJIBRIL CISSÉ, STRIKER, FRANCE)
MEATBALLS
MAMMA MIA.
FORK
THE MONK
(ZINÉDINE ZIDANE, MIDFIELDER, FRANCE)
(THE AFOREMENTIONED)
MULLET.....
(FERNANDO TORRES, STRIKER, SPAIN)
The Italian JOB
(PAOLO MALDINI, MIDFIELDER, ITALY)
GOOOOOOOOOOOOLD!
BECKHAM
ACCORDING TO FORBES, DAVID BECKHAM IS STILL THE WORLD'S TOP-EARNING SOCCER PLAYER, BRINGING HOME $32 MILLION IN SALARY AND ENDORSEMENTS LAST YEAR.
2
RONALDO
RONALDO, BECKHAM'S BRAZILIAN TEAMMATE AT REAL MADRID, IS SECOND, WITH $23 MILLION.
AMERICA'S BIGGEST STAR, LANDON DONOVAN, IS THE HIGHEST-PAID PLAYER IN THE US-BASED MAJOR LEAGUE SOCCER BUT STILL MAKES JUST $900,000 A YEAR.
AMERICA'S LOWEST WAGE EARNER: CLINT DEMPSEY,
DONOVAN
$0
WHO MAKES JUST $75,863.

2004
Lives in Montreal, PQ temporarily for two months. Travels to NY for first solo show in NY at the Adam Baumgold Gallery. Fantagraphics publishes *Worn Tuff Elbow*, a comic book of some of his weekly strips.

2005
Quits weekly comic strip. Travels to NY for *Bloo Chip*. Organizes the exhibition *From The Private Collection Of Gerard Doody* with Amy Lockhart. Travels to California for summer residency at CSSA (Cal Arts). Works on *The Collagist* with Lockhart there. Picture Box, Inc. publishes *The Hobbit* by Bell and Thompson which is very loosely based on the J. R. R. Tolkien novel. (p. 218)

2006
Assembles *Nog A Dod*, a survey of "Canadian Psychedoolia" (artist–created booklets by his peers, 1995–2005). Travels to NY for a launch/art show for *Nog A Dod* at Giant Robot. Sadly, many original *Nog A Dod* artworks are lost in the mail. Residency with Amy Lockhart at Struts in Sackville, NB.

2007
Travels to NY for *Egypt Buncake* at Adam Baumgold. Moves to Toronto and lives in "Hassle Castle." Travels to Chicago and vists the Roger Brown Study Collection.

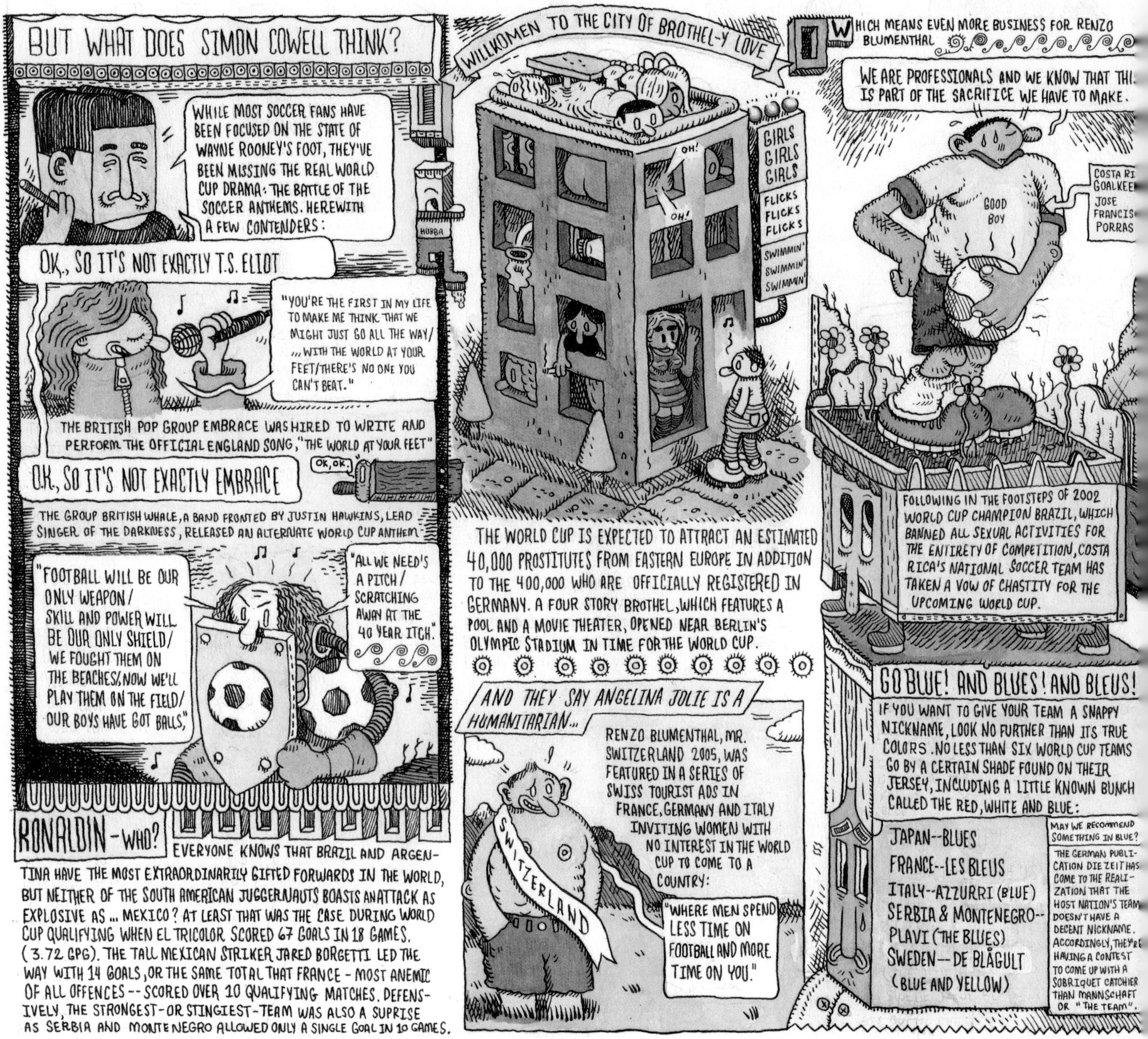

BUT WHAT DOES SIMON COWELL THINK?
WHILE MOST SOCCER FANS HAVE BEEN FOCUSED ON THE STATE OF WAYNE ROONEY'S FOOT, THEY'VE BEEN MISSING THE REAL WORLD CUP DRAMA: THE BATTLE OF THE SOCCER ANTHEMS. HEREWITH A FEW CONTENDERS:
HUBBA
O.K., SO IT'S NOT EXACTLY T.S. ELIOT
"YOU'RE THE FIRST IN MY LIFE TO MAKE ME THINK THAT WE MIGHT JUST GO ALL THE WAY/ ,,, WITH THE WORLD AT YOUR FEET/THERE'S NO ONE YOU CAN'T BEAT."
THE BRITISH POP GROUP EMBRACE WAS HIRED TO WRITE AND PERFORM THE OFFICIAL ENGLAND SONG, "THE WORLD AT YOUR FEET"
OK, OK.
O.K., SO IT'S NOT EXACTLY EMBRACE
THE GROUP BRITISH WHALE, A BAND FRONTED BY JUSTIN HAWKINS, LEAD SINGER OF THE DARKNESS, RELEASED AN ALTERNATE WORLD CUP ANTHEM
"FOOTBALL WILL BE OUR ONLY WEAPON/ SKILL AND POWER WILL BE OUR ONLY SHIELD/ WE FOUGHT THEM ON THE BEACHES/, NOW WE'LL PLAY THEM ON THE FIELD/ OUR BOYS HAVE GOT BALLS,"
"ALL WE NEED'S A PITCH/ SCRATCHING AWAY AT THE 40 YEAR ITCH."
RONALDIN-WHO?
EVERYONE KNOWS THAT BRAZIL AND ARGENTINA HAVE THE MOST EXTRAORDINARILY GIFTED FORWARDS IN THE WORLD, BUT NEITHER OF THE SOUTH AMERICAN JUGGERNAUTS BOASTS AN ATTACK AS EXPLOSIVE AS ... MEXICO? AT LEAST THAT WAS THE CASE DURING WORLD CUP QUALIFYING WHEN EL TRICOLOR SCORED 67 GOALS IN 18 GAMES. (3.72 GPG). THE TALL MEXICAN STRIKER JARED BORGETTI LED THE WAY WITH 14 GOALS, OR THE SAME TOTAL THAT FRANCE - MOST ANEMIC OF ALL OFFENCES -- SCORED OVER 10 QUALIFYING MATCHES. DEFENSIVELY, THE STRONGEST-OR STINGIEST-TEAM WAS ALSO A SUPRISE AS SERBIA AND MONTENEGRO ALLOWED ONLY A SINGLE GOAL IN 10 GAMES.
WILLKOMEN TO THE CITY OF BROTHEL-Y LOVE
OH!
OH!
GIRLS GIRLS GIRLS
FLICKS FLICKS FLICKS
SWIMMIN' SWIMMIN' SWIMMIN'
THE WORLD CUP IS EXPECTED TO ATTRACT AN ESTIMATED 40,000 PROSTITUTES FROM EASTERN EUROPE IN ADDITION TO THE 400,000 WHO ARE OFFICIALLY REGISTERED IN GERMANY. A FOUR STORY BROTHEL, WHICH FEATURES A POOL AND A MOVIE THEATER, OPENED NEAR BERLIN'S OLYMPIC STADIUM IN TIME FOR THE WORLD CUP.
AND THEY SAY ANGELINA JOLIE IS A HUMANITARIAN...
RENZO BLUMENTHAL, MR. SWITZERLAND 2005, WAS FEATURED IN A SERIES OF SWISS TOURIST ADS IN FRANCE, GERMANY AND ITALY INVITING WOMEN WITH NO INTEREST IN THE WORLD CUP TO COME TO A COUNTRY:
SWITZERLAND
"WHERE MEN SPEND LESS TIME ON FOOTBALL AND MORE TIME ON YOU."
WHICH MEANS EVEN MORE BUSINESS FOR RENZO BLUMENTHAL
WE ARE PROFESSIONALS AND WE KNOW THAT THI IS PART OF THE SACRIFICE WE HAVE TO MAKE.
GOOD BOY
COSTA RI GOALKEE JOSE FRANCIS PORRAS
FOLLOWING IN THE FOOTSTEPS OF 2002 WORLD CUP CHAMPION BRAZIL, WHICH BANNED ALL SEXUAL ACTIVITIES FOR THE ENTIRETY OF COMPETITION, COSTA RICA'S NATIONAL SOCCER TEAM HAS TAKEN A VOW OF CHASTITY FOR THE UPCOMING WORLD CUP.
GO BLUE! AND BLUES! AND BLEUS!
IF YOU WANT TO GIVE YOUR TEAM A SNAPPY NICKNAME, LOOK NO FURTHER THAN ITS TRUE COLORS. NO LESS THAN SIX WORLD CUP TEAMS GO BY A CERTAIN SHADE FOUND ON THEIR JERSEY, INCLUDING A LITTLE KNOWN BUNCH CALLED THE RED, WHITE AND BLUE:
JAPAN--BLUES
FRANCE--LES BLEUS
ITALY--AZZURRI (BLUE)
SERBIA & MONTENEGRO--PLAVI (THE BLUES)
SWEDEN--DE BLÅGULT (BLUE AND YELLOW)
MAY WE RECOMMEND SOMETHING IN BLUE?
THE GERMAN PUBLICATION DIE ZEIT HAS COME TO THE REALIZATION THAT THE HOST NATION'S TEAM DOESN'T HAVE A DECENT NICKNAME. ACCORDINGLY, THEY'RE HAVING A CONTEST TO COME UP WITH A SOBRIQUET CATCHIER THAN MANNSCHAFT OR "THE TEAM".

2008
Travels to Japan for *Nomadic: Shayne Ehman and Friends* at the Tokyo Wonder Site and shows a series of collaborations created with Seth Scriver (p. 236). Relocates to Montreal.

2009
Hot Potatoe is released to great acclaim everywhere except for the home of Dan Quayle. "He didn't get it right at all," Dan tells *The Comics Journal.*

2010
Releases the 10th Anniversary edition of *The Stacks*, which contains a "pop-up" *Canada Council Brick Snake* and several more references to *Sleep Country*. A sound chip claims "This booklet contains several reproductions of artwerks" when the front cover is opened.

2011
Despite an ever–challenging economic climate, Bell travels frequently to Brooklyn, NY to organize and open his very own chain of high–end cupcake shops. That June, *Marc Bell's #1 Cupcake Shop* opens in Williamsburg to rave reviews despite an already flooded (and failing) designer cupcake market. The shop is voted "New Cupcake Shop of the Year" in *The New York Times*. Some local detractors (suspected to be Bell's cupcake competitors) author scathing letters to the editor regarding the matter. These are mostly viewed as sour grapes by the cupcake-eating public.

2012
Bell divides his time between Montreal and NY on the continued success of his shop and

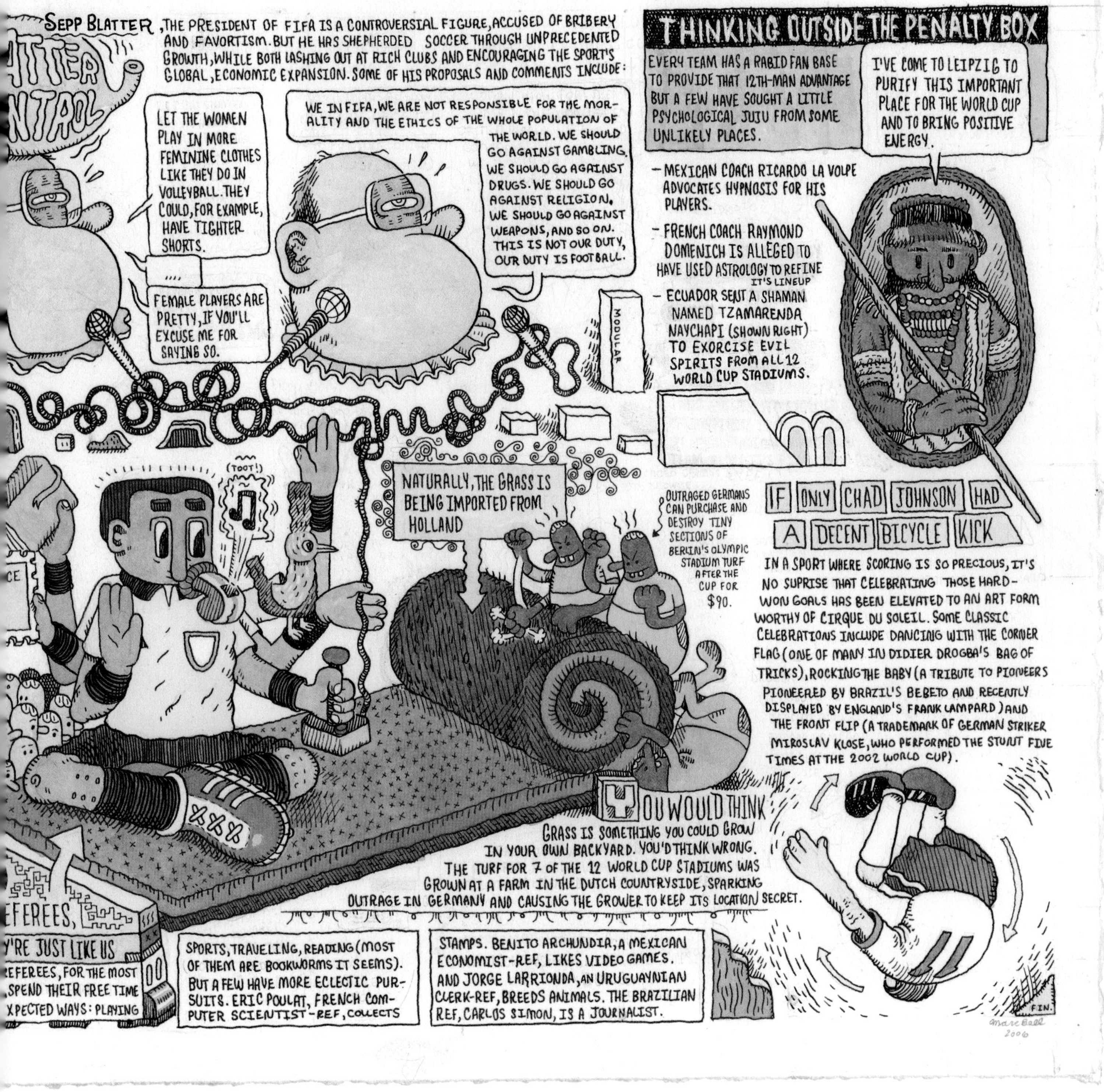
SEPP BLATTER, THE PRESIDENT OF FIFA IS A CONTROVERSIAL FIGURE, ACCUSED OF BRIBERY AND FAVORTISM. BUT HE HAS SHEPHERDED SOCCER THROUGH UNPRECEDENTED GROWTH, WHILE BOTH LASHING OUT AT RICH CLUBS AND ENCOURAGING THE SPORT'S GLOBAL, ECONOMIC EXPANSION. SOME OF HIS PROPOSALS AND COMMENTS INCLUDE:
LET THE WOMEN PLAY IN MORE FEMININE CLOTHES LIKE THEY DO IN VOLLEYBALL. THEY COULD, FOR EXAMPLE, HAVE TIGHTER SHORTS.
WE IN FIFA, WE ARE NOT RESPONSIBLE FOR THE MORALITY AND THE ETHICS OF THE WHOLE POPULATION OF THE WORLD. WE SHOULD GO AGAINST GAMBLING. WE SHOULD GO AGAINST DRUGS. WE SHOULD GO AGAINST RELIGION, WE SHOULD GO AGAINST WEAPONS, AND SO ON. THIS IS NOT OUR DUTY, OUR DUTY IS FOOTBALL.
FEMALE PLAYERS ARE PRETTY, IF YOU'LL EXCUSE ME FOR SAYING SO.
MODULAR
THINKING OUTSIDE THE PENALTY BOX
EVERY TEAM HAS A RABID FAN BASE TO PROVIDE THAT 12TH-MAN ADVANTAGE BUT A FEW HAVE SOUGHT A LITTLE PSYCHOLOGICAL JUJU FROM SOME UNLIKELY PLACES.
I'VE COME TO LEIPZIG TO PURIFY THIS IMPORTANT PLACE FOR THE WORLD CUP AND TO BRING POSITIVE ENERGY.
- MEXICAN COACH RICARDO LA VOLPE ADVOCATES HYPNOSIS FOR HIS PLAYERS.
- FRENCH COACH RAYMOND DOMENICH IS ALLEGED TO HAVE USED ASTROLOGY TO REFINE IT'S LINEUP
- ECUADOR SENT A SHAMAN NAMED TZAMARENDA NAYCHAPI (SHOWN RIGHT) TO EXORCISE EVIL SPIRITS FROM ALL 12 WORLD CUP STADIUMS.
(TOOT!)
NATURALLY, THE GRASS IS BEING IMPORTED FROM HOLLAND
OUTRAGED GERMANS CAN PURCHASE AND DESTROY TINY SECTIONS OF BERLIN'S OLYMPIC STADIUM TURF AFTER THE CUP FOR $90.
IF ONLY CHAD JOHNSON HAD A DECENT BICYCLE KICK
IN A SPORT WHERE SCORING IS SO PRECIOUS, IT'S NO SUPRISE THAT CELEBRATING THOSE HARD-WON GOALS HAS BEEN ELEVATED TO AN ART FORM WORTHY OF CIRQUE DU SOLEIL. SOME CLASSIC CELEBRATIONS INCLUDE DANCING WITH THE CORNER FLAG (ONE OF MANY IN DIDIER DROGBA'S BAG OF TRICKS), ROCKING THE BABY (A TRIBUTE TO PIONEERS PIONEERED BY BRAZIL'S BEBETO AND RECENTLY DISPLAYED BY ENGLAND'S FRANK LAMPARD) AND THE FRONT FLIP (A TRADEMARK OF GERMAN STRIKER MIROSLAV KLOSE, WHO PERFORMED THE STUNT FIVE TIMES AT THE 2002 WORLD CUP).
YOU WOULD THINK GRASS IS SOMETHING YOU COULD GROW IN YOUR OWN BACKYARD. YOU'D THINK WRONG. THE TURF FOR 7 OF THE 12 WORLD CUP STADIUMS WAS GROWN AT A FARM IN THE DUTCH COUNTRYSIDE, SPARKING OUTRAGE IN GERMANY AND CAUSING THE GROWER TO KEEP ITS LOCATION SECRET.
EFEREES,
Y'RE JUST LIKE US
EFEREES, FOR THE MOST SPEND THEIR FREE TIME XPECTED WAYS: PLAYING
SPORTS, TRAVELING, READING (MOST OF THEM ARE BOOKWORMS IT SEEMS). BUT A FEW HAVE MORE ECLECTIC PURSUITS. ERIC POULAT, FRENCH COMPUTER SCIENTIST-REF, COLLECTS
STAMPS. BENITO ARCHUNDIA, A MEXICAN ECONOMIST-REF, LIKES VIDEO GAMES. AND JORGE LARRIONDA, AN URUGUAYNIAN CLERK-REF, BREEDS ANIMALS. THE BRAZILIAN REF, CARLOS SIMON, IS A JOURNALIST.
FIN.
Marc Bell 2006

takes a prolonged break from his artwork to write about the financial crisis in North America. Bell also travels to Mexico and South America with fellow artist Ned "Ba Bing" Mitchell and critic Mrs. Stanley Clarke of East Bradenton, Florida, but refuses to participate in the destruction of several remaining Mayan and Aztec ruins with them, stating, "leave them alone, it's their year." Bell travels to Gerard Doody Projects in British Columbia, Canada to work on a commission for several site–specific pieces at the Surrey Art Ranch and Animal Hospital.

2013

A difficult year for Bell as the success of his cupcake empire takes a sharp downturn. The art market is mostly flat. He also fails to find a publisher for his completed book on financials, *My Inner Foot Tells Me the Fundamentals Are Out of Wack*. The title is taken from his 2006 drawing of the same name. Bell spends some time in Newfoundland where he learns to __________.

2014

Bell's cupcake enterprise crumbles officially and he is forced to sell his flagship Williamsburg digs, literally for a song, unloading the building and the shop's hand–painted sign in exchange for the rights to Thor's "Keep the Dogs Away" and a sword from the Spanish Civil War. As a sad reminder of the harsh economic times, a "bring your own spoon" Oatmeal Shoppe takes over the space, offering such unspectacular but affordable flavors as "potatoe n' spice" and "regular." As the politics of snacking become increasingly volatile, cupcake eaters across the continent are suddenly viewed as pariahs, if not traitors. Bell escapes to neutral Switzerland to fine–tune his book on financials and "leverage a new drawing strategy going forward."

2015

Working from a hotel in idyllic Montreux (in the district of Vevey in the canton of Vaud, Switzerland), Bell is finally able to find a home for his financial musings. The fledgling "Simply Scrumptious Press" offers Bell a handsome advance on condition that he, A: remove all bitter and/or coarse references to the cupcake industry, B: not refer to himself as "Kid Cupcake" and C: chill the fuck out.

2016

Bell initiates a return to the art world, unleashing the giant 20 x 30 foot drawing *Cupcakes for Fucks Sake* at the Venice Biennale. It is here that he manages to find a place for his scathing criticisms of all things cupcake. Unfortunately, the work's simple, casual style disappoints his European audience who describe it as "lazy" or "sehr viel zu Küchleinisch" and offends waffle and bacon art patrons everywhere. Long–suffering Bell fans at home feel equally betrayed by the work and begin to question how much longer they're willing to wait to find out just who, indeed, wears "the white denim"…or if it even matters at all.

2017

Bell is offered a show at the newly founded DoodyHaus in Berlin (an extension of Doody's Vancouver enterprise: part gallery, part electric auto repair shop). There is only one condition: that the work contain no complaining whatsoever. Bell agrees but pushes the show to 2018 or later stating, "I'll have to get these little cakes out of my system first."

2018

P.S. Sweater Vest opens to quiet acclaim at DoodyHaus. The opening gala is an interesting affair in which Bell reunites with musical group White Whisker (formerly Smooth, Fat and Funky) and they perform a cover of "Keep the Dogs Away" as well as several songs about the German housing market. Refreshingly, the work itself contains no text and no references to food.

2021

Commissioned by the Brazilian government to build a giant three–dimensional version of his 2006 drawing *Comics Ain't Buttah* in Rio de Janeiro's Botanical Gardens. Intensified public interest in his work there leads to several television appearances, including a guest host slot on a newly revived version of "De Auditório" dressed as the "Grand Poobah" of the "Water Buffaloes" (a fictional men's club from popular 20th century cartoon "The Flintstones") for his 50th Birthday. Fellow artist Peter Thompson makes a surprise appearance on the show and attacks Marc with a Weed Eater™.

2022

Delves deeper into three–dimensional work, collaborating most notably with some hot–shit architects on Toronto's "Root Beer Hall of Fame." The design is poo–poohed in fusty Canadian design circles, mainly due to its edible HVAC system, but, despite this, becomes the benchmark for a rash of soda pop–inspired buildings that sprout up across Midwestern America. Bell is employed as a consultant on a number of these buildings, but distances himself from the movement after Akron, Ohio's "Yoo–Hoo Pavilion" lifts itself out of the ground and decides to walk to Columbus with the cleaning person still inside.

2023

In the aftermath of the Akron incident, Bell retreats once again to Montreux, citing a nagging premonition of dying at 52 years old and a general need to get loose. Bell waits out the rest of the year in his usual hotel room, and, on the advice of a psychic, drinks 52 cups of hot chocolate daily in a superstitious effort to ward off death. This gambit proves effective and, in November, Bell celebrates his 53rd birthday by taking the entire hotel staff on a sleigh ride. Unfortunately, Bell's premonition of the sleigh being attacked by a bear prevents him from enjoying the day, and he spends the entire outing talking skittishly to his psychic on a cellular phone.

2025

Bell begins another period of disillusionment with the art world and his place in it. In a disturbing move, he announces that he has decided to stop drawing altogether and gradually turn himself into a version of one of his own characters using modern surgery. The process begins by him having a plastic "Bloo Chip" installed onto his shoulder and waffle-textured arm skin grafts. Friends and family stage an intervention after learning that he plans to become a six-legged "creature" with a fence built onto one side of his body, a "Bad Mon Tonne" hat and several permanent "cookies" installed onto his back.

2026

Less and less is heard from Bell in the art world or anywhere for that matter. Some drawings of angry bears closely resembling renderings in Bell's "Cupcake Eurostyle" are spotted in Galérie Tête Carré's booth at the Zimbabwe International Art Fair under the nom de plume "The Turquoise Turkey." However, upon further examination, these turn out to be the works of a younger, virtually unknown, three–headed artist from Greenland.

2045

In a bizarre gesture, Bell mails a box of paper scraps and random unfinished works to Mount Allison University, addressed to the "Students of the Fine Art Dept." A letter inside invites the students to "carry on" with his work. This is especially strange given that the department hasn't existed for 20 years, and the one in its place now focuses exclusively on the training of audio–digital–cellular–brain–phone–game–interface production workers. In fact, at this time, most traditional artists are either non–existent or produced digitally in North Korea for propaganda purposes.

2075

Bell dies in Hamilton, Ontario after former Prime Minister George Stroumboulopoulos invades his home and strikes him with the soapstone sculpture Bell tried to defend himself with. Curiously, Bell had just turned 104, exactly twice the age at which he had predicted he would meet his end. Seventeen illegitimate children surface, all wearing brown pants, and begin to fight over his estate, which amounts to nothing but a mummified stack of cupcakes locked in a safe in a Montreux hotel.

2076

Realizing there was nothing to be gained by anybody in Bell's estate, the brown–panted kinfolk put their differences aside and host the first annual *Hot Potatoe BBQ and Clothes Swap* at Springbank Park in Bell's hometown of London, Ont.

2081

After the extinction of the waffle in the early part of the 21st century, food anthropologists and art historians begin to re–evaluate Bell's work. Suddenly seen as containing clues to unlocking key nutritional secrets, Bell's catalogue is deemed the most important food art of the late 20th and early 21st century and he is granted a large, posthumous retrospective at the Gerard Doody Jr. Waffle Museum in Houston, Texas.

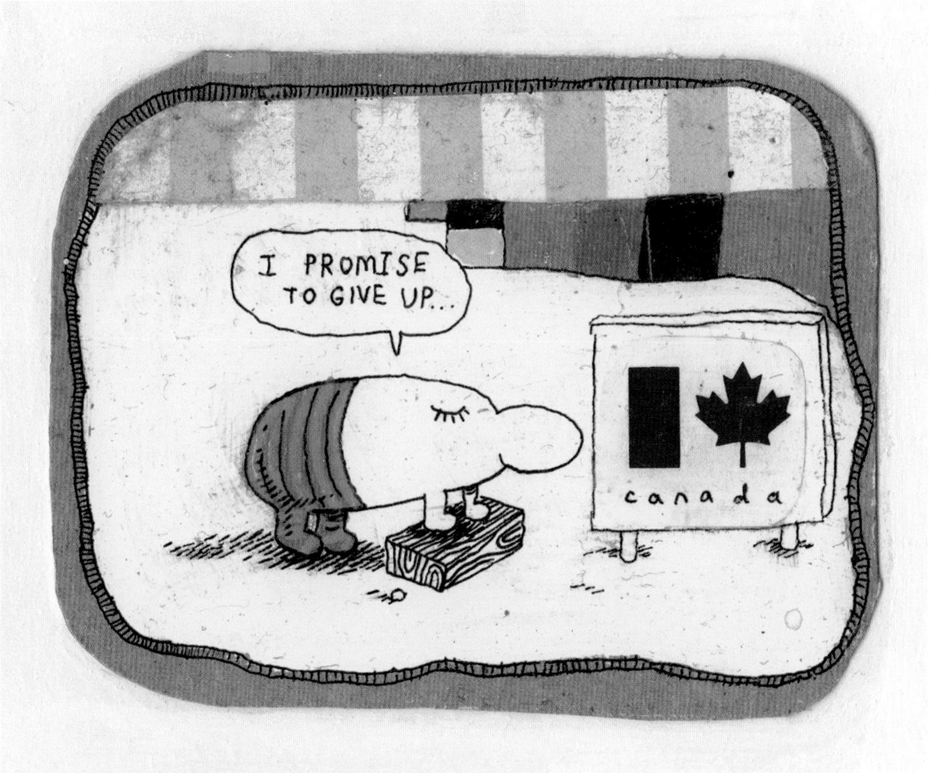
I PROMISE TO GIVE UP...
canada

I Promise To Give Up, 2000-2005
Mixed media on board

The Following Details:

254: *Whut Do They Wont? (Pilin' 'Em High)*, 2004
Mixed media on paper

255: *Kuh Kuh Kuh Kuh, I'm a Buncake*, 2006
Mixed media on Contemporary Art Gallery invitation

256: *Totem,* 2003
Mixed media on paper

258: *Trendy Brown Nose,* 2004
Mixed media construction

259: *End Of An Era,* 2005
Mixed media on envleope

260–261: *Farm Equipment,* 2005
Mixed media construction

262: *A.U.,* 2003
Mixed media construction

263: *Cucumber,* 2003
Mixed media construction

264: *Secret Sid Dickens,* 2003
Mixed media construction

265: *Calm Centrepiece,* 2003
Mixed media on cardboard

266, 269, 270, 271, 272: *Fresh From Kiev #2,* 2006
Ink and watercolour on paper

267, 268: *My Inner Foot Tells Me (The Fundamentals Are Out of Wack),* 2007
Mixed media on paper

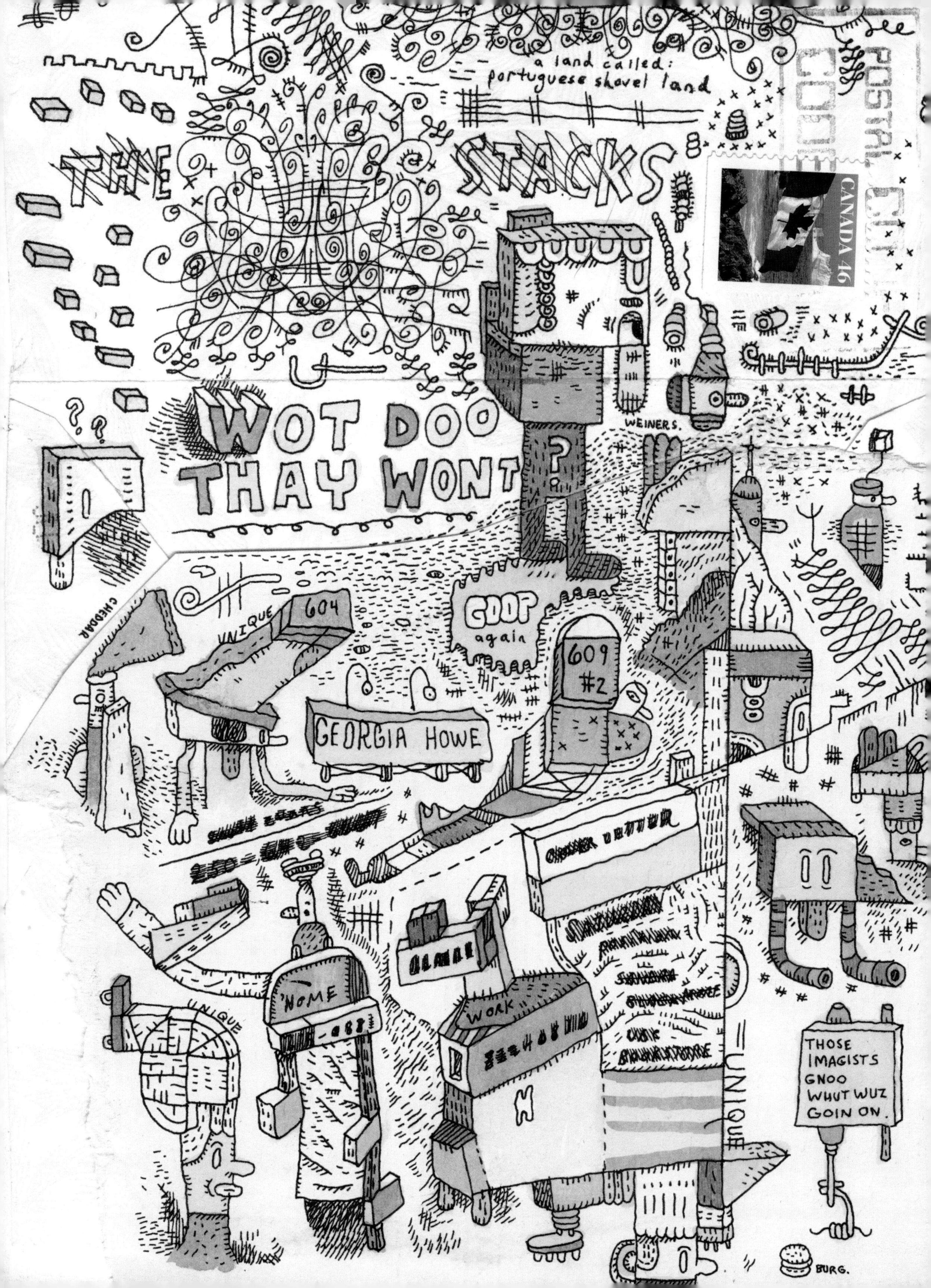
a land called:
portuguese shovel land
THE STACKS
POSTAL CODE
CANADA 46
WOT DOO THAY WONT ?
WEINERS.
CHEDDAR
UNIQUE
604
GOOP again
609 #2
GEORGIA HOWE
HOME
WORK
UNIQUE
UNIQUE
THOSE IMAGISTS GNOO WHUT WUZ GOIN ON.
BURG.

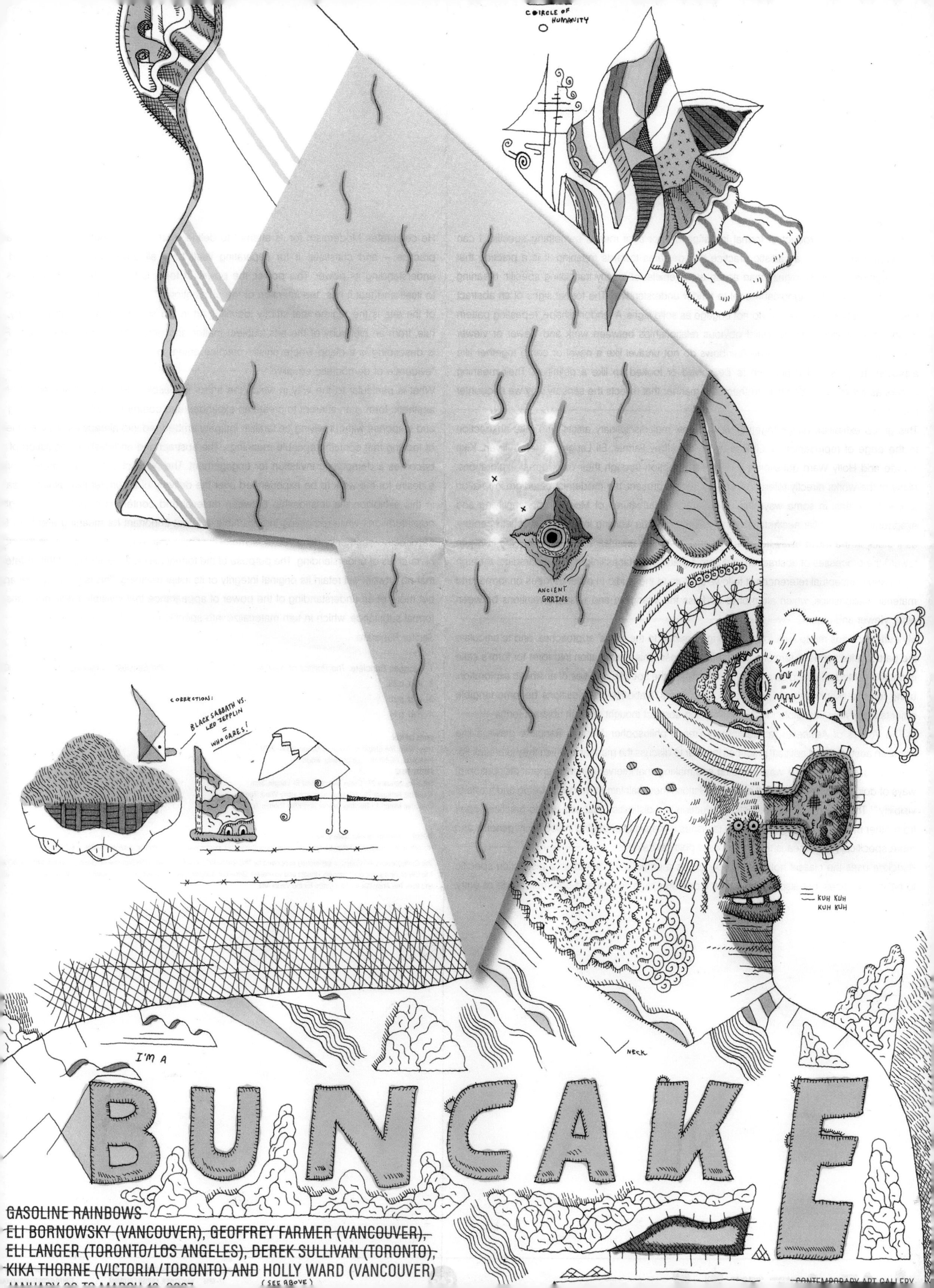
CIRCLE OF HUMANITY
ANCIENT GRAINS
CORRECTIONS:
BLACK SABBATH VS. LED ZEPPLIN = WHO CARES!
KUH KUH KUH KUH
I'M A
NECK
BUNCAKE
GASOLINE RAINBOWS
ELI BORNOWSKY (VANCOUVER), GEOFFREY FARMER (VANCOUVER),
ELI LANGER (TORONTO/LOS ANGELES), DEREK SULLIVAN (TORONTO),
KIKA THORNE (VICTORIA/TORONTO) AND HOLLY WARD (VANCOUVER)
(SEE ABOVE)
CONTEMPORARY ART GALLERY

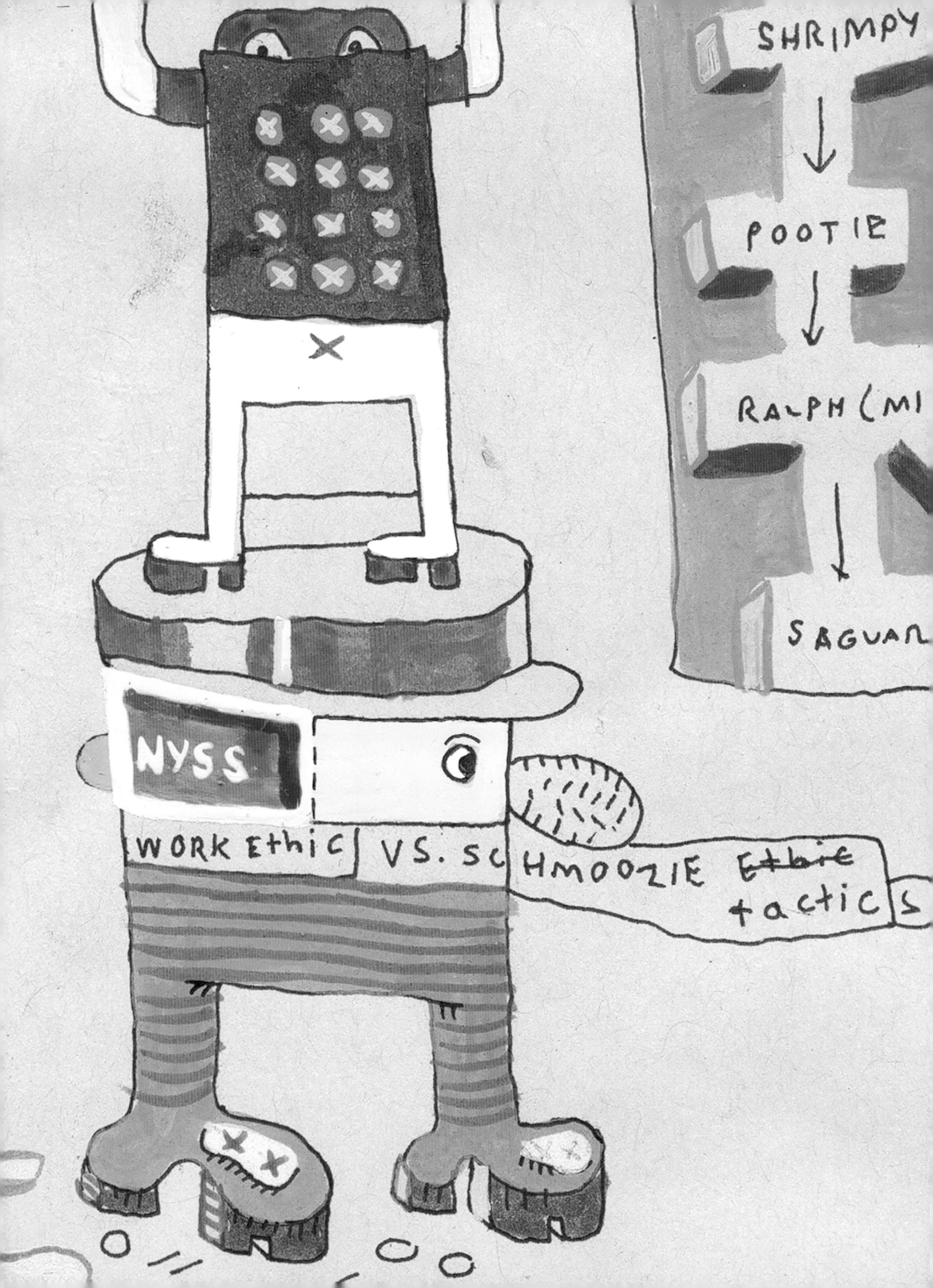
SHRIMPY
POOTIE
RALPH (MI
SAGUAR
NYSS
WORK Ethic VS. SCHMOOZIE ~~Ethic~~ tactics

Selected Exhibitions

One Person Exhibitions

2008
Illustrated Cartoon Videos, Paul Bright Gallery, Toronto, ON
Illusztraijuns For Brain Police, Librairie D & Q, Montreal, PQ

2007
Egypt Buncake, Adam Baumgold Gallery, New York, NY

2005
Bloo Chip, Adam Baumgold Gallery, New York, NY

2004
The Stacks, Adam Baumgold Gallery, New York, NY

2002
Calm Center, The Blinding Light!! Cinema, Vancouver, BC

Two Person Exhibitions

2003
L.O. (We Grow 'Em Big Here), w/Jason Mclean, Forest City Gallery, London, ON

2001
Giant Marshland Masher, w/ Peter Thompson, Struts Gallery, Sackville, NB
Bell/Mclean Workout, w/Jason Mclean, Tracey Lawrence Gallery, Vancouver, BC

2000
Giant Masher, w/ Peter Thompson, Gallery 396, London, ON

1999
Ja Ja Lipp & Sons, w/ Jason Mclean, Helen Pitt Gallery, Vancouver, BC

1994
The Waffle, w/ Libby Schnauzer, Gallery Sansair, Vancouver, BC

Selected Group Exhibitions

2009
About Face, Adam Baumgold Gallery, New York , NY
Life Drawing, Magic Pony, Toronto, ON

2008
Pulp Fiction, Museum London, London, ON
White Noise Drawn Together, V1 Gallery, Copenhagen, DM
Nomadic: Shayne Ehman and Friends, Tokyo Wonder Site, Tokyo JP

2007
Going Postal, Art Metropole, Toronto, ON
In Full Cry, New Image Art Gallery, Los Angeles, CA
Hey You Guys, Commmunity Outreach, Toronto, ON
Macronauts, Andreas Melas/Athens Biennale, Athens, Greece
GR Snack Aisle, Giant Robot, New York, NY
It's A Wonderful Life, Owens Art Gallery, Sackville, NB
Strange Brew, BLVD Gallery, Seattle, WA
No North/Big Blood, Gaff Gallery, Vancouver, BC
Drawn To The Edge, Adam Baumgold Gallery, New York, NY
8 x 10, Giant Robot SF, San Francisco, CA
Many Happy Returns, High Energy Constructs, Los Angeles, CA
Tales From The Cyclops Library, Third Space, Saint John, NB
tinyvices.com, Collette, Paris, France
Kramers Ergot, Macalester College Art Gallery, St. Paul, MN
These Bagels Are Gnarly, Cinders Gallery, Brooklyn, NY

2006
tinyvices.com, Studio Bee, Tokyo, Japan
On Sundays, Watari Museum of Contemporary Art, Tokyo, Japan
You Gave Me Hope When I Was At The End/Schlumberger, Struts Gallery, Sackville, NB
Selections From Nog A Dod, Giant Robot, New York, NY
Fantagraphics, Museum Of American Illustration, New York, NY
The Panic Room –Works from The Dakis Joannou Collection, Deste Foundation, Athens, Greece
Post It Deux, Giant Robot, Los Angeles, CA
Bit By Bit, Blackwood Gallery, Toronto, ON
The New Collage, Pavel Zoubok Gallery, New York, NY
One Is Never Enough, The Or Galllery, Vancouver, BC
tinyvices.com, Spencer Brownstone Gallery, New York, NY
Grand Union, The Front Room, Brooklyn, NY
Hairorama, The Peanut Gallery, Easthampton, MA

2005
Bit By Bit, Contemporary Art Gallery, Vancouver, BC
Up The Waterspout, New Image Art Gallery, Los Angeles, CA
The Cartoonists Eye, A + D Gallery, Columbia College, Chicago, IL
Comicology: The New Magic Real, Slought Foundation, Philidelphia, PA
Psyclops Dreams, Access Artist Run Centre, Vancouver, BC
In A Series, Adam Baumgold Gallery, New York, NY
Collage Party, Anti–Social Gallery, Vancouver, BC
The Infinity Show, Helen Pitt Gallery, Vancouver, BC
Words In Pictures, Adam Baumgold Gallery, New York, NY

2004
Ohh! Ah! Shangri–La, Cassius King, San Diego, CA
Post It Show, Junc Gallery, Los Angeles, CA
Regal Beast #2, Magic Pony, Toronto, ON
Untold Tales, Adam Baumgold Gallery, New York, NY
Watercolour, DFN Gallery, New York, NY

2003
Freee Matrusss, Pond Gallery, San Francisco, CA
From The Private Collection of Gerard Doody, Space 1026, Philadelphia, PA
Word Works, Adam Baumgold Gallery, New York, NY
Original Comic Art, Buenaventura Gallery, San Diego, CA
The Ganzfeld (Unbound), Adam Baumgold Gallery, New York, NY

2002
Visions…of the Future, Meltdown Comics, Los Angeles, CA
Ink Pushers!, Balazo Gallery, San Francisco, CA

2000
Low–Tech Time Capsules: Book Art for the New Millenium, Port of Seattle, Seattle, WA

1999
Lost, Anna Leonowens Gallery, Halifax, NS
Luck of the Drawn, Reactor Gallery, Toronto, ON
Fistfull Of Coins Box Full Of Flowers, The Khyber, Halifax, NS
My Duck Is Still Better Than Your Duck, Struts Gallery, Sackville, NB
Return Of The Corpse, Presentation house Gallery, North Vancouver, BC
Nog A Dod, Moonbase Gallery, Vancouver, BC

1996
Molitov Koktail, CGEP, Montreal, PQ

1995
My Duck Is Better Than Your Duck, Struts Gallery, Sackville, NB

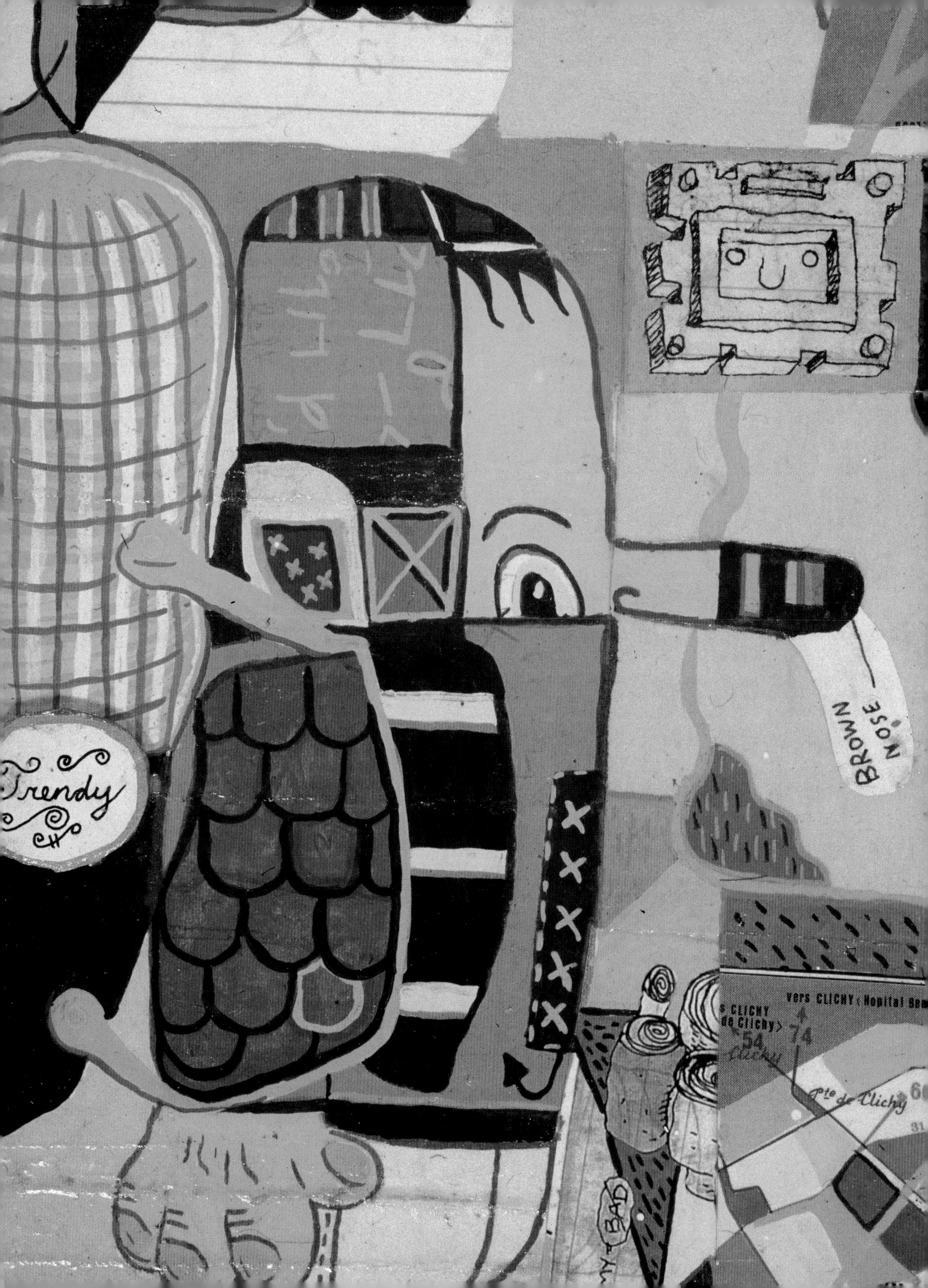
Trendy
BROWN NOSE
vers CLICHY
Pte de Clichy
BAD

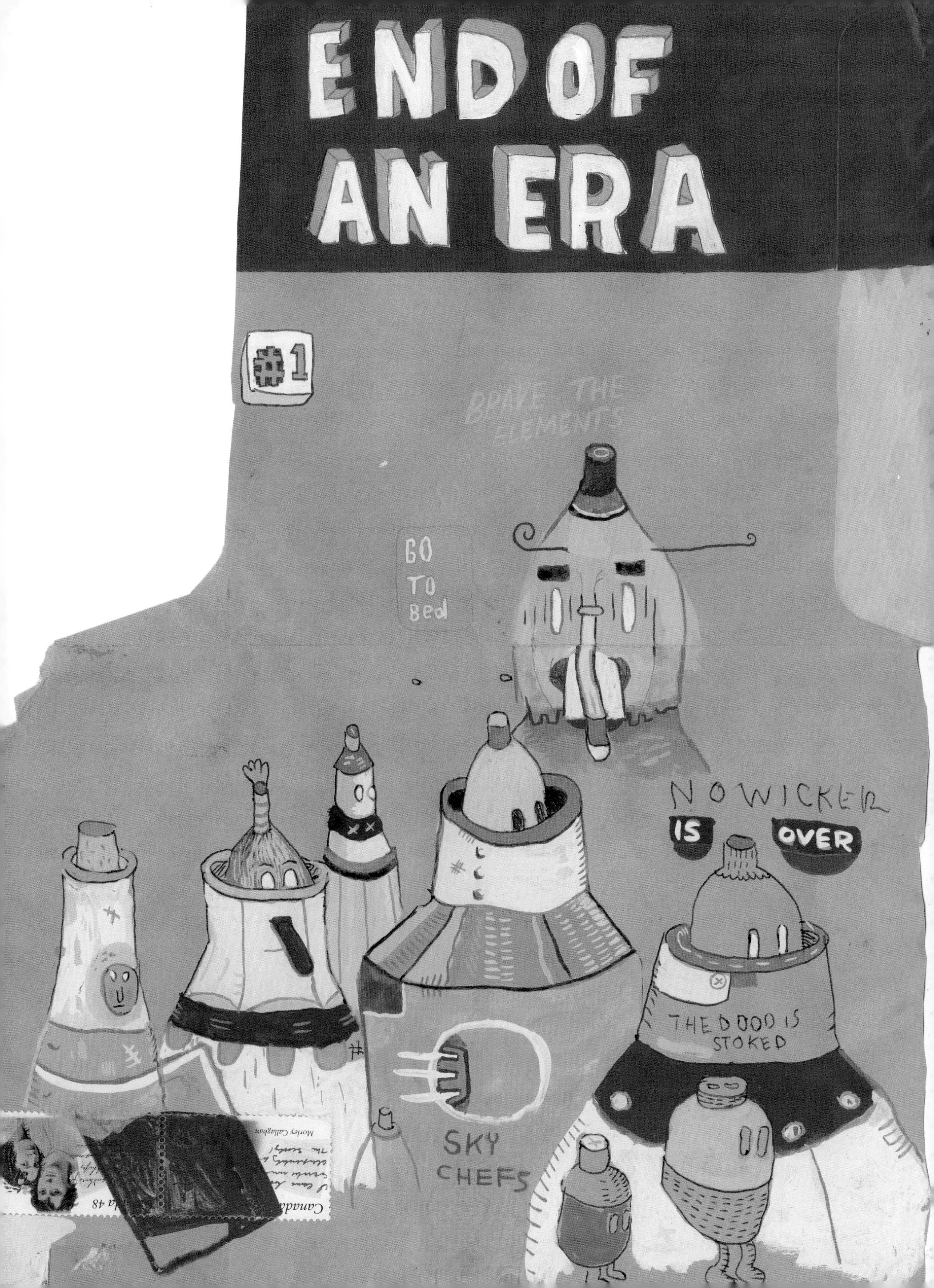
END OF
AN ERA
#1
BRAVE THE ELEMENTS
GO TO Bed
NOWICKER
IS
OVER
THE DOOD IS STOKED
SKY CHEFS

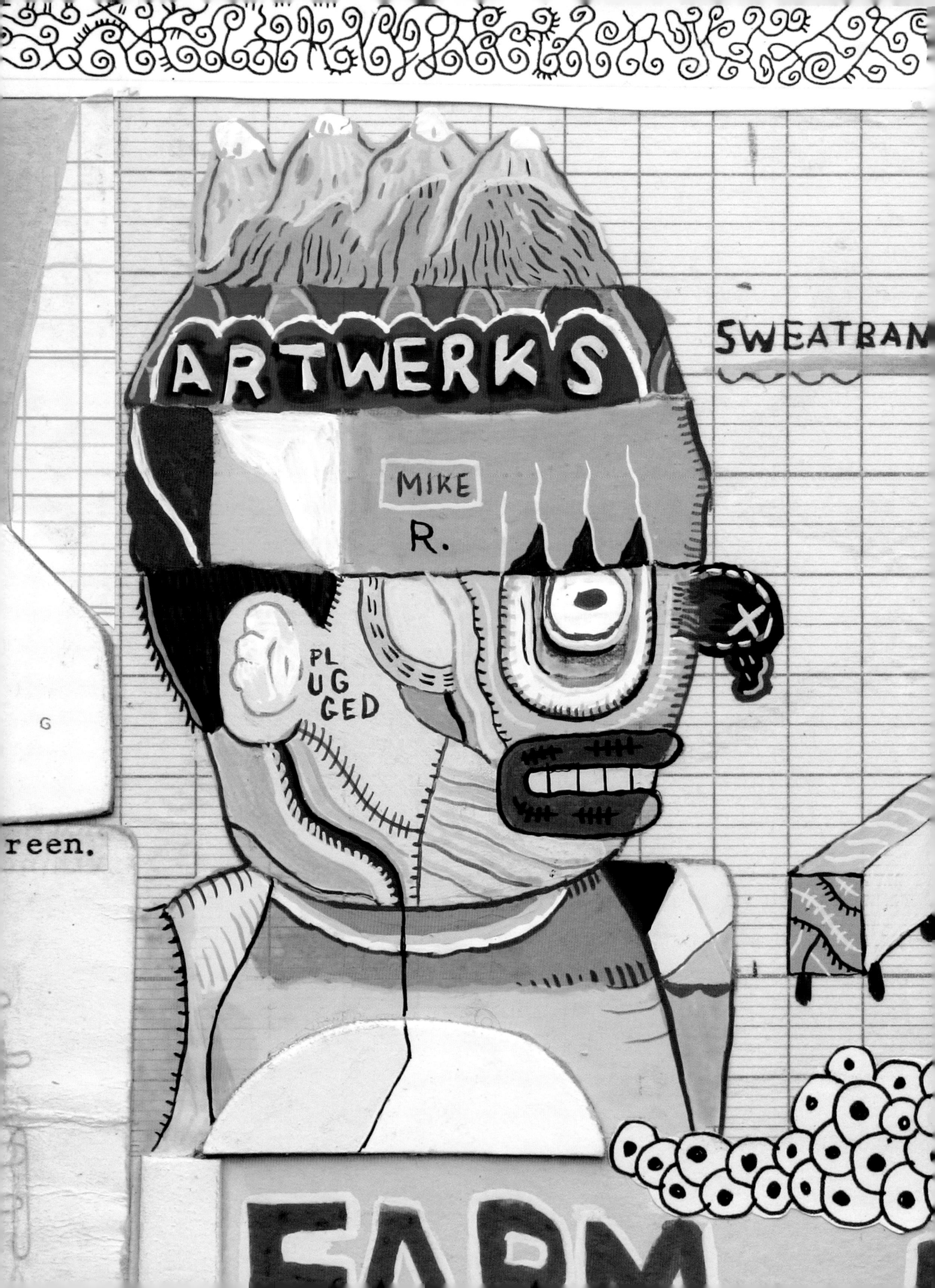

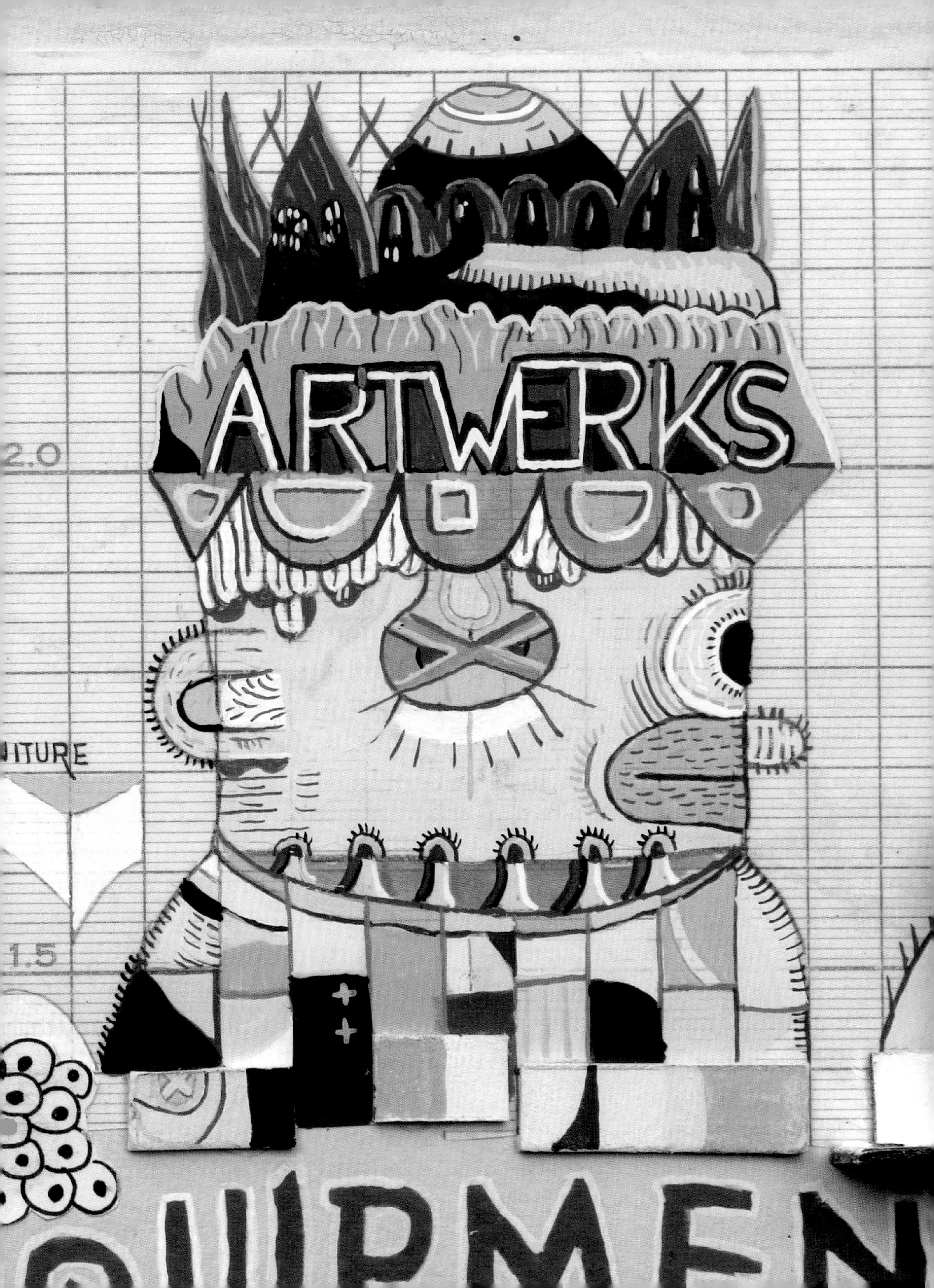
ARTWERKS
2.0
ITURE
1.5

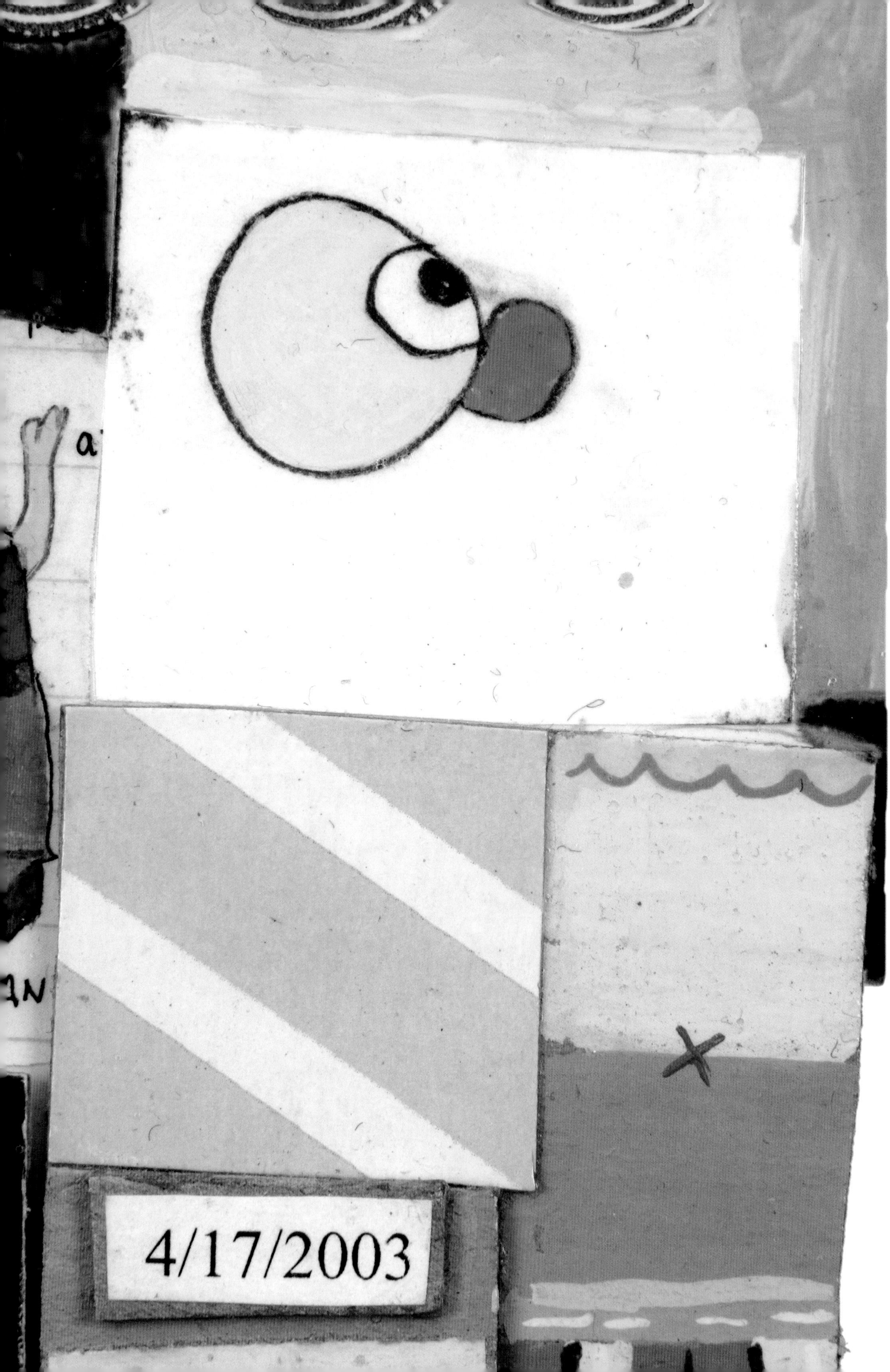
4/17/2003

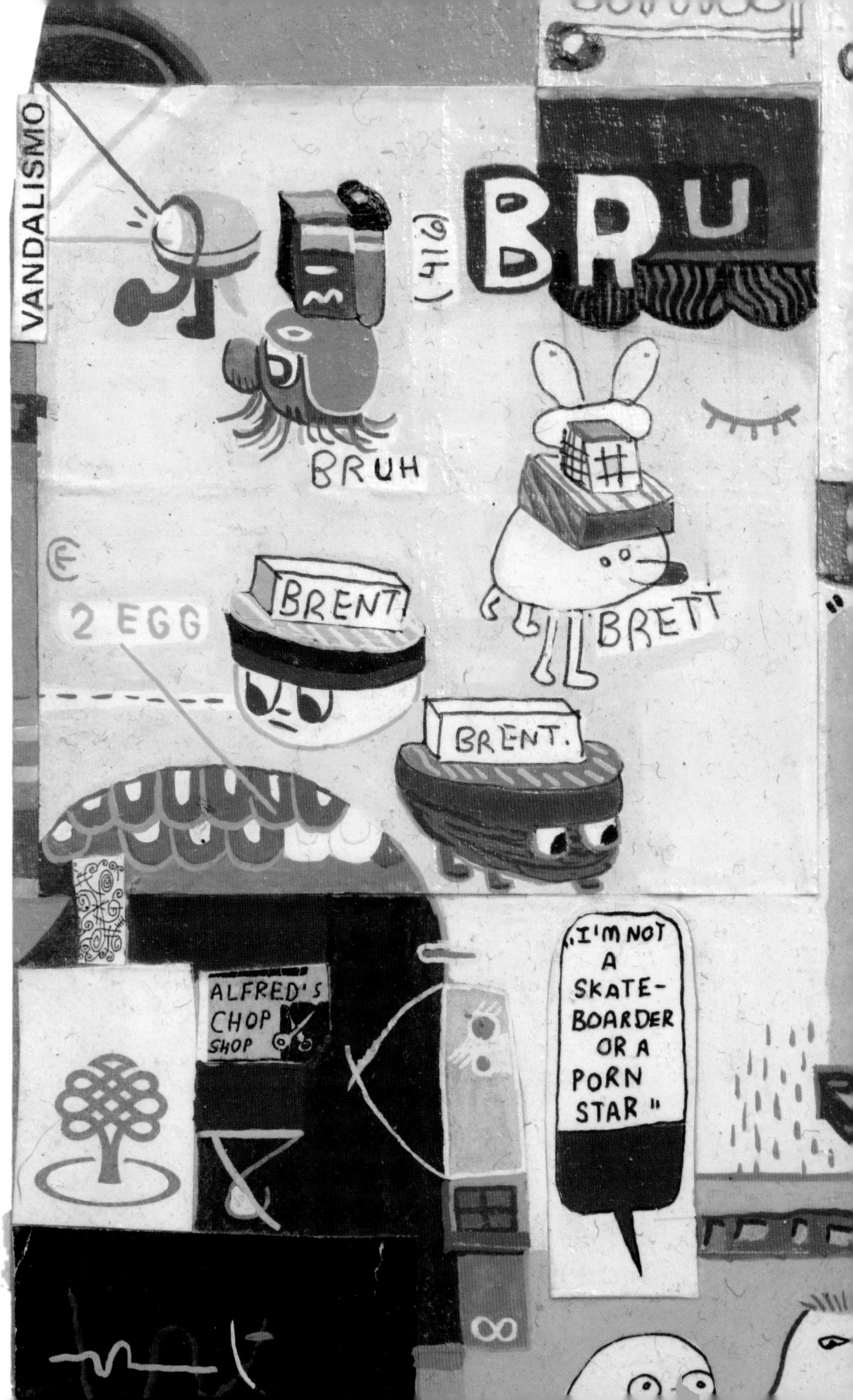

VANDALISMO
(416)
BRU
BRUH
2 EGG
BRENT
BRETT
BRENT.
ALFRED'S CHOP SHOP
"I'M NOT A SKATE-BOARDER OR A PORN STAR"

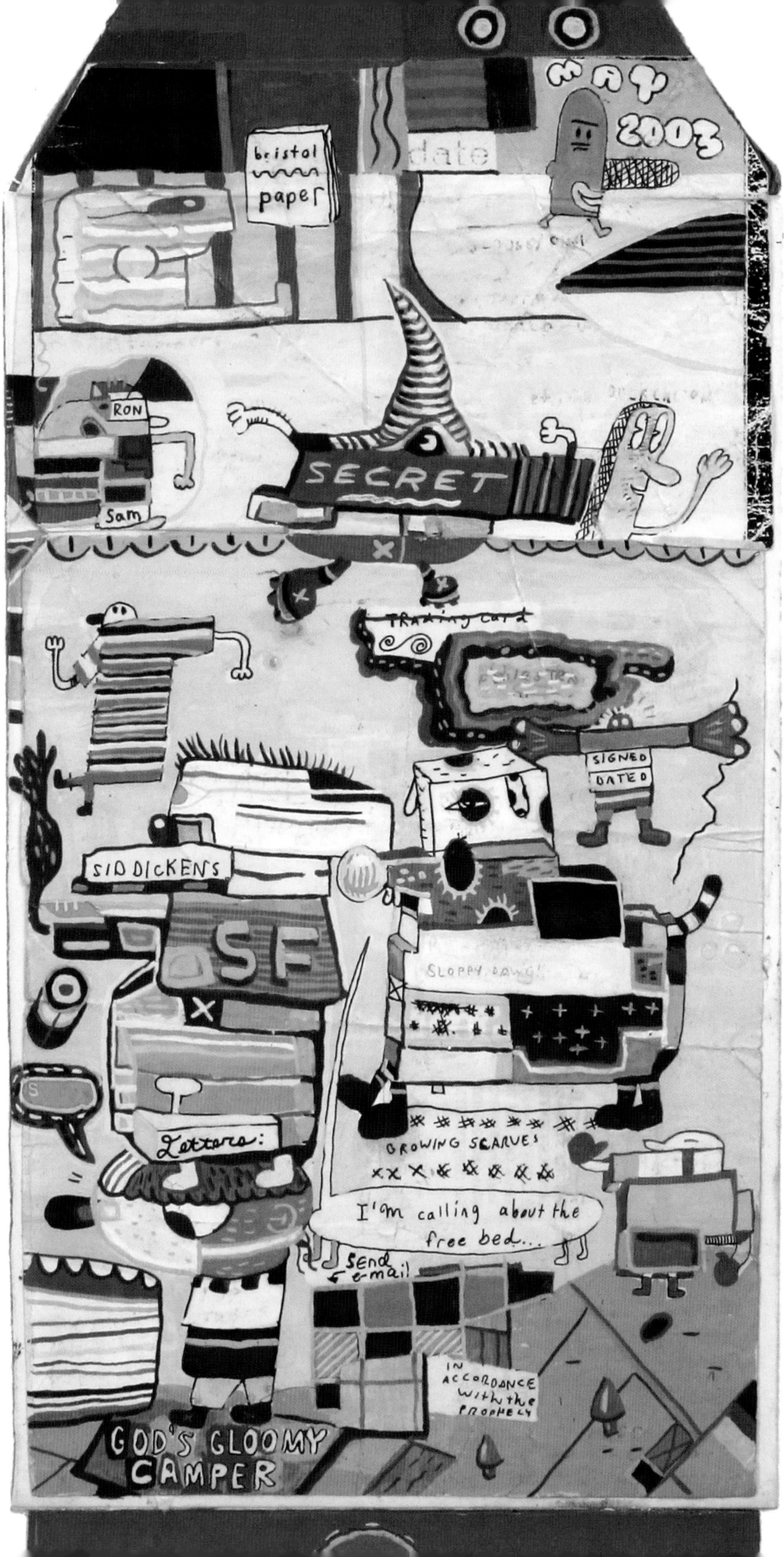
MAY 2003
bristol paper
date
RON
Sam
SECRET
SIGNED DATED
SID DICKENS
SF
SLOPPY DAWG!
Letters:
GROWING SCARVES
I'm calling about the free bed...
send e-mail
IN ACCORDANCE with the PROPHECY
GOD'S GLOOMY CAMPER

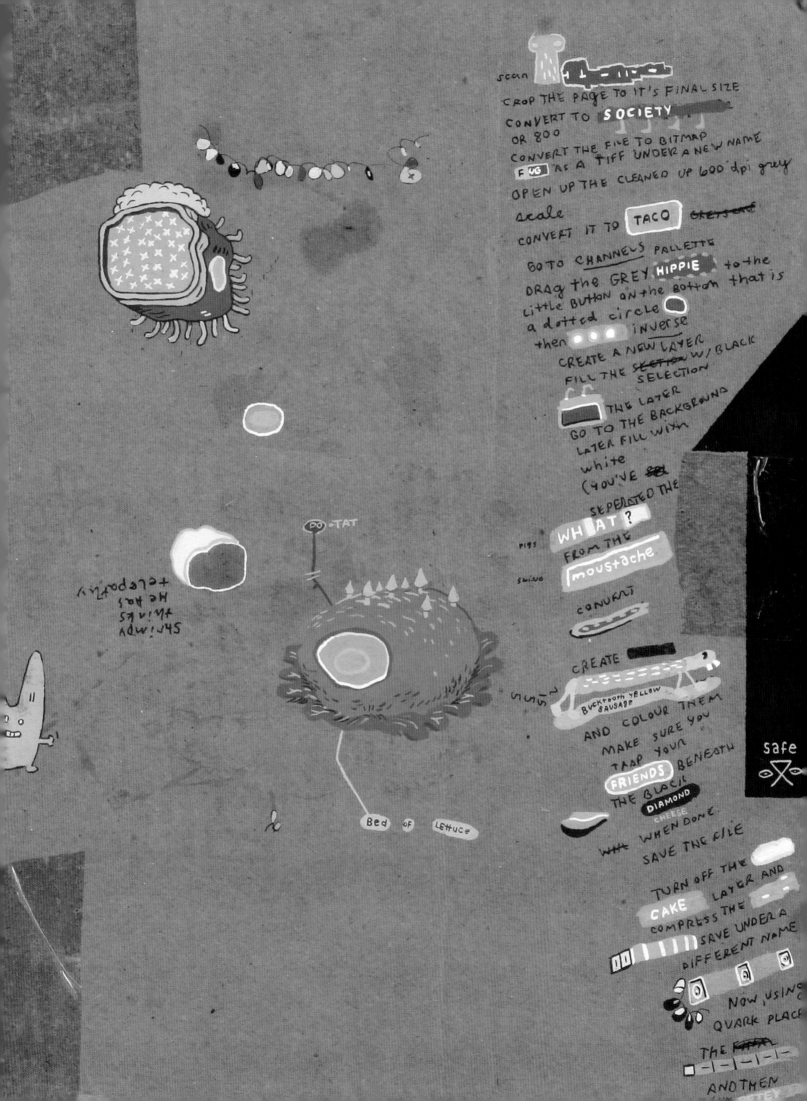

scan

CROP THE PAGE TO IT'S FINAL SIZE
CONVERT TO SOCIETY
OR 800
CONVERT THE FILE TO BITMAP
FUG AS A TIFF UNDER A NEW NAME
OPEN UP THE CLEANED UP 600 dpi grey
scale
CONVERT IT TO TACO GREYSCALE

GO TO CHANNELS PALLETTE
DRAG the GREY HIPPIE to the
little BUTTON ON the Bottom that is
a dotted circle
then ••• inverse
CREATE A NEW LAYER
FILL THE SELECTION W/ BLACK
SELECTION
THE LATER
GO TO THE BACKGROUND
LATER FILL WITH
white
(YOU'VE
SEPERATED THE

PIGS   WHAT ?
        FROM THE
SWINE   moustache

        CONVERT

        CREATE
UNISIS
        BUCKTOOTH YELLOW
        SAUSAGE
        AND COLOUR THEM
        MAKE SURE YOU
        TRAP YOUR
        FRIENDS BENEATH
        THE BLACK
        DIAMOND
        CHEESE
        WHEN DONE
        SAVE THE FILE

        TURN OFF THE
        CAKE LAYER AND
        COMPRESS THE
        SAVE UNDER A
        DIFFERENT NAME

        NOW USING
        QUARK PLACE
        THE
        —|—|—|—|—
        AND THEN

PO -TAT

Shrimpy
thinks
he has
teleported

Bed of LETTUCE

safe

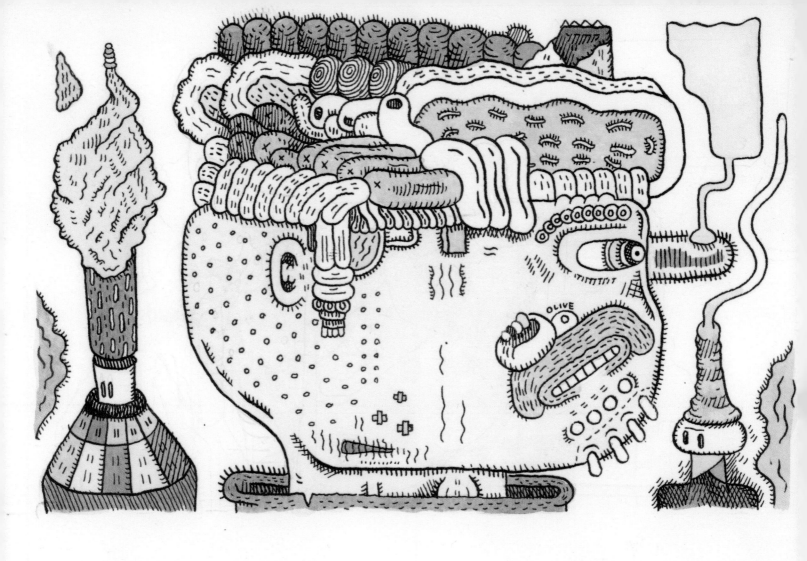

Thank You:

Tara Azzopardi, Sabine Beisser and Kip Jackson, Jason Bellchamber, Rebecca Bird, Peter Birkemoe, Rupert Botttenberg, Paul Bright, Alvin Buenaventura, Jessica Campbell, Geneviève Castrée, Michael Comeau, Mark Connery, Julie and Dave Cooper, Jordan Crane, Robert Dayton, Gabriel Deerman, Shayne Ehman, Gabriel Fowler, Fredette Frame, Adam Frank, Denis Gaugain, Stefan Gruber, Paul G and Helen Hill, William Habington, Joey Haley, Sammy Harkham, David Heatley, David Hirshey, Graham Hollings, Kevin House, Keith Jones, Gemey Kelly, Tommy Lacroix, Drue Langlois, David Larsen, Ben Jones, Trish Lavoie, Matt Leines, Gabe Linder, Sean Madden, Billy Mavreas, Gavin McInnes, Scott McIntyre, Jason Mclean, Mennonite Dan, John Murchie, Dan Nadel, Tim Olive, Lulu Peabody-Sherman, Jonathan Petersen, Dominique Pétrin, Terry Piercey, Terry and Owen Plummer, Ron Regé, Jr., Eric Reynolds, Jamie Shannon, Christian Schumann, Seth Scriver, Mark Slutsky, Fiona Smyth, Kevin Spenst, Trixy Sweetvittles, Aya Takada, Peter Thompson, Hannah Thomson, Matthew Thurber, Spencer "Sweet Mr. C." Tripp, Morris Twance-Morris, Barry T. Walsh, Sunny Wong, Etienne Zack, The All Star Schnauzer Band, The Blinding Light!! Cinema, The Nog A Dod Appreciation Society Of Canada, Owens Art Gallery, New Leaf Editions, Struts Artist Run Centre, and all the rest of my friends and my family.

Special Thanks:

Adam Baumgold, Peggy Burns, Jonathan Desbarats, Tom Devlin, Amy Lockhart, Chris Oliveros, Neil Rough, and Matthew P. Soucie.

This Book is Dedicated to:

Mr. Tacky Halo

Some of this material previously appeared in:

B.U.L.B. Comix, *Bloo Chip*, *The Coast*, *The Drama*, *Exclaim! Magazine*, *Expo*, *Fish Piss*, *The Ganzfeld*, *The Georgia Straight*, *An Anthology Of Graphic Fiction*, *The Hobbit*, *L'enfance Du Cyclope*, *Illusztraijuns For Brain Police*, *It's A Wonderful Life*, *Kramers Ergot*, *The Layer Of The Ea_th* (vol. 1 and 2), *Made Magazine*, *The Montreal Mirror*, *The New Collage*, *The New York Times Magazine*, *The Portable Conundrum*, *Showpaper*, *The Stacks*, *Swindle Magazine*, *Tab*, *These Thungs* (Japanese Export), *This Booklet Contains*, *The Toe Toddler*, and *Vice Magazine*.

STOLEN FROM

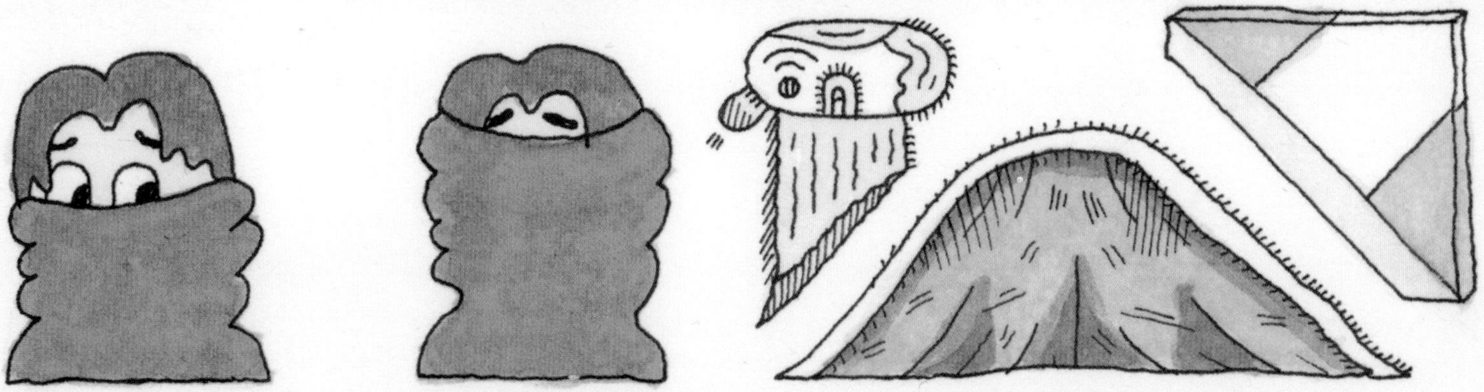

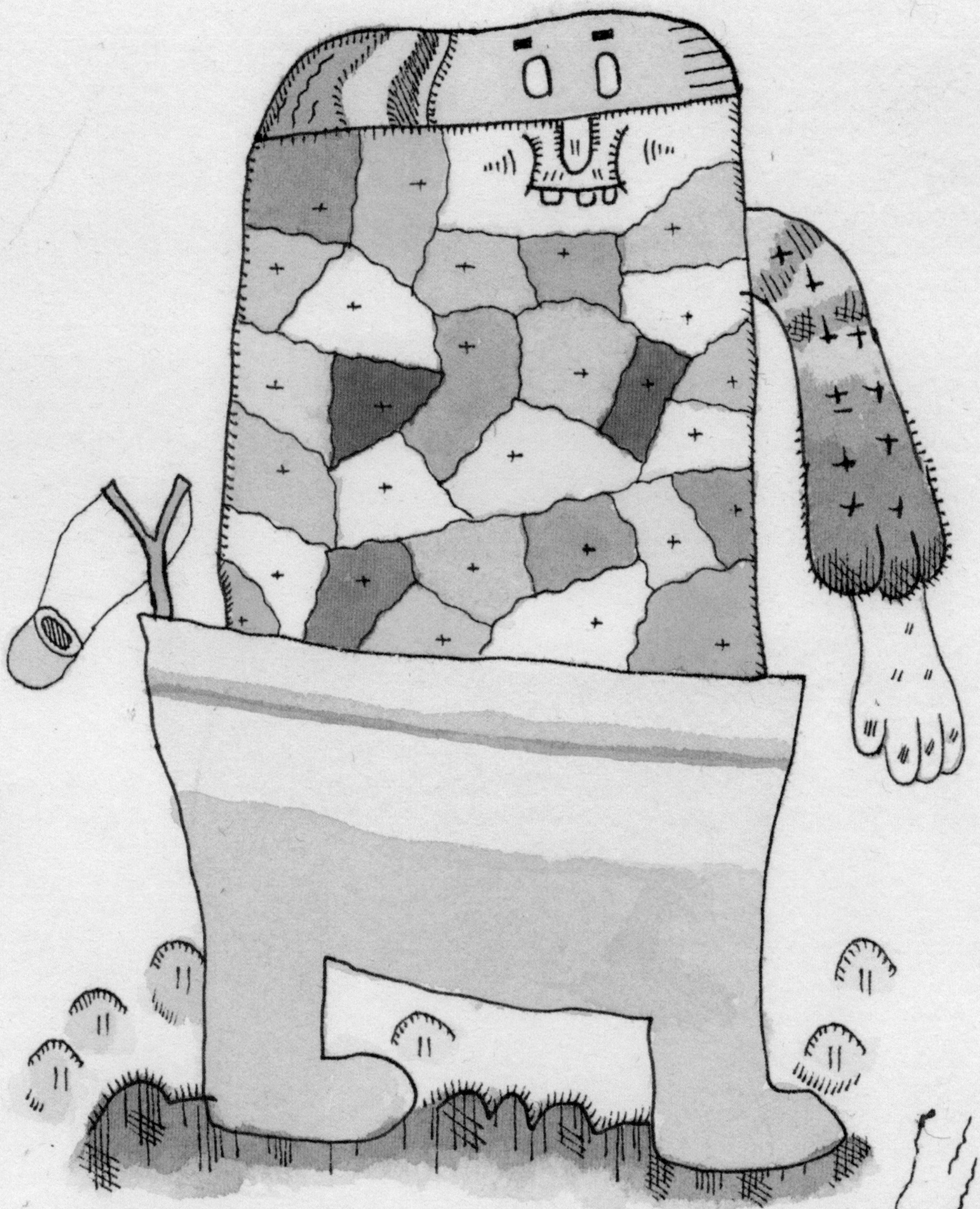

" THE WORLD IS TURNING TO DUST "

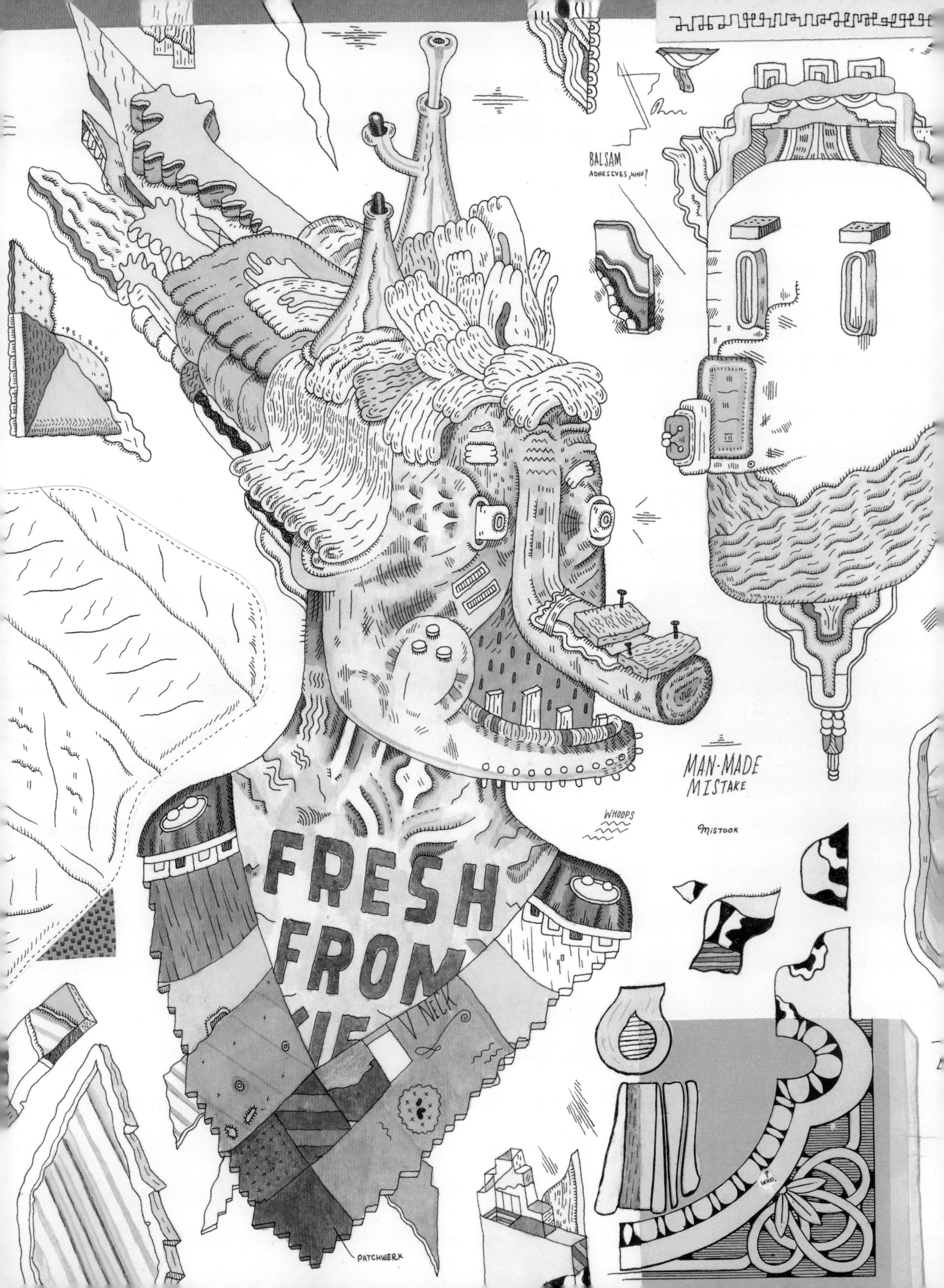
PET ROCK
BALSAM
ADHESIVES, WHU?
FRESH
FROM
V NECK
MAN-MADE
MISTAKE
WHOOPS
MISTOOK
PATCHWERK

(NOT A SELF-PORTRAIT)
HEY MAN!
ADDS
PLUSSES
TO
HIS:
(NOT A PORTRAIT OF FRIEND OR FAMILY)

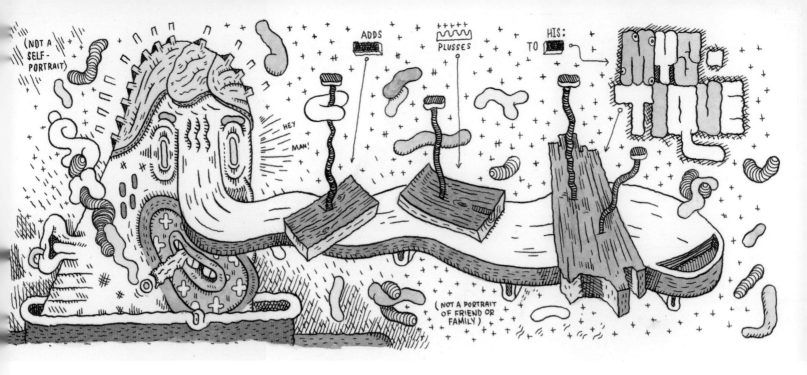

Other Books Available by Marc Bell:

Illusztraijuns For Brain Police
Nog A Dod (editor)

Other Books Sort of Available by Marc Bell:

Illustrated Cartoon Videos
Shrimpy And Paul And Friends

Other Books Not Available by Marc Bell:

Big Pile Comics
Bloo Chip
Call Larry about the Ironing Board
The Canadian Clean-Up Crew
Construkt
Corn Comics #1
Fresh From Kiev
Gooma
Hippy #1
Knoze Clippah! (various varied editions)
The Layer Of The Ea_th (vol. 1: Land Muss and 2: Nowicker)
Log Interpretation
The Mojo Action Companion Unit (Issues #1–9)
The Mojo Action Companion Unit #1 (Exclaim! Edition)
Puttoo
The Stacks #1
The Stacks (D & Q edition)
There Is Nothing + More!
These Thungs (Japanese Export)
This Booklet Contains
The Toe Toddler #1 (editor)
Worn Tuff Elbow #1

(note: some omissions for general quality have been made, collaborative books were not considered, for more info contact: balsamadhesives@yahoo.ca)

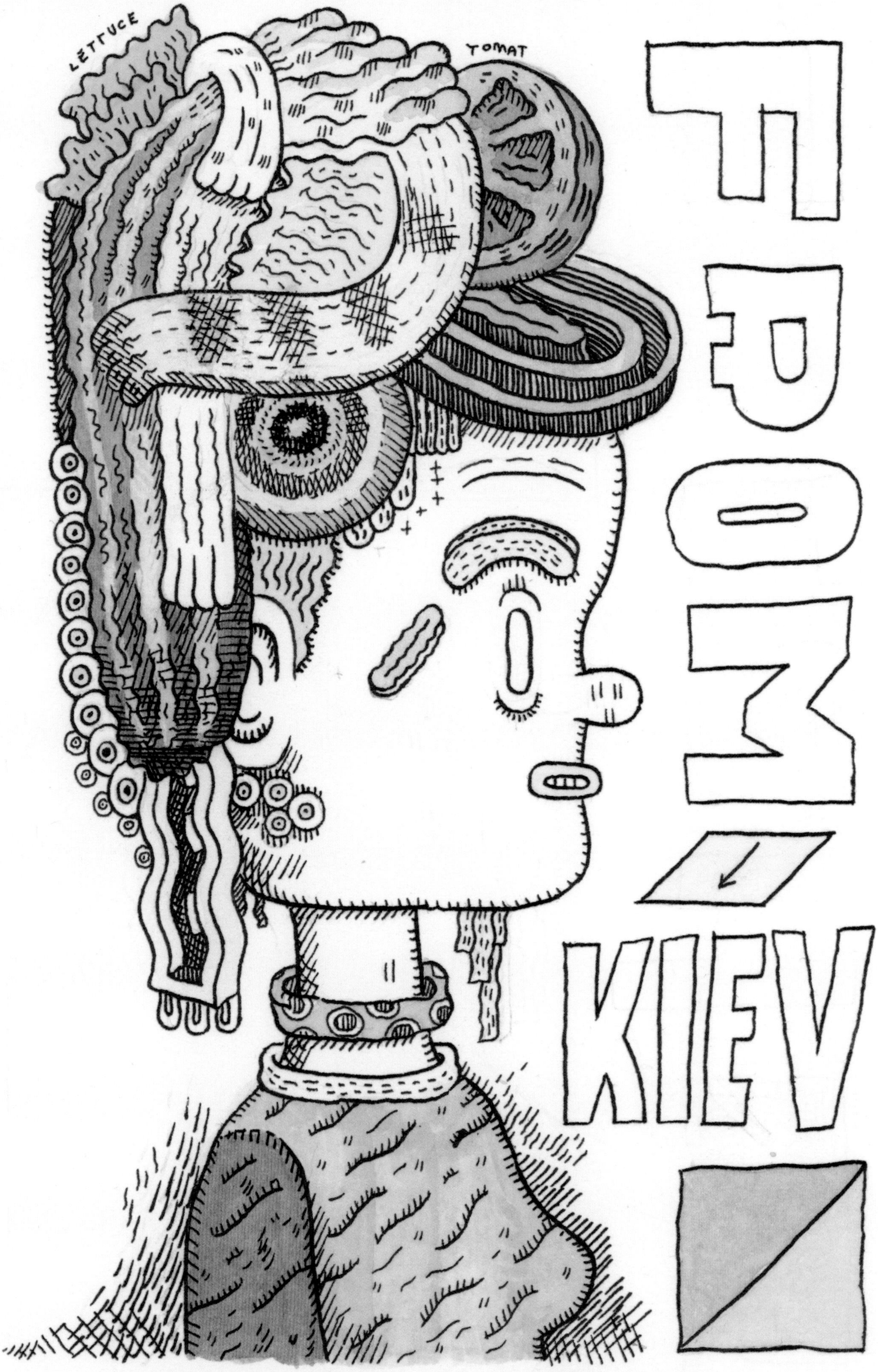
LETTUCE
TOMAT
FROM
KIEV

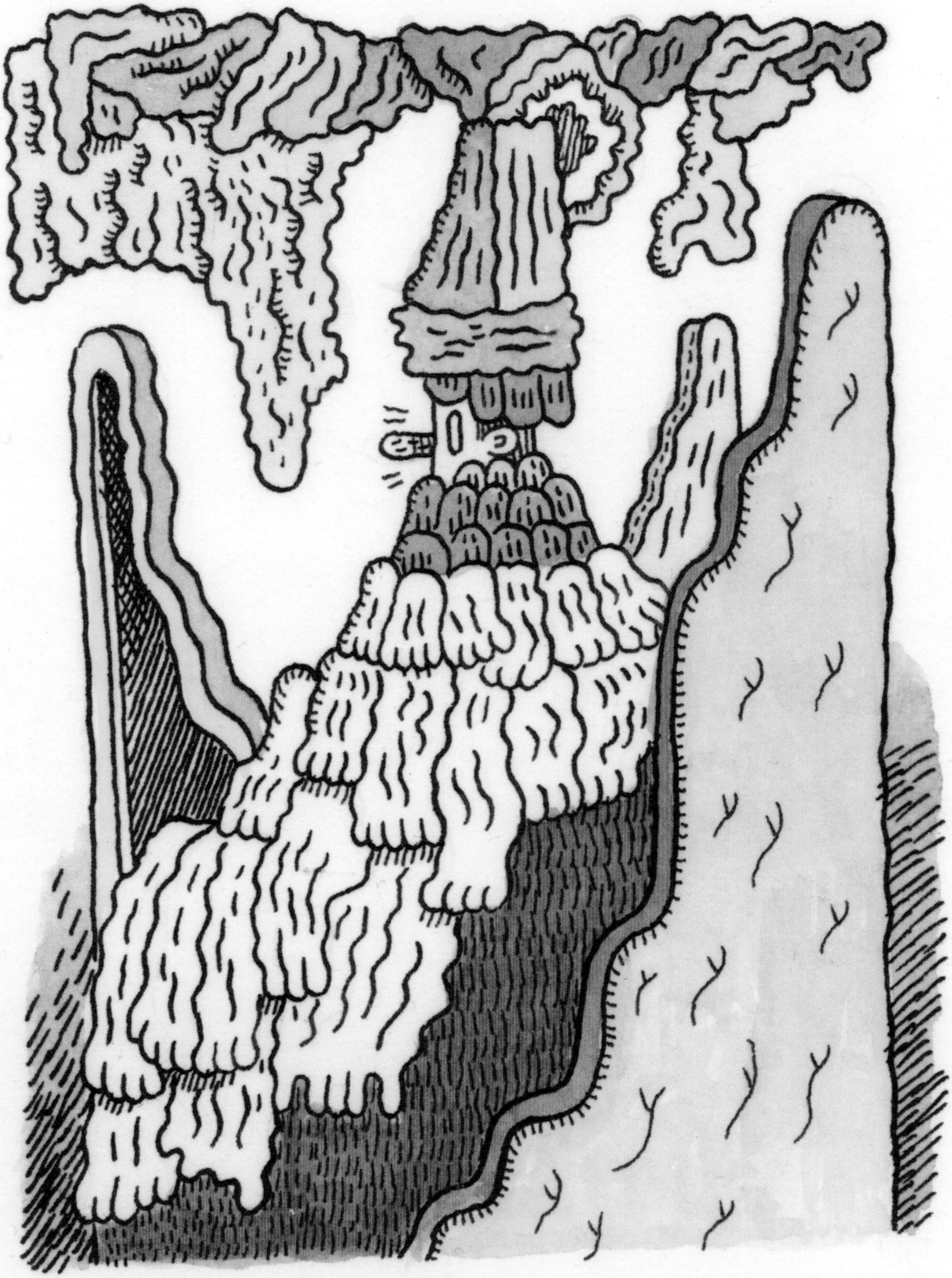

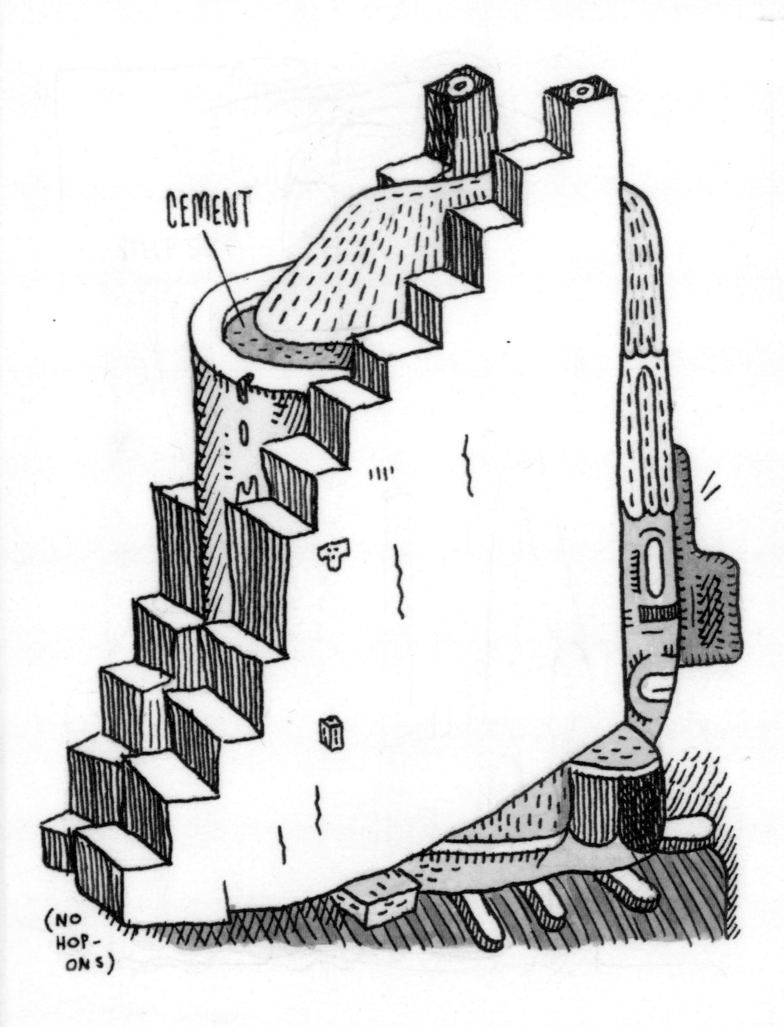

CEMENT

(NO
HOP-
ONS)

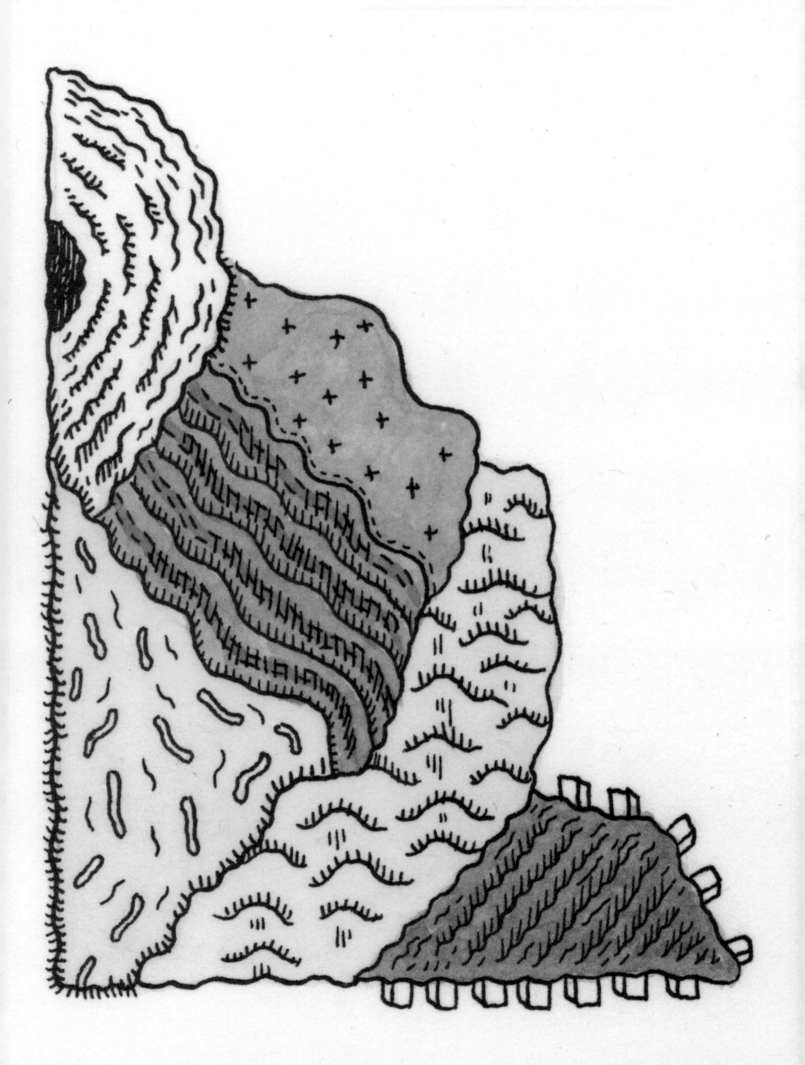

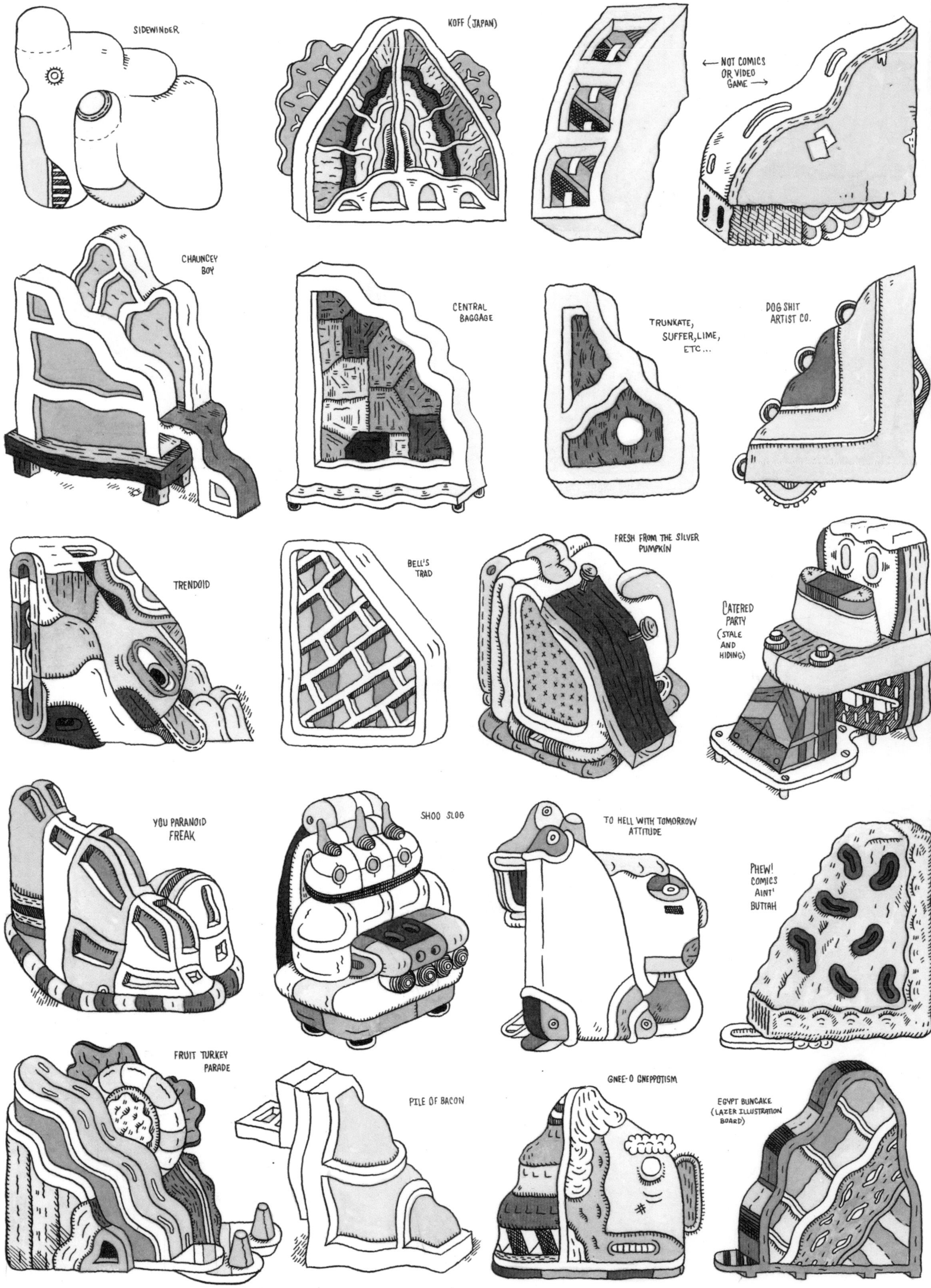

SIDEWINDER
KOFF (JAPAN)
← NOT COMICS OR VIDEO GAME →
CHAUNCEY BOY
CENTRAL BAGGAGE
TRUNKATE, SUFFER, LIME, ETC...
DOG SHIT ARTIST CO.
TRENDOID
BELL'S TRAD
FRESH FROM THE SILVER PUMPKIN
CATERED PARTY (STALE AND HIDING)
YOU PARANOID FREAK
SHOO SLOG
TO HELL WITH TOMORROW ATTITUDE
PHEW! COMICS AINT' BUTTAH
FRUIT TURKEY PARADE
PILE OF BACON
GNEE-O GNEPPOTISM
EGYPT BUNCAKE (LAZER ILLUSTRATION BOARD)